Oxford University Press
Digital Course Materials
for

Directions for accessing your
Oxford University Press Digital Course Materials

World in the Making

A Global History

Volume One: To 1500

SECOND EDITION

Bonnie G. Smith
Marc Van De Mieroop
Richard von Glahn
Kris Lane

Carefully scratch off the silver coating to see your personal redemption code.

This code can be redeemed only once.

Once the code has been revealed, this access card cannot be returned to the publisher.

Access can also be purchased online during the registration process.

The code on this card is valid for two years from the date of first purchase. Complete terms and conditions are available at learninglink.oup.com

Access Length: 6 months from redemption of the code.

OXFORD
UNIVERSITY PRESS

Your OUP digital course materials can be delivered several different ways, depending on how your instructor has elected to incorporate them into his or her course.

BEFORE REGISTERING FOR ACCESS, be sure to check with your instructor to ensure that you register using the proper method.

VIA YOUR SCHOOL'S LEARNING MANAGEMENT SYSTEM

Use this method if your instructor has integrated these resources into your school's Learning Management System (LMS)—Blackboard, Canvas, Brightspace, Moodle, or other

Log in to your instructor's course within your school's LMS.

When you click a link to a resource that is access-protected, you will be prompted to register for access.

Follow the on-screen instructions.

Enter your personal redemption code (or purchase access) when prompted.

VIA OXFORD learning link

Use this method if you are using the resources for self-study only. **NOTE:** *Scores for any quizzes you take on the OUP site will not report to your instructor's gradebook.*

Visit oup.com/he/smith2e

Select the edition you are using, then select student resources for that edition.

Click the link to upgrade your access to the student resources.

Follow the on-screen instructions.

Enter your personal redemption code (or purchase access) when prompted.

VIA OXFORD learning cloud

Use this method only if your instructor has specifically instructed you to enroll in an Oxford Learning Cloud course. **NOTE:** *If your instructor is using these resources within your school's LMS, use the Learning Management System instructions.*

Visit the course invitation URL provided by your instructor.

If you already have an oup.instructure.com account you will be added to the course automatically; if not, create an account by providing your name and email.

When you click a link to a resource in the course that is access-protected, you will be prompted to register.

Follow the on-screen instructions, entering your personal redemption code where prompted.

For assistance with code redemption, Oxford Learning Cloud registration, or if you redeemed your code using the wrong method for your course, please contact our customer support team at **learninglinkdirect.support@oup.com** or 855-281-8749.

About the Cover Image

Street Market in Guatemala City

These indigenous Maya vendors are among hundreds who have traveled from the countryside to sell their fresh produce, colorful textiles, traditional clothing, and more at this bustling street market in Guatemala City, the capital of Guatemala and the largest city in Central America. Perhaps annoyed by his intrusive camera as she plies her livelihood, the young woman in the lower left corner gives the photographer a hard look. Still, she and the two women next to her—relatives, the viewer assumes, given their physical closeness and similar dress—reveal a fact of global history, the centrality of women to the agricultural economy.

World in the Making

World in the Making

A GLOBAL HISTORY | SECOND EDITION

VOLUME ONE: TO 1500

Bonnie G. Smith
Rutgers University

Marc Van De Mieroop
Columbia University

Richard von Glahn
University of California, Los Angeles

Kris Lane
Tulane University

OXFORD
UNIVERSITY PRESS

OXFORD
UNIVERSITY PRESS

Oxford University Press is a department of the University of Oxford.
It furthers the University's objective of excellence in research, scholarship,
and education by publishing worldwide. Oxford is a registered trade mark
of Oxford University Press in the UK and certain other countries.

Published in the United States of America by Oxford University Press
198 Madison Avenue, New York, NY 10016, United States of America.

For titles covered by Section 112 of the US Higher Education Opportunity
Act, please visit www.oup.com/us/he for the latest information about
pricing and alternate formats.

Library of Congress Cataloging-in-Publication Data
Names: Smith, Bonnie G., 1940- author. | Van de Mieroop, Marc, author. |
    Von Glahn, Richard, author. | Lane, Kris E., 1967- author.
Title: World in the making: a global history/Bonnie G. Smith, Rutgers
    University, Marc Van De Mieroop, Columbia University, Richard von Glahn,
    University of California, Los Angeles, Kris Lane, Tulane University.
Description: Second edition. | New York: Oxford University Press, [2023] |
    Includes bibliographical references and index. | Contents: v. 1. Volume
    one: to 1500—v. 2. Volume two: since 1300. | Summary: "A higher
    education history textbook on World History"—Provided by publisher.
Identifiers: LCCN 2022006291 (print) | LCCN 2022006292 (ebook) | ISBN
    9780197608296 (v. 1) | ISBN 9780197608289 (v. 1 ; paperback) | ISBN
    9780197608371 (v. 2) | ISBN 9780197608364 (v. 2 ; paperback) | ISBN
    9780197608319 (v. 1 ; epub) | ISBN 9780197648506 (v. 1 ; epub) | ISBN
    9780197608302 (v. 1 ; pdf) | ISBN 9780197608395 (v. 2 ; epub) | ISBN
    9780197648537 (v. 2 ; epub) | ISBN 9780197608388 (v. 2 ; pdf)
Subjects: LCSH: World history—Textbooks.
Classification: LCC D21 .S626 2023 (print) | LCC D21 (ebook) | DDC
    909—dc23/eng/20220210
LC record available at https://lccn.loc.gov/2022006291
LC ebook record available at https://lccn.loc.gov/2022006292

9 8 7 6 5 4 3 2 1
Printed by Lakeside Book Company, United States of America

Brief Contents

Contents

PART 1 The Ancient World, from Human Origins to 500 CE

CHAPTER 1 | Peopling the World, to 4000 BCE 6

The Major Global Development in this Chapter: *The adaptation of early humans to their environment and their eventual domestication of plants and animals*

CHAPTER   **2** ▍ **Temples and Palaces: Birth of the City 5000–1200 BCE   44**

The Major Global Development in this Chapter: *The rise of urban society and the creation of states in Southwest Asia*

CHAPTER **3** | Settlers and Migrants: The Creation of States in Asia 5000–500 BCE   80

The Major Global Development in this Chapter: *The rise of large urban states in Asia and the interactions between nomadic and settled peoples that shaped them*

CHAPTER 4 ▌ Empire and Resistance in the Mediterranean 1550–330 BCE   120

The Major Global Development in this Chapter: *The rise of empires and the variety and consequences of imperial rule*

CHAPTER 7 | Reading the Unwritten Record: Peoples of Africa, the Americas, and the Pacific Islands 3000 BCE–500 CE   234

The Major Global Development in this Chapter: *The evolution of ancient cultures without writing and their fundamental role in world history*

Backstory   235

PART 2   Crossroads and Cultures 500–1450 CE

CHAPTER   8   The Worlds of Christianity and Islam 400–1000   274

The Major Global Development in this Chapter: *The spread of Christianity and Islam and the profound impact of these world religions on the societies of western Eurasia and North Africa*

CHAPTER   **9** | Religion and Cross-Cultural Exchange in Asia 400–1000   314

The Major Global Development in this Chapter: *The cultural and commercial exchanges during the heyday of the Silk Road that transformed Asian peoples, cultures, and states*

CHAPTER **10** | **Societies and Networks in the Americas and the Pacific 300–1200   352**

The Major Global Development in this Chapter: *The formation of distinctive regional cultures in the Americas and the Pacific Islands between 300 and 1200*

CHAPTER   **11** | **The Rise of Commerce in Afro-Eurasia 900–1300   392**

The Major Global Development in this Chapter: *The sustained economic expansion that spread across Eurasia and Africa between the tenth and fourteenth centuries*

CHAPTER

12 | Centers of Learning and the Transmission of Culture 900–1300   432

The Major Global Development in this Chapter: *The expansion of learning and education across Eurasia from 900 to 1300 and its relationship to the rise of regional and national identities*

CHAPTER **13** **Crusaders, Mongols, and Eurasian Integration 1050–1350   470**

The Major Global Development in this Chapter: *The Eurasian integration fostered by the clashes of culture known as the Crusades and the Mongol conquests*

CHAPTER **14** **Collapse and Revival in Afro-Eurasia 1300–1450 508**

The Major Global Development in this Chapter: *Crisis and recovery in fourteenth- and fifteenth-century Afro-Eurasia*

PART 3   The Early Modern World, 1450–1750

CHAPTER   15 | Empires and Alternatives in the Americas 1430–1530   550

FEATURES

Maps

Studying with Maps

World history cannot be fully understood without a clear comprehension of the chronologies and parameters within which different empires, states, and peoples have changed over time. Maps facilitate this understanding by illuminating the significance of time, space, and geography in shaping a world constantly in the making.

Map Key

Maps use symbols to show the location of features and to convey information, such as the movement of commodities, ideas, or people. Each symbol is explained in the map's *key*.

Projection

A map *projection* portrays all or part of the earth, which is spherical, on a flat surface. All maps, therefore, include some distortion. The projections in *World in the Making* include global, continental, and regional perspectives. Special "spot maps" in each chapter depict information at a local, or even city, level.

Inset

The maps in *World in the Making* include *insets* that show cities, localities, or regions in detail.

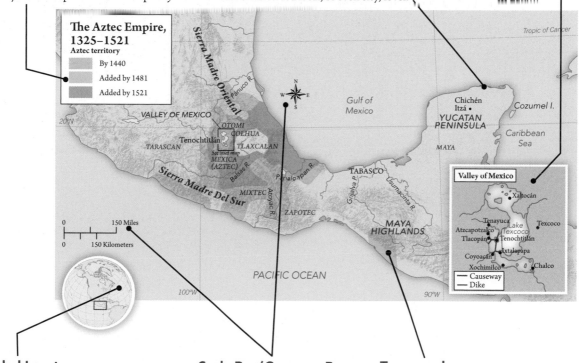

Global Locator

Many of the maps in *World in the Making* include *global locators* that show the area being depicted in a larger context.

Scale Bar / Compass Rose

Every map in *World in the Making* includes a *scale bar* that shows distances in both miles and kilometers, and in some instances, in feet as well. The *compass rose*, included on most maps, shows the map's orientation.

Topography

Many maps in *World in the Making* show *relief*—the contours of the land. Topography is an important element in studying maps because the physical terrain has played a critical role in shaping human history.

Features

Seeing the Past

Doing History

Chapter 12 Contextualization
Evaluate how the different political, religious, and intellectual contexts of Latin Christendom, the Islamic world, and the Chinese empire reshaped the social elites in each society.

Chapter 13 Claims and Evidence in Sources
Consider the reliability of eyewitness accounts as historical sources.

Chapter 14 Argument
Appraise the consequences of the Black Death for European and Muslim societies to assemble arguments that explain these differences.

Chapter 15 Making Connections
Compare the Aztec and Inca empires to better understand the development of cities in the Americas.

Preface

"I once met a little girl tenderly carrying a puppy in the bark [-fiber] carrying-strap that her mother used for her little sister. 'Are you stroking your baby dog?' I asked her. She solemnly replied, 'When I am big, I will kill wild pigs and monkeys; I will club them all to death when he barks!'"

The world-famous French anthropologist Claude Lévi-Strauss spent much of the mid-twentieth century scouring Brazil's backlands in search of native Americans whose cultures remained largely unchanged by contact with Europeans and others. He wanted to catalogue and analyze their unique customs, myths, and material culture before they disappeared. Made rich by global demand for coffee and other raw commodities, Brazil was rapidly industrializing, encouraging prospectors, ranchers, and homesteaders to transform what had for over 10,000 years been "Indian country."

In the late 1930s, Lévi-Strauss spent time among the Nambikwara of western Mato Grosso State, near the border with Bolivia. As he recalled in his best-selling 1955 memoir *Tristes Tropiques*: "Although the Nambikwara were easy-going, and unperturbed by the presence of an anthropologist with his notebook and camera, the work was complicated by linguistic difficulties." Long isolated, the Nambikwara spoke no Portuguese. Lévi-Strauss nevertheless learned to communicate in the Nambikwara language, such that he felt comfortable quoting the unnamed little girl with the puppy, future hunter of boars and monkeys.

Was *Tristes Tropiques* a summary of scientific observations or a personal narrative shot through with romantic views? Reflecting on these encounters in his memoir, Lévi-Strauss referred to Nambikwara territory as "the lost world," its society the least complex he had ever seen. They wore no clothes, slept on the cold ground beneath the stars, and produced no pottery, weavings, or much else beyond basic gathering and hunting tools. Lévi-Strauss concluded: "I had been looking for a society reduced to its simplest expression. That of the Nambikwara was so truly simple that all I could find in it was individual human beings."

Not long after, in 1959, Lévi-Strauss famously proposed that human societies were either "cold" or "hot," the former stuck in time or reliant on the ordering principles of origin stories whereas the latter were dynamic, always changing; in a word, history-making. The proposal spurred debate, and over the past five or six decades, scholars have almost universally rejected Lévi-Strauss's division of humanity into those who make history and those who live outside of it. Even so, the idea of "lost tribes" lives on in the popular imagination, often used as it was by Renaissance and Enlightenment thinkers as a foil against the real or perceived iniquities of "modern" societies.

World in the Making: A Global History is a textbook by four historians who assume all societies are "hot" and all people make history and always have. We feel the best way to understand the global endeavors of human beings in aggregate is to embrace change as the rule, to emphasize how all societies, all cultures, have been "making history" since the age of early hominids. The ancient concept of *Homo faber*, or humans as fundamentally makers of things—be they tools or weapons, dwellings or watercraft, nuclear bombs or iPhones—is what inspires us as world historians.

We argue in our emphasis on lives and livelihoods for a world constructed, altered, renovated, remade by ordinary people even as we acknowledge the genius of individual innovators, disruptors who broke the mold or struck out in some new direction. For us, world history is constantly exciting precisely because it is never predictable, much like the little Nambikwara girl's response to Claude Lévi-Strauss. Who knows if some other little girl in the backlands of Brazil in some earlier time broke away from her people to establish an entirely new culture dominated by woman hunters and warriors?

World in the Making is not an attempt to celebrate progress or despair over lost innocence, but rather to embrace the uncertain and jarring past. The book's Counterpoint discussions are meant in part to check our own tendency as historians to slot all the messy "stuff" of history into tidy, logical narratives. We recognize structures, some of them long-lasting, as things that humans make or construct—even as our narratives in this book are constructions—but we also marvel at history's unexpected twists; for example, when an apparently "weak" culture like that of the maroons of Suriname foiled a mighty adversary. Long-range paths may also prove surprising, as when a "great" culture like that of ancient Egypt simply did not conform to broad regional patterns.

In addition to our fascination with uncertainty and seeming chaos in the vast yet fragmentary record of our shared past, we are struck by the webs of interconnections, movements, mutual discoveries, and unexpected clashes—the crossroads where peoples meet—that also seem to define the human experience. In many cases, we are inclined to flip Lévi-Strauss's categories. We will see that an allegedly "hot" society was the one that appears to have gone cold, stuck in a mire of cherished myths, whereas the "cold" or "primitive" society adapted readily to changing conditions. Its people proved most flexible, ready to shove off for a new shore.

We may hope that the little Nambikwara girl who replied forcefully to the French anthropologist in the backlands of Brazil on a crisp morning in 1938 did not grow up to club wild pigs or monkeys, but that may be more a reflection of our tastes than of the truth about history. To survive the changing world of Brazil, that girl needed all the strength and smarts she could muster. For us, the authors of *World in the Making: A Global History*, that is "hot" stuff.

Organization

Author teams of world history textbooks typically divide the work based on geographic specialty, but we were determined to take responsibility for eras, not regions. Defining our subject matter by time period enabled us to see the connections or parallel developments that make societies part of world history—as well as the distinctive features that make them unique. Our approach also ensured a unified perspective to the many stories that each part tells. Marc Van De Mieroop covers the period from human origins to 500 CE (Part 1); Richard von Glahn the period 500 to 1450 (Part 2); Kris Lane the period 1450 to 1750 (Part 3); and Bonnie G. Smith the period 1750 to the present (Part 4).

Pedagogy and Features

We know from our own teaching that students need help in absorbing and making sense of information, thinking critically, and understanding that history itself is often debated and constantly revised. With these goals in mind, we bolster our narrative with a variety of learning and teaching aids, all intended to foster comprehension and analysis and to spark the historical imagination.

Part introductions provide students with an overview of the period they are about to encounter. **Chapter introductions** include **Backstory** sections to remind them of where they last encountered the peoples discussed in the chapter; **outlines** that preview the chapter's content; opening **vignettes** chosen to draw them into the atmosphere of the period and introduce the chapter's main themes; and **Overview Questions** that frame the main issues to consider while reading. Each major chapter section opens with a **Focus Question** intended to guide students' comprehension and—along with all three levels of questions in our book—to promote close reading and dynamic class discussion.

The **Counterpoint** section that ends each chapter breaks the grip of overgeneralization that often characterizes world history. It shows political movements; social, cultural, and economic trends; and everyday experiences that go against the grain. The Counterpoint feature allows students to see and learn from historical diversity. They can get a sense that historical experience—and even our own behaviors—reveal valuable divergences from general patterns at any one time.

Making Connections, our third set of chapter questions, prompts students to think broadly about the history they have just read. It ends our chapter-closing **Review** section, which incorporates as well a **timeline of important events**, a list of the **key terms** defined in our **running glossary**, and a reprise of the chapter's Overview Questions. The Review section now includes **Doing History**. These brief sections, directly tied to the content in each chapter, prompt students to consider a range historical thinking skills (see "New to this Edition" on page xxxix for a more detailed description).

Each chapter also includes **phonetic spellings** for many potentially unfamiliar words and a **Conclusion** that reinforces the central developments covered in the chapter. An end-of-book **Bibliography** directs students to print and online resources for further investigation.

In addition to these learning and review aids, we offer three special features in each chapter. Illustrated **Lives and Livelihoods** essays on topics ranging from the potters of antiquity to the builders of the trans-Siberian railroad allow us to provide more in-depth study of one of our key themes—namely, how people's lives intersect with larger cross-cultural interactions and global change. Our **Reading the Past** and **Seeing the Past** features, which include excerpts from written and visual primary sources, give students direct exposure to the ideas and voices of the people we are studying. They also help students build their analytical skills by modeling how historians interpret written and visual evidence.

Throughout the book we chose **images** to match as closely as we could the themes we wanted to stress. We did not conceive of the images as mere illustrations but rather as documents worthy of close historical analysis in their own right, products of the same places and times we try to evoke in the text. And our carefully developed **map program** provides sure-footed guidance to where our historical journey is taking us—a crucial necessity, since we travel to so many places not on the usual Grand Tour! In each chapter up to six **full-size maps** show major developments while up to four **"spot" maps**—small maps positioned within the discussion right where students need them—serve as immediate locators. To sum up, we wanted a complete toolbox of pedagogy and features to meet the needs of all kinds of learners.

New to This Edition

We are grateful for the enthusiastic response to the first edition. We are especially pleased that the book's emphasis on lives and livelihoods has been embraced by a wide range of schools with students from different backgrounds. In response to feedback from both users and nonusers, we have worked to make the text both more inclusive and more thought provoking. We have also updated many chapters with the most recent scholarship.

Doing History. This new feature, located in the Review section at the end of each chapter and based on a framework developed by the College Board™, prompts students to consider the skills that world historians employ. Tied to the content in each chapter and organized around seven key concepts, Doing History shows students the reasoning processes historians use to construct the historical past.

1. Developments and Processes: Identify and explain historical developments and processes.
2. Sourcing and Situation: Analyze sourcing and situation of primary and secondary sources.
3. Claims and Evidence in Sources: Analyze arguments in primary and secondary sources.
4. Contextualization: Analyze contents of historical events, developments, or processes.
5. Making Connections: Using historical reasoning processes to analyze patterns and connections between and among historical developments and processes.
6. Argumentation: Develop an argument.
7. Perspectives: Assess historical developments at macro and micro scales.

Historical-thinking skills increasingly matter to instructors seeking strategies that embrace the teaching of historical competencies for student success and life-long achievement. We hope Doing History will spark discussion, debate, and a deeper appreciation of the historical past.

New Features. The second edition presents several new Lives and Livelihoods, Seeing the Past, and Reading the Past features, including insights into religious practices in Stone Age Turkey (Chapter 1); ecology, production, and power in the Hawaiian Islands (Chapter 10); domestic life in Byzantium (Chapter 11); views of Alexander the Great in the East and West (Chapter 12); gender roles in late colonial Mexico (Chapter 21); wartime propaganda (Chapter 25); and the Cultural Revolution in China (Chapter 27).

New Counterpoint sections. We are pleased that many instructors have incorporated the Counterpoint sections into their teaching, and we are delighted to offer these new ones in the second edition:

- The Prophets of Israel and Judah (Chapter 5)
- Jewish Moneylenders in Latin Christendom (Chapter 11)
- Sufism in South Asia (Chapter 13)
- Njinga: An African Queen Fights Back (Chapter 17)
- National Unity in an Age of Migration (Chapter 24)

New photographs and maps. Consistently praised by users, the rich illustration and map program for *World in the Making* has been enhanced with fifty-seven new photos and four new maps. Several maps have been corrected.

New chapter opening vignettes and new scholarship. World history is a dynamic field, with new ways of thinking about the past constantly emerging. We have sought to incorporate the most recent perspectives while preserving the text's strong narrative flow. Chapter 1 includes the very latest research on human evolution and early human history, including a new vignette on the discovery of the oldest footprints outside of Africa. Chapter 3 includes substantially revised information on the Oxus people spotlighted in that chapter's Counterpoint section. Chapter 6 presents a revised discussion on the Roman Republic. Chapter 13 now opens with an account from Usamah ibn Minqidh that offers a Muslim view of Crusaders. Chapter 16 incorporates the now widely accepted term "global biological exchanges" to describe the floral, faunal, and microbial exchanges since c. 1500 CE. Chapter 17 provides a greatly expanded treatment of southwestern Africa in the period 1450–1800. Chapter 19 opens with a vignette about the sixteenth-century Spanish visionary Lucrecia de León whose life story reminds us that prescribed gender roles in early modern Europe could be stretched, challenged, or even reversed. Chapter 20 begins with the story of Zheng Zhilong, whose twisting life trajectory captures the flux of the mid-seventeenth century in much of East and Southeast Asia. Chapter 22 now examines the 1760 popular uprising in Jamaica known as Tacky's Revolt. The contributions of Shamil, the Muslim leader and resister to Russian imperialism, are now included in Chapters 23 and 24. Chapter 26 includes discussion of Rukmini Lakshmipathi, the first woman marcher arrested in Gandhi's "Salt March" of 1930. Chapter 27 offers a revised account of how colonized peoples achieved their independence from imperialist powers after World War II and presents new coverage of the global Cold War. Chapter 28 has been thoroughly rewritten to reflect the impacts of climate change, the COVID pandemic, and women's rights on twenty-first-century lives and livelihoods. The chapter opens with a new vignette on K-pop music and its global influence.

Digital Learning Resources for *World in the Making*

Oxford University Press offers instructors and students digital learning resources that increase student engagement and optimize the classroom teaching experience.

Oxford Learning Link (OLL) and Oxford Learning Link Direct (OLLD)

This online resource center www.learninglink.oup.com is available to adopters of *World in the Making*, and offers a wealth of teaching resources, including an enhanced eBook, a test-item file, a computerized test bank, quizzes, PowerPoint slides, videos, and primary sources. Oxford Learning Link Direct (OLLD) makes the digital learning resources for *World in the Making* available to adopters via a one-time course integration.

Adopters also have the option of delivering the learning tools for *World in the Making* within a cloud-based courseware platform (OLC). Contact your local OUP representative for a demo of either Oxford Learning Link Direct or Oxford Learning Cloud.

Uncovering World History

Users of Oxford Learning Link Direct have complimentary access to Uncovering World History. Edited by award-winning teacher Trevor Getz, Uncovering World History offers eight carefully designed digital-learning modules that are delivered to students in an engaging, active-learning environment. Uncovering World History makes history meaningful and memorable for students by teaching them the skills to "Do History." Contact your OUP representative for a demo or go to https://pages.oup.com/he/us/uncovering-world-history/ for more information.

- *Sources for World in the Making: Volume 1: To 1500* (**9780190849337**): Edited by the authors of *World in the Making* and designed specifically to complement the text, it includes over one hundred sources that give voice to both notable figures and everyday individuals. The Contrasting Views feature presents sources with divergent perspectives to foster comparative analysis.
- *Sources for World in the Making: Volume 2: Since 1300* (**9780190849344**): Edited by the authors of *World in the Making* and designed specifically to complement the text, it includes over one hundred sources that give voice to both notable figures and everyday individuals.

The Contrasting Views feature presents sources with divergent perspectives to foster comparative analysis.

- *Mapping the World: A Mapping and Coloring Book of World History*: This two-volume workbook includes approximately thirty-five color maps, each accompanied by a timeline, that chart global history from the Paleolithic to the present, as well as approximately fifty outline maps with exercises. An answer key is available to instructors.
- **Enhanced eBooks.** Digital versions of *World in the Making* are available at many popular distributors, including RedShelf and VitalSource. Videos, quizzes, flashcards, and other media directly embedded into the enhanced eBook increase student engagement.

Acknowledgments

It has taken a world of people with diverse perspectives and talents to craft this new edition of *World in the Making*. Our sincere thanks go to the following instructors, who helped us keep true to our vision of showing connections among the world's peoples and of highlighting their lives and livelihoods. The comments of these scholars and teachers often challenged us to rethink or justify our interpretations. Importantly for the integrity of the book, they always provided a check on accuracy down to the smallest detail of the vast history of world-making:

Editorial Reviewers of the First Edition

Kris Alexanderson, University of the Pacific

Abbe Allen, Sandhills Community College

Sara Black, Christopher Newport University

Kathy J. Callahan, Murray State University

Milton Eng, William Paterson University

Nancy Fitch, California State University

Andrei Gandila, University of Alabama in Huntsville

Steven A. Glazer, Graceland University

David Fort Godshalk, Shippensburg University

Rebecca Hayes, Northern Virginia Community College

Shawna Herzog, Washington State University

Aaron Irvin, Murray State University

Erin O'Donnell, East Stroudsburg University

Kenneth J. Orosz, Buffalo State College

Nicole Pacino, University of Alabama in Huntsville

Patrick M. Patterson, Honolulu Community College

Daniel R. Pavese, Wor-Wic Community College

Christian Peterson, Ferris State University

Nova Robinson, Seattle University

Nicholas Lee Rummell, Trident Technical College

Eric Strahorn, Florida Gulf Coast University

Bianka R. Stumpf, Central Carolina Community College

Brian Ulrich, Shippensburg University

Class Testers and Market Development Participants of the First Edition

Alem Abbay, Frostburg State University

Heather Abdelnur, Augusta University

Andreas Agocs, University of the Pacific

Kris Alexanderson, University of the Pacific

Stephen Auerbach, Georgia College

Tom Bobal, Adirondack Community College

Gayle K. Brunelle, California State University, Fullerton

Kathy Callahan, Murray State University

Aryendra Chakravartty, Stephen F. Austin State University

Celeste Chamberland, Roosevelt University–Chicago

Karen Christianson, Depaul University

Aimee Duchsherer, Minot State University

Peter Dykema, Arkansas Tech University–Russellville

Jennifer C. Edwards, Manhattan College

Robert Findlay, Solano Community College

Nancy Fitch, California State University, Fullerton

Arthur FitzGerald, San Jacinto College–North

Richard Forster, Hawaii Community College

Lucien Frary, Rider University

Tara Fueshko, William Paterson University

Jay Harrison, Hood College

Tim Hayburn, Rowan University–Glassboro

Michael Heil, University of Arkansas at Little Rock

Cecily Heisser, University of San Diego

Timothy Henderson, Auburn University at Montgomery

Gail Hook, George Mason University

Anne Huebel, Saginaw Valley State University

Kathryn Johnson, Northern Michigan University

Michael Johnson, University of Hawaii–Manoa

Thomas Jordan, Champlain College

David Longenbach, Penn State University–Lehigh Valley

Ann Lupo, Buffalo State College

Aran MacKinnon, South Georgia College

Joseph Marcum, Southeast Kentucky Community and Technical College–Middlesboro

David McCarter, Indiana State University

Ashley Moreshead, University of Central Florida

Philip Nash, Penn State University–Shenango

Kimberly Nath, University of Delaware

Lance Nolde, California State University, Los Angeles

Kenneth Orosz, Buffalo State College

Patrick Patterson, Honolulu Community College

Gregory Peek, Pennsylvania State University

David Raley, El Paso Community College–Mission Del Paso

Scott Seagle, University of Tennessee–Chattanooga

Michael Skinner, University of Hawaii at Hilo

Cynthia Smith, Honolulu Community College

Colin Snider, University of Texas at Tyler

Catherine Stearn, Eastern Kentucky University

Sylvia Taschka, Wayne State University

David Toye, Northeast State Community College

Richard Trimble, Ocean County College

Heather Wadas, Shippensburg University

Peter Wallace, Hartwick College

Gary Wolgamott, Pittsburg State University

Kirsten Ziomek, Adelphi University

Editorial Reviewers of the Second Edition

Mary Block, Valdosta State University

Nathan Brooks, New Mexico State University

Ulrich Groetsch, University of North Alabama

Rebecca Hughes, Seattle Pacific University

Sarah Mass, Sam Houston State University

Erin O'Donnell, East Stroudsburg University

Jason Ripper, Everett Community College

Scott Seagle, University of Tennessee at Chattanooga

Matthew Gantt Stanard, Berry College

Matthew E. Stanley, Albany State University

Brian Ulrich, Shippensburg University

Heather Wadas, Shippensburg University

Can Bahadır Yüce, University of Tennessee

Our special, heartfelt thanks go to Charles Cavaliere, executive editor at Oxford University Press, without whom this new edition would not have appeared in its fresh, updated form. Charles rethought the needs of today's students and teachers and pushed for our team to do likewise. His enthusiasm has kept the book evolving and its author team on its toes, especially as he gave us the benefit of his own erudition and wide-ranging interests. We surely join Charles in thanking Danica Donovan, assistant editor, for her invaluable help on many essential tasks—from communicating and guiding the authors' tasks to many behind-the-scenes efforts that we hardly know about. We also appreciate the schedules, supervision, and layouts senior production editor Cheryl Loe juggled so efficiently and effectively. We appreciate that the book's content has been laid out in the appealing design of Michele Laseau, who succeeding in enhancing the authors' text. We thank this world of talented people for such skilled efforts and happy results.

World in the Making has a wealth of materials for students and teachers as resources for supporting the text. We urge our readers to benefit from the classroom experience and imagination that went into creating them. Sheryl Adams, marketing manager, has woven the many strands of the *World in the Making* story into a unified and compelling message. Sheryl and her team have ensured that the book is in the best shape to benefit the diverse audience of users. We are deeply grateful for all the hard thinking they have done to advocate for the success of *World in the Making* in today's global classrooms.

Among the authors' greatest world-making experience has been their long-standing and happy relationship with brilliant editor Elizabeth M. Welch. More than a decade ago Beth brought her historical, conceptual, and publishing talent to the original *Crossroads and Cultures* just as she had so successfully guided so many other world history texts before that. We are more than ever grateful to have the privilege of once again working with the learned, witty Beth, this time at Charles Cavaliere's side, on *World in the Making*.

Finally, our students' questions and concerns have shaped much of this work, and we welcome all of our readers' suggestions, queries, and criticisms. We know that readers, like our own students, excel in spotting unintended glitches and in providing much excellent food for thought. Please contact us with your thoughts and suggestions at our respective institutions.

Bonnie G. Smith
Marc Van De Mieroop
Richard von Glahn
Kris Lane

Notes on Dates and Spelling

Where necessary for clarity, we qualify dates as BCE ("Before the Common Era") or CE ("Common Era"). The abbreviation BCE refers to the same era as BC ("Before Christ"), just as CE is equivalent to AD (*anno Domini*, Latin for "in the year of the Lord"). In keeping with our aim to approach world history from a global, multicultural perspective, we chose these neutral abbreviations as appropriate to our enterprise. Because most readers will be more familiar with English than with metric measures, however, units of measure are given in the English system in the narrative, with metric and English measures provided on the maps.

We translate Chinese names and terms into English according to the *pinyin* system, while noting in parentheses proper names well established in English (e.g., Canton, Chiang Kai-shek). Transliteration of names and terms from the many other languages traced in our book follow the same contemporary scholarly conventions.

About the Authors

Bonnie G. Smith (AB Smith College, PhD University of Rochester) is Board of Governors Distinguished Professor of History Emerita, Rutgers University. She has taught world history to both undergraduate and graduate students and has been supported in her research through awards and fellowships from the Guggenheim Foundation, American Council of Learned Societies, National Humanities Center, Shelby Cullom Davis Center (Princeton), European Union, and American Philosophical Society. She has published books in world, European, and women's history, among the most recent *Modern Empires: A Reader* (Oxford University Press, 2017), and currently studies cultural hybridity.

Marc Van De Mieroop (PhD Yale University, 1983) is Professor of History at Columbia University. A specialist in the ancient history of the Middle East, he has published numerous books including *A History of Ancient Egypt*, 2nd ed. (Wiley-Blackwell, Oxford, 2021) and *A History of the Ancient Near East, ca. 3000–323 B.C.*, 3rd ed. (Wiley-Blackwell, Oxford, 2016). His next book, *Before and After Babel: Writing as Resistance in Ancient Near Eastern Empires,* is soon to appear with Oxford University Press. He has received grants from the National Endowment of the Humanities, the American Council of Learned Societies, the John Simon Guggenheim Memorial Foundation, and several European institutions. He is the recipient of Columbia University's Lenfest Distinguished Faculty Award for excellence in teaching. Marc covers the period from human origins to 500 CE (Part 1) in *World in the Making.*

Richard von Glahn (PhD Yale University, 1983) is Professor of History at UCLA. Richard is the author of numerous books and articles on Chinese economic and social history, including *Fountain of Fortune: Money and Monetary Policy in China, 1000–1700* (University of California Press, 1996), *The Sinister Way: The Divine and the Demonic in Chinese Religious Culture* (University of California Press, 2004), and most recently *The Economic History of China from Antiquity to the Nineteenth Century* (Cambridge University Press, 2016). His research has been supported by fellowships from the National Endowment for the Humanities, the American Council of Learned Societies, and the John Simon Guggenheim Memorial Foundation. Richard is also a senior editor for the Oxford Research Encyclopedia for Asian History.

Kris Lane (PhD University of Minnesota, 1996) holds the France V. Scholes Chair in Colonial Latin American History at Tulane University in New Orleans. An award-winning teacher, he is author of *Potosí: The Silver City that Changed the World* (University of California Press, 2019), *Colour of Paradise: The Emerald in the Age of Gunpowder Empires* (Yale University Press, 2010), *Pillaging the Empire: Global Piracy on the High Seas, 1500–1750* (Routledge, 2015), and *Quito 1599: City & Colony in Transition* (University of New Mexico Press, 2002). Lane has also published articles on the history of slavery, witchcraft, crime, and mining in early modern Spanish America. He is also the author of textbooks on Latin American history and Atlantic history. Lane is completing a book about the global consequences of a mid-seventeenth-century mint fraud at Potosí, a world-famous silver mining town high in the Andes Mountains of present-day Bolivia. Kris treats the period 1450 to 1750 (Part 3) in *World in the Making.*

World in the Making

PART 1

The Ancient World, from Human Origins to 500 CE

≡ Unassuming small clay objects such as this one show human beings' earliest ability to record information for the future. Dating to around 3200 BCE, this tablet from southern Mesopotamia is impressed with cuneiform signs that record the transfer of goods in the city of Uruk. Writing was one of many Uruk innovations that announced the birth of the first urban society in world history. (NYPL/Science Source)

The story we tell in this book begins around 4 million years ago, when the lines of human ancestors diverged from those of the great African apes, and our exploration of the ancient period of world history ends at about the year 500 CE. If one wrote a 400-page book that gave equal space to every century in all of world history, the period from 500 CE to today would take up only one-sixth of the final page. All previous pages would treat what we call the ancient world.

It would be hard to write such a book, however. The first 399 pages would describe peoples who left little evidence for us to study, all of it archaeological—that is, the material objects humans left behind. Archaeological remains provide much information, but they have limitations: they do not reveal what languages people spoke, their names, and many other things we may discern from written records. Only late in the ancient period, some 5,000 years ago, did some peoples invent writing, but even in cultures that developed writing, its use was restricted by social class and to a small number of people.

This was the era of origins, the period in which human populations invented all the major elements we associate with culture. The modern human species itself originated over millions of years, and our ancestor species invented basic tools, some of which—such as the needle—we still use. About 10,000 years ago, modern humans invented agriculture, which remains today the main livelihood for most of the world's people. Agriculture allowed villages and, later, cities to arise, where people with special skills had an opportunity to invent new technologies. As communities grew larger and people interacted more closely, they needed means of regulating their societies. This gave rise to such developments as laws, diplomacy, and tools for managing financial transactions, among many others.

All the writing systems we use today had their roots in these early times. Some ancient scripts, such as Egyptian hieroglyphs, died out before 500 CE. Others, such as Chinese script, have remained in use since the second millennium BCE. The alphabet invented in western Asia in the second millennium BCE had particularly widespread success, with many peoples modifying it to serve their specific needs.

Peoples of the ancient world also developed a wide variety of political structures. The overall trend was toward larger and more complex organizations, from small bands of gatherer-hunters to enormous empires. Eurasia's classical empires—so called because the revolutionary ideas that shaped these empires long outlived them and gave rise to the fundamental, or "classical," cultural traditions of Eurasia—flourished from about 500 BCE to 500 CE. Their histories inspired ideas of political domination up to modern times. We consider the ancient period to have ended at the time when many empires disappeared: the Roman in the Mediterranean, the Sasanid in the Middle East, the Gupta in India, and the Han in China.

The ancient world produced the classical eras of the literate cultures of Eurasia. Many religions and philosophies begun in this period remain influential to this day, for example, Indian Buddhism, Chinese Confucianism, and in the Mediterranean region, Greek philosophies. Likewise many works of literature from this period are still read today, including Greek and Sanskrit epics and tragedies, and the Five Classics of Chinese literature, among many others.

World history was not a uniform process, however, as people everywhere chose the lifestyles and livelihoods best suited to their environments. Sometimes that led them to abandon techniques that most others saw as advances. People in Polynesia stopped making pottery; people in Australia opted not to farm. Perhaps the primary characteristic of early world history is the sheer variety of the cultures that flourished in this period. ■

Peopling the World,

to **4000** BCE

≡ **World in the Making** Among uniquely human activities is artistic expression, which relays a message only other humans can understand. The earliest objects thought to be artworks were found in South Africa in the Blombos Cave. Between 75,000 to 72,000 years ago *Homo sapiens* left behind objects onto which they traced lines in ochre (a mixture of earth and iron residue), as well as shells and pieces of ochre that were decorated. The object shown here is an example of the latter, an about three-inch-long plaque onto which a geometric design was traced on purpose. What message the maker tried to convey remains a mystery to us.

Human Origins

↘ **FOCUS** *What physical and behavioral adaptations and innovations characterized human evolution?*

Paleolithic Food Gatherers, 2,000,000–9000 BCE

↘ **FOCUS** *In the absence of written sources, what have scholars learned about the Paleolithic economy, adaptations to the natural world, and technological innovations?*

The First Neolithic Farmers, 9000–4000 BCE

↘ **FOCUS** *In what ways does the Neolithic agricultural economy reveal humans' increasing intent and ability to manipulate the natural world to their advantage?*

COUNTERPOINT: Gatherer-Hunters by Choice: Aborigines of Australia

↘ **FOCUS** *Why did Australian Aborigines, in contrast to many of the world's other peoples, choose not to farm?*

backstory

About 4.5 billion years ago the earth came into being. For 99.9 percent of the time since then, the planet only gradually developed the conditions in which humans evolved. Humans with all the physical characteristics we have today have lived on the planet only for the past 50,000 years, a short blip in the immense period that the earth has existed. The era we can study through our ancestors' written records is much shorter still. Less than 5,000 years ago people in a few places invented writing, a skill that very gradually spread over the globe. Writing is the source that provides people's names and gives us access to their actions and thoughts.

We start this book by examining the period before people invented writing, however: at the moment when a separate species of uniquely human ancestors originated. With its appearance began world history—not the history of the world, but of humans acting in the world. Over time, people's interactions with one another and their environment caused fundamental changes not only in their physical features and behavior but also in the natural world. We are one of the most recent species on the earth, but we are also the one whose impact on the planet has been the greatest.

IN MAY 2013 A STORM SWEPT the beach at Happisburgh (pronounced HAZE-borough) on the east coast of England some 140 miles north of London, and it briefly revealed what looked like footprints. Archaeologists knew that this area had been home to human ancestors because they had found ancient stone tools there starting ten years before. So they immediately took digital photographs of the impressions from many different angles, which allowed them to produce three-dimensional models of the feet that had made them. They determined that the prints came from a group of adults and children between three feet and five feet, seven inches tall who had walked in the mud at the mouth of a river. By analyzing the pollen inside the prints, they found out that this happened between 850,000 and 950,000 years ago. The impressions at Happisburgh are the oldest footprints ever found outside Africa and indicate that a species of human ancestors lived in northern Europe 350,000 years earlier than previously thought.

The study of human evolution is filled with such chance discoveries that force a radical rewrite of history. Scholars regularly find fossils of human species unheard of before or in regions where previously they were not known to have lived. All the evidence is fragmentary and extremely fragile, and it is detected accidentally or by the close investigation of areas where fossils had been found before. It includes parts of skulls, a few bones, sets of footprints, and, increasingly, DNA sequences often obtained from bits and pieces such as a single tooth. Numerous new ideas have emerged in the reconstruction of human evolution in the past forty years, and our entire perception of the process has changed. While not that long ago a cartoon-like linear sequence from ape to man was the common image, today we recognize that multiple species existed at the same time and even in the same regions. But, only one of those ultimately survived, that is, the *Homo sapiens* species to which all modern humans belong.

The idea of human evolution is relatively recent and received scientific recognition only some 160 years ago when Charles Darwin published his book *On the Origin of Species* in 1859. Darwin argued that the species of all living beings had evolved over millions of years through adaptation to their environment. He wrote in his *Autobiography*, "Natural Selection . . . tends only to render each species as successful as possible in the battle for life with other species, in wonderfully complex and changing circumstances."[1] His ideas were much contested then and are still not accepted by everyone, but the great majority of scientists agree that humans developed over millions of years and that a number of species preceded the modern human.

The wide range of evidence we explore in this chapter reveals that each species had distinctive characteristics that resulted from adaptations to different environments. Gradually, our ancestors acquired the skills to manipulate the natural surroundings for their own purposes. After millions of years of gathering foodstuffs available in the wild, they began to control the growth of plants and animals through farming and herding. The implications of this development were profound. Farming made settled communities possible, which in turn led to the development of increasingly complex societies.

Not all humans decided to practice agriculture, however. In some parts of the world, such as Australia, they continued to forage even after they knew farming was possible. Examples like this show that natural conditions always influenced people's choices: they had to work with the resources available. To a great extent, the world's diverse geography explains the various forms of livelihood we observe in human history.

OVERVIEW QUESTIONS

The major global development in this chapter: The adaptation of early humans to their environment and their eventual domestication of plants and animals.

As you read, consider:

1. What caused humans to introduce technological and other innovations?	**2.** How did these innovations increase their ability to determine their own destinies?	**3.** How did the relationship between humans and nature change?	**4.** How have historians and other scholars reconstructed life in the earliest periods of human existence despite the lack of written records?

Human Origins

⬎ FOCUS What physical and behavioral adaptations and innovations characterized human evolution?

Over the past two centuries archaeologists have uncovered fossils all over the world that show a startling range of human ancestors. Scholars use a large number of names to refer to these species and regularly add new ones to the list when the remains of a previously unknown variant are discovered. All fossils are now subjected to DNA analysis, which has seen major advances in recent years. It enables researchers to establish genetic connections among various population groups, such as a now extinct human ancestor, the Neanderthal, and modern humans. These data have given rise to many schools of interpretation, but there is much support for the idea that Africa was the home of the modern human species. From that continent, especially the eastern part, comes the oldest and largest variety of fossils (see Map 1.1).

Human evolution was not a process of constant, steady development. It unfolded unevenly, as bursts of change interrupted long periods of overall stability. Scholars understand human evolution in the context of alterations in the natural environment due to climate change, which often triggered and shaped physical and behavioral changes in our ancestors. Although today all humans belong to the same species, in the past different species of our ancestors coexisted. The sole surviving species, *Homo sapiens*, was the one best adapted to new conditions. Thus, from the very beginning, environmental adaptation and its consequences have been at the heart of the story of human history.

Evolution of the Human Species

The great African apes are the closest relatives of the human species. Indeed, we share 98 percent of our genetic makeup with them. Around 7 million years ago, human ancestors with distinct characteristics, or **hominids**, appeared. Climate change had turned dense forests into more open woodlands and grasslands in eastern Africa and forced hominids to adapt to the new environment. This led to several changes in their physical appearance and behavior. Three main physical traits came to distinguish humans from apes and other primates: upright walking, flexible hands, and larger brains.

Apes walk on two legs only in unusual circumstances, but people do so easily. We are the only mammal whose body is fully adapted to such way of moving. Probably because of the transformation of forests into grasslands, this characteristic was the first of the three to develop, and evidence from skeletons shows this happened between 4.5 and 4.3 million years ago. That human ancestors were able to walk upright is confirmed by fossilized footprints left around 3.6 million years ago in Laetoli in northern Tanzania. They show that an adult man and a woman carrying a child in her arms used the same foot movements as modern humans, although their stride was shorter, probably because they had shorter legs. Animal footprints found nearby indicate that they walked alongside big game.

Upright walking shifted the body's weight to a vertical axis, and it reduced the space available for digestive organs, which led to a need for food that was easier to

hominid The biological family that includes modern humans and their human ancestors.

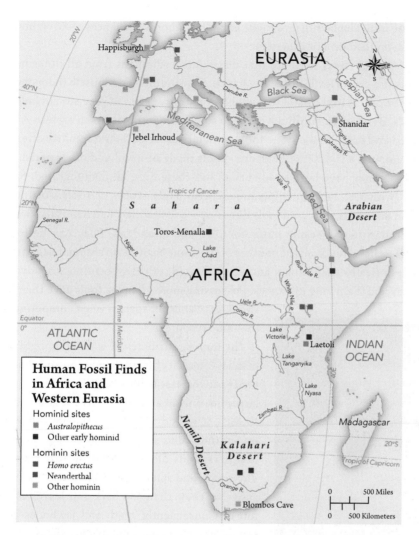

≡ **MAP 1.1   Human Fossil Finds in Africa and Western Eurasia**   Archaeologists continue to find the remains of skeletons of human ancestors, so they can determine where and when different species lived. Many of the earliest hominid remains have been found in Northeast Africa; the earliest are from 4.4 million years ago. Southwestern Eurasia has also produced many hominid finds, from 1 million to 30,000 years ago. Isolated finds complicate our reconstruction of the history of human evolution, such as the single find in Toros-Menalla in central Africa, dating to 7 million years ago.

digest and more nutritious. Instead of eating hard plant materials, human ancestors now ate fruits and nuts. Moreover, the upright posture freed the hands for uses other than walking, such as carrying food, stones, and children. Thus, upright walking created conditions favorable to the further evolution of human hands because individuals with more agile hands had improved chances of surviving and passing on their genetic inheritance.

Another physical attribute that distinguishes humans from all other mammals is the great flexibility of the hands. Our thumb has a muscle independent from the others in the hand that enables great strength and precision in holding objects. By about 3.3 million years ago some human ancestors in eastern Africa created and used simple stone tools, which because of their durability offer the archaeologist a rich set of evidence. Tools made of wood and other perishable materials may have been used earlier, but these have all disintegrated. Some other primates, such as chimpanzees, also apply stones as tools, so finding human ancestors who used tools does not prove that they had hands like we do. But human tools became more complex and abundant. They can be found much farther away from the sources of the stone than those chimpanzees make, which indicates that human ancestors thought of their usefulness in advance and carried them long distances. Possessing more complex tools gave them advantages over other species when competing for the same resources.

The human attributes of walking upright and manual versatility both depended on and contributed to an increase in brain size. The brain became larger not only in absolute terms but also relative to the entire body. To accommodate the larger organ, the skull's shape had to change, and the new grasslands diet helped make that possible. The fruits and nuts human ancestors ate were easier to chew than the bark and leaves of the forest. Consequently, teeth and jawbones grew smaller, which changed the shape of the skull. The very structure of the brain changed, too, as new areas developed, such as the one that controls speech and language. Thus, changes in human brains, like other key human characteristics, evolved out of a complex set of environmental pressures and corresponding adaptations.

Larger brains gave human ancestors the intelligence to interact with more individuals than chimpanzees, for instance, do. Bigger groups

≡ **Fossilized Footprints** In 1978, the archaeological team led by Mary Leakey discovered these revealing sets of footprints at Laetoli in northern Tanzania. Made by a man and a woman carrying a child who walked through volcanic ash some 3.6 million years ago, they were preserved after the ash solidified. They are the earliest evidence of human ancestors walking upright with the same stride we use today. (John Reader/ScienceSource)

provided safety, which was necessary as humans were relatively small, weak, and slow, and thus easy targets for predators. Cooperation offered their only defense. For example, they coordinated the throwing of rocks, a uniquely human and highly efficient skill. The need to cooperate made better communication essential, and humans took another step forward when they developed speech—the capacity to speak and to understand what others say. Speech gave them the ability to work more effectively in groups and to pass on the benefits of experience to their offspring. It is difficult to determine when this capacity appeared on the basis of skeleton remains, but observable changes in the larynx suggest around 300,000 years ago.

Scholars have developed detailed charts of the various species they have recognized in human evolution placed on a time frame that stretches back 7 million years ago. What has become obvious is that every new find can impel a revision about what species existed when and where. Some finds stand out because they caused substantial revisions and have become famous among the general public. One such find is Lucy, whose skeleton archaeologists discovered in 1974 in what is now northern Ethiopia. Lucy lived 3.2 million years ago and died when she was nineteen to twenty-one years old. She was about four feet tall and weighed no more than sixty pounds. She could walk upright because her foot had the arch-like structure of the modern human. She was muscular, and her long arms indicate that Lucy still climbed trees. Her hands were humanlike, and her brain was about the size of a chimpanzee's. Her teeth resembled those of modern humans, and the wear on them suggested that she ate mostly fruits, berries, and roots.

Lucy and the individuals who left footprints at Laetoli belonged to one species of human ancestors classified as *Australopithecus* (aw-strah-loh-PITH-uh-kihs), a term that literally means "southern ape." The *Australopithecus* lived in eastern Africa about 3.7 to 3 million years ago and may be the ancestor to all later hominids. Evolution continued with various branches developing. Then around 1.9 million years ago, a species emerged that had modern humanlike body proportions, that is, long legs and short arms when compared to the size of the torso. These proportions indicate that they lived on the ground, could no longer easily climb trees, and were able to walk and possibly run long distances. Scholars use the term *Homo erectus* ("upright person") to refer to them.

They were the first human ancestors who moved out of Africa, and they reached Southeast Asia 1.8 million years ago. Remains of their campsites show that they collaborated to kill large animals and they were the first to make fires. In fact, the use of fire made migrating out of Africa possible because it allowed human ancestors to survive in colder climates, seeking shelter in caves. Fire also enabled them to cook, so they could soften otherwise inedible plants and more easily remove the meat from bones. In this way, the invention of cooking meant that the frontal teeth could grow even smaller. *Homo erectus* existed in Asia until perhaps 30,000 years ago. At the same time that they colonized Asia, a related branch of human ancestors moved into Europe. If the Happisburgh footprints mentioned at the start of this chapter are as old as scholars believe, members of this group of human ancestors reached this far north 350,000 years earlier than previously thought. To survive the cold, they would have had to wear clothing.

Starting some 400,000 years ago a species very close to the modern human, the **Neanderthals**, lived all over Europe and southwestern to central Asia. They may have been descendants of the species that walked in Happisburgh. No remains of Neanderthals have been found in Africa or East Asia. They had long, large faces that projected sharply forward, and they had bigger front teeth than modern humans, which allowed them to consume the large amounts of meat they hunted using sharp wooden spears. Their brains were slightly larger than those of modern humans, and their bones show that they were shorter and stockier. They used sophisticated tools and fire, lived in shelters, and made and wore clothing. Occasionally they made symbolic or ornamental objects, and they buried their dead in special places, perhaps now and then giving them offerings.

While Neanderthals lived outside Africa, in Africa the earliest forms of the final species of human evolution developed around 300,000 years ago: ***Homo sapiens*** ("consciously thinking person"). The earliest evidence known today is a skull excavated at Jebel Irhoud in modern Morocco in 1961 and redated to about 300,000 years ago in 2017. This species continued to evolve slowly until it attained the physical characteristics humans have today, perhaps as recently as 50,000 years ago. *Homo sapiens* is especially distinct from other hominids in the structure of the brain. While their brains were not larger than those of the Neanderthals, they were more sophisticated. This allowed them to improve skills such as toolmaking and communication, giving the species a marked advantage over others.

Homo sapiens may have used these abilities to monopolize available resources. For millions of years, various hominid species had coexisted, and *Homo sapiens* and Neanderthals did so for some 30,000 to 50,000 years in western Asia as well, seemingly with little contact and without conflict. But about 45,000 years ago, *Homo sapiens* moved into Europe and started to use the same environments as the Neanderthals. The two species were similar, and there is genetic evidence that they interbred, although the research on this is very recent and controversial.

Neanderthal
A hominid species that inhabited Europe and southwestern to central Asia from 400,000 to 30,000 years ago.

Homo sapiens The species of hominids to which modern humans belong; "*sapiens*" refers to the ability to think.

In 2010, DNA analysis of remains found in Siberia revealed the existence of an extinct human species, the Denisovan, which was close to the Neanderthal and whose DNA is present in modern humans. These Denisovans may have lived all over Asia and interacted with *Homo sapiens*. They and the Neanderthals competed for the same resources with *Homo sapiens*, who gained the upper hand—not necessarily because they killed off the Neanderthals and the Denisovans, but perhaps because they adapted better to a change in the climate. It is possible that a cold spell reduced the food supply to such an extent that Neanderthals and Denisovans were unable to survive with the technologies available to them while *Homo sapiens* managed to gather and hunt enough.

In any case, by 30,000 years ago, *Homo sapiens* became the sole human species on earth. It is remarkable that no other species still exists, unlike all other living species on earth, which have many variants. Also remarkable is that the genetic makeup of all human beings is very similar, especially of those outside sub-Saharan Africa. Scholars now estimate that between 50,000 and 20,000 years ago there were no more than 4,000 to 10,000 female *Homo sapiens* of reproductive age alive at one time in the groups that had left the African continent. Most of the world's population today descends from this small number of women. It is important to keep in mind that the human species could easily have become extinct.

Out of Africa

Various human ancestors migrated out of Africa at different times—*Homo erectus* some 1 million years ago, the ancestors of the Neanderthal some 500,000 years ago, and finally *Homo sapiens* about 100,000 years ago. Climate change, a desire to follow a particular type of prey, and social pressures probably triggered these movements. Even if a group moves only some twenty to thirty miles a year, this soon adds up to hundreds, then thousands of miles after a few generations. Scholars reconstruct these migrations when finding fossils with the same DNA in various parts of the world, and new discoveries regularly upset accepted theories. Thus controversies and disagreements abound over when migrations happened and what routes they took.

There is no doubt that the migration of *Homo sapiens* was a remarkable success, spreading to all corners of the earth, even into the most inhospitable environments such as polar regions and desert fringes. The movement of early peoples from Africa into Eurasia was relatively easy, but to colonize the distant regions of the Americas, Australia, and other islands, humans had to take advantage of changes in the physical environment—as they did with the advent of the ice ages.

Out of Africa

■	Area of early hominid habitation, c. 5,000,000 to 1,000,000 years ago
■	Additional area of modern *Homo sapiens* habitation, c. 7000 years ago
■	Hominid site, c. 7,000,000–4,400,000 years ago
■	Early human species site, c. 1,600,000–50,000 years ago
■	*Homo sapiens* site, c. 50,000–8000 years ago
→	Migration of *Homo erectus*, c. 1,000,000–500,000 years ago
→	Migration of *Homo sapiens*, c. 100,000–50,000 years ago
■	Ice sheets, c. 16,000 years ago

≡ **MAP 1.2   Out of Africa** Several species of human ancestors migrated out of Africa at different times, ultimately settling in almost every part of the globe by 5000 BCE, about 7,000 years ago. Their ability to spread depended in part on ecological conditions such as the expansion of the Arctic ice cap and low sea levels, but it also involved such technological achievements as the construction of boats to reach islands. The first species to migrate were the ancestors of *Homo erectus* some 1 million years ago; the last was *Homo sapiens*, about 100,000 years ago.

PACIFIC
OCEAN

*Zhoukoudian
Cave*

E U R A S I A

AUSTRALIA

INDIAN
OCEAN

C A

Laetoli

Blombos Cave

In climatic terms, the earth's last 700,000 years saw a series of dramatic fluctuations between warm and cold conditions. During the ice ages the absorption of water into massive glaciers at the polar caps led to a drastic drop in the sea level. As ocean waters receded into the ice sheets, landmasses previously separated by water became connected. The last ice age started 110,000 years ago and lasted almost 100,000 years. At its height the sea level was 300 feet lower than it is today. *Homo sapiens* seems to have moved out of Africa into western Asia around 100,000 years ago and then moved farther east, reaching Southeast Asia perhaps some 63,000 years ago. After learning how to build boats to cross the sea, they reached Australia and its surrounding islands around 40,000 years ago. By 30,000 years ago they had settled all over the Eurasian continent (see Map 1.2).

No convincing evidence exists that any hominid species other than fully developed *Homo sapiens* entered the Americas. The earliest Americans had fire, stone tools, and the means to obtain clothing, food, and shelter. They most likely arrived 15,000 years ago when the last ice age lowered sea levels to produce a land bridge between Northeast Asia and North America. Possibly others migrated by boat to the Americas from other parts of Asia. Kennewick Man, so called from the site in the state of Washington where he was discovered in 1996, anatomically seems unlike other early humans of the continent, although he appears to have lived some 8,000 years ago. His physical characteristics resemble those of inhabitants of Southeast Asia rather than of Northeast Asia. Was he a descendant of another migration or not? The question remains unanswered.

The remarkable adaptability of *Homo sapiens* allowed the species to deal with differences in heat, sunlight, and other climatic and geographical conditions. One adaptation was a change in skin color. The pigment melanin, present in relatively high concentration in dark skin, protects against the ultraviolet in sunlight. This protection is essential in sun-drenched regions but not in the north, where it can even be counterproductive because it prevents absorption of vitamin D. Thus, through adaptation, inhabitants of most northern regions developed lighter skin to avoid vitamin deficiency.

Such distinctions are minor, however, when compared with the biological similarities that humans all over the globe share. The human genetic makeup is much more uniform than that of other species: two chimpanzees living in proximity to one another have ten times as much variability in their DNA as two humans living on different continents.

A second vehicle for humans' adaptation to new environments is change in the languages they speak. The work of linguists—specialists in the study of language—suggests that on average, people who originally spoke the same language would preserve only 85 percent of the common features after living in separate communities for a thousand years. Linguistic variety develops in part because populations focus on different activities. Hunters, fishermen, farmers, and herders develop vocabularies to suit their circumstances. Any aspect of a language—including pronunciation, grammar, and vocabulary—can change. Grammatical forms are abandoned or newly created; words change their meanings, disappear, or are invented.

Word meanings can differ even among speakers of the same language. For example, *corn* in the United States refers to maize, whereas in England the word refers to wheat. People will drop the names of animals and plants from their language if these species do not appear in their environment. They borrow terms from other languages to indicate new tools or foods. The diversity of languages is one of the main features that distinguish human populations, and it shows how people adjust habits to their local situations. It also demonstrates that evolution is an ongoing process. Just as human language continues to develop in response to changing circumstances, humans themselves continue to evolve in response to new environmental conditions, whether those new conditions are the result of natural processes or of the impact of humans on their environment.

Paleolithic Food Gatherers 2,000,000–9000 BCE

➘ **FOCUS** In the absence of written sources, what have scholars learned about the Paleolithic economy, adaptations to the natural world, and technological innovations?

To study the distant human past, scholars rely on archaeological remains, primarily tools made of hard stones such as flint and obsidian that leave a sharp edge when chipped. Items made of other materials, such as bone and wood, survive much less often. Scholars commonly divide the period that used stone as the main material for tools into the **Paleolithic** ("Old Stone Age") and the **Neolithic** ("New Stone Age"). Based on the type of tools people used, these terms indicate critical differences in people's livelihoods as well: in the early period they hunted and gathered their food; in the later period they farmed. The transition from one livelihood to the other was not simultaneous worldwide. On the contrary, agriculture was invented in different parts of the world at different times, and it often took many millennia for the technology to spread from these regions to others. In some parts of the world people did not farm until the modern period.

Paleolithic Literally, "Old Stone Age"; the period when modern humans and their ancestors used stone tools and lived as foragers.

Neolithic Literally, "New Stone Age"; the period when humans developed a special set of stone tools to harvest cultivated plants.

For close to 2 million years during the Paleolithic, our predecessors collected food from their environments. Seasonal cycles determined what was available and when. Only in the recent past, starting 11,000 years ago, did people in some parts of the world take a next step in manipulating the environment by controlling food supplies through farming.

The Gatherer-Hunter Economy

All living things need food to survive, and they use resources in their natural surroundings to secure it. Humans are the most versatile of all living primates in this respect. If necessary, they are willing to consume anything with nutritional value. This flexibility allowed humans to adapt to new environments as they migrated all over the globe.

A major breakthrough in the quest for food occurred around 2 million years ago with the use of stone tools, which gave human ancestors enormous advantages. They could pierce animal skins, cut meat from bones, and crush bones for marrow, increasing the availability of highly nutritious food. As we have seen, eating such foods allowed greater brain expansion, which in turn facilitated toolmaking abilities.

At first, Paleolithic people did little to modify the stones they employed as tools. They chipped off flakes that had very sharp edges, allowing them to cut, and they used the cores as hammers to crush bones. Starting around 1.65 million years ago, however, they began to shape cores much more extensively, flaking off pieces symmetrically on both sides to create sharp hand axes that resembled large teardrops. Hand axes were extremely popular and were an important part of the human tool arsenal until around 250,000 years ago. Human ancestors who migrated from Africa into Eurasia took the technology with them.

Homo sapiens expanded toolmaking dramatically, creating a wide variety of stone tools that were much sharper and easier to handle. They also fashioned tools from previously neglected materials, working antlers, bones, and ivory into various implements and inventing the needle, which made sewing possible. With these tools, they hunted, cut meat off bones, scraped skins, shaped wood, and turned dried tendons into strings. They used their creations to prepare food and to make clothing, shelter, and weapons. In short, increasingly sophisticated tools expanded their ability to manipulate the environment, which made possible the emergence of human society and culture.

For the entire Paleolithic era, humans foraged for their food—that is, they gathered and hunted edible resources in their surroundings. The common idea that early humans were great hunters is a myth. Indeed, until *Homo sapiens*, they probably obtained meat only by competing with other scavengers for the flesh of dead animals. *Homo sapiens* dared to attack large animals only after they had developed a growing arsenal of tools—including sharp spears, bows, and arrows with stone tips—and could communicate through language.

Once early hominids had learned how to build and maintain fires some 1.5 million years ago, they cooked meat, making it much easier to chew. Much of their diet, however, consisted of other natural resources, including seeds, nuts, fruits, roots, small animals, fish, and seafood, depending on the area. They gathered food daily, but such

≡ **Evolving Stone Tools** The development of tools, especially those of stone, which have survived much better than others, tells archaeologists about important changes in the technological abilities of human ancestors and early humans. The Oldowan tool shown here (left), used between 2.5 and 1.5 million years ago, was only slightly altered from the original rock in the effort to sharpen it. In contrast, the Acheulian ax (right), used between 1.65 million and 100,000 years ago, was made by carefully flaking off pieces all over the original stone to turn it into a versatile hand tool. (© Werner Forman Archive/British Institute of History and Archeology, Dar-es-Salam/HIP/Art Resource, NY)

work was not necessarily arduous, and Paleolithic gatherer-hunters probably had much more free time than many people today. Observations of modern gatherer-hunters also show that women collect most foods, so world historians increasingly place woman, the gatherer, not man, the hunter, at the center of the Paleolithic economy.

Life in Paleolithic Communities

Paleolithic gatherer-hunters typically lived in groups of fifteen to forty adult males, females, and children. Larger groups would have needed more resources than the surroundings could provide. Males probably supplemented gathered resources by providing food for the mothers of their children, strengthening emotional attachments and encouraging long-term relationships. Close connections developed not only between sexual mates but also between parents and children. This is because much maturation takes place outside the womb and children need to be nurtured and protected for many years. These various aspects of Paleolithic life led to close-knit communities that stayed together for long periods.

Paleolithic communities were egalitarian in character, largely because constant migration prevented individuals from accumulating much wealth. Because groups were small, conflicts were relatively easy to settle, and all adults, including women, could participate in most activities. When a group became too large for the region to support it, bands separated and found new places to live. Neighboring bands must have collaborated to a degree—determining borders, for example—and exchanged reproductive partners to maintain social ties.

Early humans needed shelter, of course, especially when they moved into cold regions. At first they took advantage of natural features such as caves and overhanging rocks, often visiting them year after year for protection from the elements. Members of *Homo erectus* used the Zhoukoudian (choo-koot-jehn) cave in northern China, for example, from 600,000 to 230,000 years ago. They left behind archaeological deposits 120 feet deep, which included some 100,000 artifacts. Living in caves was made possible by the ability of the *Homo erectus* to control fire, a skill already acquired 1.8 million years ago. Fire had many advantages: it made it possible to see in the dark and provided warmth and protection against animals. It also encouraged social interaction as people gathered around the fire.

≡ **Mammoth Bone Dwelling** Human ingenuity in exploiting local resources is clear from circular huts built from the tusks, leg bones, and jaw bones of mammoths (extinct elephants) in Eastern Europe. This example from Mezhirich in Ukraine dates to about 17,000 years ago, and it would have taken fifteen workers some ten days to build it. Covered with hides, it allowed people to live outside caves in a cold climate.

Paleolithic peoples often improved natural shelters by building screens made of branches at the entrances of caves. They could also construct tent-like temporary shelters. When wood was scarce, they built shelters by digging pits and constructing domes with mammoth bones or tusks, over which they draped animal skins. The earliest free-standing man-made shelters were round or oval with central hearths to keep inhabitants warm.

The emotional ties that held communities together also fostered a respect for the dead. Starting 100,000 years ago, Neanderthals began to bury their dead, at first in simple shallow pits in caves but with increasingly elaborate graves over time. Careful excavations at Shanidar Cave in the mountains of modern Iraq uncovered a Neanderthal skeleton surrounded by large amounts of flower pollen. The archaeologists who found him believe that survivors covered the buried person with garlands of flowers. Other burials contain gifts of small objects such as pendants and beads, suggesting that people believed in the survival of some aspect of the individual after death. The evolution of burial rites also suggests a growing sense of the connections between generations. A community was more than its current members; it also included those who had come before, as well as the generations to come.

Like burial rites, Paleolithic art gives us a glimpse of early human values and beliefs. Only humans create decorative objects. When did art first appear, where, and why? In the past twenty years archaeological research at the Blombos Cave in modern South Africa has upset previously held views that the first artwork appeared in Europe around 40,000 years ago. The excavations there revealed many layers dating to about 75,000 to 72,000 years ago with objects that were intentionally decorated. They include a small stone flake, less than two inches long, onto which cross-hatchings were drawn with ochre and two pieces of ochre with lines traced in them. These are the oldest purposefully decorated objects ever found. Was the design merely ornamental, or did the *Homo sapiens* who carved them want to record something? Such questions continue to excite debate. Especially after 40,000 years ago, humans started to embellish objects and shape them to represent some of the living creatures that surrounded them. Typically, the first portable art objects were modified natural items onto which people scratched geometric motifs. Later they shaped stones and bones to resemble living beings. Around 25,000 years ago, people all over western Eurasia sculpted small figurines of women with greatly exaggerated breasts and hips. Although speculation is rife about the meaning of these figurines, their focus on female sexuality suggests that the people who owned them thought they would improve fertility (see Seeing the Past: Paleolithic Statuettes of Women).

Between 35,000 and 11,000 years ago, people also painted elaborate scenes on walls and ceilings of caves. Archaeologists have found remains of portable art objects all over the modern European continent, but for unknown reasons, cave paintings appear almost exclusively in southern France and northern Spain. Found in nearly 250 caves, sometimes miles from the entrance, these paintings are the most dramatic example yet discovered of Paleolithic art. The artists worked by the light of lamps burning animal fat, and they even built scaffolding to reach the ceiling. The images range from small handprints to life-size representations of

SEEING THE PAST

Paleolithic Statuettes of Women

Paleolithic peoples of western Eurasia produced carved figurines of women for thousands of years, most abundantly between 26,000 and 23,000 years ago. They are found from Spain to central Russia and are made from materials such as mammoth ivory and soft stones. Among them is what is called the Venus of Willendorf. Discovered in the late nineteenth century CE, it is nine and three-eighths inches tall and made from limestone. The representation focuses on the woman's hips, breasts, and vulva. Other parts of the body, such as arms and legs, are very sketchily fashioned, and the figure has no face at all.

Assessments of these figurines may say more about the interpreter than about the ancient people who made them. To call this statue a "Venus" after the Roman goddess of love connects it to sexuality and religion, and originally most scholars thought these statuettes were magical objects connected to fertility and childbirth. Recent interpretations are more varied. Some think the statues represent women in different stages of life, not just when pregnant; others stress a role in social negotiations or think pregnant women carved these statuettes to communicate their experiences. Unfortunately, the early archaeologists who found the statuettes did not record what other objects lay nearby and whether there were architectural remains. Such information could have helped explain the function of these figurines.

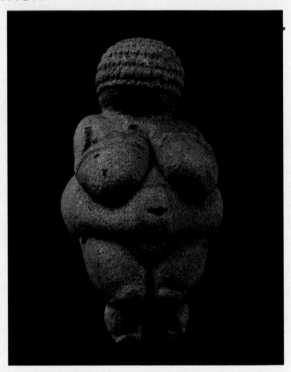

Venus of Willendorf

Examining the Evidence

1. Why is the interpretation of these figurines so difficult?

2. How would better archaeological observation have helped in understanding the purpose of these female figurines?

animals, such as horses and bison. Sometimes they sculpted three-dimensional images of animals in clay against the walls. The focus on animal images suggests the central importance of hunting to life in Paleolithic Europe. The paintings reveal the emergence of a new dimension in human communication. Artwork and the meanings it embodies can survive long after its creator has perished, allowing the artist to connect with future generations. Thus art, like religion, contributed to the increasing sophistication and cohesion of human communities.

≡ **Paleolithic Cave Art from Lascaux** In the later Paleolithic, inhabitants of southern France and northern Spain decorated numerous caves with vivid wall paintings, mostly depicting animals that lived in the area. Caves in Lascaux, France, decorated some 15,000 years ago, display one of the most elaborate examples of this art.

The First Neolithic Farmers 9000–4000 BCE

↘ **FOCUS** In what ways does the Neolithic agricultural economy reveal humans' increasing intent and ability to manipulate the natural world to their advantage?

The invention of agriculture was one of the most important technological developments in human history. Daily life as we know it today depends on agriculture and the domestication of animals. Yet for most of their existence, human beings obtained their food by collecting what was naturally available. Even today a few populations have not turned to agriculture for their survival, and in many regions some people remained foragers while others farmed.

Agriculture places humans in control of the growth cycle and makes them responsible for the domestication of plants and animals. Those who plant must sow seeds at the right moment, protect plants during growth, harvest them on time, safely store the harvest, and save enough seed for the next season. Those who raise animals must protect them against predators and provide fodder. These techniques developed independently in various areas of the world between 10,000 and 1000 BCE and then spread from these core areas to almost all other parts of the globe (see Map 1.3).

The shift to a fully agricultural livelihood began the period scholars call the Neolithic. The shape of stone tools most clearly shows the transition to the Neolithic. Producers elaborately shaped stone flakes to turn them into sharp harvesting tools. Many other technological innovations occurred as well, and the equipment of Neolithic farmers was very different from that of earlier foragers. The processes behind the invention of agriculture are best understood by studying evidence from Southwest Asia, where farming probably originated first, between 10,000 and 9000 BCE.

The Origins of Agriculture

Out of thousands of plant species that humans potentially could have domesticated, humans selected very few to become the main staples of their diet. The skills to cultivate these plants developed separately in various parts of the world and at different times. Today many scholars share the view that people developed farming independently in seven regions: Southwest Asia, China, New Guinea, sub-Saharan Africa, Mesoamerica, the Andes, and eastern North America (see Table 1.1). In each area, people learned to control the growth of local crops, and the technology they developed quickly spread to neighboring areas. In most places where people learned to control plant growth, they also began to domesticate selected local animals. However, this was not always the case, so most scholars of the rise of agriculture focus primarily on the interactions between humans and plants.

The advent of farming involved a long-term change in interactions between humans and naturally available resources, a change so gradual that people at the time probably barely noticed it. In Southwest Asia, the **Fertile Crescent** sweeps northward along the eastern Mediterranean coast into present-day southern Turkey and winds south again along the border between modern Iraq and Iran. Around 10,000 BCE it was covered with rich fields of wild wheat and barley and inhabited by wild sheep, goats, pigs, and cattle. It is these resources that humans first learned to cultivate. We have to keep in mind that the rise of agriculture was a very slow and gradual process that took thousands of years. During it humans changed their relationship with the natural environment, not only in practical terms but also intellectually (see Seeing the Past: A Stone Age Sanctuary?).

Wild wheat and barley are difficult to gather and consume because of their natural characteristics, such as thick husks. Yet humans did collect their seeds, probably because other foods were insufficient. By doing so, they became familiar with the

Fertile Crescent
The region of Southwest Asia with rich natural resources arching along the Mediterranean coast and modern southern Turkey and eastern Iraq.

Table 1.1 The Rise of Agriculture

Region	Main Plant Crops	Approximate Dates
Southwest Asia	Wheat, barley	10,000–9000 BCE
China	Rice, millet	8000–6000 BCE
New Guinea	Taro, yams, banana	7000–4000 BCE
Sub-Saharan Africa	Sorghum	4000–3000 BCE
Mesoamerica	Maize, beans, squash	4000–3000 BCE
Andes	Potato, manioc	3000–2000 BCE
Eastern North America	Squash	2000–1000 BCE

growth patterns of the plants—and they inadvertently changed the plants' characteristics to allow easier harvests. They favored species with tougher stalks (which could be more easily harvested and would remain upright when harvesters walked through the fields) and thinner husks (allowing easier preparation of food), and over many years these varieties became the only ones remaining in the area. Thus, even before deliberate farming began, humans exerted evolutionary pressure on the natural world, changing the environment and their own societies in the process.

At the same time, humans' relationships with certain animals changed. Whereas hunters continued to pursue deer and gazelles, early farmers nurtured and protected sheep, goats, pigs, and cattle. Neolithic peoples probably recognized animals' breeding patterns and understood that they required fewer males than females. Farmers selectively slaughtered young males for meat and kept females for reproduction and for milk. Like domesticated plants, domesticated animals changed in ways that better suited them to human needs. The protected animals generally became smaller and therefore easier to work with.

Further, as Neolithic peoples took their domesticated animals into regions where they did not live in the wild, the animals had to adjust to the new environments. Animals were also a convenient way to store calories; farmers could feed them extra plants that would otherwise be discarded, and in times of need slaughter them for their meat. They had many other practical uses, too. Sheep wool and goat hair were used to make

The Fertile Crescent, c. 7000–6000 BCE

Fertile Crescent   ■ Neolithic settlement

≡ **The Fertile Crescent, c. 7000–6000 BCE**

≡ **MAP 1.3** **The Origins of Agriculture** In several places across the globe early humans started to cultivate plants and herd animals, selecting from the locally available species. Most scholars agree that people invented agriculture independently in at least seven distinct regions at different times between about 9000 and 1000 BCE. The crops listed here became the main staples of the local diets.

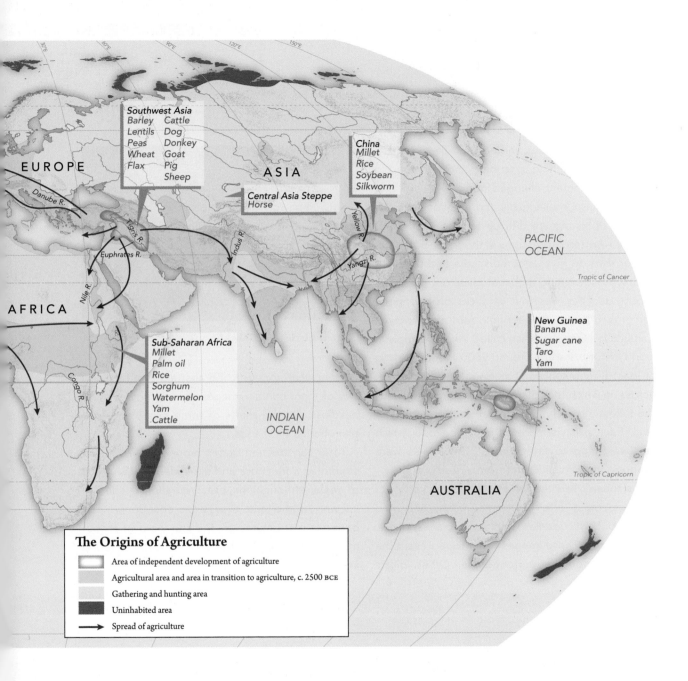

Southwest Asia
Barley	Cattle
Lentils	Dog
Peas	Donkey
Wheat	Goat
Flax	Pig
	Sheep

China
Millet
Rice
Soybean
Silkworm

Central Asia Steppe
Horse

New Guinea
Banana
Sugar cane
Taro
Yam

Sub-Saharan Africa
Millet
Palm oil
Rice
Sorghum
Watermelon
Yam
Cattle

EUROPE

ASIA

AFRICA

PACIFIC OCEAN

Tropic of Cancer

INDIAN OCEAN

AUSTRALIA

Tropic of Capricorn

Danube R.
Tigris R.
Euphrates R.
Nile R.
Congo R.
Indus R.
Yangzi R.
Yellow R.

The Origins of Agriculture

- Area of independent development of agriculture
- Agricultural area and area in transition to agriculture, c. 2500 BCE
- Gathering and hunting area
- Uninhabited area
- → Spread of agriculture

SEEING THE PAST

A Stone Age Sanctuary?

When human societies shifted their lifestyle from gathering and hunting to farming, their relationship to the environment changed not only in practical terms but also intellectually and emotionally. Such aspects of history are difficult to study in the absence of written expressions of thoughts, but material remains do give us some access to them. One of the most exciting archaeological discoveries in recent decades was that of a complex of stone carvings in the southeast of modern-day Turkey at a site called Göbekli, often called the first temple in world history. Starting around 9600 BCE people dug at least fifteen sunken chambers up to thirty feet across, in which they placed T-shaped stone pillars, the tallest of which are eighteen feet, in a circle or oval. Each pillar is made of a single stone, which can weigh up to fifteen tons. The stones were dragged for some 300 feet from a nearby quarry.

On these pillars are carved images of a variety of animals, most often serpents, foxes, and wild boars, but also gazelles, wild asses, cranes, ducks, and vultures. These images seem to represent the wild fauna of the surroundings. Other pillars

A Stone Circle from Göbekli

contain what appear to be abstract symbols, and two of them contain images of men, one of them headless. On the shafts of some pillars appear a pair of arms and hands.

After construction began around 9600 BCE, the structures were in use and expanded for hundreds of years, although the exact duration is still unknown. At the end they were abandoned and buried. All structures on the site were of monumental nature, and archaeologists have not found any evidence of dwellings.

textiles, milk products were an excellent source of protein, and animal skins, bones, horns, hoofs, and sinews could be turned into a large array of utensils and other items.

Although scholars have determined that these changes took place, they are less certain about why humans started to farm. Many suggest that the end of the last ice age around 10,000 BCE brought drier conditions to Southwest Asia, drastically reducing wild food supplies. According to this theory, humans tried to

How does one interpret these pillars and the function of the entire site? Their T-shape and the images of arms and hands suggest that the pillars were schematic representations of human beings. If this was the case, it is remarkable that there is no indication of the sex of the humans represented in contrast to the prominence of sexual organs on statuettes like the Venus of Willendorf. The carvings on the stones seem to stress the relationship with the animals in the natural environment. The excavated remains of animal bones show, however, that these were not the animals eaten at the site, so these are not representations of game the people wanted to hunt. Were the images intended to protect people from dangerous animals such as snakes? Some scholars interpret the abstract symbols as precursors of writing—what they would indicate is a mere guess, however.

The function of the entire site must have been symbolic, yet its exact nature is unclear. Some scholars have suggested astronomical purposes; others that this was a location where gatherer-hunters from the area came together to feast; yet others that this was a place for people to communicate with divine beings. To the people who built and visited it, the site was clearly very important as they spent much time and effort to construct the circles and buried them carefully when they no longer wanted to use them. One feature that shows how the relationship of human beings with the natural environment was changing in this period is the fact that they constructed the monuments on purpose. Whereas previously people had chosen natural settings, such as the Lascaux caves, for purposes that were not purely practical, they now manipulated the countryside to establish a special site on a location that they chose.

Examining the Evidence

1. Why is it so hard for us today to interpret the meaning of a place like Göbekli?

2. How does the site fit within the context of changes in human interactions with the natural environment?

3. How much can you speculate about the purpose of the Göbekli site?

compensate for losses by moving plants to land where the plants did not reproduce naturally. Other scholars propose that human behavioral changes encouraged the shift to farming. A desire to stay longer in one place may have pushed early peoples to more closely observe the growth cycles of the plants and animals around them. They may have learned the benefits of storing seeds and planting them for future harvests. Meanwhile, the permanence of their new way of life may have led to larger communities that could survive only if they grew food.

The archaeological record of Southwest Asia shows these processes at work in the period from 10,000 to 9000 BCE. The inhabitants increasingly left evidence of plant harvesting and processing in the form of flint and obsidian blades, pestles, mortars, and grinders. Although people still gathered and hunted extensively, by 9000 BCE some lived in fully sedentary communities, where they relied on a combination of foraged and cultivated food.

Once Neolithic people developed agriculture, the technology spread rapidly into regions surrounding the Fertile Crescent, introducing crops and animals that had not existed in the wild. In the north and west, farming spread into the regions that are today Turkey and Europe. By 4000 to 3000 BCE the technology had reached Britain and Scandinavia. Farmers also moved into regions of Southwest Asia where rainfall was insufficient for farming. Their invention of irrigation agriculture made settlement possible even in the most arid zones (see Chapter 2).

Not all populations of the world learned farming techniques from Southwest Asia. In China, people developed the skills independently several millennia later, focusing on locally available plants. In the middle part of the Yangzi (YANG-zuh) River Valley, where much water is available, local residents at first collected wild rice, but in the period from 8000 to 3000 BCE they gradually used more cultivated rice, and by the end of that period they lived in villages, fully depending on their crops.

Agricultural life was more difficult than that of the gatherer-hunter. Early farmers had to work many more hours, especially in certain seasons, and were more vulnerable to epidemic diseases because they lived together more closely. But farming had advantages. Cultivated crops produced much larger yields than wild plants, so farmers could live in larger communities than foragers. The increased permanence of agricultural communities led to expanded social interactions and a better survival rate for newborn babies. Whatever the reasons for the turn to agriculture, this livelihood became dominant over most of the world in the millennia after it developed.

Life in Neolithic Communities

As people began living year-round in the same location, their dwellings changed. The earliest houses, imitating the temporary shelters of migratory foragers, were round or oval. As agricultural communities spread over the world, however, the layout of houses evolved into a rectangular form, a layout that

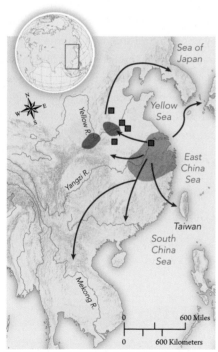

Early Agriculture in China, c. 6000–5000 BCE

▮ Area of early millet cultivation
▮ Area of early rice cultivation
→ Spread of rice cultivation
■ Settlement site, 6000–5000 BCE

≡ **Early Agriculture in China, c. 6000–5000 BCE**

remains dominant in residential structures to the present day. This innovation allowed builders to create rooms with specialized functions, such as kitchens and bedrooms. In this light, scholars see increasing complexity of design as a sign that the social organization of communities had become more complex.

The house became the center of people's activities, the place where they kept the harvest and turned it into food. Because grain must be ground before it can be consumed, grinding stones are common in the archaeological record. Grinding was backbreaking. The first farmers used mortars and pestles, which permitted only small amounts to be ground at a time. Later, they crushed the grain between a flat or convex bottom stone and a smaller, handheld round stone. The millers, mostly women, rubbed the stone back and forth until the flour was fine enough to use to prepare food. They sat bent over on their knees for such long periods that their wrists, toes, knees, and lower backs became deformed, as some excavated skeletons show. As farming developed, the labor associated with it was increasingly gendered, with some tasks seen as suitable for men and others for women.

Early farmers probably cooked gruel or mash from the flour, but by 3500 BCE people consumed grain principally as bread and beer in Southwest Asia. They were probably invented accidentally. When roasted grains are mixed with water, they form a paste that can easily be baked on a hot stone, and in brewing the grain mixture was soaked in water to ferment. Like milling, cooking and brewing became women's work in many regions.

When early farmers realized the strength of baked clay, they started to create pots. Easily produced from local resources in all shapes and sizes, pottery provides both safe storage of grains against pests and moisture and a means to heat and cook food over a fire. First appearing in East Asia about 13,000 BCE, pottery was independently invented in Southwest Asia around 6500 BCE. Because pottery is also easily decorated with carved incisions or painted designs, and because decorative styles changed rapidly, pottery finds have become the main evidence by which archaeologists date settlements.

The first farmers also made small decorative objects out of metal; natural ore deposits, especially of copper, exist in many parts of Southwest Asia. Although copper ore could be hammered cold, by 5000 BCE people had learned to heat ore to extract pure copper and pour it in liquid form into molds. They later expanded these techniques for use with other metals, and by 4000 BCE people began to mix various metals to make stronger alloys. The most important was bronze, which they manufactured from copper and tin. The development of metallurgy was, in a sense, made possible by farming, because specialization of labor was an important feature of settled communities.

Another vital innovation that agriculture made possible was textile weaving. Domestication made new fibers available, which people learned to twist into threads and wove into clothing, blankets, and many other fabrics. Some fibers derived from domesticated animals—sheep wool and goat hair—and others came from plants grown for the purpose, especially flax, used to make linen thread. The earliest pieces of cloth found so far are from the cave of Nahal Hemar (nak-hal HEY-mar) in modern Israel, dating to around 6500 BCE.

The earliest written documents available to us, written long after the invention of agriculture in Southwest Asia, show that women were mostly responsible for turning raw agricultural products into usable goods. They ground cereals and cooked food, and they wove textiles and made pots. They could perform these tasks while staying at home to take care of young children. Scholars assume that this was true in other early agricultural societies as well.

Whereas bands of gatherer-hunters were probably egalitarian, in sedentary societies inequalities grew on the basis of wealth, status, and power. Some families accumulated more goods than others because, for example, they were able to harvest more. Because the communities of the Neolithic period were larger and lived together for prolonged periods, they needed a means to settle conflicts peacefully, and wealthier men may have gained authority over the rest. The archaeological record shows differences in wealth of the inhabitants, albeit on a small scale, as early as 7000 BCE. Thus farming and the development of a hierarchical social structure seem to go hand in hand.

Çatal Höyük (cha-TAHL hoo-YOOK) in modern central Turkey is the largest Neolithic settlement yet excavated (see Lives and Livelihoods: The People of Çatal Höyük). Here, archaeologists found stone and clay figurines of women with enormous breasts and thighs. As with Paleolithic figurines of women, scholars and others understand these statues in different ways, but the idea that they are fertility symbols is very popular. It is possible that early peoples considered women to form the primary line of descent from one generation to the next and that family property passed along the female line—a system called **matrilineal**. But it is risky to conclude that women were in charge and had greater authority than men—a system called **matriarchy**. Nonetheless, a woman's ability to give birth was a force of nature that the people of early agricultural societies depended on for survival, and we can imagine that early farmers honored such forces of nature as being greater than themselves.

Among Paleolithic foragers the nomadic band was the primary social unit; in Neolithic farming communities the unit shifted to single families comprising several generations. The new rectangular form of the house made it possible for settled farmers to live together, close to other families yet separate from them. Neolithic people's burial practices reflect the more intimate family connections in that they buried at least some of the dead under the floors of their houses. It was common to detach the head from the rest of the body and bury it separately. They often placed

matrilineal A system of family descent and the passing on of property that follows the female side of the family.

matriarchy The social order that recognizes women as heads of families and passes power from mother to daughter.

heads in groups and decorated some of them. Sometimes they filled the eyes with shells and modeled facial features with plaster. The exact interpretation of these practices is not certain, but it seems likely that they are the earliest evidence for a cult of ancestors, a way to preserve their presence in the house. They may even have received food offerings. People of many early cultures in world history maintained similar ties to the deceased.

In short, in religious practices, social structures, and technological and architectural innovations, we see evidence that the advent of settled agriculture produced a set of developments that led to increasingly complex human societies. This process was not inevitable, however, and not all ancient peoples considered it desirable. The gatherer-hunter lifestyle has certain advantages, and it is in no way obvious that settled agriculture represents a clearly superior alternative.

COUNTERPOINT: Gatherer-Hunters by Choice: Aborigines of Australia

↘ **FOCUS** Why did Australian Aborigines, in contrast to many of the world's other peoples, choose not to farm?

Although agriculture spread rapidly across the globe, it was not universally practiced in ancient times. Until relatively recently, in fact, many people did not farm. Sometimes the local environment necessitated a forager lifestyle, such as in the Arctic Circle. But in some locales where *both* livelihoods are possible, people chose to continue a gatherer-hunter way of life. In this Counterpoint we consider one such group: Australian Aborigines.

Understanding the History of Aborigines

The largest landmass in which people did not rely on agriculture was Australia (see Map 1.4). Before European settlers first arrived in 1788 CE, no one in this vast region farmed; the native inhabitants, or **Aborigines**, numbering perhaps 1 million at the time, lived as foragers. We have written descriptions and other sources of information about encounters between the Aborigines and modern Europeans. Their European authors often saw Aborigines as primitive people who lacked the intelligence to farm, but when historians took into account the Aborigines' rich archaeological remains, they concluded that Australian Aborigines consciously decided not to practice agriculture because they knew that foraging was more suitable for their environment.

Aborigines
Indigenous inhabitants of regions that Europeans colonized starting in the fifteenth century CE; the word is used especially in reference to Australia.

LIVES AND LIVELIHOODS

The People of Çatal Höyük

One of the most intriguing archaeological sites of the Neolithic era is Çatal Höyük, located in the south of modern Turkey. Most densely occupied between 6500 and 5000 BCE, Çatal Höyük was an unusually large Neolithic settlement, about thirty-two acres, and it was home to perhaps as many as 8,000 inhabitants. Some were farmers, who grew wheat and barley and herded sheep and goats. Numerous bones of wild animals discovered in the houses show that people also hunted the rich wildlife of the surroundings.

Çatal Höyük is remarkable for several reasons. Its mudbrick houses stood side by side without streets in between them and without doors or large windows. Those on the outside of

≡ **The Houses of Çatal Höyük**   Although this reconstruction is hypothetical, it integrates the excavators' ideas about how the people of Çatal Höyük in southern Turkey lived. The remains of the houses suggest that residents entered them from the roofs, and it is clear that they decorated certain rooms with paintings of local animals.

By 35,000 years ago, gatherer-hunter immigrants from Southeast Asia had settled the whole of the Australian continent. The water level was much lower due to the last ice age, and they had been able to cross the sea by boat. The ensuing ice melt, which started around 12,000 years ago, widened the distance between Australia and adjacent islands and increased its population's isolation. The end of the ice age also caused the climate to dry considerably.

the settlement formed a continuous wall for protection against intruders. The unusual layout forced residents to enter their homes by a ladder through a hole in the roof. The interiors of the houses were even more extraordinary for their time because of their extensive decoration. Many contained a room with paintings, engravings, or modeled reliefs, mostly representing wild animals of the surrounding countryside. Some of the scenes seem bizarre to us, including vultures attacking headless human corpses and women giving birth to bulls. These images must reflect the beliefs and perhaps the anxieties of Çatal Höyük's inhabitants, but their interpretation remains elusive.

We can explain the wealth and size of Çatal Höyük in terms of its location. A nearby volcano provided the hard rock obsidian, which craftsmen chipped and polished into tools and ornaments. Based on chemical analysis of such stone objects excavated all over Turkey, Syria, and Cyprus, archaeologists have determined that they originated at Çatal Höyük and that the town's inhabitants were in contact with people of these distant regions. They bartered the obsidian products for shells from the Mediterranean Sea and flint from Syria. Çatal Höyük's natural environment was so rich that some inhabitants could focus on obsidian work; others collected and grew food to support them. Given the vivid imagery of their work, the painters of the decorations inside the houses may also have been specialists.

Questions to Consider

1. What factors explain the relatively large size of Çatal Höyük for a Neolithic settlement?
2. What materials reveal information about the inhabitants' ideas?
3. Why do you think the inhabitants created such an unusual layout and architecture?

For Further Information:

Balter, Michael. *The Goddess and the Bull: Çatalhöyük—An Archaeological Journey to the Dawn of Civilization.* London: Routledge, 2016.

Hodder, Ian. *The Leopard's Tale: Revealing the Mysteries of Çatal Höyük.* New York: Thames & Hudson, 2006.

A Lifestyle in Harmony with the Natural World

Despite Australia's enormous variety of natural environments, ranging from tropical rainforests to desolate deserts, the foragers' lifestyles shared certain characteristics. Although their existence was migratory, they were strongly attached to the regions they inhabited, and their migration patterns were fixed. The whole

≡ **MAP 1.4**   **Early Settlement in Australia**   Although the vast Australian continent was separated from Southeast Asia by sea, humans had migrated there by 35,000 years ago and settled in the various ecological zones. Unlike their neighbors in New Guinea, with whom they had contacts, the Australian Aborigines never adopted agriculture, instead choosing to gather and hunt the multiple wild resources available to them.

community shared ownership of the land and its resources. In collecting food, they divided labor by gender. Women gathered plants and small animals such as lizards and turtles; men hunted large animals such as kangaroos and wallabies. The division of labor sometimes led men and women to be separated for prolonged periods.

So great is the ecological diversity of Australia that inhabitants could exploit a large variety of local resources, as foragers throughout world history have done.

Yet the case of Australia shows especially vividly the enormous adaptability of humans and our willingness to take advantage of all potential food sources. In the Australian summer months, for example, moths migrate to the southeastern highlands and gather in rock crevices in huge numbers. Local people scraped them off by the hundreds and grilled them on hot stones. After removing the moth's inedible parts, they had a high-protein, peanut-sized nugget that tasted like a roasted chestnut.

Another expedient use of local resources was the processing of macrozamia nuts for food. Poisonous when not treated, the kernels must be detoxified by soaking them in water, after which they were ground into flour used to bake a highly nutritious bread. Aborigines on the coasts used marine resources intensively but responsibly, taking care, for example, to harvest shellfish so that a species would not become extinct. Coastal people fished in canoes, with men using spears and women using fish lines and hooks. These examples illustrate the resourcefulness of gatherer-hunters and another important fact: far from being unsophisticated, gatherer-hunters develop highly effective specialized tools to harvest nature's resources.

Beyond collecting what nature provided, Aborigines manipulated the environment to increase the foodstuff available in the wild. In this effort, fire was an important tool. They burned areas with shrubs because they learned that the regenerative process produced a wide variety of edible plants. These plants were useful not only in their own right but also because they attracted animals that could be hunted. Selective burning also allowed certain desirable plants to grow better and to ripen simultaneously. For example, burning increased production of macrozamia nuts up to eight times. The Aborigines were thus well aware of the growth patterns of the plants and animals that surrounded them and adjusted natural circumstances so the desired species would thrive.

The Conscious Choice to Gather and Hunt

Australia was not fully isolated before the Europeans' arrival in 1788 CE. Its inhabitants were in regular contact with those of neighboring regions such as Indonesia and New Guinea, who farmed crops, including plants such as yams that can grow in Australia as well. Scholars thus believe that the absence of domestication was a conscious choice. Australian Aborigines were content with the resources nature provided, which were adequate and easily available except in rare years of scarcity. Moreover, because much of Australia is dry and has poor soil, farming is difficult in many parts of the continent and does not guarantee a stable food supply. It also is arduous and labor intensive compared with foraging. A woman harvesting and processing macrozamia nuts, for example, can feed herself for the whole day after only two hours of work. The relatively relaxed lifestyle of Aborigines made an impression on

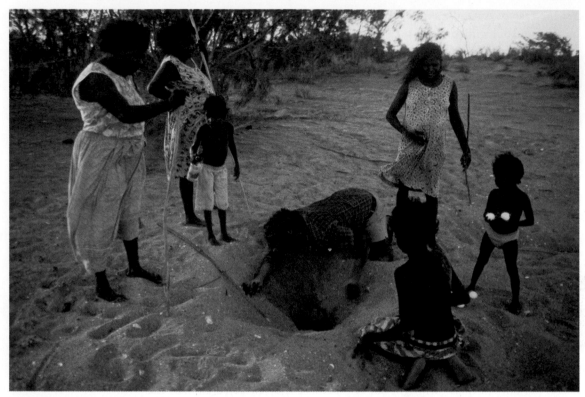

≡ **Gathering Turtle Eggs** Gatherer-hunters develop great awareness of plants and animal behavior. These Australian Aboriginal women and children, who know that sea turtles come ashore to bury their eggs, collect the eggs before they hatch.

some of the earliest Europeans, who observed Australia before they started to settle there. In 1770 CE, the English explorer James Cook wrote the following account:

> The Natives of New Holland [Australia] . . . may appear to be the most wretched people upon Earth, but in reality they are far more happier than we Europeans. . . . The Earth and sea of their own accord furnishes them with all things necessary for life, they covet not Magnificent Houses, Household-stuff &ca, they lie in a warm and fine Climate and enjoy a very wholesome Air, so that they have very little need of Clothing and this they seem to be fully sensible of, for many of who we gave Cloth &ca to, left it carelessly upon the Sea beach and in the woods as a thing they had no manner of use for. In short they seem'd to set no Value upon any thing we gave them, nor would they ever part with any thing of their own for any one article we could offer them; this in my opinion argues that they think themselves provided with all the necessarys of Life and that they have no superfluities.[2]

Religious Life and Social Organization

Aborigines had a complex religious life and social organization centered on the concept of "Dreaming" or "Dreamtime," which connected past, present, and future. According to Aboriginal belief, mythic beings created the land and its inhabitants and left rules on how humans should interact with one another and with nature. Then they withdrew into the spiritual world, but they continue to send messages through dreams and other altered states of consciousness. Humans needed to maintain contacts with these Dreaming beings through rituals and dances, for which Aborigines donned elaborate clothing, such as cloaks made of possum and wallaby skins. Ritual activity was primarily the domain of initiated men, who often temporarily withdrew from their communities for the purpose.

In Aboriginal society, a person gained respect through ritual knowledge, not wealth. Social interactions, including sexual intercourse and friendship, were allowed only between individuals with a specific family relationship. Marriages were often reciprocal—for example, men exchanged their sisters—and families arranged marriages before birth. Likewise, gifts of tools, skins, ornaments, and the like were a crucial way to maintain good relations.

The history of Australian Aborigines thus reveals that a nonagricultural life is possible, indeed preferable, under certain conditions. Native Australians' gatherer-hunter livelihood led to a distinctive historical development on the continent, with unique technologies and social, economic, and cultural practices.

Conclusion

The hominids who left their footprints on the beach at Happisburgh, as we noted at the start of this chapter, differed greatly from modern humans. Alive some 900,000 years ago, not only did they not look like us, but they also led a very different existence from ours. We should remember, however, that they too were a product of millions of years of evolution that had transformed human beings repeatedly.

Four million years ago, our ancestors depended entirely on the natural resources available in their immediate surroundings. They collected and ate plants and animals without tools or fire, relying only on their hands and teeth. But over long spans of time, they adapted to changes in their environments, acquired new skills, and started to modify what was available in their surroundings. Importantly, these developments allowed them to change physically, and they began to walk upright, hold things in their now-agile hands, speak, and think abstractly. Tools and other inventions helped them in their quest for successful livelihoods. After millions of years, some began to domesticate plants and animals and to manage the forces of nature. Others consciously decided to rely primarily on food available in the wild, for which they foraged.

By 4000 BCE, peoples in various parts of the world had learned to manipulate resources so that they could survive periods without naturally available food. As they lived in increasingly large communities, their social interactions, means of communication, and working conditions changed. The forces of nature were much more powerful than human abilities, but with a great deal of effort some people had developed the skills needed to spend their entire lives in one place. These early settlers went on to create other aspects of human culture that are still with us today, such as cities and writing, the focus of our next chapter.

review

Major global development in this chapter: The adaptation of early humans to their environment and their eventual domestication of plants and animals.

Important Events	
c. 7 million years ago (mya)	Oldest hominid on record lives in central Africa
c. 3.3 mya	First stone tools
c. 3.2 mya	Species that includes Lucy lives in the region of modern Ethiopia
c. 1.8 mya	*Homo erectus* reaches Southeast Asia
c. 500,000 BCE	Ancestors of Neanderthal migrate out of Africa
c. 400,000–30,000 BCE	Neanderthal lives in Europe and southwestern to central Asia
c. 300,000 BCE	First evidence of *Homo sapiens* in Africa
c. 45,000 BCE	*Homo sapiens* enters Europe
c. 35,000–11,000 BCE	Paleolithic cave paintings
c. 30,000 BCE	*Homo sapiens* becomes the only human species
c. 15,000 BCE	*Homo sapiens* enters the Americas
c. 10,000–9000 BCE	Development of agriculture in Southwest Asia

KEY TERMS

Aborigines (p. 35)
Fertile Crescent (p. 26)
hominid (p. 10)

Homo sapiens (p. 14)
matriarchy (p. 34)
matrilineal (p. 34)

Neanderthal (p. 14)
Neolithic (p. 19)
Paleolithic (p. 19)

CHAPTER OVERVIEW QUESTIONS

1. What caused humans to introduce technological and other innovations?
2. How did these innovations increase their ability to determine their own destinies?
3. How did the relationship between humans and nature change?
4. How have historians and other scholars reconstructed life in the earliest periods of human existence despite the lack of written records?

MAKING CONNECTIONS

1. What hominid species migrated across the globe, and for what reasons? How did natural conditions influence their migrations?
2. How did Neolithic peoples' livelihoods and daily lives compare with those of Paleolithic peoples?
3. What gender-specific roles can we discern in early human history, and how did they emerge?

DOING HISTORY

Perspectives

Ever since earth came into being, about 4.5 billion years ago, the years on it have more or less been of equal length. Yet our perception of time when we deal with the distant past is very different from how we see it today. The human species has lived on earth for only a moment in that planet's history, while in the history of the species, the modern human developed very recently. In order to visualize the different time scales with which world historians work, imagine the 4.5-billion-year history of earth laid out on a 100-yard football field. All the history of *Homo sapiens* would occupy the final quarter inch.

Calculate the distance on the football field of various periods in world history on different scales:

1. The history of *Homo sapiens*, 300,000 years ago, since the appearance of the first human ancestor, 7 million years ago.
2. The rise of agriculture, 10,000 years ago, since the origin of *Homo sapiens*, 300,000 years ago.
3. The start of writing, 6,000 years ago, since the origin of *Homo sapiens*, 300,000 years ago.
4. The years 2000 to 2020 CE since the U.S. Declaration of Independence issued in 1776.

For further research into the topics covered in this chapter, see the Bibliography at the end of the book.

2

Temples and Palaces:
Birth of the City

5000–1200 BCE

≡ **World in the Making** Unassuming small clay objects such as this one show human beings' earliest ability to record information for the future. Dating to around 3200 BCE, this tablet from southern Mesopotamia is impressed with cuneiform signs that record the transfer of goods in the city of Uruk. Writing was one of many Uruk innovations that announced the birth of the first urban society in world history. (NYPL/Science Source)

backstory

As we saw in Chapter 1, people in Southwest Asia were the first in world history to invent agriculture, which allowed them to live in the same place for prolonged periods. The abundant natural resources of the Fertile Crescent, which runs from the eastern Mediterranean shore to the mountains between modern Iraq and Iran, allowed people to live in larger communities, where social interactions became increasingly complex. In short, settled agriculture in Southwest Asia led to the birth of the city and the state.

In time, cities became major crossroads for peoples, goods, and ideas. It was in cities that the inhabitants of Southwest Asia developed a number of innovative concepts and technologies, including new forms of communication and political organization that remain important to this day. These changes did not happen in the Fertile Crescent itself, however, but in the adjacent river valleys, where natural challenges were much more severe. In this chapter we examine the origins and implications of urbanization, exploring the new patterns and connections that emerged as cities became central to Southwest Asian society and government.

45

AROUND 1800 BCE, scribes from Sumer wrote down the tale of Enmerkar and the Lord of Aratta. This Sumerian epic recounts the rivalry between Enmerkar, king of the Sumerian city of Uruk, and his unnamed counterpart in Aratta, a legendary city in what is today Iran. The two kings communicated through a messenger, but at one point the message became too difficult for him to memorize, so the tale says:

> His speech was very great, its meaning very deep.
>
> The messenger's mouth was too heavy; he could not repeat it.
>
> Because the messenger's mouth was too heavy, and he could not repeat it,
>
> The lord of Uruk patted some clay and put the words on it as on a tablet.
>
> Before that day, there had been no putting words on clay;
>
> But now, when the sun rose on that day—so it was.
>
> The lord of Uruk had put words on a tablet—so it was![1]

This passage describes in mythical terms the invention of the first writing system on earth, **cuneiform**. The invention reflected profound social and cultural developments and created a myriad of new connections, including connections between the present and the distant past. Hundreds of thousands of cuneiform tablets have survived, enormously expanding scholars' access to the lives and thoughts of peoples.

The evidence from ancient Sumer reveals the origins of the world's first urban culture. Before we begin exploring that evidence, however, we need to define what we mean by "city." Scholars characterize a **city** not just in terms of its size and large population but also by its role in the life of the region. People who lived many miles away may have venerated a god in the city temple, for instance, or they may have traveled there to obtain tools. At the same time, inhabitants of cities relied on nearby rural areas for basic needs, such as food, which they could not grow themselves. The growth of cities often led to a type of political organization we call the **city-state**: an independent urban center that dominates the surrounding countryside. Thus, as cities developed their own distinct economic, social, and political structures, they functioned as regional crossroads, connecting people with communities.

Accordingly, it is not surprising that many people have equated cities with civilization, seeing nonurban people as backward and unsophisticated. Formerly, historians also equated urban societies with civilization, but we now realize we must be more flexible in applying terms. Although complex social and economic interactions and technological and cultural innovations often developed in cities, the many other forms of social and economic organization that have evolved over world history cannot be considered "uncivilized." As we examine developments in Southwest Asia, it is important to recognize that we are exploring the rise of cities, *not* the rise of civilization.

---

cuneiform The dominant writing system of ancient Southwest Asia, which uses combinations of wedge-shaped symbols for words and syllables.

---

city A place where a dense population resides year-round and that provides specialized services to people from surrounding areas.

---

city-state A form of political organization that incorporates a single city with its surrounding countryside and villages.

Moreover, although cities were the focus of cultural development in many regions, that was not universally true. In Egypt, cities developed very early, but as the Counterpoint to this chapter will show, cities there had a limited role. The king was at the center of political, economic, and cultural life. Thus, the central role of cities in Southwest Asia reflected a specific set of historical and environmental circumstances; it was not the product of a universal pattern followed by all complex societies.

The rise of cities in Southwest Asia was a long-term process marked by many social, economic, and technological advances that combined to fundamentally alter living conditions. Once cities had developed, they became the sites of the characteristic culture of ancient Southwest Asia and provided the basis for further developments in every aspect of life.

OVERVIEW QUESTIONS

The major global development in this chapter: The rise of urban society and the creation of states in Southwest Asia.

As you read, consider:

1. What types of political and social organization appeared in the early history of Southwest Asia?

2. What new technologies appeared, and how did they affect people's livelihoods?

3. How do urban societies differ from village societies?

4. How did the early states of Southwest Asia interact with one another?

Origins of Urban Society: Mesopotamia 5000–3200 BCE

↘ **FOCUS** How do historians explain the rise of cities?

Sumer, the land where the tale of Enmerkar and the Lord of Aratta took place, was located in southern Mesopotamia, an ancient region that occupied much the same territory as modern Iraq. It was in Mesopotamia that the first urban cultures arose. Abundant archaeological findings provide evidence of the earliest processes in city development, and many cuneiform tablets provide information on later stages. Together these sources allow scholars to reconstruct the development of an urban society, an evolution that occurred over several millennia.

First Appearance of Cities	
c. 3200 BCE	Southwest Asia
c. 3000 BCE	Egypt
c. 2600 BCE	Indus Valley
c. 2000 BCE	Northern China
c. 1500 BCE	Nubia
c. 1200 BCE	Mesoamerica
c. 100 CE	Sub-Saharan West Africa
c. 1000 CE	Sub-Saharan East Africa

The Environmental Challenge

Southern Mesopotamia is an extremely arid region where rain alone is insufficient to grow crops. It also lacks certain basic natural resources, including trees, metal, and hard stone for building. So southern Mesopotamia may seem like an unlikely region to develop the world's first urban culture—but it did, mainly due to the inhabitants' ingenuity in facing the region's challenges. Two major rivers ran through the countryside, the Tigris and Euphrates, and people invented irrigation agriculture to use them to water fields (see Map 2.1).

By 8000 BCE, people in the Fertile Crescent zone of Southwest Asia had developed agriculture, which enabled them to reside year-round in villages with a few hundred inhabitants. Scholars speculate that some of them visited the arid areas nearby to graze herds and saw the opportunities this region provided—although rain was inadequate in Mesopotamia, the soil is extremely fertile. People discovered that when they guided water from the rivers into fields, barley grew abundantly. This innovation allowed farmers using irrigation to establish small villages throughout the southern Mesopotamian plain starting around 5000 BCE.

Irrigation and Its Impact

Once they had invented the basic concept of irrigation, farmers dug canals to carry water over greater distances. Because flooding was a serious threat in the extremely flat Mesopotamian countryside, the canals and fields needed to be lined with strong dikes, which required maintenance. Such tasks demanded organization and cooperation, as well as a system to resolve conflicts over water rights. From the very beginning, irrigation farming stimulated development of new forms of social organization.

≡ **MAP 2.1   The Ecology of Southwest Asia**   Southwest Asia includes many different ecological landscapes. In this map, the heavy line labeled "southern limit of nonirrigated agriculture" makes a critical distinction between zones that have enough rainfall for agriculture and zones where agriculture requires irrigation. The cultures of early Mesopotamia and Egypt developed where irrigation was always needed; ultimately, then, their rise depended on the Nile, Tigris, and Euphrates Rivers.

Cooperation brought substantial benefits. In southern Mesopotamia, irrigation farmers could reap enormous yields and earn much more income than farmers elsewhere who relied on rainfall. Moreover, the region had several other rich natural resources. Near the rivers and canals, date orchards flourished, and they provided shade for vegetable gardens. In the rivers and marshes at the head of the Persian Gulf, inhabitants could catch loads of fish and other sources of protein. Herdsmen guided large flocks of sheep and goats to seasonal pastures. These diverse resources fueled the growth of larger communities and attracted outsiders, and the population of southern Mesopotamia rapidly increased after 5000 BCE.

The earliest settlers of Mesopotamia established villages like those of the surrounding Neolithic societies (see Chapter 1). All family members worked at agricultural tasks. Because they cared for children, women had stronger ties to the house than men and performed duties such as cooking and grinding grain. They made pottery and wove sheep wool and goat's hair into clothing, blankets, and other textiles.

To maintain a close relationship with their ancestors, people buried the dead beneath the house floors and gave them food and drink offerings. They also provided grave goods—items buried with the dead. These goods provide evidence of social change in the villages during the centuries from 5000 BCE to the time of the origin of cities, 3200 BCE. Certain tombs came to include more and richer goods, indicating that their owners had a special status in life. Thus, even at this early stage, we see evidence of the social hierarchy that would come to characterize Mesopotamian cities.

Another important development occurred during the same period: **specialization of labor**, which made production more efficient. Specialist farmers, gardeners, herdsmen, and fishermen produced higher yields than families who undertook these tasks on their own. As labor became more specialized, a new necessity arose: families that were formerly self-sufficient had to trade to meet some of their basic needs. This crucial need for exchange was a major stimulus to the development of cities. People needed a central place to meet, a crossroads where they could connect with potential trading partners and exchange goods.

Many of the world's early urban cultures grew up in the valleys of mighty rivers, most notably in Mesopotamia along the Tigris and Euphrates, in Egypt along the Nile, in South Asia along the Indus, and in China along the Yellow (Huang He) and Yangzi Rivers. With this in mind, many historians make a connection between irrigation agriculture and the centralized authority and social hierarchy typical of many ancient urban cultures. This line of argument suggests that irrigation depends on a strong central authority to coordinate its construction, use, and maintenance. Archaeological research does not, however, support this argument. Rather, the evidence shows that small communities initiated and maintained irrigation projects; centralized authority developed only long after such projects had begun. Nonetheless, it was the rich agricultural potential of the river valleys that led people in many parts of the world to establish densely populated urban centers.

specialization of labor The organization of work such that individuals concentrate on specific tasks rather than engage in a variety of activities.

The First Cities 3200–1600 BCE

> ⟩ **FOCUS** How and why did the rise of the city lead to a more hierarchical society in early Mesopotamia?

A crucial element in the definition of a city is that it serves communities in the surrounding countryside and that these communities provide goods to people in the city. The city is the center for many activities, including exchange of goods. Archaeological remains throughout Mesopotamia show that during the fourth millennium BCE such central places grew increasingly large. This process culminated around 3200 BCE at Uruk—the home of Enmerkar in the Sumerian tale quoted at the start of the chapter (see Map 2.2, page 54). The population there became so large (perhaps 30,000 individuals or more) and provided so many services to the surrounding region that we can consider it the first true city in world history.

Uruk exerted its influence in many ways. It was the economic hub for the exchange of goods and services. It was the religious center with temples for the gods. It was home to political and military powers who governed people, represented them in relations with others, and protected and controlled them.

Soon similar centers arose throughout southern Mesopotamia, organizing the inhabitants of cities and surrounding villages into the political structure historians call the city-state. In later centuries this form of political organization spread from Mesopotamia to the rest of Southwest Asia, characterizing the early history of the region from 3200 to 1600 BCE.

The Power of the Temple

What motivated the residents of Uruk and its surroundings to embrace the city as a hub of exchange? One reason they accepted the arrangement was that it had the support of an ideology—that is, a set of ideas and values—to explain and justify it. That ideology was Mesopotamian religion.

In the center of Uruk was a gigantic temple complex, which must have required many community members to build and decorate. Not only did it house the city's gods and goddesses, but its staff also administered the economy. People contributed the products of their labor to the gods, whom they trusted to give something in return in the near or distant future. The head of the temple organization was the priest-king, the gods' representative on earth. A stone vase of the period, known as the Uruk vase, depicts the guiding ideology (see Seeing the Past: The Uruk Vase). Uruk's main goddess, Inanna, received the agricultural products of her people with the city-ruler as intermediary. In return, as the goddess of procreation, Inanna was expected to guarantee fertility and bountiful crops. Thus, city and country were connected by a divine cycle of exchange that benefited both.

SEEING THE PAST

The Uruk Vase

Archaeologists found this alabaster vase in the ruins of the Sumerian city of Uruk. It is over three feet high and dates to about 3200 BCE. Its surface is completely carved in an elaborate relief. Images in the bottom section represent the agriculture of the region (a); in the middle frame, a procession of naked men carry agricultural products in bowls, vessels, and baskets (b). The high point of the relief's story occurs where a female figure is presented with these products (c). Originally the city-ruler's image was carved behind the nude man visible here, but his depiction was cut out of the scene at some point.

The female figure is the goddess Inanna, identified by the two symbols standing behind her, which were the basis for writing Inanna's name in later cuneiform script. Beyond those symbols are the images of animals and storage jars and of statues, one of which holds an object in the shape of the cuneiform sign for "lord" in Sumerian (invisible in this photograph). Scholars believe this sign, the most common in tablets from the period, represents the highest temple official and that the scene indicates that the local lord provided the agricultural produce of the region to the goddess.

Uruk Vase

Examining the Evidence

1. What does the image tell us about the resources of the Uruk region?

2. What is the relationship among common people, secular ruler, and deity as expressed in this relief?

3. How can we interpret the image as representing the ruling ideology of the time?

Like almost all other ancient peoples, the Mesopotamians honored numerous deities, a system we call **polytheism**. Their gods and goddesses mostly represented aspects of the natural environment. There was a god of the sky, An; of the moon, Nanna; of grain, Ashnan; and many more. Some deities were the patrons of occupations, such as Dumuzi, the god of herding. Others were responsible for abstract concepts: the sun god, Utu, oversaw justice, and Inanna was the goddess of fertility, love, and war.

The rise of the city had fundamental consequences for all the local people living in the vicinity; every aspect of life became more complex. In economic terms, specialization of labor soon extended beyond agriculture. The farming sector produced a surplus that could support people who were not farmers. Weaving, for example, became the full-time occupation of teams of women who received food as compensation. Artisans in temple workshops worked faster and turned out standardized products. Archaeologists have excavated thousands of vessels produced by stamping clay into a mold. These simple bowls are very different from the wheel-made and painted vessels of the preceding centuries, which took much longer to make and varied in size and decoration. Thus, urbanization and labor specialization changed the focus of Mesopotamian economic life. Instead of working to meet the needs of a self-sufficient family, people increasingly produced goods and services for a growing marketplace.

Artisans manufactured not only practical items but also luxury products using exotic materials from abroad, such as the semiprecious blue stone lapis

polytheism A religious system that accepts the existence of many gods.

≡ **Ubaid and Uruk Pottery** Because archaeologists can see distinctions among pottery vessels from different periods, they rely on pottery to date the other remains they excavate. Production techniques can reveal features of the potter's culture as well. Compare the two bowls here. The potter used great care to shape and decorate the one on the left, from the Ubaid period in the fifth millennium BCE. (Image copyright © The Metropolitan Museum of Art. Image source: Art Resource, NY). The bowl on the right, from the later Uruk period of the fourth millennium BCE, was made quickly and left undecorated, demonstrating the ancient origin of mass production.

lazuli (LAP-is LAZ-uh-lee), which they could obtain only through trade contacts with the distant mountain regions of modern Afghanistan. They also imported copper from what is today the country of Oman in the Persian Gulf and tin from present-day Iran (see Map 2.2). Mixed together, these produce bronze, which is much more durable and versatile than the stone and copper earlier people had used to make tools. That this new metal was invented soon after the first cities arose is no surprise. Only cities had the collective resources to coordinate the import of ingredients from two separate distant sources. Cities became crossroads not only for their immediate surroundings but also for the people and products of different societies.

≡ MAP 2.2   Sumer's Trade Contacts, c. 3200–1600 BCE Because Sumer's heartland in southern Iraq lacked metals, wood, and hard stone for building and toolmaking, its inhabitants had to import them from as far away as Afghanistan and Egypt. The precious materials we find in the Royal Cemetery of Ur and elsewhere all came from distant sources. Even more important for the economy, however, were tin and copper, which the Sumerians combined to make bronze for tools and weapons.

The Might of the Palace

From its beginnings, the ideology of urban power had a military dimension, as evidenced by early art that shows the priest-king in battle or inspecting bound prisoners. But before 3000 BCE, artists emphasized nonmilitary functions. That imagery changed, however, as multiple urban centers emerged alongside Uruk, often as little as twenty miles apart. These cities housed fast-growing populations who needed ever-larger agricultural zones for food, and when both sides claimed an area their demands led to battles. Around 3000 BCE, the basis of power in cities began to shift from religion to the military. Neighboring city-states fought wars over territory and resources, and military leaders gained prominence, finally taking full control over political life; they absorbed some earlier religious functions as well. In archaeological sites, we see this change in the appearance of palaces next to temples and in massive walls built to protect cities.

Temples remained important institutions in Mesopotamian cities, and military leaders used them to legitimize their own rule. They created hereditary **dynasties**—that is, successions of rulers who belonged to different generations of the same family—claiming that the gods had chosen them to lead their city. Around 2450 BCE, for example, Eanatum (AI-an-na-TOMB), king of Lagash, declared that several gods had selected and nurtured him to lead his city in war, especially against the neighboring city of Umma. Both cities wanted control of an agricultural zone and repeatedly fought wars over it. Eanatum claimed his victory was a result of the gods' favor (see Reading the Past: Royal Inscriptions from Early Mesopotamia).

Militarism thus became a fundamental element of political power and a driving force behind historical change in Mesopotamia. Each Mesopotamian city-state had an army commanded by its king, who consolidated his power at home and abroad through warfare. Some rulers grew so powerful that they could claim the lives of others for their own benefit. Around 2400 BCE, members of the royal house of Ur demanded that human attendants and soldiers accompany them to the afterlife. In a few tombs of the Royal Cemetery of Ur, occupants were surrounded by incredible luxuries and by the bodies of dozens of sacrificed men and women. Other rulers took their special connections to the divine world to a different extreme, professing to be gods themselves. These practices of human sacrifice and divine kingship were short-lived, however, and for most of Mesopotamian history kings were considered mortal representatives of the gods on earth. Nonetheless, these examples of extreme claims to power reflect a general trend toward the concentration of political authority in the hands of a single individual or family.

dynasty A succession of rulers from the same family.

READING THE PAST

Royal Inscriptions from Early Mesopotamia

Inscriptions carved on stone or pressed into clay first appeared in southern Mesopotamia around 2500 BCE. They honor the king's military feats and his patronage of public works, such as the construction of temples and irrigational canals. The inscriptions tie the king closely to the gods of the city, who are sometimes represented as his physical parents or as his caretakers in his youth. One such king was Eanatum of Lagash, who around 2450 BCE left several such inscriptions, among them the following example.

> For the god Ningirsu—Eanatum, ruler of Lagash, whom the god Enlil named, whom the god Ningirsu gave strength, whom the god Nanshe selected, whom the goddess Ninhursag nourished with good milk, whom the goddess Inanna gave a good name, whom the god Enki gave wisdom,

whom the god Dumuzi'abzu loves, whom the god Hendursag trusts, son of Akurgal, ruler of Lagash, restored the city Girsu for the god Ningirsu and built the wall of the city Uruku for him. For the god Nanshe he build the city Nina.

> Eanatum . . . defeated the city Umma, and made twenty burial mounds of it. He gave back to the God Ningirsu the Gu'edena, his beloved field. He defeated the city Uruk, he defeated the city Ur, and he defeated the city Kiutu. He sacked the city Uruaz and killed its ruler. He sacked the city Mishime and he destroyed the city Arua. All the foreign lands trembled before Eanatum. Because the king of the city Akshak attacked, Eanatum removed him from the Antasura field that belonged to the god Ningirsu and destroyed the city Akshak.
>
> After all that, Eanatum dug a new canal for the god Ningirsu.

Source: J. S. Cooper, trans., *Sumerian and Akkadian Royal Inscriptions* (New Haven, CT: American Oriental Society, 1986), 1:41–42.

EXAMINING THE EVIDENCE

1. How does King Eanatum establish his relationship with various gods?

2. What are his achievements, according to this text?

3. What does the inscription reveal about the relationship among Mesopotamian city-states?

The political situation became more complex throughout Southwest Asia as a variety of peoples with different cultures and languages developed city-states in Mesopotamia and in adjacent regions. These city-states were regularly in conflict, and some energetic rulers and dynasties gained great fame for conquering large territories. Their successes were short-lived, however, and the city-state remained the basis of political organization for centuries. This changed in the eighteenth century BCE, when Hammurabi (r. 1792–1750 BCE) created a large state around the city of Babylon. He molded southern Mesopotamia into a single political unit, which fundamentally shifted the base of power from the city-state to the territorial state. Although Hammurabi's kingdom soon disintegrated, the **territorial state**, not the city, would be the most important unit of political power in Southwest Asia during the second half of the second millennium BCE.

The New Order of Society

As in any ancient society, the great majority of people in Mesopotamia spent most of their energy producing food: they farmed, herded, hunted, and fished and often lived in outlying villages. But because they depended on the city's central institutions, its temples and palace, their lives differed from those of their ancestors who never experienced cities. As part of a large social structure, they had both responsibilities and benefits. They had to provide assistance to the state, and in return, they counted on its material support.

A special characteristic of early Mesopotamian society is the ration system. Every man, woman, and child who depended on the central institutions received predetermined amounts of barley, oil, and wool. The amounts depended on one's status and gender. Leaders received larger payments than their supporters, and men received more than women. Despite its inequities, the system offered a safety net for individuals in economic trouble. It also helped widows and orphans who had no family support. Everyone but the old had to work, however, to qualify for these rations. This system of rations thus reflected both Mesopotamian social structure and Mesopotamian religious beliefs, with their emphasis on cycles of offerings and rewards. People worked for the city, and, in exchange, the city rewarded them in proportion to their perceived contribution to the general well-being.

Kings came to play a key role in maintaining the health of this exchange society. If the powerful completely ignored the needs of those below them in society, the whole system would collapse. With the growth of secular power (that is, worldly rather than religious authority), it became part of royal ideology that kings should protect the weak. The earliest written records of royal activities already express this idea. King Uruinimgina (ou-ROU-e-NIM-ge-na) of Lagash, for example, stated that he "would never subjugate the orphan and the widow to the powerful."

territorial state A highly centralized form of political organization that unites inhabitants of a geographical area that may include multiple cities and regions.

The idea that a good king guaranteed justice to his people remained part of Mesopotamian ideology for many centuries. Its most elaborate expression appeared in the laws of Hammurabi of Babylon. Carved on a seven-and-a-half-foot-tall stone stele are some 300 laws, all phrased in the same two-part form: an "if" action followed by consequences. The phrasing of the statements suggests general rules that judges needed to follow in court cases, but they are not abstract statements of principles. In cases of physical injury, for example, several laws describe distinct body parts:

> If a member of the elite blinds the eye of another member of the elite, they shall blind his eye. If he breaks the bone of another member of the elite, they shall break his bone (§§196–197).[2]

The concept underlying this system of justice is one of retribution: an eye for an eye. Hammurabi's law code was more complex than this, however, and penalties were related to the social structure. Only when a victim and a transgressor were of the same social level was the punishment equal. When the victim was of a lower class, a monetary fine was imposed; if the victim was of a higher status than the transgressor, the punishment was more severe.

Hammurabi's laws and other contemporary sources indicate clearly that Mesopotamian society was a **patriarchy**: women were always subject to a man. They moved from the father's house to the husband's upon marriage. A man could even sell his wife into servitude to pay off a debt. Women were somewhat protected, however. The wife's dowry was her own and could not be taken away upon divorce. A man could marry several women, but the woman's wealth went to her natural children alone. While their status was certainly below that of men, Babylonian women had more rights and protection than women in many other ancient societies.

Although protecting the weak was a central part of the ideology of power in Hammurabi's Babylon, that does not mean it was a society of equals. As we have seen, Babylonian law recognized and codified great inequalities rooted in gender and social status. When the number of people living together increased, social inequalities increased, and the new urban society that developed in Mesopotamia had a clear social hierarchy.

≡ **Hammurabi's Stele** This tall stone pillar is one of several that Hammurabi set up throughout his kingdom to proclaim his famous laws. The top of the monument shows the king receiving symbols of justice from the seated sun god. More striking is the lengthy, carefully carved inscription, which lists some 300 laws that present Hammurabi as a just ruler.

patriarchy A social system in which men hold all authority within the family and transfer their powers and possessions from father to son.

City Life and Learning

↘ **FOCUS** Why did ancient peoples develop writing systems, and what has been the enduring impact of this invention on intellectual expression?

The rise of cities also fundamentally changed how humanity expressed itself intellectually. The invention of writing—the ability to express thoughts in a permanent form—was an enduring contribution of the first citizens of Mesopotamia. Because writing and reading required a group of well-trained specialists, it remained an urban phenomenon for all of Mesopotamian history. These specialists were relatively few in number, but they left us innumerable rich examples of the literature and scholarship of the time.

The Invention of Writing

The need for writing derived from the urban economy, which had become increasingly complex and required a system of record keeping. Administrators had to keep track of income and expenditures, and they needed a means of reviewing transactions that involved large quantities of goods. To address this need, the Sumerians developed a revolutionary invention: writing. Writing requires a connection between spoken language and the symbols written down. It enables someone who was not present to reconstruct events from the written account alone. The challenge to its inventors was to represent oral expression in graphic form.

The Sumerian epic tale about the origins of writing at the beginning of this chapter explains in mythical terms the physical characteristics of writing: the clay tablet into which cuneiform signs were pressed. Clay tablets did indeed appear with the emergence of the first city, Uruk, around 3200 BCE. They were pillow-shaped objects a person could hold in one hand.

The earliest scribes were mainly accountants, and it is no surprise that numbers were the most common characters on the first tablets. The tablets demonstrate that the Sumerians counted, weighed, and indicated the values of a great variety of items, registering the names with a set of signs understood by everyone who handled the records. In the earliest stage of writing, each word was represented with one sign. It could be a graphic representation of the entire item, such as a drawing of a fish for the word *fish*, or of an emblematic part, such as the head of an ox for the word *ox*. The sign could also be purely abstract, such as a circle with a cross for *a sheep*. It was also crucial that written records express actions. For this purpose, the writers logically extended the meaning of items that they could draw. For example, the foot could communicate the verb *to go*. Sometimes they used similarities in sounds to make the drawing of an object represent an action. A word pronounced *ti* meant both *arrow* and *to receive* in Sumerian. Scribes thus could use the arrow sign to indicate the action of receiving. The signs developed from elaborate drawings to a handful of straight lines made by pushing a small piece of reed into the clay. The use of reeds created the impression of a wedge, a triangular head joined to a thin line, which inspired the modern name of the script, *cuneiform*, wedge-shaped (see Figure 2.1).

Soon the scribes invented signs that represented not only entire words but also the sounds of syllables. This allowed them to reduce the number of signs in the script because a limited number of syllable signs could be used to form many words; each word no longer required a distinct sign. A further benefit of the increased flexibility of script was that scribes could write down languages other than Sumerian. Throughout the long history of cuneiform, people used it to record many languages, not only in Mesopotamia but also in neighboring regions. The cuneiform script dominated written culture in Southwest Asia for some 3,000 years.

					SAG Head
					NINDA bread
					GU₇ eat
					AB₂ cow
					APIN plough
					SUHUR carp
c. 3100 BCE	c. 3000 BCE	c. 2500 BCE	c. 2100 BCE	c. 700 BCE (Neo-Assyrian)	Sumerian reading + meaning

FIGURE 2.1   Cuneiform Writing The earliest known form of writing originated in Sumer around 3200 BCE, when people began linking meaning and sound to signs such as these. Cuneiform was used for numerous ancient Middle Eastern languages and continued to be written for 3,000 years. During this period the shape of the signs changed and became increasingly abstract.

After the Sumerians invented script around 3200 BCE other cultures independently came up with different writing systems: the Egyptians around 3000 BCE, the Chinese after 2000 BCE, the Maya after 400 BCE, and many others throughout history.

Inventions of Writing Systems	
c. 3200 BCE	Mesopotamian cuneiform
c. 3000 BCE	Egyptian hieroglyphs
c. 2600 BCE	Indus Valley script
c. 2000–1200 BCE	Chinese writing
c. 1850 BCE	Cretan Linear A
c. 1800 BCE	Earliest alphabetic script, western Syria
c. 400 BCE	Mesoamerican glyphs

Scholars in each case debate what motivated people to invent writing, but the economic needs that arose with the birth of urban societies seem to have been the main inspiration in most places. Writing vastly increased the power of communication in the societies that possessed it. It allowed ideas and information to be preserved and disseminated in ways that were previously impossible. Further, it created a community of readers who shared a familiarity with common texts, texts written by authors of both their generation and generations before. In this way, written documents created connections that were crucial to the expansion of knowledge.

The Expansion of Knowledge

Although scribes originally wrote for the practical purpose of administering the complex economies of urban societies, they soon extended writing into all spheres of life. Kings commissioned inscriptions carved in stone to proclaim their accomplishments as military leaders, builders, and caretakers of their people. They also encouraged the creation of poetry, at first to sing praise to themselves and to the gods and heroes of the past. Most authors remain unknown because they did not sign their works, but there are a few remarkable exceptions. The earliest known author of world literature is Princess Enheduanna (ehn-hoo-DWAHN-ah), the daughter of King Sargon. In the twenty-fourth century BCE she composed a long plea to the goddess Inanna to reinstate her as high priestess of the city Ur after her father's enemy had deposed her:

≡ **Princess Enheduanna, the World's First Known Author** The first author known by name in world history is Princess Enheduanna, who around 2400 BCE wrote several poems in the Sumerian language, which were copied out by students centuries later whose manuscripts acknowledge her by name. She is also known to us through this image carved in stone in her lifetime, where she is shown participating in an offering, one servant or priest standing in front or her and two behind her. On the back of this disk is carved a brief inscription that identifies Enheduanna as high priestess, spouse of the god Nanna, and daughter of Sargon, and states that she commissioned the making of the altar.

He stood there in triumph and drove me out of the temple. He made me fly like a swallow from the window; I have exhausted my life-strength. He made me walk through the thorn bushes of the mountains. He stripped me of the rightful crown of the high priestess.[3]

Students, mostly the sons of priests but also some girls, copied out these poems and many others. We have a detailed view of the teaching profession from a set of cuneiform tablets dated from 1821 to 1789 BCE that document the activities of Ku-Ningal, a schoolmaster who taught in his house near the main temple in the city Ur. He lived in a neighborhood densely populated with people attached to the temple as priests and administrators. In addition to working as an archivist, Ku-Ningal taught his neighbors' children to write. His house was small, so he probably offered instruction to only a few students at a time. In his home he kept literary manuscripts, copies of royal inscriptions, mathematical texts, and lists of words students had to reproduce. Ku-Ningal may have had literary talents himself and probably composed a hymn in honor of the king, copies of which were found in his house. Thus, writing was the central activity of Ku-Ningal's profession, a skill he passed on to others, and a means of self-expression.

The early second millennium BCE brought the beginnings of literature written in Akkadian, including an early form of the *Epic of Gilgamesh*, which describes the hero's search for immortality. Gilgamesh (GIHL-gah-mehsh) was a king of Uruk—the third successor of Enmerkar of the epic at the start of this chapter—who saw his friend Enkidu die and refused to accept that fate for himself. He traveled to the edge of the world to find the only humans to whom the gods had given immortality: Utnapishtim (UHT-nuh-PISH-teem) and his wife, who had survived a universal flood. A woman he met on his travels told Gilgamesh, "When the gods created humankind, they gave death to humans and kept life for themselves."

Gilgamesh's search was ultimately futile because physical immortality cannot be attained. But eternal fame is possible. If one's deeds are recorded, they will be remembered forever, something that writing can ensure. In that way, Gilgamesh did succeed.

Students also had to study mathematics, and they did so in the same way they learned language, by copying out increasingly complex texts. They started with standard lists of capacity, weight, area, length, division, and multiplication. Then they moved to mathematical problems formulated in words, such as how to determine the height of a pile of grain based on its circumference and shape. Early Mesopotamian mathematics was highly developed and had a lasting impact on world history. Its basis was a mix of the decimal (base-10) and sexagesimal (base-6) systems. The numbers 6, 60, 360, and so on indicated new units of measure. This convention still influences us today; it is why, for example, there are 60 minutes in an hour and 360 degrees in a full circle.

The First International Order 1600–1200 BCE

↘ **FOCUS** What were the main features of the first international order, and what developments explain its rise and fall?

No state exists in isolation. Throughout world history we see many instances when contacts between neighboring states produced similarities in political and social structures. Such was the case from 1600 to 1200 BCE in Southwest Asia and adjacent regions, where an international system of states developed. Although these states had similar social organization and culture and exerted increasing influence on one another, they remained distinct. Their close connections did not end their capacity to produce independent innovations.

From City-States to Territorial States in the Eastern Mediterranean

As we have seen, from the beginning of urbanism in 3200 to 1600 BCE, the city-state had been the dominant form of political organization throughout Southwest Asia. After 1600 BCE, however, a new political order emerged in the region, one characterized by territorial states. Territorial states controlled much larger landmasses and included several dependent cities. The king controlled his territory through a hierarchy of officials, governors, and others, who were personally beholden to him. The primary focus of political loyalty was now the ruler, not the city.

In the centuries between 1600 and 1200 BCE, territorial states existed from western Iran to the Aegean Sea and from the Black Sea to south of Egypt (see Map 2.3). The elites who ruled these states knew they belonged to a collective system and maintained constant contact with one another. The development of their individual states became intertwined, and an international system emerged that bound them in

≡ **MAP 2.3   Territorial States of the Eastern Mediterranean, c. 1600–1200 BCE**   Between 1600 and 1200 BCE the region from the Aegean Sea to Iran and from Anatolia to Nubia was the site of a system of powerful states—Babylonia, Egypt, Mycenae, the Hittite realm, and others. Although local cultures would continue to flourish, the entire region shared a common elite culture that collapsed around 1200 BCE.

a shared history. Yet, as we will see, the region was diverse in every respect, including ecology, economy, political organization, and culture.

On the western edge of this international system was the Bronze Age Aegean world, which historians know primarily from archaeological material. In the second millennium BCE two main cultures appeared in the region: the Minoan, centered on the island of Crete, and the Mycenaean, which flourished in southern mainland Greece.

Minoan Cretan society revolved around palaces, which served as the economic hubs of larger regions. Best known is the palace at Knossos (K-NOSS-oss), a sprawling building centered on a large open court and decorated with colorful wall paintings. The Knossos building and other Cretan palaces lacked defensive structures, which suggests that warfare played a small role in this society. Like Mesopotamian cities, Cretan palaces served as crossroads, places where people collected and exchanged resources such as grain, wine, and oil. The Cretans kept track of the exchanges that took place with an as-yet undeciphered writing system called **Linear A**. Although the signs in the Linear A system do not resemble those of Southwest Asia at all, they were traced onto clay tablets in imitation of the cuneiform records. Crete's central location in the northeastern Mediterranean gave it a prominent role in maritime trade, making it a regional crossroads.

On the southern and eastern mainland of Greece a very different tradition developed. People here built fortresses, such as Mycenae (my-SEE-nee) and Tiryns (TIHR-ihnz), constructed with stones so large that later Greeks thought only giants could have built them. Nearby burials contained great riches, including weapons, golden masks, and jewelry. Around 1450 BCE, the people of this world, the Mycenaeans, expanded their influence throughout the Aegean Sea, including Crete. The regional economic activity of the Mycenaeans was focused on fortresses, from which officials controlled agriculture and craft production. Scribes recorded activities on clay tablets incised with a script that scholars call **Linear B**.

Linear B tablets do not reveal much about the social and political organization of the area, but they do mention a number of political and military titles, including one, *wanax*, that historians interpret as "ruler." The fortresses probably housed military leaders and their entourages, and Mycenae probably had several coexisting rulers. It seems likely, too, that rulers joined in alliances and accepted one man among them as overlord. The famous Greek poet Homer portrayed this world in the epics he wrote in the eighth century BCE. His *Iliad* tells how Greeks joined forces to attack Troy, a city on the west coast of modern Turkey, under the leadership of Agamemnon. Although Homer certainly interpreted what were even in his time events from a distant past, his depiction may reflect the actual political situation in the Mycenaean world.

Linear A The administrative writing system of the Minoans, which is still not deciphered.

Linear B The administrative writing system of the Mycenaeans, used to record an early form of the Greek language.

≡ **The Minoan Palace at Knossos** This is the throne room from the palace at Knossos, built around 1450 BCE, and much restored after excavations at the start of the twentieth century. It vividly illustrates aspects of Minoan culture. The colorful wall paintings show mystical creatures, griffins, beside an alabaster throne in front of a central fireplace. Scholars debate the function of this room, but all agree it must have been central to palace life at the time.

International Relations

In the regional system of the eastern Mediterranean, state relations ranged from peaceful to hostile. Scholars could write the entire history of the period as a sequence of battles and conquests; these are the focus of the ancient record. But states were connected by important diplomatic and economic ties as well.

Around 1600 BCE, the introduction of the horse-drawn chariot fundamentally changed warfare in Southwest Asia. The use of fast, light vehicles allowed warriors to move rapidly over the battlefield. The equipment was expensive, however, and charioteers needed special training. The mass of the armies consisted largely of infantrymen, mostly farmers and others who performed military service for their states. Official inscriptions report on numerous battles and glorify the king's success in war, but historians should remember that warfare caused misery for many.

The official inscriptions and new nature of warfare both reflect the increasingly hierarchical nature of militarized Southwest Asia.

At the same time, however, diplomatic activity thrived. Kings exchanged letters, which scribes all over Southwest Asia wrote in Mesopotamian cuneiform on clay tablets. The letters show that the kings traded valuables to reinforce friendly relations based on mutual respect. They also exchanged women, and many princesses married foreign kings. The Egyptians did not reciprocate in this respect, however. They loved to receive princesses from abroad but never gave one of their own in return. This angered other kings, who complained bitterly about it in writing.

Women of the courts, especially queens, were also in contact with one another during this era. We know of several letters that Egypt's Queen Nefertari (nehf-uhr-TAHR-ee) wrote Queen Puduhepa (Poo-doo-KHE-pa) in the thirteenth century BCE. Puduhepa was queen of the Hittite state that dominated modern-day central Turkey and northern Syria. The writers called each other "sister" to indicate their equal status, as if they were all part of the same large family.

> Thus speaks Nefertari, the great queen of Egypt, to Puduhepa, the great queen of the Hittites: My sister, I am well and my country is well. May you, my sister, be well and may your country be well. I have heard that you, my sister, have written to me to inquire about my well-being and that you write to me because of the peaceful relations and the good brotherhood that exists between the great king, king of Egypt, and the great king, king of the land of the Hittites, his brother.
>
> The sun god and the storm god will raise your head and the sun god will let goodness flourish and he will preserve the brotherhood between the great king, king of Egypt, and the great king, king of the Hittites, his brother. I am in peace with you, my sister. Now I send you a present for well-wishing to my sister, and you, my sister, should know about the present I send to you with the royal messenger: 1 multicolored necklace of good gold made up of 12 strings and weighing 801 grams; 1 multicolored linen garment from the city Byssos; 1 multicolored linen tunic from the city Byssos; 5 multicolored linen garments with good thin weave; 5 multicolored linen tunics with good thin weave, a total of 12 linen textiles.[4]

This letter exemplifies how the elites of eastern Mediterranean societies saw themselves as equals with a shared culture and ideology. Both queens communicated in Akkadian, a language neither of them spoke, and appreciated luxuries that often could be obtained only in foreign countries.

Alongside court exchanges, a lively trade in luxury goods connected the societies of the eastern Mediterranean. Seafaring merchants conducted much of this trade, and some shipwrecks reveal what they carried. A prime example is a ship found on the south coast of modern Turkey at Uluburun, dating to around 1300 BCE (see again Map 2.3). The array of goods the ship carried was so diverse that it is impossible to identify its origin. The main load consisted of ten tons of copper and one ton of tin. The merchants probably picked up these metals in Cyprus and southern Turkey, intending to exchange them for other goods in various harbors along the route. The ship contained tropical African ebony logs, obtained in Egypt, and cedar logs from Lebanon. The cargo's ivory tusks came from Egypt, and marine snail shells, prized for the dye they contained, were a special product of Syria. The ship also carried manufactured goods, such as jewelry from Syria, pottery from Cyprus, and beads of gold, agate, and colored glass, each type from a different source. There was even a jeweler's hoard on board, with scraps of gold and silver and an amulet with the name of the Egyptian queen Nefertiti. The cargo was truly cosmopolitan in origin and reflected the desire for luxury items of elites throughout the region.

The frequent contacts and shared interests extended to culture and art as well. Although each state had its own traditions, often many centuries old, the elites imported the literate culture of Mesopotamia. Palaces all over the region employed scribes who could read and write Akkadian. Their libraries contained works of Mesopotamian literature, sometimes adapted to local tastes. In the Hittite capital, for example, the *Epic of Gilgamesh* was read in both a Mesopotamian version and an abbreviated translation in the local Hittite language.

The spread of Mesopotamian culture did not destroy local traditions; rather, a multiplicity of languages, scripts, and literatures flourished. In western Syria a new type of script had developed around 1800 BCE, and its use expanded at this time. The writing was **alphabetic script**. Instead of using signs to indicate entire words or syllables, a sign represented each consonant of the language. Vowels were not indicated. This type of writing required fewer than thirty characters. Various alphabetic scripts coexisted, but the system that survived into later periods had a set of characters whose pronunciation was based on a simple principle: each character was a drawing of an item, and the first sound of that item's name gave the character its pronunciation. For example, a drawing of a house represented the sound /b/, the first sound in the Semitic word for house, *baytu*. This system of writing would spread enormously in the first millennium BCE, and it is the basis of alphabetic scripts in use today all over the world.

alphabetic script A type of writing with a limited number of characters, each one representing a single sound.

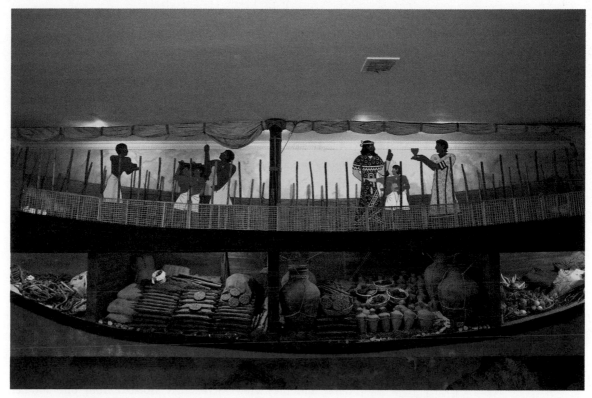

≡ **Uluburun Shipwreck** The contents of ships like the one excavated at Uluburun in southern Turkey show how traders
traveled throughout the eastern Mediterranean with a cargo that included items from all the regions they visited.
Shown here is a reconstruction of the ship and the items it transported, including metal ingots, vessels containing
liquids such as olive and wine, and other valuable goods.

Kings and Commoners: An Unequal System

The heads of the leading states were like members of a club whose membership was
restricted to "Great Kings," the term they used to refer to one another. Always included in this elite group were the kings of Babylonia, the Hittite state, and Egypt.
Other rulers joined when resources and fortune enabled them to do so. Around
1350 BCE, for example, the king of Cyprus was included on the basis of his control
of copper mines.

Throughout this world existed a similar social structure, one with greater inequality than in the past. The leading elites accumulated enormous wealth, whereas the
general population lived in poverty. This social disparity was reflected in the contents
of elite tombs, which especially in Egypt show the amazing wealth reserved for a tiny
ruling class. During their lifetimes, too, the elites basked in luxury, which they

enjoyed in palaces in secluded walled sections of their cities. Kings often ordered their subjects to build entirely new, and often gigantic, cities for themselves and their entourages. Removed from the masses of the lower classes, they restricted their company to the palace household. Thus, just as kings emphasized their membership in an exclusive elite in their diplomatic relations with other kings, they built walls around themselves in their day-to-day lives to underscore the vast distance between the powerful and the powerless.

The rulers' lavish lifestyles were funded, in part, by the spoils of military conquest. Yet it was local populations who bore the brunt of the unequal social system. Primarily farmers, the lower social classes throughout the eastern Mediterranean were compelled to produce surpluses for their urban ruling elites. Although they were not enslaved, they were tied to the land and forced to hand over much of their produce. The kings of this era may have been engaged in almost constant warfare, but they recognized a common interest in maintaining strict control over their subjects, who were the true source of their wealth and power.

The inequality that characterized the international system may have been the primary cause of its collapse around 1200 BCE. The success of the system had relied on collaboration and sustained contacts among the various states, even if those interactions involved warfare. After 1200 BCE individual states gradually failed to sustain their social and political systems, and they grew increasingly isolated from one another. Historians have difficulties determining what happened, but revolts from the lower classes seem to have initiated the process. Documentation from Egypt attests to the earliest workers' strikes on record in world history.

These uprisings prompted outsiders from the northern shores of the Mediterranean to immigrate to the unstable kingdoms. Their attacks on coastal cities made sea travel unsafe and unraveled the connections among the various states. Reports of these attacks speak of "Sea Peoples," migrants who forced their way into the rich areas of the eastern Mediterranean. The chaos that ensued changed life fundamentally all over this region. People of the Aegean abandoned their Mycenaean fortresses, and the Hittite state disintegrated. Many cities along the Syrian coast were destroyed, and states such as Egypt and Babylonia lost influence outside their borders and went into economic decline. The rapid and simultaneous decline of the region's states reflects the vital nature of their close connections. Just as these states rose together, the disintegration of connections brought with it the collapse of the states themselves.

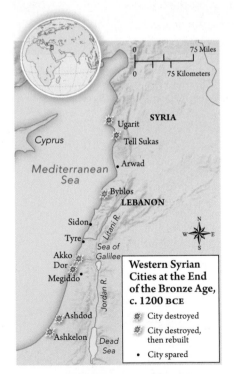

≡ **Western Syrian Cities at the End of the Bronze Age, c. 1200 BCE**

COUNTERPOINT: Egypt's Distinct Path to Statehood

↘ FOCUS In what ways did the early history of Egypt contrast with that of the ancient states of Southwest Asia?

In the evolution of societies documented in Southwest Asia, the city played a decisive role. It was the earliest unit of social and political organization, and cities dominated all aspects of life in the region for more than 1,500 years. The city-state was a stepping-stone to the formation of larger political units. This was the case in nearly all the regions Mesopotamia was in contact with, with one notable exception: Egypt. Egypt never had city-states. It was a highly centralized territorial state from the very beginning.

Egypt's Geography and Early History

Egypt's farmers, like their counterparts in Mesopotamia, China, and elsewhere, had to rely on river water to grow their crops, because the region receives almost no rain. They were more fortunate than others, however. Every year the Nile rose at just the time when the crops needed water, turning large areas of land along its banks into rich and extremely fertile fields (see Map 2.4). By monitoring the height of the annual flood, the Egyptians could determine exactly how much land could be farmed each year.

Egypt's territory along the Nile River, 700 miles long, comprises two regions, which the ancient Egyptians clearly distinguished. In the northern delta area the Nile separates into numerous branches in a flat countryside. Scholars call this region Lower Egypt because it lies where the river drains into the sea. To the south the river runs through a narrow valley in a clearly demarcated basin, the region called Upper Egypt. Prior to 3000 BCE, the long country stretching beside the Nile was dotted with villages, whose inhabitants farmed the fertile soil the annual floods created.

Then, quite suddenly around 3000 BCE, a state arose that was very different from the city-states that emerged in Mesopotamia at about the same time. The earliest state in Egypt incorporated a large territory from the Mediterranean Sea to the northernmost place where rapids interrupt the Nile River, called the first cataract. The Egyptians portrayed the emergence of the Egyptian state as the result of a campaign of military conquest. The earliest Egyptian historical document shows the victory of a king of Upper Egypt, Narmer, over his Lower Egyptian counterpart. The document reflects an ideal that would survive throughout Egyptian history: the king held the two parts of the country together through his military might. Modern historians distinguish two types of periods in the 3,000-year history of the country: when Upper and Lower Egypt were united, they speak of

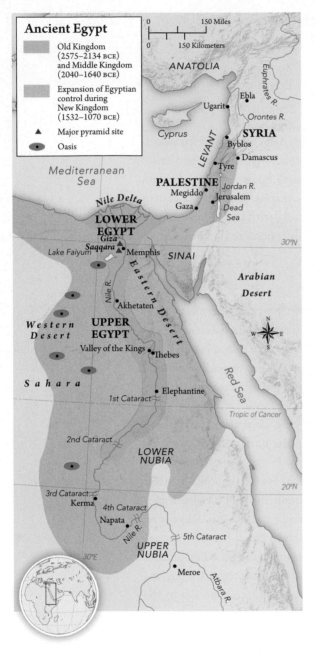

≡ **MAP 2.4   Ancient Egypt** Egypt stretches along the Nile River for some 700 miles and has depended on it from the start of its history. When the ancient state was strong and unified, its influence reached out from its heartland in the Nile Valley and the delta to the deserts nearby, as well as to areas in western Asia and Nubia.

Kingdoms (Old, Middle, and New), and when political fragmentation existed, they speak of Intermediate Periods (First, Second, and Third).

Egyptian Ideology of Kingship

Cities did arise in Egypt, but unlike those in Mesopotamia, they did not become the center of political life and cultural development. Instead, the king played that role. He guaranteed the success and welfare of the country, and in return the entire population supported him and his entourage. The earliest Egyptian monumental remains are massive tombs from around 3000 BCE with offerings that show that the persons buried in them, the earliest kings, received grave goods that originated from all over the country. The wealth of these and later tombs show a tremendous concentration of Egypt's economic resources in the ruler's palace.

The difference between the role of cities in Egypt and in Mesopotamia is reflected in the palaces of the two societies. In Mesopotamia, palaces gained prominence through their connection to the cities in which they were located. In contrast, the palaces of Egyptian rulers gained prominence through their connection to the king. The linkage of the palace with the king led the Egyptians to use the term for palace, *per-o*, for the title of king—hence our use today of the term **pharaoh** to refer to the ancient Egyptian king.

The Egyptians' ideology of kingship was closely tied to their religious ideas. Like the Mesopotamians, they honored a large number of gods, many of whom represented aspects of the universe. For example, Geb was the earth, Nut the sky, and Re the sun. The Mesopotamian gods had human forms, but the Egyptians visualized many gods as wholly or partly animal. The goddess Hathor was a cow or woman with a cow's head, the god Horus a falcon or falcon-headed man, and so on. Why this was the case we do not know, but many animals became objects of cults.

The king fit into this system, in that he was considered the earthly embodiment of the god Horus, who in mythology had inherited the throne from his father Osiris. To the Egyptians, history was the sequence of kings, each of whom was related to his predecessor just as Horus had been related to Osiris. The Egyptian king was not a god, nor was he a simple human; his status was somewhere in between. As such, he served as a connection between his people and the divine.

The majority of the Egyptian population seems to have accepted this system without much difficulty. Food and other resources were plentiful along the Nile, and they saw the king as a source of stability and peace who would help preserve their fortunate circumstances. In return for his safeguarding the country, they contributed their labor to the monuments that today remain the greatest testimonies of Egypt's past: the pyramids and Great Sphinx of Giza, built between 2550 and 2500 BCE (see Lives and Livelihoods: The Pyramid Builders of the Pharaohs).

pharaoh The ancient Egyptians' title for their king.

≡ **Egyptian Women Weaving** Images such as this one from an Egyptian tomb represent an idealized view of daily life, yet they show that weaving was an important activity performed by women. The two weavers depicted here use a horizontal loom. Because the Egyptian artistic convention was to show all the important elements of an object, regardless of perspective, the painter depicted the loom from above, allowing us to see the weavers' tools and techniques. (Image copyright © The Metropolitan Museum of Art. Image source: Art Resource, NY)

Most Egyptians lived in simple circumstances in villages. They farmed plots of land, which often belonged to the palace or a temple, and they paid part of their harvests as a rental fee. The Nile provided them with fish, and they hunted small animals and caught birds for food as well. Unlike in Southwest Asia, where people made their clothes from wool, Egyptians wore mostly linen textiles, which they made from the flax plant that grew throughout the country. Artistic representations show women weaving the cloth. As in Mesopotamia, weaving was an important domestic task in Egypt.

The New Culture of Statehood

The Egyptians developed their own script, which we call **hieroglyphics**. The signs were distinct in form from those of Mesopotamian cuneiform, but they shared the same principles in how they rendered words. Hieroglyphic signs were pictorial and were painted on papyrus and pottery or carved in stone. The script stayed in use from about 3000 BCE to 400 CE and never lost its basic characteristics (see Figure 2.2). However, because hieroglyphs were elaborate and cumbersome to write, over time the Egyptians developed derivative scripts.

As in Mesopotamia, the first writings Egyptians produced were limited to business transactions and short inscriptions celebrating the deeds of kings. Then people started to write down compositions, such as hymns and prayers to the gods. Around 2000 BCE creativity flourished as authors composed the tales considered classics of Egyptian literature for centuries afterward. Among the most notable early Egyptian compositions are texts on death and burial.

The Egyptians viewed death not as an end, but as the beginning of a new existence that resembled life in many respects, one that required material goods such as food if the dead were to thrive. Thus, a tomb was more than a depository for the body—it also contained a chapel where surviving family members offered food to the dead. Egyptians expected to use their bodies after death, so they had to be preserved intact. To achieve this goal, they turned corpses into mummies, which are some of the most remarkable remains of ancient Egyptian culture: today we can still see the bodies of famous kings and queens such as Ramesses (RAM-ih-seez) II and his wife Nefertari. They removed all perishable parts (lungs, intestines, etc.) and treated the other remains in such a way that they maintained their shape. Then they wrapped the bodies in linen and deposited them in coffins to protect them against possible damage. The dryness of the desert where the tombs were located aided in preservation as well.

From the start of Egyptian history kings had enormous tombs, a practice that culminated in the great pyramids of Giza (see again Lives and Livelihoods: The Pyramid Builders of the Pharaohs). The masses of stone eloquently demonstrate how much

hieroglyphics The writing system of ancient Egypt, which used detailed pictorial symbols to indicate words and syllables.

energy the Egyptians would expend to guarantee the king a safe and impressive burial. Common people had the same hopes; they too wanted to be buried safely and to receive gifts into eternity. Royal cemeteries such as the one at Giza reflect the distinct nature of the early Egyptian state. The royal pyramids lie in the center, massive in size and bordered by temples for the cults of the dead kings. Numerous tombs of officials and others surround them. Just as the king was the center of power in life, it was desirable to be near him in death.

Although Egypt became part of the international system in the eastern Mediterranean after 1600 BCE, its earlier history contrasted notably with that of its neighbors. The king of Egypt was the center of power over the entire territorial state, which he personally held together. The strong unity of Egypt's territorial state led it to become the earliest empire in this part of the world, which we will discuss in Chapter 4.

Conclusion

After the rise of agriculture, the historical development of the world's peoples continued to unfold in Southwest Asia and North Africa, where the Eurasian and African continents meet. We have focused in this chapter on Mesopotamia and Egypt, which rapidly developed socially and economically complex cultures that left behind many remains for historians to study. Their invention of writing, which the mythical tale at the start of the chapter portrayed as a simple act to aid a messenger, had a fundamental impact on our understanding of people's lives in that era. These are the first cultures in history we can study through the written expressions of the people themselves. We see a clear difference between these two regions: in Mesopotamia (and many other ancient cultures) the city was crucial to political life; in Egypt, it was the king.

After hundreds of years of separate developments, from about 3200 to 1600 BCE, the countries of Mesopotamia and Egypt united with others in the eastern Mediterranean region to form a much larger system of exchange in diplomacy, trade, and culture. Their fortunes were intertwined, and around 1200 BCE they all suffered decline. In the new world that would develop after 1000 BCE, the

Hieroglyph	Meaning
	vulture
	flowering reed
	forearm and hand
	quail chick
	foot
	stool
	horned viper
	owl
	water
	mouth
	reed shelter
	twisted flax
	placenta (?)
	animal's belly
	door bolt
	folded cloth
	pool
	hill
	basket with handle
	jar stand
	loaf

≡ **FIGURE 2.2 Egyptian Hieroglyphs** Ancient Egyptians used pictures such as these to create their own system of writing around 3000 BCE. Because Egyptians used this formal script mainly for religious inscriptions, Greeks referred to it as *hieroglyphica* ("sacred carved letters"). Eventually Egyptians also developed the handwritten cursive script called demotic (Greek for "of the people"), a much simpler and quicker form of writing.

LIVES AND LIVELIHOODS

The Pyramid Builders of the Pharaohs

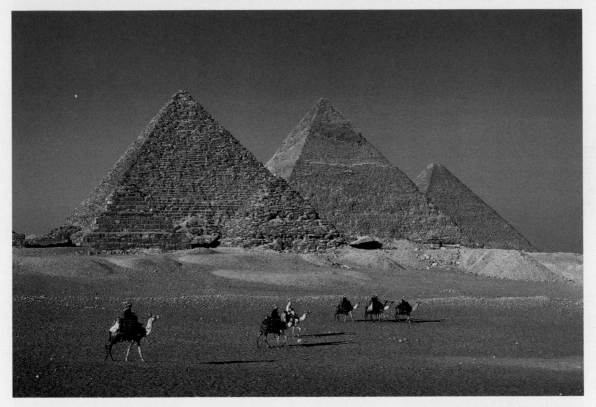

≡ **The Pyramids at Giza** To build the Giza pyramids the ancient Egyptians transported, carved, and set into place massive amounts of stone, using tools that were themselves made of stone or of the soft metal copper. Archaeologists wonder how they managed to accomplish this work in less than a century. It is no surprise that the greatest of the three pyramids—the tomb of King Khufu—was considered one of the wonders of the ancient world.

The three pyramids of Giza on the outskirts of modern Cairo are among the most awe-inspiring monuments of early world history. Archaeologists estimate that the largest of the three, the tomb of King Khufu, contained 2,300,000 blocks of stone with an average weight of two and three-quarter tons, some weighing up to sixteen tons. Khufu ruled

for twenty-three years, which meant that throughout his reign 100,000 blocks had to be quarried, transported, trimmed and finished, and put in place every year. That comes to about 285 blocks a day, or one for every two minutes of daylight.

The pyramids themselves are just one part of a much larger burial complex that included temples for offerings to the dead king, a ramp to transport the body to the pyramid, secondary burials for queens and others, and statuary. The latter could be as monumental as the Great Sphinx of Giza, the largest monolith (made from a single large block of stone) sculpture in the world.

Because the logistical requirements for these gigantic projects were daunting, the question of manpower is especially intriguing. Every district of Egypt had to supply laborers, which meant that some had to travel hundreds of miles. Scholars estimate that about 10,000 workers were active at a time, and they infer from later records of state enterprises that they worked three-month stints. Archaeologists have discovered the remains of a worker's village near the building site, which show how they were provided with housing, food, and tools. They left their families behind and slept in crammed dormitories, each laborer assigned a narrow space. They received rations of bread and beer, which were prepared on a massive scale in bakeries. Also the remains of workshops where tools were manufactured and repaired have been found. Metal tools were mostly made of copper, which is soft, and they must have been sharpened often.

Although no ancient Egyptian description exists of how the pyramids were built, the massive stones could have been moved into place only by dragging them on ramps constructed from wooden beams, stone rubble, and mud. The Giza plateau has little open space, so the architects must have laid out the ramps in circles around the pyramid base. They had to construct new ramps for every pyramid, and space must have become increasingly cramped as temples and secondary tombs surrounded earlier pyramids. From fractures found in the skeletons buried in a cemetery near the worker's village, it is clear that some workers suffered injuries; some must have died on the job.

The willingness of Egyptians to participate in this massive enterprise tells us much about the king's position in society. The inhabitants of the entire country regarded him with so much respect that they willingly undertook these tasks. The projects required many years of work, and people had to forsake other responsibilities to work on them. After finishing their stint of pyramid building, these workers would resume their livelihoods as farmers, fishermen, or some other occupation, but with the memory of having contributed to the glory of their king.

Questions to Consider

1. How do scholars estimate the number of people involved in constructing Khufu's pyramid?

2. What were the logistical problems of the project?

3. Where did the workers come from, and how were they convinced to participate?

For Further Information:

For general information on Egyptian pyramids: Pyramids. http://www.pbs.org/wgbh/nova/pyramid/excavation

Lehner, Mark, and Zahi Hawass. *Giza and the Pyramids: The Definitive History.* Chicago: University of Chicago Press, 2017.

balance of power that undergirded the first international system no longer existed. The inhabitants of Southwest Asia and North Africa were the first in world history to develop the elements of culture we studied in this chapter, but soon afterward peoples elsewhere in Asia also did so. In the next chapter we will turn to these peoples living farther east.

review

Major global development in this chapter: The rise of urban society and the creation of states in Southwest Asia.

Important Events	
c. 5000 BCE	First permanent settlement in Mesopotamia
c. 3200 BCE	Uruk, the first Mesopotamian city; invention of Mesopotamian cuneiform script
c. 3000 BCE	Creation of the Egyptian state; invention of Egyptian hieroglyphic script
c. 3000–1800 BCE	Competing city-states in Mesopotamia
c. 2550 BCE	Khufu's pyramid at Giza
c. 1800 BCE	Development of alphabetic script in Syria
c. 1800–1700 BCE	Hammurabi's unification of southern Mesopotamia
c. 1650 BCE	End of the Minoan culture
c. 1600–1200 BCE	First international order in the eastern Mediterranean
c. 1450 BCE	Mycenaean expansion throughout the Aegean

KEY TERMS

alphabetic script (p. 68)
city (p. 46)
city-state (p. 46)
cuneiform (p. 46)
dynasty (p. 55)

hieroglyphics (p. 74)
Linear A (p. 65)
Linear B (p. 65)
patriarchy (p. 58)
pharaoh (p. 73)

polytheism (p. 53)
specialization of labor (p. 50)
territorial state (p. 57)

CHAPTER OVERVIEW QUESTIONS

1. What types of political and social organization appeared in the early history of Southwest Asia?
2. What new technologies appeared, and how did they affect people's livelihoods?

3. How do urban societies differ from village societies?
4. How did the early states of Southwest Asia interact with one another?

MAKING CONNECTIONS

1. How did the development of agriculture in Southwest Asia lead to the first urban culture there?
2. What were the roles of cities in political developments in the regions discussed here?

3. What was the relationship between gods and humans in Mesopotamia and Egypt?
4. What are similarities and differences between Mesopotamian and Egyptian writing systems, and how do they differ from alphabetic writing?

DOING HISTORY

Developments and Processes

Although human history has never been a simple process of development at a standard, steady pace, it is true that general trends can be recognized in specific regions or even the world in its totality. One trend we can observe in the earliest history of the eastern Mediterranean world is the growth of increasingly large units of interaction. In political organization states grew in size, and their regular interactions with other states reached farther over time.

1. Explain this development in the cultures discussed in this chapter. What were the different stages?
2. What kinds of interaction could have encouraged such expansions of horizon?
3. Can you think of events and processes that would contradict this trend?

For further research into the topics covered in this chapter, see the Bibliography at the end of the book.

3

Settlers and Migrants: The Creation of States in Asia

5000–500 BCE

≡ **World in the Making** The vast expanses of Central Asia opened up when people started to use domesticated horses extensively around 2000 BCE and could quickly cross large, arid areas. Central Asian horsemen connected the urban cultures at the fringes of Eurasia and may have introduced technologies such as bronze manufacture to China. This decorated textile, dating to around 500 BCE, comes from Pazyryk, on the modern border between Russia and northern China. It depicts a man riding on horseback using a saddle and a bit, tools that revolutionized the use of horses and have not gone out of use since.

backstory

In Chapter 1 we saw how humans developed, spread across the globe, and invented agriculture, which enabled them to establish permanent settlements. Societies in various parts of the world evolved differently, often in response to varying environmental challenges and opportunities. But wherever large numbers of people started to live together, they needed institutions and social arrangements to regulate their interactions. The peoples of Southwest Asia and Northeast Africa were the first to form large states around 3000 BCE. This ultimately led to a complex system of states throughout the region interconnected by diplomatic relations (discussed in Chapter 2). Sometime after the founding of Southwest Asian states, peoples in other parts of Asia also created large political and social entities, each in accordance with their particular circumstances. It is to these early states that we turn in this chapter.

AROUND THE YEAR 100 BCE, the Chinese historian Sima Qian (sih-muh chee-en), in a massive work on the early history of his country, wrote these words about nomadic people living on the fringes of the Chinese state whose emperor he served:

> We hear of these people, known as Mountain Barbarians . . . wandering from place to place pasturing their animals. The animals they raise consist mainly of horses, cows, and sheep. . . . They move about in search of water and pasture and have no walled cities or fixed dwellings, nor do they engage in any kind of agriculture. . . . They have no writing and even promises and agreements are only verbal. . . . All the young men are able to use a bow and act as armed cavalry in times of war. It is their custom to herd their flocks in times of peace and make their living by hunting, but in periods of crisis they take up arms and go off on plundering and marauding expeditions. This seems to be their inborn nature.[1]

This is a stereotypically negative portrayal of nomadic people by an author living in an urban society. Settled people provided almost all the written sources with which the historian works, and typically they did not like, or even understand, those who did not live like themselves. The ancient history of Asia shows, however, that settled and nomadic peoples were connected in numerous and important ways. As alien as nomads may have seemed to urban peoples, the contacts, conflicts, and exchanges among nomadic and settled peoples profoundly influenced world history, shaping the lives of nomads and city dwellers alike.

Asia is a vast landmass with numerous natural environments, which support primarily two types of livelihood: farming and herding. Where sufficient rain fell or rivers allowed for irrigation, farmers worked the soil and lived in the same location year-round. The earliest urban cultures of Asian history arose especially in the river valleys, that is, in Southwest, South, and East Asia. In all these areas people developed large states with urban and literate cultures, but key differences distinguished them. The states of Southwest Asia show continuity from about 3000 BCE to 600 CE. In South Asia the urban Indus Valley culture arose around 2600 BCE and ceased to exist after some 700 years. Several centuries later, the new Vedic culture provided the basis of all the region's later history. In East Asia the Shang (shahng) state of 1570 to 1027 BCE was the first in a long series of Chinese dynasties that continued into modern times. Elsewhere on the Asian continent, such as in the Oxus River Valley, some early urban cultures flourished only temporarily, however, and when people abandoned them, they left no traces for later history.

Beyond Asia's river valleys agriculture was often impossible, and people survived instead as **pastoralists**, nomadic animal herders who moved with their flocks in search of grazing land. The widespread use of domesticated horses by around 2000 BCE greatly increased the mobility of pastoralists, enabling some to migrate over great distances and create links among the urban states of Asia. Especially important were the migrations of speakers of Indo-European languages, whose nomadic lifestyle brought them to western China, Europe, and the Indian subcontinent. Many other nomadic groups flourished as well, and the interactions between settled and pastoral peoples powerfully shaped the history of Asia from its beginning until recent times.

pastoralist Animal herder who moves around with a flock to find grazing land; the lifestyle of such people is called *pastoralism*.

OVERVIEW QUESTIONS

The major global development in this chapter: The rise of large urban states in Asia and the interactions between nomadic and settled peoples that shaped them.

As you read, consider:

1. How did peoples living in far-flung regions of Asia develop societies that had many similarities?

2. What were the unique characteristics of the cultures studied here?

3. Which features of ancient Indian and Chinese society and culture shaped later developments most fundamentally?

4. What common trends in the interactions between settled and nomadic peoples can you discern?

Early Agricultural Societies of South and East Asia 5000–1000 BCE

⬎ **FOCUS** How did Asia's diverse natural environments shape the different lifestyles of its inhabitants?

After people in Southwest Asia had developed agriculture by 8000 BCE, inhabitants of other regions of Asia started to farm as well, especially in river valleys, where the soil was fertile and people could use river water to irrigate crops when rainfall was insufficient. Over the millennia farmers settled throughout the valleys of the Yellow River (Huang He) and the Yangzi River in China, and in parts of the South Asian subcontinent, including the Indus Valley. Out of those communities the earliest urban cultures of East and South Asia would develop. Simultaneously, pastoralists survived by herding animals, grazing them on the continent's steppes, vast areas of semiarid and treeless grasslands. After some pastoralists domesticated the horse, they could cover long distances, which led to their migration over the entire Eurasian continent. These people became the nomads of Central Asia.

Settled Farmers of the River Valleys

Most of the regions with agricultural potential in the Asian continent lie along mighty rivers whose waters make the adjoining fields very fertile. Besides the Tigris and Euphrates Valleys in Southwest Asia, the valleys of the Indus and Ganges in South Asia and those of the Yellow River and Yangzi to the east in China were home to early agricultural societies with intensive food production (see Map 3.1). The first farmers appeared by 7000 BCE in East Asia and by 6500 BCE in South Asia. In China they cultivated rice in the southern Yangzi Valley because the large amounts of water the crop required were available there. In the northern Yellow River Valley, people grew millet because that hardy grain could survive the region's chronic droughts. In the western Indian subcontinent people cultivated wheat and barley, plants that need a modest, yet annually recurring, amount of water.

The early farmers lived in villages and produced pottery in which to store produce and liquids and to cook. Studies of their pottery show that the early inhabitants of various regions of modern-day China had distinct customs and practices. On the coast of eastern China, for example, they made delicate vessels on potter's wheels in colored clay, whereas in the central Yellow River Valley they made large bulky vessels by placing bands of clay on top of one another and painting decorations on the upper half. Thus, although each agricultural region emerged in response to similar environmental opportunities, each developed distinct cultural characteristics.

Over time these diverse populations across China increased contacts and started to share cultural elements. Some of the interactions were violent, so inhabitants of northern China began to protect their villages with walls. They employed a unique building technique that would remain characteristic for many centuries in the region. They filled a wooden frame with layers of earth, which they pounded until the wall became as solid as cement. When the builders removed the boards, straight and strong walls remained.

≡ **MAP 3.1   The Nomads and Settlers of Early Eurasia** Throughout history, migrants crisscrossed the vast grasslands in the center of Eurasia. This map shows the situation around 2000 BCE, when the urbanized regions of Egypt, the Middle East, and the Indus Valley, as well as the village culture of China, coexisted with Indo-European migrants, whose spread brought radical changes to Eurasian societies and cultures.

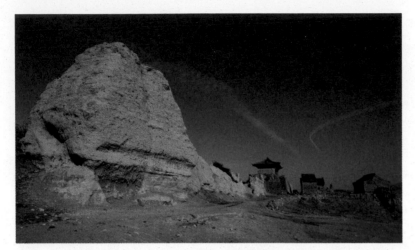

≡ **Pounded Earth Walls** The earliest agricultural communities in China invented a building technique that survived for millennia. After constructing a wooden frame, they pounded moistened earth mixed with clay and pebbles until the mixture became a solid mass that could stand on its own when the frame was removed. Walls of this type could be massive and with proper care could stand for centuries.

The construction of such walls and other large projects in early China required organized communal labor and a hierarchical social structure. By 2000 BCE social differences became evident in people's burials. While the vast majority of people were buried with only a few objects, a small number of elites took many gifts with them to their graves. That great power conferred special status was made very clear by the human sacrifice of people of lower status to serve members of the elite in the afterlife. Archaeologists regularly find skeletons with their feet cut off placed near the principal occupants of rich Chinese graves.

Grave goods are not the only evidence we have of social stratification. As some members of Chinese society grew wealthy, they demanded new and more luxurious products. One typically Chinese luxury product, silk cloth, provides an example of the specialization of labor that went along with social stratification. Starting in the third millennium BCE, Chinese women began weaving cloth from the cocoons of silkworms. They fed the worms masses of mulberry leaves to make them grow fast. The women unraveled the cocoons to obtain the delicate silk threads and wove them into valuable textiles. The silk trade became a key component of the Chinese economy, and silk production remained a Chinese monopoly until the sixth century CE. Thus, silk production both reflected Chinese social structure and helped make China a global trading crossroads.

Similarly, villages appeared by 6500 BCE in the northwestern part of the Indian subcontinent, where farmers grew barley and wheat using techniques probably imported from Southwest Asia. They gradually spread out into regions such as the Indus River Valley, where the rich soil allowed increased agricultural production and, hence, population growth. Over time South Asian farmers extended the range of plants they grew and started to cultivate cotton, which they used to weave textiles. By 3500 BCE village life was common in the fertile river valleys of South and East Asia.

Nomadic Herders of the Steppe

At the same time that they learned to domesticate plants, the early inhabitants of Asia became responsible for the survival of selected animals. They bred them, protected them against natural predators, milked and sheared them, and guided them to pastureland where they could feed. The search for pasture required herders to move around for at least part of the year because most natural environments in Asia do not provide sufficient food for herds in the same place year-round.

From about 3000 BCE on, sheep, goats, and cattle were the most important domesticated animals throughout Asia. The settled farmers and nomadic herders exchanged the specialized goods they each produced. Farmers traded grains, pottery, and other craft goods for the herders' dairy products, wool, and skins. But tensions could arise between the two groups, especially in summer when herders drove their flocks from the dry steppe to the lush river valleys where their animals could graze. At just that time, the farmers' crops were nearly ready for harvest, so allowing flocks near them could prove disastrous. Many ancient accounts focus on these tensions and ignore the cooperation, but both were important, and the need for exchange created a web of connections between nomadic and settled peoples that shaped both cultures.

The pastoral lifestyle originally did not allow people to range over great distances as they moved on foot. A dramatic change occurred when they started to use domesticated horses. There are many scholarly disagreements about this innovation: When did it happen and was it a development in one place that spread over the entirety of Eurasia or did people in various regions think of it independently? Horses became truly important in world history around 2000 BCE only when they were hitched to chariots and wagons. For both settled and pastoral populations, the two-wheeled horse-drawn chariot was an essential piece of equipment, used in warfare and for other purposes. By 1000 BCE, chariot technology had spread throughout Asia, and in pastoral societies charioteers became elites with great wealth and power.

When people started to ride horses using saddles and bits, rather than bareback, their mobility increased even more, and the distances they could cover expanded drastically. By 500 BCE, animal herders on horseback roamed the Asian steppes. Their speed and agility made them feared in battle, but the armies of settled populations soon imitated their techniques. The use of the horse revolutionized warfare throughout Asia and beyond.

The mobility of mounted horsemen had a remarkable consequence: during the first millennium BCE, shared cultural elements appeared over a vast region, from eastern Russia to western China. From the Black Sea to Siberia, nomadic people used similar burial mounds. They placed the dead in a central chamber of wood or stone, over which they piled an earthen mound. As gifts, they included weapons and sacrificed animals. These burial items reveal the people's preoccupations in life with warfare and animal husbandry.

The best examples of such tombs are found on the modern border between Russia and northern China at the site of Pazyryk (PA-zee-rick) (see again Map 3.1). The builders covered the tomb chambers with earthen mounds, on top of which they piled loose rocks. The tombs housed the bodies of horses and of people whose skins had dried naturally, some of them completely tattooed. They also contained textiles, leather, and felt, all decorated with images of humans, animals, and other special motifs, as well as weapons and precious goods, including imports from China, India, and Southwest Asia.

The people buried in them were leaders of nomadic groups. Among them was a young blond woman, covered with body tattoos, who died around 500 BCE. She was placed in a wooden coffin wearing a blouse imported from India and a

≡ **Chariot from Pazyryk Burials in Central Asia** The people of Central Asia who relied on the horse for transport invented a new set of tools and equipment to use with the animal, including chariots. This chariot, found in one of the burials at Pazyryk, was reconstructed from pieces of wood and leather. The distance between the front and back wheels is only two inches, which suggests this was a ceremonial object.

three-foot-high felt headdress onto which gilded wooden birds had been sewn. Six horses accompanied her in death, which showed her wealth in life as well as the profound importance of the horse for Asian nomads.

Between 5000 and 1000 BCE, Asians had thus developed two basic means of survival, as nomadic herders and as settled farmers. Interactions between the two groups would have an enormous impact on all of Asia's subsequent history.

The Indus Valley Culture 2600–1900 BCE

↘ **FOCUS** What were the main characteristics of South Asia's early urban culture?

In the third and second millennia BCE, the villages of South and East Asia had developed major urban societies in the valleys of the powerful Indus and Yellow Rivers. The two regions were strikingly different, however. The Indus Valley had cities earlier than China, but they disappeared after 1900 BCE, whereas in China the building of the first cities started a long history of urban life. The Indus culture is also less accessible to us because its script has not yet been deciphered. Further, no later native Indian sources describe Indus elites and their activities. Archaeological remains fill some of the gaps, but uncertainties about their interpretation have led to competing theories about many features of the Indus Valley culture.

Urban Society in the Indus Valley

Archaeological evidence shows that the geographical spread of the Indus culture was enormous, stretching some 1,100 miles from the northernmost reaches of the Indus River to the Arabian Sea and some 800 miles from east to west (see Map 3.2). The Indus culture existed in varied natural environments, including fertile agricultural zones with abundant rainfall near the mountains, a large alluvial plain that is naturally fertilized by annual flooding, and a marshy coastal area with islands and peninsulas.

Around 2600 BCE the mature Indus culture emerged. For unknown reasons numerous people moved into cities surrounded by villages. We know of five very large urban centers, whose inhabitants may have numbered 30,000 (similar to the population of Uruk, discussed in Chapter 2), and more than thirty smaller cities. At the same time, the number of villages remained very high as well: archaeologists have identified more than 15,000 of them. Despite the great distances between them, the urban settlements were remarkably similar. Scholars often refer to them as *Harappan*, after the modern name of one of the large cities.

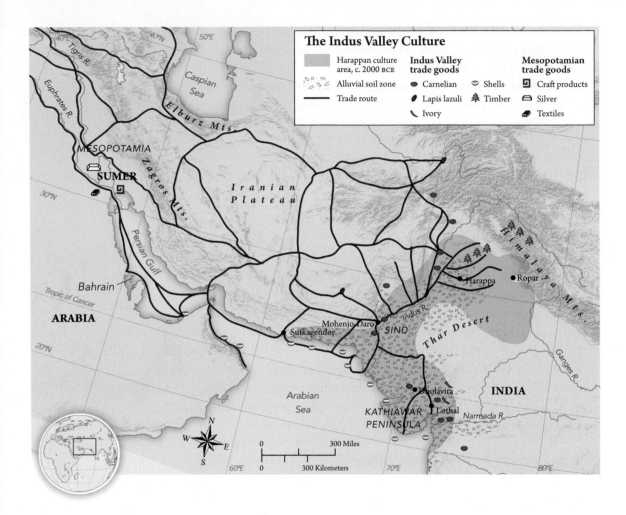

≡ **MAP 3.2**   **The Indus Valley Culture**   Stretched over a vast area along the Indus River, the earliest urban culture in South Asia is remarkable for the consistency of archaeological finds in many cities and villages. Trade in valuable goods was partly responsible for the shared cultural elements, some of which reached far beyond the Indus Valley into Mesopotamia.

Each of the five large cities had a high sector, set on a mud-brick platform, with monumental buildings, and lower sectors with residences and workshops. The interior layout of each sector was planned on a grid pattern oriented north to south and east to west. In some residential areas, streets up to thirty-three feet wide created city blocks, which were subdivided with narrower streets. Evidence that smaller settlements had the same layout indicates that people consciously planned cities and villages using an established pattern.

Mohenjo-Daro (moe-hen-joe-DAHR-oh) in the east of modern Pakistan is the best-known and largest site of the culture. Its monumental buildings on the high sector are relatively well preserved. They include the Great Bath, twenty-three feet wide by thirty-nine feet long and eight feet deep, made of baked bricks and lined with plaster. Around the outside of the bath was a three-inch layer of bitumen, a kind of asphalt used as waterproofing. People may have used the small rooms next to the bath to change clothing. Next to the Great Bath was a vast storehouse for grain, ninety-nine by ninety-nine feet, and the platform also supported a large pillared hall. These structures indicate a communal effort to construct special edifices.

In the residential areas—which also housed the shops and craft workshops—people built their homes using uniformly sized bricks. The Harappan cities show a greater attention to sanitation than was seen anywhere else in the ancient world.

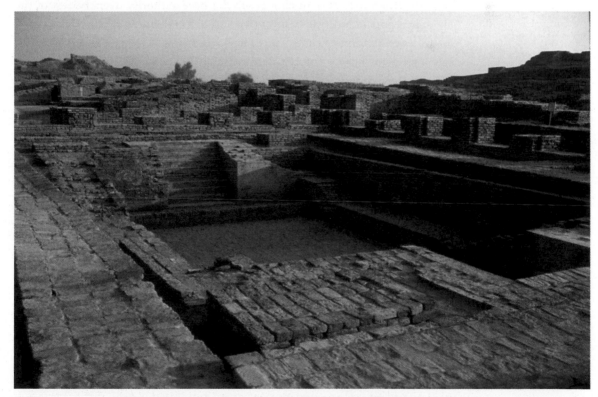

The Great Bath at Mohenjo-Daro This building in the center of Mohenjo-Daro clearly had a use related to water; the bricks are neatly fitted together and sealed with plaster, and the outside is covered with bitumen, a waterproofing substance. Because of the stairs and the bench-like ledge, most archaeologists think it was used for ritual bathing.

Houses had private bathrooms and wells, and their sewage systems were connected to main channels underneath the streets. All cities had large artificial basins to collect water. Scholars believe that the Indus people planned these elaborate systems to protect themselves against flooding rivers and heavy rains. They could have used some of the basins as harbors as well.

The archaeological remains of Harappan cities present many problems of interpretation. They suggest political and social structures that are very unlike those of other early urban cultures in which an elite holds power over the mass of the population, often by military means. The remains of the Indus society show no military activity. The people never depicted warfare, and none of their tombs contained weapons. Further, houses or tombs show no grandiose displays of wealth. The archaeological material from the Indus Valley creates the impression (perhaps falsely) that the majority of people shared wealth equally.

The existence of massive public works, however, suggests that, as was the case in other urban societies, an elite group did have authority over the rest of the Harappan population. The basis of that authority remains a mystery, as there is no evidence of military control or, as far as we know, of temples that could indicate a religious basis of power. Because long-distance trade was crucial to the Indus Valley economy, many historians propose that a merchant class governed. Others speculate that the Indus Valley culture featured certain people who gained respect by renouncing material goods and luxuries, as people in later Indian history did.

How do we explain that the cities of the Indus Valley culture show an amazing cultural uniformity even though they are located 200 to 400 miles apart? The idea that one unified territorial state would have imposed the cultural norms seems improbable, as such a state would have been enormous. The cultural similarity indicates that the cities were in close contact with one another. Trade most likely played a key role in creating and reinforcing the contacts and connections that resulted in the uniformity of Indus culture.

Harappan Crafts and Long-Distance Trade

The archaeological evidence is more secure when we look at the role of crafts and trade in the Indus Valley culture. The people imported prized stones, such as carnelian and lapis lazuli, to carve valuable objects, including seals and beads. Wherever archaeologists find such objects, the objects are similar in shape and size, showing that craftsmen throughout the Indus Valley followed standard patterns. All the settlements used a unified system of weights and measures, which greatly facilitated transactions among people of different towns.

SEEING THE PAST

Inscribed Seals from the Indus Valley

The people of the Indus Valley created a script that emerged around 2600 BCE, remained in use until around 1900 BCE, and then disappeared forever. Some 4,000 texts are known, mostly incised on stamp seals, pottery, or pieces of jewelry. People of the Indus Valley used the stone stamps to make an impression on a piece of soft clay, so they cut the inscriptions in mirror image. On these seals the signs often appear next to the image of a single standing animal. Archaeologists have found lumps of clay into which such seals were pressed, often on several sides.

The inscriptions were usually very short, on average containing about five signs. Thus they did not record long sentences or tales, but most likely administrative information, such as the amount of a commodity and the name of the person who supervised the transaction. There are about 400 signs, which suggests that each sign expressed an entire word.

Seals from Mohenjo-Daro

Examining the Evidence

1. Although we cannot understand the writing on them, what do these seals tell us about record-keeping in the Indus culture?

2. Comparing the two seals, what similarities do you observe? How would you describe the differences?

3. How do the Indus Valley seals differ from the first writings we discussed for other early cultures?

For Further Information:

An Indus Seal. https://www.khanacademy.org/humanities/art-asia/south-asia/x97ec695a:indus-valley-civilization/a/an-indus-seal

Writing is another indicator that trade was important in the Indus Valley. Although we cannot decipher the texts, all scribes over the vast region of the culture used the same signs and carved them on the same types of objects. Indus script appeared in two contexts that seem connected to trade. People inscribed vessels, probably to indicate who owned the contents; more dramatically, writing appears on stone seals that appear throughout the Indus Valley (see Seeing the Past: Inscribed Seals from the Indus Valley).

Traders also exported Indus Valley craft items to distant places, including Mesopotamia and the Persian Gulf. Inhabitants of the island of Bahrain adopted the Indus system of weights and measures and produced seals in the Harappan style, sometimes inscribing them with signs of the Indus script. Thus Indus cities served as crossroads, connecting communities to one another and to the larger world.

The End of the Indus Valley Culture

Around 1900 BCE people throughout the Indus Valley started to leave the great cities and other settlements, and they abandoned shared cultural practices. Many historians theorize that the arrival of Indo-European-speaking migrants forced them to change their lifestyles completely. But there is no clear evidence of conquest. The cities were not burned down or sacked, and there are no signs of violence.

The end of the Indus Valley cities was more likely due to a combination of factors. It is possible that the climate became drier in the early second millennium BCE and that urban residents could no longer grow enough food to live in large groups. People moved into villages, which required smaller concentrations of food, or migrated eastward, where the climate was wetter. This movement disrupted the trade networks that had tied the vast region together, and by 1700 BCE people used a variety of local traditions. The great cities of the Indus Valley ceased to exist, and many centuries passed before urban culture returned to that area of the world.

The Indo-Europeans 3000–1000 BCE

⬊ **FOCUS** What does the concept "Indo-European" mean, and how important is it for the study of Eurasia?

We just considered the theory that the Indus Valley culture ended because of the immigration of people speaking an Indo-European language. The scholarly disagreement over exactly what happened illustrates how difficult it is to understand the process by which Indo-European languages came to be spoken over a vast area of Eurasia. However, the fact that by 100 BCE people from western China to western Europe spoke related Indo-European languages certainly was the result of a crucial process in Eurasian history—a process likely connected to the interactions between farmers and pastoralists.

Indo-European Languages

The term *Indo-European* does not refer to a race or an ethnic group but to a group of languages that are related in vocabulary and grammar. In the eighteenth century CE, European scholars first observed links between Sanskrit, the sacred language of ancient India, and the European classical languages, Greek and Latin. Note, for example, how English, Sanskrit, Greek, and Latin use the same words to express mother, father, and house (domicile):

English	Sanskrit	Greek	Latin
mother	matar	meter	mater
father	pitar	pater	pater
domicile	dama	domos	domus

Hence linguists reasoned that the languages evolved from an original, ancient language that spread when its speakers migrated. They grouped the languages derived from this ancient one under the name *Indo-European*. When Indo-European groups separated, they adjusted to new natural environments and interacted with populations who spoke non-Indo-European languages. Consequently, their languages developed differences but maintained clear common Indo-European roots.

Indo-European Migrations

Speakers of an Indo-European language who called themselves *Arya*, "noble," arrived in South Asia shortly after 2000 BCE and started to displace the local people, who spoke non-Indo-European Dravidian languages. Where the speakers of Indo-European speakers came from and what motivated them to migrate remain unresolved (see again Map 3.1). The two principal explanations for these migrations show how scholars can interpret the same set of evidence very differently. Some researchers suggest that Indo-European languages spread together with agriculture from the area of modern Turkey where farming originated, a process that started already between 7500 and 6000 BCE. Farmers would have altered not only the local populations' means of survival but also their languages, in a process parallel to that of the Bantu migrations in Africa (see Chapter 7). Other scholars believe the speakers of Indo-European languages were pastoralists who moved into farming areas starting around 4000 BCE. Many believe these migrants originated in the southern Russian steppes and that their arrival entailed the conquest and domination of local populations. The conquerors would have benefited greatly from their expertise in horsemanship. It is equally possible, however, that pastoralists often integrated peacefully into existing farming communities.

Whatever the correct explanation, it is important not to see the Indo-European migrations as a massive wave of people who moved across Eurasia changing everything in their path. There were many different types of interactions with existing populations that had an effect not only on the languages that resulted from these interactions but also on other aspects of people's lives. These processes took place over many centuries, in many different environments, and with diverse outcomes.

Indo-European Speakers and Eurasian History

Indo-European languages gradually came to dominate Eurasia. The earliest definitive evidence of an Indo-European language is from what is now Turkey, where, as we saw in Chapter 2, the Hittites had established a powerful state by 1800 BCE whose official court language was Indo-European Hittite. In Greece, evidence of Indo-European first appears in Linear B tablets from 1500 to 1200 BCE that include Greek words. The presence of Indo-European languages farther west and north in Europe is clear from the earliest written remains found there, that is, from about 500 BCE onward.

In Asia, Indo-European speakers did not become as dominant as they were in Europe. In the Middle East outside Turkey (where people today speak Turkish, the non-Indo-European language of later immigrants), people continued to use Semitic languages, such as Akkadian. But migrants speaking Indo-European languages moved into southern Asia, arriving on the Iranian plateau in the second millennium BCE.

The easternmost evidence of Indo-European languages appears in the Central Asian provinces of modern China, in the Tarim Basin, where texts from much later centuries are in an Indo-European language. Excavations have uncovered burials there with naturally mummified human bodies, for some of which the burials date back to 2000 BCE. The dead people had European physical features, including fair skin and light hair, and some scholars believe that they were Indo-European speakers. They arrived in western China when the chariot first appeared in Shang China, and the two events seem to be related.

The spread of Indo-European languages was one of the most important events in the early history of the entire Eurasian continent. As a result, by the beginning of the Common Era, if not before, peoples from the Atlantic Ocean to the western regions of China spoke a variety of related languages that had a common source. The spread of Indo-European languages is but one example of the profound impact of migrants on the societies of Eurasia.

India's Vedic Age 1500–500 BCE

◥ FOCUS How did cultural developments in early Indian history shape the structure of society?

By 1500 BCE the Aryas had entered the Indian subcontinent from the Iranian plateau. They migrated into the fertile river valleys in search of land, first in the northwest of India and later farther east. The mixture of peoples, traditions, and languages that resulted led to changes in customs and lifestyles that affected all, and this fusion became the foundation of classical Indian culture (see Map 3.3).

Vedic Origins

Ancient Indian literature contains many references to the new society that developed when Indo-European speakers migrated into the subcontinent. Unfortunately for historians, the accounts were written down long after the events they describe, raising questions about their accuracy. The oldest compositions are the **Vedas**, collections of hymns, songs, prayers, and dialogues. The term *Veda* literally means "sacred knowledge," and the texts are written in a very early form of the Indo-European Sanskrit language. Priests probably composed the *Rig Veda*, a collection of 1,028 hymns organized in ten books and addressed to various deities, between 1500 and 900 BCE. The hymns were not written down until after 300 BCE, however, and the later authors likely modified their contents.

The authors depicted the Aryas as light-skinned nomadic warriors who conquered the local dark-skinned population, the *Dasa*, which means "enemy." The Aryas fought on horse-drawn chariots against the Dasa, who often lived in fortified settlements, and also against each other. According to the Vedas, the Aryas greatly valued cattle and needed access to grazing areas for their animals. Although the Vedas focus on military feats, many scholars now believe that the Aryas spread across India through peaceful interaction and intermarriage with local populations.

Rise of a New Society: Families, Clans, and Castes

People in early Vedic society belonged to extended families organized along patriarchal lines, the leading men having full control over other members of the family. Women had little authority and did not inherit family wealth unless there were no male heirs. The *Lawbook of Manu*, although written down much later in the first century BCE, gives an idea of the low status of women in the Vedic age:

Vedas Early collections of Indian hymns, songs, and prayers that contain sacred knowledge; initially preserved in oral form, they were recorded in writing at an unknown date, probably after 300 BCE.

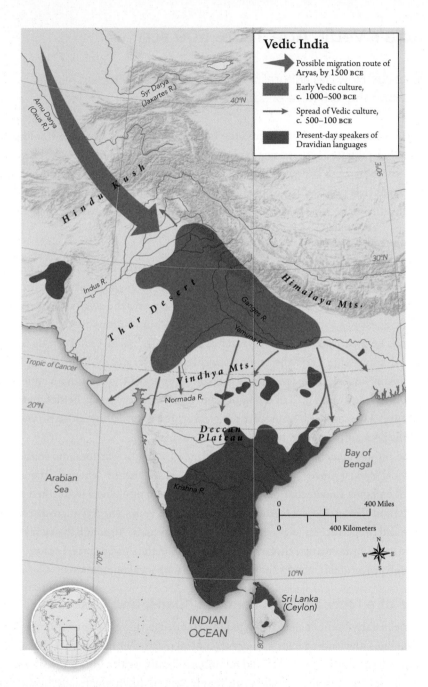

≡ **MAP 3.3   Vedic India** The migration around 1500 BCE of Indo-European-speaking Aryas into South Asia introduced radical changes in culture and society, which gradually spread from the northwest throughout much of the subcontinent.

Day and night women must be kept in dependence by the males of their families, and, if they attach themselves to sensual enjoyments, they must be kept under one's control. Her father protects her in childhood, her husband protects her in youth, and her sons protect her in old age; a woman is never fit for independence.[2]

Extended families joined together in **clans**, which were the basis of the early Vedic political structure. Family heads met in assemblies and accepted the leadership of a **raja**, a word that corresponds to the Latin *rex*, "king," although a translation of "chief" is more accurate. Clan members shared their resources and maintained strong social ties. Clashes between clans were frequent, and the rajas had to be great military leaders to gain the respect of their people. This explains the atmosphere of conflict in the Vedas.

Around 1000 BCE, after the composition of the *Rig Veda*, different categorizations arose. One involved the concept of **varna**, which literally means "color," but the word came to mean something like "class." Originally the varna system had four levels: Brahmins (BRAH-mihns), or priests; Kshatriyas (shuh-TREE-uhs), the warriors; Vaishyas (VYSH-yuhs), landowning peasants and merchants; and Shudras (SHOOD-ras), by far the largest group, composed of artisans, landless farmers, and laborers. Later on came the addition of a fifth group, the Untouchables, who worked with materials that others refused to touch, such as animal skins. Entire families belonged to the same varna, and they stayed in the same category over many generations, as people were supposed to marry within their own varna.

This rigorous system of social hierarchy required justification, and a hymn added late to the *Rig Veda* provided it in these terms:

> When the gods . . . divided the Man . . .

> His mouth became the Brahmin; his arms were made into the Warrior (Kshatriya), his thighs the People (Vaishya), and from his feet the Servants (Shudra) were born.[3]

Just as each part of the human body serves a specific purpose, each varna served a specific purpose in society and had a fixed place in the social hierarchy. This social order, like the body itself, had been created by the gods and could not be questioned or changed.

Over time the structure of Vedic society became more complex, however. Labor became more specialized, and by 500 BCE subdivisions of the varna system developed. These became known as **jati**. Although varnas continued to determine people's position in the social hierarchy, specific occupations grouped them into jatis.

clan Group of families related to a real or presumed common ancestor.

raja Chief of Indian clan; the term is related to the Latin word for "king," *rex*.

varna Group identity in early Indian society, related to the concept of class; people belonged to one of four varnas as a result of their birth.

jati Division of Indian society that identifies an individual's occupation and social standing.

Every specialized occupation could create a new jati, each with its specific tasks and duties. Members of a jati lived together, married each other, and ate together.

When Portuguese visitors to the Indian subcontinent in the sixteenth century CE observed these social groups, they gave them the name *casta*, which means "breed." That categorization led to the English designation of the **caste system**, a social structure in which everyone had an allotted place. There were clear rules of behavior, which, if broken, would lead to expulsion from the caste—hence the term *outcast*. Social mobility was very difficult in Vedic society. Jatis could improve their lot as a group, but individuals rarely moved into a higher caste. The system had a particular advantage, however: it facilitated the integration of newcomers into Indian society, even those with different faiths. Many immigrants to the subcontinent could establish themselves as a defined jati.

Vedic Religion

The Vedas portray a rich religious system, one that shares ideas and gods described in other Indo-European writings, especially those from Iran and Greece. The atmosphere of conflict dominates in the divine world of the Vedas, and many of the gods represent forces of nature admired because of their strength.

As was true among humans, male gods dominated the Vedic divine world. Their leader was Indra, the war god, often violent and fond of drink. The sky god, Varuna, maintained cosmic order and justice. The god of fire, Agni, was the intermediary between humans and gods because, as fire, he made it possible for people to give sacrifices. Trained priests burned offerings to urge the gods to be kind. Sacrifice was so central in the Vedic culture that it became connected with creation itself. According to tradition, the gods had created the universe by sacrificing a Lord of Beings, the primeval man who had existed before the universe. Consequently, every time the priests performed a sacrifice, they repeated creation and thus became responsible for the order of the universe.

The most important sacrifices, especially those of horses, demanded the presence of the raja. Over time, the raja became the sole patron of sacrifices, and the priests gave him attributes of divinity. In this way a division of authority developed: the Brahmins gained superiority in the ritual world, and the raja became the political, military, and administrative head of the clan. Women were fully excluded from this power structure. Thus Vedic religious practices and beliefs reinforced the social and political order.

The Brahmins' central role in sacrifices confirmed their uppermost status in the caste system and also had a unique effect on the spread of literacy in India. Only they knew the Vedic hymns that were essential during sacrifices, and they may

caste system Indian organization of society that identifies people's position and status on the basis of the group into which they were born.

have prevented their written recording and the use of writing in general. This monopoly on literacy strengthened the power of the Brahmins, but it slowed the spread of writing throughout Indian society. Only by 500 CE did writing become widespread in India, whereas in other equally complex societies—such as Mesopotamia, where, as we saw in Chapter 2, writing first served administrative functions—it caught on much earlier.

Developments in Vedic Ideas

Early Vedic society was primarily centered in the river valleys of northwest India, as the dense forests farther east in the Ganges plain originally prevented extensive agriculture and herding there (see again Map 3.3). It was only after 1000 BCE, when people began to use iron tools, that forests could be cleared. Aryas spread eastward, and during this period of expansion they encountered indigenous traditions that affected their own religious doctrines. Starting around 500 BCE groups of people started to reject the structures of Vedic society and began to formulate new interpretations of the Vedas in a new type of texts, which were only written down much later. Called *Upanishads* (oo-PAHN-ih-shhad), they combined indigenous and Vedic traditions and shifted the strong focus on sacrifice toward an emphasis on living a righteous life. This shift was connected to changes in the beliefs about the afterlife and to the concept of **reincarnation**—rebirth in a new form.

The belief arose that every living creature had an immortal essence, something like a soul. Upon death this soul would leave the body and be reborn in another body. When people had behaved well, their souls reincarnated into higher bodies. But when they had misbehaved, they reincarnated into a lower life form, either a lower caste or an animal or plant. The outcome depended on a person's **karma**, his or her behavior in the former life. The idea of reincarnation supported the caste system—a person's position in the hierarchy was the result of earlier behavior and hence one's own responsibility.

The belief in reincarnation tied all forms of life together into a single system, a universal and eternal entity called **Brahman**. The aim of the Upanishads was to make people conscious of their connection to the Brahman. In this view, each being has a Self, called the **atman**, understanding of which liberates people from the constant cycle of reincarnation. They would first attain a state of deep sleep without dreams, unaware of any physical reality. After achieving deep sleep, an individual could reach a level beyond this dreamless trance, in which he or she realizes that his or her Self is identified with the eternal entity (Brahman). One does

reincarnation Belief system that every living being's soul can be reborn in another life form after death in an eternal cycle of existence.

karma In Indian thought about reincarnation, the consequences of one's behavior in an earlier life that influence events in the present.

Brahman In Indian thought, a universal and eternal soul that binds all life forms together.

atman In Indian thought, the immortal essence of a living creature.

not reach the higher stage through active life but by meditating, that is, reflecting on religious questions.

We see, then, that the expansion of the Aryas across India did not result in the simple dissemination of Vedic ideas. Rather, contact with indigenous traditions led to changes in Vedic ideas. A religion that emphasized individual transcendence replaced one that emphasized the role of social elites in divine sacrifice. It is within this later Vedic world that further developments in Indian religious thought would take place (which we will explore in Chapter 5).

The Early Chinese Dynasties 2000–771 BCE

⬊ FOCUS What factors account for the remarkable cultural continuity of early Chinese states?

In India of the second millennium BCE, we have seen how the arrival of new people caused sweeping social and religious changes. By contrast, in the region of East Asia that would develop into China, cultures in the early and later periods were linked by continuities. From the start of agricultural life in the vast landmass that constitutes modern China, multiple cultures coexisted, and through increased contacts and exchange they acquired common features. The middle Yellow River Valley was the seat of a succession of dynasties, and archaeological information from that region allows us to study how states governed by a powerful elite developed.

Re-creating Early China: Literary Traditions and the Archaeological Record

Around 100 BCE, Sima Qian, whom we met at the beginning of the chapter, wrote a history of his country up to his own day, the *Records of the Historian*. Because he lived in a time when a single dynasty, the Han, ruled China, he depicted the earlier history of his country as a sequence of similar dynasties. According to Sima Qian, after a period in which heroes and sages established the elements of culture, three dynasties governed in succession: the Xia (shah), Shang, and Zhou (joe).

Archaeology tells a somewhat different story. Excavations provide evidence that from about 2000 to 771 BCE, a sequence of large urban centers flourished in China; they were probably the capital cities of states. In those cities lived elites who surrounded themselves with luxury goods in life and were buried in lavish tombs, similar to those we have seen in Southwest Asia and Egypt.

China's early history becomes clearer with the appearance of bones and turtle shells incised with mostly short inscriptions, using early characters of Chinese script. Some 200,000 such inscriptions have been discovered. These were used in **divination**—that is, the prediction of the future—and modern scholars refer to them as *oracle bones*. The names on them, which Sima Qian also listed, reveal that they derive from the reigns of the last nine kings of the Shang dynasty—that is, from about 1200 to 1027 BCE (see Lives and Livelihoods: Chinese Diviners, page 108).

The script of the oracle bones uses a principle followed in the cuneiform and hieroglyphic writings we discussed in Chapter 2: a single sign represents an entire word. Some of the characters were pictures of the item they indicated (for example, a kneeling human for a woman), whereas conventional symbols conveyed abstract ideas (for example, a mouth for "to call"). Although many words in Chinese sound alike, each had its own representation in writing, and until the twentieth century CE, Chinese script did not rely much on syllabic signs. In this respect, it departed from the early scripts of Southwest Asia and Egypt.

The Chinese script has a unique history. After the first emperor, Shi Huangdi (shee huang-dee, discussed in Chapter 5), ordered its standardization, its basic elements and characters did not change, although the shape of the signs evolved over time. The script had a deep effect on Chinese history in that it connected people from a wide geographical area to the same ancient past.

The Growth of States 2000–1570 BCE

Soon after 2000 BCE the village cultures that had characterized China for millennia developed into a more uniform culture in which bronze played a major role. Scholars disagree about how bronze working arrived in China. Some argue for an indigenous invention, whereas others believe that Indo-European nomads brought the technology from western Asia to China.

Bronze production in ancient China was unparalleled in the ancient world. Demand was so great that around 1500 BCE large-scale production started. Workers manufactured numerous objects. Many were giant—one tomb from around 1200 BCE contained 3,520 pounds of the metal, and the largest surviving bronze vessel from antiquity, which weighs 1,925 pounds, is also from this era. All the bronze objects were cast in molds with intricate decorations. Mining the metals, transporting them, and casting them required the handicraft of hundreds of workers, many with specialized skills. Thus, the desires of elites stimulated bronze production and required the specialized labor that went along with social stratification.

divination The practice of seeking information about the future through sources regarded as magical.

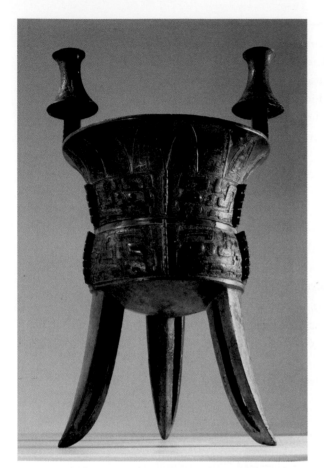

≡ **Shang Dynasty Bronze Vessel** To produce a vessel like this one, Shang artists made a clay model of the desired object to create a mold, which they cut into pieces. They cast bronze segments in the clay molds and reassembled them before filling in the details. This process enabled them to produce large items with elaborate decoration. (Werner Forman Archive/Private Collection London. Location: 07/HIP/Art Resource, NY)

The earliest large urban site in China is Erlitou (er-lee-toh), dating from around 1900 BCE (see again Map 3.1). In its center on top of a pounded-earth platform archaeologists found the remains of a monumental building, measuring about 110 by 117 yards. The objects found at the site of Erlitou resemble those that later clearly showed political control and ritual activity, such as weapons and bronze vessels. Archaeologists also found many animal shoulder blades, which, although not inscribed, may have been oracle bones.

The archaeological remains from Erlitou belong to a culture that spread over the central Yellow River Valley and adjacent zones. Scholars used to believe that Erlitou was the capital of the dynasty that Sima Qian called Xia, but today most historians think that the Xia dynasty did not exist and that Sima Qian imposed an image of the state of his day onto an earlier period. Many of Erlitou's cultural elements survived into the succeeding period, which may characterize the start of what Sima Qian called the Shang dynasty. Historians feel that they are on firmer ground in the study of that dynasty, as oracle bones confirm its existence and contain information that archaeology on its own cannot provide.

The Shang Dynasty and the Consolidation of Power 1570–1027 BCE

Several major cities in the Yellow River Valley seem to have been successive centers of political power in the second half of the second millennium BCE (see Map 3.4). They differed from early cities in Southwest Asia and the Indus Valley; they covered a much larger area and had zones with clearly distinct functions that housed a hierarchy of social classes. The centers of the early Chinese cities

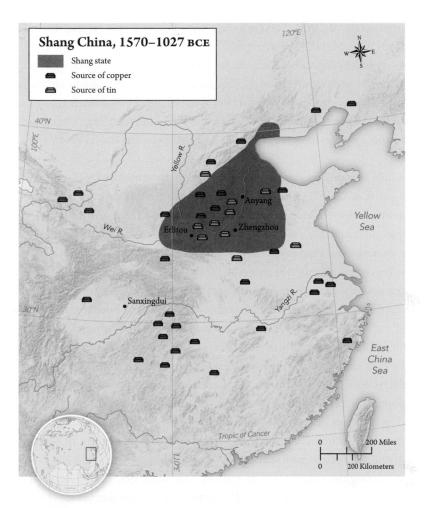

≡ **MAP 3.4   Shang China, 1570–1027 BCE** The Shang dynasty ruled the Yellow River (Huang He) Valley and its surroundings. They repeatedly moved the capital to sprawling new cities with massive earthwork constructions and impressive royal tombs. Famed for its bronzes, Shang China needed continued access to copper and tin, whose sources the state sought to control.

contained large buildings on top of pounded-earth platforms reserved for the elites. Surrounding them were industrial areas with workshops that produced goods for these elites. The common people lived in the outer rings of the cities in small houses partly dug into the ground. On the outskirts of the cities were located the tombs for rulers and other elites, and nearby were sites for rituals related to the dead, such as the reading of oracle bones. Thus, Chinese cities were physical manifestations of Chinese social structure.

The city of Anyang shows the culmination of a process of increasing concentration of power and wealth in early China. Stretching over a huge area of some twenty square miles, it most likely was a capital of the Shang state. Anyang's cemetery shows the riches that elites accumulated. It had thirteen large tombs, dug into the ground up to forty-three feet deep and with wooden burial chambers at the bottom.

The only remaining intact tomb from Anyang belonged to Queen Fu Hao (foo HOW), wife of King Wu Ding, who lived in the thirteenth century BCE. Previously known oracle bones had already revealed that she was a highly unusual woman for her time, although she was only one of Wu Ding's many consorts. Some oracle bones state that Fu Hao prepared them, evidence that she took a leading role in divination, which was usually reserved for the king. The oracle bones also indicate that she actively participated in her husband's wars, raising troops and leading them into battle. The finds in the tomb confirmed her unusual status. They included over a hundred weapons—very uncommon for a woman's burial—and some were inscribed with her name. Several bronze vessels were also inscribed with Fu Hao's name or title. The splendor of her tomb goods was magnificent. They included more than 460 bronze objects, some seventy stone sculptures, nearly 705 jade objects, numerous bone hairpins, and roughly 7,000 cowrie shells, which served as currency at the time. Alongside Fu Hao lay six sacrificed dogs and sixteen sacrificed humans. As in other ancient societies, the tombs of the Chinese elites displayed their wealth and power.

Surrounding the royal tombs of Anyang were more than 1,200 pits containing the remains of people and animals. Human skeletons were the most numerous by far, but there were also twenty pits with horses and fewer pits with other animals. The human sacrifices were usually young men, who were often beheaded or otherwise dismembered, with the heads buried apart from the bodies. Although some of these sacrifices were made at the time of a king's burial, most occurred later, as gifts to the dead. They were part of interactions between the king and his ancestors, which dominated the ritual life of the Shang state.

The cult of ancestors dominated Shang's ritual and religious ideas; the deceased were thought to have enormous powers over the living. A god called *Di* (dee) presided over hierarchically organized powers, which included natural phenomena and people who had lived in the past. These included male and female Shang ancestors of the king, pre-Shang ancestors, and former regional lords. When an important person died, he or she became an ancestor and joined the group of powers. The honors awarded to these people while still alive continued after death and may even have expanded.

Their high respect for ancestors also explains the care the Shang gave to burials and the subsequent sacrifices. The living king had to keep ancestors satisfied so that they would not cause harm, and he constantly consulted them through oracle bones to divine the future. Oracle reading evidently took place continuously and required an infrastructure of specialists. These included people to slaughter the animals; individuals to select and prepare the bones and shells; and scribes to record the questions, predictions, and other information on perishable materials before carving the text on the actual bones or shells (see Lives and Livelihoods: Chinese Diviners). Ancestor worship reinforced the power of kings by connecting them to a host of notable people stretching back through the generations to the beginning of time.

The king enforced his rule through military means as well as rituals. Devotion to warfare was a Shang hallmark. The core of the army fought on chariots pulled by two horses and ridden by three men: a warrior, an attendant, and a driver. The introduction of chariots after 1500 BCE marked a major technological change in Chinese society. Because the earliest chariots in China were fully developed, many scholars think the innovation came from western Asia. Once again, nomads were key to this development. Indo-European-speaking nomads of Central Asia were probably the intermediaries between the two regions.

All the monumental remains relate to the top level of Shang society, whose members had access to great wealth and power. The large majority of people, however, lived in poor conditions, working the fields, mining metals, building tombs and monumental residences, and providing other services to their masters. Many were enslaved persons captured during military campaigns, and as we have seen, their lives could be sacrificed to benefit the Shang elites.

Sima Qian's focus on the Shang dynasty, along with Anyang's status as the only city to provide written evidence of this period, creates the false impression that the Shang state was the only important one in late-second-millennium BCE China. Recent archaeological work shows that other regions had their own cultures, which sometimes produced artwork as impressive as that of Anyang, but stylistically distinct. The people of some of these regions must have created states as well. It was one of these centers that ended the Shang dynasty.

LIVES AND LIVELIHOODS

Chinese Diviners

Like other ancient peoples, the Chinese were preoccupied with predicting the future. In the Shang period, this stimulated a massive enterprise based on oracle bones. Numerous people were involved, including the preparers of bones or shells, the scribes, and the diviners themselves, a post reserved for noblemen. In most of the preserved oracle bones the Shang king was the principal figure, as the questions and interpretations derived their authority from his person. Recently excavated collections show that also non-royals could initiate the divination. The basic idea behind the practice was that ancestors could give guidance about the future and communicate their advice through oracle bones.

In typical practice, the king or his diviners first formulated a statement such as "We will receive millet harvest." The diviner then touched a previously prepared animal shoulder bone or turtle shell with a hot metal point until the bone or shell cracked. He numbered the cracks, and the king interpreted them as being auspicious—that is, indicating a good omen—or not. He then made a prediction such as "Auspicious: We will receive harvest." Next, a scribe carved the original

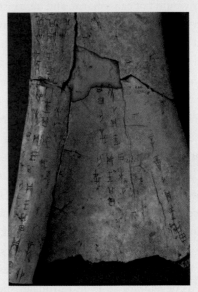

≡ **Oracle Bone** Bones inscribed with early Chinese characters present the first examples of Chinese writing dating to the late Shang period, 1200 to 1027 BCE. This oracle bone is one of the about 100,000 that have been found near the Shang capital of Anyang.

question on the bone or shell, sometimes with the king's prediction and more rarely with a statement of what happened in reality.

The Early Zhou Dynasty and the Extension of Power 1027–771 BCE

During the Shang period many distinct groups controlled parts of northern China as either allies or opponents of Shang rulers. According to Sima Qian, the leader of one such group, the Zhou, defeated Di Xin, the last Shang ruler, at the Battle of

The questions posed often involved the success of harvests or whether the queen would give birth to a boy or a girl. They ranged over a wide area of royal activities, however. Whom should the king appoint to a bureaucratic post? When should he make an offering? Will an act of his incur the displeasure of the Powers? One group of early diviners often listed alternatives side by side. For example:

Divined: "On the next day, day 31, (we) should not make offering to Ancestor Yi."

Divined: "On the next day, day 31, (we) should make offering to Ancestor Yi."

Some statements contained an appeal for good luck or asked for guidance in the interpretation of an event or a dream. Others aimed to predict disasters, as in this example:

Crack-making on day 30, Que divined: "In the next ten days there will be no disasters." The king read the cracks, and said: "Not so. There will be trouble!" And so it was. On day 31, the king went to hunt buffaloes and the chariot of officer Zi hit the royal chariot. Prince Yang fell to the ground.

Oracle bone divination is closely tied to the Shang dynasty. It may have originated earlier in Chinese history, but archaeologists cannot determine from the uninscribed bones and shells whether they were consumed for food only or had uses in divination. The Shang dynasty elevated oracle bone divination to a major state enterprise, as the numerous remains show. With the Zhou, however, people turned to other means to find out what the future held in store.

Source: Redouan Djamouri, trans., "Écriture et divination sous les Shang," in *Divination et rationalité en Chine ancienne*, ed. Karine Chemla, Donald Harper, and Marc Kalinowski (Saint-Denis, France: Presses Universitaires de Vincennes, 1999), 19.

Examining the Evidence

1. What areas of life did Shang divination cover?
2. How did oracle bones bolster the king's role in society?

Muye in 1027 BCE. King Wen, the Zhou ruler, justified the rebellion by stating he had received the **Mandate of Heaven** to replace an evil and oppressive ruler. An ode in his honor from the *Book of Poetry* (see page 112) explains:

Great, indeed, was the Mandate of Heaven.
There were Shang's grandsons and sons.

Mandate of Heaven
Concept in Chinese
thought that Heaven
gave the right to rule
to a king or emperor
and could withdraw
that right were the
ruler to behave badly.

Was their number not a hundred thousand?
But the High God gave his Mandate,
and they bowed down to Zhou.[4]

As a supreme divine force Heaven gave the right to rule to a just and honorable man. When that man maintained order and harmony on earth, the entire cosmos was harmonious. If he misbehaved, however, Heaven withdrew the mandate, natural disasters occurred, and the people were allowed to rebel. The idea of the Mandate of Heaven thus became a check on rulers and allowed the possibility of political change.

The Zhou was the longest ruling dynasty in Chinese history (1027–221 BCE), although, as we will see, its powers were only nominal after 771 BCE. The territory Zhou kings ruled was larger than that of the Shang, but their control was indirect. Zhou kings did not personally annex and govern all the regions included in the state but appointed family members to do so on their behalf or established alliances with local lords who were willing to accept the kings' supremacy. By around 800 BCE there existed some 200 regional lords in the Zhou state. According to convention, they all belonged to one extended family, with the Zhou king being the oldest brother who deserved the most respect (see Map 3.5).

This structure provided a very strict hierarchy to Zhou society. Each local lord and state official had a well-defined rank and position assigned by birth. Sacrifices to ancestors continued. The king made offerings to the ancestors of the royal family, and local lords honored their own ancestors. By participating in these rituals, they reinforced their social ties.

Under the Zhou, however, the ritual practices associated with ancestor cults changed. Instead of performing sacrifices, nobles contacted their ancestors by donating bronzes, which they inscribed with short texts listing the names of the donors. In return, the ancestors were expected to provide favors to the living. The consultation of oracle bones also ended, and in its place kings determined the wishes of ancestors by reading messages in the lines sticks created when thrown down.

Some statements kings made in interpreting cast sticks became part of the major literary works of subsequent Chinese history. Later works, especially the *Book of Poetry*, include poems from the early Zhou period that reflect court life at the time (see Reading the Past: *Book of Poetry*). It is clear that many later generations in China saw the Zhou period as very special, with an ideal government and social

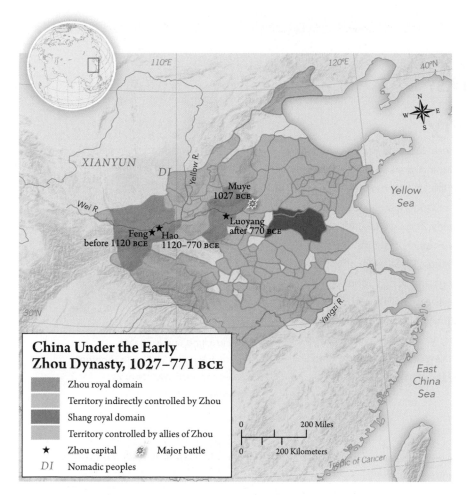

≡ **MAP 3.5   China Under the Early Zhou Dynasty, 1027–771 BCE** Although less centralized than the Shang, the power of the Zhou dynasty reached a larger area of China as many regional lords pledged their allegiance to the Zhou kings.

structure. Just as ancestors provided models for the living to emulate, the Zhou provided a model for the current Chinese state.

The Zhou political organization fell apart in 771 BCE, when leaders of dependent states started to ignore the king's commands and to fight one another, ushering in a long period of internal warfare. Nonetheless, in the many preceding centuries, a large part of China had become organized culturally and politically along similar lines, and a distinctive Chinese identity had arisen. The cultural developments

READING THE PAST

Book of Poetry

In its 305 poems the Chinese *Book of Poetry* covers a large variety of topics, including praise of the king and commentary on the daily life of commoners. It is the oldest collection of poetry in world history. and many of its poems date from the early Zhou period. All authors are anonymous, and the voices represented are multiple: kings, noblemen, soldiers, peasants, men, and women. There are love songs and songs about betrayal and sorrow. This example was originally a love song, but later Chinese thinkers interpreted it as a contest song by farmers who urge each other to escape government oppression, metaphorically referred to as the north wind.

> Cold is the north wind,
> the snow falls thick.
> If you are kind and love me,

take my hand and we'll go together.
You are modest, you are slow,
but oh, we must hurry!
Fierce is the north wind,
the snow falls fast.
If you are kind and love me,
take my hand and we'll go home together.
You are modest, you are slow,
but oh, we must hurry!
Nothing is redder than the fox,
nothing blacker than the crow.
If you are kind and love me,
take my hand and we'll ride together.
You are modest, you are slow,
but oh, we must hurry!

Source: Burton Watson, trans., in *Sources of Chinese Tradition*, 2nd ed., ed. Wm. Theodore de Bary and Irene Bloom (New York: Columbia University Press, 1991), 1:40.

EXAMINING THE EVIDENCE

1. How can one read this poem both as a love song and as a contest song?

2. How does it use the natural environment to convey its message?

were the result of indigenous processes, but technological innovations from the nomadic outsiders had played a significant role. Although settled Chinese such as Sima Qian saw these intruders as "barbarians," they had been crucial in the evolution of Chinese culture.

COUNTERPOINT: The Oxus People: A Short-Lived Culture in Central Asia 2250–1700 BCE

⬊ **FOCUS** What are the unique characteristics of the Oxus culture in the early history of Asia?

≡ **The Oxus Culture**

The urban cultures and early states discussed in this chapter—those the Aryas created in India and those of China starting with the Shang state—established long traditions with much continuity into modern times, despite ups and downs and many changes over the centuries. Similarly, the early states of Southwest Asia and Egypt considered in Chapter 2 were at the beginning of millennia-long traditions. Not all cultures in history show this type of continuity, however. Some arose, prospered magnificently, and then disappeared, leaving no traces in later cultures.

One such culture emerged around 2250 BCE in the Central Asian valleys of the Amu Darya and Syr Darya Rivers. It was remarkably wealthy and closely connected to other cultures in Asia. But it lasted for only some 550 years and disappeared without an impact on subsequent inhabitants. Scholars refer to it as the Oxus (OX-uhs) culture, after the Greek name *Oxus* for the Amu Darya River. Remains of the culture have been discovered in a wide area that encompasses parts of modern-day Iran, Pakistan, Afghanistan, and the Central Asian states of Turkmenistan, Uzbekistan, Tajikistan, and Kyrgyzstan. Archaeologists started to find evidence of the Oxus culture only about fifty years ago, and so far no texts written by its people have appeared. There are thus many uncertainties in the interpretations of its remains.

We do know that the Oxus culture existed in an arid environment where agriculture was impossible except in oases along rivers whose water was used to irrigate fields. Unlike in Mesopotamia, the people did not construct extensive irrigation systems, but still they left behind hundreds of settlements. In contrast to those in other parts of the world we have studied, the Oxus culture settlements were mostly occupied briefly, with people moving to other locations rather than building on the same site. In only a few places did they stay for prolonged periods of time.

The architecture of these settlements is remarkable. People built walled fortresses with guard towers and reinforced gates and constructed large storage areas inside the fortresses. They may have wanted to protect their resources from hostile

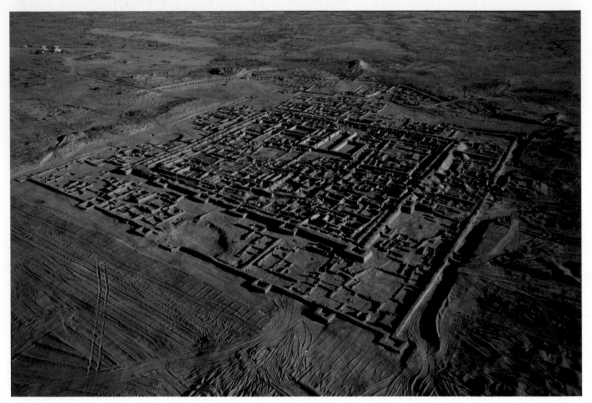

☰ **Oxus Fortress** The settlements of the Oxus culture were typically heavily fortified, surrounded by straight rectangular walls with guard towers. This is Gonur Tepe in modern Turkmenistan, which was fully excavated so that its entire plan is visible.

outsiders. Many historians believe that each fortress was the base of a clan leader who lived in its center and had authority over the local population. This view that elite members of society controlled others is evidenced by the presence of human sacrificial victims in some tombs.

Alongside the settlements archaeologists discovered many cemeteries, which especially show the wealth of at least some of the people of the Oxus culture. Some tombs contained sophisticated artwork made of various metals and stones: elaborately decorated axes, stamp seals, and vessels. The region's artisans also produced sculptures of women and men composed of a mixture of costly light and dark stones. These works are distinctive in style, and it is clear that the artisans who made them were highly skilled and produced them as expensive luxury goods.

The artwork also reveals wide-ranging connections between the Oxus culture and other parts of Asia. Objects produced there were found in the Indus Valley, Iran, and the Persian Gulf area, while some, albeit few, objects from places like Babylonia made their way into the Oxus region. More tellingly, there are many similarities between the works produced in the Oxus culture and those from South Asia to Egypt in imagery, style, and production techniques. Art historians believe that the artisans from those regions inspired those of the Oxus culture in various ways. There were also influences in pottery production from areas farther north in Central Asia, and the find of a piece of silk suggests contacts with China.

Those connections with other parts of Asia suggest that the Oxus culture was at the center of a network of trade, which was the source of the people's wealth. It is not certain what the Oxus people traded, however. The region had sources of metals such as copper, tin, gold, and silver, and of

≡ **Oxus Sculpture** Among the finds of the Oxus culture are a group of small figurines of women represented without the details of arms and so on. They seem to be seated and wrapped in cloaks made of sheepskin. These figurines are always made of two types of stone, the bodies of green chlorite or steatite and the heads of white limestone.

semiprecious stones, especially lapis lazuli, which was much desired in Southwest Asia, Egypt, and the Indus Valley. Perhaps the culture also acted as a transit point for farther-reaching contacts.

What explains the sudden appearance of the Oxus culture and its disappearance, especially as the region is far from ideal for permanent settlement? Some scholars suggest that an improvement of the climate around 2250 BCE caused people to settle there and that drier conditions some 550 years later forced them to leave. But the conditions there were always difficult, and the constant shift of settlements suggests that people had learned to adjust to the fluctuations in water supplies by moving. It seems that the rise of a network of long-distance connections including the urbanized areas of Southwest Asia and the Indus Valley may have inspired the settlements in the Oxus region. Likewise, the breakdown of those contacts may have taken away the sources of the Oxus people's wealth. The culture did not disappear overnight, and traces of it remained until around 1500 BCE. But after then, permanent settlement in the region ceased for centuries, and when it returned no one knew about the Oxus culture. This culture, however short-lived, shows how throughout world history humans have been able to take advantage of strategically located regions to forge long-distance connections even if the effort required moving into a highly challenging environment.

Conclusion

The historian Sima Qian had a very low opinion of the nomadic people living on the edges of the Chinese state whose ruler he served. His disparaging remarks were misguided, however. Contacts between the settled and the nomadic people of Asia were constant, and throughout the entire history of the continent, the interactions between these two groups with distinct livelihoods were important to both. Their uses of the natural environment were complementary, and cultural exchanges went both ways. The boundaries between the two groups were also not absolute. Many nomadic groups became sedentary, as we saw with the Indo-European speakers in India, just as sedentary people could turn to nomadism, as was possibly the case at the end of the Oxus culture. To understand the history of the region, we must take both groups into account.

The ancient histories of India and China show how long cultural traditions can last—their influences are still felt today. But historical differences between the two regions are clear. In India, an early urban culture of the Indus Valley ceased to exist before newly arrived Aryas, together with indigenous people, created the foundations of the region's culture. In China the earliest states—the Shang and Zhou—introduced elements such as a script and political ideology that survived into modern times.

Historians do not, however, find such continuity everywhere in Asia. Some ancient cultures, such as the Oxus culture, disappeared completely. In the next chapter we will return to the western parts of Asia to see how its urban cultures developed new structures, political and otherwise. We will investigate how the first empires in world history evolved.

review

Major global development in this chapter: The rise of large urban states in Asia and the interactions between nomadic and settled peoples that profoundly shaped them.

Important Events	
c. 7000 BCE	Earliest farmers in East Asia
c. 6500 BCE	Earliest farmers in South Asia
c. 5000 BCE	Agriculture throughout Yellow River and Yangzi River Valleys in China
c. 3000 BCE	Agriculture throughout South Asia
c. 2600–1900 BCE	Mature Indus Valley culture
c. 2250–1700 BCE	Oxus culture
c. 2000 BCE	Widespread use of domesticated horses throughout Asia
c. 2000–1570 BCE	Earliest Bronze Age cultures in China
c. 2000 BCE–100 CE	Indo-European migrations
c. 1570–1027 BCE	Shang dynasty in China
c. 1500–500 BCE	India's Vedic age
1027 BCE	Battle of Muye in China
1027–771 BCE	Early Zhou dynasty in China

KEY TERMS

atman (p. 101)
Brahman (p. 101)
caste system (p. 100)
clan (p. 99)
divination (p. 103)

jati (p. 99)
karma (p. 101)
Mandate of Heaven (p. 109)
pastoralist (p. 83)
raja (p. 99)

reincarnation (p. 101)
varna (p. 99)
Vedas (p. 97)

CHAPTER OVERVIEW QUESTIONS

1. How did peoples living in far-flung regions of Asia develop societies that had many similarities?
2. What were the unique characteristics of the cultures studied here?

3. Which features of ancient Indian and Chinese society and culture shaped later developments most fundamentally?
4. What common trends in the interactions between settled and nomadic peoples can you discern?

MAKING CONNECTIONS

1. How did the development of Indus Valley cities compare with the processes in Southwest Asia and China?
2. How does the social structure of Vedic India compare with those of other ancient Asian and North African cultures?

3. In what ways do the interactions between settled and nomadic peoples explain the historical development of Asia?
4. What are the similarities in burial practices of the ancient cultures we have discussed so far, and what do they suggest about attitudes toward class and religion in these societies?

DOING HISTORY

Sourcing and Situation

In this chapter we have studied ancient cultures for which no textual sources exist (the Oxus culture) or whose writings are incomprehensible to us (the Indus Valley culture). We have also looked at cultures from India and China that are discussed in ancient texts, but those texts were not written down in the periods they describe. The earliest manuscripts that contain the texts of the Vedas, the Upanisads, and the *Book of Poetry* are used as sources for the periods when these texts are thought to have been composed, but they were written centuries later.

1. How could the contents of these texts have been altered, and why would such changes have been made?

2. How does this issue with sources complicate the work of the historian who tries to study periods such as the Vedic age in India and the Shang and Zhou periods in China?

3. Can you think of other situations in world history where similar conditions occurred?

For further research into the topics covered in this chapter, see the Bibliography at the end of the book.

Empire and Resistance in the Mediterranean

1550–330 BCE

☰ **World in the Making** Around 500 BCE the Persian emperor Darius started to build a new capital of astonishing magnificence at Persepolis in modern Iran, where he celebrated an annual ceremony of tribute delivery from all subject peoples. The reliefs that decorate the walls show the great diversity of the peoples in his empire, indicating the Persians' awareness of the novelty of this type of political organization. Shown here are Nubians bringing products from their African region: a small jar (content unknown), an elephant tusk, an okapi (a local animal), and bracelets. The artist who made the image was careful in depicting the tribute bearers' physical characteristics and dress. (Diego Delso, delso. photo, License CC-BY-SA)

backstory

In Chapters 2 and 3 we saw how early states developed throughout the Asian continent and in North Africa. From its very beginnings, the state of Egypt incorporated a wide territory centered on the king; in Southwest Asia, India, and China, states first grew up around cities and then expanded rapidly. Although a number of these states were quite large, their populations were relatively homogeneous, sharing a common culture and history.

Starting around 1550 BCE, however, the rulers of some of these early states began wide-ranging foreign conquests, creating empires that brought together a great diversity of people under the same political structure. In the first millennium BCE, the first empires of Southwest Asia and North Africa dominated the eastern Mediterranean. To the west, however, inhabitants of Europe initiated changes—especially in politics and culture—that would have far-reaching effects on world history.

121

IN THE LATE SIXTH CENTURY BCE, the Persian king Darius commissioned the carving of a long inscription that described his rise to power in Persia, an empire made up of twenty-three countries from central Asia to Egypt. He had acquired these territories by defeating men who, in his words, had falsely claimed kingship over those states. He proclaimed,

> Thus says Darius, the king: These are the countries that listen to me—it is under the protection of the god Ahuramazda that I am their king: Persia, Elam, Babylonia, Assyria, Arabia, Egypt, the Sealand, Sardis, Ionia, Media, Urartu, Cappadocia, Parthia, Drangiana, Aria, Choresmia, Bactria, Sogdiana, Gandhara, Scythia, Sattagydia, Arachosia, and Maka, in total twenty-three countries. . . .
>
> I captured . . . the Magian Gaumata, who lied saying: "I am Bardiya, son of Cyrus, king of Persia," and who caused the lands of Persia and Media to rebel; . . . the Babylonian Nidintu-Bel, who lied saying: "I am Nebuchadnezzar, son of Nabonidus, the king of Babylon," and who caused Babylonia to rebel.[1]

Darius was aware of the cultural and ethnic diversity of his vast empire, a fact he acknowledged by presenting his message in three different languages: his own, Old Persian; Babylonian, the language of Mesopotamia; and Elamite, the language of western Iran. He knew that the Persian Empire had brought together these and other regions in a single unit of unprecedented size. He also knew, however, that it was political and military power that held his empire together. His subjects did not see themselves as Persians, but as distinct peoples.

History has seen many empires, and their diversity makes it difficult to devise a definition of **empire** that encompasses all their variety. A common characteristic is clear, however: empires are very large political units that rule over diverse countries, peoples, and cultures. Relations between empires and their subjects are complex and influence many spheres of life—political, economic, social, and cultural—so we can study empires from a range of perspectives.

Because the definition of what constitutes an empire is not simple, it is hard to say when the empire first appeared. Historians agree, however, that a set of large states that incorporated many countries and peoples in much of North Africa and Southwest Asia from 1550 to 330 BCE deserve the title. Thus, in this chapter we focus on the imperial efforts of the Egyptians, Nubians, Assyrians, and Persians. These empires, while extremely powerful, did not always succeed in their military aims, however. As an example, we will see how on the western border of the Persian Empire the inhabitants of Greece successfully resisted its expansion. In doing so, they established new political systems and cultural traditions that would have a radical impact on world history.

empire A large political unit that imposes its rule over diverse regions, peoples, and cultures; it can take many different forms.

OVERVIEW QUESTIONS

The major global development in this chapter: The rise of empires and the variety and consequences of imperial rule.

As you read, consider:

1. What were the main characteristics of the early empires?

2. How did the empires affect the peoples who created them and their subject populations?

3. How did imperial rulers adapt their control to local circumstances?

4. How did people resist empires?

Imperial Egypt and Nubia 1550 BCE–350 CE

↘ **FOCUS** How did Egyptians and Nubians interact in the two imperial periods that united them politically?

In Northeast Africa, where that continent borders Southwest Asia, the kingdoms of Egypt and Nubia dominated the Nile Valley from around 3000 BCE. From about 1550 to 660 BCE, first Egypt and then Nubia formed the core of the earliest empires in this part of the world (see Map 4.1). Egypt in its New Kingdom period expanded beyond its borders both northward into Asia and southward into Nubia, annexing huge territories. The empire thrived for more than 400 years.

Several centuries later, Nubia itself became the dominant power in the region, ruling over Egypt for some seventy years. Thus a region once dominated by a powerful neighbor itself developed into a force and overtook its master. Despite this reversal of political fortune, Egyptian culture continued to have a powerful influence in Nubia. The Egyptians had almost completely ignored Nubian culture, but the Nubians promoted Egyptian culture in both the conquered Egyptian state and the Nubian homeland. In the case of the Nubian Empire, this **assimilation**—absorption of the cultural traditions of others—produced a unique mix of local and foreign influences that characterized the region for many centuries after Nubia's empire had faded away.

The Imperial Might of New Kingdom Egypt 1550–1070 BCE

Around 1550 BCE, the Egyptians started a sustained period of expansion. In the north, large armies pushed deep into Asiatic territory, confronting states that belonged to the international system described in Chapter 2. The especially

assimilation The process by which one group absorbs the cultural traditions of another group.

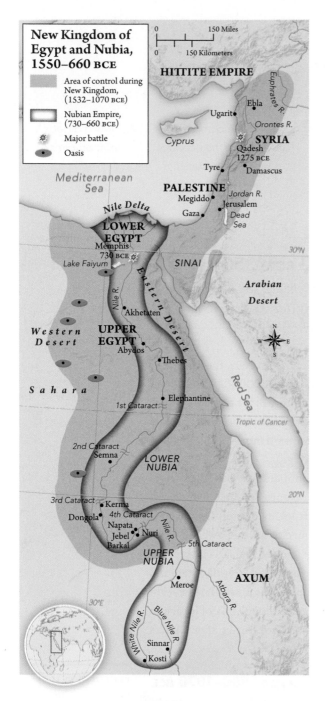

≡ **MAP 4.1 New Kingdom of Egypt and Nubia, 1550–660 BCE** After ruling supreme in the northern Nile Valley and western Syria from 1550 to 1070 BCE, Egypt was conquered by one of its earlier subjects, Nubia, whose kings extended their power up to the Mediterranean Sea from 730 to 660. Each empire controlled a massive area centered on the Nile.

aggressive empire builder King Thutmose III (r. 1479–1425 BCE) drove his troops into Syria seventeen times to force local rulers into submission. Resistance remained strong, however, and 200 years later King Ramesses (RAM-ih-seez) II (r. 1279–1213 BCE) still had to fight massive battles to maintain control over the region. The most famous of these clashes was Ramesses's battle at Qadesh (KA-desh) in northern Syria (1275 BCE) against the Hittites, which in large relief carvings on several monuments he depicted as a great victory for the Egyptian army.

At the same time, Egypt expanded south into Nubia, annexing some 700 miles south of its border along the Nile River. There, the opposition was less organized, and once Egypt occupied the region after a century of campaigning, troops were more involved with peacekeeping than with further conquest (see again Map 4.1).

Conquest brought tremendous riches to Egypt, something we can best see today in the items that were deposited in tombs, which, as we saw in Chapter 2, were extremely important to ancient Egyptians, who regarded them as their dwellings for eternity. The most astonishing example of a royal tomb is Tutankhamun's (r. 1333–1323 BCE), which archaeologists discovered intact in the early twentieth century CE. It was packed with objects made of gold, silver, precious stones, ivory, and other very valuable materials, all exquisitely crafted. Tutankhamun's inner gold coffin alone weighs 243 pounds—and he was only a minor king. The gold came from Nubia, then under direct control of New Kingdom Egypt. The mines were located deep in the harsh desert east of the Nile Valley and required grueling labor to extract the gold. Men had to break up and pulverize blocks of stone from which the gold dust was then washed, likely by women and children who accompanied them. It has been estimated that at most a third of an ounce of gold could be extracted in this way from one metric ton of rock. Yet royal records report that hundreds of pounds a year came into Egypt.

There were numerous other magnificent projects financed through the assets the empire accrued. Many of the great temples of Egypt one can still see today were first constructed or massively expanded in the New Kingdom period, and countless works of art displayed in museums all over the world—statues, jewelry, wall paintings, and so on—were made then. An illustrious example is Queen Hatshepsut (hat-SHEP-soot), who seized power in 1473 BCE when the legitimate heir Thutmose III was still a young boy, and she ruled Egypt until 1458 BCE, the probable year of her death. To honor her after death, she ordered that a temple be constructed on the west Nile bank of the capital Thebes. Relief sculptures on the walls celebrate her accomplishments.

Determined to leave behind grand monuments, Egypt's pharaohs employed many specially trained craftsmen, including the men who dug and decorated tombs in the Valleys of the Kings and the Queens in the mountains facing the capital Thebes. We are particularly well-informed about these craftsmen because archaeologists have excavated the village where they lived, called Deir el Medina (dare uhl meh-DEE-nah) today.

King Tutankhamun's Golden Inner Coffin The enormous wealth the Egyptians obtained through imperial expansion is perhaps best illustrated by the treasures found in Tutankhamun's tomb. This is a detail of his inner coffin, made of gold that could be obtained only in Nubia. Despite its opulence, the inner coffin was merely a small part of the gifts placed alongside the dead king.

One was a sculptor called Qen, who had two wives and at least ten children. Because the village was in the desert, the family could not grow its own food; instead, it was delivered from the state's storehouses. They received grains, vegetables, fish, oil, and milk, as well as water and firewood. When Qen worked in the tombs, which were several hours by foot from Deir el Medina, he stayed overnight in a camp. Each day he and his colleagues worked two shifts of four hours each, with a lunch break in between. After the men had dug and plastered long tunnels and a draftsman had traced the figures, Qen sculpted religious images and hieroglyphic texts to help the king on his way to the underworld, a journey central to Egyptian religious beliefs (discussed in Chapter 2). Over the years the pharaoh had rewarded him well for his work, so Qen had acquired

≡ **Western Thebes**

precious objects, some of which accompanied him in his own tomb for use in the afterlife.

Not only royalty benefited from the empire's existence. A large group of officials and priests also acquired tombs in western Thebes to keep them comfortable in the afterlife. On the tomb walls artists painted colorful scenes of what the Egyptians considered to be an idyllic existence. They showed lush farms with abundant harvests, sumptuous meals with the dead and their families being entertained by musicians and dancers, and other scenes of daily life. Although these may seem realistic, we have to remember that they show an idealized world. Historians cannot know for certain how the majority of Egyptian people fared at this time because we have few remains from them. We imagine, however, that all of them benefited to some extent from the empire's existence, at least insofar as it produced internal peace and economic stability. Like Qen, they were all part of an imperial system that connected Egypt to its territories, a system that allowed Egypt's rulers to draw resources from many distant lands to glorify themselves and to enrich their homeland.

All the magnificent monuments New Kingdom Egyptians constructed reveal how deeply committed the people were to the country's religious ideas. The temples were used to venerate the many gods of the pantheon, and those of the leading deities were enormous in size, with many kings and queens expanding them and adding elements such as chapels, obelisks, statues, and altars. The great temple of the main god of Thebes, Amun, became very large and wealthy in this period because great military conquerors, such as Thutmose III (r. 1479–1425 BCE), donated massive amounts of loot obtained in their campaigns. As the existence of the gods was considered to parallel that of humans—with the major exception that gods were immortal while people had to die—Amun's wife Mut and their son Khonsu were also venerated in his temple. The temples of other deities throughout the country received the attention of the kings as well, and when the empire annexed territories, new temples were regularly constructed in the Egyptian gods' honor.

In the tombs of western Thebes the religious ideas about the afterlife were expressed in texts and images painted on the walls; the god Osiris as lord of the netherworld received much attention, as did his wife Isis and son Horus. Excerpts from what is often called the *Book of the Dead* today, although there are many different versions of the text, were written out in order to help the dead person reach a paradise-like place where Osiris ruled. The path was filled with dangers, and the

Book of the Dead provided spells to ward off evils and prayers to beg various gods for help. The goddess Isis was prominent in them because, according to myth, through magic she had revived her husband and protected her son in his battles for kingship against the god Seth. The Egyptians did not leave behind systematic accounts of the ideas behind their beliefs or of the myths that informed them on how gods were related to one another and interacted. Yet the texts and images fit within a coherent context that involved multiple gods known from the beginning of Egyptian history. The number of gods increased during the New Kingdom because several gods from western Asia entered the pantheon—none from Nubia, however.

The New Kingdom Empire was so large and included such diverse peoples and countries that the Egyptians were obliged to adjust their attitude toward subjects in response to local conditions. In Southwest Asia, Egypt participated in the eastern Mediterranean system described in Chapter 2, using diplomacy to interact with rulers they considered equals. Vassal rulers, who paid taxes and allegiance to the Egyptian king, governed small kingdoms in the southern part of the Syria-Palestinian area. These vassals were politically dependent on Egypt, but the Egyptians treated them with respect, sometimes adopting elements of their cultures. For example, New Kingdom Egyptians started to honor various Syrian gods and adopted certain artistic motifs from the region as well as the technology of glassmaking.

In contrast, the Egyptians showed no respect for the Nubians, whom they considered inferior and uncivilized. Their primary interest in Nubia was its gold mines. Egyptian governors ignored the local culture and founded Egyptian-style settlements with administrative buildings and temples devoted to Egyptian gods. But still they needed local Nubians to help in the administration, who then adopted an Egyptian lifestyle. One such man in the fourteenth century BCE was Prince Hekanefer. His tomb near his hometown presents him in full Egyptian attire, and the accompanying hieroglyphics call him an admirer of the Egyptian god of the netherworld, Osiris. Interestingly, Hekanefer also features in paintings in a tomb in Thebes, where he appears with Nubian physical features and clothes, prostrating himself in front of an Egyptian official. Clearly, the Egyptians saw Hekanefer very differently from how he saw himself. He seems proud to have adopted the dominant Egyptian culture, but for Egyptian elites his most important characteristic was submission to their rule.

When the eastern Mediterranean system collapsed around 1200 BCE, the Egyptian Empire also disintegrated and gradually lost its foreign territories. By 1070 BCE Nubia had become an independent kingdom. The Nubians used the practices they had observed among the Egyptians to develop a culture distinct from the rest of Africa, continuing such elements as writing and monumental building and maintaining a more centralized state organization than existed elsewhere on the continent.

Nubia's Rise and Rule of Egypt 1000–660 BCE

The Nubians had their capital in Napata (nah-PAH-tuh), which had been the major Egyptian town in the region (see again Map 4.1), and they developed a strong centralized state shortly after 1000 BCE, at a time when Egypt was divided among several competing dynasties and chiefdoms. In Egypt's south, the Theban high priest of Amun ruled as if he were king. In the eighth century BCE, political control over Thebes shifted to a new system that centered on the women of the royal court. The highest religious office became that of the high priestess of Amun. She was always a princess of the most powerful political house in Egypt at the time of her selection. To maintain political control over her possessions, she could not marry and have children. Instead, she passed on her office by adopting her successor, again a princess from the strongest dynasty.

The growing power of Nubia in the region became clear when, in 736 BCE, the sister of King Piye (py) became high priestess and in effect ruled southern Egypt. Northern Egyptians refused to accept Nubian authority and threatened to attack Thebes. In response, around 730 BCE. Piye led his troops northward from Napata all the way to Memphis at the tip of the Nile delta, forcing local rulers to submit (see again Map 4.1). Egypt and Nubia reunited—but this time Nubia was in control.

The succession of Nubian kings who ruled this new empire behaved in every respect like the earlier Egyptian pharaohs. Nubian kings can be distinguished from native Egyptian rulers only because they retained their Nubian names. They used Egyptian titles and promoted Egyptian culture throughout their empire. In the Nubian capital Napata, the Nubian rulers substantially enlarged and embellished the temple to Amun, the highest Egyptian god, to rival the one at Thebes, his main sanctuary. Nubian burial customs, inscriptions, and statues also showed devotion to Egyptian traditions—after the conquest of Egypt, Nubian kings were buried in pyramids rather than the earlier round mounds of earth. Nubians also decorated the tomb chambers with scenes from the Egyptian books of the underworld. As in Egypt, they mummified corpses and set them in human-shaped coffins, placing hundreds of small statuettes in the tombs to assist the dead in the afterlife. The Nubians also used the Egyptian language and hieroglyphic script for their official inscriptions, and in statues of kings the poses matched those of the

Egyptian pharaohs. Thus, in a myriad of ways, Nubian rulers demonstrated that their conquest of Egypt was not predicated on a sense of their own cultural superiority. Rather, they saw Egyptian culture as a key source of imperial power and unity, and they sought to use the cultural connections the Egyptians had created to reinforce the legitimacy of their own rule.

Nonetheless, some local Nubian traditions survived. For example, in depictions of Nubian kings, artists rendered their African physical features. A very un-Egyptian element in the Nubian burials was the interment of horses along with the king. The Nubians greatly admired the animals, which had contributed to their military victories, and due to Nubian success in battle the horses they bred were in high demand in other countries.

Egypt flourished economically, and in many respects the Nubians oversaw a period of prosperity. Although we have no evidence of popular resentment of

☰ Statues of Nubian Kings These statues of Nubian rulers of the first millennium BCE, some up to ten feet high, were found in a pit, where they were preserved after a raiding Egyptian king had smashed them in 593 BCE. Reassembled, they show that in depicting kings, Nubian artists followed many Egyptian conventions, such as the posture, but they also reveal typically Nubian elements, such as physical features, the royal crown, and the lion face on one of the belts.

≡ **The Kingdom of Meroe, c. 400 BCE–350 CE**

Nubian rule among Egyptians, some elites, particularly in the north, seem to have wanted independence but lacked the military might needed to resist the Nubians. Then, around 660 BCE, the Assyrians of Southwest Asia invaded Egypt and drove the Nubians out of Egypt. When the Assyrians' grip on the country loosened a few years later, a family from the north of Egypt established itself as the new ruling dynasty.

The Nubian Kingdom of Meroe 400 BCE–350 CE

Although driven from Egypt, the Nubians continued to rule their homeland. By 400 BCE they moved their political capital to Meroe (MER-oh-ee), some 700 miles upstream from Napata. This shift took advantage of the greater fertility of the region surrounding Meroe and of the intersection of trade routes in the city, which reached into regions of Africa farther south, east, and west.

Over time, the political situation in Egypt changed as first the Greeks (332–30 BCE) and then the Romans (30 BCE–395 CE) occupied it. The Meroites had mostly friendly contacts with the Greeks and Romans, who fancied African luxury goods such as gold, ivory, spices, animals, and enslaved persons. During a long period of peace, the enormous Roman appetite for luxury items brought fantastic wealth and a flood of Mediterranean goods into Nubia.

After the first century CE, however, Meroe's commercial advantage gradually declined. The kingdom of Axum, to Meroe's east on the Red Sea in what is today Ethiopia, became Rome's preferred center for access to African trade. As Axum's wealth grew, so did its military power, and in 350 CE, the Axumites conquered Meroe.

After the political separation of Nubia from Egypt in the seventh century BCE, Egyptian influences in Nubia remained strong. The Nubians continued to honor Egyptian gods such as Amun, to bury kings in pyramids, and to depict themselves in an Egyptian style. Nonetheless, important changes occurred. In the second century BCE, for example, the Meroites started to write their own language, rather than Egyptian.

Women enjoyed a high status in the social structure of Meroe. In royal succession a king was followed by his sister's son, and from the second century BCE on, several women became rulers themselves. Like their male counterparts, they were represented on monuments as defeating enemies and honoring gods. Classical

Greek and Roman authors mistakenly concluded from these depictions that queens had always ruled in Nubian society (see Seeing the Past: The Queen of Meroe in Battle). As this example illustrates, the economic connections between Rome and Nubia facilitated cultural exchange and inquiry but did not eliminate misunderstandings and misinterpretations.

Rise and Fall of the Assyrian Empire 900–612 BCE

⬊ **FOCUS** What kind of power structure did the Assyrians impose on their subjects, and how did it lead to cultural assimilation in the empire?

As we have seen, it was not Egyptians but the Assyrians who drove the Nubians out of Egypt. Waging unrelenting wars of conquest, the Assyrians built the first empire to encompass much of Southwest Asia. Assyria's martial character dominates our modern view of the empire, and the Assyrian state was indeed organized around the demands of warfare. But the Assyrian kings also commissioned engineering projects, built new cities, sponsored the arts, and powerfully influenced cultural developments in the empire. Despite their military successes, structural weaknesses in the empire would ultimately thwart the Assyrian kings' dreams of integrating the conquered territories into a coherent whole. Their conquests did, however, lay the groundwork for later empires in the region.

Assyria: A Society as War Machine

Starting around 860 BCE, Assyria began a series of wars that would lead to 250 years of dominance in Southwest Asia. The Assyrians defeated all their rivals, and by around 650 BCE their control reached from western Iran to the Mediterranean Sea and from central Anatolia (modern Turkey) to Egypt (see Map 4.2).

The empire's militarism affected every level of Assyrian society. The state was organized as a military hierarchy with the king—the ultimate source of authority—at the top. All state officers, whatever their responsibilities, had a military rank. The army required massive amounts of weapons, clothing, and food and vast numbers of horses. But manpower was perhaps in the greatest demand: the central Assyrian state simply could not provide enough soldiers without drawing too many people away from other essential work, such as farming and building.

SEEING THE PAST

The Queen of Meroe in Battle

Naga Temple

South of the capital Meroe, the Meroites of the late first century BCE or early first century CE built a group of temples near a staging post for caravans traveling east. They dedicated one of the temples to the Meroite lion god Apedemak, and built it fully in accordance with an ancient Egyptian plan. Its decoration, however, shows a mixture of ancient Egyptian and local traditions.

The image on the front gate of the temple reveals this mixture. On the right side, the queen is battling enemies with the god's help; she is depicted as equal to her husband, who appears on the left. Both stand in the pose that Egyptian rulers used to show their victories, wielding arms over opponents bunched together. Underneath them are rows of bound enemies representing defeated countries. Short Egyptian hieroglyphic inscriptions identify the figures as Queen Amanitore and King Netekamari. Above them, traditional Egyptian gods appear as birds.

The Assyrians filled their need for manpower through a policy of deporting conquered people. After the army defeated a region that had resisted Assyrian dominance, the troops forced large numbers of people to resettle elsewhere in the empire. These dislocated men, women, and children labored for the Assyrian state, working on farms and construction projects. Some of the men enlisted in the Assyrian army. Besides providing the state with workers, the policy of deportation effectively thwarted opposition to Assyrian expansion and rule. The Assyrians also used the threat of deportation as a scare tactic to cow opponents into submission. The policy thus aimed both to supply laborers and to reduce the chance of rebellion in the conquered territories.

These Egyptian motifs are mixed with Meroitic details. The king and queen wield swords rather than the axes or maces that Egyptians would have used. Their dress and jewelry are local, and the lion god Apedemak (unknown in Egypt) assists them. Moreover, unlike Egyptian queens in images, Queen Amanitore is quite chubby, which may have been the local ideal of beauty.

Examining the Evidence

1. Which decorative features of the front gate would most have startled Egyptians, and which would they have recognized as normal?

2. How does the temple illustrate contacts between Egypt and regions to its south?

For Further Information:

To see the modern investigation of the temple complex: http://naga-project.com

Queen Amanitore

Assyria's military culture was dominated by men, allowing most women a limited role in Assyrian society. The available evidence reveals little about ordinary women and focuses instead on queens and princesses. As wives and mothers, royal women could shape political affairs. Queen Naqia (na-KEE-ah) married King Sennacherib (sehn-AK-er-ihb) (r. 704–681 BCE) before he ascended the throne, and she bore him a son called Esarhaddon (ee-sahr-HAD-in). He was not the first in line for succession, but after Sennacherib's eldest son was murdered, Naqia convinced Sennacherib to declare the young Esarhaddon his heir. Older sons by another wife rebelled and assassinated Sennacherib. This started a civil war, which Esarhaddon won after months of fighting. During Esarhaddon's subsequent rule

≡ MAP 4.2 The Empires of Assyria and Babylonia, 900–539 BCE From its small core in northern Mesopotamia, Assyria gradually extended its control over most of the Middle East and at times even Egypt, turning the entire region into a vast land-based empire by 650 BCE. By 610, however, the Babylonians had taken over most of Assyria's territory. Both peoples used the enormous influx of resources to embellish their homelands, creating two of the most impressive cities of the ancient world, Nineveh and Babylon.

from 680 to 669 BCE, the queen mother Naqia became his staunchest ally. She corresponded with high officials of the empire, who paid her the same respect they gave the king. Even after Esarhaddon's death she remained prominent. Her last known act was to impose an oath on court officials to obey her grandson as king.

Despite Naqia's power, however, note that it ultimately derived from her status as the mother of a prince, not from her own independent political position.

Imperial Governance

All imperial powers face the challenge of administering territories after conquering them. The Assyrians were not eager to impose direct rule on defeated countries—it would have required large investments in infrastructure and administrators. Moreover, because the empire was centralized around a king who made all decisions, urgent issues in territories far from the king would have been difficult to deal with. Thus, when the military forced a population to submit, they left the local king on the throne but demanded obedience and annual contributions. If the region rebelled—a common occurrence—troops returned to install a pro-Assyrian ruler in the local king's stead. If this arrangement also failed, Assyria annexed the region as a **province**, a territory fully administered by the empire. The Assyrians usually hesitated to take this drastic step, however.

The Assyrians' preference for indirect rule was linked to their motives for expansion. They were not interested in ruling other peoples, but in acquiring the wealth and resources of other lands. With each conquest, the army captured huge amounts of booty, and the empire required yearly contributions, or **tribute**, from conquered territories. In an annual ceremony, ambassadors from Assyria's subject peoples renewed their states' loyalty oaths and brought tribute, often goods that were the region's special assets. In this way, Assyrian palaces became centers for collections of the empire's diverse resources and products.

Deported subjects gave Assyrian rulers the manpower to construct magnificent cities and to enlarge existing towns to serve as capitals. On these sites the kings erected monumental palaces and temples and decorated them with such materials gathered from the entire empire. Although not the largest in the world at that time—Chinese cities were spread over vaster areas—the new Assyrian cities were too gigantic for the surrounding countryside to support. Because agriculture in the Assyrian core produced too little food to feed the city, products from elsewhere in the empire had to be imported. Assyria thus became an enormous drain on the resources of the conquered territories.

Culture and Identity in the Assyrian Empire

Through its far-reaching conquests, the Assyrian Empire brought people from a wide territory together under the same political structure. They spoke a variety of languages, followed different religious systems and customs, and must have been visually distinguishable to the people of the time. The Assyrians displayed different attitudes toward this cultural variety, depending on the region.

province In an empire, a region or country directly governed by an imperial official answering to the central administration.

tribute Payment made from one state to another as a sign of submission.

In the core of the empire, the Assyrians enforced assimilation. They relabeled existing cities with Assyrian names, built public buildings in the Assyrian style, and forced the people to support the cult of their leading god, Assur, the divine commander of the army. But beyond this central zone, the Assyrians did not demand that people change their ways of life. Their only concern was that the subjects provide tribute and pay taxes.

Naturally, assimilation occurred because of the imperial deportation policy. When the Assyrians resettled an entire population in a foreign part of the empire, these immigrants maintained their identity for a while, but over generations they adopted local customs. Yet they also influenced the customs of their conquerors, leaving a cultural imprint on Assyria, especially in the realm of language. Many of the deportees came from the west and spoke Aramaic, which may have become the primary spoken language in the empire. They also affected writing practices. Arameans used an alphabetic script with only twenty-two characters, which they had adopted from their neighbors on the Mediterranean coast, the Phoenicians.

As we have mentioned, the Assyrians shrewdly recognized that it was often preferable to grant independence to their subject peoples so that they could freely carry on activities that would benefit the empire economically. One such people was the Phoenicians, the inhabitants of Mediterranean port cities including Sidon (SIE-duhn), Byblos (BIB-loss), and Tyre (TY-er), which had been important hubs of trade for thousands of years.

The Phoenicians' extensive trade contacts inspired the use of their alphabet by many foreign peoples (see Figure 4.1). To the east of Phoenicia, these included speakers of the Semitic languages Aramaic and Hebrew, and to the west, the Indo-European-speaking Greeks. Because both Aramaic and Greek adopters of the Phoenician alphabet later had broad cultural influence in the Mediterranean and

Semitic name of letters	Phoenician	Hebrew	Greek name of letters	Greek	Roman
alef	𐤀	א	alpha	A	A
beth	𐤁	ב	beta	B	B
gimel	𐤂	ג	gamma	Γ	C, G
daleth	𐤃	ד	delta	Δ	D

≣ **FIGURE 4.1 Comparative Alphabets** In the Phoenician alphabet we can find the roots of our own. Our alphabet is based on that of the Romans, who borrowed their letter forms from the Greeks, who adapted the Phoenician alphabet.

Middle Eastern worlds, that script gained enormous reach. Today the Phoenician alphabet is the basis of all alphabetic scripts in the world.

The Assyrians willingly accepted cultural influences from the conquered territories. This openness to foreign ways is most notable in literature and scholarship, but outsiders also influenced architecture, crafts, and religion. In the second millennium BCE, the country of Babylonia to the south of Assyria had been the center of literary and scholarly creativity in Southwest Asia. When the Assyrians conquered it in the late eighth century BCE, Babylonian scribes were still very actively composing and duplicating cuneiform texts. King Assurbanipal (ah-shur-BAH-nee-pahl) (r. 668–631 BCE) used their output to build up the richest library of ancient Southwest Asia in his palace at Nineveh. He ordered his officials in Babylon to search for early, well-preserved manuscripts of texts of literary and scholarly character. With its thousands of manuscripts, Assurbanipal's library gives us the most complete record of the Babylonian written tradition. Among its many treasures are multiple manuscripts of the *Epic of Gilgamesh* (see Chapter 2).

In other forms of cultural expression, too, the Assyrians readily accepted outside influences. In architecture they imitated the palaces they saw in Syria, and the jewelry and ivory carvings found in Assyrian palaces were either produced in Syria or made locally using Syrian designs. The influx of expensive goods from foreign sources reveals not only that the Assyrian court was a rich market but also that the Assyrians were very willing to accept foreign styles.

In religion, the Assyrians remained true to their old cults, but they attempted to harmonize them with Babylonian ideas. In Babylonian religion, the god Marduk was supreme, and common belief credited him with creating the universe. This event was the subject of a myth, the *Babylonian Creation Story*. It describes how Marduk defeated the forces of chaos and organized the universe, and how the other gods rewarded him by making him their king. The Assyrians wanted to integrate their leading god Assur into this myth, and they either made him a forefather of Marduk or directly equated Assur with Marduk. Thus, in many ways, the Assyrian attitude toward foreign cultures mirrored their attitude toward foreign wealth and resources: they were interested in taking anything, and everything, that seemed valuable.

Failure of the Assyrian System

In 663 BCE King Assurbanipal invaded Egypt, looted its rich cities, and removed Nubian control over the country. By this time, the Assyrian Empire encompassed an enormous territory, and huge amounts of wealth flowed from dependent peoples to the Assyrian homeland. Just fifty years later, however, it would no longer exist. The collapse of the empire was precipitated by attacks launched by previously subjected peoples, but its causes lay in the structure of the system itself.

The military events are clear: after the death of Assurbanipal in 631 BCE, Babylonia regained its independence under a local dynasty, which we call Neo-Babylonian or Chaldean (chal-DEE-uhn). In 612 BCE Chaldean troops, with the help of some other people resentful of Assyria's rule, destroyed the empire's capital, Nineveh. The Assyrians would resist a few years longer in northern Syria, but soon the Chaldeans had taken over almost their entire territory.

At the heart of Assyria's failure to rise to the military challenge from the Chaldeans was a serious structural weakness. The centralized power structure required a strong king at the helm, and after Assurbanipal, internal struggles for the throne produced instability and uncertainty. Moreover, the empire relied heavily on the conquered territories to sustain itself—it could not survive without their goods and manpower. When Assyria's military power faltered, the sources of Assyrian wealth dried up, further undermining the state and leading to collapse of the imperial system.

Assyria's successor, the Neo-Babylonian dynasty, soon restored order and extended the empire by annexing more territory (see again Map 4.2). The most famous Neo-Babylonian ruler was King Nebuchadnezzar II (NAB-oo-kuhd-nez-uhr) (r. 604–562 BCE), who captured the kingdom of Judah in 587 BCE and deported its people to Babylonia. This period became known as the Babylonian Captivity, or the **Exile**.

Like his Assyrian predecessors, Nebuchadnezzar used the resources of conquered territories to embellish the cities of his homeland. Under Nebuchadnezzar's direction, Babylon became the most fabulous city in the western Eurasian world. We can still see remains from his time on the site and in museums around the world (see Lives and Livelihoods: Mesopotamian Astronomers). The Neo-Babylonian Empire did not last long, however. Less than one hundred years after its creation, it was conquered by a far mightier force—the Persian Empire.

The Persian Empire 550–330 BCE

Exile In the history of ancient Judah, the period when the Neo-Babylonians deported the Judeans to Babylonia, c. 587–530 BCE.

↘ **FOCUS** What imperial vision and style of government marked the rise of the vast Persian Empire and allowed it to endure for over 200 years?

In the sixth century BCE, the Persians, starting from what is today southern Iran, united all the existing empires and states from the Mediterranean coast to the Indus Valley. Remarkably, they were able to integrate an enormously diverse group of peoples and cultures into an imperial whole. Although they demanded obedience to their king, the Persians respected local cultures and identities, and this respect was key to their success. Their empire—unprecedented in its scale—lasted for more than 200 years partly because of their tolerance. Although others replaced the Persians, the practices of government they initiated survived for many centuries.

The Course of Empire

The Persian Empire was established by Cyrus the Achaemenid (a-KEY-muh-nid) (r. 559–530 BCE), who in the sixth century rapidly annexed his neighbors' territories, including the large Neo-Babylonian empire and the states of central Iran. His son and successor, Cambyses (kam-BIE-sees) (r. 530–522 BCE), added Egypt to the empire, and for another fifty years the Persians campaigned in all directions to conquer new lands. By 480 BCE, the Achaemenid Empire incorporated the area from western India to the Mediterranean coast and from Egypt to the fringes of Central Asia. Indeed, for more than a millennium, four ruling dynasties—the Achaemenids (559–330 BCE), Seleucids (323–83 BCE), Parthians (247 BCE–224 CE), and Sasanids (224–651 CE)—maintained imperial rule over much of Southwest Asia (see Maps 4.3 and 4.4).

Although they were foreign occupiers, the early Persian kings presented themselves as legitimate heirs to local thrones. Thus when Cambyses became king of Egypt, he adopted an Egyptian throne name and was represented with traditional Egyptian royal garments and crowns. These men had to be strong individuals to assert their authority over various conquered peoples, who yearned for independence and the return of a native ruler. These feelings boiled over at the death of Cambyses in 522 BCE, and only after much campaigning—described in the passage at the beginning of this chapter—did the new Persian king, Darius (r. 521–486 BCE), gain full control of the empire.

The difficulties Darius faced led him to undertake a program of reorganization and reform. In place of a collection of states held together by the person of the king, Darius created an imperial structure comprising twenty provinces, called **satrapies** (SAY-trap-eez), thereby extending a uniform system of government over an area of unprecedented size. Each satrapy had a Persian administrator (satrap) and was forced to provide tribute and troops. Imperial authorities exploited the skills of their subject peoples: Phoenicians manned the navy along with Cypriots and Ionians; in the army, Arabian camel drivers fought next to North African charioteers.

Despite Persia's enormous power and military success, there were limits to its ability to expand. Most famous is the empire's failure to conquer Greece despite repeated attempts (see Counterpoint). Resistance to Persia continued throughout the empire's history, and Egypt, for example, was able to gain independence from 404 to 343 BCE.

satrapy A province in the Achaemenid Persian Empire, administered by a satrap.

LIVES AND LIVELIHOODS

Mesopotamian Astronomers

Like the Chinese in the Shang period (see Chapter 3), the Mesopotamians were obsessed with predicting the future. But instead of asking specific questions and finding the answers in the cracks of oracle bones as the Chinese did, the Mesopotamians saw signs from the gods everywhere: in the birth of a malformed animal, the appearance of a large flock of birds, the occurrence of a lunar eclipse, and so on. The challenge to the people was to know how to read these omens.

From early in Mesopotamian history, scholars had compiled lists of guidelines for interpreting omens. The items were phrased in the same way as the Laws of Hammurabi (see page 58), as "if-then" statements. The "if" part could be any observable phenomenon. The second part indicated what the observation foretold. For example, "If a white cat is seen in a man's house, then hardship will seize the land." Often observations involved slaughtering a sheep to investigate the liver, an organ with many variations in color and shape, any of which could present a sign. For example, "If the left lobe of the liver is covered by a membrane, the king will die from illness."

In the first millennium BCE, astronomical observations became very important to the Mesopotamians, and the longest lists of omens relate to events in the sky, such as planetary alignments, eclipses, and the appearance of stars. One series of omens, *Enuma Anu Enlil* ("When the gods Anu and Enlil"), was copied out on seventy clay tablets and included some 7,000 entries. It described omens

≡ **Assyrian Astronomy** The best evidence of the Assyrian reliance on the stars and other heavenly bodies to predict the future is written lists of astronomical omens, but their art reflects the same interest. This stele from Assurnasirpal II (r. 883–859 BCE) shows the king under the protection of the sun, the moon, and the planet Venus.

dealing with the moon, the sun, the weather, and the planets. For example, one omen warned, "If the moon makes an eclipse in Month VII on the twenty-first day and sets eclipsed, they will take the crowned prince from his palace in fetters."

Although every Mesopotamian consulted omens, most of those recorded in writing deal with the king. They cover everything important to him personally and to his rule: the outcome of battles, deaths, births, illnesses, the success of the harvest, and many more concerns. Kings ordered scholars from all over the empire to examine anything that could be an omen and to report it to them. From their constant observation of phenomena in the sky, astronomers became aware of cyclical patterns. For example, they learned to calculate when events such as eclipses would occur and when a specific star would appear on the horizon. Ancient Mediterranean peoples thus regarded astronomy as a Mesopotamian science, and they considered the Babylonians its greatest experts.

The observation and interpretation of astronomical and other omens were not goals in themselves, however. Rather, Mesopotamians believed it was possible to change a predicted negative outcome. They aimed to produce this change mostly by appeasing the gods with prayers and offerings. But when an omen foretold the death of the king, the people would place a substitute on the throne and hide the real king in a safe place. They enacted a ritual in which the substitute was crowned, dressed in royal garb, and even provided with a queen. When they considered that the evil had passed, they removed the substitute (most often killing him to indicate that the prediction had been accurate) and restored the real king to the throne.

Omen readers, and especially astronomers, were thus very important, highly respected people in ancient Mesopotamia. They probably had to study for long periods to become familiar with the extensive writings that guided the interpretation of signs, and they had to master the intricacies of the cuneiform script and of Babylonian mathematics, which were at the basis of the analysis. The astronomers' accomplishments as observers of planetary behavior were remarkable, and their predictions of eclipses and the like were accurate. They were also meticulous record keepers, and to this day we identify many of the constellations they were the first to discern.

Questions to Consider

1. What was the purpose of omen reading in ancient Mesopotamia?
2. How did astronomers obtain their data?
3. What was the relationship between political rule and omen reading?

For Further Information:

Bottéro, Jean. *Mesopotamia: Writing, Reasoning, and the Gods.* Translated by Z. Bahrani and M. Van De Mieroop. Chicago: University of Chicago Press, 1992.

Rochberg, Francesca. *The Heavenly Writing: Divination, Horoscopy, and Astronomy in Mesopotamian Culture.* Cambridge: Cambridge University Press, 2004.

☰ **MAP 4.3** **The Persian Empire, 559–330 BCE** Building on the work of Assyrians, Babylonians, and Egyptians before them, the Persians merged their lands with the areas of Iran and beyond. Ruling a wide variety of peoples and states from the Indus Valley to the Mediterranean Sea, they ran one of the most successful empires in world history. When at last the empire fell to the Greeks in 330 BCE, Greek generals carved up the empire's territory, most of which initially was ruled by the Seleucids.

Yet these rebellions did not destroy the empire. That occurred only with the arrival of a young ruler, Alexander the Great, from Macedonia, the region just north of Greece. With his highly skilled troops, Alexander defeated the Persian king Darius III in three crucial battles. These events did not allow Alexander to inherit the entire empire at once, however. As we will see in Chapter 5, victory came only after he led his troops on a long series of campaigns from Egypt to Iran and farther east, to claim control over these territories.

Administering a Multicultural Empire

At Persepolis, in the heartland of Persia, Darius constructed a magnificent city where he annually celebrated the delivery of tribute. The ceremony had an ideological as well as economic value, for it showed the ruler as master of the subject

≡ **MAP 4.4** **The Parthian and Sasanid Empires, 247 BCE–651 CE** Iranian peoples reestablished control over the eastern parts of the Seleucid Empire and developed into formidable opponents of the Mediterranean powers of the Seleucids, Romans, and Byzantines. The Parthians and Sasanids preserved the Persian language, Zoroastrian religion, and ideals of kingship, and, although we know much less about them than about their western neighbors, they had a crucial impact on Eurasian history.

regions, each dependent people offering him the specialties of their lands. Bactrians, for example, brought camels; Armenians, gold vessels; and Nubians, ivory tusks.

Because communication was of utmost importance in administering this colossal empire, the Persians developed an extensive road system to connect the capital to the provinces. The king used messengers, known as "the eyes and ears of the king," to inspect his provincial officials and to make sure they obeyed his orders. The most famous road was the Royal Road from Susa in western Iran to Sardis in western Turkey, covering a distance of 1,600 miles, which a traveler could cover in ninety days (see again Map 4.3). Rest houses along its route accommodated the king's representatives.

Given the empire's vast size and enormous bureaucracy, the efficiency-minded Persians readily adopted existing practices in the conquered territories, including writing and language. In Babylonia they continued to record on clay tablets; in Egypt they wrote on papyri. For affairs that crossed the borders of these earlier states, they used Aramaic language and script. Unfortunately, Aramaic records were written on papyrus or parchment, which easily disintegrate, and therefore few such documents have survived.

The Persians' adoption of the Aramaic alphabet spread that system's use far to the east, and it inspired later alphabets as far east as India. Before their empire, the Persians did not have a script. They spoke an Indo-European language, Old Persian, in which they may have had a flourishing oral literature. When Darius became king, he instituted the use of a new script to write Old Persian, an alphabetic cuneiform intended for royal inscriptions. These inscriptions appeared in three languages—Old Persian, Babylonian, and Elamite, the last being the official

≡ **View of Persepolis** The imperial city of Persepolis (the Greek name meaning "the Persian City") dominated the countryside, to be seen from afar and stand as a symbol of the empire's power.

language of the Elamite state that had ruled western Iran for centuries until about 700 BCE. The intent was to show that the empire integrated several great literate cultures.

An innovation that simplified trade and spread widely over the empire was the use of coins—small, portable disks of precious metal stamped by official mints to guarantee their value. Around 650 BCE, before the Persian Empire, people from the country of Lydia in western Anatolia had invented coinage. They made the earliest coins of electrum, a locally available mixture of silver and gold. Sometime later, others minted coins of pure gold and silver; each region or city could produce its own coins with distinctive stamps. Coins facilitated trade by providing an easily portable, guaranteed means of exchange.

The First Coins Because people who received payment in precious metals ran the risk of receiving inferior metal, around 650 BCE inhabitants of Lydia developed the idea of casting pieces with a mark stamped on them. Recipients would recognize the distinctive image from an authority that guaranteed the value. The earliest coins were of electrum, as are the examples shown here, but soon coins of pure gold and silver were more common. The Persian Empire's need to pay soldiers promoted the use of coinage all over its vast territory and beyond.

Persia's empire had a distinctive attitude toward local traditions and beliefs. In contrast to other imperial elites, the Persians adopted the lifestyles and ideologies of the territories they annexed and integrated themselves into existing structures. As we have seen, the Persian king behaved as a local ruler, participating, for example, in traditional rituals to local gods. Further, the Persians restored local traditions that their imperial predecessors had recently disrupted. Most famous is Cyrus's decision to allow Judean deportees to return from Babylonia to Jerusalem. The Hebrew Bible depicts Cyrus as the savior of the Judean people sent by their god Yahweh. Other literatures, too, presented the Persians as more devoted to the local gods than the rulers they replaced. Such observations may have been propagandistic, but they did contain a grain of truth. By respecting local identities and adopting local customs, the Persians reduced resistance to their rule and claimed political legitimacy in terms the local population understood. They saw themselves as heads of a multicultural empire and did not seek to impose a common Persian identity on their subject peoples.

Zoroastrianism in a Polytheistic World

Persian religion followed the teachings of Zoroaster (the Greek rendering of the Iranian name Zarathushtra), who is often called a **prophet**; therefore we call it **Zoroastrianism**. He taught through **Gathas** ("Songs"), which are contained in the Avesta, a collection of writings recorded around 500 CE. The Gathas depict a world inhabited by pastoralists, probably located in eastern Iran, similar to the world described in the Indian Vedas (see Chapter 3). The languages of the Gathas and Vedas are closely related, and they both belong to the Indo-Iranian branch of Indo-European.

It is unclear when Zoroaster lived; scholars have suggested dates from 1700 to 500 BCE. Persian religion was **polytheistic**—they believed in the existence of many gods—but according to Zoroaster, the universe was divided into the two opposing forces, good and evil, represented by two spirits. A line in his teachings says, "Yes, there are two fundamental spirits, twins which are renowned to be in conflict. In thought and in word, in action, they are two: the good and the bad. And between these two, the beneficent have correctly chosen, not the maleficent."[2] Everything in the Zoroastrian world was characterized by this dualism—good versus evil, truth versus lies, light versus darkness—and all humans had to choose between them. The god Ahuramazda (ah-HOOR-uh-MAZZ-duh) ("wise lord") was the father of both the beneficent and the hostile spirit and the force for keeping evil in check. The creator of heaven and earth, day and night, light and darkness, Ahuramazda provided ethical guidance to humans to seek truth, goodness, and light.

Because Zoroaster's teachings stressed that individuals had to seek purity in nature, the cult focused on the pure forces of fire and water. Unlike other peoples of Southwest Asia and neighboring regions, Zoroastrians did not build temples, and they burned sacrifices on altars standing in the open. As in Vedic India, priests, called Magi in Greek texts on Persia, played a key role in the sacrifices, and they drank a stimulant, haoma (HOW-muh), that was related to the Vedic drink soma.

It is unclear whether the Persian rulers were Zoroastrians, but historians know that they recognized Ahuramazda as the god who placed them on the throne and guided them in their search for truth. Representations of the king commonly show him next to a winged sun disk containing the upper body of a man, most likely the god Ahuramazda.

Zoroaster's teachings became the basis of the official religion of later Iranian dynasties (the Parthians and the Sasanids, as we will see in Chapter 6). But the ancient Persians did not force their subjects to honor Ahuramazda or adopt Persian cult practices. The focus on choosing between good and evil and on worshipping only the god Ahuramazda had a significant impact on Judaism, however, and through it on Christianity and Islam.

prophet Someone who speaks for a god or by divine inspiration.

Zoroastrianism The religion founded in the ancient Persian Empire by the prophet Zoroaster.

Gathas The songs that contain the prophet Zoroaster's teachings.

polytheism A religious system's belief in the existence of many gods.

COUNTERPOINT: On the Edge of Empire: The People of Ancient Greece 800–500 BCE

⬊ FOCUS What significant political and cultural developments emerged in Greece in the early first millennium BCE?

In this Counterpoint we focus on a territory that was at first marginal in terms of political and military power but became a center of cultural and technological innovation: Greece in western Eurasia. In close contact with the nearby empires of Southwest Asia and North Africa, yet politically independent, the Greeks stimulated many political and cultural developments during the first millennium BCE. Although Greek city-states were in almost perpetual military competition with one another, people throughout the region shared a common culture, and all experimented with new intellectual endeavors.

Greek Colonization of the Mediterranean 800–500 BCE

The Greeks inhabited a world dominated by mountains that made overland travel difficult, and where only limited agriculture was possible. The sea, however, was dotted with many small islands. By sailing small ships that almost never lost sight of the coastline, the inhabitants maintained contacts among the Greek mainland, the Aegean islands, and the west coast of Anatolia (modern Turkey). The combination of lack of resources at home and access to the sea encouraged the Greeks to have an outward look and seek contacts with the wider Mediterranean world (see Map 4.5). They did so by establishing **colonies** eastward to the modern Turkish coast and the Black Sea and westward to southern Italy, Sicily, southern France, and Spain. They also settled on the Libyan coast in North Africa. The Greek colonies' economic bases varied, as did their importance to their hometowns. Settlements in fertile agricultural zones shipped grain back home, while other outposts provided commodities such as timber and tin. Some special trading ports facilitated commerce with the great states of Assyria and Egypt. Hence, in numerous ways, but most directly through trade, colonization strengthened the connections between Greeks and the larger world.

The presence of Greeks abroad naturally led to a brisk exchange of ideas, practices, and people in the eighth century BCE. Because the East had much older and more developed traditions than the West, most of the inspiration went from east to west, and various Eastern cultural elements entered the Greek world. Most consequential perhaps was the Greeks' adoption of the Phoenician alphabet, perhaps as early as the ninth century BCE. The Phoenician origin of Greek letters is clear from

colony A settlement or administrative district in a foreign country established and governed by people who intend to exploit the resources of that country.

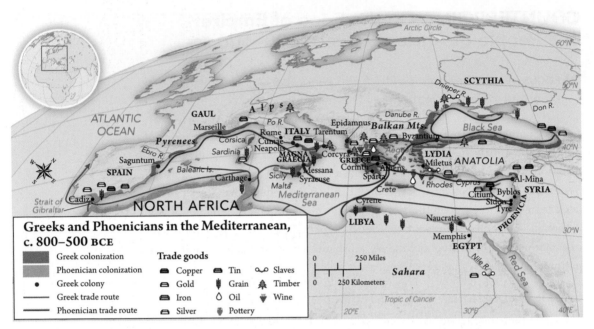

≡ **MAP 4.5   Greeks and Phoenicians in the Mediterranean, c. 800–500 BCE**   Throughout most of the first millennium BCE, Phoenician and Greek traders sailed the Mediterranean Sea, competing to bring natural resources from the west to urban centers in the east. The Phoenicians focused especially on the south coast and the far west, while the Greeks settled mostly in the northern Mediterranean and explored the Black Sea coast.

polis The Greek city-state, in the ideal a self-governing community of citizens. The plural of the word is poleis.

phalanx A formation of soldiers who overlap their shields and swords to protect one another; developed in ancient Greece.

the names, which are Semitic (see again Figure 4.1, page 136). The Greeks introduced a crucial innovation in the alphabet, however: they wrote down the vowels, which were not expressed in Semitic writing. A speaker of a Semitic language knows what vowels to use from the grammatical context, but in Indo-European languages such as Greek, the context does not provide this clue and the vowels need to be explicitly indicated.

In the eighth to sixth centuries BCE, increasing prosperity from manufacturing and trade enabled the Greeks to buy art from foreign regions, which inspired potters, painters, and other artists. Sculptors carved human figures in imitation of Egyptian statues, and architects borrowed from Egypt techniques for constructing large buildings in stone. In the other direction, west to east, the Greeks provided manpower. Greek mercenaries appeared in Egypt in the seventh century BCE and soon afterward in Southwest Asia, where they remained a fixture for centuries. How and why had the Greeks developed such fighting skills? We find the answer in the emergence of powerful Greek city-states.

Growth of the City-State in Early Greece 800–500 BCE

Population growth in the mid-eighth century BCE led to fundamental changes in the political organization of the Greek world. Village communities expanded or merged to form city-states, which became the characteristic political unit of Greek society. The Greeks referred to the city-state using the word **polis**, from which the modern term "politics" derives. The polis was a self-governing community of citizens. It was administered by officials (who were themselves citizens) with defined responsibilities. There were numerous poleis, each controlling a relatively small territory comprising the city and its immediate surroundings. We have encountered city-states before—in Mesopotamia, for example (see Chapter 2)—but the Greeks added a further ideal to this concept. The citizens of the polis shared power rather than depending on a king. It must be emphasized, however, that most inhabitants of a polis were not citizens. That status was originally reserved for native-born men who owned land, while women, the landless, enslaved persons, and foreigners were all excluded from Greek government.

Neighboring Greek poleis often competed with one another over scarce resources. As a result, one of the most important duties of the citizen was to fight in the army. The eighth century BCE saw radical changes in military tactics. Instead of a few heavily armed men riding to battle in chariots, the soldiers formed **phalanxes**. Fighting on foot, these tightly organized groups relied on strict cooperation, every soldier, called a *hoplite*, holding a shield in his left arm to protect the right side of his neighbor. This teamwork created the strong sense of community that characterized the ideal of the polis.

≡ **Women's Statue in the Orientalizing Style** This statue, sculpted in Crete between 640 and 620 BCE, reveals how much styles from Egypt and the Middle East influenced early Greek art. The woman's posture, dress, and hairstyle resemble those that Egyptian or Syrian sculptors of the same period would have shown.

The early city-states were dominated by aristocrats, a small group of people from wealthy families who inherited their status and made most of the important decisions for the community. When more people acquired wealth, the base of politically engaged men gradually expanded to include all citizens, with elected officials administering the state. Flouting the ideal of elected officials, from around 650 to 500 BCE individuals seized power in many city-states. The Greeks called these men *tyrants*, which was at first a value-neutral term indicating "lord." People grew to resent this form of government, and rule by **tyranny** largely gave way to two other types of political organization. Many cities were controlled by an **oligarchy**, a small group of men who were usually wealthy, but not always from the old aristocratic families. Other cities embraced a more radical political system—the ideal of **democracy**, or rule by the people.

Athens and Sparta, the two most prominent Greek city-states of the sixth and fifth centuries BCE, illustrate the two political systems best (see again Map 4.5). The basic principle of Athenian democracy was most eloquently expressed in a speech the Athenian leader Pericles delivered in 430 BCE (see Reading the Past: Pericles Praises the Democratic Ideal): all citizens could and should participate in government. All men over the age of eighteen who had completed their military training decided on policy in an assembly that met four times every month. They considered the most important matters of state, listened to one another's arguments, and truly governed as a people. They also stood in judgment over one another—each citizen had the right to be judged by his peers. It is important to remember, however, that few individuals qualified as citizens and that the majority of the population—women, children and adolescents, foreign-born residents, freed enslaved persons, and those still enslaved—were denied these rights.

Because the Athenian assembly was too large to manage daily business, they created a smaller body for this purpose. Each year 500 men who were at least thirty years old were selected by lot to join a council, and they served in groups of fifty for a period of thirty-six days each. The council prepared laws for consideration by the assembly and executed the assembly's decisions. To prevent someone from gaining too much executive power, no man was allowed to serve on the council for more than two years.

The ideal of the democratic system was clear: every citizen had the ability to make intelligent decisions and perform official duties. But not everyone thought this was true. Ancient philosophers such as Plato (see Chapter 5) doubted that all men were equally capable of governing, and modern scholars often depict an Athenian assembly that was easily swayed by the false arguments of great orators. Yet despite the shortcomings Athenian democracy displayed in practice, its ideals have inspired political thinkers throughout world history.

tyranny A political system in which one person holds absolute power; originally value-neutral, the term has acquired the negative connotation of severe abuse of power.

oligarchy A political system in which a small group of people holds all powers.

democracy The political ideal of rule by the people.

READING THE PAST

PERICLES PRAISES THE DEMOCRATIC IDEAL

The ancient Greeks greatly admired the power of rhetoric, and certain speeches recorded from the time have become classics emulated to this day. Athens's leader Pericles delivered one such speech at the end of the first year of the Peloponnesian War, in 431 BCE. When he honored those who had fallen in battle, he extolled the virtues of the city of Athens and the institutions in whose defense they had died:

> Let me say that our system of government does not copy the institutions of our neighbors. It is more the case of our being a model to others, than of our imitating anyone else. Our constitution is called a democracy because the power is in the hands not of a minority but of the whole people.

When it is a question of settling private disputes, everyone is equal before the law; when it is a question of putting one person before another in positions of public responsibility, what counts is not membership of a particular class, but the actual ability which the man possesses. No one, so long as he has it in him to be of service to the state, is kept in political obscurity because of poverty. And, just as our political life is free and open, so is our day-to-day life in our relations with each other. We do not get into a state with our next-door neighbor if he enjoys himself in his own way, nor do we give him the kind of black looks which, though they do no real harm, still do hurt people's feelings. We are free and tolerant in our private lives; but in public we keep to the law. This is because it commands our deep respect.

Source: Thucydides, *History of the Peloponnesian War*, ed. M. I. Finley, trans. Rex Warner (London: Penguin Classics, 1972), 145.

Examining the Evidence

1. What characteristics of the Athenian political system does Pericles praise? Do you think his claims reflect the reality of life in ancient Athens?

2. Why was this speech pertinent in a period of war?

3. How do the ideals expressed here still echo in political discourse today?

In Sparta, too, all citizens—again, the male inhabitants of the city—sat in an assembly. The institution had much less power than the Athenian assembly, however, because it had to work in concert with an elected council of thirty men, all over sixty years old. A group of five officials, annually elected from among all citizens, held executive power. The highest Spartan officials were two kings, men from two wealthy families, who ruled simultaneously for life. Real power in Sparta was thus in the hands of an oligarchy.

Spartan oligarchy and Athenian democracy shared several elements, but to us today their ideals seem very different. Athenians declared that citizens, however restricted that group was, could and should be involved in politics, whereas Spartans believed that only select men had the ability to govern. The Spartan economy depended on the control and exploitation of the nearby land and population. Athenians, in contrast, emphasized the sea and trade. The opposition of the two systems would grow over time and, as we shall see, lead to conflict.

Struggle Between Persia and Greece 500–479 BCE

To the mighty Persian Empire conquest of the small and divided city-states of Greece must have seemed like a minor challenge. Successive invasions, however, ended in disaster for Persia. In 490 BCE, the Athenians defeated the Persians soundly at the Battle of Marathon, relying on their heavy armor and tight battle formation (see Map 4.6). Ten years later, the Persians once again invaded Greece on land and by sea with a gigantic army. They reached central Greece and sacked Athens, which its citizens had evacuated without trying to resist a siege. Despite the destruction of their city, the Athenians continued the fight at sea. They lured the massive Persian fleet into the narrow bay at Salamis, where, unable to maneuver, it fell prey to the smaller Greek ships. The next year, in 479 BCE, the Greeks defeated the remainder of the Persian force and ended further threats of invasion.

The Persian Wars had tremendous consequences for the Greeks. Some thirty city-states had formed an unprecedented coalition, and for the rest of the fifth century BCE Sparta and Athens, which had distinguished themselves militarily, used their fame to command the respect and gratitude of the other Greek city-states. The wars also raised the Greek self-image, which they emphasized by portraying themselves in opposition to outsiders. They scorned those who did not speak Greek as "barbarians," a term derived from "bar bar," after the sound of foreign languages to Greek ears. They depicted non-Greeks as lacking the sense to have proper political institutions, customs, and social behavior. This contrast led to a skewed view in the historical record of the relationship between Greeks and foreigners. Stressing their own uniqueness, the Greeks downplayed the significant

≡ **MAP 4.6   The Eastern Mediterranean**   Carved up by the sea and mountain ranges, Greece was home to many city-states, each with its own political structure and organization. But the threat of the mighty Persian Empire pushed them to join forces to withstand repeated invasions. The subsequent rivalry between Sparta and Athens, which dominated the later fifth century BCE, led to the creation of the land-based Peloponnesian League under Sparta and the sea-based Delian League under Athens.

role that Southwest Asia and Egypt had played in inspiring many of their cultural achievements.

Athens and Sparta used their special status to gain allies, by free will and by force. Each formed a league of allies (see again Map 4.6). Sparta, which had risen to power by exploiting land resources, allied itself primarily with states on the Greek mainland that had strong infantries. The Spartans dominated most of the city-states of the Peloponnese, that is, the southern Greek peninsula. Their coalition was called the Peloponnesian League. Athens, in contrast, looked outward to the sea, where its navy had crushed the Persians. The Athenians allied themselves with states on the Greek islands and the Ionian coast. They created the Delian League, so named because the coalition originally kept its treasury on the island of Delos. At first, members delivered contributions mainly in the form of ships and their crews, but over time this arrangement developed into silver payments to

Athens, which used the money to build and crew ships of its own. Soon Athens had by far the region's largest navy, with which it imposed its will on the members of the Delian League, presenting itself as the protector of democracy against the oligarchic regimes of the Peloponnesian League. The wealth the city accumulated enabled revolutionary developments in the arts and intellectual life, as we will see in Chapter 5.

The Peloponnesian War and the End of Athenian Supremacy 431–404 BCE

Over time, Athens's ever-expanding power led to resentment among its rivals, especially Sparta. The tensions erupted in a generation-long conflict known as the Peloponnesian War (431–404 BCE), which impoverished Greece and undermined its society. During the war years, the Athenians became increasingly authoritarian, extracting ever higher contributions from members of the Delian League, forcing other cities to choose sides, and punishing those who refused to join. They could be ruthless. When the inhabitants of the island of Melos asked to remain neutral, Athens massacred all the men and enslaved all the women and children. Despite such desperate acts, Athens failed to defeat its enemies, and in 404 BCE Sparta prevailed.

Sparta's hegemony, however, did not last long, and the fourth century BCE saw fierce struggles among Greek cities for preeminence. The power that ended this period of civil strife was Macedonia, a kingdom to the north of Greece. In many respects Macedonia's relationship to Greece was like that of Nubia to Egypt: it owed much of its culture to Greece, yet ultimately it came to dominate its neighbor. Inspired by Greek practices, the Macedonian king Philip (r. 359–336 BCE), father of Alexander the Great, improved his army's strength and tactics by arming his foot soldiers with ten-foot-long spears and coordinating their actions with those of the horse-mounted cavalry. With this military advantage, in 338 BCE Philip defeated the city-states of southern Greece and forced them into an alliance under Macedonian leadership. The age of independent Greek poleis was over.

Conclusion

The earliest empires in world history arose in North Africa and Southwest Asia, beginning in the second millennium BCE. Their emergence prompted peoples with separate cultures and habits to interact, and they exchanged ideas and influenced one another in enduring ways.

The degree to which they assimilated and the sources of the most influential traditions varied enormously. Political domination could lead to cultural supremacy, as when Egypt conquered Nubia, but sometimes rulers eagerly adopted the practices and ideas of their subject people, as when Nubians ruled Egypt. Some imperial powers—Persia, for example—permitted their subjects to continue cultural practices and even promoted them. Others, such as Assyria, did not interfere with cultural matters and local customs as long as their subjects obeyed them. Whereas these empires may have seemed invincible, some people successfully resisted them, most notably the Greeks. The interactions led to cultural exchanges, however, and had radical consequences for later world history. In the next chapter we will see how the cultural developments in western Eurasia had parallels throughout the continent.

review

Major global development in this chapter: The rise of empires and the variety and consequences of imperial rule.

Important Events	
c. 1700–500 BCE	Scholarly estimates for life of Zoroaster, founder of Zoroastrianism
c. 1700–330 BCE	Development and spread of the alphabet in western Asia
c. 1550–1070 BCE	Egyptian New Kingdom Empire
c. 1070 BCE	Nubian independence from Egypt
c. 900–612 BCE	Assyrian Empire
c. 775 BCE	First evidence of alphabetic writing in Greece
750–550 BCE	Main period of Greek colonization of the Mediterranean
c. 730–660 BCE	Nubian Empire
c. 626–539 BCE	Neo-Babylonian (Chaldean) Empire
c. 550–330 BCE	Achaemenid Persian Empire

Important Events	
500–479 BCE	Persian Wars
443–429 BCE	Pericles leads Athens
431–404 BCE	Peloponnesian War
c. 400 BCE–350 CE	Kingdom of Meroe
330 BCE	Alexander the Great defeats Persia

KEY TERMS

assimilation (p. 123)
colony (p. 147)
democracy (p. 150)
empire (p. 122)
Exile (p. 138)
Gathas (p. 146)

oligarchy (p. 150)
phalanx (p. 148)
polis (p. 148)
polytheism (p. 146)
prophet (p. 146)
province (p. 135)

satrapy (p. 139)
tribute (p. 135)
tyranny (p. 150)
Zoroastrianism (p. 146)

CHAPTER OVERVIEW QUESTIONS

1. What were the main characteristics of the early empires?
2. How did the empires affect the peoples who created them and their subject populations?
3. How did imperial rulers adapt their control to local circumstances?
4. How did people resist empires?

MAKING CONNECTIONS

1. How would you describe the different attitudes of the imperial elites discussed in this chapter toward the cultures of the conquered?
2. What languages and scripts were used in the different empires described in this chapter?
3. How did imperial policies and trade contacts influence the spread of writing systems?
4. What characteristics make these empires different from the earlier political structures we have studied?

DOING HISTORY

Making Connections

When studying political formations in a broad geographical context, it becomes clear that the appearance of one type of organization in a region often triggers its development in neighboring areas. In this chapter we looked at sequences of empires in North Africa and Southwest Asia and considered as well the adjoining region of Greece. Can you explain the connections in the political developments in the following cases?

1. New Kingdom Egypt and Nubia
2. The Assyrian, Neo-Babylonian, and Persian Empires
3. The Persian Empire and Greece

For further research into the topics covered in this chapter, see the Bibliography at the end of the book.

Thinkers and World Empires of Eurasia

500 BCE–500 CE

≡ **World in the Making** According to tradition, in 260 BCE Emperor Ashoka built thousands of stupas across India to cover ashes of the cremated Buddha. This example from Sanchi is known to have a simple hemispherical brick core to hold the remains. In later centuries people turned the stupa into an elaborate construction with a large stone mound and entrance gates. The monument is still in use today.

backstory

We left the discussion of South and East Asia in Chapter 3 in 500 BCE. By this point, centuries of development in India and China had laid the foundations for the two regions' subsequent histories. In India, many had accepted the Vedic traditions and the caste system, whereas in China the ideal of political unification and dynastic rule had been firmly established. By contrast, in questioning inherited practices and beliefs, the early Greeks (Chapter 4) created an environment that was unique politically, socially, and intellectually. We return now to Eurasia to study how its peoples both built on and challenged their cultural inheritance.

AROUND 300 BCE, A MAN from Athens in Greece, Clearchus, traveled to a city, now called Ai Khanoum, that Greeks had recently founded on the northern border of modern Afghanistan. He covered a distance equivalent to crossing the continental United States. At some point after he arrived, Clearchus inscribed on a rock sayings he had brought from the god Apollo's sanctuary at Delphi back home:

> When a child, show yourself well behaved;
> When a young man, self-controlled;
> In middle age, just;
> As an old man, a good counselor;
> At the end of your life, free of sorrow.[1]

The inscription shows us that Clearchus brought wisdom from his homeland with him, reflecting the spread of characteristic Greek values over a vast area. He could do so while staying in an area under the political control of Greeks, because some thirty years earlier Alexander the Great had created an enormous empire that connected Greece to distant places in the east, reaching the Indus River. Clearchus and others were interested not just in political dominance, however. They also sought to spread ideas developed in their homeland.

The Greeks were not alone in this. Across the continent of Eurasia in the centuries shortly before and after the year 1 CE stretched a series of empires, with their centers in China, India, and the Mediterranean (see Map 5.1). Each of these empires enabled the ideas of great thinkers, who had lived either just before their creation or at their height, to influence the inhabitants of vast areas. Their ideas appealed to people with various backgrounds and cultural traditions, and the spread of them was facilitated by trade networks throughout Eurasia. The periods when these ideas flourished are considered to be the **classical** ages for these regions because the ideas were preserved and treasured into modern times. Their impact was so momentous and lasting that the entire era has been called the **Axial Age**; that is, a time of pivotal intellectual shifts.

There was an exception to this universalist context, however, in the ideas developed in the small states of Israel and Judah. Those were intended for a distinctive group of people who considered themselves descendants of a common ancestor and strongly focused their religious belief on one god alone.

classical The traditional authoritative form of a culture.

Axial Age Historians' term for the centuries shortly before the common era when radical intellectual shifts occurred in Eurasian powers that would have profound consequences for these regions and beyond.

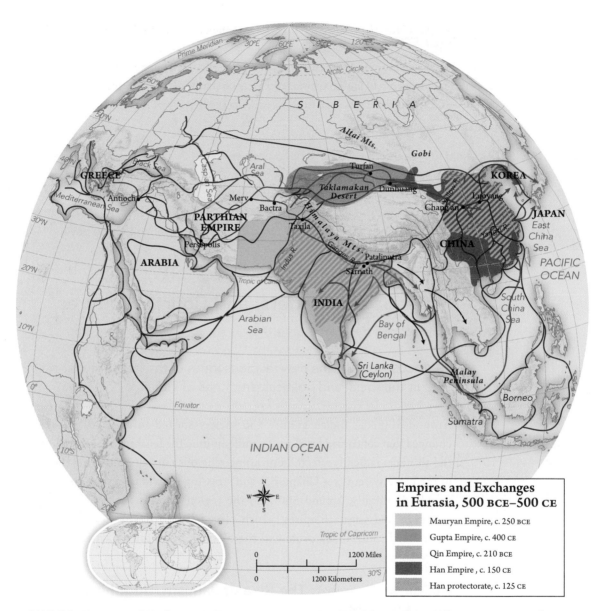

≡ **MAP 5.1 Empires and Exchanges in Eurasia, 500 BCE–500 CE** For a thousand years, the vast territories of Eurasia were connected through a vibrant trade of goods and ideas regardless of the multiple political powers that dominated parts of the region. Qin and Han China in the east, Mauryan and Gupta Empires in South and Central Asia, and ancient Greece, followed by the Roman Empire, in the west, were all hotbeds for the development of new ideas and technologies, many of which had a great impact on their regions and beyond throughout later history.

The major global development in this chapter: The revolutionary religious and cultural developments in India, China, and Greece that took place between 500 BCE and 500 CE and that remained fundamental to the history of Eurasia.

As you read, consider:

1. How did new social circumstances stimulate changes in religious beliefs and cultures?

2. What processes encouraged close connections among the various regions of Eurasia?

3. In what ways did the revolutionary thinkers discussed here have a lasting impact on the histories of the regions they inhabited and beyond?

India: Sages, Traders, and Courtly Cultures 500 BCE–500 CE

⬊ **FOCUS** How did the new religious ideas of the last centuries BCE suit the social and political structures of India?

Around 500 BCE, Indian culture and society started to undergo fundamental changes that continued for almost a millennium. The teachings of several influential thinkers radically affected prevailing religious currents, changing the nature of the caste system (see Chapter 3) and stressing individual responsibility for all people. Politically, around 300 BCE, the region saw the successive rise of the Mauryan and Gupta Empires, which placed large parts of South Asia under centralized control, and promoted the blossoming of Indian arts and scientific investigation.

Religious Ferment: The Rise of Jainism, Buddhism, and Hinduism

The rigor of the Vedic caste system, which assigned people a place in society at birth, was ill suited to the Indian society of 500 BCE. By that time, some merchants and craftspeople from lower castes had gained great wealth and were unhappy with their secondary status. In their discontent, they turned to religious teachers who stressed individual behavior over caste. These teachers often prescribed **asceticism**, that is, a lifestyle of indifference to physical comfort. Thus, a variety of new and profoundly influential religions emerged.

asceticism A rejection of physical pleasures that, in its extreme, can lead to deprivations and even starvation.

One of the most important of these new religions was based on the teachings of Vardhamana Mahavira (mah-hah-VEER-uh), who according to tradition was born around 540 BCE in northern India. Mahavira became known as the Jina (JYN-uh), "the conqueror," and the religion he inspired was Jainism (JYN-ihz-uhm). The Jains' belief that everything—humans, animals, plants, and inanimate objects—had a soul led devotees to complete nonviolence. They believed that no creature should be killed, even accidentally. Jains call the moral virtue that inspires such behavior **dharma**. They also tried to end the cycle of reincarnation (rebirth in a different form), which bolstered the caste system, and to free the soul from the body through ascetic behavior such as fasting.

Few could adhere fully to such a rigorous lifestyle, but Jainism was especially popular among urban merchants and artisans who were attracted to its rejection of castes. Its pacifism also had great appeal, inspiring men and women ever since its inception, including the twentieth-century Indian statesman Mahatma Gandhi, who grew up in a region where Jainism was widespread. Some political elites promoted Jainism, but the religion never spread beyond India.

In sharp contrast, another religion that originated in India, Buddhism, had a powerful impact on the entire Asian continent. Buddhism is based on the teachings of the Buddha, a title that means "the Awakened One"—that is, the one who awakened from a sleep of ignorance to find freedom from suffering. According to traditions written down centuries after his death, the Buddha was Prince Siddhartha Gautama from a small kingdom in southern Nepal, who lived according to various traditions from 563 to 483 or from 480 to 400 BCE. Originally shielded from the evils of life, when Gautama was twenty-nine years old, he insisted on leaving the palace and was shocked to witness old age, illness, and death. When his father told him that these conditions were inescapable, he moved into the forest to search for a state beyond birth and death. At first Gautama joined other ascetics, but after six years of self-mortification he realized that was not the answer (see Seeing the Past: The Fasting Buddha). He then sat down in a yoga position for meditation, which ultimately led him to formulate the idea of "the middle way." A balanced way of life, avoiding the extremes of indulgence in sensual pleasures and of asceticism, was the answer to human suffering. Having thus become the Buddha, he established the Four Noble Truths: (1) existence is suffering, (2) the cause of suffering is negative deeds of the body inspired by desire, (3) desire can be eliminated, and (4) the way to end desire lies in the eightfold path—right belief, resolve, speech, behavior, occupation, effort, contemplation, and meditation.

Buddhism's appeal relied on the "three jewels": (1) the charismatic teacher, the Buddha; (2) his teachings, the Buddhist interpretation of dharma; and (3) the community, **sangha**. For forty-five years after his awakening, the Buddha traveled

dharma A term with slightly different meanings in various Indian religions; it refers in Jainism to moral virtue, in Buddhism to the teachings of the Buddha, and in Hinduism to duty.

sangha In Buddhism, the community of monks and nuns, who see themselves as the successors of the people who traveled with the Buddha in his lifetime.

SEEING THE PAST

The Fasting Buddha

The figure of the Buddha was of central importance to Buddhism, and details of his life were explored and recounted in stories originally transmitted orally and later written down. These stories and texts were the inspiration of many works of art, which in the first century BCE started to be carved in stone and used to decorate public shrines such as the round stupas that were built across South Asia. Visitors could walk around them and see key moments in the story of the Buddha from birth to death. The Buddha was also represented in numerous statues that range in size from less than small scale to gigantic. The sculptures were not intended to be realistic but focused on important elements of the Buddha's ideas.

Statue of the Buddha

The stone statue shown here, only eleven inches high, depicts the Buddha when he was fasting for six years before he found his awakening, and the ravages of the asceticism on his body are vividly shown. But the statue also represents other aspects of his life. His position is one of meditation, with his legs in the lotus position and his hands on his lap. According to the story of his life, he meditated sitting on a bed of cut grass, which is carved here underneath him. The base of the statue shows another moment in his life, when he started to teach five men who previously were ascetics too. The sixth man, standing on the right, is probably the person who donated the statue.

Examining the Evidence

1. How does the statue combine multiple elements of the Buddhist ideas?

2. What would the purpose of such a statue have been?

3. How does the image emphasize specific aspects of the Buddha's life?

throughout northeastern India to teach the religion, which allowed for levels of commitment to an ascetic life. Most followers remained laypeople who engaged in everyday business, but some devoted their lives to Buddhism, becoming monks and nuns and founding **monasteries**. There they strove to reach **nirvana**, a state without desire, hatred, and ignorance and, ultimately, without suffering and re-birth, in which the physical was completely removed from the spiritual. Any man or woman who acquired freedom from suffering and postponed nirvana to teach it to others was a called a **bodhisattva**, an "enlightened being," who in turn became an object of veneration.

After the Buddha died, followers cremated his remains and distributed them over large parts of India, where they were buried underneath earthen mounds called **stupas**. Pilgrims visited sites that had been important in the Buddha's life and spread the new religion, reaching a wide audience by using vernacular dialects rather than literary Sanskrit. By promising an escape from the cycle of reincarna-tion and by rejecting the caste system, Buddhism appealed powerfully to the new wealthy mercantile class.

The support of royals and merchants greatly facilitated the spread of Buddhism. Kings sent out missionaries, and traders carried Buddhist manuscripts to distant places, where scholars translated them into local languages and adapted them to local tastes. The spread of Buddhism beyond India proved crucial to the religion's survival. Hinduism eventually replaced Buddhism as India's dominant religion, but Buddhism continued to flourish abroad.

Buddhism and Jainism challenged the Vedic tradition and drew believers away from the older religion. In reaction, the Vedic tradition evolved rather than with-ered away. In a centuries-long process the Vedic tradition widened its appeal by abandoning its special treatment of the upper-caste Brahmins. These develop-ments coincided with the production of written Sanskrit versions of the Vedas, as well as of a large literature, both secular and religious. The new religion, Hinduism, found ways to emphasize the value of the individual within a caste framework. All people had an obligation to carry out the activities and duties of their caste, but proper behavior could free any individual from the cycle of reincarnation. Hence, Hinduism combined essential elements of the Vedic tradition with some of the beliefs and ideals of the tradition's critics, creating a stronger and more pop-ular religion.

The Hindu way of life encouraged a balanced pursuit of devotion and pleasure. People should seek righteousness, virtue, and duty, but they could also pursue ma-terial gain, love, and recreation. The poem known as the *Bhagavad Gita* ("Song of the Lord") explains how a person could attain the ideal balance in an active life. The poem is a dialogue between the hero Arjuna and his charioteer Krishna. When Arjuna is reluctant to fight his family members and friends, Krishna convinces

monastery A community of adherents to a particular religion, who often live in seclusion from general society.

nirvana In Buddhism, the goal of religious practice, a state of existence without desire, hatred, ignorance, suffering, and, ultimately, reincarnation.

bodhisattva In Buddhism, a person who found enlightenment and teaches others.

stupa A Buddhist monument to hold a part of the Buddha's remains or an object connected to him.

him that he will hurt only their bodies, which are renewable, and not their souls, which are immortal:

> Just as man, having cast off old garments, puts on other, new ones, even so does the embodied one, having cast off old bodies, take on other, new ones.
>   . . . He is eternal, all pervading, stable, immovable, existing from time immemorial.[2]

As a warrior, Arjuna has a specific role in society, just as everyone does: the duty of the Brahmin was to provide wisdom; of the warrior, valor; of the Vaishya, industry; and of the Shudra, service.

The centuries after 500 BCE thus witnessed remarkable intellectual activity in India as thinkers reinterpreted the ancient Vedic ideals and sought to make them accessible to all people. Hinduism continued to stress the caste system, but people on every level could find spiritual liberation. In contrast, Buddhism and Jainism focused on the individual quest for salvation outside the caste system. All three religions proved to have widespread and long-lasting appeal, and they continue to inspire millions of people to this day.

Unity and Fragmentation: The Mauryan and Gupta Empires

With its vast size, varied ecology, and diverse population, it was not easy to bring the Indian subcontinent under central political control. Nevertheless, between 300 BCE and 500 CE the Mauryan and Gupta Empires controlled large parts of India. They encouraged the merging of traditions throughout their realms and used the new religions to inspire a regional sense of community.

For many centuries South Asia had been divided into a number of kingdoms, such as the one in which Siddhartha Gautama grew up, and these were often at war with one another. Eventually these civil struggles ended, perhaps in part due to outside pressures. In 326 BCE Alexander of Macedonia crossed the Indus River and confronted Indian armies. Greek sources say that a rebellious Indian prince, whose name they render in Greek as Sandracottos (san-droh-KOT-uhs), met Alexander and urged him to conquer the kingdom of Magadha in the Ganges Valley. Alexander's men refused to go farther east, however, and retreated.

Later Indian sources do not mention Alexander, but they do describe the Indian prince, using his Indian name, Chandragupta. He started out as a penniless servant but established himself as ruler of the kingdom of Magadha. Through conquest and clever diplomacy, he created the largest empire in Indian history—called

≡ **MAP 5.2   The Mauryan and Gupta Empires, 324 BCE–540 CE** After centuries of political fragmentation, the Mauryan dynasty unified the South Asian subcontinent except for its south, initiating a long sequence of empires that controlled broad territories. Most prominent were the conquests of the Mauryan emperor Ashoka, who, shocked by the violence of his own campaigns, converted to Buddhism and announced his intentions for good governance in inscriptions he set up throughout the region.

Mauryan after the name of Chandragupta's dynasty—bringing the entire subcontinent except for the very south under his control (see Map 5.2).

Chandragupta relied on his chief adviser, Kautilya, to create the empire's administration, which became famous for its efficiency. Kautilya left behind a handbook on government, the *Arthashastra*, or "Treatise on Material Gain," as a guideline for future officials. The king was the sole guarantee against disorder and could use any means necessary to avoid it, including spies and political assassination. For much of his reign, Chandragupta followed Kautilya's advice, consolidating his own power and eliminating potential sources of opposition. He came to regret his ruthless policies, however, and around 297 BCE, Chandragupta abdicated the throne, became a Jain monk, and starved himself to death in absolute asceticism.

The religious climate of his day also deeply influenced Chandragupta's grandson and successor, Ashoka. Buddhist ideals inspired his government, and he announced his reforms publicly throughout the empire through the use of carved inscriptions, which are the oldest preserved writings from India, after the Indus Valley texts (see Chapter 3). Ashoka ruled his empire in a way that was unique for his time. He urged nonviolence, humane treatment of servants, and generosity to all. He did not force his views on his people, instead leading through example, as seen here, in one of his statements:

> All the good deeds that I have done have been accepted and followed by the people. And so obedience to mother and father, obedience to teachers, respect for the aged, kindness to Brahmins and ascetics, to the poor and weak, and to slaves and servants, have increased and will continue to increase.[3]

The emperor promoted general welfare by lining roads with fruit trees for shade and food, digging wells, and building rest houses. He provided medicine to people and animals. He hoped to bring together his varied subjects under an ideology of tolerance, seeking universal principles that all of his diverse subjects could accept.

Ashoka's empire did not long outlast the death of this charismatic leader in 232 BCE. By 185 BCE, the Mauryan Empire was no more, and the various regions of India had regained independence. The breakup of India was temporarily reversed when a dynasty from the Ganges Valley, the Guptas, unified the north and parts of the center between about 320 and 540 CE (see again Map 5.2). The dynasty's founder took the name Chandra Gupta to recall the Mauryan Empire of the past, but his state was smaller. The Guptas replaced the direct administration of the Mauryans with a system that relied on the cooperation of allies and vassals.

≡ **Inscription of King Ashoka** After his conversion to Buddhism around 260 BCE, King Ashoka broadcast his message of good governance in a series of inscriptions on pillars and rock facades. He used local languages and scripts to do so, and these inscriptions are the earliest evidence of writing in India after the Indus Valley script. This fragment of a pillar is inscribed in the Brahmi script, the ancestor of all modern Indian scripts.

Much of the conquest was the work of Chandra Gupta's son, Samudra Gupta (c. 330–380 CE), who used violence and the threat of violence to hold his empire together. This strategy proved effective, and he could control his subjects while expanding his empire. Inscriptions from his reign claim that he received tribute from places as distant as Central Asia in the north and Sri Lanka in the south. But under increasing pressure from Central Asian nomads, by 540 CE the Gupta Empire disappeared. Not until the Mughal dynasty in the sixteenth century CE would empire return to India.

A Crossroads of Trade

Like people all over the ancient world, most Indians devoted their lives to agricultural tasks. They lived in small villages, enjoying few if any luxuries. The work of this rural labor force was nonetheless crucial to India's cultural and material development. Food produced in the countryside made possible the growth of cities, which were at the heart of both internal and external trade. Indian urban artisans created products that appealed to elites all over India. Moreover, its location at the crossroads of land and sea trade routes across Asia and beyond placed India at the center of an enormous and dynamic international trading system. Despite the region's political turmoil from 500 BCE to 500 CE, long-distance trade continued to grow. India was in contact with far-flung lands, from China and Southeast Asia to East Africa and the Mediterranean world. As both importers and exporters of luxury goods, its merchants accumulated enormous wealth. Indian rulers, who also benefited financially from this trade, sent ambassadors to distant lands, promoting an exchange of ideas and styles as well as goods.

India's merchants looked both east and west to trade with Asia's great empires. Caravans to and from China took advantage of the age-old trade routes that crossed Asia to India's north, which later became known as the **Silk Road**. The name is somewhat misleading as it was neither a single road nor was silk the main product transported over it. Running 4,000 miles through lush regions, deserts, and mountain ranges, various routes connected China to western Asia and the Mediterranean coast in ancient and medieval times (see Map 5.3, page 175). Few traveled the entire distance, instead passing goods on to others in trading stations in oases, near mountain passes, and in other strategic locations.

The name "Silk Road" derives from the Chinese monopoly on silk, which lasted until the fifth century CE. People throughout Eurasia coveted the cloth so much that they shipped large amounts of gold, silver, and other products east to obtain it. But many other goods moved along the road, ranging from very precious items to basic agricultural products. Many crops that are now widespread originated in one region of Eurasia and were introduced elsewhere as a result of travel along the Silk

Silk Road The caravan route with various branches that connected China in the east to the Mediterranean Sea in the west, passing through regions such as South and Southwest Asia.

Road. It is often not easy to date when exactly this happened, but sometimes it is recorded. The Chinese historian Sima Qian reports, for example, that a late second-century BCE Chinese diplomat brought back a grape vine from the region of modern Uzbekistan. Peaches and apricots, fruits that originated in China, appeared in the Mediterranean area in the last centuries BCE. The introduction throughout Eurasia of more basic crops such as barley, wheat, millet, and rice was the outcome of interactions along the Silk Road's forerunners. The Silk Road was also very important for the spread of ideas carried by merchants and missionaries. It was the route by which Buddhism spread into China and several of the other intellectual innovations discussed in this chapter achieved their world historical importance.

Literary and Scientific Flowering

Despite the region's shifting political circumstances, the era from 500 BCE to 500 CE was a period of great literary production for India, its own classical age. This flowering involved religious and secular poetry, drama, and prose. In the Mauryan period scribes started to write down the Vedas and their interpretations in the *Upanishads* (see Chapter 3), and Ashoka's use of various languages and scripts in the third century BCE encouraged the use of spoken dialects in writing.

The language of the Vedas inspired the primary literary language of ancient India, Sanskrit. Used for much of Indian literature until the nineteenth century CE, Sanskrit texts fall into a wide range of genres, but most prominent are the epics, or warrior songs, which began to be recorded in writing after 100 BCE. Perhaps the longest single poem in world literature is the *Mahabharata*, the "Great Epic of the Bharata Dynasty," with 100,000 stanzas (among them the *Bhagavad Gita*). It describes the contest between two branches of the same royal family, which culminated in an eighteen-day-long battle with both parties supported by a large number of allies from all over India. The epic showed how people of all ranks should behave, following the rules of dharma, which in Hindu thought refers to "duty."

A shorter epic, the *Ramayana*, the "Story of Prince Rama," shows the adherence to dharma in practice. Rama's wife Sita was kidnapped, taken to the island of Sri Lanka, and forced to reside in another man's house. After many adventures, Rama freed her, but because people doubted her chastity, she had to live in the forest despite his great love for her. There she gave birth to Rama's twin sons. In the end, the family was reunited, but Sita asked to be returned to her mother, the goddess Earth. The *Ramayana* and the *Mahabharata* enjoyed great popularity across India, providing common cultural touchstones for the continent's diverse peoples.

Indian poetry was not limited to sweeping epics. Most notable are the works of Kalidasa, who probably lived in the Gupta period between 390 and 470 CE. In one short poem, the "Cloud Messenger," he describes how an exiled man asks a cloud to carry a message to his wife, whom he misses deeply. He declares:

> In the vines I see your limbs, your look
> in the eye of a startled doe, the loveliness
> of your face in the moon, in the peacock's plumage your hair,
> the playful lift of your brows in the light ripples
> of rivers, but, O, sadly, nowhere, my passionate girl,
> is the whole of your likeness in any one of these.[4]

Kalidasa was also famous for his dramatic works, which featured gods, heroes, and courtiers who suffered a good deal of intrigue and hardship but always prevailed in the end.

Scholarship also flourished during India's classical period. In linguistics, Panini developed a grammar of the Sanskrit language around the fifth century BCE, recording more than 4,000 grammatical rules. Investigations in astronomy, medicine, physics, and chemistry brought technological wonders. Probably about 400 CE, ironsmiths set up a pillar near Delhi that was made of a single piece of iron so chemically pure that it has not rusted. And Indian mathematicians would have a great impact on the world by inventing the concept of zero. The Indian number system, with its symbols from 0 to 9, spread east and west in the seventh century CE, and western Europeans adopted it from the Middle East as "Arabic" numerals around 1000 CE.

China: Intellectuals and the Qin and Han Empires, 221 BCE–220 CE

◥ **FOCUS** How did the early Chinese philosophers come to have a long-lasting influence on the intellectual development of the region?

In East Asia, the unified Zhou (joe) kingdom of the early first millennium BCE started to disintegrate around 800 BCE (see Chapter 3). Historians still see the

≡ **Delhi's Iron Pillar** Near Delhi in modern India stands an iron pillar whose characteristics demonstrate the great technical skills of Gupta craftsmen. Probably erected around 400 CE, the pillar is more than ten-feet tall and weighs about six tons. The iron is 98 percent pure, which is possible only when extremely high heat has been applied. The ability to work this enormous mass of metal was unparalleled in early world history and was not attained in Europe until the nineteenth century CE.

China's Warring States, 480–221 BCE

≡ **China's Warring States, 480–221 BCE**

period from 770 to 221 BCE as part of the Zhou dynasty, but the political situation differed greatly from those of earlier centuries; instead of a united country under Zhou kingship competing dynasties each controlled small principalities. The later Zhou dynasty is divided into the Spring and Autumn period (770–481 BCE) and the period of the Warring States (480–221 BCE). The name "Spring and Autumn period" derives from a book called *The Spring and Autumn Annals*. It depicts a world of more than one hundred states routinely involved in wars, both among themselves and with inhabitants of the surrounding regions. Conflicts increased even more in the period of the Warring States.

Perhaps inspired by the volatility of the time, revolutionary thinkers such as Confucius, Mencius (mehng-tsi-uz), Laozi (low-ZUH), and Lord Shang Yang founded intellectual movements that questioned human nature, the state, and political behavior. The implementation of their ideas led to a reconfiguration of political life that paved the way for the first Chinese empires, the Qin (chin), which was followed by the Han (hahn). From about 500 BCE to 200 CE, culture flourished in China, especially scholarly writings on law, medicine, divination, philosophy, and many other topics. In contrast to Indian thinkers, who generally focused on religious issues, Chinese scholars turned their attention to secular subjects and concerns. Therefore, we tend to label their teachings as philosophy—as we do for Greek thinkers of the time—rather than religion. Nonetheless, Indian, Chinese, and Greek thinkers were engaged in a common project. They all sought to understand and improve the societies in which they lived.

Intellectual Churning: Confucians, Daoists, and Legalists

Confucius (traditionally dated 551–479 BCE) dominates the intellectual history of this period, and his teachings have crucially influenced Chinese society and political life to this day. The son of an impoverished aristocrat, Confucius (from the Chinese name Kongfuzi, "Master Kong") in his thirties turned to education, supporting himself by tutoring young men. His followers grew in number, and the historian Sima Qian claims that, when Confucius died at the age of seventy-three, 3,000 followers were studying with him.

It was these students who preserved his teachings in writing; Confucius himself did not write down his ideas. Probably compiled by 100 BCE in the form known today, so centuries after his death, Confucius's *Analects* document the philosopher's ideas about human nature, behavior, and the state. He taught that proper conduct in all social interactions instilled in individuals a humaneness that emphasized benevolence and kindness. Confucius urged that behavior adhere to a moral code: "For the gentleman integrity is the essence; the rules of decorum are the way he puts it into effect; humility is the way he brings it forth; sincerity is the way he develops it. Such indeed is what it means to be a gentleman."[5] Confucius especially urged children to take care of their parents in old age and to obey those above them in the social hierarchy.

Proper behavior, Confucius believed, should also be taught to highborn men who desired to become good rulers. He did not want to institute a new political system but to return to the centralized rule of the Zhou dynasty. He stressed that doing good would stop the forces of evil, including war. Confucius renounced coercion in government because it produced resentment among subjects rather than respect. Thus his teachings went beyond establishing moral guidelines for individuals. He believed that proper behavior by all men and women could help produce a more peaceful and prosperous society.

After Confucius's death, a number of philosophers interpreted and further developed his teachings. Among the most influential was Mencius (c. 372–289 BCE), who emphasized the importance of human compassion and believed all human beings shared the capacity to empathize with one another. The philosopher Xunzi (shoon-zuh) (c. 300–230 BCE), by contrast, saw humans as basically greedy and selfish, and he urged leaders to adopt strict rules to prevent their subjects from doing evil.

Confucius taught that proper behavior involved active participation in society. In contrast, those who came to be known as Daoists urged people to withdraw from society and meditate, forsaking the pursuit of wealth and prestige and seeking a peaceful inner life. If many people behaved well, the world would be in harmony and follow its natural course. These teachings are ascribed to a sixth-century BCE sage, Laozi, but they probably represent the work of more than one philosopher collected in the third century BCE under Laozi's name. In the Later Han period after 25 CE, Daoism became an official religion, closely associated with Buddhism, with which it shared many ideas, and Laozi was depicted as a god.

Rather than stressing practical guidance to rulers and officials, Daoism emphasized personal introspection. On the opposite end of the spectrum was a school of thought called Legalism, which focused on the ruler, the social hierarchy, and practical aspects of government. At the height of the political turbulence of the Warring States period, Lord Shang Yang (c. 390–338 BCE) put legalistic ideas into practice in the then small state of Qin, paving the way for the later unification of

China. He believed every man should have an occupation that benefited the state, so he introduced compulsory military service and forced others to become farmers. He established strict laws—hence the name *Legalism*—that harshly punished even the smallest crime. He assumed that fear would prevent people from wrongdoing; the only reward they could expect for correct behavior was absence of punishment. Lord Shang also introduced the principle of collective responsibility: if a soldier disobeyed, his entire family was executed. When the Later Qin state forced Lord Shang's ideas onto the entire population of China, its ruler became so unpopular that the people overthrew the government.

Unification and Centralization: The Worlds of Qin and Han

Although the Zhou kings nominally ruled the entire region, after 771 BCE China was actually carved into numerous small principalities. It was only after 500 years of fragmentation that rulers, inspired by the teachings of Confucius, Lord Shang, and others, restored China's political unity (see Map 5.3).

Two innovations dramatically changed the nature of warfare in the period of political fragmentation. First, chariotry had been the core of the Shang army, but it lost its effectiveness in mountainous or marshy terrain. In its place, infantry rose in importance and local leaders forced thousands of farmers and other commoners to fight. The chariot-based aristocracy disappeared in favor of a more meritocratic army in which a soldier from any social background could rise up the military ranks. Second, iron became the preferred metal for weapons. Iron weapons were not only much stronger than bronze, but iron ore was also much more widely available than copper and tin. Archaeological evidence shows that several states organized the mass production of iron weapons that were more deadly than the bronze ones previously in use.

As the military aristocracy declined and family ties became less important in determining social status, bureaucracies arose to administer the states. Inspired by Legalism, lords instituted centralized systems of taxation and a military draft. A new educated elite arose among the administrators, trained in the ideas Confucius had introduced.

The state that most successfully applied Legalism was Qin in western China, where Lord Shang had been minister of state. In 237 BCE, the Qin ruler started an all-out war, and after fifteen years he had unified an immense part of China (two-thirds of today's territory) under his rule. He succeeded because his state had a strong economic base and he could raise numerous troops and arm them with iron weapons. In 221 BCE, proclaiming himself Shi Huangdi (shee huang-dee), "First August Emperor," he began a series of reforms that would determine the political organization of China for more than 400 years and inspire the norms of

The Qin and Han Empires, 221 BCE–200 CE

- Qin state, c. 350 BCE
- Qin Empire, c. 210 BCE
- Han Empire, c. 150 BCE
- Han protectorate, c. 59 BCE–23 CE and 73–127 CE
- ⌁⌁⌁ Wall or fortification, 3rd century BCE
- —— Silk Road, 1st century CE
- —— Trade route, 1st century CE

≡ **MAP 5.3 The Qin and Han Empires, 221 BCE–200 CE** During the political unification of China that ended the divisive Warring States period, Qin and Han rulers established rigorous governmental practices and bureaucracy, which allowed them to extend their powers over wide areas. Qin and Han both imposed centralized control over China itself, but the Han also created political dependencies along the routes that connected China to regions farther west, facilitating the flourishing trade between east and west.

centralized rule in China up to the early twentieth century CE. The modern name *China* derives from *Qin*.

Shi Huangdi (r. 221–210 BCE) considered the expansion of China's agriculture the basis of progress, and like the Babylonians and others we have discussed he ordered large irrigation canals to be dug. He also sponsored the exploitation of new territories by giving land to farmers. He forced people to construct 4,000 miles of roads to connect the regions to one another and to the capital Xianyang (shan-yahng). Another large-scale public work was the building of defensive walls at the northern border of the state, the forerunner to the Great Wall of China (see again Map 5.3). All these projects were facilitated by the use of iron tools.

≡ **Han Farmers at Work** Like that of all ancient states, the Han Empire's success depended to a great extent on agricultural development. The first emperor instituted reforms that expanded China's farming abilities. Although the subject is not glorious, it merited representation in art. Shown here is a stone relief of two men plowing with an ox-drawn plow. The relief was originally part of the decoration of a tomb built between 200 BCE and 200 CE. (Werner Forman Archive/Yang-tzu-shan, Szechwan. Location: 05/HIP/Art Resource, NY)

The First August Emperor did not tolerate dissent. Indeed, according to late Han sources, Shi Huangdi assassinated 460 Confucian scholars who had criticized him, and in 213 BCE he ordered that all books be burned except practical works on agriculture, medicine, and divination. The great classics of Chinese literature and philosophy would have disappeared had copies not been hidden or memorized by people who transmitted them orally. Shi Huangdi saw in diversity the potential for disorder, chaos, and rebellion, and first and foremost he sought political centralization. He standardized the script his bureaucrats used to record the variety of languages spoken in the empire, and he imposed a single system of weights and measures and of coins.

One of the most massive building projects of Shi Huangdi's reign is his tomb near his capital at Xianyang. The emperor created an underground palace, surrounding himself with an army of 7,300 life-size terra cotta statues. They depict footmen, archers, charioteers, and cavalry, and although the bodies were mass-produced, the faces show individual characteristics. Sima Qian described the central tomb (so far unexcavated) and claimed that it had a bronze foundation to protect against underground water, representations of seas and rivers composed of mercury made to flow by special mechanisms, and crossbow traps that the motion of an intruder would trigger. According to legend, 700,000 men built the tomb and were imprisoned in it when they finished. Childless royal concubines also accompanied their master in death. Moreover, the tomb was filled with treasures from all over the land. The entire complex seems to have been intended to continue the emperor's rule in the afterlife.

The death of Shi Huangdi in 210 BCE effectively meant the end of his dynasty, as subsequent palace intrigues weakened the central hold of the state. Resentful of the Qin's harsh rule, mobs sacked the court and killed imperial officials. But China did not once again fall into pieces—a determined and popular rebel leader, Liu Bang (lee-OO bangh), managed to establish full dominance in 206 BCE. Liu Bang created a new nobility by giving two-thirds of the empire as kingdoms to relatives and supporters. His generosity generated support for himself and his dynasty, which he named Han after his home region (see again Map 5.3). The Han Empire governed

China for 400 years (206 BCE–220 CE) with only a short interruption (9–24 CE). Historians refer to the first half of the Han period, in which the capital was at Chang'an in the west, as Former, or Western, Han (206 BCE–25 CE); they call the second half, in which the capital was at Luoyang farther east, Later, or Eastern, Han (25–220 CE).

The success of the Former Han was due to the fact that it combined the pragmatism of Legalism with Confucian traditions that were instilled upon a bureaucratic Chinese elite. Highly centralized and well organized, the Former Han state relied on agricultural resources for its support. In addition, a state monopoly on iron and salt allowed the emperor to charge artificially high prices for these vital products. Trade of luxury goods, especially silk and lacquerware, also brought substantial income to the empire.

A combination of causes led to the collapse of the Han Empire. By the end of the first century BCE, a few local families had acquired huge estates and reduced the population to the status of enslaved persons. A usurper seized the throne in 9 CE, temporarily discontinued the Han dynasty, and freed the enslaved. When the Han regained the throne by 25 CE, the local landed gentry became even more powerful than before. In consequence, large numbers of peasants from several provinces rose in rebellion. Although the state crushed the uprisings, they weakened the central government, and by 220 CE the Han dynasty fell, leaving China politically fragmented once again.

≡ **Shi Huangdi's Terra Cotta Army** The tomb of the first emperor of China near his capital at Xianyang is one of the greatest archaeological sites of the ancient world, and it is still mostly unexcavated. A massive army of soldiers surrounds the tomb, each life-size figure made from baked clay and shaped to show the individual warrior's features. Created shortly before 200 BCE, the complex reveals a commitment to the dead emperor on a par with what we see in Egypt and other ancient cultures.

In both the Qin and Han dynasties, a government bureaucracy applied uniform practices throughout the empire. State-trained officials, chosen for their abilities rather than family connections, staffed the administration. Their allegiance to the state created a powerful unifying force. The pressures of decentralization remained strong, however—especially the resilience of aristocratic families, whose wealth allowed them to control local populations. The competing forces of centralization and decentralization led those in power to exploit the general population, who, pushed to the limit, grew to resent all authority and ultimately overthrew both empires.

Preserving and Spreading the Written Word

The Chinese political elite placed special value on the written word. Members of the bureaucracy buried themselves with their libraries, which consisted of manuscripts written on bamboo and silk. The physical objects themselves were very valuable. The use of bamboo forced the scribes to write the characters in long vertical columns, a layout that survived in Chinese writing until the twentieth century CE, when writers began to use horizontal lines in letters and books.

A tomb excavated in the 1970s at Mawangdui in the Hunan province of southern China reveals the high value that the Chinese elite accorded manuscripts. It contained an extensive library. On bamboo strips appear numerous medical treatises, some with recipes to enhance sexual pleasure. The silk manuscripts include several classic works of ancient Chinese philosophy, as well as books on astronomy, astrology, politics, military affairs, culture, science, and technology. The fact that the dead man had his library buried with him suggests that he wanted to show off his ability to read and write, a rare skill that was the hallmark of the upper levels of Chinese society.

The Former Han period was crucial to the preservation of the Chinese literature of the earlier Zhou and Warring States periods—works that would determine the form of literary production for millennia. Confucius's teachings became mandatory reading for all Chinese bureaucrats, but they also read works such as Laozi's *Classic of Integrity and the Way*, a discussion in verse of a tranquil and harmonious life.

The writing of history in prose flourished under the Han dynasty. China's first historian was Sima Qian (c. 145–90 BCE), whose *Records of the Historian* has defined our modern understanding of early Chinese history. Sima Qian developed the idea that a sequence of dynasties had always ruled all of China, a tradition that has continued in Chinese historical writing until modern times. He started with a mythological distant past, when sages brought civilization to humanity. Afterward the Xia, Shang, and Zhou dynasties (discussed in Chapter 3) ruled the country as a whole. He even calculated the dates when kings ruled and gave details on battles and other events. By suggesting that unified centralization under a dynasty was normal for the region, Sima Qian wanted to show that Han efforts at empire building were in keeping with tradition.

Sima Qian's history stops at around 100 BCE, but a family of scholars from the first century CE carried on the tradition of dynastic history. The father, Ban Biao (bahn bi-ah-ow), started a work called *History of the Western Han Dynasty*, and his son, Ban Gu (bahn gu), continued it. Finally, the emperor ordered Gu's sister, Ban Zhao (bahn jow), to finish the work, giving her access to the state archives. Ban Zhao took the narrative up until the interruption of the Han dynasty in the first decade CE. Others continued the genre of dynastic history, and in 1747 CE the combined work of this family and subsequent authors amounted to 219 volumes, an unparalleled continuous record of the history of a country.

Ban Zhao (c. 45–120 CE) was a remarkable woman in a period when most families saw their daughters as little more than economic burdens. Coming from a scholarly family, she was well educated before her marriage at the age of fourteen. Still young when her husband died, she joined the court at age thirty, where she gained great influence and was given the task of finishing the official history of the Han dynasty. At the same time she taught young women, including a girl called Deng, who, when she later became empress, remained under Zhao's influence. Zhao also wrote numerous literary and scholarly works. At first, her fame derived primarily from her *History*, but from about 800 CE on, her *Lessons for Women* gained enormous popularity (see Reading the Past: Women in Han China). Men used it to justify the inferior role of women in society, but in reality Zhao had written practical advice to her daughters on how to survive in their husbands' family homes.

From 500 BCE to 200 CE, then, the foundations of Chinese culture were established in arts and sciences as well as politics. The chaos and disorder of the Spring and Autumn and the Warring States periods inspired many of these developments and thinkers hoped to restore the order that had existed in the past. They developed philosophies with long-lasting influence, and politicians gave these philosophies practical applications in statecraft. The newly created empires promoted the wide spread of the new ideas over the vast territories they controlled. Politically, imperial administrations were highly centralized and harsh, but the forces of decentralization also remained strong. Both the central administration and the local elites demanded much from the general population, and in the end their excessive demands may have led to the collapse of the entire system.

Greece: Philosophers, Scholars, and Poets, 500–30 BCE

↘ **FOCUS** What were the cultural innovations of classical Greece, and how did they affect the peoples of Greece, North Africa, and Southwest Asia?

READING THE PAST

Women in Han China

Ban Zhao's *Lessons for Women* of the early second century CE made her the most famous female author in Chinese history. Although she wrote the work as personal advice to women, men later used the book to prescribe how women ought to behave in relation to men.

A woman ought to have four qualifications: 1. womanly virtue, 2. womanly words, 3. womanly bearing, and 4. womanly work. Now what is called womanly virtue need not be brilliant ability, exceptionally different from others. Womanly words need be neither clever in debate nor keen in conversation. Womanly appearance requires neither a pretty nor a perfect face and form. Womanly work need not be work done more skillfully than that of others.

To guard carefully her chastity, to control circumspectly her behavior, in every motion to exhibit modesty, and to model each act on the best usage—this is womanly virtue.

To choose her words with care, to avoid vulgar language, to speak at appropriate times, and not to weary others with much conversation may be called the characteristics of womanly words.

To wash and scrub filth away, to keep cloths and ornaments fresh and clean, to wash the head and bathe the body regularly, and to keep the person free from disgrace and filth may be called the characteristics of womanly bearing.

With wholehearted devotion to sew and to weave, to love not gossip and silly laughter, in cleanliness and order to prepare the wine and food for serving guests may be called the characteristics of womanly work.

These four qualifications characterize the greatest virtue of a woman. No woman can afford to be without them. In fact they are very easy to possess if a woman only treasure them in her heart. The ancients had a saying: "Is Love far off? If I desire love, then love is at hand." So can it be said of these qualifications.

Source: Chao, Pan, and Nancy Lee Swann. "Lessons for Women." In *The Shorter Columbia Anthology of Traditional Chinese Literature,* edited by Victor H. Mair (New York: Columbia University Press, 2000), 323–24.

EXAMINING THE EVIDENCE

1. What are the basic tenets of Ban Zhao's advice to women?

2. Why can this passage from the independent and politically influential Zhao be interpreted as an argument for women's secondary role in society?

As we saw in Chapter 4, under the leadership of Athens and Sparta the city-states of Greece had successfully resisted the expansion of the Persian Empire in the early fifth century BCE. Especially in Athens the subsequent prestige and wealth created fertile conditions for thinkers to develop new ideas concerning all aspects of life, including politics, science, and literature. Greece's later integration into the empire of Alexander the Great promoted the spread of these ideas, which had a radical impact on intellectual developments in western Eurasia.

Pericles's Athens, c. 430 BCE
——— Wall   ——— Road

≡ Pericles's Athens, c. 430 BCE

Athens's Golden Age 500–400 BCE

In the fifth century BCE Athenian democracy reached its high point under the leadership of Pericles (443–429 BCE), who sought to ensure that all Athenian citizens were able to take an active role in government. Hence, he arranged for men who sat in council or on a jury to receive a daily stipend from the state so that less well-to-do citizens could take time off from work to fulfill their civic duties. As important as Pericles's policies were, we must remember that they aimed to increase the number of citizens who took part in civic life, not to increase the total number of citizens, a group that excluded women, adolescents, resident foreigners, freed enslaved persons, and those still enslaved. Pericles instituted a rule that only men whose parents were both Athenians could be citizens.

Those Athenian men with political rights obviously wanted to present convincing arguments, and the art of rhetoric, or public speaking, gained importance unprecedented in world history. The need to speak persuasively created a niche for a new type of teacher, called a **sophist** ("wise man"), who offered instruction in rhetoric for a fee. The term *sophist* has a negative connotation today, suggesting someone who makes an invalid argument with the appearance of truth. But in ancient Athens, these men subjected intellectual and religious traditions to a rigorous examination that pushed Greek thinking in new directions. Above all, sophists believed in the power of human reason, which they saw as *the* crucial tool for explaining the workings of the universe. Many sophists came from outside Athens. Because of its wealth and vibrant cultural life, the city became an intellectual crossroads and the center of the new field of **philosophy**, a word literally translated as "love of wisdom."

sophist Originally an ancient Greek teacher of rhetoric; today the term has the negative connotation of someone who convinces through false argument.

philosophy The systematic intellectual endeavor of explaining basic concepts in human existence, such as truth, knowledge, reality, and ethical behavior.

The three most famous and influential Greek philosophers of antiquity were Socrates, Plato, and Aristotle. Although the three men were closely linked (Socrates taught Plato, who in turn taught Aristotle), each made distinctive contributions to Greek philosophy. Socrates developed a mode of questioning designed to help separate truth from assumption. Plato developed the notion of universal ideals. Aristotle analyzed everything from literature to the natural environment by classifying their elements. Together they laid the foundation of education and scientific investigation as practiced in the Middle East and Europe until the modern period (see Lives and Livelihoods: Philosophers of Athens's Golden Age).

Other Athenians explored the events that shaped Greek life, notably the wars that occupied much of fifth-century BCE Greece (see Chapter 4). Herodotus (c. 485–425 BCE) wrote on the Persian Wars, which ended when he was a young boy, and Thucydides (c. 460–400 BCE) documented the Peloponnesian War between Athens and Sparta, in which he had fought. The elder of the two, Herodotus, became known in the West as the Father of History ("inquiry" in Greek) because he was the first who studied the past to find the causes of historical events.

Thucydides explained the war between Athens and Sparta as an unavoidable clash between two expansionist states, the former focusing on sea power, the latter on control of land. He used his work as a vehicle to express his support for democratic rule under a strong leader, connecting Athens's problems to deviations from this ideal. The works of Herodotus and Thucydides were revolutionary because they presented historical events as the consequences of human actions, not simply the result of divine intervention. Moreover, they personified the general curiosity about the structure and causes of things that swept Athens in its Golden Age.

Athens was also the hub of an extraordinary literary production including, most prominently, works of drama. The most famous tragic poets—Aeschylus (525–456 BCE), Sophocles (c. 496–406 BCE), and Euripides (c. 485–406 BCE)—examined human nature and society in all their aspects. A common subject was human *hubris*, the Greek term for excessive pride and self-confidence, which led to the hero's downfall. For example, in *Oedipus the King*, Sophocles explored how the main character's certainty that he could uncover the truth through his own intellect caused his utter ruin: he blinded himself and his mother committed suicide. Another emotion regularly depicted was the desire for vengeance. In the *Oresteia*, Aeschylus demonstrated how it becomes an endless cycle, as Clytaemnestra killed her husband Agamemnon because he had slaughtered their daughter. In retaliation, their son Orestes murdered her. The cycle ended only when a jury in Athens's law court decided guilt. The *Oresteia* explained how a new

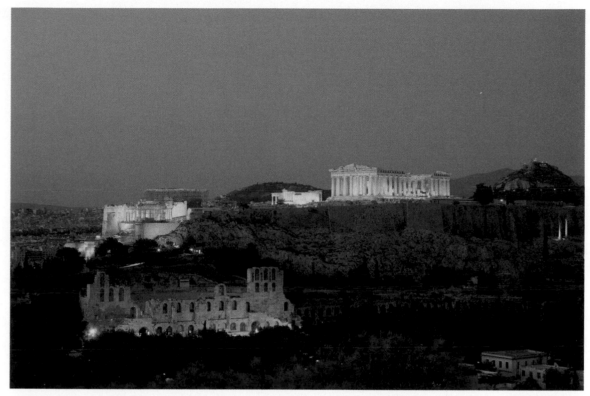

≡ **The Acropolis of Athens** The remains of the Acropolis ("top of the city") of Athens, towering over the modern city, include the Parthenon—the majestic temple to Athena, divine protectress of the city, at the center of this photograph—and the elaborate entrance gate on the left. Built under the world's first democratic government system, the Acropolis stands as a symbol of the Greeks' accomplishment in the first millennium BCE.

institution based on the judgment of humans superseded the older system of never-ending revenge.

Remarkably for a society that treated women as inferior, women were often the central characters of Greek tragedies. Sophocles's heroine Antigone, for example, stood against her uncle's decree that her brother should not be buried. She proudly obeyed divine laws and was willing to die for doing so:

> And so, for me to meet this fate, no grief.
> But if I left that corpse, my mother's son,
> Dead and unburied I'd have cause to grieve
> As now I grieve not.
> And if you think my acts are foolishness
> the foolishness may be in a fool's eye.[6]

LIVES AND LIVELIHOODS

Philosophers of Athens's Golden Age

Three early Athenians stand out as giants in the history of Western philosophy: Socrates, Plato, and Aristotle. For some one hundred years their teaching and writing inspired intellectual life in the city and beyond, and ever since their ideas have engaged philosophers. Socrates (c. 470–399 BCE) did not leave any written work; we know of his teachings primarily through his student Plato. Socrates's chief aim was to find justice, which he equated with truth. Questioning people who claimed to be wise in such a way that they realized the limitations of their knowledge, Socrates sought ways to discover true wisdom. Probably because he was, as he himself said, a gadfly constantly reproaching the Athenians, he was condemned to death in 399 BCE, ostensibly because he corrupted youth. He chose to commit suicide by drinking hemlock, rather than flee from prison as his friends had arranged.

It is hard to determine how much of Plato's writing reflects Socrates's teaching and how much records his own philosophy. Plato (c. 428–348 BCE) used the dialogue form to communicate his ideas. He portrays Socrates as questioning persons in such a way that his ideas were arrived at as the only logical conclusion. The dialogues assume that all knowledge is innate in human beings and can be revealed by asking the right questions, through the so-called Socratic method. In one dialogue, Socrates takes an enslaved young man through a geometrical proof as if he knew the answer all along. In this view, the soul naturally possesses all knowledge; the philosopher needs only to find the key to unlock it. The Socratic method can be used to investigate all aspects of life, from mathematics to love.

Plato stressed the distinction between the physical, which he saw as imperfect, and the spiritual, which he viewed as perfect. Only the immortal human soul knows the spiritual, Plato believed. He also commented on political life in his dialogue *Republic*, in which he questioned the democratic ideal on the grounds that not all men have the skills needed to make the right decisions. He proposed a hierarchy instead: on top would be "guardians," who are wise and well educated; in the middle, "auxiliaries" would provide protection; on the bottom, "producers" would provide food and manufactured goods. Laws would be the instruments to enable the guardians to carry out their decisions.

Plato founded a school, the Academy, that drew students from all over Greece, including his most famous pupil, Aristotle (384–322 BCE), who would go on to tutor the young Alexander of Macedonia. In 335 BCE Aristotle started his own school, the Lyceum, where he taught a vast array of subjects, from the natural sciences to literary criticism. He abandoned Plato's distrust of the physical, focusing instead on observing particulars, from which one could derive general conclusions through logical induction. Aristotle wrote many analytical treatises, including the famous work *Politics*, in which

≡ **Aristotle in Medieval Islamic Tradition** The great classical Greek philosophers were remembered long after antiquity. In the Middle Ages they were especially treasured in the Islamic world, where scholars translated their works into Arabic. This manuscript from the thirteenth century CE depicts the philosopher Aristotle teaching Alexander the Great. The manuscript contains a medical text called "The Usefulness of Animals," which draws from classical works such as Aristotle's.

he described a state in which the virtues of people guided government. He disapproved of both tyranny and democracy (rule by the masses in his eyes) and wanted a middle road with an assembly directed by able experts. Aristotle thought that slavery was a natural condition for some people and that these individuals should be captured for the benefit of the state. In the field of ethics, Aristotle warned against extremes and argued that people should strive for balance.

Because the three philosophers sought rational explanations and (especially Aristotle) formulated ideas very systematically, they became the models for scholarly investigation in the Hellenistic world. Philosophers in Alexandria and elsewhere turned to them for inspiration for centuries. When Christianity and Islam emerged, the thinkers who laid their intellectual foundations merged classical Greek philosophical ideas with biblical concepts. The works of Plato and Aristotle were translated into other languages, notably Arabic, which is how they survived, and for centuries they provided the foundation of scientific investigation in Europe and the Middle East. Even today no philosopher working in the Western tradition can ignore these thinkers.

Questions to Consider

1. How and why did approaches to philosophical inquiry differ among Socrates, Plato, and Aristotle?

2. Why did these three philosophers have such influence on later intellectual history?

For Further Information:

Ancient Greek Philosophy: http://www.iep.utm.edu/greekphi/.

Annas, Julia. *Ancient Philosophy: A Very Short Introduction.* New York: Oxford University Press, 2000.

These female characters do not fight their inferior status but often uphold values that are more personal than those of the publicly oriented men.

Hellenism: The Expansion of Greek Ideals and Institutions 323–30 BCE

After establishing dominance over Greece, the new power of Macedonia conquered the vast Persian Empire and created in its stead a system of kingdoms ruled by Greeks. As the Greeks moved into Egypt, Southwest Asia, and beyond, contacts between Greeks and local population led to a cultural fusion known as **Hellenism**, from *Hellas*, the native term for Greece. Although the precise mix of Greek and local culture varied from place to place, people throughout the Hellenistic world were connected through exposure to common language, literature, and intellectual and political ideas. Historians date the Hellenistic age from the death of Alexander in 323 BCE to 30 BCE, when the Roman Empire (discussed in Chapter 6) conquered Egypt, the last major Hellenistic state.

In 336 BCE twenty-year-old Alexander succeeded his father Philip as king of Macedonia and leader of the league of Greek states. As we saw in Chapter 4, almost immediately he invaded the Persian Empire, which for 200 years had dominated an enormous territory stretching from the Mediterranean coast to India. Defeating the Persians in a quick succession of battles, Alexander proclaimed himself the new master of the empire. The swift military successes earned him the title "the Great" in later tradition.

To thwart challenges to his rule, however, Alexander had to take his troops to every corner of his realm. When his troops refused to go farther, as we saw earlier in this chapter, Alexander settled in Babylon, where he died in 323 BCE. His death triggered long battles over succession among Alexander's generals, who ultimately carved the giant territories he had conquered into several states (see Map 5.4). The two largest kingdoms were the Seleucid Empire, which initially included lands from Syria to the Indus, and the Ptolemaic Empire, which controlled Egypt and the Libyan coast. Seeking legitimacy as kings within the indigenous traditions, the generals celebrated local religious festivals, supported cults, and commissioned inscriptions in cuneiform (Seleucids) and hieroglyphics (Ptolemies). In Egypt they had themselves represented as traditional Egyptian kings and queens. They also maintained the existing bureaucracies, although Greek gradually took over as the language of administration.

For common Egyptians and Babylonians, little changed. They worked the land and produced goods, interacting with their new authorities only through local

Hellenism The culture that derived from the merger of Greek, Southwest Asian, and Egyptian ideas through the creation of Alexander the Great's empire.

≡ **MAP 5.4   The Hellenistic Kingdoms, c. 300 BCE**   Soon after Alexander's death in 323 BCE, his generals carved his empire into competing kingdoms, whose borders shifted constantly. In 300 BCE the Seleucids in Southwest Asia and the Ptolemies in Egypt controlled the largest areas and fought over the territories of the eastern Mediterranean. The smaller kingdoms in Greece and Anatolia had to deal with the pressures from Celts to their north and the rising power of Rome to the west.

government agents; the ruling elite remained mostly in the region's large cities. The Greeks, however, faced fundamental changes both at home and in the new empires. Before they had belonged to small political and social groups in which (ideally) everyone knew each other, but they now lived in immense empires and regularly mingled with people with whom they at first could barely communicate. The political system changed fundamentally: kingdoms in which absolute power passed from father to son (and also to daughters in the case of the Ptolemies) replaced city-states ruled by citizens.

The ideal of the polis survived, however; in his march through the former Persian Empire, Alexander founded some seventy cities, which he used to help establish his local dominance. As his successors continued the policy, new cities

≡ **Cleopatra as an Egyptian Queen** While the Ptolemaic rulers of Egypt prided themselves on being Greek and descendants of the general who helped Alexander of Macedonia conquer the country, they also wanted their Egyptian subjects to see them as legitimate rulers. Therefore they were shown in many works of art in fully Egyptian fashion. This relief shows Queen Cleopatra, ruler of Egypt 51–30 BCE, making an offering to the goddess Isis, who is breastfeeding her son Horus. Showing styles and motifs that date back millennia, the image is thoroughly Egyptian. The inscription, however, is in Greek and states that a man with the Egyptian name Onnophris set up the relief in a sanctuary he directed.

took root across the Hellenistic world. Taking the form of city-states, they resembled Greek cities in layout, buildings, and government structures. One such outpost was the city whose ruins are called Ai Khanoum (eye KHA-nuum) today, which was built to defend the northeastern border at the Oxus River. It was here that Clearchus, whom we met at the beginning of this chapter, arrived around 300 BCE, bringing with him wise sayings from Delphi.

The most prominent new city was Alexandria, which Alexander had founded as the capital of Egypt in 331 BCE and whose population soon rose to half a million. Located on the Mediterranean Sea, Alexandria dazzled both in appearance and as a center of learning and culture. It was laid out on a plan of straight streets that intersected at right angles. Palaces, temples, theaters, and an enormous library lined the streets; these were constructed in the Greek style, but the city was also clearly Egyptian. Kings and queens followed traditional styles as they filled the city with monumental statues of themselves as rulers.

Royal patronage drew scholars and artists from all over the Greek-speaking world and beyond to Alexandria. The city became a center of learning, which it actively promoted through the Library and Museum (literally, "House of the Muses"; the Muses were nine sister goddesses who presided over poetry, history, science, and the arts). The Museum housed poets and scientific researchers in all fields. The Library's aim was to collect copies of every known work of Greek literature; it held 490,000 volumes, probably the largest collection of writings in the ancient world.

The promotion of learning epitomized by the Library at Alexandria stimulated intellectual innovation. Scientific inquiry relied on older traditions, and mathematics and astronomy, well-developed sciences in Babylonia (as seen in Chapter 4), influenced Greek science anew. Researchers made remarkable advances, which were often lost after antiquity and rediscovered only in more recent times. For example, Aristarchos of Samos (c. 310–230 BCE) correctly recognized that the planets revolved around the sun, not earth.

Philosophy flourished in the Hellenistic world. When the polis disappeared as the center of political and social life, philosophers focused more on the individual, exploring ways to live a good and proper life. They presented a wide range of options. The Epicureans, for example, taught that one should enjoy every moment in the pursuit of simple pleasures and a quiet life. Cynics urged the rejection of social norms and conventional behavior, often living as beggars without any physical comfort. The Stoic school was the most influential throughout Greek and Roman antiquity. It encouraged intellectual inquiry to provide guidance in moral behavior, which would eliminate the anxieties of daily life and desire. "Freedom is secured not by the fulfilling of one's desires, but by the removal of desire," a Roman Stoic wrote. Such words resemble the somewhat earlier teachings of men like the Buddha and Laozi in India and China. Although we cannot know if Hellenistic philosophers encountered these teachings directly, we can say that similar ideas developed in various parts of the ancient world.

The Hellenistic world brought together an enormous variety of religious traditions and their gods. Although people maintained their indigenous cults, they also adopted foreign gods and they merged the identities of different ones: Egyptian Osiris (see Chapter 2), for example, was identified with the Greek god Zeus. Historians debate how much all this cultural mixing influenced the majority of the people. A Persian, Babylonian, Egyptian, or Greek farmer would still have been illiterate and would have adhered to old traditions and ideas. Even so, gods could and did achieve an unprecedented popularity outside their original place of worship, and people throughout the Hellenistic world were exposed to new ideas. As in China, the vast empire that Alexander had created and its Hellenistic successors promoted the wide spread of newly formulated concepts as well as scholarly and literary explorations. As the story of Clearchus at the beginning of this chapter shows, educated people from Greece to Afghanistan could understand the same words of wisdom.

COUNTERPOINT: The Prophets of Israel and Judah

Ancient Israel and Judah

Kingdom of Israel
Kingdom of Judah

0   30 Miles

0   30 Kilometers

Sidon

Tyre

PHOENICIA

Litani R.

SYRIA

Damascus

Sea of Galilee

Megiddo

Mediterranean Sea

Samaria
Sacked by
Sargon II,
722 BCE

PALESTINE

PHILISTINES

Ashkelon

Gaza

Hebron

Jericho

Jordan R.

AMMON

Jerusalem
Sacked by
Nebuchadnezzar II,
587 BCE

Dead Sea

MOAB

EDOM

Negev Desert

≡ **Ancient Israel and Judah**

FOCUS How did the intellectual and religious developments in Israel and Judah take place in an environment very different from that in the world empires?

Most of the new ideas that thinkers in India, China, and Greece elaborated in the later centuries of the first millennium BCE spread rapidly over wide geographical areas and among peoples with different cultural backgrounds. The development of world empires and flourishing long-distance trade promoted this diffusion. For example, the conversion of the Mauryan king Ashoka to Buddhism helped disseminate its ideas over much of South Asia, while trade relations along the Silk Road brought them to China. Likewise, Greek philosophical approaches caught on through the entire Hellenistic world because of political circumstances and the movement of goods and people. The nature of the new ideas with their focus on individual behavior made their adoption by diverse people possible. They were universal.

In contrast, in the small eastern Mediterranean countries of Israel and Judah the religious and philosophical ideas prophets and others expressed were not intended for a universal audience. Instead, they were envisioned for a single people; that is, those who descended from three generations of patriarchs—Abraham, Isaac, and Jacob. The latter's twelve sons were the ancestors of the twelve tribes of Israel, whose members were the only people to whom the message was addressed.

The beliefs developed over centuries in the first millennium BCE, when Israel and Judah first existed independently and later were absorbed in succession by the Assyrian and Babylonian Empires. They were probably codified in the form known to us today during the Exile (c. 587–530 BCE) and in the subsequent period when the Persians allowed the Judeans to return home (see Chapter 4). They are mostly contained in speeches by men we call prophets, speaking on behalf of god or under divine inspiration. The prophets often attacked kings and others for not obeying the god's commands and predicted disaster as the outcome.

These ideas are expressed in one of the most monumental works of ancient literature, the **Hebrew Bible**, or Tanakh and Old Testament in Jewish and Christian traditions, respectively. It is actually a collection of books, including myths and tales, historical narratives, king lists, wise sayings, and laws; some are written in prose, others in poetry. The first five books, which in Jewish thought are the most important, the **Torah**, narrate the origins of the people of Israel from the moment of the creation of the universe until they left Egypt for the land of Israel. The Torah describes how god gave them laws he demanded they obey, and it explains how these people were distinct from all other humans because of their ancestry and their special relationship to their god, Yahweh (YAH-way). Anonymous writers and adapters composed these and the other books of the Bible over the centuries of the first millennium BCE, and they continued to modify the text into the first centuries CE. Modern scholars hold a wide range of opinions on when specific parts of it were originally written and when to date the evolving ideas that they document. Nonetheless, the fully developed ideas show a unique religious ideology.

The members of the tribes of Israel were unique in the world at that time because of their devotion to one god only, the god of Israel Yahweh, in a **monotheistic** belief system, Judaism. Judaism declared that Yahweh was not just the supreme god—such was the norm with the pantheons of other cultures at the time, for example, Zeus in Greece—but that he was also the only god in the universe. No other god or divine being existed, nor could there be any other cults, and the god of Israel demanded full obedience from his people. If they provided it, he would reward them with a homeland—that is, the land of Israel—and guarantee that they would be numerous and successful. The god of Israel was also very different from others at the time in that he was never represented in statues or other images.

The prophets constantly reminded the people of their duties, which were not limited to honoring one god alone but also included ethical behavior and adherence to divine laws. When the prophets saw that the people strayed, they foretold punishment that was often at the hands of outsiders, such as the Assyrian and Babylonian armies. They also promised that god would relieve them from their suffering, for example, by sending a savior who would allow them to return from Exile.

Although these ideas developed when Israel and Judah were integrated into the large empires of the Persians and Seleucids, there was no desire to spread them beyond the select group of the Jewish people. It is even the case that the priests of

Hebrew Bible The sacred books—in prose and poetry—that document the religious ideas of the peoples of Israel and Judah.

Torah The first five books of the Hebrew Bible, which in Jewish thought are considered to be the most important as they explain the origins of the people of Israel and the special relationship to their god.

monotheism A religious system that tolerates the existence of one god only.

Jerusalem used them against the internationalism and multiculturalism of the Hellenistic kingdoms and hoped to bring about a Jewish state based on the religion's principles. It was only later that the ideas of the prophets of Israel and Judah obtained a universal character. This happened when the teachings of Jesus, rooted in Jewish thought, started Christianity and that religion spread throughout the Roman Empire and beyond (see Chapter 6), and when Muhammed presented the Qur'an as the completion of earlier divine revelations in the Torah and Christian gospels (see Chapter 8).

Conclusion

The centuries from roughly 500 BCE to 500 CE were of critical importance to the cultural histories of societies across Eurasia: the classical traditions of India, China, and Greece were formulated at that time as were the thoughts of the prophets of Israel and Judah. Modern scholars have called this the Axial Age, meaning a turning point in world history. Across Eurasia men and women came up with new ideas and understandings of themselves and their place in the universe. They reflected on what caused events around them, such as wars and social conflict, and they investigated the human condition through scientific, religious, and philosophical inquiry. While earlier peoples surely asked such questions, it was in this era that individuals started to discuss them explicitly and that they or their students wrote the answers down. Thus we know the names of these thinkers—Siddhartha Gautama, Confucius, Socrates, and so on—while earlier thinkers remain mostly anonymous.

These intellectual developments took place in a period when various large territorial empires rose and disappeared across Eurasia. While these thinkers did not all live in such empires, the spread of their ideas often benefited from the fact that people over wide distances lived under the same rule. This was also a time when long-distance trade contacts flourished and ideas traveled together with people and goods along routes such as the Silk Road. The simultaneous appearance of these approaches to thinking is astounding. Did these cultures influence one another? Although, as we saw, there were many contacts, we cannot determine securely that intellectual practices of one end of the Eurasian continent triggered those elsewhere. There is no evidence, for example, that Socrates would have known of Confucius's teachings or Lord Shang Yang of Aristotle's writing (or vice versa). Each of these developments needs to be seen within the context of the regions where they took place.

Many of these ideas could, however, spread among people with different backgrounds and cultural traditions because their authors wanted them to have universal appeal. This was not always true, and some thinkers addressed only a specific audience. In the case of Israel and Judah, where the monotheistic belief system was closely tied to the identity of a single group of people, the prophets spoke to those people alone and wanted only them to follow their teachings. It was only when those teachings were reformulated later on in Christian thought that they obtained a universal character. That happened in the Roman Empire, to which we turn in the next chapter.

review

Major global development in this chapter: The revolutionary religious and cultural developments in India, China, Greece, Israel, and Judah that took place between 500 BCE and 500 CE and that remained fundamental to the history of Eurasia.

Important Events	
c. 600–500 BCE	Possible century for the life of Laozi, who inspired Daoism
c. 587–530 BCE	Judean Exile in Babylonia
563–483 BCE	Possible dates for the life of Siddhartha Gautama, the Buddha
551–479 BCE	Traditional dates for the life of Confucius
c. 500–400 BCE	Athens's Golden Age
480–221 BCE	Period of the Warring States in China
c. 390–338 BCE	Lord Shang Yang, who developed Legalism
331 BCE	Alexander the Great defeats Persia; Alexandria founded in Egypt
323–30 BCE	Hellenistic period

Important Events	
321–185 BCE	Mauryan Empire
c. 260 BCE	Mauryan Emperor Ashoka converts to Buddhism
221–206 BCE	Qin Empire
206 BCE–220 CE	Han Empire
c. 320–540 CE	Gupta Empire

KEY TERMS

asceticism (p. 162)
Axial Age (p. 160)
bodhisattva (p. 165)
classical (p. 160)
dharma (p. 163)
Hebrew Bible (p. 191)

Hellenism (p. 186)
monastery (p. 165)
monotheism (p. 191)
nirvana (p. 165)
philosophy (p. 181)
sangha (p. 163)

Silk Road (p. 169)
sophist (p. 181)
stupa (p. 165)
Torah (p. 191)

CHAPTER OVERVIEW QUESTIONS

1. How did new social circumstances stimulate changes in religious beliefs and cultures?
2. What processes encouraged close connections among the various regions of Eurasia?

3. In what ways did the revolutionary thinkers discussed here have a lasting impact on the histories of the regions they inhabited and beyond?

MAKING CONNECTIONS

1. What ideas that emerged in classical India, China, and Greece remained fundamental to the later histories of these countries?
2. How would you describe cultural and intellectual interactions among the various Eurasian countries?

3. How did the cultural innovations in India and China compare with those in Greece of the first millennium BCE?

DOING HISTORY

Claims and Evidence in Sources

Virtually none of the thinkers whose ideas we studied in this chapter wrote them down, nor did they leave us any autobiographical accounts of their lives. Yet there are many stories about them that narrate their entire lives, as in the case of the Buddha, or give details, such as how Socrates was able to drink vast amounts of wine without getting a hangover. Those stories could be written by people who knew the thinkers, such as Plato as a student of Socrates, or develop over time with the input of many who lived centuries later, as in the case of the Buddha.

1. How can historians use these accounts and verify these claims?

2. Describe how stories about famous individuals develop over time and become more elaborate, not because of new evidence but because people were fascinated by them. Use examples from any period of world history.

For further research into the topics covered in this chapter, see the Bibliography at the end of the book.

The Unification of Western Eurasia

500 BCE–500 CE

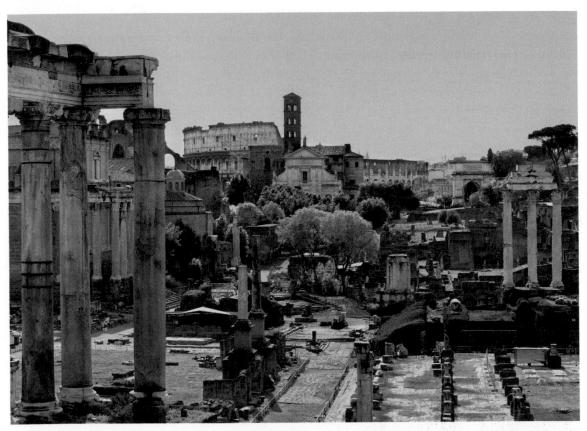

≡ **World in the Making** Over the centuries from 500 BCE to 500 CE, Rome grew from a small village in the heart of the Italian peninsula into the crossroads of a vast empire dominating all of western Eurasia. Pictured here is the Roman Forum, the ancient square that was for centuries the center of Roman public life. Temples and government buildings surround the Forum, and looming in the background is the Colosseum, a massive amphitheater constructed for gladiatorial contests and other public spectacles. Completed in 80 CE, the Colosseum is now imperial Rome's most iconic symbol.

backstory

As the Mauryan, Gupta, Qin, and Han Empires were bringing vast areas of Asia under one rule (see Chapter 5), a similar political unification occurred in western Eurasia, merging two regions with previously separate histories. In the Middle East and eastern North Africa, empires had existed since the second millennium BCE. New Kingdom Egypt, Nubia, Assyria, and Persia, for example, had all brought large and diverse populations under their rule (see Chapter 4). However, the peoples of the western Atlantic zone of modern-day Europe and the Mediterranean areas to its south had never known political union. The citizens of Rome would change that, creating an empire that would profoundly influence the history of the world.

AROUND 100 CE, THE ROMAN historian Tacitus (c. 56–117 CE) described how inhabitants of Britain, encouraged by the Roman governor Agricola, took on the habits of their Roman occupiers:

> To induce a people, hitherto scattered, uncivilized and therefore prone to fight, to grow pleasurably inured to peace and ease, Agricola gave private encouragement and official assistance to the building of temples, public squares, and private mansions. . . . Furthermore, he trained the sons of the chiefs in the liberal arts. . . . The result was that in place of distaste for the Latin language came a passion to command it. In the same way, . . . the toga was everywhere to be seen.[1]

The Romans built their empire through military conquest, taking over new lands in order to dominate them. Roman expansion spread Roman culture, for, as this passage from Tacitus makes clear, conquered peoples were often as eager to adopt Roman practices as the Romans were to encourage their adoption. From North Africa to Britain and from the Atlantic coast to the Euphrates River, numerous peoples were "Romanized," leaving behind aspects of their previous cultural identities to acquire the benefits of participating in the empire. This process worked both ways because incorporating new cultures into the empire changed what it meant to be Roman. Conquered territories were fully integrated into Roman political and administrative structures. In time, subject peoples gained the opportunity to become Roman citizens. Men from the provinces could even become emperors, which has no parallel in the earlier empires we have studied.

At the heart of the vast empire was the city of Rome. From its foundation—traditionally said to be in 753 BCE—to its establishment as an imperial capital, Rome underwent a remarkable political evolution. After a period of rule by kings, the most common type of government in the ancient world, the Romans set up institutions with the aim of preventing one man from holding all power. In spite of these carefully crafted institutions, the Roman Republic failed and descended into the chaos of civil war until one man, Augustus, assumed full control around 27 BCE.

Because the Romans had such a great impact on the history of western Eurasia, many of the political concepts and terms in use today derive from ancient Rome. Indeed, the word *empire* itself comes from the Romans' designation *imperium*, which means "rule." Similarly, the Republic as a political organization for the common good, the Senate as a place of deliberation and representative government, and many other concepts and terms are rooted in ancient Roman ones, although the exact meaning and functioning of them are no longer the same. The aim to imitate the Romans is often expressed in the architecture and names of buildings connected to government, such as the U.S. Capitol in Washington D.C. Even though Roman history itself shows how these institutions can fail, the principles behind them continue to inspire admiration.

The standardization of imperial practices that Tacitus evokes in this chapter's opening lines also explains the success of a new religion, Christianity. Spreading from a small community in the Middle East via the empire's network of roads and sea routes, Christianity eventually became the official state religion, and its institutions merged with those of the state. Once this happened, the power of the state helped bring Christianity to all the empire's peoples.

As powerful and important as the Roman Empire was, it was not without its peers, and ultimately it could not defeat its rivals to the east, the Parthians and Sasanids from Iran. Although in the history of Europe the Roman Empire was a watershed, in a global perspective it was one of a series of world empires that stretched across Eurasia from around 500 BCE to 500 CE.

OVERVIEW QUESTIONS

The major global development in this chapter: The unification of western Eurasia under the Roman Empire.

As you read, consider:

| **1.** How are Roman political institutions still important to us today? | **2.** How did the Romans face the challenge of creating and maintaining an empire? | **3.** What impact did Rome have on the lives of the people it conquered? | **4.** How did Christianity's rise benefit from the Roman Empire? | **5.** What were the limits of Roman imperialism? |

Rome: A Republican Center of Power 500–27 BCE

 FOCUS What were the political ideals of Republican Rome, and how did they intersect with the military successes of Rome?

Although ancient Rome's ideals and practices were not unique in its time, Rome achieved something unprecedented with the unification of western Eurasia based on a combination of two principles. First, Rome rejected the idea of kingship and replaced it with a system of representative government that imposed strict term limits on political offices. Second, it was a highly militaristic state whose successes depended on the leadership of individual men who often used their military accomplishments to gain political power. Ultimately these two principles would prove incompatible.

Society and Politics in the Republic

When Rome was still a village located on the Tiber River in the center of the Italian peninsula, its government was a monarchy, albeit with elected kings. According to later historians, around 509 BCE members of prominent families rose up against the king and exiled him because he had diminished their political influence and his son had raped one of their daughters. They set up a structure of government called *res publica,* a term often translated as commonwealth and the basis of the word "republic." It was a legal system that applied to all citizens and gave them rights and responsibilities. In this system all decisions were made after deliberation in assemblies, and magistrates elected for only one year implemented them.

However, as was the case in Athenian democracy, access to political rights was very restricted. It was rooted in the Roman idea of the family, the essential unit of Roman society whose head was the oldest man, the **pater familias**. The family incorporated not only those related by blood but also enslaved persons and individuals the Romans called **clients**. The latter were persons of a lower social rank who were economically attached to the family and received assistance from the pater familias. In return he expected clients to support him, by voting for him in an election, for example, or by serving in his private militia. The pater familias had unlimited powers over the other members of the family. Adult sons with children of their own did not have an independent legal status and could not own property. Hence, the Roman family was like a miniature society, with the eldest male holding absolute authority over all his dependents.

Women had a secondary role, although over time they gained financial power. At first, in the usual marriage a woman entered her husband's family and was under full control of its leader. But in the second century BCE so-called free marriages became common: a married woman remained a member of her father's family and inherited a share of his property. Upon her father's death she became financially independent, and several affluent women acquired much influence in this way.

The heads of old Roman families, the **patricians**, held all political power in the Republic's early days. The origins of this class are unclear, but they were the richest members of Roman society and passed on their privileged status from father to son. They were the only ones who could sit in the most important consultative body, the **Senate**, and only they could become government officials, or **magistrates**. They were a minority of the population, however. Most people were **plebeians**, the

---

pater familias The head of a Roman household, with full power over other family members and clients.

client Within the early Roman social structure, a person who was economically dependent on an influential family head.

patrician The Roman aristocratic class.

Senate The Roman assembly of elderly men, usually patricians, whose main function was to deliberate important issues of state and give advice.

magistrate A Roman government official.

plebeian The Roman class of commoners.

commoners of society—craftsmen and so on—who had assemblies and magistrates as well, but much less powerful than those of the patricians. In the beginning of the Republic plebeians were forbidden to marry patricians. Their struggle to acquire political influence and their share of public assets dominated Rome's political and social life throughout the Republic.

With the creation of the Republic, the Romans aimed to make it impossible for a single man to acquire absolute power, so they created a number of government officials (magistrates) who had different responsibilities. In order to limit their power even further, the Romans restricted the offices to one-year terms and placed two men in each office. The two most prominent magistrates were the **consuls**, who led the army and convened and chaired the Senate and other assembly meetings. Patricians monopolized the office of consul until 367 BCE, when plebeians forced passage of a law requiring one consul to come from their ranks. As the state and the number of people governed expanded, other magistracies had to be created to carry out special tasks, but the concept of power sharing between two men remained a firm rule. The only exception occurred in times of crisis, when the Senate gave absolute power to a single magistrate, the dictator. The term *dictator* did not have the negative meaning then that it has today. He was someone who could make decisions on his own, and he returned to his former status after six months or when the emergency had passed, whichever came first.

Rome's wars of conquest and the need to control conquered territories continually increased reliance on the military. The growing army depended on plebeian recruits, and the plebeians used this to extract concessions from patricians. They forced the Senate to create the new government office of **tribune** to protect plebeians from arbitrary decisions by patrician magistrates. Tribunes could veto (a Latin term that means "I prohibit") acts by consuls and the Senate.

This increase in the political power of the plebeians did not, however, lead to social equality in Rome. In fact, inequality increased. Some businessmen became extremely rich from state contracts to construct Rome's enormous public works. Their wealth enabled them to join the order of **equestrians**, officially cavalrymen but in reality men with a certain amount of property who were not in the Senate. Many Romans, however, did not fare so well. The wars on Italian soil had ruined the livelihood of countless farmers. Rich men—patricians and equestrians—bought up their lands

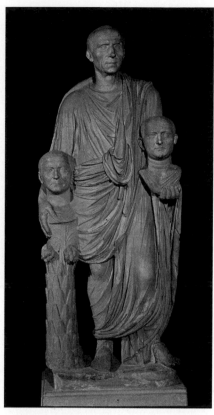

≡ **A Roman Patrician** In this typical example of Roman sculpture dating from around 25 BCE, the subject wears a toga that identifies him as a senator. Because family was so crucial for patrician leaders' social status, he holds the busts of his ancestors in his hands.

consul In the Roman Republic, one of the two highest magistrates.

tribune The Roman magistrate whose role was to protect the interests of the plebeians.

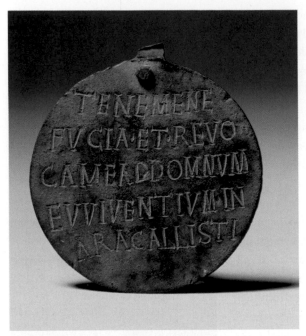

≡ **Roman Enslavement Tag** Roman enslaved persons were clearly identified as someone's personal property and wore metal collars with tags attached such as the one shown here, dating to the fourth century CE. The text on it states, "Stop me from running away and return me to my master, Viventius, who lives in Callistus's court."

equestrian
The class of wealthy businessmen and landowners in ancient Rome, second only to the patricians in status and political influence.

latifundia Vast rural estates in ancient Rome whose owners employed a large number of tenant farmers and sometimes enslaved people.

and turned them into **latifundia**, large estates on which they raised cattle and produced cash crops (wine, olive oil, and various fruits). After the conquest of Sicily and North Africa, wheat from their rich farmlands was shipped to Rome rather than being produced near the city. Italian farmers who stayed on the land did so as tenants or day laborers. Other farmers left the land and joined the ranks of the urban poor or the army. Thus, as Rome grew, becoming the crossroads of the Mediterranean, one result was social and economic dislocation in Italy.

The extensive use of enslaved foreigners exacerbated the problems for landless, free Romans to find employment. Each new conquered territory added to the flood of the enslaved who saturated the labor market, and scholars estimate that of the 6 million people in Italy around 100 BCE, 2 million were enslaved. Some were domestic servants in rich Roman households. Such enslaved people were often freed by their owners, although they remained clients. The majority of the enslaved were less fortunate, however. They worked in silver mines and stone quarries, farmed the latifundia, and manned workshops. Because they were so plentiful and so cheap, they were often treated harshly. It is not surprising, therefore, that the period from 150 to 70 BCE witnessed several revolts of enslaved people. The most famous took place between 73 and 71 BCE. Led by a fugitive named Spartacus, tens of thousands of enslaved people rose in a revolt that devastated the Italian countryside. They defeated three Roman legions before they were crushed and Spartacus was killed.

It would be a mistake, however, to conclude that the Romans and their subjects were connected only by mutual animosity. Roman expansion created new cultural connections throughout the Mediterranean, and the peoples of the empire had a profound and multifaceted impact on Roman life. Among the enslaved the Romans brought to Italy were educated Greeks who became physicians, secretaries, and tutors. The Romans were skilled warriors, but they had given little attention to intellectual pursuits. Thus, when they encountered Greek culture, they eagerly absorbed many elements of it. A Roman poet of the first century BCE wrote, "Greece was captured but it captivated its wild conqueror."[2] The Romans imitated Greek styles in their buildings and artwork. They equated Roman gods with Greek ones: the Roman Jupiter with the Greek Zeus, the Roman goddess Minerva with the Greek Athena, and so on. Elite Roman children learned the Greek language, and Greek scholars came to Rome to form philosophical schools of the type that had existed earlier in the Hellenistic world. Familiarity with Greek culture became a hallmark of Roman education.

From Village to World Empire

As we noted earlier, in addition to its establishment of a republic, a second achievement of ancient Rome was its military might. While it started out as a small settlement in the center of Italy, surrounded by states that were often much more powerful, by 30 BCE Rome was the hub of a massive empire that centered around the Mediterranean Sea—which the Romans could call "our sea," *mare nostrum*—and incorporated a large area of western Europe to the north (see Map 6.1). During

≡ **MAP 6.1   Roman Expansion Under the Republic, 500 BCE–14 CE**   From a village founded around 500 BCE, over the next 500 years Rome grew into a world power that encircled the Mediterranean and reached far into modern western Europe. The expansion at first took place under republican leadership with elected officials, but especially in the last century BCE ambitious men built up power bases that they used to force their will upon the people and institutions of Rome. This process ended when Octavian, who annexed the wealthy country of Egypt, acquired every powerful office, and became Rome's first emperor, Augustus.

centuries of continual warfare, Rome annexed states and tribal territories system-atically, overpowering one competitor after the other, some of whom took decades to defeat. There were times when Rome's very survival was at risk. In 390 BCE Gauls from across the Alps sacked and burned the city and laid siege to its remaining fortress. Only after malaria struck the Gauls and the Romans paid a large ransom of gold was the siege lifted. In 218 BCE Carthage's general, Hannibal, crossed the Alps with two dozen elephants and ransacked the Italian countryside for sixteen years. He delayed an attack on Rome for too long, however, which enabled the city to mount a counterattack and defeat the Carthaginians.

Early military setbacks inspired the Romans to fund and organize a large well-dis-ciplined army that made the defeat of these and other enemies possible. The army was the central institution in Roman society, the backbone of the empire. Scholars estimate that more than 10 percent of the adult male population typically served in active duty at one time. The core of Rome's army consisted of **legions**, infantry units of 6,000 men each, divided into ten cohorts of six centuries—one hundred men—each. While at first only Roman-born citizens could serve in the army, with the growth of the territory Rome controlled the legionaries were predominantly non-Romans, who received Roman citizenship when they enlisted. Alongside the legionaries fought auxiliaries, non-Roman soldiers who often excelled in a special skill such as archery. They fought under a Roman officer in cohorts of 500 or 1,000 men each. Upon retirement they, too, as well as their sons, became Roman citizens, and their female family members acquired the rights of Roman women. Thus the army facilitated the fuller integration of provincials into Roman life. Military ser-vice was long and arduous. A legionary served twenty years, an auxiliary twen-ty-five. To keep soldiers loyal, their salaries were regularly increased, and they received a share of the booty, as well as special gifts and a retirement bonus.

The detailed descriptions of Rome's wars by its ancient historians allow us to map its territorial expansion step by step (see again Map 6.1). After it had unified the Italian peninsula by 275 BCE, its major competitor in the western Mediterranean was Carthage in North Africa. It took Rome seventy years to defeat Carthage in several wars that are known as the Punic Wars, sometimes fought on Italian soil, as when Hannibal invaded. Once Hannibal was defeated in 202 BCE Rome was a power on a par with the Hellenistic states of the eastern Mediterranean (see Chapter 5) and increasingly interfered in the competition between those. Because of its military expertise, it was frequently asked to support one side or another, which often turned into the annexation of the original ally. Greek cities, for exam-ple, requested Roman help against the Seleucid Empire but in the end were con-quered by the Romans, who did not hesitate to do so ruthlessly. The sack of Corinth

legion A military unit in the Roman army consisting of 6,000 infantry soldiers.

in 146 BCE was so violent that it sent shock waves throughout the Mediterranean world. Most of Corinth's inhabitants were killed or enslaved, and the city was systematically looted before it was left abandoned.

The final major military feat of the Roman Republic was its annexation of Egypt. This extremely wealthy Hellenistic state was in Roman eyes as exotic as decadent. Its ruler, the famous Queen Cleopatra, represented the opposite of what the Roman alleged to be their traditional values: a woman in control, the proud display of great wealth, and absolute lifelong monarchical power that was inherited. Cleopatra's affairs with successive Roman generals fascinated people then and now but also show how and why the Republic failed.

Failure of the Republic

Rome's military successes depended on generals, who the Senate initially selected for only one campaign so they would not acquire too much power. Yet, victories were celebrated in triumphal parades that showed off the military leader with the booty and enslaved he had captured. Consequently these men acquired popular acclaim, often became very wealthy, and gained the loyalty and support of their legionnaires. This enabled them to interfere in the political struggles in Rome and demand privileges and powers that the creators of the Republic had hoped to avoid.

By 100 BCE social tension and political intrigue pervaded Roman society. The struggles between patricians and plebeians over political influence had led to assassinations, and military men and provincial administrators bought political influence with the wealth they looted from conquered regions. They broke the ancient rules on who could hold offices and for how long, forcing the Senate, for example, to elect them as consuls or to give them the position of dictator for several years in a row. Because the legions were often more loyal to their commanders than to the state, generals did not hesitate to use their armies to advance their personal political ambitions. Several civil wars broke out in the first century BCE, bringing enormous devastation. By the end of the century, the people were so war-weary that they granted one man, Octavian, supreme power.

Julius Caesar, who lived from 100 to 44 BCE, is a good example of the famous men who struggled for power in the first century BCE. He started his political career by allying himself with powerful men to win a number of offices and managed to gain the governorship of northern Italy. He used this position as a springboard for the conquest of Gaul, which brought him unparalleled personal wealth and turned the Atlantic zone into his personal power base. Caesar used this wealth to broaden his political influence in Rome and to remain in elected offices despite legal restrictions. Others opposed him, however—at one point the Senate ordered him to lay down his army command. In response, on January 10, 49 BCE, Caesar led his troops across the Rubicon River, the northern border of Italy, which was an act of treason as no provincial army was allowed to pass that point. The ensuing civil war lasted four years before Caesar won the often brutal conflict. Back in Rome in 44 BCE, he tried to restore order, but he did not have time. On March 15— known in the Roman calendar as the Ides of March—opponents assassinated Caesar on his way to the Senate.

Caesar's assassination led to another thirteen-year-long civil war, fought in various battlefields throughout the Mediterranean. The final contest was between Octavian, who portrayed himself as the representative of ancient Roman values, and Antony, who relied on the support of his mistress, Queen Cleopatra of Egypt. She had been Caesar's mistress before, and she ruled the only remaining major power independent from Rome in the Mediterranean. This was to no avail as Antony and Cleopatra's navy was crushed at the Battle of Actium in 31 BCE. After fleeing to Egypt, both committed suicide—Cleopatra famously by having an asp bite her and Antony by his own sword. After Octavian annexed Egypt he expanded Roman territory at the edges until it reached natural borders that his armies could more easily defend: the Sahara and Syrian Deserts, the Danube, and the Atlantic coast from Gibraltar to the Rhine (see again Map 6.1).

The people of Rome had grown so tired of war and chaos that they did not object to Octavian taking full control, as long as he would bring peace and stability. He created the Roman Empire by developing a system in which he and his successors exercised absolute control. Octavian obtained overall command of the army and of the provinces. He could propose and veto any legislation, overrule provincial governors, and sit with the highest magistrates, the consuls. In 27 BCE the Romans awarded him the title *Augustus*, "noble one," suggesting he was closer to the gods than to humans.

Augustus's dominance of government was unprecedented in Roman history, but he cloaked his ambition by appearing to accumulate traditional Republican offices, which he held without the usual term limits. He called himself *princeps*, "the first citizen," not "king" or another title that would have indicated absolute rule. In that sense, Augustus was a master of diplomacy: he offered the war-weary people of Rome a new and efficient system of government without casting it as the monarchical system they had traditionally rejected. When he died in 14 CE, he had ruled Rome as de facto emperor for forty-two years, and few Romans remembered life without him. Augustus's political acumen and the length of his reign contributed to the durability of the system of government he created. His successors would maintain it for the next 200 years.

Rome: The Empire 27 BCE–212 CE

↘ **FOCUS** How did the Roman Empire bring administrative and cultural unity to the vast territory it ruled?

Starting with Augustus, a succession of powerful Romans ruled an enormous territory that brought together numerous peoples with diverse cultural backgrounds and traditions. In a process known as Romanization, universal administrative and economic practices fused the regions of the Roman Empire into a cohesive whole. Retired Roman soldiers routinely moved to the provinces, and people from the provinces moved to Rome to work at running the empire. The system of government that dominated Roman life for several centuries became the archetype of an empire in world history. Even though its structure contained weaknesses that would lead to its decline in the west, the Roman Empire was highly successful and fundamentally changed the histories of all the regions it controlled.

Emperors and Armies

As in the Republic, the military played a substantial role in Roman imperial politics. Thus the emperor's relationship to the army was pivotal, and most Roman emperors were active soldiers. The continuous campaigns sometimes extended the empire beyond its Augustan borders—for example, Claudius (r. 41–54 CE) annexed much of Britain—which could bring the emperor great wealth and glory (see Map 6.2). War could also lead to disaster, as when the Sasanid Persians captured the emperor Valerian (r. 253–260 CE) in 260 CE and tortured him to death (see Counterpoint: Rome's Iranian Rivals in the Middle East).

The emperor's civilian duties required his constant attention. He was flooded with requests for guidance and favors, and his answers, communicated by letter, had the force of law. The emperor controlled a massive treasury, which received income mostly from customs duties and taxes on sales, land, and agricultural products. The emperor also had enormous personal wealth, from his own estates, which he could extend by confiscating property, and from gifts by those who wished to obtain his favor.

One way Roman emperors shaped Roman life was by commissioning extensive public works, many of which still stand today (see Lives and Livelihoods: Roman Engineers). They built majestic theaters and huge amphitheaters and erected triumphal arches to celebrate their military victories. They laid out forums—open places with temples, shops, and public buildings in which citizens conducted government business. An elaborate road system extended from Scotland to the Sahara

Roman Expansion Under the Empire, 14–212 CE

- Roman Empire at death of Augustus, 14 CE
- Roman Empire at death of Hadrian, 138 CE
- Territory gained and lost, with dates held
- Parthian Empire, c. 200 CE

≡ **MAP 6.2 Roman Expansion Under the Empire, 14–212 CE** Roman emperors attempted to enlarge the empire through repeated campaigns, but mostly they succeeded only in securing the borders along natural boundaries, such as the Sahara Desert and the Rhine and Danube Rivers. Their activities consolidated Roman rule over the territory, however, and increased the integration of non-Italians into the imperial governmental structure.

Desert. The roads ran straight for miles, extending over stone bridges when needed, and their surfaces were carefully paved to resist all weather. By building and improving the empire's transportation network, the emperors connected their provinces to Rome, making their capital the crossroads of the Mediterranean.

Because of the emperor's pivotal role in the political system, the empire's power centers viewed the choice of emperor with the utmost concern, and succession was highly contested. Rarely did a natural son succeed his father as emperor. This was true from the start of the empire: Augustus had no sons, so he groomed several relatives, including his daughter's sons, to succeed him. When they all died before him, he reluctantly chose Tiberius, his last wife's son from a previous marriage, as heir and adopted him as a stepson (see Seeing the Past: The Augustan Cameo Gem).

From the early history of the empire, generals contested succession, relying on armies to enforce their claims. When Augustus's dynasty ended with the suicide of the childless Nero (r. 54–68 CE), four men in quick succession claimed the throne, each with the support of provincial troops. Because real power now derived from military support, the emperor's direct connection to the city of Rome and its aristocratic families vanished. The general who gained the upper hand, Vespasian (ve-hs-PAYZ-ee-an) (r. 69–79 CE) was not born in Rome, but in provincial Italy to humble parents. Ten years later a Spaniard, Trajan (r. 98–117 CE), became emperor. Soon afterward the rulers began to come from other regions of the empire—Gaul, North Africa, Syria, and the Balkans.

Nonetheless, because it was the capital of the empire, many emperors focused attention on the city of Rome. Augustus reportedly boasted that he found Rome a city of brick and left it a city of marble. Workers and artisans from all over the empire flocked to the city to provide labor and craftsmanship. Its population grew to around a million. Many inhabitants lived in squalid conditions, in city blocks packed with multiple-story wooden buildings. When in July 64 CE a fire erupted, it took almost a week to put it out; ten of the fourteen urban districts were damaged, and three were burned to the ground.

Because many Roman residents were poor and unemployed, emperors sought to ward off restlessness with "bread and circus games": food handouts, performances, races, and contests between gladiators—that is, enslaved men fighting to the death for public entertainment. (Spartacus had been a gladiator before leading his rebellion.) The Roman Colosseum, built in the first century CE for such games, could seat 50,000 spectators. The games and food handouts diverted people's attention and made them feel as if the emperor cared about them.

In return for such benefits, the people awarded the emperor divine status. The Senate had declared Augustus a god after his death, and soon the idea took hold that the living emperor was a deity. Other members of the imperial family were likewise deified to exalt their status. Visual imagery such as statues, relief sculptures, and coins that appeared throughout the empire broadcast the idea that the emperor was a god, and in the provinces temples existed for his cult (see again Seeing the Past: The Augustan Cameo Gem).

Despite the frequent changes of emperors and their often erratic behavior and military adventures, the peoples of the empire enjoyed substantial periods of peace and prosperity. In particular, the second century CE was a time of **Pax Romana**, or Roman peace: a sequence of competent rulers held power, the borders were secure, and internal tranquility generally prevailed. In this climate of peace and prosperity, Roman culture spread rapidly throughout the empire.

Pax Romana Literally, "Roman peace," the period in the second century CE when the empire was stable and secure.

LIVES AND LIVELIHOODS

Roman Engineers

Throughout the territory of the former Roman Empire, we can still see the impressive remains of constructions put up some 2,000 years ago. Numerous landmarks in the modern city of Rome date to ancient times. Visitors admire monuments such as the Colosseum, the giant amphitheater opened for gladiatorial games in 80 CE (see again the chapter-opening illustration), and the Pantheon, whose present form dates to around 120 CE. A temple for the veneration of all Roman gods, the Pantheon had the largest dome on earth until modern times, 142 feet wide.

Roman engineers are famous not because of their originality—they mostly continued to use Greek inventions—but because they developed techniques to their fullest extent. They also left behind the most detailed writings on engineering in the ancient world. Most elaborate is the work of Vitruvius from the first century CE. His *On Architecture* is ten volumes of information on materials, construction methods, water management, town planning, and many other subjects.

Engineers and skilled builders were organized in associations that grouped together specialists. The variety of these associations shows that skills were highly specialized: stonemasons, demolition experts, brick makers, plasterers, painters, and many others had their own associations. Only people who belonged to the association could do the job. Access was restricted, however, and often only the sons of existing members could join. Young workers had to undergo a long apprenticeship before they could work independently. The associations also provided assistance to their members—for example, to pay for funerals or tombs. They worked under the supervision of architects, who were highly respected.

As groups of engineers traveled and worked in different regions, they contributed to the unity of the empire. They used the same techniques to create Roman buildings and monuments of similar appearance everywhere, from modern-day Britain to Syria. Among the most impressive Roman remains still standing are aqueducts—man-made channels that brought water from distant sources. Constructed in stone and concrete (lime, sand, and water poured into molds to obtain the desired shape), the aqueducts relied on gravity to move the water. Their builders sometimes used massive constructions to bypass natural obstacles. One example is the Pont du Gard ("Bridge over the Gard") in the south of modern France. To allow passage over the Gard River, Roman engineers built three tiers of stone arches rising 180 feet above the riverbed. The water runs through a channel on top that is four and a half feet wide and five and a half feet deep, covered with stone slabs to protect against the sun and pollution. Many aqueducts supplied Rome with water, and some still feed fountains in the city today, including the landmark Trevi Fountain.

Military engineers were especially important in Rome's extensive wars. They devoted much effort to the development of artillery. One typical Roman piece of equipment was the ballista, a large crossbow,

≡ **Pont du Gard** The Romans are famous for their engineering skills. A key concern was guaranteeing the water supply to cities throughout the empire, and several aqueducts still stand as major signs of their accomplishment. This is the Pont du Gard, part of an aqueduct in the south of France that was built in the first century CE. The structure remained in use as a bridge into the eighteenth century.

mounted on wheels, that could propel a projectile for 1,000 feet or more with a high degree of accuracy.

Many of the techniques Roman engineers used were forgotten after the end of the empire, but once Europeans of the fifteenth and later centuries CE rediscovered the writings of Vitruvius and others and investigated the remains still standing, they used them as the basis for their constructions. Roman engineering is thus another connection between antiquity and modern times.

Questions to Consider

1. How did Roman engineers serve the needs of the empire?
2. In what ways did they contribute to the Romanization of the empire?
3. How did their organization help preserve techniques?

For Further Information:

Hodge, A. Trevor. *Roman Aqueducts and Water Supply*. 2nd ed. London: Duckworth, 2002.

Oleson, John Peter, ed. *The Oxford Handbook of Engineering and Technology in the Classical World*. Oxford: Oxford University Press, 2008.

SEEING THE PAST

The Augustan Cameo Gem

Probably around 50 CE, an anonymous artist cut this stone (seven and a half inches high, nine inches wide) in honor of Augustus, visually expressing the new idea of rule introduced by the first emperor of Rome. Although officially Augustus was only "a first citizen," in this piece the artist conveys the idea that he was a king linked to the gods. It may have been possible only after Augustus's death in 14 CE to express such an idea.

In the center of the top register we see the goddess Roma, along with Augustus as a heroic seminude; his image is based on that of statues representing Jupiter, head of the Roman pantheon. To the right are Gaia, goddess of the earth, and Neptune, god of the sea, to express the idea that Augustus's rule encompassed both land and sea. Oikumene (oy-ku-MEHN-ay), the personification of the civilized world, holds a crown over the emperor's head. On the left is Tiberius, Augustus's

designated successor, descending from his chariot after he defeated the barbarian threat represented on the bottom register. Next to Tiberius stands a young man in military dress; he represents Germanicus, Tiberius's adopted son, who had died before Tiberius. The image thus represents the idea of a royal dynasty in which generations of the same family rule in succession.

Examining the Evidence

1. What ideals of rule does the artist express in this piece?

2. How does this representation of Augustus diverge from his official status in society as *princeps*, "the first citizen"?

≡ **A Roman Mosaic in England** With the military expansion of the Roman Empire throughout western Eurasia came the spread of Roman culture. The mosaic shown here, dating to around 350 CE, is a typical example of Roman floor decoration. Not only is the architectural style Roman but so is the story illustrated, the tragedy of Dido and Aeneas, two lovers separated by the gods, as told in Virgil's *Aeneid*. The mosaic shows that the poem was known at the edges of the empire.

The Provincial System and the Diffusion of Roman Culture

The presence of legionaries and Roman bureaucrats in the provinces fundamentally altered the local societies, especially in the west. The impact of this process is still visible today. Modern inhabitants of places that were once Roman provinces speak Romance languages—languages that developed from Latin—rather than Germanic and Slavic tongues. Moreover, many ancient Roman settlements are important western European cities today, including London and Paris.

Provincials who wanted to participate in the empire's business had to learn Latin in the west and Greek in the east and to dress and behave like Romans. Their material goods and houses reflected Roman styles, and provincial craftsmen produced items that imitated Italian products for local consumption. But **Romanization**, the process through which Roman culture spread into the provinces, was not wholesale adoption of Roman practices. Rather, local and imperial traditions merged as people retained the parts of their own culture they valued most. Consequently, the east and the west of the empire were very different. Much of the western empire had been

Romanization The process by which Roman culture spread across the empire.

inhabited by nonliterate societies with few cities, and when the Romans annexed these regions, they introduced urban life, which naturally had a strong Roman character. In contrast, in the eastern territories, Hellenistic cultures had flourished before the Roman conquest, and many inhabitants were urban, literate, and educated (see Reading the Past: A Young Woman Laments Her Premature Death). Cities in the eastern empire remained Greek in character.

The diffusion of Roman culture coincided with the spread of citizenship. Only citizens could hold office, so non-Romans who wanted to participate in government had to become citizens. Over time the empire granted citizenship to more and more people, including other Italians, officials from the provinces, and former soldiers of foreign origin. Finally, in 212 CE, Emperor Caracalla (cahr-ih-CAHL-ah) (r. 211–217 CE) gave nearly all free men in the empire Roman citizenship and all free women the same rights as Roman women. This created a new sense of unity, but at the same time it reduced the appeal of citizenship because it became less exclusive. Moreover, men from the provinces no longer needed to enlist in the army to become citizens, so to meet the constant demand for soldiers, the army increasingly turned to Germanic mercenaries.

Another means of unifying the empire was through law, which was evenly applied throughout the territories. From the Republican period on, legal experts had developed comprehensive procedures, mainly for private law, that is, interactions between individuals. Laws laid out rules for transactions in every aspect of life. They stipulated, for example, that a woman who married or divorced retained her property. They determined whether a neighbor could pick fruits from a tree overhanging his garden or collect water that ran off a roof. For transfers of property, they indicated what documentation was needed and whether witnesses had to be present. The laws had such an impact that people based their legal practices on them even after the empire's collapse. Roman law is the foundation of the continental European legal system to this day.

Christianity: From Jewish Sect to Imperial Religion

↘ **FOCUS** Why did imperial policy toward Christianity shift from persecution to institutionalization as Rome's state religion?

Roman culture profoundly influenced life throughout the empire, but as we have seen, cultural diffusion was a two-way process. In the first centuries CE, the teachings of Jesus, a Jewish preacher in Palestine, fundamentally changed the religious

READING THE PAST

A Young Woman Laments Her Premature Death

To reconstruct Roman history we often rely on the extensive writings of ancient historians and official records. But many common people in the Roman Empire left documents as well, including business correspondence, letters, and the like, written on parchments and papyri that have survived only in Egypt, thanks to the region's dry climate. They also carved inscriptions on gravestones. This example of such an inscription comes from Egypt and was written in Greek. In it, a young woman asks passersby to mourn her premature death.

What profit is there to labor for children, or why honor them above all else, if we shall have for our judge not Zeus, but Hades [god of the underworld]?

My father took care of me for twice ten years, but I did not attain to the marriage bed of the wedding chamber,

Nor did my body pass under the bridal curtain, nor did the girls my age make the doors of cedar resound throughout the wedding night.

My virginal life has perished. Woe for that Fate, alas, who cast her bitter threads on me!

The breasts of my mother nourished me with their milk to no purpose at all, and to those breasts I cannot repay the favor of nourishment for their old age.

I wish I would have left my father a child when I died, so that he would not forever have an unforgettable grief through remembrance of me.

Weep for Lysandre, companions of my same age, the girl whom Philonike and Eudemos bore in vain.

You who approach my tomb, I implore you very much, weep for my youth, lost prematurely and without marriage.

Source: Jane Rowlandson, ed., *Women and Society in Greek and Roman Egypt* (Cambridge: Cambridge University Press, 1998), 347.

Examining the Evidence

1. What would have been expected from the deceased Lysandre had she lived longer?

2. What does this inscription tell us about the role of women in Roman society?

3. What does it tell us about the role of children in Roman society?

≡ **Roman Depiction of the Egyptian Goddess Isis** Especially in the time of the empire, the Romans often adopted the religious cults of conquered peoples and incorporated foreign gods into their pantheon. Very popular was the goddess Isis, the mother of Horus who, according to millennia-old traditions in Egypt, protected her son and revived her dead husband. This statue of her, probably set up in Rome in the first century CE, has many attributes of Greek and Roman sculpture, such as her dress. But it also has elements that are typical Egyptian, notably the sun disk decorated with a serpent on her head and the musical instrument, the sistrum, which was used in her cult.

outlook of many inhabitants of the Roman Empire, and by 325 CE his ideas would become the basis for a new state religion, Christianity. Christianity's absorption of classical Greek philosophical tradition and the merging of the church hierarchy with that of the imperial bureaucracy explain the new religion's remarkable success. These intellectual and bureaucratic foundations enabled the Christian church to survive the collapse of the Roman Empire in the west and to dominate the religious life of Europe for centuries.

Religions in the Roman Empire

Even if officially the Roman Senate and the emperors often forbade and persecuted new religious ideas, the Roman people readily adopted foreign cults and religions, whose spread was facilitated by migration, trade, and military campaigns. As a result, foreign gods found new adherents far from the regions where they originated. In the first century CE especially, eastern mystery religions, or religions of salvation, gained followers throughout the empire. The cult of the Egyptian goddess Isis, for example, reached Rome already under the Republic and gained many adherents among women, the poor, and enslaved persons. Because in Egyptian myth she had revived her slain husband Osiris and helped her son Horus in his battles with Seth through magic (see Chapter 4), she was considered the protector of the family, especially of women and newborns, with the power to bring good fortune to her followers, even escape from death. While the Senate ordered the destruction of chapels in her honor and Augustus linked her cult with sexual misbehavior—with Cleopatra as the reincarnation of Isis—by the mid-first century CE the empire accepted the cult and Emperor Vespasian made Isis and her divine husband Serapis (the Romans' name for Osiris) his personal protectors. Cults of Isis existed from Britain to Afghanistan, and she was the main character in several works of Latin literature that emphasized her magical powers. Her success shows that popular sentiments could change cultural and religious habits, even in the face of resistance by the authorities.

At the same time that new gods entered the Roman pantheon, a strong tendency arose to merge the gods of various cultures. Isis's husband Serapis, for example, came to be equated with Jupiter, the supreme god of the Roman pantheon, and Emperor Caracalla built a massive temple for Serapis and had him depicted on coins. It became common to place gods that were merged from various cults at the center of Roman religion as if there was only one deity. Thus the process of religious experimentation and exchange produced a Roman tendency toward monotheism, the belief in the existence of only one true deity.

Although monotheism may have been a new concept to many Romans, in some parts of the empire it had a long history. In Palestine in the east of the empire, the monotheistic religion of Judaism had survived (see Chapter 5), and its temple hierarchy was integrated into the Roman administrative structure. Several interpretations of Judaism coexisted, however, some focusing on adherence to established law, others more open to foreign cultural traditions. Certain Jewish groups wanted to overthrow Roman rule, among them the Zealots (originally a Greek term that indicates a zealous follower), some of whom were willing to assassinate Roman sympathizers. Thus in Palestine the process of Romanization was contested, with some Jewish groups choosing to adopt Roman ways and others seeing Roman rule and culture as totally incompatible with the survival of an authentic Jewish identity.

It was in this context of competing Jewish interpretations that the teachings of one preacher, Jesus of Nazareth, became popular. Focusing on personal faith, Jesus reached out to the disenfranchised of society, including women and the poor. Although the dates are uncertain, scholars estimate that he lived from about 4 BCE to 30 CE. Accounts of his life, which we call the New Testament gospels today, show that the traditional Jewish urban hierarchy rejected Jesus and that the Romans, who thought he advocated independence from the empire, executed him as a subversive and a rebel.

After his execution, a small community of Jesus's followers preserved his message and identified Jesus with the messiah, the "anointed one," whom earlier prophets had announced. Jesus's disciples started to teach his message to other Jews. Initially their greatest appeal was to Jews who had partly assimilated into the Greek-speaking communities of Syria, and the gospels were written in Greek rather than Aramaic, the most common spoken language in the region. They used the Greek term *Christ* for messiah, which led to the word *Christians* for their followers.

Christianity's Spread Outside the Jewish Community

The earliest Christians saw themselves as Jews who could teach only those who obeyed the laws of circumcision and of the Jewish diet. A teacher from Anatolia called Paul especially advocated an end to that restriction, and around 50 CE he began to spread Christianity among non-Jews. Paul established numerous Christian communities throughout the eastern Roman Empire, work greatly facilitated by the Roman communication and transportation network (see Map 6.3).

Initially, Christian communities existed in harmony with the Jewish temple hierarchy in Jerusalem, but when the Christians failed to back a Jewish rebellion against the Romans in the years 66 to 74 CE, many Jews considered Christians to be traitors. By 90 CE, the two religions had split apart. At that time, a substantial number of Christian communities prospered in the regions of Syria-Palestine, Anatolia, and Greece. The two largest cities of the empire, Rome and Alexandria, also housed numerous Christians.

≡ **MAP 6.3   The Spread of Christianity, 40–500 CE**   Crucial to the spread of the religious ideas of Jesus were the early missionary travels of his disciple Paul and, later, the adoption of Christianity as a state religion in 325 CE. At first it was embraced mostly by urban residents, but the religion had spread to most people in the Roman Empire by 500 CE, when the Christian church hierarchy had taken over many tasks of the imperial government.

The early Christians were mostly urban merchants and members of the lower classes, drawn to the church because of its focus on human equality and support for the poor. That equality extended to women, who at first seem to have made up a large part of the congregations and to have held prominent roles. Paul often addressed his letters to women. When the Christian church became more institutionalized, however, the role of women decreased, and the new church selected its leaders from among old men, the literal meaning of the Greek title given to them, *presbyteros*. By the early second century CE, each Christian community elected one such elder as "overseer," *episkopos* in Greek, which became the title *bishop*.

Toward a State Religion 50–324 CE

Because they refused to honor other gods and formed close-knit communities, the early Christians grew apart from others in society—a development that made them an easy target for persecution. Although the Romans were willing to accept foreign religions, the authorities did not want such religions to inspire rejection of the Roman community and state. At first, acts of persecution were tied to specific events, such as the burning of Rome in 64 CE, which Emperor Nero blamed on Christians. When the empire subsequently encountered military setbacks, the idea that the Christians' refusal to honor traditional gods had caused divine displeasure led to more general persecutions. In the mid-third century CE, officials traveled across the empire and forced people to make offerings to Roman deities. If they refused, as Christians often did, they were killed.

Persecution led to **martyrdom**, the execution of Christians who refused to renounce their faith. Such acts of defiance became a sign of great devotion, to be admired and praised. Early Christian writings recount in detail the suffering of the faithful, which often included women. One early record is the account of Vibia Perpetua (WIHB-ee-ah pehr-PEHTCH-u-ah), the earliest preserved Christian diary authored by a woman. The twenty-two-year-old woman described her imprisonment in the city of Carthage in the year 203 CE. She and four other Christians were thrown to the animals: a wild cow trampled her, and a soldier killed her with his sword.

Perpetua described three visions she had in prison. In the final vision she saw herself in an arena:

> The crowd began to shout and my assistants started to sing psalms. Then I walked up to the trainer and took the branch. He kissed me and said: "Peace be with you, my daughter!". . . I awoke. I realized that it was not with wild animals that I would fight but with the Devil, but I knew that I would win the victory.[3]

martyrdom The suffering of death for one's religious beliefs.

In 313 CE, about a century after Perpetua's death, Emperor Constantine issued the Edict of Milan, which allowed Christians to practice their faith openly. Now that martyrdom was no longer necessary, early Christians focused on an ascetic lifestyle as they believed that rejecting physical pleasure would stimulate the soul's perfection. The dislike of the body was especially acute in the domain of sexuality. Abstinence from sexual relations, especially for women, became an obsession in

The Early Christian Martyr Perpetua The stories of early Christians who were tortured and killed for their beliefs led to their popular admiration in later periods, as evidenced by numerous representations of them, including many of women. This mosaic made around 500 CE is from a church in Ravenna in Italy and shows Vibia Perpetua, who had become a saint by then and was included in a series of images of apostles and other martyrs. She is depicted as resigned to her fate and at peace with herself over the terrible tortures she was to face.

the second century CE. Women who remained virgins were thought to carry an intact soul in an intact body. Sexual abstinence was encouraged even in marriage. At this time the church started to promote the idea that Jesus's mother Mary had been a perpetual virgin and removed references to his siblings from official literature.

How could Christianity, with its focus on austerity, appeal to a wide public? Although there are no definitive answers to this question, some historians point to the humanity of Christ's teachings: unlike the distant Roman gods, the Christian God was so concerned with humans that he sacrificed his son for their salvation. In Christian doctrine, God became human in Jesus, and Jesus was the force through which God influenced human history. Such closeness between humans and god was absent in other religions.

Moreover, Jesus preached love and compassion for one's peers, and his followers actively built a sense of community that transcended social and cultural boundaries and was much stronger than that of other religious groups. The new community served very well in a Roman world in which people moved around and often ended up in large cities with mixed populations. Furthermore, the early Christian church was well organized to provide services otherwise missing. It protected widows, fed the poor, and provided education for some. Many of the empire's bureaucrats were Christians who knew how to read and write. Some historians see the church's organizational skills as its major strength.

Christianity's guarantee of success came under Emperor Constantine (r. 307–337 CE). When he won a crucial battle in 312 CE, Constantine credited his victory to the Christian God and converted to Christianity. A year after his military victory, he promulgated the Edict of Milan, guaranteeing freedom of worship to Christians and all others. Historians debate whether Constantine was spiritually motivated or a pragmatist who recognized the growing influence of the religion in the empire and sought to win the support of its adherents.

Constantine used the Christian church as an institution to unify the empire. He granted land to build churches, especially in places significant to the religion's history. In this cause, his mother, Helena, traveled through Palestine and financed the building of memorials in locations where, according to the gospels, crucial events in Jesus's life had taken place. Thus, Christians used the roads and sea routes that connected the empire to spread their message and establish new outposts for their religion. By Constantine's day, Christianity had grown to such an extent that the empire turned to Christian institutions and networks to reinforce imperial unity.

Institutionalization of the Christian Church

After Constantine, the institutions of the empire and Christian church were increasingly intertwined, and the power of the church within the empire was irreversible. Changes in the imperial administration, which had become fully focused on the emperor's authority, confirmed the religion's grip. Whereas the empire's earlier administration had been decentralized, by 300 CE the emperor's court had taken over most administrative tasks. According to one estimate the imperial court controlled 30,000 to 35,000 government offices by 400 CE. The Christian church mirrored the centralized imperial bureaucracy when it stabilized its structure and hierarchy. The imperial and Christian administrative structures coincided, and soon religious leaders also adopted civilian roles.

As Christianity spread over the wide empire with its multiple cultural traditions, differences of opinion about aspects of the religion emerged. Especially controversial was the question of the relationship between Jesus's divine and human natures. A doctrine called Arianism (AYR-ee-an-ihz-uhm), which originated with Arius, a priest of Alexandria, claimed that Jesus could not have been divine because he was born from the will of God and had died. Only God, the father, was eternal and divine. Constantine, to whom religious disagreement meant civil disorder, called a council of bishops at Nicaea in Anatolia in 325 CE to determine the official doctrine. The council rejected Arianism, but disagreements remained over such questions as exactly when in the year Jesus died and whether priests should remain celibate, among many others. Over the next centuries several councils followed, as we will see in Chapter 8. Opinion differed especially between eastern and western church leaders, who became more distant from each other as the eastern and western halves of the empire increasingly diverged.

At the same time, intellectuals refined the philosophical basis of the Christian creed. Particularly important in this context was the North African bishop Augustine (354–430 CE), who connected Christian thought to Plato's notion of universal ideals (see Chapter 5). Just as Plato believed that rigorous intellectual searching revealed the ideal form of the good, Augustine saw reading the Bible as a way to comprehend God's goodness. To explain the military difficulties Rome encountered in his lifetime, Augustine reinterpreted the history of the world in his *City of God* (written between 413 and 425 CE). He contrasted the "city of man," in which people pursue earthly pleasures, with the "city of God," in which they dedicate their lives to the promotion of Christian ideals. Roman gods and non-Christian philosophers had failed to provide true happiness to humanity; only the Christian God could do so. Although Augustine attacked earlier philosophers, he was very familiar with their works and used their systems of reasoning. By helping merge the Roman and Christian traditions, Augustine did much to cement the place of Christianity in Roman life.

Rise of Christianity	
c. 20–30 CE	Jesus teaches in Palestine
45–58 CE	Paul spreads Christianity in the eastern Mediterranean
64 CE	Nero persecutes Christians in Rome
c. 90 CE	Split between Judaism and Christianity
312 CE	Constantine converts to Christianity
313 CE	Edict of Milan establishes freedom of worship for Christians
324 CE	Constantine makes Christianity the official state religion
325 CE	Council of Nicaea labels Arianism a heresy
354–430 CE	Life of Augustine
c. 400–500 CE	The Roman imperial and Christian church bureaucracies merge

The merger of Christian ideas with Roman imperial ideology and bureaucracy led to ultimate success for the religion, even while the empire collapsed in the west. Emperors became the upholders of the faith, persecuting non-Christians and dissenting voices within the church. Civil and religious bureaucracies were combined—bishops were also judges, for example. Thus, to understand fully the success of Christianity, we must further explore political developments in the late Roman Empire.

Transformation of the Roman Empire 200–500 CE

↘ **FOCUS** How and why did the eastern and western parts of the Roman Empire develop differently?

In the third century CE, severe social and economic crises gripped Rome. Divisions between the eastern and western parts became more acute, and despite attempts to keep the empire together, a definitive partition took place in 395 CE. In the following century, the pressures on the Western Roman Empire became too great, and it collapsed for reasons that are much debated. What is undeniable is that fundamental changes took place, and that western Eurasia in 500 CE was a very different place from that in 200 CE.

Division Between East and West

The peace and stability of the Pax Romana was shattered when, in the third century CE, generals using their legions in fights over the imperial throne devastated the land. It was during this chaotic period that the eastern and western parts of the empire split—they had often served as distinct power bases for contenders to the throne. As we have seen, they had dissimilar cultural histories, and in religious terms they grew further apart because their inhabitants interpreted Christianity differently.

In 324 CE, Emperor Constantine turned the old city of Byzantium in the eastern part of the empire into a majestic new capital, which he called Constantinople ("city of Constantine"). Strategically located near the empire's borders and situated on major trade routes, Constantinople soon became the most important city of the east. Its rise exacerbated the growing division between the two parts of the empire, however, and by 395 CE a single ruler could no longer govern the Roman Empire. Rather, one emperor resided in Constantinople in the east; in the west another emperor ruled, at first from Rome and later from the Italian cities Milan and then Ravenna. The two halves had different histories thereafter: the western part declined and fell prey to Germanic invaders, but the eastern part remained an imperial power for centuries.

Economic Strains and Social Tensions

Throughout its existence, the costs of running the Roman Empire had been enormous, and they increased in the third century CE when the army, which had always been large, grew massive, and emperors gave soldiers increasingly high pay to gain their support. Moreover, already expected to commission public works and monumental buildings, after the official conversion to Christianity, emperors were obliged to donate property and build numerous churches. Financial concerns mounted.

≡ **Division of the Roman Empire, c. 395 CE**

To guarantee state income the emperors took steps to limit economic and social mobility. Peasants were tied to the land, unable to leave to pursue other economic opportunities. Artisans were similarly tied to their workshops and had to pass on their occupations to their sons, and when soldiers retired their sons replaced them. This new arrangement facilitated tax collection, because social class determined the level of taxation, but it severely limited people's freedom. In the country, peasants sought protection against the state from the landowners they worked for. In the cities, the poor turned to bishops, who had gained special prominence and who could act as people's patrons—in the fifth century CE, bishops became the masters and protectors of entire cities, especially in the western empire. Thus, as the problems of the empire intensified, its inhabitants increasingly saw the imperial government as a threat rather than a protector, and they tried to establish a new set of social and political connections to guarantee their safety and security.

This transformation was accelerated by the decline of cities and towns in the west. They were victims of insufficient funds for public works, a disappearing imperial administration, and diminished trade. Economic power shifted to the landed estates, whose owners were masters over the people working for them and produced all they needed by themselves. Many regions became virtually autonomous. By contrast, in the east the cities were more resilient, and the peasants resisted forced settlement and retained their independence.

Collapse in the West and Revitalization in the East

After 200 CE, outside pressures exacerbated the internal problems of the Roman Empire. In the east, the empire fought over border territories with the centralized states of Parthia and, after 224 CE, Sasanid Persia. Because these wars involved two equal powers, they regularly ended in negotiated settlements. In the west, Rome confronted various Germanic tribal groups, which acted independently of one another.

The tribal threat had loomed since the beginning of the empire, and the Romans had strengthened the western border with a long line of walls and fortresses. Some tribes infiltrated imperial lands, however, and officials allowed them to settle there. Because German tribes themselves were under pressure from Central Asian nomadic Huns, they increased their efforts to enter the empire and broke down Rome's resistance. The Huns entered the fray themselves under their king, Attila, who acquired the epithet "scourge of God." He invaded Gaul in 450 and then assailed Italy, where the bishop of Rome had to pay him off. Although an emperor remained enthroned in the western empire, his influence was minor, and he watched feebly as various German leaders struggled for power.

Despite the Germanic presence, there was much continuity in daily life in the western empire. The older inhabitants kept obeying Roman law, while the Germans followed their own legal traditions. Bureaucrats were still needed, and those of the empire continued to serve. Because many Germans converted to Christianity upon entering the empire, religious practices remained the same, and the church even increased its influence. Thus when in 476 CE Odoacer (OH-doo-way-sahr), the German king whose territory included Italy, forced the last Roman emperor, Romulus Augustulus, to abdicate, the event did not affect most people's lives. The western empire ceased to exist, and several Germanic kingdoms arose in its place, as we will see in Chapter 8.

The history of the eastern empire was very different from that of the west. Notwithstanding outside pressures, Constantinople's emperors governed large territories that remained urban and economically successful. The court saw itself as the protector of the Christian faith and of Roman civilization. A distinct eastern culture of late antiquity developed; today historians call it Byzantine. The eastern empire and its culture would continue into the fifteenth century CE, when, as we will see in Chapter 14, the Turks captured Constantinople.

COUNTERPOINT: Rome's Iranian Rivals in the Middle East

↘ **FOCUS** What were the differences in organization between the Iranian and Roman Empires?

To ancient Romans, their empire may easily have seemed the strongest power on earth, invincible and unlimited. In reality, however, Rome's dominion of western Eurasia was just one of a string of empires that stretched across Eurasia from the South China Sea in the east to the Atlantic Ocean in the west. Bordering Rome was a Southwest Asian power that never yielded to Roman armies. Centered in Iran and heirs to the ancient Persian Empire, two empires in succession withstood the forces of Roman expansion (see again Map 4.4, page 143). From the moment

Rome started to annex regions of the eastern Mediterranean in the first century BCE, it confronted the Parthians. The Sasanids overthrew the Parthians in 224 CE and continued the competition with Roman Byzantium until their defeat by Muslim armies in the seventh century (discussed in Chapter 8).

In contrast to the Roman style of control, which imposed a uniform system over subject territories, the Iranian empires were conglomerates of kingdoms and provinces whose kings and governors owed obedience to a "king of kings." These empires successfully ruled a vast area for more than nine centuries.

The Parthians 247 BCE–224 CE

Soon after Alexander of Macedonia's death in 323 BCE, the territories he had conquered from the Mediterranean Sea to the Indus Valley had become the Seleucid Empire (see Chapter 5). Gradually, however, various regions of the Seleucid state gained independence. In the north, to the east of the Caspian Sea, was the province of Parthia, where in 247 BCE a new people came to power under a leader called Arsaces (ar-SAY-sez). The Seleucids recognized Parthia's independence around 210 BCE, and in succeeding decades Parthians annexed parts of Iran and Mesopotamia. When Rome conquered the remains of the Seleucid Empire in the eastern Mediterranean, it found itself faced with a formidable new opponent in the Parthians.

The Euphrates River formed a natural border between the two empires, but several Roman generals sought fame and fortune by leading their forces across the river. Likewise the Parthians regularly tried to annex Roman-controlled western Syria, without lasting success. For 250 years the wars continued: several Roman emperors of the second century CE made gains in northern Syria and Mesopotamia, but the territories were never truly integrated into the Roman Empire.

The Parthians could manage these territorial gains and losses because they saw their ruler as a "king of kings," a master of vassals from various states, an idea that had already existed in the Persian Empire. As in the past, the empire's cohesion depended greatly on the strength of the Parthian ruler; the local kings had a local power base and sufficient independence to switch allegiance at times. The cities, the hubs from which the Seleucids had governed the territory, also maintained the sovereignty they had before. Nonetheless, the structure gave flexibility and resilience to the Parthian Empire: the loss of one territory would not have disastrous effects on the whole.

Despite the numerous wars, Parthians and Romans maintained important economic connections. Parthia controlled a large part of the overland trade route that brought silk and other luxuries from the East to Rome. The Parthians contributed to this trade, exporting foods such as pomegranates and alfalfa to China, as well as Iranian horses, which the Chinese greatly admired.

The Sasanids 224–651 CE

In 224 CE, Ardashir (ARda-shear), the leader of a Parthian vassal kingdom, defeated the last Parthian king in battle and asserted supremacy over the entire empire. A native of the southwestern Iranian region of Fars, Ardashir claimed descent from a man named Sasan, and his dynasty is thus called the Sasanids. The structure of the Parthian Empire allowed for such a change of ruler; in essence, a new "king of kings" had arisen. The Sasanids inherited their concept of kingship from the Parthians but added increased centralization of power to it.

≡ **Shapur Celebrates the Capture of Valerian** In 260 CE the Sasanid ruler Shapur defeated the Roman army in northern Syria and captured its emperor Valerian alive, a feat unparalleled in Roman history. This relief, carved on a rock near the tombs of the ancient Persian kings seven miles from Persepolis, depicts the Roman emperor kneeling in submission. According to tradition, after the Roman emperor was killed, Shapur had him skinned and preserved.

Diplomatically, the Sasanids carried on as the Parthians had, their trade with Rome being an enormous source of income. Simultaneously, wars with the Romans continued with some notable Sasanid successes: for example, in 260 CE King Shapur I defeated the Roman army of Valerian and captured the Roman emperor alive. The wars did not end with the division of the Roman Empire, and Byzantine and Sasanid forces regularly fought each other, despite threats to both from the Huns of Central Asia. The end of the Sasanid dynasty would come from the south when Muslim armies from Arabia invaded Iran in the seventh century CE (see Chapter 8).

So for almost a thousand years the Parthians and Sasanids successfully ruled Iran and the surrounding regions. They enforced control through armies that were especially effective because of the cavalry. The core of the army consisted of mounted archers and heavily armored mounted spearmen, their horses covered with armor as well. The Romans were in awe of these opponents. One soldier wrote in 362 CE,

> The Persians opposed us with squadrons of mounted armored soldiers drawn up in such serried ranks that their movements in their close-fitting coats of flexible mail dazzled our eyes, while all their horses were protected by housings of leather.[4]

A Tapestry of Cultures and Religions

The Parthians and Sasanids brought together people with diverse cultural backgrounds and religions, who spoke many languages and used different scripts. They tolerated these various traditions and even promoted them. The emperors spoke Aryan languages of Iran (Parthian and Middle Persian), which they used for official inscriptions often carved on rock surfaces and written in alphabetic scripts derived from Aramaic. They also used Greek as an official language. The Semitic Aramaic language, written in its own script, was very important for administration. The use of a variety of Semitic (for example, Hebrew) and Indo-European (for example, Bactrian, Armenian) languages persisted throughout the entire period.

Although the kings relied on Zoroastrianism (see Chapter 4) to support their rule, the variety of religions in the empire was equally great. A Zoroastrian priest wrote in the third century CE that the empire housed "Jews, Buddhists, Hindus, Nazarenes, Christians, Baptists, and Manicheans,"[5] that is, followers of the various religions from India and the eastern Roman Empire, including various Christian sects.

A new religion that originated in Iran perfectly illustrates a coalescence of various spiritual influences. Its founder, Mani (MAH-nee), was born in 216 CE in the Babylonian part of the then Parthian Empire. At age twenty-four, Mani started to preach a religion he hoped would appeal universally. He saw the Buddha, Zoroaster, and Jesus as his precursors in a long line of prophets and borrowed from all their teachings. Like Zoroaster, Mani saw a strict opposition between soul and body, good and evil, and light and dark. To him life was painful, and the human soul had succumbed to evil. Only true knowledge would free the soul and return it to its original state of goodness, which it would share with God.

Mani's teachings were so flexible that they could easily merge with existing religions. In the west they inspired many Christians of the Roman Empire, including Augustine, who followed Manichaean teachings for nine years, but the church hierarchy saw them as heresy. In Iran, too, the original toleration of Manichaeism gave way to persecutions. Mani himself died in prison sometime between 274 and 277 CE, and his severed head was impaled on a pole for public display. His religion survived, however, until persecutions in the Roman Empire in the fifth century and in the Middle East in the tenth century almost extinguished it.

Conclusion

When the Roman historian Tacitus wrote around the year 100 CE that the empire he inhabited changed the way people lived as far away as Britain, he was not bragging groundlessly. Rome had created a world in which people from North Africa and Syria to Britain and France shared habits and tastes. A man born in one corner of the empire could make a career hundreds of miles away. The cohesion of the Roman Empire explains why the ideas of a small Jewish sect could spread over an enormous area and why the Christian church it inspired could obtain an encompassing structure once it assimilated with the imperial bureaucracy. The Roman Empire was a crucial milestone in the history of western Eurasia, a structure that fundamentally shaped the region with effects still visible today. Its own development is a fascinating story of how strong republican institutions with elected officials and term limits failed to prevent the consolidation of power in the hands of one man. In European tradition, the Roman Empire became the embodiment of the ancient world, a period of the past that produced great human achievements that needed to be recovered.

A subject of the empire may have imagined that Rome was unique and dominated the entire world. But students of world history today realize that it was merely part of a system of empires that stretched throughout Eurasia. For each region, the empire constituted a finishing point of developments that had started thousands of years earlier, as politically united regions grew larger and cultural uniformity increased. These empires represent the culmination of ancient history throughout Eurasia.

review

The major global development in this chapter: The unification of western Eurasia under the Roman Empire.

Important Events	
753–509 BCE	Roman monarchy
509 BCE	Start of the Roman Republic
210 BCE	Parthians gain independence from Seleucid Empire
73–71 BCE	Enslaved persons rebellion led by Spartacus
49 BCE	Julius Caesar crosses the Rubicon
44 BCE	Assassination of Julius Caesar
31 BCE–**14** CE	Reign of Augustus
c. 30 BCE	Rome controls entire Mediterranean region
27 BCE	Augustus establishes full dominance over Roman affairs
c. 4 BCE–**30** CE	Life of Jesus
100–200 CE	Pax Romana; height of the Roman Empire
212 CE	Caracalla grants citizenship to nearly all free inhabitants of the empire
224 CE	Sasanids overthrow Parthians
313 CE	Constantine issues Edict of Milan, legalizing Christianity
395 CE	Roman Empire divided into eastern and western parts
410 CE	German tribes sack Rome
476 CE	German leader Odoacer forces last western Roman emperor to step down

KEY TERMS

client (p. 200)
consul (p. 201)
equestrian (p. 201)
latifundia (p. 202)
legion (p. 204)

magistrate (p. 200)
martyrdom (p. 219)
pater familias (p. 200)
patrician (p. 200)
Pax Romana (p. 209)

plebeian (p. 200)
Romanization (p. 213)
Senate (p. 200)
tribune (p. 201)

CHAPTER OVERVIEW QUESTIONS

1. How are Roman political institutions still important to us today?
2. How did the Romans face the challenges of creating and maintaining an empire?
3. What impact did Rome have on the lives of the people it conquered?

4. How did Christianity's rise benefit from the Roman Empire?
5. What were the limits of Roman imperialism?

MAKING CONNECTIONS

1. How did the political and cultural achievements of Republican Rome compare with those of classical Greece (see Chapter 4)?
2. How did the world empires of the centuries from 500 BCE to 500 CE facilitate the spread of new ideas and religions? Compare, for example, the Han (see Chapter 5) and Roman Empires.

3. How does the level of cultural integration in the Roman Empire compare with that of the Eurasian empires we studied in earlier chapters?
4. In what sense did Christianity merge earlier traditions of the eastern Mediterranean world?

DOING HISTORY

Contextualization

By definition empires overpower large territories, and they tend to leave behind much more textual and archaeological information than weaker states do. It is thus not surprising that historians studying a specific empire are so immersed in the evidence available that they forget the context in which the sources existed. A student who looks at the history of the world around the year 1 CE may think that the Roman Empire, which Augustus just created with his conquest of Egypt, dominated everything. But was that really the case?

1. If we place the Roman Empire in the context of Eurasia and the other states and empires there, does the image that it ruled the entire world make sense? Why or why not?

2. Can you think of other periods in world history when placing a major empire in a broader context changes how we perceive that empire?

3. Can you look at other nonpolitical aspects of history in the same way? Explain your response.

For further research into the topics covered in this chapter, see the Bibliography at the end of the book.

Reading the Unwritten Record:

Peoples of Africa, the Americas, and the Pacific Islands

3000 BCE–500 CE

≡ **World in the Making** The ancient populations of South America developed textiles into an art form, experimenting with fiber materials and decorations. In the first millennium BCE, the people of Paracas in the southern Andes revolutionized textile production by introducing tapestry weaving and new techniques of dyeing. The fragment shown here, part of a mummy wrapping produced in the first century BCE, depicts a mythical monster we call the "Decapitator."

backstory

At the start of this book we looked at the evolution of the human species and our ancestors' migration throughout the globe. As the setting for the lives of the earliest humans, Africa played a major role in these events. Vast oceans separated Africa and its original human inhabitants from places such as the Americas and the islands of the Pacific Ocean. But over broad expanses of time, the significance of these gaps between the earth's far-distant realms diminished as African peoples responded to changes in their physical environment and migrated to other parts of the world. In this chapter, we shift our focus from the ancient cultures of Eurasia to sub-Saharan Africa, the Americas, and the Pacific in the period 3000 BCE to 500 CE. In so doing, we explore a unique challenge these regions present to the historian: reconstructing the history of societies that did not leave a written record.

IN 1769 CE THE ENGLISH explorer Sir Joseph Banks, who kept a journal of his visits to the Polynesian islands of the South Pacific, remarked:

> The people excell much in predicting the weather, a circumstance of great use to them in their short voyages from Island to Island. They have many various ways of doing this but one only that I know of which I never heard of being practisd by Europaeans, that is foretelling the quarter of the heavens from whence the wind shall blow by observing the Milky Way, . . . and in this as well as their other predictions we found them indeed not infallible but far more clever than Europaeans. In their longer voyages they steer in the day by the Sun and in the night by the Stars. Of these they know . . . the time of their annual appearing and disapearing to a great nicety, far greater than would be easily believed by an Europaean astronomer.[1]

The ancestors of these Polynesians had boldly spread over the myriad of islands in the Pacific Ocean, but the people Banks observed had maintained many of their customs:

> From the similarity of customs, the still greater of Traditions and the almost identical sameness of Language between these people and those of the Islands of the South Sea there remains little doubt that they came originally from the same source.[2]

Banks was among the handful of early European explorers who drew the peoples of Polynesia into history by recording some of their customs, practices, and languages. Because these people did not write, our only records of their early histories are the accounts of literate visitors. Often, however, European observers' comments were derogatory or patronizing, depicting the peoples of Africa, the Americas, and the Pacific Islands as savages without culture.

All peoples of the world have a history, but in ancient times very few people wrote. Thus there are limits to what historians can say about people who left no written documents, such as the early Polynesians, or about cultures such as the Olmec of Mesoamerica, whose writings they do not comprehend. To explore the lives of such populations, researchers must rely on material remains. Scholars usually refer to this type of archaeological study as **prehistory**, a discipline that focuses on the remains of nonliterate peoples or peoples with early writing systems that are still not fully deciphered.

In this chapter we consider prehistoric cultures from various parts of the world as examples of historical developments in such societies. The

prehistory The scholarly discipline that studies peoples' histories before they left behind written evidence; also the time period during which cultures had no writing.

examples show that they could reach high levels of social and technological development and acquire many features of what we call civilization, including cities.

This is not to say that these societies closely resembled those of Eurasia in the same period. Some purposely rejected technologies that were almost universally used elsewhere in the ancient world, such as pottery. The prehistoric peoples we study here were more physically isolated from other cultures than those treated before, and local conditions had more impact than outside influences on their cultural development. Yet some of these small groups—especially among the Polynesians and Africa's Bantu speakers—migrated vast distances and in this way spread technologies and cultural traditions to a range of new environments.

As in Eurasian societies, in this period the inhabitants of sub-Saharan Africa, the Americas, and the Pacific Islands laid the groundwork for later developments. In a sense, they are the voiceless peoples of early world history, for the absence of writing that we can comprehend makes them less approachable than other cultures we have studied. But it is important to remember that throughout the ancient world, very few people speak to us directly—as in every society we have discussed so far, the great majority of people were illiterate and remain equally voiceless.

OVERVIEW QUESTIONS

The major global development in this chapter: The evolution of ancient cultures without writing and their fundamental role in world history.

As you read, consider:

1. How does the presence or absence of writing influence how we study ancient cultures?

2. Why did the ancient cultures of sub-Saharan Africa, the Americas, and the Pacific often show similar developments in spite of their isolation from one another?

3. How is the spread of peoples, languages, and technologies interrelated, and in what ways can we study these processes?

Peoples of Sub-Saharan Africa

↘ **FOCUS** How have scholars reconstructed the histories of early Africans, and what do their sources reveal about the livelihoods and cultures of these peoples?

The human species originated in Africa, the continent with the longest history in the world. But except in northern Africa, the study of early African history must be based primarily on material remains because there were no native writing systems, and accounts by foreign visitors are scarce until European reports from the seventeenth century CE. Thus, we mainly reconstruct developments in sub-Saharan Africa in ancient times through archaeology, with some help from linguistics. These sources show a long-term process during which the livelihoods of most people changed from gathering and hunting to agriculture, as was the case in the Eurasian regions we studied before. In many parts of Africa, migrations by peoples speaking Bantu languages were responsible for the shift to settled farming, which was made easier by the use of iron tools. In the African context, the spread of languages, agriculture, and iron-working are closely related.

Early Hunters and Herders

Although sub-Saharan Africa had been the starting place of several migrations of early humans, for millennia after the last ice age contacts with other parts of the world were rare (see Chapter 1). The earliest inhabitants of sub-Saharan Africa, as elsewhere, survived by gathering and hunting local resources. Africa has several ecological zones that provide a diversity of wild resources for small groups of people to survive comfortably (see Map 7.1).

Around the equator lies a tropical rain forest. The area has few food sources and the climate promotes tropical diseases such as malaria, so in ancient times human occupation was very limited there. But **savannas**—grasslands with scattered trees and shrubs where plenty of animals reside and plant life is rich—cover large parts of Africa. Wild food supplies were especially plentiful near lakes, and ancient peoples who lived near them could spend most of the year in the same settlement by fishing, hunting, and collecting plants and nuts. Also in the very northern part of Africa, where the Sahara Desert is today, people could survive this way as the climate was cooler and wetter than it is now. It is important to remember that access to the outside world varied enormously in different regions of the continent. While the Indian Ocean on the east African coast was easily crossed with small boats, the Atlantic Ocean on the west coast was a huge natural barrier. The great variety of

savanna Tropical or subtropical grassland with scattered trees and shrubs.

Sub-Saharan Africa, c. 6000 BCE–400 CE

- Tropical rain forest
- Savanna
- Desert
- Mixed forest
- Scrubland
- Coniferous forest
- Extent of the Sahara, c. 600 BCE
- Ancient lake, c. 6000 BCE
- Bantu homeland
- Bantu migrations, c. 3000 BCE–400 CE
- Selected iron-working site
- Iron-age sheep herding site
- Yam   Site of crop domestication

MAP 7.1   Sub-Saharan Africa, c. 3000 BCE–400 CE A fundamental development in ancient African history was the Bantu migration, which took place in various waves between about 3000 BCE and 400 CE. The migrants spread the use not only of Bantu languages but also of agriculture and iron technology into the many different ecological zones of sub-Saharan Africa. Note that some of the natural features we now take for granted were not present in ancient times, such as the vast size of the Sahara, which was much less arid before 2500 BCE and sustained a rich pastoral culture.

environments in Africa led to a diversity of challenges and opportunities and many different human responses to them.

Sometime after 5000 BCE, some people in the Sahara region moved from gathering and hunting to herding cattle, sheep, and goats. Wild cattle were native to the region. Sheep and goats were not, however, so the Saharan people must have imported them from the Middle East, where these animals had been herded since 8000 BCE. The pastoral lifestyle spread farther south over the centuries and was combined with a more intensive collection and care of wild plants. Throughout the various ecological zones, pastoralism provided the most enduring means of survival, as the animals turned all sorts of vegetation into consumable goods for humans. The ownership of herds was thus a sign of wealth and security.

Bantu Migrations

Today tens of millions of people in Africa speak some 500 related languages that originate from one common source. Scholars call the linguistic group they belong to **Bantu**, after a native term for "persons" or "people." The expansion of Bantu languages all over the continent is related to the spread of agriculture and the use of iron and is fundamentally important to African history. It is a mistake to see it as a systematic movement in a single direction with Bantu speakers spreading their language and technologies. There was a continuous back and forth between different population groups that in the end led to a shared culture with much diversity in it.

Linguistic analysis identifies similarities and differences among the various languages to determine how closely they are related and to estimate when their speakers became separated. As these examples from four central African languages show, the similarities are great, but there are clear differences.

English	Asu	Bemba	Koyo	Yao
husband	ume	lume	lomi	lume
house	umba	nganda	ndago	njuumba
cattle	ngombe	ngombe	(not used)	ngoombe

Bantu The name for some 500 closely related languages spoken in sub-Saharan Africa and for the speakers of these languages.

Most scholars accept that the first Bantu speakers had a single homeland in the southern region of modern-day Cameroon and eastern Nigeria. From this core, people migrated in multiple movements south and east in a long-term process, until their descendants inhabited most of sub-Saharan Africa (see again Map 7.1). There is much debate over when these migrations happened, but they were certainly a long-term process that may have started about 3000 BCE and completed by 400 CE. The details of how they took place are impossible to reconstruct as we can rely only on the degree of linguistic similarities to estimate when two Bantu languages diverged and some archaeological remains to identify common practices among different groups of speakers. The speakers of Bantu languages had very diverse forms of social, political, and economic organization, but all based their economic lives on agriculture. The Sahara Desert started to dry up after 5000 BCE, pushing people into the sub-Saharan savanna, and it was probably on the edges of the rainforest that they learned how to farm crops. The yam, the root of a tropical vine, proved especially important. After the men cut down trees and other large plants, leaving some remains to screen the soil from heavy rains, the women made narrow furrows in the earth in which they planted yam cuttings. Similarly, the inhabitants of the savanna learned to farm sorghum and millet, local grasses that produce grains, and they promoted the growth of a palm tree whose nuts they could press for oil.

Possibly around 3000 BCE these agriculturalists started to migrate. It was a slow process, and it did not begin for any one reason. Probably the most common cause was that a community grew too large for the local area to support, so part of the population had to leave, searching for new areas suitable to their agriculture. Wherever the Bantu migrants settled, their villages became the focal point for the smaller groups of gatherer-hunters in the area. These local groups were probably most attracted by the settlers' use of pottery, which made cooking easier (see Lives and Livelihoods: Potters of Antiquity, p. 244). The gatherer-hunters exchanged their fish or meat with the settlers for farmed food, and Bantu languages were probably crucial to their interactions. Bantu speakers started to adopt non-Bantu words and expressions, and the original populations adopted agriculture and other Bantu practices. There was an exchange not only of languages but also of practices and ideas.

Bantu speakers moved everyplace in eastern and southern Africa where farming was possible, but they did not enter zones too dry to cultivate their crops. Into these areas they pushed people who maintained a gathering-and-hunting lifestyle until modern times. Prominent among them were the Khoisan (KOI-sahn), gatherer-hunters and pastoralists from southern Africa who spoke languages in which a clicking sound is used for consonants.

Farming became more efficient with the arrival of iron technology, which deeply influenced sub-Saharan African society and agriculture. Iron has several advantages over other metals: iron ore is found in numerous locations, and the metal is stronger than the bronze that many cultures used before iron. The first evidence for working iron ore in world history comes from about 2000 BCE in the Middle East, but people in the region started to use the metal extensively only about 800 BCE. By about 500 BCE iron technology appeared in sub-Saharan Africa. Most scholars think it arrived from the Middle East through Egypt, because to work iron one must know how to regulate air flow in furnaces; people in sub-Saharan Africa did not melt any metals before, and without experimenting with softer metals it seems unlikely that they would have developed the skills to work iron. They mastered the technology fast, however, and iron manufacture became an important activity in the earliest urban centers of sub-Saharan Africa. The oldest known city of the region was Jenne-jeno in modern-day Mali, where slag deposits show that the earliest settlers worked iron around 250 BCE despite that the nearest source for iron ore was thirty miles away. The replacement of stone tools with iron tools had a radical impact on agriculture. It became much easier to clear trees in the previously impenetrable rain forest, rendering new areas fit for farming.

Bantu Society and Culture

Matrilineal descent was the cornerstone of Bantu social organization. Status, goods, and political office were inherited from mothers, and a man usually moved to his wife's village upon marriage. Childbearing, not marriage, signified a woman's entry into full adulthood. Although men cleared forests for cultivation, women did virtually all the farming. This division of labor encouraged polygamy. Women's labor made valuable contributions to household wealth, and a man with several wives could farm more land, produce more food, and raise more children. Despite the prevalence of matrilineal descent and the central place of women in production as well as reproduction, decision-making authority within families was usually a male privilege.

With the migrations, Bantu social and political institutions changed significantly, especially in East Africa. The dislocations of migration and the intermarriage with indigenous peoples caused a steady shift away from the Bantu tradition of matrilineal descent and inheritance to patrilineal descent and strict gender roles in food production. This change resulted from the growing importance of herding, especially cattle raising. Cattle was the crucial form of wealth in East African societies, and this wealth went to the men who tended the cattle. Agriculture remained a woman's task with little prestige. As cattle herds increased in size, ownership of cattle conferred status as well as wealth. Men who owned large herds of cattle could attract many followers and dependents and assume positions of leadership in their communities. Moreover, the authority of chiefs derived increasingly from wealth; previously, it had depended heavily on ties to the spirits of their ancestors residing at the ancestral burial grounds. Thus, the cultural exchanges that accompanied Bantu migrations changed the societies of both the Bantu migrants and the peoples they encountered.

Because sub-Saharan Africans did not write until their encounters with Europeans in the modern period, we have no texts on Bantu religious beliefs. Accordingly, to reconstruct early Bantu ideas, historians of religion use tales and customs that exist today or that earlier visitors recorded. Just as scholars use similarities in language to trace Bantu migrations, they use similarities in myths and beliefs among distant African peoples to identify the original, common set of religious ideas. For example, many modern Bantu speakers think that proper human conduct was part of the natural order established at the time of creation, but that the creator has remained distant ever since. They believe that natural disasters and evil arise from human transgressions that disturb the cosmic order. To restore the essential positive nature of things, mortals must perform rituals to clear away anger and calm the spirits. Although these views are widespread and probably originated with the earliest Bantu, scholars accept that ideas and rituals change over time, so they cannot firmly establish what the Bantu speakers of antiquity believed and how they expressed those beliefs.

The archaeological remains of ancient Africa are largely devoted to basic human needs such as food and housing. But the early sub-Saharan Africans also produced nonutilitarian goods. From around 800 BCE to 200 CE, for example, people of the Nok culture in modern northern Nigeria created remarkable artwork in terra cotta. Their baked clay human heads, often life-size, show unique skills of representation (see Lives and Livelihoods: Potters of Antiquity). Throughout their history, the Khoisan people of southern Africa produced many cave paintings, representing their lives as hunters of local animals such as giraffes and elands (a type of antelope). People from sub-Saharan Africa undoubtedly fashioned many other objects of art as well, but they were often made of materials that have now decomposed.

Thus, ancient Africa produced diverse and dynamic communities, connected by a common thread of Bantu culture, society, and technology. The cultural richness of sub-Saharan Africa in ancient times had parallels in other parts of the world where prehistoric cultures flourished. Those of the Americas will draw our attention next.

LIVES AND LIVELIHOODS

Potters of Antiquity

With very few exceptions, people in agricultural societies produce pottery, that is, containers made of clay that have been baked to keep their shape. In antiquity all pottery was fired at a relatively low temperature, between 1652° and 2192°F, and needed to be glazed (coated with a special layer) to become waterproof. Archaeologists find broken and whole pots in large quantities in almost every excavation. These remains are crucially important to our understanding of ancient societies because of their enormous variety in shape and decoration.

Pottery manufacture began in Japan in around 13,000 BCE. From the start, people shaped pots in different ways and decorated them according to local tastes. They molded them into countless forms, painted them with various pigments, and incised them or added such elements as knobs. Shapes and decorations changed rapidly, giving the archaeologist an effective means for dating. Variations in the quality and care of pottery decoration inform historians about class differences, and the presence of foreign pottery in certain places reveals trade contacts. Beyond their importance

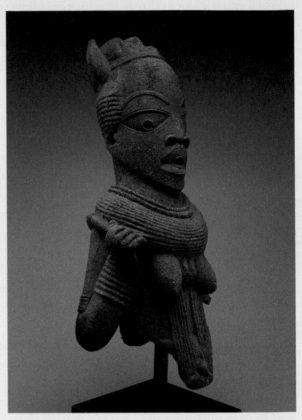

≡ **A Nok Clay Statue** In the centuries between 500 BCE and 200 CE, the Nok culture of western Africa produced impressive statues of terra cotta (baked clay), the oldest known figurative sculpture south of the Sahara. Most of the remains are parts from large statues that were close to life-size when complete but, because the statues were hollow, often broke over time. While the heads were not naturalistic portraits, each preserved one is unique.

to the modern scholar, potters were crucial contributors in ancient societies, creating valuable utensils as well as expressing ideologies and esthetic values.

Pottery revolutionized cooking, allowing people to heat liquids and other food products such as fats and store them for prolonged periods. This feature of pottery had the greatest effect on women's lives. It is likely that pottery was mainly the work of women who shaped, decorated, and baked basic pots as part of their domestic chores. Because basic pots are easy to make, the earliest potters worked at home or in simple communal installations. From the beginning, these women showed imagination and the desire to make something beautiful. The creative possibilities of working with clay are almost limitless because it is flexible and easy to decorate, and so for peoples all over the world, pots are often the most prominent and plentiful art forms.

Artistic experimentation with pottery inspired other forms of creativity. The earliest preserved sculptures of sub-Saharan Africa are the terra cotta heads of the Nok culture in Nigeria. Potters' work with clay must have been instrumental in teaching the sculptors of these striking figures what shapes they could obtain.

Thus, the potters of antiquity were not mere artisans who provided for basic needs. They were also artists who imaginatively expressed their societies' ideas and tastes, which we can study today through their enduring creations.

Questions to Consider

1. In what ways is pottery useful to the scholar?
2. How can pottery reveal the social conditions of an ancient society?

For Further Information:

Barnett, William K., and John W. Hoopes, eds. *The Emergence of Pottery: Technology and Innovation in Ancient Societies*. Washington, DC: Smithsonian Institution Press, 1995.

Orton, Clive, and Michael Hughes. *Pottery in Archaeology*. 2nd ed. New York: Cambridge University Press, 2013.

Peoples of the Americas

↘ FOCUS What kinds of evidence have scholars used to recreate the experience of ancient American peoples, and what do we know about these cultures?

As we saw in Chapter 1, the most widely accepted theory about the peopling of the world holds that migrants crossed into North America from northeastern Asia during the last ice age about 15,000 years ago and then spread throughout the Americas. When the glaciers gradually melted, rising sea levels cut off the Americas from the rest of the world. Although sailors from Europe and perhaps from Africa could still reach American shores, these visits did not introduce lasting changes until the sixteenth century CE. Thus, all technological and social developments after people arrived in the ancient Americas were due to internal processes until European contact.

In Central and South America, societies developed first into states and later into empires. Despite the difficulties of overland contacts and the region's enormous ecological diversity, cultural similarities emerged over wide areas, and a number of populations seem to have shared ideologies and religious beliefs. In Central America, or Mesoamerica, and the Andes Mountains of South America, archaeological evidence reveals a variety of advanced cultures. By contrast, the peoples of North America remained mostly isolated from their southern neighbors and pursued a gatherer-hunter lifestyle for much longer.

The Olmecs 1200–400 BCE

Volcanoes in the narrow strip of land that connects North and South America created high mountain barriers between numerous valleys and coastal zones. It is thus no surprise that several centers of cultural development arose (see Map 7.2). One such area occupies the modern Mexican states of Tabasco and Veracruz, south of the Gulf of Mexico. Between 1200 and 400 BCE, this region had a flourishing common culture that influenced others for hundreds of miles beyond its heartland. Scholars today call the culture *Olmec*.

The Olmecs, or their ancestors, were one of the few peoples on earth who invented agriculture independently, sometime between 3000 and 2000 BCE. Their crops differed from those of Eurasia and North Africa, however, because their indigenous plants were different. The cereal they cultivated was maize (corn), and beans and squash were also very important. Moreover, unlike Eurasia and Africa, the Americas had no large native mammals that could be domesticated for food.

Mesoamerica, c. 1200 BCE–250 CE

- Olmec heartland, c. 1200–400 BCE
- Olmec site
- Early Maya culture area, c. 400 BCE–250 CE
- Maya site
- *Beans* Domesticated crops and animals

Gulf of Mexico

Beans
Maize
Squash
Dogs
Turkeys

YUCATAN PENINSULA

La Mojarra •

Tres Zapotes

La Venta

NORTHERN LOWLANDS

El Mirador

Cerros

San Bartolo

Caribbean Sea

Balsas R.

Papaloapan R.

San Lorenzo

Usumacinta R.

Grijalva R.

Sierra Madre

ZAPOTEC

SOUTHERN LOWLANDS

MAYAN HIGHLANDS

PACIFIC OCEAN

0   150 Miles
0   150 Kilometers

≡ **MAP 7.2 Mesoamerica, c. 1200 BCE–250 CE** Mesoamerica forms a land bridge between North and South America, yet it is fragmented by mountain ranges and valleys. It was home to a variety of highly developed cultures between 1200 BCE and 250 CE, Olmec and Maya prominent among them.

So the main sources of protein for all Mesoamerican people were hunted animals (rabbits, deer, and iguanas), domesticated turkeys and dogs, and fish.

Although agriculture was not as productive in Mesoamerica as in the river valley cultures of Asia and northern Africa, the Olmecs could concentrate enough resources to construct elaborate ceremonial centers. The earliest such center, San Lorenzo, was inhabited beginning in 1500 BCE. Around 1200 BCE, the people leveled the mountaintop where the settlement was situated and created a platform some 2,500 by 3,300 feet in size and 165 feet higher than the surrounding countryside. On top of this platform they built podiums and pyramids of clay and erected numerous sculptures, including ten massive stone heads, made of the volcanic rock basalt, which the Olmecs could have obtained only in mountains some fifty miles away. The stone heads represented men who must have been important to the people of San Lorenzo, but we do not know their identity.

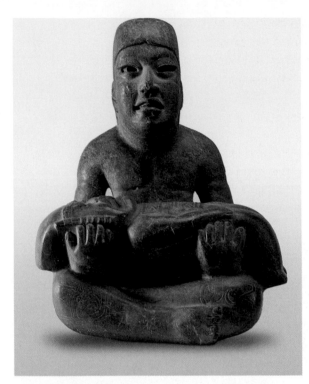

Around 900 BCE, the Olmecs shifted the focus of their building activity fifty-five miles to the northeast to the site that is now called La Venta. Between 800 and 400 BCE, they developed the locale into their most elaborate ceremonial center. At its core stood a clay pyramid with a base measuring 420 by 240 feet and a height of over 108 feet. Bordering the pyramid to the north and south were plazas that contained magnificent stone monuments: colossal heads, massive thrones, stelae decorated with carved relief sculptures, and statues. Also carved from imported stone, the heads in some cases are eleven feet high and weigh twenty tons.

The remains at La Venta tell an intriguing and puzzling story. The stone sculptures were regularly damaged on purpose: faces were erased, arms and heads cut off, and pieces removed. The Olmecs then buried the sculptures and displayed new ones, which indicates that they were responsible for the mutilations. It is possible that the monuments' destruction was part of a ceremony performed at the death of the person portrayed. Speculation about the reasons for these acts continues, however.

Just as we cannot offer verified explanations of Olmec practices, it is difficult to explain the overarching purpose of the complexes at San Lorenzo and La Venta. Although they share certain elements with the cities of Eurasia, they seem not to have been large population centers, as those cities were. They appear instead to have been primarily ceremonial in character, and ideas about what ceremonies took place there often depend on theories about the relationship between the Olmecs and later Mesoamerican cultures, especially the better-known Maya. Ceremonial centers with pyramids and intricate sculptures remained a part of Mesoamerican culture until the Spanish conquest in the sixteenth century CE, and later practices are easier to understand because we have early European accounts and some written Maya evidence. For example, in the classical Maya period of 250–900 CE (discussed in Chapter 10),

☰ **An Olmec Statue** This twenty-two-inch-high statue shows a young man holding a baby-like figure that is usually interpreted as a mythological creature connected to fertility. Babies appear regularly in Olmec art with a downturned mouth and a cleft head. On the basis of later Mayan parallels, scholars think they are associated with maize. The statue is carved from a greenish stone that was reserved for special objects. On the body of the person holding the baby are carved four glyphs (figurative symbols) that are thought to represent other mythological figures.

the ballgame ritual was very important. It appears very likely that the Olmecs played the ballgame, as a dozen rubber balls were found as ritual deposits in a spring to the east of San Lorenzo. Because the game may have been important to the Olmecs, some scholars interpret the culture's colossal sculpted heads as representations of ball players.

There are indications that the Olmec had a system of writing, although the evidence is very limited and its interpretation controversial. A unique stone slab, dating to around 900 BCE according to archaeologists, is covered with what may be written signs, but these do not resemble any other signs from later and better-known scripts. The text is thus fully incomprehensible. Somewhat later Olmec objects contain individual symbols that scholars relate to later Mesoamerican **glyphs**—symbolic characters used to record a word or a syllable in writing—but they cannot decipher them. They resemble the glyphs of later Maya texts, and the inscriptions may or may not have contents similar to the later ones.

It is clear that Olmec society was hierarchical, with an elite who had the power to demand labor from the general population. Based on Maya parallels, many archaeologists believe that the elites could even claim the lives of commoners and that they regularly practiced human sacrifice. The source of the elite's authority is debated. Many Olmec representations show men involved in rituals, which leads some scholars to suggest that Olmec leaders derived command from their role as **shamans**, individuals who have the ability to communicate with nonhuman powers and who safeguard the community's prosperity. Shamans appear in many parts of the world, and throughout history various societies have seen certain persons, often with unusual physical characteristics, as crucial to communication with greater powers. The leaders' authority probably had more secular aspects as well. The ceremonial centers gave prominence to stones imported from distant places, and it is likely that only elites could obtain them. This privilege must have confirmed their special status.

The validity of these scholarly interpretations of Olmec culture and ideology depends strongly on the Olmecs' connection to later Mesoamerican societies. Because their monuments are similar, many scholars see Olmec as the "mother culture" and inspiration of all subsequent Mesoamerican cultures. In this interpretation, the Olmecs would have spread their ideas and practices through trade to regions as distant as the Mexican west coast and El Salvador to the south, where later Mesoamerican cultures flourished. The appearance of Olmec objects and artistic motifs in these regions supports this view. Others disagree, however, and consider the various cultures of Mesoamerica to be of local origin, the result of internal developments.

glyph A figurative symbol, usually carved in stone, that imparts information.

shaman A tribal member who acts as an intermediary between the physical and spiritual worlds.

The Early Maya 400 BCE–250 CE

Olmec culture had disappeared by 400 BCE, for reasons that are unclear to us, and several major Mesoamerican cultures developed to the east and west of the Olmec heartland. One of the best-documented Mesoamerican cultures in the archaeological record was that of the Maya, centered in the Yucatan peninsula in the southeast corner of the Gulf of Mexico (see again Map 7.2). Although the culture achieved its height after 250 CE, it originated earlier, in a time when various early Maya kingdoms existed side by side (see Reading the Past: The La Mojarra Stele). Beginning around 800 BCE, in an area of dense forest, the early Maya developed a number of complexes that included massive stone buildings, pyramids, and platforms. The largest was at El Mirador in the remote jungle of Guatemala, where between 150 BCE and 50 CE the inhabitants built numerous tall pyramids, plazas, platforms, causeways, and elite houses in stone, decorating them with stone reliefs. How such a complex came to be constructed remains a mystery because the area has insufficient agricultural land to support a large labor force.

El Mirador was not the only large Mayan religious complex. Around 50 BCE, the site of Cerros (SEHR-rohs), in a more hospitable environment near the sea, suddenly grew from a small village into a major center. The inhabitants leveled existing houses and on top of the rubble they erected a temple, surrounding it with plazas, pyramids, causeways, and other monuments characteristic of Mayan settlements. The transformation occurred so abruptly that it must have resulted from the arrival of some powerful authority, who ordered the construction of a new settlement.

Early Mayan sites contain a few glyphs that scholars can connect to a later stage of the Mayan script. Much of the interpretation of the early inscriptions remains uncertain, but they clearly focus on the deeds of kings, especially in war. By understanding the calendar, scholars can assign precise dates to some early Mayan monuments. For example, one stele (stone tablet) was carved in the year 197 CE. It shows a leader, whose name in the accompanying text is expressed by the combination of a bone and a rabbit skull, which scholars read as Bak T'ul. He is dressed as the rain god and surrounded by scenes of human sacrifice, fertility, and renewal. Beneath his hand are the severed bodies of three victims going down into the underworld.

As in Eurasia, all the evidence indicates that a political and social elite in Mesoamerica held power over the mass of the population whose labor they commanded. The leaders of these societies commissioned representations showing them participating in rituals that often involved bloodletting and human sacrifice and probably gave them a special connection to the gods. Men and women pierced

READING THE PAST

The La Mojarra Stele

Although the first Mesoamerican writing dates to about 900 BCE, historians cannot read the earliest inscriptions with certainty, because they often do not know what language the texts record. As we saw, there are traces of Olmec writing and several subsequent Mesoamerican cultures left us inscribed objects. Scholars do find continuity between these writings and the later, better-known classic Mayan script. For example, many topics addressed in classic Mayan inscriptions, such as warfare and the glorification of the leader, also appear much earlier. Moreover, the calendar used was the same, which allows scholars to date inscriptions with confidence.

In 1986 archaeologists discovered one early inscription on this stele, or stone tablet, at La Mojarra (la moh-HAH-rah), in the province of Veracruz in eastern Mexico, a region the Olmecs had occupied before the inscription was carved (see again Map 7.2). It contains two dates, 143 and 156 CE. The language of the inscription is a matter of debate among scholars, as is the exact content, but all agree that the man with the elaborate cloak and headdress must be some kind of leader. They speculate that the stele deals with issues of sacrifice and war in parallel with later Mayan inscriptions, which often deal with these concerns. The

The La Mojarra Inscription, c. 160 CE

man's ornate headdress resembles that of Maya war leaders. The La Mojarra inscription raises various puzzling questions, however. Why is this the only lengthy inscription from early Mesoamerica so far discovered? Is its language related to that of the Olmecs? And what is the relationship between this script and the later Mayan?

Examining the Evidence

1. In the absence of knowledge of the language, by what means have scholars sought to interpret the La Mojarra inscription?

2. What enables scholars to relate the inscription to the Olmecs?

themselves with stingray spines, thorns, or lancets, especially through the tongue, ears, and genitals. They usually collected the blood on cloth-like paper, which they burned so that the gods could consume the blood in the form of smoke.

The early Mayan cultures arose in a range of natural environments, as Map 7.2 reveals, and people's choice of a particular location for settlement was probably connected to their ideas about the universe and the king's role in connecting the human and supernatural worlds. We can scarcely imagine the massive amounts of labor and coordination involved in early Mayan building projects; they were undertaken either without bureaucratic accounting records or with documents that have been lost over time. Such accomplishments as these led to the network of Mayan city-states in the classical age, which we will study in Chapter 10.

Andean Peoples 900 BCE–600 CE

Along the west coast of South America runs a narrow finger of land that contains an amazing variety of ecological zones (see Map 7.3). Here the Pacific Ocean and the tops of the Andes Mountains, which can reach heights of over four miles, are only sixty miles apart. The coastal area is arid except where rivers run through it, but marine resources are abundant, because the current that brings cold water from the South Pole carries vital nutrients that feed a wide variety of fish, shellfish, and sea mammals. Thanks to this sea life, early Andean coastal residents did not need to practice agriculture.

At irregular intervals this cold-water current is reversed by a global climatic event called *El Niño* (ehl NEEN-yoh) (Spanish for "the Christ Child," as the name derives from its occurrence around Christmas). When El Niño appears, warm water from the north chases away the marine life, while rainstorms sweep across and devastate the countryside. These times of crisis may have led to social and political upheaval among Andean peoples throughout history.

Perhaps to offset the uncertainties of marine supplies, the peoples of the Andes started to farm plants on the mountain slopes, potatoes possibly as early as 4400 BCE and maize after 1500 BCE. Farther up the mountains they herded alpacas and llamas, the only domesticated beasts of burden in South America. The tops of the Andes Mountains are so high that only people who have physically adjusted to the scarcity of oxygen can be active there. As the peoples of the Andes adapted to local conditions and environmental change, unique communities evolved that reflected the challenges and opportunities the region's ecology presented.

Early Andean peoples developed complex societies with a large array of intricate cultural expressions. One such local culture emerged in valleys of the Norte

El Niño A periodic change in the sea current in the Pacific Ocean west of South America, which brings about severe climatic change in regions in and near the Pacific.

≡ **MAP 7.3   South America, c. 3000 BCE–600 CE** Perched on steep mountain slopes overlooking the Pacific Ocean, inhabitants of the Andes Mountains established a sequence of cultures, each one characterized by unique remains. After a period of diversity, the Chavín culture unified the region from around 900 to 200 BCE, apparently on the basis of shared ideology. The subsequent Moche state, flourishing from around 200 to 600 CE, used military might to impose itself upon multiple populations.

Chico region on the coast some one hundred miles north of Peru's modern capital, Lima, where between 3000 and 1800 BCE people constructed some twenty large ceremonial centers. They built platforms on artificial mounds with circle-shaped plazas partially sunken into the ground. The people of this culture did not yet make pottery, but they used gourds as containers, sometimes deco-rated with the image of a god holding a staff. They lived off the resources from the sea and practiced agriculture inland, including cotton, which they grew with irrigation.

Around 900 BCE, the cultural diversity of the Andes gave way to relative uni-formity when a new culture, called Chavín (cha-BEAN), came to dominate a wide area of north and central Peru. In the Chavín culture, people used the same style of pottery decoration, similar artifacts, and the same architecture for about 700 years. The ceramics of Chavín show remarkable skill; the artisans shaped the vessels in many different forms, including elaborately decorated human and animal figures. The animals came from different ecological zones within the region, including on the east side of the Andes, which indicates that the Chavín people traveled widely. They also refined metalworking techniques, using pure gold or alloys of gold with silver or copper. At the site that gave the culture its name, Chavín de Huantar, 170 miles north of Lima, stood a stone temple com-plex with galleries, stairs, and ramps looking out over a plaza that was partly sunken into the ground. Fantastical stone carvings decorated the complex, including sculpted heads of humans, birds, and canines, as well as reliefs of felines, serpents, and supernatural beings made up of the body parts of various creatures.

The Chavín culture inspired peoples over a wide stretch of the Andean region, including those of the south-central Peruvian peninsula of Paracas (pah-RAH-kas), 150 miles south of Lima. This area is especially famous for its long history of textile production. Even before the introduction of agriculture, people in this region wove fibers from cacti, grasses, and other plants into textiles. When they domesticated cotton around 3500 BCE, it became the main plant fiber for weaving, but people also used alpaca and llama hair.

In the late first millennium BCE, the introduction of tapestry weaving and new techniques of dyeing revolutionized textile production. The weavers pro-duced intricate patterns and figures using multicolored threads and further decorated the cloth with feathers, metal strips, and other embellishments. The most remarkable textiles produced by the inhabitants of Paracas are those used in the burials of wealthy people. The dead sat in a fetal position, wrapped in thick layers of multicolored cotton garments. These included embroidered mantles, tunics, and headbands that depicted mythical creatures and humans in ornate dress. The resulting mummy bundles were covered with white cotton sheets and placed in an underground vault, with up to forty individuals in one vault.

The similar artistic motifs in the Chavín area and beyond suggest the region shared a common belief system that accorded great significance to animals and the forces of nature. Because there is no evidence of military conquest, most likely ideology produced this cultural unity. Around 200 BCE, however, this unity ended, and the appearance of massive defensive structures around settlements suggests that wars may have torn the different peoples apart. After a period of disintegration, a new set of states arose, but the basis for control differed dramatically from that of the Chavín culture. One such state, in northern Peru, is called Moche (MOH-che) today, after the river in its center (see again Map 7.3). Flourishing from around 200 to 600 CE, the Moche state was highly militaristic and hierarchical, as evidenced by its art, which teems with brutal images of warfare, torture, and other forms of violence.

Moche Vessel The Moche from the South American Andes are particularly famed for the skills of their potters. Many vessels represent human heads, probably those of the men who commissioned the potters. They show them as warriors, strengthening the view that the Moche were a militaristic society.

The Moche economy was based on an elaborate system of irrigation agriculture. The farmers cultivated a mixed crop of maize, beans, squash, and chili peppers and fertilized the fields with guano (bird dung). With increased resources gained through agricultural development and military muscle, more people could live in cities, where they constructed huge ceremonial complexes.

At the Moche capital in Cerro Blanco, in northwestern Peru, the people built two enormous mud-brick temples in pyramid shapes: the Pyramid of the Sun and the Pyramid of the Moon. The leaders of Moche society lived on top of these giant pyramids. But the structures also formed a ceremonial complex in which human sacrifice was central, as was the case in Mayan culture. Excavations of nearby plazas have revealed the remains of seventy individuals who were killed and dismembered, their body parts having been thrown off the platforms. Human sacrifice is also prominent in the representational arts of the Moche. Humans in bird costumes slit the throats of prisoners, drank their blood, and cut off their heads, feet, and hands. The goal of the many wars the Moche appear to have waged was probably not to kill enemies on the battlefield but to capture them and bring them home for these sacrifices.

Other Moche archaeological sites had similar ceremonial complexes. At Sipán (SHEE-pan) in northern Peru, tombs were also connected with human sacrifice. Their occupants were buried with enormous amounts of grave goods—including pottery, jewelry, and textiles—as well as other humans. In the richest tomb, said to be of "the lord of Sipán," eight individuals accompanied the dead, including three adult men, one adult woman, three young women, and one child. On top of the burial chamber lay the body of a young man whose feet had been amputated, seemingly to prevent his escape. The garments of the tomb occupants suggest that they were the central figures in the sacrificial ceremonies, as represented in Moche art.

The Moche state went into decline in the sixth century CE, probably due to natural disasters. By 800 CE other states would arise to replace it. Around 1400 the entire Andean zone would be incorporated into the Inca Empire (discussed in Chapter 15), which would continue some of the practices the Moche people had begun.

Gatherer-Hunters of North America 800 BCE–400 CE

The vast North American continent contains many varied natural environments, and for millennia after humans arrived the relatively few inhabitants survived by hunting and collecting wild resources (see Map 10.3, page 374). Hunters in the Great Plains, for example, killed large bison herds after driving them into closed-off canyons. At times the meat was so abundant that they butchered only the best parts. These folk also gathered plants and hunted small game, however; the bison were caught mostly in the fall to provide meat for the winter months.

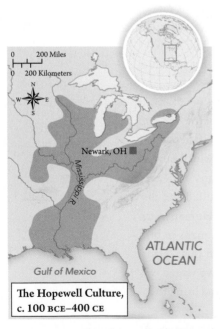

The Hopewell Culture, c. 100 BCE–400 CE

≡ **The Hopewell Culture, c. 100 BCE–400 CE**

Eastern North America, between the Great Plains and the Atlantic Ocean, was a vast wooded region with a network of rivers centered on the Mississippi Valley. Although this region had great agricultural potential because of its rich alluvial soils, until 400 CE most inhabitants survived by hunting and gathering the rich wild resources. They made simple pottery and crafted artwork, often using materials that had to be imported. These materials were traded among the small communities that lived throughout the region. The men who arranged for the trade became community leaders and settled disputes in the mostly egalitarian societies. They or others may also have been shamans.

The people of these communities joined forces to construct large earthworks, mostly low mounds that covered tombs, but also fortifications and platforms for buildings. The areas inside these fortifications were used for ceremonial rather than residential purposes. The largest known site of the period, at Newark in modern Ohio, belonged to what archaeologists call the Hopewell culture, which lasted from about 100 BCE to 400 CE. This site contains geometric earthworks spread over an area of four and a half square miles, which include a Great Circle, an Octagon, and near perfect square enclosure, the Wright Earthworks. Throughout the site are burial mounds, that contained many crafted objects, often in hoards. The materials came from distant sources: shell from the Gulf of Mexico, copper from the Great Lakes, mica from the Carolinas, and obsidian (a glasslike volcanic rock) from the Rocky Mountains. The earthworks were connected through pathways, and the entire complex seems to have had ritual functions with pilgrims guided in a specific sequence. The find of a stone sculpture thought to represent a shaman dressed as a bear suggests that people came to honor the dead who held leading positions in the society. Archaeologists interpret features of the site to display intricate knowledge of geometry, as the circumference of the Great Circle is equal to the perimeter of the Wright Earthworks, and possibly astronomy.

≡ **A Shaman of the Hopewell Culture** This small ceramic figurine was discovered near the Ohio River and dates between 200 BCE and 500 CE. The knot on the man's forehead may be a horn and probably represents a shaman, someone who acted as an intermediary between humans and the forces of nature and the gods.

Thus, in ancient times various regions in the Americas developed cultures of different levels of complexity. All this took place without an extensive written tradition—in Mesoamerica the few examples of writing are brief official statements regarding wars and kingship, and in the Andes and North America no documents are preserved for this period. Although the absence of writing denies us access to many aspects of these cultures, archaeology provides us with abundant evidence of the energy and diversity of ancient American societies.

Peoples of the Pacific Islands

↘ **FOCUS** What do their material remains tell us about Pacific Islanders' society and culture?

The Pacific Ocean, stretching 12,500 miles along the equator, is dotted with a myriad of small islands, mostly of volcanic origin or taking the form of **atolls**, rings of coral (see Map 7.4). Although their natural resources are limited, humans inhabit some 1,500 of the 25,000 islands, the result of a colonization process that spanned millennia. These people did not create scripts, so their written histories begin with European descriptions from the eighteenth century CE, such as the account by Sir Joseph Banks quoted at the start of this chapter. Archaeology shows that people in this part of the world had the initiative and courage to sail across enormous distances to discover new lands—and that they brought their agricultural lifestyle with them.

Agricultural Livelihoods

The early inhabitants of the Pacific Islands derived much of their food from the sea, but they also cultivated plants and herded animals that their ancestors brought with them during migrations. Only a few native plants and fruits of the Pacific Islands became important foods; the islanders' main crops—coconut, taro, yam, banana, and breadfruit—were not native: farmers had imported them from elsewhere. The peoples of the Pacific Islands promoted their growth using simple yet efficient techniques. For example, taro, a plant with an edible root, requires a very wet soil, so in some places the islanders created irrigation systems. By contrast, the yam, another root plant, needs a much drier soil, and the people drained marshes to grow it. Their domesticated animals were few—chickens, pigs, and dogs—but they were found on all inhabited islands. We see, then, that human needs profoundly shaped the ecology of the Pacific Islands.

Scholars believe that much of the colonization of new islands was deliberate, displacing the earlier theory that drifters settled the islands by accident. As with Bantu migrants in Africa, Polynesian peoples set out with the plants and animals they intended to grow and breed, and they established permanent dwellings soon after arriving in the new land. Their migration required sailing, sometimes across great distances. In some cases they encountered populations that had settled there before, and the interactions between the two groups varied with mutual

atoll A small ring-like island made of coral.

≡ **MAP 7.4   The Pacific Islands, c. 4000 BCE–200 BCE**   One of the most remarkable migrations of ancient times was that of speakers of Austronesian languages, who over many centuries expanded from southern China and Taiwan to colonize islands throughout the Pacific Ocean. They often set sail in small boats, crossing seas without knowing when they would encounter new land. They took domesticated animals and plants with them and thus spread agricultural practices throughout the vast island region.

influences. In other cases they were the first to colonize an island and continued their practices without outside influences. So in the Pacific Islands, too, a great diversity of cultural practices is visible.

Peopling the Islands

All reconstructions of prehistoric migrations rely on a mixture of linguistic and archaeological evidence to determine which modern populations share common ancestors and when they became separated from one another. The dating of events is especially problematic because it relies on scant archaeological evidence.

The peoples of the Pacific Islands speak languages that belong to the Austronesian family. Some 1,000 Austronesian languages exist, and they show many similarities. For example, the inhabitants of three island groups in Polynesia use almost all the same terms for the following English words:

English	Society Islands (includes Tahiti)	Tonga	New Zealand
two	rooa	looa	rooa
five	reema	neema	reema
eye	matta	matta	matta
to drink	ainoo	ainoo	ainoo

The indigenous peoples of Taiwan and of some areas in southern China also speak Austronesian languages, as do the inhabitants of Madagascar, an island off the southeast coast of Africa. Linguistic analysis indicates that Austronesian speakers migrated in several waves. The first speakers of Austronesian languages lived in southern China and Taiwan, where the largest variety of such languages exists today. These early Austronesians were farmers who grew millet, rice, and sugar cane; they lived in wooden houses, used boats, and kept pigs, dogs, and chickens. They knew how to make pottery but did not use metals, and they had a typical Neolithic lifestyle that they shared with the people of farther inland China (see Chapter 3). Around 3000 BCE this homogenous population started to break up, and some people migrated south by sea to the Philippines, where they discovered tropical plants for cultivation, such as breadfruit, coconut, bananas, yams, and taro (see again Map 7.4). They improved the canoes they used, probably by adding sails and outriggers (beams on the side that greatly increased stability). These new technologies enabled the people to spread rapidly and widely. In subsequent centuries Austronesian speakers settled on the islands of Southeast Asia to the west and of Melanesia and western Polynesia to the east, a process that seems to have ended around 750 BCE. Then there was a pause of about a thousand years before further expansion occurred around 400 CE, as we will see in Chapter 10. Many of the islands at which the Austronesians arrived had only small gatherer-hunter communities that were easily displaced. On the large island of New Guinea, however, indigenous people had developed agriculture in the highlands long before the arrival of the Austronesians, and with their larger numbers they restricted Austronesian settlement to areas on the shores.

The migrating Austronesians took with them a mixture of technologies and styles that gives us another means of using the archaeological record to trace their movements. From 1400 to 200 BCE, those living in Melanesia surrounded themselves with material goods that archaeologists identify as belonging to the Lapita (lah-PEE-tah) culture. Most distinctive is the pottery—although the pots were poorly made and not well fired, they were extensively decorated by incising lines or impressing comb-like toothed instruments, which left a series of dots. The lines formed geometric motifs and occasionally human features such as faces. The designs resembled the body tattoos popular among Austronesian speakers.

The pottery, fishhooks, and other implements of the Lapita culture spread eastward from Melanesia into western Polynesia by 1000 BCE. The migration was amazingly fast: scholars estimate that they explored 2,800 miles of the ocean over as few as fifteen to twenty-five human generations. In the end, Lapita culture appeared across 4,050 miles, from northeastern New Guinea to Samoa. Although some pots were traded among islands, local artisans produced most pottery using the same techniques as their forebears. After 750 BCE the quality of their pottery declined even further, however, and by the beginning of the common era some Polynesians stopped producing pottery altogether.

The Polynesians' decision to abandon the use of pottery is unique in world history. It is easily understandable, however, because atolls lack the clay needed to make it. On other islands, however, people consciously decided to stop using pots even when clay was present. Instead of boiling foods, they baked them in underground ovens, and for storage, drinking cups, and the like, the islanders used coconut shells, which were readily available. In short, they had no need to continue using advanced pottery technology.

The people of the Lapita culture inhabited small villages, living in houses they sometimes built on stilts (see Seeing the Past: The Archaeological Site of Talepakemalai). They grew taro, yams, and other tropical plants and kept dogs, pigs, and chickens. They were mostly self-sufficient, with trade in obsidian for stone tools the only essential link among the islands. Because of their self-sufficiency, and the influence of the indigenous populations on the settlers, Lapita communities developed many local characteristics, making Melanesia a highly diverse world.

☰ **The Lapita Culture, c. 1400–200** BCE

SEEING THE PAST

The Archaeological Site of Talepakemalai

In the absence of written texts, scholars reconstruct the history of past peoples by examining the physical remains they left behind. As an example, we can look at the Lapita site of Talepakemalai on the coral island of Eloaua off Papua New Guinea, which archaeologists excavated with great care (see again Map 7.4). In the center of this atoll they discovered the remains of the largest Lapita settlement known to date, covering some 870,000 square feet (or twenty acres), the size of fifteen U.S. football fields. Although the remains today are fully on the island, archaeologists discovered that when it was first built, around 1500 BCE, the village had two distinct sections: one on land, the other in the sea. Up to sixty-six feet offshore were houses on stilts whose inhabitants reached them either by canoe or over short bridges. They dumped their waste in the lagoon around the houses, which allowed archaeologists to determine that they were relatively well off. They owned elaborately decorated Lapita pottery, but neighbors who lived in houses on the island had only plain pots. The inhabitants of the stilt houses also discarded food waste, and analysis of the seeds and shells shows that they ate coconuts, candlenuts (the seed of a tropical tree), pandanus (conelike fruits from a tree of the same name), and other fruits. They also ate shellfish, turtles, birds, porpoises, and occasionally pigs.

Archaeologists also determined that the sea level dropped around 800 BCE, which forced these people to shift the location of the stilt houses farther out to open water. Eventually they abandoned the village completely and moved to another part of the island. Although many questions remain about the inhabitants of Talepakemalai, the reading of their archaeological remains gives us some fascinating insights into their lives.

COUNTERPOINT: The Voiced and Voiceless in Ancient Literate Societies

⬎ **FOCUS** To what extent does a society's literacy or nonliteracy affect our study of it?

When we study peoples of the ancient past, we find a wealth of visible, physical artifacts, which can be astonishingly rich and appealing and tell us much about their

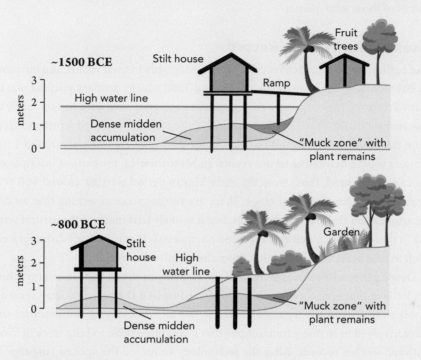

Examining the Evidence

1. Why would the wealthier people of this community have lived offshore?

2. How does the history of Talepakemalai show the effect of changes in the natural environment on human behavior?

3. Generally speaking, what can archaeological remains tell us, and in what respect will they always remain silent?

creators. But historians are especially attracted to written documentation because it can reveal elements of ancient cultures about which there is no other evidence, such as the languages people spoke, the names they gave themselves and the things that surrounded them, their literary creativity, and much more. The advent of writing in the various cultures of the world is thus an important turning point because it opens new pathways for us to approach the peoples of the past.

We should not, however, overestimate the impact of writing on ancient societies. In all the cultures we have studied so far, literacy remained a rare skill. The inequality of access to literacy can distort the historian's picture of the past because the voices of those who wrote are so much clearer and so much louder than the voices of those who did not.

Uses of the Written Record

The earliest known written records vary considerably in their nature and purpose. In Babylonia, where script appeared around 3200 BCE, its primary purpose was to record the exchange of goods. The Egyptians soon afterward used script mainly to commemorate the deeds of kings. In China, the earliest preserved written sources were the oracle-bone inscriptions that kings started to commission around 1200 BCE as a way to determine future events. In Mesoamerica, the earliest inscriptions we can understand, those from the early Mayan period starting around 400 BCE, dealt with the heroic acts of kings. These are the purposes of writing that we can ascertain from the preserved records. But it is likely that much of the earliest writing in these and other cultures appeared on materials that have since disintegrated, such as tree bark, and are thus lost from the historical record.

Despite these differences in focus of the earliest preserved writings, many scholars believe that economic needs everywhere inspired the desire to keep records. Those needs began when people started to live together in large communities and were involved in so many transactions that it was impossible to keep track of them without written records. After the technology to record the spoken language in written form had been invented for administrative purposes, people could write down anything, and in most cultures the purposes of writing multiplied quickly after script came into use.

The Voiceless Many

To learn how to read and write required training, from which most people were excluded. Moreover, there are degrees of literacy that require different periods of training. In a culture such as that of classical Greece, for example, many citizens of Athens may have been able to read basic words such as signs and the names of people. But they might not have managed to comprehend a treatise of Aristotle. And consider this: the citizenry of Athens was a highly select group of landowning men. Among those excluded from citizenship, literacy was even more restricted.

Whether a person was included in or excluded from literate life depended mostly on economic factors. Only those who were involved with activities beyond a subsistence level would have needed to record anything in writing. These people would join large-scale organizations such as palaces, temples, and monasteries that kept accounts of their holdings. Furthermore, some of those propertied individuals, or people supported by them, could engage in activities that did not produce economic benefit, such as composing plays and epics. The large majority of these people were men because, for the most part, males alone received an education.

In all early literate societies some women did write, however, and their writings constitute a small portion of the material that historians use as sources. A handful of the earliest figures in world literature are women. The first known author in history is Enheduanna, a Babylonian princess, who around 2400 BCE composed several poems in the Sumerian language (see Chapter 2). Likewise, in China of the first century CE, the historian Ban Biao gave his daughter a literary education. As we saw in Chapter 5, Ban Zhao finished her father's *History of the Han Dynasty* and wrote other works of literature.

One of the most renowned poets of Greek antiquity was Sappho (c. 630–570 BCE). The daughter of an aristocratic family, Sappho wrote poetry about religious festivals, military celebrations, and life at court. In her moving poems she focused on her emotions, which often involved the young women who were her friends and companions. Due to a military coup, her family was forced to leave their home on the Aegean island of Lesbos for a period of exile in Sicily, which she described with anger. But she was already so famous that the inhabitants of Sicily welcomed her with great ceremony.

Much of Sappho's poetry has been lost through the ages, but the pieces that remain show a remarkable sensitivity and ability to describe human feelings. Fortunately, scholars continue to discover some of her poems on fragmentary manuscripts preserved in the dry sands of Egypt. One such discovery on a papyrus from the third century BCE, made in 2004, contains a description of old age:

> (You for) the fragrant-bosomed (Muses') lovely gifts
> (be zealous,) girls, (and the) clear melodious lyre:
> (but my once tender) body old age now
> (has seized;) my hair's turned (white) instead of dark;
> my heart's grown heavy, my knees will not support me,
> that once on a time were fleet for the dance as fawns.
> This state I oft bemoan; but what's to do?
> Not to grow old, being human, there's no way.
> Tithonus once, the tale was, rose-armed Dawn,
> love-smitten, carried off to the world's end,
> handsome and young then, yet in time grey age
> o'ertook him, husband of immortal wife.[3]

Outside the urban centers, in the villages and temporary pastoral settlements where most ancient peoples lived, very few, if any, were literate. Thus their lives are often not revealed to us, or we view their experience only through the eyes of urban

A Fragment of Sappho's Poetry The dry climate of Egypt allowed numerous papyri to be preserved, including many that contain ancient Greek literature. The fragmentary papyrus shown here, dating from the third century BCE, contains the text of a poem that Sappho wrote around 600 BCE. It was only in 2004 that a scholar recognized that the fragment recorded a previously unknown work from the famed Greek poet.

dwellers with very different concerns and lifestyles. Sima Qian's quote about pastoral nomads at the beginning of Chapter 3 is just one of many statements of this nature.

These exclusions from the technology of writing limit modern historians' view of the peoples of the past. Scholars can rarely close this gap through the archaeological record: archaeologists seldom excavate the remains of villages, and the temporary camps of nomads left virtually no traces. In investigations of urban remains, historians can focus on aspects traditionally associated with women, such as kitchens in the houses. But they must be careful not to impose a presumed gender division of labor upon all peoples of the past. Within ancient literate societies there are always large numbers of people whose voices we cannot hear.

Conclusion

Were we to imagine a woman making a tour around the world in the year 1 CE (an improbable adventure), we could reconstruct who her hosts would have been and how she would have been received for many stages of the voyage. She would have stayed in a city only very rarely, but when she did we can picture her as the guest of a courtier of the Roman, Parthian, and Han emperors as she made her way across Eurasia, and we could even think of a name for that courtier. In Mesoamerica she might have seen the ceremonial centers of the early Maya, people whose names we do not know. Most days, however, she would have visited people in small villages or in temporary settlements whose names we cannot even guess. Many of her hosts in Eurasia, Africa, the Pacific Islands, and the Americas would have been farmers, but others would have foraged or raised herds of animals to feed themselves.

At a distance of more than 2,000 years, the details of the histories of most of the world's inhabitants in the year 1 CE are vague to us, but there is much that we do know. A crucial distinction in our ability to study the peoples of that past is whether they wrote. Few literate cultures existed. The archaeological remains of cultures without writing show us, however, how much they could accomplish, even in areas where in other cultures writing was crucial. The Polynesian sailors Joseph Banks described at the start of this chapter could navigate without the written records or maps that were indispensable to that eighteenth-century European explorer.

All over the world, the foundations of later histories developed in the long period from the evolution of the human species to 500 CE. For their cultural and intellectual lives, people in Europe, the Middle East, and South and East Asia still rely on the creations of their ancestors. So, too, do people whose ancestors did not write. In ancient times, people all over the globe contributed to the world that we live in today.

review

The major global development in this chapter: The evolution of ancient cultures without writing and their fundamental role in world history.

Important Events	
c. 3000 BCE	Start of migration of the Bantu in Africa
c. 3000–1800 BCE	Norte Chico culture in the Andes
c. 3000–750 BCE	First wave of Austronesian migrations
c. 1400–200 BCE	Lapita culture in the Pacific Ocean
c. 1200–400 BCE	Olmec culture in Mesoamerica
c. 900–200 BCE	Chavín culture in Mesoamerica
c. 800 BCE–**200** CE	Nok culture in West Africa

Important Events	
c. 400 BCE–250 CE	Early Maya culture in Mesoamerica
c. 100 BCE–400 CE	Hopewell culture in eastern North America
c. 200–600 CE	Moche culture in the Andes
c. 400 CE	Bantu arrival in southern Africa
c. 400–1200 CE	Second wave of Austronesian migrations

KEY TERMS

atoll (p. 258)

Bantu (p. 240)

El Niño (p. 252)

glyph (p. 249)

prehistory (p. 236)

savanna (p. 238)

shaman (p. 249)

CHAPTER OVERVIEW QUESTIONS

1. How does the presence or absence of writing influence how we study ancient cultures?

2. Why did the ancient cultures of sub-Saharan Africa, the Americas, and the Pacific often show similar developments in spite of their isolation from one another?

3. How is the spread of peoples, languages, and technologies interrelated, and in what ways can we study these processes?

MAKING CONNECTIONS

1. Consider the agricultural techniques and resources of the inhabitants of Africa, the Americas, and the Pacific. What do the similarities and differences reveal about the development of their cultures?

2. Why did Eurasian societies develop the features we associate with civilization before their counterparts elsewhere in the world?

3. What are the similarities and differences between the major cities of Eurasia and the ceremonial centers of the Americas?

DOING HISTORY

Argument

Certain aspects of human behavior appear constantly throughout world history, and they always had important repercussions and continue to have so today. An example of this is migration, the movement of a substantial number of people from one part of the world to another. We have seen how migrations out of Africa spread human ancestors and the modern human species across the globe and have encountered several other population movements in other chapters. The phenomenon will reappear in later chapters of this book and remains a major issue in contemporary affairs.

1. Many of the migrations discussed so far, including those of the Bantu and Polynesians, happened without any written sources about them. Can you make an argument for how later and better-documented migrations can help us explain these particular cases in the past?

2. Is it valid to use knowledge about migrations in the past in modern debates about migration? Why or why not?

For further research into the topics covered in this chapter, see the Bibliography at the end of the book.

PART 2

Crossroads and Cultures
500–1450 CE

≡ No mere spectator sport, the Mesoamerican ballgame, which spread as far as northeastern North America, was charged with powerful ritual and religious meaning. Maya myths associate the ballgame with the Hero Twins' triumph over the gods of the underworld and with the gift of agriculture. This stone disk, which dates from about 590 and once marked the site of a ball court in the modern Mexican province of Chiapas, displays a ballplayer striking the ball with his hip. The headdress and inscriptions suggest that the ballplayer is a royal figure reenacting the feats of the Hero Twins.

The new age in world history that began around 500 CE marked a decisive break from the "classical" era of antiquity. The passing of classical civilizations in the Mediterranean, China, and India shared a number of causes, most notably invasions by nomads from the Central Asian steppes. As the once mighty empires of Rome, Han China, and Gupta India fragmented into a multitude of competing states, cultural revolutions ensued. Confidence in the values and institutions of the classical era was shattered, opening the way for fresh ideas. Christianity, Buddhism, Hinduism, and the new creed of Islam spread far beyond their original circles of believers.

The spread of foreign religions and the lifestyles and livelihoods they carried with them gave birth to distinctive regional societies. By 1000, Europe had taken shape as a coherent society and culture even as it became divided between the Roman and Byzantine Christian churches. Modern East Asia—rooted in the literary and philosophical traditions of China but assuming distinctive national forms—likewise emerged during the first millennium CE. Indian civilization expanded into Southeast Asia and acquired a new unity expressed through the common language of Sanskrit. The rapid expansion of Islam across Asia, Africa, and even parts of Europe demonstrated the power of a shared religious identity to transcend political and cultural boundaries.

We also see the formation of regional societies in other parts of the world. Migrations, the development of states, and commercial exchanges with the Islamic world transformed African societies and brought them into more sustained contact with one another. The concentration of political power in the hands of the ruling elites in Mesoamerica and the Andean region led to the founding of mighty city-states. Even in North America and the Pacific Ocean—worlds without states—migration and economic exchange fostered common social practices and livelihoods.

Nomad invasions and political disintegration disrupted economic life in the old imperial heartlands, but long-distance trade flourished as never before. The consolidation of nomad empires and merchant networks stretching across Central Asia culminated in the heyday of the overland "Silk Road" linking China to the Mediterranean world. The Indian Ocean, too, emerged as a crossroads of trade and cultural diffusion. After 1000, most of Eurasia and Africa enjoyed several centuries of sustained economic improvement. Rising agricultural productivity fed population expansion, and cities and urban culture thrived with the growth of trade and industry.

Prosperity and urban vitality also stimulated intellectual change. Much of the new wealth was channeled into the building of religious monuments and institutions. New institutions of learning and scholarship—such as Christian Europe's universities, the madrasas of the Islamic world, and civil service examinations and government schooling in China—spawned both conformity and dissent. Yet cross-cultural interaction also brought conflict, war, and schism. Tensions between Christians and Muslims erupted into violent clashes with the onset of the Crusades. The rise of steppe empires—above all, the explosive expansion of the Mongol Empires—likewise transformed political and cultural landscapes. In the 1340s the Black Death pandemic devastated the populations and economies of Europe and the central Islamic lands.

By 1400, however, signs of recovery were conspicuously visible. Powerful national states emerged in Europe and China, restoring some measure of stability. Strong Islamic states held sway in Egypt, Anatolia (modern Turkey), Iran, and India. The European Renaissance—the intense outburst of intellectual and artistic creativity envisioned as a "rebirth" of the classical civilization of Greece and Rome—flickered to life, sparked by the economic vigor of the Italian city-states. Maritime Asia, spared the ravages of the Black Death, continued to flourish while Eurasia's agrarian economies struggled to regain their earlier prosperity.

In 1453, Muslim Ottoman armies seized Constantinople and deposed the Byzantine Christian emperor, cutting the last thread of connection to the ancient world and posing a direct threat to Latin Christendom as well. Denied direct access to the rich trade with Asia, European monarchs and merchants shifted their attention to the Atlantic world. Yet just as Columbus's discovery of the "New World"—in fact, a very ancient one—came as a surprise, so too the idea of a new world order centered on Europe—the modern world order—was still unimaginable. ■

The Worlds of Christianity and Islam

400–1000

≡ **World in the Making** The emperors of Constantinople had grand ambitions to rebuild the Roman Empire on new foundations of Christian faith. They displayed special devotion to the Virgin Mary, the patron saint of their capital. This mosaic in the Hagia Sophia ("Holy Wisdom"), Constantinople's greatest Christian church, shows Emperor Constantine (right) offering a model of the city to Mary and the infant Jesus. Emperor Justinian I (left) presents a model of the Hagia Sophia, which he rebuilt in 562.

backstory

As we saw in Chapter 6, the Roman Empire enjoyed a second lease on life in the early fourth century under Constantine, who reinvigorated imperial rule and adopted Christianity as an official religion. But the western part of the empire, wracked by internal conflicts and Germanic invasions, crumbled in the fifth century. By contrast, the emperors at Constantinople, buoyed by the diverse and resilient economy of the eastern Mediterranean, continued to preside over a strong state, which historians call the Byzantine Empire. The resurgent Persian Empire of the Sasanid dynasty struggled with the Romans for control of Syria, Mesopotamia, and Armenia. The rise of Islam in the seventh century would transform political, religious, and economic life from the Mediterranean to Persia.

IN 550, MÉDARD, the bishop of Noyon, northeast of Paris, faced a dilemma. Radegund, the pious wife of the Germanic king Clothar, had come to him seeking to become a nun. But Médard was reluctant to offend Clothar, his patron and benefactor, and the king's men had threatened to drag him from his church should he attempt to place a nun's veil on their queen. According to her biographers, Radegund, sizing up the situation, entered the sacristy, put on a monastic garb, and proceeded straight to the altar, saying, "If you shrink from consecrating me, and fear man more than God, pastor, He will require [my] soul from your hand." Chastened, Médard ordained her as a deaconess.

Radegund (520–587) was the daughter of a rival German king who was a bitter enemy of Clothar's tribe, the Franks. When Radegund was eleven, the Franks slaughtered her family and took her prisoner. Later she was forced to marry Clothar and became, in her words, "a captive maid given to a hostile lord." Raised a Christian, Radegund took refuge in religion. Even before renouncing secular life, "she was more Christ's partner than her husband's companion."[1] Her biographers describe in great detail the physical torments she inflicted on herself, her ministrations to the poor and the sick, the miracles she performed, and the rich gifts she bestowed on the church and the needy. After Clothar's death, Radegund founded a convent at Poitiers and took up a life of full seclusion.

By Radegund's day, Christianity had become deeply entrenched in all of the Roman Empire's former territories and beyond. Pagan societies on the fringes of the old empire, such as the roving Germanic tribes and the Slavic peoples of eastern Europe, gradually adopted the Christian religion as well. Even the Norse Vikings, at first reviled as the mortal enemies of Christianity, remade themselves into models of Christian piety.

Unity proved elusive in Christendom (the realm of Christianity), however. Radegund's contemporary Justinian I (r. 527–565), the emperor at Constantinople, tried to reunify the old Roman Empire through military conquest. But Justinian's triumphs barely outlasted his death in 565. New adversaries in the east—above all, the rising religion of Islam—drew the emperors' attention away from the western provinces of the old empire. The rulers of Constantinople began to identify themselves exclusively with their capital's Greek heritage, spurning Roman traditions and replacing Latin with Greek as the official language of the empire. By 600 the religious and cultural gulf between the Latin west and the Greek east had so widened that historians speak of the latter as the Byzantine Empire (from *Byzantium*, the Greek name for Constantinople).

At the same time that the Latin west and the Greek east took increasingly divergent paths, a new and powerful culture arose that would challenge both. The emergence and spread of Islam in the 600s occurred with astonishing speed and success. The Muslim conquests sowed the seeds of Islamic faith and Arab institutions in diverse societies in Africa, Europe, and Asia. The pace of conversion varied greatly, however. Islam quickly made deep inroads among urban merchants and among pastoral nomads such as the Berbers of North Africa. In agrarian societies such as Syria, Mesopotamia, and Spain, the Arabs long remained a tiny elite ruling over Christian majorities, who only gradually accepted Islam. Local conditions shaped cultural exchange among Muslim conquerors, subject peoples, and neighboring states.

Like Christianity, Islam claimed to be a universal religion. Both religions offered a vision of common brotherhood that brought a new religious sensibility to daily life and integrated different peoples into a community of faith. Both were also beset by tension between sacred and secular authority. The Christian church preserved its autonomy amid political disorder in the Latin west, whereas the Byzantine emperors yoked imperial power and clerical leadership tightly together. The vision of a universal Islamic empire combining spiritual faith with political and military strength was crucial to the initial expansion of Islam. In the ninth and tenth centuries, however, the Islamic empire fragmented into numerous regional states divided by doctrine, culture, and way of life. Nonetheless, the economic vibrancy and religious ferment of the far-flung Islamic world created a vast territory through which Muslim merchants, missionaries, and pilgrims moved freely. Islamic cities and ports became global crossroads, centers for the exchange of goods and ideas that helped create cultural connections stretching from the Iberian peninsula to China.

OVERVIEW QUESTIONS

The major global development in this chapter: The spread of Christianity and Islam and the profound impact of these world religions on the societies of western Eurasia and North Africa.

As you read, consider:

1. How and why did the development of the Christian church differ in the Byzantine Empire and Latin Christendom?

2. In what ways did the rise of Christianity and Islam challenge the power of the state?

3. Conversely, in what ways did the spread of these faiths reinforce state power?

4. Why did Christianity and Islam achieve their initial success in towns and cities rather than in the countryside?

Multiple Christianities 400–850

↘ FOCUS In what ways did Christianity develop and spread following its institutionalization in the Roman Empire?

In the century following the Roman emperor Constantine's conversion to Christianity in 312, Christian leaders were confident that their faith would displace the classical Mediterranean religions (see Chapter 6). Yet the rapid spread of the Christian religion throughout Roman territories also splintered the Christian movement. Christian communities did not readily yield to any universal authority in matters of doctrine and faith. Efforts by the Byzantine emperors to impose their will on the Christian leadership met strong resistance.

The Christian Church in Byzantium

In the eastern Mediterranean, where imperial rule remained strong, the state treated the Christian church and clergy as a branch of imperial administration. Although the Christian communities of the eastern Mediterranean welcomed state support, they also sought to preserve their independence from the emperors' direct control. In the late fourth century a council of bishops acknowledged the special status of the bishop of Constantinople by designating him as patriarch, the supreme leader of the church. But the bishops of Alexandria in Egypt and Antioch in Anatolia (modern Turkey) retained authority and influence nearly equal to that of Constantinople's patriarch (see Map 8.1). The urban elite of imperial officials and wealthy merchants adopted the new religion, but alongside such new Christian practices as prayer, repentance, and almsgiving they often continued to uphold the old forms of Greek religion. Their vision of Christianity reflected the strong influence Greek culture continued to exert on Byzantine city life.

In Syria and Egypt, however, rural inhabitants embraced a more austere form of Christian piety. Some of the most impassioned Christians, deploring the persistence of profane Greco-Roman culture in the cities, sought spiritual refuge in the sparsely inhabited deserts, where they devoted themselves to an ascetic life of rigorous physical discipline.

While also serving as spiritual guides for the Christian population at large, other ascetics founded monasteries that attracted like-minded followers. The monastic movement began sporadically in Egypt and Syria in the late third century and surged in the fourth and fifth centuries. The austerity of monastic life endowed

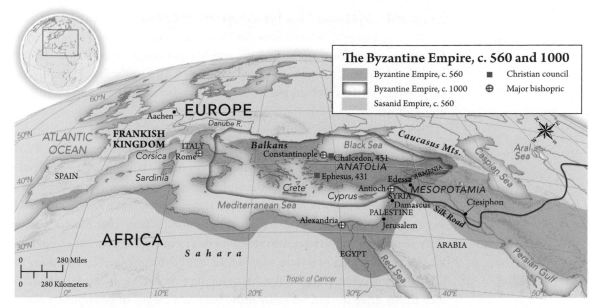

≡ **MAP 8.1   The Byzantine Empire, c. 560 and 1000**   Emperor Justinian I, bent on restoring the Roman Empire to its former glory, had recovered Italy and much of North Africa by 560. But a century later, Muslim Arab armies seized the Byzantine possessions in the Middle East and North Africa and extinguished the Sasanids, Byzantium's chief rival. By 1000, a strengthened monarchy supported by a unified Orthodox church had revived the fortunes of a much smaller Byzantine Empire.

monks with an aura of holiness that outshone the pomp and finery of church leaders in the cities.

The divisions within eastern Christianity went beyond differences in style and presentation to disagreements over basic Christian beliefs. Already in the time of Constantine, the bishops had been locked in debate over the divinity of Jesus (see Chapter 6). Nestorius (neh-STORE-ee-us), elected patriarch of Constantinople in 428, renewed this controversy by proclaiming that Jesus had two natures, one human and one divine. Nestorius especially objected to the idea that a human woman, Mary, could give birth to the son of God. But Nestorius's views outraged Cyril, the bishop of Alexandria, who insisted that Jesus had a single, fully divine nature, a principle that became known as the Monophysite ("single nature") doctrine. Councils of bishops held at Ephesus (431) and Chalcedon (KAL-suh-dahn) (451) denounced Nestorius's views as heresy (see again Map 8.1). To counter the claims of Nestorius, the Ephesus council formally declared Mary "mother of God." The Chalcedon council, in an effort to heal the split among the clergy, adopted a compromise position, that Jesus was both "fully divine and fully human." But the bishops of Alexandria remained committed to their Monophysite views, whereas the Nestorian doctrine gained a considerable following among local clergy in Syria and Mesopotamia. At issue was the very nature of Jesus and, thus, the essential nature of Christianity. It is, therefore, not surprising that this debate led to long-lasting divisions within the Christian community.

There were, however, countervailing pressures for Christian unity. Justinian I (r. 527–565) used the powers of the imperial state to impose religious unity, refusing to tolerate heretics and nonbelievers. Born a peasant but schooled in political intrigue while rising through the ranks of the palace guard, Justinian believed himself to have been divinely ordained to restore order to the Roman world. He began his campaign to impose religious uniformity soon after his coronation. "His ambition being to force everyone into one form of Christian belief, Justinian wantonly destroyed everyone who would not conform," wrote Procopius, the great historian of Justinian's reign.[2] He also put the content of Christianity in service to his drive toward religious orthodoxy as a means of promoting political unity. The theology elaborated at Constantinople during the next several centuries reiterated the principles of order and hierarchy on which the imperial state was built.

Christianity in Asia and Africa

Far from restoring unity, though, Justinian's often strong-arm tactics widened the fractures within the church. Alexandria resisted imperial domination, and the Nestorian heresy became entrenched in the easternmost provinces. Justinian's vision of a unified Christian empire was not matched by the power to impose his will.

Armenia, at the frontier between the Roman Empire and the Persian Sasanid Empire, nurtured its own distinctive Christian tradition. Christianity had advanced slowly in Armenia following the conversion of its king in the early fourth century. But after Armenia was partitioned and occupied by Roman and Sasanid armies in 387, resistance to foreign rule hardened around this kernel of Christian faith. Christianity became the hallmark of Armenian independence.

Except in Armenia, where Christians suffered political persecution, the Sasanids generally tolerated Christianity. The Nestorian church enjoyed a privileged position at the Sasanid capital of Ctesiphon (TEH-suh-fahn), south of modern Baghdad, and a number of Nestorian clergy attained high office at court. Nestorian missionaries traveled eastward and established churches along the trade routes leading from Persia to Central Asia. Merchants from the caravan settlements of Sogdia carried their adopted Nestorian faith eastward along the Silk Road as far as China, as we will see in Chapter 9.

Christianity also gained a foothold in Ethiopia, at the northern end of the Rift Valleys in eastern Africa, and once again trade played a key role. Both Jewish and Christian merchants settled in the Ethiopian towns that served this trade, chief of which was Axum (AHK-soom). By the first century

≡ Justinian and His Court This mosaic from the San Vitale church in Ravenna, Italy, depicts Justinian surrounded by his civil, military, and ecclesiastic officials—a clear effort to project the emperor's identity as head of both state and church. The mosaic was commissioned around 550 by Maximian, archbishop of Ravenna, the only figure labeled by the artist.

CE, Axum was a thriving metropolis connected to the Mediterranean trade network through the Red Sea port of Adulis (ah-DOOL-iss). Axum was the chief marketplace for precious African goods such as ivory, gold, gems, and animal horns and skins. Although the majority of the population consisted of herders and farmers, townsmen made pottery, worked leather and metal, and carved ivory.

Commercial wealth led to the creation of a powerful monarchy. During the early fourth century the rulers of Axum officially recognized Christianity as their state religion. Intolerance of other creeds hardened as the pace of conversion to Christianity accelerated. But the Islamic conquests in the seventh century disrupted the lucrative trade on which Axum's vitality depended. Trade routes shifted away from the Red Sea to Syria, and Damascus became the new commercial capital of the eastern Mediterranean. When the Axum monarchy declined, a class of warrior lords allied with Christian monasteries gained both economic and legal control of the agrarian population. As in Europe, most of the population was reduced to servile status, and much of the produce of the land supported Christian monasteries, which remained the repositories of learning and literate culture.

In the twelfth and thirteenth centuries, new royal dynasties arose in the highlands of Ethiopia that became great patrons of Christianity. These dynasties claimed direct descent from the ancient kings of Israel, but they also drew legitimacy from African traditions of sacred kingship. Ethiopia endured as a Christian stronghold down to modern times. Not surprisingly, isolated as it was from the larger Christian world, the Ethiopian church developed its own distinctive Christian traditions.

Christian Communities in Western Europe

≡ **Pope Gregory I** Pope Gregory I exercised firm leadership over the Latin Christian church through his voluminous correspondence with bishops, missionaries, and noble laypeople. At least 20,000 letters were dispatched from Rome under his name. This ivory carving shows the pope at his writing desk, with scribes below copying his writings.

While the Christian movements in Asia and Africa strove to maintain their independence from Constantinople, the collapse of the imperial order in the west posed different challenges for the Christian faithful. With imperial Rome in ruins, local communities and their leaders were free to rebuild their societies on the pillars of Christian beliefs and practices. When the Frankish king Charlemagne achieved military supremacy in western Europe at the end of the eighth century, his contemporaries heralded their new emperor as having been chosen by God "to rule and protect the Christian people."[3]

Amid ongoing warfare and violence, the beleaguered Christian communities in Gaul and Spain turned for leadership to provincial notables—great landowners and men of the old senatorial class. The bishops of Rome proclaimed their supreme authority in doctrinal matters as popes (from *papa*, or "grand old man"), the successors of St. Peter, who represented the universal ("Catholic") church. But Christians in the provinces of western Europe entrusted their protection to local men of wealth and family distinction, whom they elected as bishops. Bred to govern in the Roman style, these aristocrats took firm control of both secular and religious affairs. In time, with the assistance of zealous Christian missionaries, they negotiated settlements with their new Germanic overlords—the Franks in Gaul, the Visigoths in Spain, and the Saxons in Britain.

In an increasingly uncertain and violent world, the bishops of the west rallied their followers around the cults of saints. From at least the second century, Christians had commemorated beloved and inspiring martyrs and bishops as saints. Christians viewed saints as their patrons, persons of power and influence who protected the local community, and they regarded the bodily remains of saints as sacred relics. Thus, worship of saints at the sites of their tombs became a focal point of Christian life.

In the 460s, the bishop of Tours built a huge and ornate basilica at the site of the grave of the martyr St. Martin (335–397) that attracted pilgrims from throughout Gaul and beyond. When the Frankish king Clovis challenged the Visigoth ruler Alaric for control of southern Gaul in 507, he sought divine blessing at St. Martin's shrine. After defeating the Visigoths, Clovis returned to Tours laden with booty that he donated to the shrine. Similar cults and networks of pilgrimage and patronage sprung up around the relics of other saints.

Pope Gregory I (540–604) typified the distinctive style of leadership in the western Christian church. Born into a prominent Roman aristocratic family, Gregory entered the imperial service in 573 as the governor of Rome. Pulled by a strong religious calling, however, he soon retired to become a monk. After achieving fame for his devotion to learning and ascetic lifestyle, Gregory returned to public service. He spent a decade as the papal envoy to the Byzantine court before returning to Rome upon his election as pope in 590. Keenly aware of the divisions within the Christian world, Gregory strove to make the papacy the centerpiece of a church administration that stretched from Britain to North Africa. Mindful, too, of the limited penetration of Christian religion in the countryside, he worked tirelessly to instill a sense of mission among the Christian clergy. "The art to end all arts is the governing of souls," wrote Gregory, insisting that the contemplative life of the monastery must be joined to the pastoral duty of saving sinners.[4]

Slowly but surely, Gregory's vision of the Christian clergy as the spiritual rulers of the humble peasantry gained converts. By the eighth century, social life in the western European countryside revolved around the village church. Still, Latin Christendom was far from united. Distinctive Christian churches and cultures had emerged in Italy, Gaul, Britain, and Spain. Moreover, conversion to Christianity proceeded fitfully, and for long afterward Christian beliefs and practices among the Germanic peoples and in Anglo-Saxon Britain remained deeply influenced by pagan religion, myth, and folklore (see Seeing the Past: Interweaving Christian Belief and Germanic Folklore). During the eighth century, however, the rise of the Carolingian dynasty would bring these regional Christendoms into a single European form.

SEEING THE PAST

The Franks Casket: Interweaving Christian Belief and Germanic Folklore

In 597 Pope Gregory I dispatched Benedictine monks as missionaries to the Anglo-Saxon kingdoms founded by Germanic warriors who invaded England after the demise of Roman rule. At first the Anglo-Saxon kings were wary of an unfamiliar religion they associated with their Frankish foes. As the kings expanded their domains and consolidated power over the course of the seventh and eighth centuries, however, they began to value alliances with Christian bishops and monasteries and competed for ecclesiastic patronage. As conversion to Christianity progressed, Germanic traditions and folklore were revised to reflect Christian teachings and messages—as we see in the tenth-century epic poem *Beowulf* (discussed on pages 308–309).

The juxtaposition of Christian piety with Germanic legends is vividly displayed in the Franks Casket, a box encased in carved whalebone panels depicting narrative scenes drawn from Roman, Christian, and German sources. The box, probably made in northeastern England in the early eighth century for a royal benefactor, also bears inscriptions in Old English—with snatches of Latin—written in Anglo-Saxon letters. The front panels depicted here divide into two separate scenes. On the right appears the common Christian motif of the Adoration of the Magi, showing the three kings (the Magi) presenting gifts of gold, frankincense, and myrrh to the infant Jesus and his mother under the guiding star that brought them to Bethlehem. The scene on the left is drawn from the Germanic legend of Weland the blacksmith, who was lamed, enslaved, and forced to work for the cruel King Nithhad. Weland exacted terrible revenge, killing the king's sons and turning their skulls into drinking cups and raping the king's daughter Beadohild, who bears Weland's child, the future warrior-hero Widia. Weland then escaped by making a feathered cloak that enabled him to fly away. Here Weland stands at left straddling a decapitated body; in one hand he holds the severed head of the king's son with a pair of tongs, while with the other hand he offers Beadohild a cup with the potion he uses to drug her. A smaller figure to the right—presumably Weland again, or his brother, the hero Ergil—captures birds to gather feathers for the magic cloak.

On the back of the casket a medley of scenes depicts the Roman sack of Jerusalem in 70 CE, the destruction of the Jewish Temple, and the flight of the Jews. The top and side panels illustrate the abandonment of Romulus and Remus, the fabled founders of Rome; Ergil's defense of a woman from armed warriors; and an unidentified but surely German legend. Strikingly dissimilar as the Christian and pagan narratives are, they share themes of suffering, exile, bloodshed, redemption, and the triumph of good over evil.

The Franks Casket

Examining the Evidence

1. The gifts brought by the three kings—gold, frankincense, and myrrh—allude to Jesus's kingship, divinity, and death. What parallels or contrasts might link the Adoration of the Magi scene with its pair, the Weland the blacksmith story?

2. The Anglo-Saxon inscription accompanying these panels reads like a riddle: "The sea cast up the fish onto the rocky high beach; the king of terror became sad when he swam onto the shingle [shore]." Consider the biblical legend of Jonah and the whale (the panels, we should remember, are made from whalebone). In light of this story, what might the riddle mean?

Source: British Museum, 1867,0120.1

Social and Political Renewal in the Post-Roman World 400–850

⬎ **FOCUS** What major changes swept the lands of the former Roman Empire in the four centuries following the fall of imperial Rome?

The Byzantine emperors in the east and the Germanic chieftains who ruled the empire's former western European provinces shared a common heritage rooted in the Roman imperial past and Christian religion. The Byzantine Empire faced a profound crisis in the sixth and seventh centuries. Protracted wars with the Sasanids, the Slavs, and the Avars were followed by the loss of two-thirds of Byzantium's realm to the rapid advance of Muslim Arab armies. Yet the Byzantine Empire survived, thanks to the revitalization of the imperial state and a resilient economy. Byzantine political institutions and especially its distinctive version of Christianity also exerted a powerful influence on the Slavic peoples and led to the formation of the first Rus state. Although Byzantium regained its political and cultural vigor in the ninth century, their fellow Christians, the Frankish empire of the Carolingian dynasty, proved to be more a rival than an ally.

Crisis and Survival of the Byzantine Empire

schism A split in any organized group (especially a church or religious community) resulting in a formal declaration of differences in doctrine or beliefs.

iconoclasm Literally, "destruction of images"; the word originates with the movement against the veneration of images in the Byzantine Empire in the eighth and ninth centuries.

Justinian I's conquests in Italy and North Africa had once again joined Constantinople and Rome under a single sovereign, but this union was short-lived. Lengthy wars and the enormous costs of Justinian's building programs sapped the fiscal strength of the empire. Although the Byzantine forces repulsed a Sasanid-led attack on Constantinople in 626, this victory was eclipsed within fifteen years by the loss of Syria, Palestine, and Egypt to Muslim armies. By 700 the Byzantine Empire was a shrunken vestige of Justinian's realm, consisting essentially of Constantinople and its immediate environs, a few territories in Greece, and Anatolia.

Accompanying Byzantium's declining power and prestige were worsening relations with Rome. Emperor Justinian II (r. 685–695) convened a council of bishops at Constantinople in 692 that affirmed the independence of the patriarch of Constantinople from the Roman pope in matters of religious doctrine. Over the course of the eighth century the religious **schism** widened. The Frankish king Charlemagne's coronation as emperor by Pope Leo III in 800 in effect declared Charlemagne to be the protector of the church, usurping the Byzantine emperor's role. Although Charlemagne negotiated a compromise in 813 that recognized the Byzantine monarch as "emperor of the Romans," Latin Christendom had clearly emerged as a separate church.

Within Byzantium, debate raged over the proper conduct of life and religion in a Christian society, especially concerning the veneration of icons—painted images of Jesus, Mary, and the saints. The powerful new faith of Islam denounced any representation of the divine in human form as idolatry. This radical **iconoclasm** (Greek for "image-breaking") struck a responsive chord among the many Byzantines who saw the empire's political reversals as evidence of moral decline. Throughout the eighth century a bitter struggle divided Byzantium. On one side were the iconoclasts, who sought to match Muslim religious fervor by restoring a pristine faith rooted in Old Testament values. On the other side were the defenders of orthodoxy, who maintained that the use of explicitly Christian images was an essential component of the imperially ordained liturgy on which social unity depended. In the mid-ninth century the proponents of orthodoxy prevailed over the iconoclasts. Henceforth Byzantine Christianity became known as the Orthodox Church, in which religious authority became tightly interwoven with imperial power.

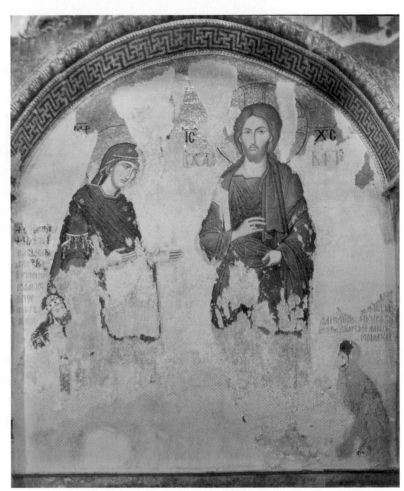

≡ **Christ and Mary, Mother of God** In this fourteenth-century mosaic from the Chora monastery in Istanbul (then Constantinople), Mary, mother of Jesus and patron saint of Constantinople, beseeches Jesus to cleanse the faithful of their sins. Likely founded by Justinian I (r. 527–565), the Chora monastery was rebuilt in 1120 by the Byzantine prince Isaac Komnenos, who is depicted at Mary's feet. At bottom right the princess Maria Palaiologos, daughter of a thirteenth-century emperor who was forced into a marriage of political convenience to the Mongol Ilkhan ruler of modern-day Iran/Iraq, kneels in prayer wearing a nun's habit.

In the second half of the ninth century the Muslim threat abated, and the Byzantine Empire enjoyed a rebirth. Resurgent economic strength at home fueled military success against the Muslims and the Slavs. The church and the army supported efforts to enhance the power and authority of the emperor and the central state. Yet as the leading classes of Byzantine society rallied around a revitalized imperial institution, the estrangement between the churches of Constantinople and Rome intensified.

The Germanic Successor States in Western Europe

At the peak of the Roman Empire, its northern frontier stretched 3,000 miles, from the British Isles to the Black Sea. As we saw in Chapter 6, provincial Romans had frequent social and economic interactions with their Celtic and Germanic neighbors. Many Germanic chieftains had previously served as mercenaries defending the territories they now ruled (see Map 8.2).

Similar patterns of livelihood prevailed among the Germanic peoples—and indeed among all the peoples of northern and eastern Europe. In most of the region, small, patriarchal farming communities predominated, in which men had full authority over their families or clans. The most important crop was barley, which was consumed as porridge, bread, and beer. Cattle raising also was important. The number of cattle a household possessed determined its wealth and prestige, and acquiring cattle was a chief objective of both trade and warfare.

Valor and success in warfare also conferred prestige. Village communities organized themselves into warrior bands for warfare and raiding, and at times these bands joined together to form broad confederations for mutual defense and campaigns of plunder. These groups were primarily political alliances, and thus they dissolved and reformed as the needs and interests of their constituent tribes shifted. Contact with the Roman world, through both trade and war, magnified the roles of charismatic military leaders, men skilled at holding together their fragile coalitions of followers and negotiating with the Roman state.

One such confederation, the Goths, arrived in Italy and Gaul as refugees, driven westward by the invasions of the Hun nomads from Central Asia in the fifth century (see Chapter 6). Expelled from their homeland in the lower Danube region, the Visigoths (Western Goths) followed their king Alaric into the Balkans and Italy. Alaric's army captured and plundered Rome in 410. In 418 the Visigoths

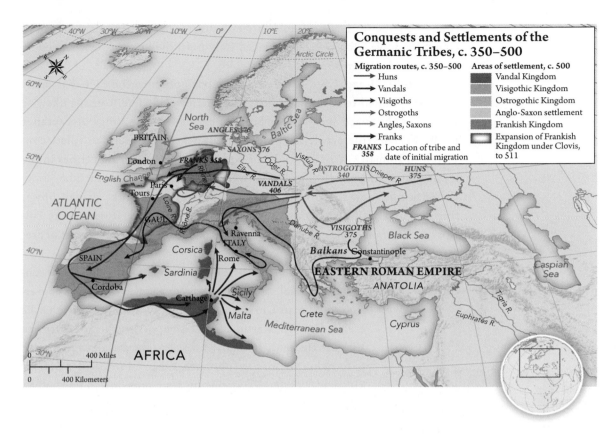

≡ **MAP 8.2   Conquests and Settlements of the Germanic Tribes, c. 350–500** In the fourth and fifth centuries, as Rome's authority disintegrated, Germanic chieftains led their followers to invade and occupy Roman territories. The new Germanic rulers such as the Franks and the Goths cultivated alliances with local leaders and the Christian church and restored a measure of stability.

negotiated an alliance with the Byzantine emperor that allowed them to occupy southern Gaul—the first Germanic people to complete the transition from confederation to kingdom.

The Ostrogoths (Eastern Goths) emerged as an independent force in the late fifth century, following the death of the Hun leader Attila, whom the Ostrogoths loyally served. After Attila's empire disintegrated, the Ostrogoths shifted their allegiance to Constantinople. In 488 the Byzantine emperor dispatched the Ostrogoth leader Theodoric to subdue Odoacer, the German king who had seized Rome and deposed its last emperor in 476. Theodoric conquered the Italian peninsula in 493 but refused to relinquish control to Constantinople. The Ostrogoths ruled Italy until they were overwhelmed by Justinian's armies in 553.

Sensational images of "barbarian invasions" obscure the fact that many Germans wanted to assimilate into the Roman world. The Romans likewise welcomed the peace and security brought by the German kings. Acceptance of "barbarian" rule accelerated most rapidly where the German rulers converted to Roman Christianity. The Franks, a league of German tribes in the lower Rhine River Valley, had long lived near the Roman world. The "long-haired kings"—as the Romans called them—of the Franks gained power through loyal military service to the empire. When the Roman state collapsed, the Frankish kings allied with Christian bishops in the interest of preserving local order.

Under the leadership of Clovis (r. 482–511), the Franks consolidated their control over the Rhineland and Gaul. Although the circumstances of Clovis's conversion to Roman Christianity are murky, we have seen that he credited to St. Martin his decisive victory in 507 over the Visigoths in southern Gaul. Clovis also issued a law code, Roman in form but German in substance. When Clovis died in 511, his kingdom was divided among his four sons, including Clothar, future husband of Radegund (whom we met at the beginning of this chapter).

The Franks added new conquests during the sixth and seventh centuries, but the pattern of decentralized rule continued. The lightning conquest of Spain by Muslim armies in 710–711 triggered a crisis that reversed this erosion of royal power. When the Muslim forces subsequently invaded southern Gaul, local nobles turned to a Frankish warlord, Charles Martel, for protection. Martel's decisive victory over the Muslims at Tours in 732 made him the undisputed leader of the Franks; his descendants would rule as the Carolingian (from *Carolus*, Latin for "Charles") dynasty of kings.

Frankish political power reached its height under Martel's grandson Charlemagne (r. 768–814). Drawing on the Roman Empire as a model, Charlemagne's conquests added substantial territories to the Frankish empire, extending from the Baltic Sea to the Adriatic Sea. Charlemagne incorporated

Empire of Charlemagne, 814

Frankish Kingdom, 768	Tributary peoples
Areas conquered by Charlemange, to 814	Byzantine Empire

≡ **Empire of Charlemagne, 814**

these new dominions into his empire by sharing power with local rulers and allowing their peoples to be governed in accordance with their own laws and customs. Thus the Carolingian Empire created new ethnic identities among its diverse subjects.

Charlemagne made protection of the pope and Roman orthodoxy an essential component of his mandate. The culmination of his efforts took place on Christmas Day, 800, when Pope Leo III placed a crown on Charlemagne's head and proclaimed him Augustus, the title of the first Roman emperor. Recognition of Charlemagne and his successors as "emperors" forged a lasting bond between the papacy and the secular rulers of Latin Christendom. Compared with Byzantium, church and state remained more independent of each other in western Europe. Nonetheless, Charlemagne established a new ideology of Christian kingship.

Economic Contraction and Renewal in Christendom

Although the Franks patronized the Christian church and monasteries, the urban culture of the Roman world withered. The nobility retreated to the security of their rural estates, and the great monasteries in the countryside, enriched by royal land grants, began to overshadow the urban bishops. The Carolingian monarchs, too, abandoned the old Roman towns, preferring to hold court at rural villas such as Charlemagne's capital at Aachen, along the modern border between Germany and Belgium. Both secular lords and monastic abbeys built up vast estates; for labor, they subjected the rural population to increasingly servile status. Throughout the Carolingian realm this new institution, the **manor**, was widely adopted. The tenants became **serfs**, tied to the land and subject to the legal authority of the lord. The obligations of serfs could vary significantly, but in general they owed labor services to the lord, as well as rents and fees for the right to graze animals and collect firewood. Women serfs also provided labor in the manor's workshops or by making cloth in their own homes.

Towns and commerce in Europe declined in part from the rise of the new rural manors, but more fundamental was the contraction of the international trading system centered on Constantinople. A terrible plague swept across the Mediterranean from Egypt to Europe in 541–542. Byzantine officials reported that 230,000 died in Constantinople alone, and Mediterranean cities from Antioch to Alexandria also suffered huge losses. In addition, the Sasanid and Muslim conquests of the seventh century deprived the empire of its richest domains. These cumulative demographic and territorial losses greatly reduced economic productivity.

manor A great estate, consisting of farmlands, vineyards, and other productive assets, owned by a lord (which could be an institution, such as a monastery) and cultivated by serfs.

serf A semi-free peasant tied to the land and subject to the judicial authority of a lord.

Political setbacks, the decline of towns, and the shrinking population led to a downturn in the Byzantine economy. Yet the Byzantine state still appropriated a significant share of agricultural surpluses, which it distributed as salaries to its officials and soldiers. Hit hardest by the waning fortunes of the empire was the landowning aristocracy. Peasants who owned their own land increased in numbers and importance, and the state benefited from the taxes they paid.

Yet even as it spiraled downward, the Byzantine economy displayed far more vigor than that of the Germanic kingdoms. Political stability rekindled population growth in both town and countryside, especially in the long-settled coastal regions. By 800 unmistakable signs of economic prosperity had reappeared: the demand for coinage increased, new lands were put under the plow, and reports of famine became less frequent and less desperate. The Mediterranean trade network centered on Constantinople began to recover as tensions with Islamic rulers eased.

The quickening prosperity of the Byzantine economy promoted commerce across the Mediterranean. Silks produced in Constantinople's workshops ranked among the most prized luxury goods in the Carolingian world (see Lives and Livelihoods: Constantinople's Silk Producers). Significant economic growth, however, would not return to the European heartland until the late tenth century, well after the expansion of the Byzantine economy was under way.

Origins of the Slavs and the Founding of Rus

During its crisis of the sixth and seventh centuries, the Byzantine Empire confronted a new people on its borders, the Slavs. Today nearly 300 million people in eastern Europe and Russia speak a Slavic language. They trace their ancestry back to peoples known as *Sclavenoi* in Greek, who first appear in sixth-century Byzantine chronicles. Early Byzantine accounts classified the Slavs, together with the Avars and the Goths, as pagan savages and mortal enemies of Christendom. Between the fifth and tenth centuries, however, Byzantine interaction with both settled and nomadic Slavic populations led to the crystallization of an identifiable Slavic culture with its own written languages and to the assimilation of the Slavs into a larger Christian civilization.

Like the Germanic peoples, most Slavs lived in small farming settlements consisting of several extended related families: "each living with his own clan on his own lands," in the words of a Russian chronicler.[5] The Slavs practiced shifting cultivation, regularly moving into wilderness areas and cutting down virgin forest to plant barley and millet, using the nitrogen-rich ash of burnt trees as fertilizer. Procopius portrayed the Slavs as leading "a primitive and rough way of life. . . . They are neither dishonorable nor spiteful, but simple in their ways, like the Huns."[6]

In the ninth and tenth centuries the Slavic peoples were strongly influenced by Byzantine and Frankish models of government, law, and religion. The uniform Slavic culture divided into separate societies and political allegiances, leading to the emergence of Serb, Croat, Polish, and other Slavic national identities. The most far-reaching change was the conversion of most Slavic peoples to Christianity. Slav rulers, pressured by hostile Christian adversaries, were the first to convert. The Slavic adoption of Christianity only heightened frictions between Rome and Constantinople, however, because the southern and eastern Slavs adhered to Byzantine rites and beliefs, whereas Latin teachings prevailed among western Slavs.

According to later (and not wholly reliable) Russian chronicles, the first state of Rus was formed in 862 when Scandinavian communities in the Novgorod region elected a Viking chieftain as their ruler. But a Rus confederation of Viking settlements engaging in slave raiding and fur trading had already emerged some decades before. Lured by the riches of the Mediterranean world, the Rus pushed southward toward the Black Sea along the Dnieper and the Volga Rivers. At some point, probably in the 930s, the Rus princes shifted their capital to Kiev in the lower Dnieper Valley. By the late tenth century Kievan Rus had emerged as the dominant power in the Black Sea region. Prince Vladimir (r. 980–1015) consolidated Rus into a more unified state and adopted the Christian religion of Byzantium. Conversion to Christianity and deepening commercial and diplomatic ties with Byzantium marked a decisive reorientation of Rus away from its Scandinavian origins.

Thus the middle centuries of the first millennium CE saw both the growth and the splintering of Christianity, as competing visions of Christianity emerged. Although the Latin and Orthodox churches continued to win new converts in eastern and northern Europe, the sudden emergence of Islam in the seventh century transformed the religious landscape of the Mediterranean world.

≡ **Slavic Territories in Eastern Europe, c. 900**

Constantinople's Silk Producers

During the heyday of the Roman Empire, when silk was said to be worth its weight in gold, Romans depended wholly on imports of silk from China. According to the historian Procopius, sericulture—the raising of silkworms to make silk—first appeared in the Byzantine Empire in his own time, during the reign of Emperor Justinian I (r. 527–565). Several Indian monks arrived at Constantinople offering to reveal the secrets of sericulture.

> When the Emperor questioned them very closely and asked how they could guarantee success in the business, the monks told him that the agents in the production of silk were certain caterpillars, working under nature's teaching, which continually urged them to their task. To bring live caterpillars from that country would be impracticable indeed, but . . . it was possible to hatch their eggs long after they had been laid by covering them with dung, which produced sufficient heat for the purpose.[1]

The monks delivered the eggs as promised, and silk manufacture subsequently became a pillar of the Byzantine economy.

Since Roman times, silk clothing had become a conspicuous mark of wealth and social distinction. The Byzantine government issued numerous decrees restricting the wearing of certain kinds of silk to the nobility. Purple-dyed silks—the "royal purple," a pigment derived from a tropical sea snail—were reserved for the emperor alone. Silk also served as a valuable tool of diplomacy. The

≡ **Byzantine Silk Shroud** Tradition has it that this silk shroud was placed in the tomb of the Frankish ruler Charlemagne after his death in 814. The design features a charioteer—probably an emperor—driving a four-horse chariot. Attendants in the background hold out crowns and whips; those at the bottom pour coins onto an altar.

Byzantine emperors regularly sent gifts of silk fabrics to the Frankish kings and the Islamic caliphs. In the Carolingian Empire, Byzantine silks were coveted luxury goods, flaunted by male aristocrats and well-born nuns no less than by royal princesses. The prominence of silk garments, furnishings, and liturgical vestments in wills, dowry and marriage contracts, and church inventories attests to both their economic value and their social prestige.

Silk manufacture involves a complex series of operations, ranging from low-skilled tasks such as raising silkworms and reeling yarn to those requiring high technical proficiency, such as weaving, dyeing, and embroidery. In late Roman times, imperial textile workers, both men and women, had been reduced to hereditary occupational castes. By Justinian's day, the standing of skilled silk artisans had risen appreciably, and government employment was considered a privilege, not a burden.

Yarn production was largely a family business. The silk clothiers, in contrast, combined weaving, dyeing, and tailoring workshops under one management, relying mostly on hired labor but employing household slaves as well. Enslaved persons also operated workshops as agents for their masters. Government workshops employed skilled craftsmen divided into guilds of clothiers, purple dyers, and gold embroiderers, who made richly decorated fabrics for the emperor and his officials. Menial tasks were relegated to servile labor, including foreign enslaved persons.

Keen to profit from the high prices its silks commanded in foreign markets, the Byzantine government feared the loss of trade secrets. Foreign merchants were prohibited from taking certain silk goods and unsewn fabrics out of Constantinople, and their cargoes were carefully inspected before they could leave the city. The city magistrate decreed that "every dyer who sells a slave, a workman, or a foreman craftsman to persons alien to the city or the Empire shall have his hand cut off."[2] But these efforts to monopolize technological know-how proved futile. By 1000, technical mastery of silk manufacture had become widely disseminated. Surviving silk specimens show that Byzantine and Muslim artisans freely borrowed weaving techniques, artistic motifs, and color patterns from each other, to the point where it is nearly impossible to distinguish their handiwork.

1. Procopius, *The History of the Wars*, 4:17.
2. *Book of the Eparch*, in *Roman Law in the Later Roman Empire: Byzantine Guilds, Professional, Commercial; Ordinances of Leo VI, from the Book of the Eparch*, ed. E. H. Freshfield (Cambridge: Cambridge University Press, 1938), 26.

Questions to Consider

1. Did the Byzantine government's measures to regulate the silk industry stimulate or discourage competition among producers?

2. How did the organization of the Byzantine silk industry serve to promote the interests of artisans, merchants, and the government?

For Further Information:

Laiou, Angeliki E., ed. *The Economic History of Byzantium from the Seventh Through the Fifteenth Century*. 3 vols. Washington, DC: Dumbarton Oaks Research Library and Collections, 2002.

Laiou, Angeliki E., and Cécile Morrisson. *The Byzantine Economy*. Cambridge: Cambridge University Press, 2007.

The Rise and Spread of Islam 610–750

↘ FOCUS In what ways did Islam instill a sense of common identity among its believers?

In the early seventh century, the Arab prophet Muhammad (c. 570–632) founded what became a new religion, Islam, rooted in the Judaic and Christian traditions but transformed by the divine revelations he proclaimed. Muhammad envisioned the community of believers as a tight-knit movement dedicated to propagating the true faith, and his successors fashioned Islam into a mighty social and political force. Within a century of Muhammad's death in 632 an Islamic empire had expanded beyond Arabia as far as Iran to the east and Spain to the west. As in Christendom, tensions arose between political rulers and religious authorities. During the tenth century the united Islamic empire fractured into a commonwealth of independent states. Yet the powerful inspiration of Muhammad's teachings and Islam's radical egalitarian ideals sustained a sense of community that transcended political and ethnic boundaries.

The Prophet Muhammad and the Faith of Islam

Muhammad's call for a renewal of religious faith dedicated to the one true God must be seen in the context of social and religious life in the Arabian peninsula. The harsh desert environment of Arabia could sustain little more than a nomadic pastoral livelihood. Domestication of the camel since about 1000 BCE allowed small, clan-based groups known as Bedouins to raise livestock. During the summer the Bedouins (BED-uh-wuhns) gathered at oases to exchange animal products for grain, dates, utensils, weapons, and cloth. Some of these oases eventually supported thriving commercial towns, of which the most prosperous was Mecca.

The Bedouin tribes regularly came to Mecca to pay homage at the Ka'aba (KAH-buh) shrine, which housed the icons of numerous gods worshipped throughout the region. Mecca thus served as a sanctuary where different tribes could gather to worship their gods in peace. The religious harmony that prevailed at Mecca also offered opportunities to settle disputes and conduct trade.

Building on its status as an Arabian crossroads, Mecca developed economic connections with the larger world. During the sixth century, it blossomed into a major emporium of international trade between the Mediterranean and the Indian Ocean. Yet clan solidarity remained paramount, and the gap between rich and poor widened. It was here that Muhammad, the founder of Islam, was born in around the year 570.

Muhammad belonged to a once prominent clan whose fortunes were in decline. As a young man he worked as a caravaner for a woman named Khadija, a rich widow older than Muhammad, whom he married when he was twenty-five. Although Muhammad seemed to have gained a secure livelihood, moral doubts and growing contempt for what he regarded as the arrogance and greed of his fellow Meccans deeply troubled him. Beginning around 610 he experienced visions of a single, true God ("Allah") who did not cater to the worldly wishes of worshippers as the pagan gods of his countrymen did but instead imposed an uncompromising moral law upon all peoples. Muhammad's revelations were suffused with a deep sense of sin inspired by Christianity. From Judaism Muhammad incorporated devotion to the one true God, a sense of personal mission as a prophet sent to warn the world against impiety, and a regimen of ritual prayer intended to instill rightful thought and conduct.

Initially, Muhammad communicated his visions only to a small group of confidants. In 613, however, a revelation instructed him to "rise and warn," and he began to preach publicly. Muhammad's egalitarian vision, in which all believers were equal before God, directly challenged tribal loyalties and clan leaders. Like Jesus, his teachings won favor among the lower classes, the poor and propertyless, while making him a pariah among the affluent and powerful clans. Persecution forced Muhammad and his followers to seek sanctuary in Medina, a nearby oasis town, in 622. Muhammad's move to Medina, known as the **hijra** (HIJ-ruh) ("migration"), subsequently marked the beginning of the Muslim calendar.

In Medina, Muhammad's reputation for holiness and fairness and his vision of a united community bound by a single faith elevated him to a position of leadership. The primary obstacle to the consolidation of his power in Medina was the town's large Jewish population, which rejected Muhammad's claims of prophethood and allied with his Meccan enemies. Muhammad began to issue new revelations accusing the Jews of breaking the covenant with God and declaring that he himself was the direct successor of the first and greatest prophet, Abraham. Muhammad vowed that his own creed of Islam ("submission") would supersede both Judaism and Christianity. Backed by Medina's clan leaders, Muhammad executed or exiled the town's leading Jewish citizens, thereby securing unchallenged authority in political as well as spiritual matters.

Subsequently Muhammad and his followers warred against Mecca—the first instance of a **jihad** ("struggle") of the sword, a holy war fought against those who persecute believers. In 630, the

hijra Muhammad's move from Mecca to Medina in 622, which marks year 1 of the Islamic calendar.

jihad Literally, "struggle"; a key concept in the Qur'an, which can refer to the individual's spiritual effort to follow "the path of God" (jihad of the soul) or to a holy war (jihad of the sword) against those who persecute Islam.

Hijra of Muhammad, 622

≡ **Hijra of Muhammad, 622**

Meccans surrendered their city to Muhammad, who destroyed the idols of pagan gods in the Ka'aba and instead established it as the holiest shrine of Islam. Most Bedouin tribes soon capitulated to Muhammad as well. Preparing in 632 for an invasion of Syria, Muhammad was struck down by an illness and died in Medina. By the time of his death, he had created the basis for a new political order founded on a universal religion and a faith in the oneness of God that transcended clan, ethnic, and civic identities.

The revelations of Muhammad were written down in Arabic in the **Qur'an**, which Muslims regard as the completion of earlier revelations from God set down in the Jewish Torah and the Christian gospels. The Qur'an elaborates the "five pillars of faith": (1) bearing witness to the unity of God and the prophethood of Muhammad; (2) daily prayers while facing the direction of Mecca; (3) fasting during Ramadan, the ninth month of the Islamic calendar; (4) giving alms to the poor; and (5) for those physically able and with the financial means, the obligation to make a pilgrimage (*hajj*) to Mecca. In the absence of a formal priesthood, the *ulama*—scholars and teachers steeped in study of the Qur'an—acted as the custodians and interpreters of divine teachings.

Although the Qur'an modified some of the prevailing norms of Bedouin society—for example, by recognizing women and children as individuals with their own needs and some limited rights—on the whole it reinforced the patriarchal traditions of clan society (see Reading the Past: Women and Property in Islam). At the same time, the charismatic leadership of clan elders yielded to the higher authority of divine will. Islam pointed toward a new understanding of community in which membership was defined not by kinship or geography but by assent to a common set of religious principles.

The Islamic Empire of the Umayyad Caliphs 661–750

Muhammad's stature as the Prophet made him unique in the Islamic community. After his death the community faced the thorny problem of choosing his successor. Eventually a compromise was reached that recognized Muhammad's father-in-law, Abu Bakr (AH-boo BOCK-ear), as **caliph** (KAY-luhf) ("deputy"). The caliph would inherit Muhammad's position as leader of the Islamic community, but not his role as prophet. As caliph, Abu Bakr led the community in wars of conquest and submission. The Byzantine and Sasanid Empires, weakened by three decades of wars against each other, were no match for the Arabs. The Arabs decisively defeated the Byzantine army in Palestine in 634 and proceeded to capture Syria, Mesopotamia, and Egypt by 641. The Byzantine Empire lost most of its territories in the east but, as we have seen, survived. The Sasanid Empire, however,

Qur'an The book recording the revelations of the Prophet Muhammad; regarded as the most sacred scripture in Islam.

ulama Scholars learned in Islamic scripture and law codes who act as arbiters of Islamic teachings.

caliph The designated successor to Muhammad as leader of the Muslim faithful in civil affairs.

utterly collapsed after Arab armies seized its capital of Ctesiphon in 637 (see Map 8.3, page 303).

Abu Bakr and his immediate successors as caliphs ruled by virtue of their close personal relationships to the Prophet Muhammad, but disputes over succession persisted. The third caliph, Uthman (r. 644–656), a Meccan aristocrat of the Umayya (oo-MY-uh) clan, sought to resolve the succession problem by creating a family dynasty. Uthman's grab for power provoked civil war, however, and he was assassinated in 656. Ali, Muhammad's cousin and husband of his daughter Fatima, was elected to replace Uthman, but he failed to unite the warring Arab tribes. In 661 Ali, too, was assassinated. Mu'awiya (moo-AH-we-yuh) (r. 661–680), a cousin of Uthman and governor of Syria, then succeeded in establishing a hereditary dynasty of Umayyad caliphs.

Although Mu'awiya cemented dynastic control over the caliphate and built up an imperial government in his new capital of Damascus, the wounds opened by the succession dispute failed to heal. When Mu'awiya died in 680, Ali's son Husayn (hoo-SANE) launched an insurrection in an attempt to reclaim the caliphate. The Umayyads defeated the rebels, and Husayn was captured and killed. Nonetheless, a faction of Muslims remained who contended that the only rightful successors to the caliphate were Ali and his descendants, known as the *imam* ("leaders"). This group, which became known as the **Shi'a**, regarded Husayn as a great martyr. The Shi'a emphasized the role of the caliph as an infallible authority in matters of religious doctrine. Supporters of the Umayyad caliphs, known as the **Sunni**, instead regarded the caliph primarily as a secular ruler. Although the Sunni believed that the chief duty of the caliph was to protect and propagate Islam, they turned to the ulama for interpretation of Islamic doctrine and law. Thus the divisions in Islam that grew out of disputes over the succession evolved into divergent understandings of the nature of the Islamic community and Islamic institutions.

When Abd al-Malik (r. 685–705) assumed the office of Umayyad caliph in 685, the Muslim world was in disarray after a half century of astonishingly rapid expansion. Abd al-Malik succeeded in quelling uprisings by Shi'a and other dissidents and restoring the caliph's authority over Arabia and Iran. He retained much of the administrative system of the Byzantine and Sasanid states, while substituting Arabic for Greek and Persian as the language of government. Abd al-Malik upheld the supremacy of Arabs in government as well as faith, but bureaucratic office and mastery of the written word displaced martial valor as marks of leadership. He thus succeeded in creating a powerful monarchy supported by a centralized civilian bureaucracy.

imam The supreme leader of the Islamic community (especially in the Shi'a tradition), the legitimate successor to Muhammad; or any Islamic religious leader.

Shi'a A branch of Islam that maintains that only descendants of Muhammad through his cousin and son-in-law Ali have a legitimate right to serve as caliph.

Sunni The main branch of Islam, which accepts the historical succession of caliphs as legitimate leaders of the Muslim community.

READING THE PAST

Women and Property in Islam

Under laws that prevailed in Latin Christendom until the nineteenth century, women had no right to inherit property, even from their deceased husbands. The Jewish legal tradition allowed only limited inheritance rights to women, generally for unmarried daughters or to perpetuate the family line when a man had no male heirs. Islamic law, by contrast, explicitly granted women certain property rights and control over their own earnings. In practice, however, the property rights of Islamic women and their access to gainful employment have been shaped and in some cases curtailed by social practices and scriptural interpretation.

Islam establishes men as the guardians of women, responsible for both their material welfare and their moral conduct, obligations that entail the right to punish women for their moral failings. At the same time, in keeping with the commandment against coveting the wealth and property of others, women are entitled to whatever earnings they receive from their work, trade, or property.

Men are the ones who support women since God has given some persons advantages over others, and because they should spend their wealth on them. Honorable women are steadfast, guarding the Unseen just as God has it guarded. Admonish those women whose surliness you fear, and leave them alone in their beds, and even beat them if necessary. If they obey you, do not seek any way to proceed against them. (Qur'an, 4.34)

In no way covet those things in which God has bestowed his gifts more freely on some of you than on others: to men is allotted what they earn, and to women what they earn. (Qur'an, 4.128)

In both the Jewish and Islamic traditions, at the time of marriage the husband must provide the wife with a dowry that becomes her irrevocable personal property. Whereas the husband has free use of this property during the marriage under Jewish law, Islamic law places the dowry entirely at the disposal of the wife. The Qur'an also guarantees women an inheritance from their parents and

---

dar-al-Islam Literally, "the House of Belief"; the name given to the countries and peoples who profess belief in Islam; in contrast to *dar-al-harb* ("the House of War"), where Islam does not prevail and Muslims cannot freely practice their religion.

Abd al-Malik and his successors continued to pursue vigorous expansion of **dar-al-Islam** ("the House of Belief") through military conquest, extending the Umayyad realm across North Africa and into Central Asia. In 710–711 a coalition of Arab and Berber forces from Morocco invaded the Iberian peninsula and quickly overran the Visigoth kingdom, stunning Latin Christendom.

At first, to preserve the social unity of the conquerors, the Arabs ruled from garrison cities deliberately set apart from older urban centers. The Arabs thus became an elite military class based in garrison cities such as Basra and Kufa close kin, though their share is usually less than the portion received by male heirs.

> [Upon marriage], give women their dowry as a free gift. If they of their own good wish remit any part of it to you, take it and enjoy it with good cheer. (Qur'an, 4.4)
>
> From what is left by parents and near relatives there is a share for men and a share for women, whether the property be small or large. (Qur'an, 4.7)
>
> God instructs you concerning your children's inheritance: a son should have a share equivalent to that of two daughters: if you have only daughters, two or more, their combined share is two-thirds of the inheritance; if only one, her share is a half. (Qur'an, 4.11)

Under Jewish law, both men and women could initiate a divorce, but one of the radical reforms of Christianity was to abolish divorce. Islamic law granted the right of divorce to men but not to women. The Qur'an allows the husband to divorce a wife without her consent, but it also requires that he provide financial support for a divorced wife, as well as a widow. Following a period of mourning, widows are free to leave their husband's household together with their property and remarry if they wish.

> A divorce may be pronounced twice [to give the parties a chance to reconcile]: after that, the parties should either hold together on equitable terms, or separate with kindness. (Qur'an 2.229)
>
> Those of you who die and leave widows should bequeath for their widows a year's maintenance and residence. (Qur'an, 2.240)
>
> For divorced women, maintenance should be provided on a reasonable scale. (Qur'an, 2.241)

Examining the Evidence

1. Did Islamic law strengthen or weaken women's economic dependence on men?

2. Did Islamic laws on divorce and women's property correspond more closely to Jewish or to Christian precedents?

(both in Iraq), Fustat (modern Cairo), and Qayrawan (KYE-rwan) (in Tunisia), and they made little effort to convert their non-Arab subjects. "Peoples of the book"—Jews, Christians, and Zoroastrians, collectively referred to as **dhimmi** (DEE-me)—were permitted to practice their own religions, which the Arabs regarded as related but inferior versions of Islam, with some restrictions. The dhimmis also had to pay a special tax (*jizya*) in return for the state's protection.

The segregation of Arabs from the conquered peoples could not be sustained indefinitely, however. After a century of trying to maintain a distinct Arab-Muslim

dhimmi The Arabic term for "peoples of the book" (i.e., the Bible), namely Jews and Christians, who are seen as sharing the same religious tradition as Muslims.

≡ **Damascus's Great Mosque** Caliph al-Walid I (r. 705–715) built grand mosques at Medina, Jerusalem, and the Umayyad capital of Damascus to display the power and piety of the Islamic empire. The small octagonal building on pillars at left served as the treasury for the Muslim community. The mosque's southern entrance at right was reserved for the caliph and led directly to his palace.

identity separate from local societies, the Umayyad caliphs reversed course and instead began to promote Islam as a unifying force. Caliph Umar II (r. 717–720) encouraged conversion of local rulers, merchants, and scholars. Although most people remained faithful to their ancestral religions, many members of the local elites were eager to ally with their Arab rulers. They converted to Islam, adopted the Arabic language, and sought places in the military and government service as equals to Arabs.

From Unified Caliphate to Islamic Commonwealth 750–1000

↘ **FOCUS** How did the tensions between the ulama and the Abbasid caliphs weaken a unified Islamic empire?

Umar II's efforts to erase distinctions between Arabs and non-Arabs and create a universal empire based on the fundamental equality of all Muslims stirred up strong opposition from his fellow Arabs. Although the creation of a unified Islamic state fostered the emergence of a cosmopolitan society and culture, rebellions by Bedouin tribes and Shi'a communities caused the collapse of the Umayyad regime in 743. A new lineage of caliphs, the Abbasids, soon reestablished a centralized empire.

Rise of the Abbasid Caliphs

In 750, the Abbasids (ah-BASS-ids), a branch of Muhammad's clan that had settled in Khurasan in northern Iran, seized the caliphate in their own name. They based their legitimacy on their vow to restore the caliphate to the imams descended from Muhammad, which won them the crucial support of Shi'a Muslims. Once securely in power, however, the Abbasids revived Umar II's vision of a pan-Islamic empire (see Map 8.3). Proclaiming the universal equality of all Muslims, the Abbasids stripped the Arabs of their military and economic privileges while recruiting non-Arab officers and administrators loyal to the new dynasty.

The Abbasid dynasty perpetuated the image of the caliph as a universal sovereign and supreme defender of Islam. When the Abbasid caliph al-Mansur (r. 754–775) began building his new capital of Baghdad on the banks of the Tigris River, near the former Sasanid capital of Ctesiphon, in 762, he claimed to be fulfilling a prophecy that a city would be built at this spot, at "the crossroads of the whole

≡ **MAP 8.3** **The Islamic World, c. 1000** Under the Abbasid caliphs the Islamic empire reached its peak of power and influence. During the tenth century, however, the refugee Umayyad rulers of the Iberian peninsula and the Shi'a Fatimid dynasty in North Africa declared their own separate caliphates, permanently fracturing the political unity of the Islamic world.

world."[7] Baghdad soon mushroomed into a giant complex of palaces, government offices, military camps, and commercial and industrial quarters.

The merchant communities of Baghdad and other cities included a mix of Jews, Christians, Persians, and Central Asians, as well as Muslims. Abbasid policies favoring conversion to Islam isolated Christians and Jews, turning them into ethnic minorities. Nonetheless, Jews and Nestorian Christians enjoyed better opportunities to earn a living and practice their religions in the Muslim world than they had under Byzantine rule.

≡ **Iconoclasm in Islamic Art** Repudiating depictions of human figures (deemed a form of blasphemous self-glorification), Islamic art instead featured geometric designs, floral imagery, and moralizing proverbs. This plate—produced in Khurasan (Iran) during the Samanid dynasty (819–1005)—presumably was made for an urban upper-class client. The two identical inscriptions read: "He who believes in recompense is generous in giving, and to whatever you accustom yourself, you will grow accustomed."

The Abbasid rulers cultivated a cosmopolitan court life that blended Persian culture and Islamic faith. The court and wealthy officials and merchants in Baghdad became great patrons of scholars, physicians, and poets. Baghdad's scholars translated numerous Greek, Persian, and Indian works on philosophy, science, and medicine into Arabic, the common language of the Islamic world.

Baghdad society also included a significant number of enslaved people. According to Islamic law, Muslims could not enslave their fellow Muslims. Thus, enslaved persons were mostly obtained by purchase from Central Asia, the Slavic lands, and Africa. Elite households employed them as domestic servants, concubines, guards, and entertainers. Despite their legal status as "slaves," they could acquire some measure of social rank in Muslim society, as the example of Arib al-Ma'muniya (797–890) shows. Sold as a young girl to a high Abbasid official, Arib was trained in singing and music, talents that were in great demand in the elite homes of Baghdad. Arib became a leading figure in the capital's musical and literary salons. Through these contacts and her love affairs with high-ranking members of the Abbasid government and army, she acquired powerful friends and patrons. By the end of her life, Arib had become a wealthy woman who owned and trained her own slave singers.

The rise of the Abbasids drew the Islamic world farther from its roots in Arabia. After the founding of their caliphate, Arabia was no longer at the center of the Islamic world. Mecca and Medina remained the holy cities, where pilgrims throughout the Muslim world gathered and intermingled. But religious leadership, like political and economic power, shifted to Baghdad and other commercial centers such as Damascus, Basra, and Cairo.

Mesopotamia, the heartland of the Abbasid caliphate, experienced extraordinary economic and urban development. Building on improvements carried out by the Sasanid Empire, the Abbasid government invested heavily in the irrigation works needed to sustain agriculture. Papermaking, learned from China, displaced the practice of writing on papyrus leaves. Cotton textile manufacture and sugar refining emerged as major industries using techniques imported from India. The Muslim world became part of a vast global trading network, with Baghdad at its center.

Rise of the Religious Scholars

Whereas the power of the caliphs rested on their wealth, their legitimacy ultimately derived from their role as defenders of Islamic orthodoxy. Yet the caliphs did not inherit Muhammad's stature as prophet. The Qur'an remained the indisputable testament of religious wisdom, and the ulama taught how to apply its lessons to the conduct of social life. Religious teachers also compiled records of the deeds and words of Muhammad, known as **hadith**, as guides to the proper fulfillment of divine commandments. The caliphs thus occupied an ambiguous space in Islamic religious life. It was their job to defend Islamic orthodoxy, but they lacked the power to define that orthodoxy.

Their position was made even more difficult by the proliferation of scriptural commentaries and hadith, which widened the scope for individual interpretation of Islamic doctrine. In response, the caliphs sought to ensure orthodoxy by creating formal legal codes (*shari'a*) and law courts that combined religious and civil authority. Schools of law sprang up in major seats of Islamic learning such as Baghdad, Basra, Fustat, and Medina (see Chapter 12). However, because no consistent body of law could be applied uniformly throughout the caliphate, this initiative only added to the profusion of scriptural commentary and legal opinion that threatened to splinter the unity of Islamic teachings.

Faced with the potential fracturing of Islam, the ulama largely reconciled themselves to the caliphs' authority to maintain unity and order. Yet beneath this acceptance of Abbasid rule simmered profound discontent. "The best ruler is he who keeps company with scholars," proclaimed a leading religious teacher, "but the

hadith Records of the sayings and deeds of the Prophet Muhammad.

worst scholar is he who seeks the company of kings."[8] For the ulama, the special privileges and riches of the caliph and his courtiers betrayed Islam's most basic principles. In their view, the role of the caliph was not to determine Islamic law but rather to ensure the just administration of the shari'a for the benefit of all.

Relations between the caliphate and the ulama sank to their lowest point during the reign of al-Mamum (r. 813–833), who launched a harsh campaign to force the ulama to acknowledge the caliph's higher authority in theological matters. His heavy-handed tactics failed, however. The spiritual leadership of the ulama rested securely on the unswerving allegiance of ordinary citizens, which the caliph was powerless to usurp.

Collapse of the Unified Caliphate

Unable to command the loyalty of its subjects and with its very legitimacy in question, the Abbasid regime grew weaker and ultimately collapsed. Al-Mamum's brother and successor as caliph, al-Mutasim (r. 833–842), made the fateful decision to recruit enslaved Turks from Central Asia to form a new military force loyal to the caliphate. The slave soldiers soon ousted civil officials from the central government and provincial posts. In 861 a regiment of Turkish troops revolted and murdered the caliph, plunging the caliphate into anarchy. Some measure of stability was restored in 945, when a Persian military strongman took control of Baghdad, reducing the Abbasid caliph to a mere figurehead. But by then rulers in Spain and North Africa had claimed the mantle of caliph for themselves.

In the early years of the Abbasid caliphate, the sole survivor of the Umayyad clan, Abd al-Rahman (ahbd al-rah-MAHN) (r. 756–788), had assembled a coalition of Berber and Syrian forces and seized power in Muslim Spain. Too far removed from the Muslim heartland to pose a threat to the Abbasids, the Umayyad regime in Spain coexisted uneasily with the Baghdad caliphate (see again Map 8.3). In 931 as Abbasid authority ebbed, the Umayyad ruler Abd al-Rahman III (r. 912–961) declared himself the rightful caliph in the name of his forebears.

Another claim to the caliphate arose in North Africa, a stronghold of a messianic Shi'a movement known as the Ismailis. The Ismailis believed that soon the final prophet, the true successor to Muhammad and Ali, would appear in the world to usher in the final judgment and the resurrection of the faithful. In 909 an Ismaili leader in Algeria proclaimed himself caliph, founding what came to be called (in homage to Muhammad's daughter Fatima) the Fatimid dynasty. In 969 the Fatimids captured Egypt and made Cairo the capital of their caliphate.

By the middle of the tenth century, then, the unified caliphate had disintegrated into a series of regional dynasties. The collapse of political unity, however, did not lead to decline of Islamic social and cultural institutions. On the contrary, the tenth century was an age of cultural flowering in the Islamic world. The doctrinal disputes of the time produced an outpouring of theological scholarship and debate, and conversion of non-Arabs to Islam accelerated. Sufism, a mystical form of Islam based on commitment to a life of spirituality and self-denial, acquired a large following (see Chapter 12). Despite its political fragmentation, the Islamic world retained a collective identity as a commonwealth of states united by faith.

COUNTERPOINT: The Norse Vikings: The New Barbarians

↘ **FOCUS** How did the Vikings' society and culture contrast with those of the settled societies of Europe?

The Norse Vikings ("sea raiders") who terrified Latin Christendom for more than two centuries originally operated as independent bands of pirates and rarely acknowledged any authority other than the captains of their ships. Their Nordic homelands did not shift to formal centralized authority until the mid-eleventh century. Ultimately, however, the Vikings were transformed by their interactions with the settled peoples whose goods they coveted.

The Viking Raids 790–1020

The earliest record of the Vikings relates that in the year 793 strange omens appeared in the skies over northeastern England, followed by a dire famine; then, "on June 8th of the same year, merciless heathens laid waste the Church of God in Lindisfarne [in northeast England], with plundering and killing."[9] By 799 the Vikings were launching raids along the coast of France. The leaders of Christendom were aghast at what they interpreted as a brutal assault on the church and true religion. The Vikings were not, however, motivated by hatred of Christianity. They wanted money, goods, and slaves, and they were just as likely to prey on their fellow pagans as on Christians.

The Viking marauders originated from the Nordic, or Scandinavian, lands ringing the Baltic and North Seas, whose thick forests, thin soils, and long winters discouraged agriculture (see Map 8.4). Given this harsh and unpromising environment, it is not surprising that many Vikings turned to military raids to acquire what they could not produce themselves.

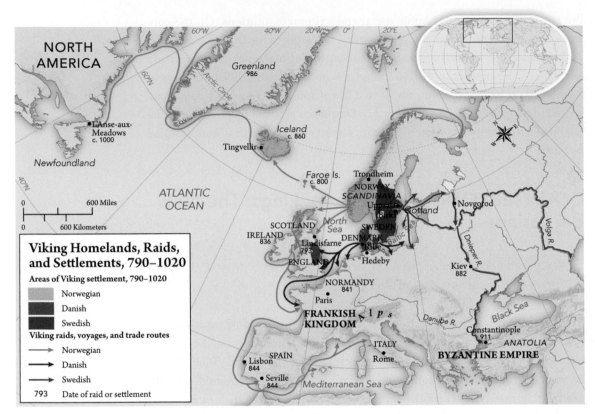

≡ **MAP 8.4   Viking Homelands, Raids, and Settlements, 790–1020** The Viking raiders were primarily interested in plunder and booty. But some Norse chieftains also led expeditions of conquest and settlement to England, France, Iceland, and the Baltic coast. Viking bands seeking the riches of Byzantium and the Islamic world also opened trade routes extending from the Baltic to the Black Sea.

Warfare had a long history in this region. The object of war was booty rather than territory. Instead of building the castles and stone fortifications that proliferated in northern Europe, the Vikings concentrated on improving their ability to launch seaborne raids. Between the fifth and eighth centuries, Norse shipbuilders developed larger and more seaworthy longboats, equipped with keels and powered by sails and by crews of thirty to sixty oarsmen. Using these vessels, roving Viking bands crossed the North Sea to pillage the coastal communities of Britain and France.

During the eighth century local chieftains all around the Nordic coasts constructed great halls, the "mead halls" celebrated in *Beowulf*, a tenth-century epic recounting the feats of a heroic Norse warrior. (Mead is a potent alcoholic beverage made from fermented honey and water.) Yet the great halls typically housed no more than thirty warriors and their families, and outfitting a single longboat required recruiting additional men beyond the chieftain's immediate retinue.

For raiding expeditions, convoys of longboats were assembled under the leadership of a king, or paramount chief.

Amid the conflict and rivalries of this warrior class few families could uphold their claim to royal authority for more than a couple of generations. The Christian missionary Ansgar, traveling in southern Sweden around 865–875, observed that although the king at Uppsala led armies overseas and conducted diplomatic negotiations with the Franks, in civil matters he deferred to an assembly of chieftains and landowners. The anonymous author of *Beowulf* boasted of a mighty Danish king who "shook the halls, took mead-benches, taught encroaching foes to fear him . . . until the clans settled in the seacoasts neighboring over the whale-road all must obey him and give tribute."[10] Yet outside of the epics and sagas, few kings commanded such awe and allegiance.

The Norse kings did not levy taxes in coin or grain. The king's role was not to accumulate wealth, but to distribute it. Extravagant banqueting in the mead halls—occasions of majesty in lands of meager and monotonous diets—lay at the heart of social and ritual life. Feasting enabled kings and chieftains to renew friendships and allay rivalries, while bestowing gifts of gold and other treasures allowed them to display their liberality and lordship.

In contrast to the settled peoples of Christendom and the Islamic world, the Vikings were indifferent town builders and traders. In the ninth and tenth centuries a few seaside trading posts—including Ribe and Hedley in Denmark and Birka in Sweden—grew into towns, with their own Christian bishops and mints, and attracted colonies of foreign merchants. But these towns remained small enclaves of at most 2,000 inhabitants. Only after 1000 did Nordic iron, furs, and slaves gain a foothold in European markets.

Islamic silver coins imported from the Black Sea began to appear in the Baltic region at the close of the eighth century. The abundance of Islamic coins found in Viking hoards should not be taken as a measure of commercial activity, however. Most likely the Vikings obtained their troves of silver from piracy rather than trade.

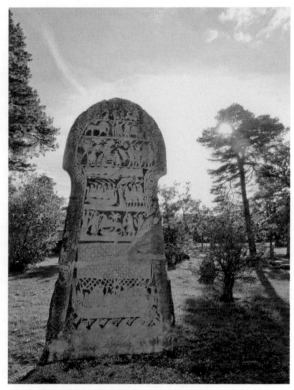

Viking Memorial Stone Viking picture stones such as this eighth-century one from the island of Gotland off the coast of Sweden are believed to have been memorials to dead warriors and chiefs. Scholars disagree about the precise meaning of the scenes shown on this stone. One interpretation suggests that they depict the death of a warrior in battle and his final journey to the underworld on the Viking longboat at bottom.

Norse Emigration and Colonization

In the ninth century the Norse chieftains began to conduct expeditions aimed at conquest and colonization. Danish marauders seized lands in eastern England and imposed their own laws and customs on the Anglo-Saxons. By about 1000, the Danes had extended their control to parts of Norway, Sweden, and, under King Cnut (Keh-NEWT) (r. 1017–1035), all of England. Vikings also occupied parts of Ireland and coastal lands on the European continent from Normandy to Denmark.

Legends relate that the island of Iceland was first colonized during 870–930 by hundreds of families fleeing the tyranny of the Norwegian king Harald Fairhair. More likely the immigrants were driven by hunger for land. Iceland, with its relatively mild winters, ample pasture for cattle, and abundant game, must have seemed a windfall. But human settlement soon upset the island's fragile ecology. Forests and fields were ruined by timber cutting, erosion, and overgrazing, while the game was hunted to extinction. By 1000 the settlers were desperately short of fuel and timber, and fishing had become the staple of their livelihood.

Around 980 Icelanders in search of virgin territories made landfall on Greenland, only to discover that this new world was even less well endowed with forests, pasture, and arable land. Subsequent foraging expeditions took them to Newfoundland, but there, too, the prospects for farming and stock raising were dim, and settlements were short-lived.

Prolonged contact with Latin Christendom eventually eroded the Viking way of life. From about 1000 on, towns and merchants proliferated, local chieftains yielded to the rule of royal dynasties, and kings submitted to baptism and the Christian church's authority. As these new forms of economic, religious, and political life permeated the Nordic world, the Vikings' plundering ceased.

Conclusion

By the year 1000 the classical civilizations of western Eurasia had been reshaped by their new dominant religious cultures, Christianity and Islam. Christianity had spread throughout the European provinces of the old Roman Empire, whereas Islam prevailed in the heartlands of the ancient Persian and Egyptian empires and among the pastoral desert tribes of Arabia and North Africa. Christianity and Islam both flourished most vigorously in the cities. By 1000 the Christian church had made a concerted effort to extend its reach into village society through its legions of parish priests, and monastic orders ranked among the greatest landowners of Europe. The penetration of Islam into the countryside in long-settled areas such as Syria, Mesopotamia, and Iran came more slowly.

From its inception, Islam became a political force as well as a religious movement, and the Umayyad caliphs created a vast Islamic empire. Despite efforts by the Byzantine emperors and the Muslim caliphs to impose religious orthodoxy, however, both Christendom and the Islamic empire fractured into competing religious traditions and a multitude of states.

At the same time, these religious faiths advanced into new frontiers. German kings and warriors followed in the footsteps of our chapter-opening heroine Radegund in embracing Christianity. Cultural, economic, and political interaction with the Byzantine Empire brought most Slavic peoples into the Christian fold. The arrival of Christianity in the Norse lands of northern Europe brought an end to the Viking menace. Although the prospects for a unified Muslim empire receded, Islamic religion and culture had become deeply implanted in a vast territory stretching from Iran to Spain. Starting around 1000, Islam again underwent rapid expansion, notably in Africa and Asia, where, as we shall see in the next chapter, the Indian religions of Buddhism and Hinduism had shaped many diverse societies.

review

The major global development in this chapter: The spread of Christianity and Islam and the profound impact of these world religions on the societies of western Eurasia and North Africa.

Important Events	
410	Visigoth sack of Rome
431	Council of Ephesus denounces Nestorianism as heresy
507	Clovis defeats Visigoth invaders and converts to Christianity
527–565	Reign of Justinian I as Byzantine emperor
570–632	Life of Muhammad, founder of Islam
589	Conversion of Visigoths to Roman Christianity
590–604	Papacy of Gregory I
622	Muhammad's hijra to Medina, marking the beginning of the Islamic calendar

Important Events	
661–750	Umayyad caliphate
680	Split between Shi'a and Sunni Islam
710–711	Muslim invasion and conquest of Visigoth-ruled Spain
732	Charles Martel halts Muslim advance into Europe
750–1258	Abbasid caliphate
793	Earliest record of Viking raids on Britain
800	Coronation of Charlemagne as emperor by Pope Leo III
868–883	Zanj revolt against the Abbasid regime
870–930	Vikings colonize Iceland
909	Fatimid dynasty founded
988	Vladimir, the Rus prince of Kiev, converts to Christianity

KEY TERMS

caliph (p. 298)
dar-al-Islam (p. 300)
dhimmi (p. 301)
hadith (p. 305)
hijra (p. 297)

iconoclasm (p. 287)
imam (p. 299)
jihad (p. 297)
manor (p. 291)
Qur'an (p. 298)

schism (p. 286)
serf (p. 291)
Shi'a (p. 299)
Sunni (p. 299)
ulama (p. 298)

CHAPTER OVERVIEW QUESTIONS

1. How and why did the development of the Christian church differ in the Byzantine Empire and Latin Christendom?
2. In what ways did the rise of Christianity and Islam challenge the power of the state?

3. Conversely, in what ways did the spread of these faiths reinforce state power?
4. Why did Christianity and Islam achieve their initial success in towns and cities rather than in the countryside?

MAKING CONNECTIONS

1. How did the political institutions and ideology of the Islamic empire of the Umayyad and Abbasid caliphates differ from those of the Roman Empire (see Chapter 6)?

2. In what ways did the spiritual authority of the Islamic ulama differ from that exercised by the Christian popes and bishops?

3. How does the Islamic conception of the community of the faithful compare with Jewish and Christian ideas of community?

4. What were the causes and effects of the Viking raids and invasions in Europe in the eighth through tenth centuries, and how did these compare with the early invasions of the Roman Empire by the Germanic peoples (see Chapter 6)?

DOING HISTORY

Perspectives

Historians engaged in world history seek to understand long-term changes in ideas, cultures, economic life, and political institutions across diverse societies around the globe. This macrocosmic perspective is a fundamental feature of writing world history. Yet at the same time we want to know how such changes affected people at the microcosmic level of the individual person. For example, we see in this chapter that the ancient empires of Rome and Persia were transformed by conversion to the new religions of Christianity and Islam. We must ask why and how entire societies adopted radically different beliefs, practices, and social institutions that affected all aspects of life. But we also want to understand the implications of conversion as a personal experience.

1. Was religious conversion a matter of personal choice?

2. Or should the spread of Christianity and Islam be better understood as social conversion—choices made by political leaders and social elites, with little room for personal convictions?

3. How might the reasons for social conversion differ from the personal motives of individuals?

For further research into the topics covered in this chapter, see the Bibliography at the end of the book.

9

Religion and Cross-Cultural Exchange in Asia

400–1000

≡ **A World in the Making** The Chinese monk Xuanzang's epic journey to India epitomized the cross-cultural exchanges that took place across Asia during the heyday of the Silk Road. In this Japanese painting commemorating Xuanzang's life, the pilgrim monk parades in triumph through the Chinese capital of Chang'an, preceded by horses bearing the precious Buddhist scriptures he brought back from India.

backstory

In China as in the Roman world, invasions and migrations by "barbarian" peoples followed the collapse of empire. After the Han Empire fell in the third century CE (see Chapter 5), endemic fighting among regional warlords weakened China and made it possible for steppe nomads to conquer the north China heartland in the early fourth century. Pressure from central Eurasian nomads also contributed to the demise of the Gupta Empire in northern India at the end of the fifth century. Yet political turmoil and the fragmentation of India and China into smaller rival kingdoms did not breed isolation. On the contrary, the Silk Road flourished as a channel of trade and cultural exchange.

IN 642, A CHINESE Buddhist pilgrim named Xuanzang (shoo-wen-zahng) (c. 602–664) was enjoying a leisurely stay at the court of the king of Assam, in the Himalayan foothills of northern India. Thirteen years before, Xuanzang had left China, where he had studied Buddhism at Chang'an, capital of the recently founded Tang dynasty (618–907). As his studies progressed, however, Xuanzang concluded that he could learn the Buddha's original teachings only by traveling to India, homeland of the Buddha, "the Awakened One." Defying an imperial decree that forbade travel abroad, Xuanzang embarked across the deserts and mountain ranges of Central Asia and spent years retracing the footsteps of the Buddha. It was these travels that had brought him to the court of Assam.

Xuanzang's visit, however, was interrupted by an urgent summons from King Harsha (r. 606–647), the most powerful Indian monarch at the time. Xuanzang's reputation as a great philosopher and skilled orator had come to the attention of King Harsha, a pious man and an earnest patron of both Hindu Brahmin priests and Buddhist monks. "He divided the day into three parts," commented Xuanzang, "the first devoted to affairs of state, and the other two to worship and charitable works, to which he applied himself tirelessly, as there were not enough hours in the day to complete his ministrations."[1] Harsha now wished to host a grand philosophical debate featuring his Chinese guest.

On the appointed day King Harsha led a vast procession of princes, nobles, soldiers, and priests to a parade ground on the banks of the Ganges River. The theological tournament lasted five days, during which the rhetorical clashes grew increasingly fierce. When Harsha declared Xuanzang the victor, his Brahmin opponents allegedly set fire to the shrine housing the Buddha's image, and one of them tried to assassinate the king. Harsha, keen to avert religious strife among his subjects, punished the ringleader but pardoned the rest of the disgruntled Brahmins. Four months later, Xuanzang departed for home. Although he had left China illegally, he returned in triumph. The Tang emperor anointed him "the jewel of the empire" and built a magnificent monastery to house the precious Buddhist icons, relics, and books that he had brought back from India.

Xuanzang's remarkable experiences were part of the larger pattern of cross-cultural encounters and exchanges that shaped Asia in the second half of the first millennium CE. Since the first century CE, Buddhist missionaries had accompanied the caravans setting out from India to seek the fabled silks of China. As we will explore in this chapter, in later centuries others traveled this Silk Road between India and China bearing goods and ideas that fertilized cross-cultural exchange, including nomad warriors, long-distance traders, and missionaries and pilgrims. A similar interweaving of commerce and evangelism also drew Southeast Asia into sustained contact with India and to a lesser extent with China.

The resulting spread of Buddhism and Hinduism from India provided the foundations for distinctive regional cultures across Asia. Political and social crises in China and India prompted serious questioning in those countries of traditional beliefs and values, creating a climate more receptive to new ideas. At the same time, the leaders of newly emerging states in East and Southeast Asia looked toward China and India for models of political institutions and cultural values. A common civilization inspired by Chinese political, philosophical, and literary traditions and permeated by Buddhist beliefs and practices emerged in East Asia. In Southeast Asia, a more eclectic variety of societies and cultures developed, one that blended Indian influences with native traditions.

OVERVIEW QUESTIONS

The major global development in this chapter: The cultural and commercial exchanges during the heyday of the Silk Road that transformed Asian peoples, cultures, and states.

As you read, consider:

1. In what ways did Asian societies respond to cross-cultural interaction during the fifth to tenth centuries?

2. What strategies did pastoral nomads adopt in their relations with settled societies, and why?

3. What patterns of political and cultural borrowing characterized the emerging states in East and Southeast Asia?

4. Why did India and China experience different outcomes following the collapse of strong and unified empires?

Steppe Peoples and Settled Societies of Central Asia

↘ **FOCUS** What strategies did nomadic steppe chieftains and the rulers of agrarian societies apply in their dealings with each other?

Neither the fall of the Han dynasty in China in the early third century nor the collapse of the Roman Empire in the West in the fifth century resulted directly from invasions by pastoral nomads from the steppes of Central Asia. In both cases, imperial decline was the cause rather than the consequence of nomadic invasions. Political instability following the demise of the Han encouraged raids by nomadic groups on China's northern frontiers. During the fifth century, one of these groups, the Tuoba (TWAUGH-bah) confederation, gradually occupied nearly all of northern China, as well as Manchuria and Mongolia.

Despite the political instability on the Eurasian steppe in this era, trade and cultural exchange flourished as never before. The heyday of the Silk Road between the fourth and the eighth centuries witnessed major changes in the societies and cultures of Asia. The empires of the Tuoba, the Turks, and the Khazars marked a new stage in state formation among the nomadic tribes. The military ingenuity and political skills these nomad confederations developed would later make possible the greatest nomad conquerors of all, the Mongols (discussed in Chapter 13).

Nomad Conquerors of China: The Northern Wei 386–534

Throughout the long-lived Han dynasty (202 BCE–220 CE), steppe nomads had shifted between a "hard" strategy of invading China and extorting tribute during times of strength and a "soft" strategy of allying with Chinese rulers and acknowledging their overlordship during times of weakness. The nomads were primarily interested in obtaining scarce resources they could not produce themselves, such as grain and silk cloth. Nomad chieftains had no desire to conquer the agrarian states. They preferred to acquire the goods they desired through tribute and trade rather than direct rule.

The demise of the Han dynasty in 220 ushered in a century of civil wars that sapped the empire's defenses and left China vulnerable to foreign invasion. In 311, steppe invaders sacked Luoyang (LWAUGH-yahng), the capital of the reigning Jin dynasty. For the next three centuries, a series of foreign rulers controlled north China. In the late fourth century, a measure of stability was restored to north China by the rulers of a new confederation of steppe peoples, the Tuoba.

The rise of the Tuoba marked the first attempt by steppe nomads to build enduring institutions for governing agrarian China, rather than merely seeking to extract booty from it. In 386 the Tuoba declared their imperial ambitions by adopting a Chinese-style dynastic name, Northern Wei (way). From 430, when the Tuoba captured the former Han capital of Chang'an, to the 530s, the Northern Wei reigned virtually unchallenged across a wide swath of Asia from Manchuria to Bactria (see Map 9.1).

To reinforce their legitimacy and further their imperial ambitions, the Northern Wei promoted assimilation between themselves and their Chinese subjects.

≡ **MAP 9.1 Nomad Steppe Empires, c. 500–650** In the fifth century the Tuoba nomads ruled over north China and the southern edge of the steppe grasslands as the Northern Wei dynasty. After the Northern Wei collapsed in the 530s, a new confederation, the Turks, emerged. Over the next century the Turks created the first great nomad empire, spanning the Central Asian steppe from Manchuria to Sogdia.

Northern Wei rulers avidly embraced the Buddhist faith that, as we will see, had spread throughout Central Asia. Emperor Xiaowen (SHI-AW-when) (r. 471–499) encouraged intermarriage between the Tuoba nobility and the leading Chinese aristocratic clans, as well as adoption of Chinese language, dress, and customs. Xiaowen sought to create a hybrid ruling class that combined the martial traditions of the steppe with the cultural prestige and administrative expertise of imperial China. Ultimately, however, his policies divided the "sinified" Tuoba—those who adopted Chinese ways—within China from the Tuoba nobles, based in the steppe grasslands, who staunchly resisted Chinese habits and values. This split widened when purist Tuoba chiefs from the steppes revolted in 524. The Northern Wei state crumbled ten years later.

Rise of the Turks

The return of tribal strife to the eastern steppe gave charismatic leaders among the pastoral nomads a chance to forge new coalitions. In Mongolia, a chieftain named Bumin (BOO-min) (d. 552) emerged as the **khan** ("lord") of a new confederation called the Heavenly Turks.

Technology played a role in the Turks' rise to prominence. Recent innovations in warfare, such as the use of stirrups, had become widespread in the eastern steppe in the fifth century. The stirrup gave horse-riding archers a steadier posture from which to shoot. Turkic warriors cloaked themselves in mailed armor and wielded large bows and curved sabers. Thus equipped, the Turkic cavalry transformed themselves into a far more deadly force than the mounted warriors of the past.

The Turks' most dramatic advance occurred in the western steppe. They swallowed up the oasis towns and principalities of the Silk Road, reaching as far west as the Black Sea. Like earlier steppe confederations, the Turks preferred tribute and trade as means of obtaining booty. The merchants of Sogdia, in modern Uzbekistan, became key advisers and agents of the Turkic leaders (see Counterpoint: Sogdian Traders in Central Asia and China).

In diplomatic negotiations with the autocratic empires of Iran and China, the Turkic khans presented themselves as supreme monarchs. Nevertheless, the Turkic confederation remained a loose band of tribes whose chieftains retained considerable autonomy. When, as we will see, a strong empire reemerged in China under the Sui dynasty in the late sixth century, the Turks lacked effective leadership to counter a resurgent China. By 603 the Sui captured the eastern portion of the Silk Road corridor, splitting the Turks into separate eastern and western groups.

A Turkic Khanate in the West: The Khazars

Following the division of the Turkic Empire in 603, local tribal identities once again came to the fore in the western part of the former empire, where few people were of Turkic ancestry. The Khazars (hus-ahr), based in the Caucasus region between the Black and Caspian seas, emerged as an independent khanate. Around 650 the Khazars conquered the rival Bulgar khanate that had been established northeast of the Black Sea (see again Map 9.1).

Following their triumph over the Bulgars, the Khazars moved their capital to Itil in the Volga River delta. Although Itil consisted of little more than a massed array of felt tents, the Khazar capital attracted merchants from distant regions. Many Muslims resided there, along with Jewish merchants who had fled Constantinople because of persecution by the Byzantine government. Commercial exchange with the Muslim world was fed by the rich mines of the Caucasus region,

---

khan The Turkish word for "lord," used especially for rulers of the nomad empires of the central Eurasian steppes.

☰ **Tuoba Mounted Warriors** The cave temples constructed between the fourth and eleventh centuries at the Central Asian oasis town of Dunhuang constitute perhaps the world's most important repository of Buddhist art. The cave murals also illustrate secular life; here, mounted Tuoba warriors, with their characteristic helmets and horses clad in mailed armor (in green), subdue a bandit force on foot. The donors of this cave temple, constructed in 538, appear in another mural, also in Tuoba dress.

the tribute of furs collected from Slavs in the Dnieper River Valley, and the steady flow of enslaved persons seized as war captives. Despite the Khazars' nomadic lifestyle, their capital became a crossroads for trade and cultural exchange.

This openness was dramatically demonstrated when, around 861, the reigning Khazar khan abruptly converted to Judaism. The khan adopted the Jewish Torah as the legal code of the Khazars, although Christians and Muslims continued to be judged according to their own laws. Subsequently the head of the Jewish community gained effective power over political affairs, relegating the khan to the role of a symbolic figurehead. The Khazar khanate did not long survive this dramatic shift. In 965 Rus armies overran Itil and other Khazar towns, bringing the khanate to an end and opening the region to settlement by Christian Slavs.

The Shaping of East Asia

↘ FOCUS How did the spread of Buddhism transform the politics and societies of East Asia?

The culture and technology of the Chinese empires—and of course their political and military muscle—could not fail to have a powerful impact on China's neighbors. The imposition of direct Chinese rule on the Korean peninsula and Vietnam during the Han dynasty (see Chapter 5) left a deep imprint on these regions. Independent Korean states arose after the Han Empire collapsed in the early third century CE, but Vietnam remained under Chinese rule until the tenth century. In the Japanese islands, contact and exchange with the continent stimulated the progress of state formation beginning in the third century.

Although both Korea and Japan preserved their independence from the resurgent Sui (sway) (581–618) and Tang (618–907) Empires in China, their societies were shaped by Chinese political and cultural traditions. The farthest-reaching cultural transformation of this era was the adoption of a foreign tradition, Buddhism, as the dominant religion within China, and subsequently in the rest of East Asia. With the waning of Tang imperial might after the mid-eighth century, however, Japan and Korea shifted away from Chinese models and developed their own distinctive political and social identities. After Vietnam gained independence in the early tenth century, the multistate system of modern East Asia assumed definitive form.

The Chinese Transformation of Buddhism

From the first century CE, Buddhist missionaries from India had crossed the steppe grasslands of Central Asia and reached China. The rise of the kingdom of the Kushans, great patrons of Buddhism, at the intersection of the trade routes linking China with India and Iran had stimulated the spread of Buddhism along these thoroughfares. The collapse of the Han Empire and subsequent foreign invasions prompted many Chinese to question their values and beliefs and to become receptive to alternative ideas and ways of life.

In its original form, Buddhism could not be readily assimilated into the Chinese worldview. Its rejection of the mundane world and its stress on a monastic vocation conflicted with the humanist goals and family-centered ethics of Confucianism. As we saw in Chapter 5, however, the **Mahayana** school of Buddhism maintained that laypeople in any walk of life had equal potential for achieving enlightenment and salvation. The figure of the **bodhisattva**

Mahayana A major branch of Buddhism that emphasizes the potential for laypeople to achieve enlightenment through the aid of the Buddha and bodhisattvas.

bodhisattva In Mahayana Buddhism, an enlightened being who delays entry into nirvana and chooses to remain in the world of suffering to assist others in their quest for salvation.

chakravartin In Indian political thought, the "wheel-turning king," a universal monarch who enjoys the favor of the gods and acts as a defender of religious orthodoxy.

(boh-dih-SAHT-vah), an enlightened being who delays entry into nirvana to aid the faithful in their own religious quests, exemplified the Mahayana ideal of selfless compassion and provided a model for pious laypeople and clergy alike. The Mahayana vision of a multitude of Buddhas (of whom the historical Buddha was only one) and bodhisattvas as divine saviors also encouraged the prospect of gaining salvation within a person's present lifetime, rather than after many lives of suffering. It was the Mahayana school of Buddhism, therefore, that made broad inroads in China.

Mahayana Buddhism's compatibility with Chinese cultural and intellectual traditions was crucial to its acceptance. The Buddhist doctrine of karma—the belief that the individual's good and evil actions determine one's destiny in the next reincarnation—was revised to allow people to earn merit not just for themselves but also for their parents and children. The pursuit of karmic merit became a family endeavor rather than a self-centered enterprise. This understanding of karma fit well with the Chinese practice of ancestor worship and view of family as the fundamental moral unit.

During the fifth century, devotion to Buddhism spread swiftly among the ruling classes in both north and south China. Several Northern Wei emperors converted to Buddhism and became avid patrons of Buddhist institutions. Buddhism also served useful political purposes. In a world fractured by warfare and political instability, its universalist spirit offered an inclusive creed that might ease social and ethnic frictions among the Chinese and the diverse foreign peoples who had settled within China. The Northern Wei rulers were especially attracted to the Buddhist ideal of

≡ **Buddhist Family Shrine** Although the Buddha had presented the pursuit of enlightenment as an individual quest, Mahayana Buddhists in China promoted devotional acts intended to earn karmic merit for the entire family. This colossal (over three meters tall) stone sculpture, dated 495, was commissioned by members of the Zhao clan, undoubtedly as a collective family project. The four rows of figures standing in a posture of adoration to the left of the figure of the Buddha represent the donors, who are depicted wearing Tuoba dress and headgear.

the *chakravartin* (chuhk-ruh-VAHR-tin), the "wheel-turning king" (controller of human destiny) who wages righteous wars to bring the true religion to the unenlightened peoples of the world. The chakravartin ideal was founded on the historical precedent of Ashoka (see Chapter 5), the great Mauryan king of the third century BCE, whose success was closely tied to his patronage of Buddhism.

In the sixth century, two interrelated developments profoundly altered the evolution of Buddhism in East Asia. First, Chinese monastic communities and lay congregations created their own forms of Buddhist theology and practices more closely attuned to their Chinese audience. Second, these new movements reached well beyond the elite and led to the emergence of Buddhism as a religion of the masses. As a reaction against the exclusivity of earlier forms of Buddhism, two new forms of Buddhism developed—**Pure Land** Buddhism and Chan (Zen) Buddhism.

Pure Land Buddhism first emerged as a coherent religious movement in China during the sixth century. Pure Land expressed deep pessimism about mortal existence. The formidable burden of sins accumulated over countless lifetimes made the possibility of attaining salvation through one's own efforts appear hopelessly remote. Yet people of sincere faith could obtain rebirth in the Pure Land, a celestial paradise, through the aid of savior figures such as Amitabha (Ah-MEE-tah-bah), the presiding Buddha of the Pure Land, or Guanyin (GWAHN-yin), the bodhisattva of compassion.

Like the later Protestant Reformation of Christianity, Pure Land Buddhism emphasized salvation through faith alone rather than good works. Thus, it offered the hope that through sincere piety all persons, no matter how humble, might attain salvation within their present lifetimes. Pure Land teachings found favor among poor and illiterate people. Its devotions focused on simple rituals, such as chanting the names of Amitabha and Guanyin, that did not require wealth, learning, or leisure. Because of the universal appeal of its message, the Pure Land movement transformed Chinese Buddhism into a mass religion focused on the worship of compassionate savior figures.

Like Pure Land, **Chan** Buddhism—better known by its Japanese name, Zen—rejected a religious life centered on recitation of scripture and performance of rituals. Chan instead embraced strict discipline and mystical understanding of truth as the genuine path of enlightenment. But in contrast to Pure Land, Chan Buddhism emphasized sublime spiritual enlightenment rather than rebirth in paradise. The Chan movement gained a widespread following among the clergy beginning in the eighth century and subsequently became the preeminent monastic tradition throughout East Asia.

Reunification of the Chinese Empire: The Sui Dynasty 581–618

The collapse of the Northern Wei in 534 once again plunged northern China into anarchic warfare. In 581, Yang Jian (yahng gee-ehn) (d. 604), a member of the mixed-blood Tuoba-Chinese aristocracy, staged a bloody coup and installed

Pure Land A school of Mahayana Buddhism, originating in China, that emphasizes the sinfulness of the human condition and the necessity of faith in savior figures (the Buddha and bodhisattvas) to gain rebirth in paradise.

Chan A Buddhist devotional tradition, originating in China, that emphasizes salvation through personal conduct, meditation, and mystical enlightenment; also known as Zen.

himself as emperor. As iron-fisted ruler of the Sui dynasty (581–618), Yang Jian quickly reasserted military supremacy. In 589 he conquered southern China and restored a unified empire.

Yang Jian was determined to resurrect the grandeur of the Han by rebuilding a centralized bureaucratic state. Although his inner circle was still drawn from the hybrid aristocracy fostered by the Northern Wei, high office was a privilege the emperor could bestow or take away as he saw fit. Yang also retained the system of state landownership that the Northern Wei had put in place. Under the **equal-field system**, the Northern Wei government allocated landholdings to individual households based on the number of able-bodied adults the household had to work the land and how many mouths it had to feed. Each household was expected to have roughly equal productive capabilities, so that the state could collect uniform taxes in grain, cloth, and labor or military service from all households. Although aristocratic families largely preserved their extensive landholdings, this system of state landownership provided the Northern Wei with dependable sources of tax revenues and soldiers.

Yang Jian's son and successor, Yang Guang (r. 604–618), further centralized control over resources by building the Grand Canal. This artificial waterway connected the Sui capital at Chang'an in northwestern China with the rice-growing regions of the Yangzi River delta. With the Grand Canal, the central government could tap the burgeoning agricultural wealth of southern China to feed the capital and the military garrisons surrounding it.

≡ **Eleven-Headed Guanyin** Guanyin, the bodhisattva of compassion, became the most popular figure in East Asian Buddhism. This tenth-century banner depicts Guanyin with eleven heads and six arms, symbolizing Guanyin's role as a savior. Guanyin is surrounded by scenes from the Lotus Sutra in which the bodhisattva rescues devout followers from perils such as fire and bandits. The donor, dressed as a Chinese official, appears at bottom right.

The Sui rulers differed sharply from their Han predecessors in their commitment to Buddhism rather than Confucianism. A devout believer in Buddhism since childhood, Yang Jian recognized Buddhism's potential to aid him in rebuilding a universal empire. Yang Jian polished his self-image as a chakravartin king and imitated the example of Ashoka by building hundreds of Buddhist shrines and monasteries throughout the empire.

Yet the Sui dynasty ended as abruptly as it began. Foreign affairs, rather than domestic problems, proved the dynasty's undoing. From the outset the Sui had

equal-field system
A system of state-controlled landownership created by the Northern Wei dynasty in China that attempted to allocate equitable portions of land to all households.

tempestuous relations with their Korean neighbors. In 612 Yang Guang launched an invasion of Korea that ended in disastrous defeat. When the emperor insisted on preparing a new offensive, his generals revolted against him, and he was assassinated in 618. One of his former generals, Li Yuan (565–635), declared himself emperor of a new dynasty, the Tang.

The Power of Tang China 618–907

Li Yuan's seizure of power was only the latest in a series of coups led by the Tuoba-Chinese aristocratic clans dating back to the fall of the Northern Wei. Yet unlike its predecessors, the Tang fashioned an enduring empire, the wealthiest and most powerful state in Asia (see Map 9.2). Given their roots in both the Chinese and Tuoba nobilities, the Tang rulers laid equal claim to the worlds of the steppe nomads and settled peoples. They extended Chinese supremacy over the oasis city-states of the eastern steppe, which further fragmented the Turkic confederation. Within China, they revived Confucian traditions while building on the institutional foundations of the Northern Wei and Sui to reestablish a strong bureaucratic state.

At its pinnacle of power in the late seventh century, the Tang dynasty was beset by a jarring crisis. During the reign of the sickly emperor Gaozong (gow dzoong) (r. 650–683), the empress Wu Zhao (woo jow) took an increasingly assertive role in governing the empire. In 690 Wu Zhao set aside the Tang dynasty and declared her own Zhou dynasty, becoming the only woman ever to rule as emperor of China. Although Confucian historians depict her in the harshest possible light, there is little evidence that the empire's prosperity diminished during her reign. Shortly before her death in 705, however, Empress Wu was forced to abdicate, and the Tang dynasty was restored.

The Tang capital of Chang'an had been built by the Sui founder, Yang Jian, near the site of the ancient Han capital. The Chinese conceived of their capital not only as the seat of government but also as the axis of cosmological order. The capital's design—laid out as a square, with its main gate facing south—expressed the principles of order and balance that imperial rule was expected to embody. Imperial palaces, government offices, marketplaces, and residential areas were symmetrically arranged along a central north–south avenue in checkerboard fashion. The bustling Western Market, terminus of the Silk Road, teemed with foreign as well as Chinese merchants. The more sedate Eastern Market catered to an elite clientele of officials and aristocrats. The cosmopolitan styles of life and culture radiating from Chang'an reverberated throughout East Asia, shaping tastes in fashion, furnishings, and pastimes, as well as music, dance, and art (see Lives and Livelihoods: Tea Drinkers in Tang China).

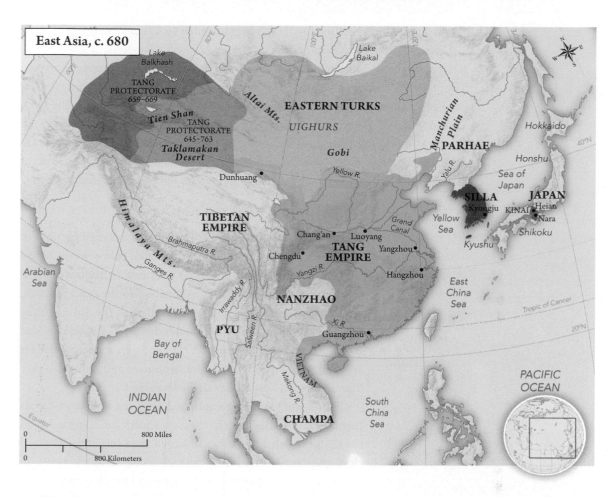

≡ **MAP 9.2 East Asia, c. 680** The early Tang emperors sought to reassert Chinese dominion over the eastern steppe, including Manchuria and Korea. Tang military assistance helped the Korean kingdom of Silla to topple Koguryo, long the most powerful of the Korean states, in 668. Although Tang China exerted a powerful cultural influence on its East Asian neighbors, Silla and the newly christened emperors of Japan retained their political independence.

Yet the gilded glory of Tang civilization masked deepening political and economic divisions. Aristocratic factions jockeyed for control of the court and the riches and privileges at its disposal. Economic prosperity and commercial growth eroded the rigid equal-field landownership system and jeopardized the state's financial stability. The gravest challenge to Tang rule came in 755, when An Lushan (ahn loo-shahn), a Sogdian general who commanded the Tang armies along the northeastern frontier, revolted. Convinced that he was about to fall victim to court intrigues, An rallied other generals to his side and marched on Chang'an. The dynasty survived, but probably only because An Lushan was assassinated—by his son—in 757. The rebellion finally was suppressed in 763, thanks to the crucial aid of Turkic Uighur mercenaries from Central Asia.

Although the Tang dynasty endured for another 150 years, it never recovered from the An Lushan rebellion. The revolt wrecked the empire's finances by forcing the government to abandon the equal-field system. The aristocratic families who had dominated government and society since the Han dynasty were perhaps the major casualties of the rebellion, as the court ceded much military and civil authority to provincial warlords. Tethered to the weakened Tang court, their estates lying in ruin, the old aristocracy clung to its prestige but never regained its power.

China and Its Neighbors

At its height in the second century BCE, the Han Empire had annexed portions of the Korean peninsula and Vietnam and established colonial rule over the native peoples of these regions. The introduction of China's political institutions and cultural heritage exerted a lasting influence on Korea and Vietnam, and later on Japan as well. The rise and fall of the Sui and Tang Empires gave birth to East Asia as a common civilization divided into separate national states. Although each state aggressively asserted its independence, Chinese policies and influences profoundly shaped how each of them developed.

Chinese rule in Korea continued until the nomad invasions that overran north China in the early fourth century CE. In 313 the Chinese-ruled territories in Korea were seized by Koguryo (koh-goo-ryuh), a recently formed confederation based in southern Manchuria. Pressure from nomad invaders soon forced Koguryo to move its capital to the site of modern Pyongyang, but it became embroiled in conflict with the states of Paekche (pock-CHAY) and Silla (SHEE-lah), which had sprung up in the southern peninsula.

The earliest reference to the Japanese islands in Chinese records concerns an embassy dispatched to the Chinese court in 238 by Himiko (hee-mee-KOH), queen of the Wa people. Himiko was described as a spinster sorceress whom the Wa had elected as ruler to instill unity and curb the violent disorder that had wracked the archipelago for generations. At the time that Himiko's envoys arrived in China, influences from the mainland had set in motion a profound transformation in the economy and society of the Japanese islands. Settled agriculture based on

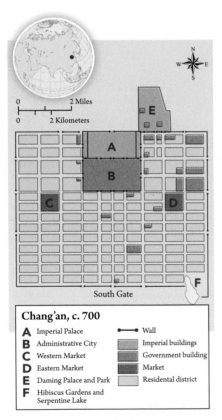

0   2 Miles

0   2 Kilometers

South Gate

Chang'an, c. 700

A   Imperial Palace

B   Administrative City

C   Western Market

D   Eastern Market

E   Daming Palace and Park

F   Hibiscus Gardens and Serpentine Lake

Wall

Imperial buildings

Government building

Market

Residental district

≡ **Chang'an, c. 700**

rice cultivation had developed in Japan since the fourth century BCE. Bronze and iron wares—chiefly weapons and prestige goods such as bronze mirrors—appeared together in the archipelago, probably in the first century CE. During the first four centuries CE, the population of the Japanese islands grew rapidly, in part because of immigration from the continent.

In the fourth century the Yamato kingdom in Kinai, the region around the modern city of Osaka, gained dominance in the Japanese islands. The Yamato "great kings" may or may not have descended from the Wa lineage of Himiko, but their power clearly derived from their success as warrior chiefs. Although the Yamato won the Chinese court's recognition as rulers of Japan, they only gradually extended their authority over the local chiefdoms scattered across the archipelago.

Buddhism first arrived in Korea in the mid-fourth century. The Koguryo kings lavishly supported Buddhist monasteries and encouraged the propagation of Buddhism among the people. Paekche and Silla adopted Buddhism as their official religion in the early sixth century. In 552 a Paekche king sent a letter to the Yamato ruler in Japan urging him to adopt Buddhism, which "surpasses all other doctrines," adding that in Korea "there are none who do not reverently receive its teachings."[2] A Koguryo monk, Hyeja (tee ay-JUH), became tutor to the Yamato regent Prince Shōtoku (SHOW-toe-koo) (573–621). Shōtoku subsequently sent missions to China, and their reports inspired him to imitate both the Sui system of imperial government and its fervent devotion to Buddhism.

The fall of the Sui dynasty did not resolve the tense confrontation between the Chinese empire and Koguryo. The Tang rulers formed an alliance with Silla, the rising power in the southern part of the Korean peninsula, against Koguryo and Paekche. The outbreak of war on the peninsula in 660 prompted the Yamato court in Japan to send a naval expedition to the aid of its Paekche allies. But the Tang warships routed the Japanese fleet and Paekche fell to the Silla forces. With Chinese support, Silla then conquered Koguryo in 668, unifying Korea under a single ruler for the first time. Although the Tang court naively assumed that Silla would remain a client state under Tang imperial dominion, the Silla kings quickly established their independence (see again Map 9.2).

The growing power of the Tang was witnessed with great trepidation at the Yamato court. In 645, after a violent succession

≡ **Korea, c. 600**

Tea Drinkers in Tang China

≡ **Tea Preparation** The tombs of the Zhang family cemetery, near modern Zhangjiakou (jahng-jyah-koh) in northern China, are decorated with murals displaying the lifestyle of an affluent Chinese family—perhaps merchants—in the eleventh and twelfth centuries. This mural from the tomb of Zhang Kuangzheng (interred in 1093) shows servants preparing tea to serve the head of the household and his family. The seated servant (center) grinds fresh tea leaves into powder, the preferred way of infusing tea at that time.

The wild tea plant is native to the mountainous borderlands between China and India. References to drinking an infusion of fresh tea leaves in hot water date back to the first century BCE, but the vogue for drinking tea made from roasted leaves became widespread during the Tang dynasty. In the mid-eighth century a Tang scholar-official named Lu Yu wrote *The Classic of Tea*, which became so widely celebrated as a handbook of connoisseurship that tea merchants made porcelain statues of Lu Yu and worshipped him as their patron deity.

Tea plants flourished best in a humid climate and in stony, well-drained soils on mountain slopes. After the outbreak of the An Lushan rebellion in 755, many peasants fled war-torn northern China and settled in the upland valleys of the south, where the rugged terrain was far better suited to tea cultivation than to rice agriculture. Over the next four centuries, as the popularity of tea drinking rose, tea cultivation spearheaded settlement of the interior provinces of southern China.

Tea was harvested in the spring. Although large tea plantations hired both men and women, in peasant households the task of tea picking fell almost exclusively to women, of all ages. "Tea comes in chopped, loose, powdered, and brick varieties, but in all cases the tea leaves are simply picked, steamed, roasted, pounded, and sealed in a ceramic container,"[1] wrote Lu Yu. In his day, roasted tea leaves usually were pressed into bricks for ease of storage and transport. Fragments of these bricks were crushed or ground into a fine powder before brewing.

Originally, drinking tea was a leisurely pastime of the elite, but over the course of the Tang dynasty, tea became a staple in all social classes. Lu Yu greatly esteemed tea for its medicinal value: "A person who [feels ill] should take four or five sips of tea. Its flavor can compare favorably with the most buttery of liquors, or the sweetest dew of Heaven."[2]

Feng Yan, a contemporary of Lu Yu, attributed the rising popularity of tea to Chan Buddhist monks, who drank tea to remain alert during their rigorous meditation exercises. Monastic regulations prohibited monks from eating an evening meal but allowed them to drink tea while fasting. The diary of the Japanese Buddhist monk Ennin, who traveled throughout China on a pilgrimage between 838 and 847, contains many references to tea as a courtesy provided to guests, as a gift, and as a religious offering.

The habit of tea drinking also spread beyond the borders of China. Feng Yan reported that "Uighur Turks who came to the capital bringing herds of fine horses for sale would hasten to the marketplace and buy tea before returning home."[3] The stock-raising nomads of Central Asia and Tibet flavored their tea with butter or fermented milk.

Lu Yu's commentary bristles with sharply worded judgments about the aesthetics of preparing and drinking tea. For example, he observed that it was common to "stew tea together with finely chopped onion, fresh ginger, orange peel, or peppermint, which is boiled until a glossy film forms."[4] But in Lu's view such vile concoctions were "like water tossed into a ditch."[5] In choosing tea bowls Lu favored the celadon (sea green) hue of the Yue porcelains of eastern China as a fitting complement to the greenish color of tea. Later generations of tea connoisseurs in China and Japan developed complex tea ceremonies that became fixtures of refined social life.

1. Translated from Lu Yu, *The Classic of Tea*, Chapter 6.
2. Ibid., Chapter 1.
3. Translated from Feng Yan, *Master Feng's Record of Things Seen and Heard*, Chapter 6.
4. Lu, *The Classic of Tea*, Chapter 6.
5. Ibid.

Questions to Consider

1. How did Buddhist religious practices promote tea drinking?
2. Why did the cultivation of tea in China increase dramatically beginning in the Tang dynasty?

For Further Information:

Benn, James A. *Tea in China: A Religious and Cultural History*. Honolulu: University of Hawai'i Press, 2015.

Sen Shōshitsu XV. *The Japanese Way of Tea: From Its Origins in China to Sen Rikyū*. Honolulu: University of Hawai'i Press, 1998.

dispute, sweeping political reforms recast the Yamato monarchy in the image of Tang imperial institutions. The court issued a law code, based on that of the Tang, that sought to adapt Chinese institutions such as the equal-field landownership system to Japanese circumstances. At the same time, the Japanese court remade its national identity by replacing the dynastic title Yamato with a Chinese-inspired name, Nihon (nee-HOHN) ("Land of the Rising Sun"). The Japanese emperors (as they now called themselves) also asserted their independence from and equality with the Tang Empire.

In the early eighth century, Tang China reached the height of its influence on its East Asian neighbors. In Korea, Japan, and Vietnam alike, the Chinese written language served as the lingua franca, or common language, of government, education, and religion. Adoption of Chinese forms of Buddhism such as Pure Land and Chan/Zen reinforced Tang China's cultural preeminence. Thus elites in China,

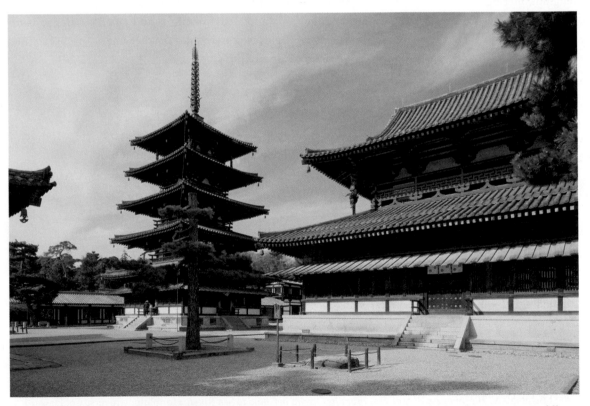

≡ Horyuji Monastery After gaining the patronage of rulers and aristocrats in China in the fourth century CE, Buddhism soon spread to Korea and Japan. The Horyuji monastery, founded by Japan's Prince Shōtoku in the seventh century, was built in a Chinese architectural style adjacent to the prince's palace. The five-story pagoda, believed to be the world's oldest wooden building, houses a statue of the bodhisattva Guanyin (known in Japan as Kannon).

Korea, Vietnam, and Japan were bound together by a common language, similar political ideas and institutions, and shared religious beliefs.

By the early tenth century, the political boundaries of East Asia had assumed contours that would remain largely intact down to the present. Silla (supplanted by the new Koryo dynasty in 935) ruled over a unified Korea. Most of the Japanese archipelago acknowledged the sovereignty of the emperor at Kyoto, the new capital modeled on the design of Chang'an and founded in 792. In 939, local chieftains in Vietnam ousted their Chinese overlords and eventually formed their own Dai Viet kingdom. At the same time, the decline of the Silk Road caravan trade and the waning popularity of Buddhism in the land of its origin loosened the ties between China and India. Henceforth, the cultural worlds of East Asia and South Asia increasingly diverged.

The Consolidation of Hindu Society in India

↘ **FOCUS** Why did Hinduism gain a broader following in Indian society than the ancient Vedic religion and its chief rival, Buddhism?

The Gupta Empire (c. 320–540) often is regarded as India's classical age. Indian historians portray the Guptas as the last great native rulers of India—a dynasty under which a revived Vedic religion surpassed the appeal of the dissident religions of Buddhism and Jainism. Yet the power of the Gupta monarchs was less extensive than that of the Mauryan emperors they claimed as their forebears. Gupta rule was largely confined to the Ganges River Valley heartland, and by the 480s nomad invasions had already dealt the dynasty a mortal blow (see Chapter 5).

The demise of the Gupta Empire, like that of the Roman Empire in Europe, resulted in the fragmentation of political power and the formation of regional states. Not until the rise of the Mughal Empire in the sixteenth century would India be unified again. The absence of a unified state did not deflect the emerging cultural and social trends of the Gupta era, however. On the contrary, in post-Gupta India, as in post-Roman Europe, common values, social practices, and political institutions penetrated more deeply into all corners of the subcontinent.

Land and Wealth

The Chinese pilgrim Xuanzang, whom we met at the start of this chapter, arrived in India during the reign of King Harsha (r. 606–647), perhaps the most powerful of the post-Gupta monarchs. Yet Harsha's kingdom depended on his own charismatic leadership, and it perished soon after his death. Nonetheless, a strikingly uniform political culture spread throughout India. Regional states expanded their reach into hinterland territories, bringing neighboring hill and forest tribes under their sway and assimilating them to the norms of caste society.

The Gupta monarchs, recognizing their limited control over local societies, had started awarding royal lands to their officials and Brahmin priests. In post-Gupta times, such land grants were often bestowed on corporate bodies such as temples, monasteries, and Brahmin communities. Xuanzang observed that "the royal lands are divided into four parts: one portion provides for the needs of the court and sacrificial offerings; the second portion is given as compensation to officers and ministers for their service; the third is awarded to men of intelligence, learning, and talent; and the fourth establishes charitable endowments for religious institutions."[3] In some cases the grants included whole villages, and the peasants fell under the jurisdiction of the grant recipients (see Reading the Past: A Copper-Plate Land Grant).

This system of royal land grants stabilized the agricultural base of society and the economy while fostering a landlord class of Brahmins who combined religious authority, caste prestige, and landed wealth. Temples and Brahmin landowners dominated the local economy, garnering tribute from the lands and peasants attached to them and controlling enterprises such as mills, oil presses, and moneylending. Beginning in the tenth

≡ **MAP 9.3   The Indian Subcontinent in the Age of Harsha, c. 640** A century after the demise of the Gupta Empire, King Harsha succeeded in restoring unified rule over most of the Gupta territories in northern India. Although tolerant of all religious faiths, Harsha became a devoted follower of Buddhism and patron to the Chinese pilgrim Xuanzang. After Harsha's death in 647, his empire disintegrated into numerous small states.

century, temples dedicated to gods such as Shiva and Vishnu were built on an unprecedented monumental scale, symbolizing the dominance of the temple over community life. Yet nothing like the large manors or serfdom characteristic of Latin Christendom at this time appeared in India. The peasant household remained the basic unit of work and livelihood. Rural society typically was governed by village assemblies that enjoyed some measure of independence from their lords.

Devotional Worship in Hinduism

Beginning in Gupta times, Brahminical religion regained its primacy, while competing religious movements such as Buddhism and Jainism retreated to the margins of Indian society. The resurgence of Brahminical religion during this period—in the form now called **Hinduism**—stemmed both from changes in religious practice and from the wealth and power Brahmin groups obtained through royal patronage.

The farthest-reaching change in Hindu practice was the emergence of forms of worship all ranks of society could participate in. Hinduism, like Buddhism and Jainism, centered on the salvation of the individual, regardless of one's caste. Personal devotion to gods such as Shiva and Vishnu replaced Brahminical rituals as the core of religious life. Devotional worship, or *bhakti*, was celebrated as the highest form of religious practice in texts known as the **Puranas**. The Puranas instructed believers in the proper forms for worshipping a specific god. Bhakti worship also encouraged more active participation by women, who previously had been excluded from religious life.

Hindu temples also joined religious piety to political power. The focus on bhakti devotion accelerated the trend of founding temples through royal land grants. Royal inscriptions also celebrated the close relationship between kings and the gods, in some cases asserting that the king was an incarnation of a god such as Shiva or Vishnu. Major temples employed large retinues of Brahmin priests, students, and caretakers. Many temples also maintained troupes of female attendants—known as *devadasis*—who were "married" to the local god. The devadasis performed rituals that combined music and dance and served as temple wardens.

The rapid growth of local temples and bhakti devotion spurred intense adoration of a multitude of new or transformed deities. People worshipped the principal Hindu gods, Shiva and Vishnu, in many different incarnations. Krishna, an incarnation of Vishnu, appeared both as the wise philosopher-warrior of the celebrated philosophical poem *Baghavad Gita* ("Song of the Lord") and as a rustic herdsman, the patron of cowherds and devoted lover of the milkmaid Radha. Kings and warriors particularly venerated Shiva, an icon of sovereign authority and wielder of terrible powers of destruction.

Hinduism The name given (first by Muslims) to the body of religious teachings, derived from the Brahminical religion of the Vedic era, that developed in response to the challenge of Buddhism.

Puranas Religious writings, derived from oral tradition and written down during the first millennium CE, that recount the legends of the gods and serve as the canonical texts of popular Hinduism.

READING THE PAST

A Copper-Plate Land Grant

This inscription from 753 records a land grant made by the king of the Pallava dynasty in southern India to the king's religious teacher, a local Brahmin. The grant was recorded on eleven copper plates that were strung together on a copper wire and stamped with the Pallava royal seal—a bull and the phallic symbol associated with the god Shiva.

The inscription begins with a eulogy written in Sanskrit lauding the king. Details of the land grant, written in the local language, Tamil, follow. This passage from the Tamil portion defines the relationship between the land grant recipient and the local village community.

> Having seen the order . . . we, the inhabitants, went to the boundaries which the headman of the district pointed out, walked around the village from right to left, and planted milk-bushes and placed stones around it. . . . The recipient shall enjoy the wet land and the dry land included within these four boundaries, wherever the iguana runs and the tortoise crawls, and shall be permitted to dig river channels and irrigation channels. . . . Those who take and use the water in these channels by pouring out baskets, by cutting branch channels, or by employing small levers shall pay a fine to be collected by the king. The recipient and his descendants shall enjoy the houses, house gardens, and so forth, and shall have the right to build houses and halls of burnt tiles. The land included within these boundaries we have endowed with all exemptions. The recipient shall enjoy the exemptions obtaining in this village without paying for the oil-mill and looms, the hire of the well-diggers, the share of the Brahmins of the king, the share of shengodi [a plant], the share of figs, the share of lamp black, the share of corn-ears, the share of the headman, the share of the potter, the sifting of [rice] paddy, the price of ghee [clarified butter], the price of cloth, the share of cloth, the hunters, messengers, dancing-girls, the grass, the best cow and the best bull, the share of the district, cotton-threads, servants, palmyra molasses, the fines to the accountant and the minister.

Source: Kasakkudi Plates of Nandivarman, South Indian Inscriptions, Archaeological Survey of India, vol. 2, part 3 (Madras: Government Press, 1896), 360–362.

Examining the Evidence

1. What services—supported by the taxes and fees explicitly exempted from this land grant—did the village community provide to its members?

2. Why did rights to water figure so prominently in this grant?

Worship of goddesses who originated in local fertility cults marked a significant departure in Hinduism from the Vedic tradition. Consort goddesses were seen as necessary complements to male gods such as Shiva, whose power and energy could be activated only through union with a female. Yet goddesses such as Lakshmi, the consort of Vishnu, and Shiva's many wives also attracted their own personal followings.

As he traveled about India, Xuanzang was appalled by the decayed state of Buddhism in its homeland. Arriving at Varanasi (the modern city of Benares), the site of the Buddha's first sermon, the Chinese pilgrim found "a densely crowded city teeming with rich and prosperous inhabitants, their houses filled with great wealth and rare goods." But "few of them revered Buddhist teachings. . . . Of Deva [Hindu] temples there were more than a hundred, and more than ten thousand adherents of the non-Buddhist sects, the great majority professing devotion to Shiva."[4] Popular devotion to Buddhism was fading, and by the thirteenth century it would vanish altogether.

New Economic and Social Trends

The land grant system and the temple-centered economy it spawned stimulated the expansion of agriculture and village settlement into frontier areas. New irrigation and fertilization techniques also promoted the growth of the agricultural economy. The encroaching agrarian states with their caste-based social order incorporated many tribal groups in the forests and hills. An inscription dated 861 celebrated the conquest of a frontier area in western India by a king of the Pratihara dynasty, boasting that he had made the land "fragrant with the leaves of blue lotuses and pleasant with groves of mango and *madhuka*-fruit trees, and covered it with leaves of excellent sugarcane."[5]

The prominence of the temple-centered economy in these centuries also reflected the decline of towns and trade. As local agricultural economies became more important, international trade declined. India was largely severed from the lucrative Central Asian caravan trade now in the hands of hostile Turkic and Muslim neighbors. Itinerant traders and local merchants remained active, however, supplying agricultural produce,

≡ **The Many Faces of Shiva** Hindus worship the god Shiva in many forms, as both a creator and a destroyer. The faces on this sculpture—which include a bust of Shiva's consort Parvati, the embodiment of feminine composure and wifely devotion—portray Shiva as both a fierce exterminator and a serene ascetic. The four faces encircle a linga, an erect phallus symbolizing Shiva's powers of fertility and procreation.

ghee (clarified butter), betel leaves (a popular stimulant), and cotton cloth to ordinary villagers and procuring ritual necessities and luxury goods for temples and royal courts.

As Brahmin religion and social norms became more deeply entrenched in village society and the frontier tribal regions, the structure of caste society underwent profound changes. Many of the upstart regional dynasties came from obscure origins. The rigid formal hierarchy of the four major caste groups—Brahmins (priests), Kshatriyas (warriors), Vaishyas (merchants and farmers), and Shudras (servile peoples)—could not contain the growing complexity of Indian society, especially with the inclusion of pastoral nomads and forest-dwelling tribes. Social status based on occupation—known as *jati*—often superseded ancestral birth, at least on the lower rungs of the caste hierarchy. Jatis developed their own cultural identities, which were expressed in customs, marriage rules, food taboos, and religious practices.

Yet the status of merchants and artisans often varied from place to place. In some localities, certain craftsmen jati—for example, butchers and shoemakers, associated with animal slaughter—were required to live outside the town walls, like Untouchables and other social groups deemed ritually unclean. However, groups of artisans who worked for royal courts, such as copperplate engravers, weavers, and masons, received special privileges.

The rights and privileges of women, like those of men, differed according to caste and local custom. As in most cultures, writers and artists often idealized women, but they did so in terms that distinguished feminine from masculine qualities. Whereas the ideal man was described in strongly positive language—emphasizing, for example, ambition, energy, mastery of knowledge, and skill in poetry and conversation—female virtues were often conveyed through negative constructions, such as absence of jealousy, greed, frivolity, and anger. These characterizations reflect prevailing notions of women's weaknesses.

Women were encouraged to marry young and remain devoted to their husbands. The fate of a widow in this patriarchal society was often grim. Unable to inherit her husband's property or to remarry, a widow depended on her husband's family for support. However, women who chose not to marry, such as nuns and devadasis, were accepted as normal members of society.

Court Society and Culture

The unraveling of the Gupta Empire left a multitude of local rulers. In this political world—referred to as the "circle of kings" in the *Arthashastra* ("The Science of Material Gain"), a renowned treatise on statecraft—each ruler pursued his advantage through complex maneuvers over war and diplomacy. Monarchs achieved political dominance by gaining fealty and tribute, not by annexing territory, as was usual in China, for example.

jati In India, a caste status based primarily on occupation.

Given the treachery and uncertainty of the "circle of kings," rulers eagerly sought divine blessings through lavish patronage of temples. They portrayed themselves as devoted servants of the supreme gods Shiva and Vishnu, and they demanded similar reverence and subservience from their courtiers and subjects. The rituals of the royal court gave monarchs an opportunity to display their majesty and affirm their authority. As we also see in Europe and the Islamic world at this time, royal courts became the main arenas of political intercourse, social advancement, and cultural accomplishment.

Attendance at court and participation in its elaborate ceremonial and cultural life were crucial to establishing membership in the ruling class. The lifestyle of the courtly elite was exemplified in the *Kama Sutra* ("The Art of Pleasure"), composed during the Gupta period. Most famous for its frank celebration of sexual love, the *Kama Sutra* was intended as a guidebook to educate affluent men in the rules of upper-class social life. It is addressed to a "man about town" who has received an education, obtained a steady source of wealth (whether from land, trade, or inheritance), established a family, and settled in a city populated by other men of good birth and breeding. The book enumerates sixty-four "fine arts" that a cultivated man should master, from dancing and swordsmanship to skill in conversation and poetry. Above all, the *Kama Sutra* exalts mastery of the self: only through discipline of the mind and senses can a man properly enjoy wealth and pleasure while avoiding the pitfalls of excess and indulgence.

The *Kama Sutra* describes an urbane lifestyle that imitated the worldly sophistication and conspicuous consumption of the king and his court. It dismisses rural society, in contrast, as boorish and stultifying. Despite such assertions that a vast cultural gulf separated the court from the countryside, courtly culture and its values permeated the entire ruling class, including local lords and Brahmin landowners.

The post-Gupta era witnessed steady cultural integration throughout the Indian subcontinent, even in the absence of political unity. Non-Brahmin religions and social values were increasingly marginalized, and by the tenth century Hindu religious culture, as well as the norms of caste society, prevailed in almost all regions.

The Spread of Indian Traditions to Southeast Asia

⬊ **FOCUS** What aspects of Indian religions had the greatest influence on the societies and cultures of Southeast Asia?

Indian culture and religions spread to Southeast Asia before the emergence of indigenous states, in a process resembling how China influenced its East Asian neighbors. Thus Indian traditions had a powerful effect on the development of

Southeast Asian ideas about kingship and social order and provided a new vocabulary to express cultural and ethical values.

Southeast Asian religious beliefs and practices integrated aspects of two Indian religions, Hinduism and Buddhism. As in East Asia, Mahayana Buddhist teachings were readily adapted to local cultures. Hinduism, with its roots in Indian social institutions, especially the caste system, proved less adaptable. Yet some elements of Hinduism, such as bhakti devotional cults and the worship of Shiva, flourished in Southeast Asia. Given the Brahmin priesthood's prominent role in Southeast Asia, it would be more appropriate to refer to this tradition as **Brahminism** than as Hinduism. Across Southeast Asia, aspects of both Buddhism and Brahminism would intermingle in novel ways, fusing with ancient local traditions to produce distinctive religious cultures (see Map 9.4).

Commerce and Religious Change in Southeast Asia

Indian religions and cultural traditions were carried to Southeast Asia by merchants and missionaries following the maritime routes from the Bay of Bengal to the South China Sea. Buddhist missionaries were crossing the Southeast Asian seas by the second century CE. But Indian law prohibited Brahmins from traveling abroad for fear of jeopardizing their purity of body and spirit. Brahminism was disseminated to Southeast Asia, therefore, largely via Indian merchant colonies, and also by Southeast Asian natives who traveled to India for study and training and returned as converts.

Historians find evidence for the diffusion of Brahminism to Southeast Asia in Funan, the first identifiable state in the region, and in Java during the early centuries CE. The Funan state, based in the lower Mekong River Valley (in present-day Vietnam and Cambodia), flourished during the first to fourth centuries CE as the principal trading center between India and China. Contemporary Chinese observers noted that Indian beliefs and practices were prevalent in Funan, as was the use of Indic script in writing.

Brahminism The distinctive Hindu religious tradition of Southeast Asia, in which the Brahmin priesthood remained dominant despite the absence of a caste system.

Brahminism also flourished in central Java. The earliest inscriptions in Old Javanese, dating from the late fourth to early fifth centuries, refer to gifts of cattle and gold to Brahmin priests and to royal ceremonies apparently derived from Indian precedents. As in India, local rulers in Southeast Asia appropriated Hindu religious ideas and motifs that meshed with their own worldviews and grafted them onto ancient local traditions. In Java, the high gods of Hinduism came to be identified with the island's fearsome volcanoes, which the inhabitants regarded as the homes of the gods.

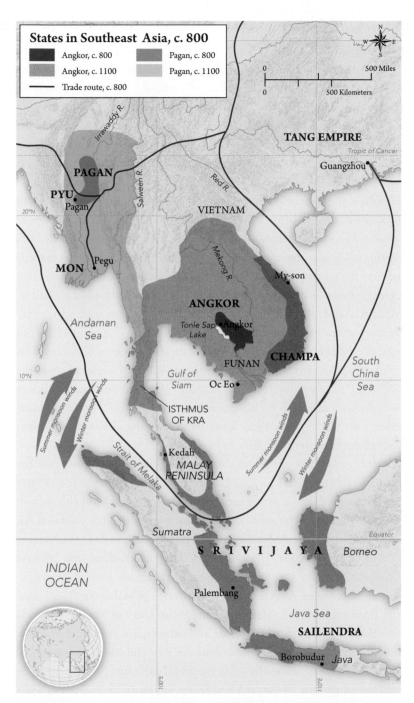

States in Southeast Asia, c. 800

- Angkor, c. 800
- Angkor, c. 1100
- Trade route, c. 800
- Pagan, c. 800
- Pagan, c. 1100

≡ **MAP 9.4   States in Southeast Asia, c. 800**   Many Southeast Asian states, such as Angkor in the lower Mekong River Valley and the Sailendra dynasty in Java, were based in fertile agricultural regions. But the Champa and Srivijaya confederations ruled the seas and derived their power from the profits of trade. During its heyday from the seventh to twelfth centuries, Srivijaya dominated the maritime trade routes linking China with India and the Islamic world.

Religion and State Power

From the beginning, Southeast Asia's borrowing of religious ideas from India was closely linked to the ambitions of local rulers. Both Buddhism and Brahminism provided models for divine blessing of royal authority. In the Buddhist tradition, the universal monarch, the chakravartin, achieved supremacy through lavish acts of piety and devotion. In the Brahminical tradition, by contrast, the king partook of divine power by identifying with the high gods, above all Shiva, and received worship from his subjects much as the gods did. This association of the king with the gods sanctified the king's role as ruler and protector of his people.

The earliest appearance of the worship of Shiva in Southeast Asia is found in Champa, where a loose confederation of local rulers shared power under a weak royal overlord (see again Map 9.4). One Champa king instituted a Shiva cult at the royal shrine at My-son, the ritual center of the Champa confederation, in the fourth century. Yet the Champa chiefdoms never coalesced into a centralized state. The Champa chieftains instead relied on piracy and plunder to obtain wealth. Thus Indian political and religious ideas alone were not enough to create a powerful king.

However, where ample resources were combined with a compelling political ideology, powerful kings did emerge. For example, worship of Shiva aided consolidation of state power in the lower Mekong River Valley of modern Cambodia. The founder of the Angkor kingdom, Jayavarman (JUH-yuh-vahr-mon) II, was proclaimed universal monarch by his Brahmin advisers in 802; he consolidated his dominion over the region's local lords by combining devotion to Shiva with homage to himself as deva-raja (divine lord).

During the early phase of the Angkor state, kings delegated control over the land and its inhabitants to officials assigned to royally chartered temples. Not until a century later did one of Jayavarman's successors, Yasovarman (YAH-suh-vahr-mon) I (r. 889–c. 910), consolidate royal authority by establishing his capital at Angkor. The many temples he founded at Angkor and elsewhere were dedicated primarily to Shiva, Vishnu, and Buddha. Depending on individual inclinations, later Angkor kings sometimes favored worship of Vishnu—the chief deity at Angkor's most famous temple complex, Angkor Wat—or patronage of Mahayana Buddhism.

Apart from Brahminism, Mahayana Buddhism was the other Indian religious tradition that initially attracted devotion and patronage in Southeast Asia. Chinese pilgrims in the seventh century described the Pyu and Mon city-states of lower Burma, which had ready access by sea to the great Mahayana monasteries in Bengal, as "Buddhist kingdoms." Mahayana Buddhism was also enthusiastically welcomed by Malay chiefs in Sumatra, who had begun to capitalize on a major reorientation of maritime trade routes that occurred between the fourth and sixth centuries.

Previously, merchants had avoided the monsoon winds that dictated the rhythms of seafaring in the Southeast Asian seas. Instead of sailing around the Malay peninsula, ships would land at the Kra Isthmus, the narrowest point along the peninsula. From there, they would carry their goods overland to the Gulf of Siam before setting sail again for the Indochina peninsula. Funan used its strategic location on the more protected eastern shore of the Gulf of Siam to become the major crossroads where merchants from the Indian Ocean could meet those from China. Beginning in the fourth century, however, Malay navigators pioneered an all-sea route through the Strait of Melaka, bypassing the Gulf of Siam altogether. Funan's prosperity abruptly ended, and the ports of southeastern Sumatra replaced Funan as the linchpin of maritime trade (see again Map 9.4).

≡ **Angkor's Greatest Temple** Most of the temples at the Khmer capital of Angkor honor the Hindu god Shiva. But King Suryavarman II (r. 1113–1150) built his great monument, Angkor Wat, as a state temple dedicated to the god Vishnu as well as his own future mausoleum. Angkor Wat's soaring towers symbolize the five peaks of Mount Meru, the home of the Hindu gods, and the temple complex is enclosed by a wide, square moat representing the oceans surrounding the inhabited world.

SEEING THE PAST

Borobudur, the World's Largest Buddhist Monument

The Sailendra kings never built palaces or cities for themselves. Instead they devoted their wealth and resources to building vast monuments displaying their devotion to the Buddhist faith. The massive stone edifice they erected at Borobudur in central Java rises from a fertile plain ringed by imposing volcanoes. Construction of Borobudur began around 760 and took seventy years to complete.

Aerial View of Borobudur

The exact purpose of the Borobudur monument, which was neither a temple nor a monastery, continues to provoke scholarly debate. Borobudur consists of ten concentric terraces of decreasing size crowned by a bell-shaped stupa, a Buddhist shrine used as a repository for relics or other sacred objects. The terraces are adorned with carved reliefs depicting episodes from the scriptures of Mahayana Buddhism and with more than 500 statues of Buddhas. The carved reliefs provide a virtual encyclopedia of Mahayana teachings. But they also include many scenes from court life, which spoke more directly of the royal majesty of

In the late seventh century, the ruler of the Sumatran port of Palembang founded the first of a series of kingdoms known collectively as Srivijaya (sree-vih-JUH-yuh). Our first image of a ruler of Srivijaya comes from an inscription of 683, which tells how the king celebrated his conquest of a rival city-state and gravely admonished his vanquished foe to accept Buddhism. The rulers of Srivijaya became great patrons of Mahayana Buddhism. The large international community of monks that gathered at Palembang included novices from China seeking instruction from Indian monks.

the Sailendras. Some scholars have suggested that the mountain-like edifice celebrated the Sailendras' exalted stature as "Lords of the Mountains" and marked the dynasty's original home.

By visiting Borobudur, the Buddhist faithful could pass physically and spiritually through the ten stages of devotion necessary to attain enlightenment. Entering from the eastern staircase, they would proceed slowly around each terrace, studying and absorbing the lessons told by the carved reliefs before passing to the next level. To see all the reliefs one must walk around the monument ten times, a distance of three miles. Reliefs at the lower levels retell well-known stories from the life of the Buddha and other holy figures. The higher levels are devoted to the pilgrim Sudhana, who visited 110 teachers in his quest for enlightenment. On the upper levels the narrow galleries of the lower levels give way to three round open terraces surmounted by numerous lattice-like stupas enclosing life-size statues of Buddhas. The devotee's ascent of the monument symbolized a spiritual progress from the world of illusion to the realm of enlightenment.

Source: John Miksic, *Borobudur: Golden Tales of the Buddhas* (Hong Kong: Periplus, 1990).

Examining the Evidence

1. How can we see the architectural design of Borobudur as a physical representation of the world, which in Buddhist cosmology is depicted as a series of circular oceans and continents surrounding a sacred mountain at the center?

2. In what ways does the monument reflect Buddhism's renunciation of worldly life?

The rise of Srivijaya was soon followed by the emergence of a lineage of kings in the Kedu Plain of central Java. Known as the Sailendra (SIGH-len-drah) dynasty, these monarchs were equally dedicated to Mahayana Buddhism. The Sailendra kings used Sanskrit sacred texts and administrative language to construct a network of religious and political allegiances under their leadership. They also founded many Buddhist shrines. The massive monument of Borobudur in central Java testifies to the Sailendra kings' deep faith in Mahayana Buddhism (see Seeing the Past: Borobudur: The World's Largest Buddhist Monument).

Allied to Srivijaya by their common faith and intermarriage between the royal families, the Sailendra dynasty flourished from 750 to 850. Around 850, however, the Sailendra were suddenly expelled from Java by an upstart rival devoted to Shiva. The royal house fled to Sumatra, where they joined their Srivijaya kin. Bereft of Sailendra patronage, the Buddhist monasteries in Java plunged into irreversible decline. Henceforth, Brahminism predominated in Java until a wave of conversions to Islam began in the fifteenth century.

Indian Religions in Southeast Asia: A Summing-Up

Indian religions were assimilated in Southeast Asia as the existing cultural and social frameworks adapted foreign ideas. The potent ideologies of the Sanskrit literary heritage and the organizational skills of Buddhist and Brahmin holy men stimulated the formation of states based on divinely sanctioned royal authority. The Angkor kingdom represents the most striking case of simultaneous patronage of both Brahminism and Mahayana Buddhism, but to a lesser degree this eclectic adoption of Indian religions occurred throughout Southeast Asia.

Royal temples and monuments became focal points for amassing wealth in service to the gods, while also serving as testaments to the kings' piety. In contrast to Islam, which exercised a powerful centralizing pull and created a common brotherhood of faith across national, ethnic, and cultural boundaries, Indian religions in Southeast Asia—as in India itself—spawned a diverse array of regional religious cultures.

COUNTERPOINT: Sogdian Traders in Central Asia and China

↘ **FOCUS** How did the social and economic institutions of the Sogdian merchant network differ from those of the nomadic confederations and the agrarian empires?

The heyday of the overland caravan routes of Central Asia—the Silk Road—lasted from the fourth to the eighth centuries. The great length of the trade routes and the harsh terrain through which they passed made it impossible for any single political power to dominate the Silk Road. Instead, rulers had to cultivate close ties with those who, in the words of a Moroccan spice merchant turned Christian monk, "to procure silk for the miserable gains of commerce, hesitate not to travel to the uttermost ends of the earth."[6] The Sogdian merchants who linked together Asia's great empires did so through economic enterprise rather than military or political might.

A Robust Commercial Economy

Sogdia (SUGG-dee-yah) (now divided between Uzbekistan and Tajikistan) was a fertile agricultural region surrounded by the grassland habitat of the Eurasian nomads. Persian in language and religion, Sogdian culture was also enriched by contact with the Indian and Greek worlds.

≡ **Sogdia, c. 600**

Sogdia's commercial economy began to develop in the first century CE. Sogdian merchants achieved success by leaving their homeland and traveling to distant regions, especially eastward to China. The dispersion of Sogdian merchants took the form of a **trade diaspora** (*diaspora* was the Greek word for scattering grain), a network of merchant settlements united by their common origins, religion, and language, as well as by family ties and business partnerships.

Nomad incursions in the fifth and sixth centuries ruined many cities in Central Asia, as the Chinese pilgrim Xuanzang observed. Sogdia's city-states were largely spared this devastation and began to enjoy unprecedented prosperity. The creation of the Turkic nomad empire in the mid-sixth century catapulted Sogdian merchants to dominance over the Silk Road trade. Sogdian merchants allied with the Turks and entered the administration, army, and diplomatic service of the Turkic khan.

Under the umbrella of Turkic military power, Sogdian merchant colonies sprouted in Mongolia and on the frontiers of China. Sales contracts found at Turfan, the principal hub of the Silk Road, show Sogdian merchants buying and selling silk, silver, gold, perfume, saffron, brass, medicines, and cane sugar. Horses ranked first among the goods they brought to China, while slaves, Siberian furs, and gems and spices from India filled the markets of Samarkand and other Sogdian cities.

As the generations passed, many Sogdians in China began to assimilate to the cosmopolitan Chinese culture. The Sogdian silk merchant He Tuo, who settled in China in the mid-sixth century, joined the entourage of a Chinese prince and amassed a great fortune. His eldest son and nephew became experts

trade diaspora A network of merchants from the same city or country who live permanently in foreign lands and cooperate with one another to pursue trading opportunities.

at cutting gemstones, and the He family is credited with introducing the techniques of glassmaking to China. The Tang emperors also frequently employed Sogdians in important civil and military offices, most notoriously the general An Lushan.

Breakdown of the Trade Network

The Muslim conquest of Sogdia in the early eighth century marked the beginning of the end of Sogdian prosperity. When Samarkand surrendered to an Islamic army in 712, the city's population was forced to pay a huge indemnity.

The An Lushan rebellion of 755–763 dealt another major blow to the Sogdian trade network. It severely damaged the Chinese economy, and after the rebels were defeated many Sogdians in China disguised their ancestry and abandoned their culture out of fear of persecution. Finally, with the rise of maritime trade routes connecting the Islamic world and China, overland traffic across the Silk Road dropped off steeply. By the late tenth century, Sogdian culture was on the verge of extinction in Sogdia itself. Samarkand, however, would enjoy a brilliant revival in the fourteenth century when the city was reborn as an Islamic metropolis (see Chapter 14).

Conclusion

Commercial and cultural exchanges across the Silk Road during the first millennium CE linked the distant agrarian empires of China, India, and Iran. The interactions that resulted transformed the peoples and cultures along the Central Asian trade routes. The Tuoba, Turks, and Khazars all transcended their original predatory purposes by creating empires that spanned both nomadic and settled societies. These empires, however, failed to create political institutions that might have perpetuated their dominion. The Sogdian merchant communities forged very different commercial and cultural linkages across Asia, but these networks, too, proved vulnerable to shifts in political fortunes and trade patterns.

The movement across the Silk Road of goods and of people such as the Buddhist pilgrim Xuanzang fostered unprecedented cosmopolitan cultural exchange throughout Asia, peaking with the rise of the Sui and Tang Empires. The spread of Buddhism to China and from there to Korea, Japan, and Vietnam provided the foundation for a common East Asian culture. The political dominance of the Chinese empires also spread China's written language, literary heritage, and social values among its neighbors. Correspondingly, the demise of Tang power after the An Lushan rebellion in the mid-eighth century undermined China's political dominance. Subsequently a new order of independent states emerged in East Asia.

In India, too, a cosmopolitan culture formed during the first millennium CE, despite the absence of political unity. This elite culture was based on Gupta political institutions and Hindu religious beliefs and social values. The royal lineages and noble classes that founded the first states in Southeast Asia during this period participated fully in creating this cosmopolitan culture. Yet by the tenth century, as in East Asia, the elite culture encompassing South and Southeast Asia had begun to fragment into more distinctive regional and national traditions.

Regional cultures in East and South Asia were formed by the movement of people and goods across trade routes, the mixture of religious and political ideas, and the spread of common forms of livelihood. The same forces were also at work in the formation of regional societies in the very different worlds of the Americas and the Pacific Ocean, as we will see in the next chapter.

review

The major global development in this chapter: The cultural and commercial exchanges during the heyday of the Silk Road that transformed Asian peoples, cultures, and states.

Important Events	
386–534	Northern Wei dynasty in north China and Mongolia
552–603	First Turkish empire
581–618	Sui dynasty in China
604	Prince Shōtoku reorganizes the Yamato kingdom in Japan

Important Events	
606–647	Reign of King Harsha as paramount ruler of north India
618–907	Tang dynasty in China
668	Unification of the Korean peninsula under the rule of the Silla kingdom
c. 670–965	Khazar khanate in Volga River delta
755–763	An Lushan rebellion in north China severely weakens the Tang dynasty
802	Consolidation of the Angkor kingdom in Cambodia by Jayavarman II
939	Vietnam wins independence from China

KEY TERMS

bodhisattva (p. 322)
Brahminism (p. 340)
chakravartin (p. 323)
Chan (p. 324)

equal-field system (p. 325)
Hinduism (p. 335)
jati (p. 338)
khan (p. 320)

Mahayana (p. 322)
Puranas (p. 335)
Pure Land (p. 324)
trade diaspora (p. 347)

CHAPTER OVERVIEW QUESTIONS

1. How did Asian societies respond to cross-cultural interactions in the period 400–1000?
2. What strategies did pastoral nomads adopt in their relations with settled societies?
3. What patterns of borrowing characterized the emerging states in East and Southeast Asia?
4. Why did India and China experience different outcomes following the collapse of empires?

MAKING CONNECTIONS

1. How and why did the spread of Buddhism from India to China and Southeast Asia differ from the expansion of Islam examined in Chapter 8?
2. Do you think that the invasions of Germanic peoples into the Roman Empire had more lasting consequences (see Chapter 8) than the invasions in China by steppe nomad peoples? Why or why not?
3. Compare the main values of Hinduism in the post-Gupta period with those of the ancient Vedic religion (see Chapter 3). How had the goals of religious practice changed, and what effect did these changes have on Indian society?

DOING HISTORY

Making Connections

A global perspective pushes us to think about how historical developments in one part of the world are connected to developments in other parts. But connection does not necessarily imply similar causes and consequences. Consider the spread of Indian religions to other Asian regions, a main theme of this chapter. Conversion to the foreign religion of Buddhism in Central Asia, China, and Southeast Asia coincided with the eclipse of Buddhism by Hinduism in India itself.

1. How can we explain the adoption of the foreign religion of Buddhism in other parts of Asia even as Buddhism disappeared in the land of its birth?

2. Why did Hinduism take root in Southeast Asia but not in Central Asia or China?

3. Do you see parallels—or, conversely, large differences—between the spread of Buddhism in Asia and the simultaneous expansion of Islam that we studied in Chapter 8?

For further research into the topics covered in this chapter, see the Bibliography at the end of the book.

Societies and Networks in the Americas and the Pacific

300–1200

≡ **World in the Making** No mere spectator sport, the Mesoamerican ballgame, which spread as far as northeastern North America, was charged with powerful ritual and religious meaning. Maya myths associate the ballgame with the Hero Twins' triumph over the gods of the underworld and with the gift of agriculture. This stone disk, which dates from about 590 and once marked the site of a ball court in the modern Mexican province of Chiapas, displays a ballplayer striking the ball with his hip. The headdress and inscriptions suggest that the ballplayer is a royal figure reenacting the feats of the Hero Twins.

backstory

As we saw in Chapter 7, during the first millennium BCE, signs of growing social complexity and a hierarchy of villages and towns had emerged in both the Olmec culture on Mexico's Atlantic coast and the Chavín culture along Peru's Pacific coast. By 200 BCE, however, the Olmec and Chavín societies had been eclipsed by the rising city-states of the Maya and Moche, respectively. These city-states concentrated political and military power by mobilizing massive amounts of labor to build monumental cities and irrigation systems for agriculture. Meanwhile, in North America, agriculture and settled societies did not appear until the first millennium CE, when native peoples began to adopt Mesoamerican food crops and farming techniques. In the Pacific Ocean, once the Lapita migrations ceased around 200 BCE, many islands remained undisturbed by human occupation. Colonization of the Pacific Islands would not resume until after 500 CE.

WHEN HOLY LORD EIGHTEEN RABBIT (r. 695–738)

became king of the Maya city-state of Copán (co-PAHN) in today's western Honduras, his society was at the peak of its wealth and strength. Eighteen Rabbit's building projects reflected Copán's power. He commissioned an impressive series of stone monuments, adding major new temples in the heart of the city and laying out the Great Plaza to the north. He rebuilt Copán's magnificent ball court, where the warriors reenacted the Maya myth of creation as a gladiatorial contest culminating in the blood sacrifice of captured nobles. The entrance to the Great Plaza was studded with carved stelae depicting Eighteen Rabbit as a multifaceted deity.

After ruling Copán for forty-three years, Eighteen Rabbit was betrayed by one of his followers. In 725 he had installed a man named Cauac (kah-WOK) Sky as ruler of the nearby city of Quiriga (kee-REE-gah). In 738 Cauac Sky captured Eighteen Rabbit and carried the Copán king back to Quiriga, where he was killed as a sacrificial victim. Yet Cauac Sky made no attempt to occupy Copán or destroy its monuments. In fact, Eighteen Rabbit's successor as Copán's ruler completed one of his predecessor's most ambitious projects, a pyramid staircase that set down in stone the history of his dynasty. The seated sculptures of earlier rulers placed at ascending intervals include an image of Eighteen Rabbit. His death—"his breath expiring in war"—was duly noted, but only as an unfortunate episode in an otherwise heroic history.

The life and death of Eighteen Rabbit recorded in his city's monuments exemplify the obsession with dynastic continuity that was central to the Maya kings' identity. Rulers of the Maya city-states devoted enormous resources to asserting their god-like power to command their subjects' labor and wealth. Their monuments wove together history and myth to tell the story of conquests, captives, slain enemies, and military alliances. Yet this wealth of historical documentation speaks in a single uniform voice. It is the speech of kings and nobles and sheds little light on the lives of the commoners who toiled under their rule.

As we saw in Chapter 7, the scarcity of written records, especially in comparison to Eurasia, complicates scholars' efforts to recover the histories of peoples of the Americas, the Pacific Islands, and most of sub-Saharan Africa. Only in Mesoamerica, stretching from central Mexico to Honduras, do we find substantial indigenous writings, which are as yet only partly deciphered. But the absence of documentary evidence does not indicate social or cultural isolation. Throughout the period from 300 to 1200, movements of peoples, goods, and ideas had far-reaching influences on these regions of the world.

The intensity of interaction and degree of cultural convergence varied with time and place. In Mesoamerica, cross-cultural interactions created a set of institutions and ideologies that knitted together local societies and cultures from the highland plateaus of central Mexico to the tropical rain forests of the Maya world. In the Andean region of South America, too, inhabitants of the coastal plains and the highlands developed common political and cultural institutions. In contrast, cross-cultural influences touched virtually all of the local societies of North America without producing a shared cultural and political identity. In the Pacific Islands, migration, trade, and social interchange fostered both the high degree of cultural uniformity of Polynesia and the remarkable cultural diversity found on the single island of Bougainville.

Equipped only with stone tools, these peoples faced formidable obstacles in their efforts to create stable agricultural economies. Landscapes as diverse as the alpine plateaus of the Andes, the barren deserts of southwestern North America, and the volcanic islands of the Pacific posed daily challenges to farming folk. Their success produced larger surpluses, greater social stratification, and more hierarchical political systems than before. In North America and the Pacific Islands, political and religious authority was dispersed among numerous hereditary chiefs. But in Mesoamerica and the Andean region, where irrigated agriculture supported denser populations, large states emerged. The rulers of these states, such as Eighteen Rabbit, expressed their ideologies not only in words but also in the design of their settlements and cities, in monumental architecture and sacred objects, and in rituals performed on behalf of both their deceased ancestors and their living subjects.

OVERVIEW QUESTIONS

The major global development in this chapter: The formation of distinctive regional cultures in the Americas and the Pacific Islands between 300 and 1200.

As you read, consider:

1. How did these societies, equipped with only Stone Age technologies, develop the social and political institutions and the patterns of exchange to tame often hostile environments and build complex civilizations?

2. How did differences in environment and habitat foster or discourage economic and technological exchanges among adjacent regions?

3. What were the sources of political power in the societies studied in this chapter, and how were they similar or dissimilar?

4. How did differences in the design of cities reflect distinctive principles of political and social organization?

The Classical Age of Mesoamerica and Its Aftermath

↘ **FOCUS** What common beliefs and social and political patterns did the various local societies of Mesoamerica's classical age share?

Historians often define the period from 250 to 900 as the classical era of Mesoamerica, which extends from the arid highlands of central Mexico to the tropical forests of modern Honduras and Nicaragua (see Map 10.1). Mesoamerica encompassed many local societies of varying scale and different degrees of integration and complexity. What united it as a regional society was a common ideology that produced similar patterns of elite status, political power, and economic control.

Between the first and ninth centuries, Mesoamerica underwent a remarkable cycle of political consolidation and disintegration. At the beginning of this period, Mesoamerica was home to numerous **chiefdoms**, in which a hereditary chief exercised political and religious authority and military leadership over a group of tribes or villages. By the third century, more complex and more steeply stratified political orders—**city-states**—dominated both the highlands and the lowlands by extracting labor and tribute from their subjects.

Bronze and iron metallurgy were unknown in Mesoamerica during this period. Despite the limitations of Stone Age technology, Mesoamericans built great cities, and their skilled craft industries flourished. Highly productive agriculture based on maize, beans, squash, and chili peppers supported some of the world's densest populations. The monumental metropolis of Teotihuacán (teh-o-tee-WAH-kahn) in central Mexico and the dozens of Maya city-states testify to the strong control the rulers wielded over their subjects' lives.

Political Power and Ideology in Mesoamerica

Scholars have traced the origins of Mesoamerican cultural and political traditions to the ancient Olmec civilization (see Chapter 7). Powerful Mesoamerican city-states emerged during the first centuries CE, and cross-cultural exchange intensified as trade and warfare among cities forged connections between the Mesoamerican peoples. Throughout the region, people came to recognize a similar array of gods— feathered serpents, lords of the underworld, and storm gods. Knowledge of the Mesoamerican calendar and writing gave rulers important tools for state-building.

In the absence of bronze and iron metallurgy, **obsidian**—a hard volcanic stone used to sharpen cutting tools—was crucial to agricultural production. The two sources of obsidian in the region, the northern part of the Valley of Mexico and highland Guatemala, emerged as early centers of economic exchange and state

chiefdom A form of political organization in which a hereditary leader, or chief, holds both political and religious authority and the rank of members is determined by their degree of kinship to the chief.

city-state A small, independent state consisting of an urban center and the surrounding agricultural territory.

obsidian A hard volcanic stone used to sharpen cutting tools and thus one of the most valuable natural resources for Stone Age peoples.

Mesoamerica, c. 250–900

- Teotichuacán culture area, c. 300
- Maya Region, c. 250–900
- Toltec heartland, c. 900
- ■ Maya city
- ■ Mexica city

Trade goods
- Cacao
- Feathers
- Jade
- Obsidian
- Pottery
- Turquoise
- Trade route

≡ **MAP 10.1   Mesoamerica, c. 250–900**   In contrast to the highly centralized state founded at Teotihuacán in central Mexico, dozens of city-states emerged in the Maya region. Each region maintained its own distinctive cultural features, while war, diplomacy, and trade all contributed to the formation of a shared Mesoamerican culture.

formation. Poor transportation limited the reach of political control, however; in the absence of draft animals (domesticated beasts of burden) and wheeled vehicles, people could transport only what they could carry on their backs. Long-distance exchange was therefore difficult, and it was restricted to the most highly desired goods. The possession of rare and exotic **prestige goods** gave rulers awesome authority, and so items such as jade, gold, jaguar skins, feathers, and cacao seeds (for making chocolate) acquired great value. Rulers of the Mesoamerican city-states constantly warred against each other, vying for control of labor resources and prestige goods and exacting tribute from their defeated enemies.

Mesoamerican political power was explained and legitimated by a political ideology that many scholars argue was rooted in memories of the great rulers and cities of antiquity. The people collectively associated these memories with a mythical city known as **Tollan** ("the place of reeds"), which they saw as a paradise of fertility and abundance, the place where human and animal life began. They believed Tollan was the earthly abode of the god Feathered Serpent (whom the Aztecs would later name Quetzalcoatl [kate-zahl-CO-ah-tal]), the creator and patron of humanity.

prestige good A rare or exotic item to which a society ascribes high value and status.

Tollan In Meso-american myths, the name of the place where the gods created human beings, and thus the place of origin for all of humanity.

≡ **Feathered Serpent and War Serpent** Teotihuacán's monuments lack the prolific historical records and portraits of royal figures found in the Maya world. But scholars think the sculpted heads shown here of the Feathered Serpent and the War Serpent on the Temple of Quetzalcoatl, constructed between 200 and 250, may represent an expression of power by a single ruler or dynasty.

Mythological lore credited the Feathered Serpent with creating the sun and moon, inventing the calendar and thus the cycles of time, and bestowing basic necessities such as maize, their staple food.

But Mesoamerican concepts of cosmic order, in which cycles of time are punctuated by violence and death, required that the Feathered Serpent sacrifice his own life to renew the creative powers of the universe. Human rulers in turn could acquire and maintain political power only through offering frequent blood sacrifices to the gods. These blood sacrifices involved both the execution of war captives and bloodletting rituals by rulers and priests. Human rulers embodied the divine powers of the Feathered Serpent and reenacted his heroic exploits through ritual performance.

Mesoamericans believed that all humans originally spoke a common language and lived under the benign rule of the Feathered Serpent. Gradually, though, groups of people developed their own languages, customs, and beliefs and went their separate ways. By building temples and cities, rulers sought to renew the community of the original Tollan. Thus political power in Mesoamerica was rooted in a shared cultural heritage and a vision of cultural unity.

The City-State of Teotihuacán

The rise of Teotihuacán, about thirty miles northeast of present-day Mexico City, as the dominant center in the Valley of Mexico was due largely to its location near the region's major obsidian mines and irrigated farmland. In the first two centuries CE, Teotihuacán's founders constructed a magnificent city with wide avenues, numerous walled residential complexes, and a massive open plaza anchored by giant pyramids and temples.

Most of the population of the valley, farmers and craftsmen alike, lived in this vast city. To house all these people, apartment-like stone buildings were constructed. The apartments usually housed members of a single kinship group, but some were for craftsmen working in the same trade. This residential pattern suggests that the city's people were divided into groups (probably based on kinship) that shared everyday life, collective rituals, and in some cases specialized trade and craft occupations. These groups may also have been the basic units of the city's economy. Although the scale of Teotihuacán's buildings and monuments shows that the state could command vast amounts of labor, there is little evidence that its rulers exercised direct control over the inhabitants' ordinary working lives.

Despite the extensive centralization of the Teotihuacán state, scholars have not found evidence of a hereditary dynasty of kings. Most believe that in its formative stages, Teotihuacán—like the city-states of Mesopotamia discussed in Chapter 2—was ruled by a cadre of priests rather than a military elite. Ritual action, including blood offerings, dominates the art and imagery of Teotihuacán, but warriors and scenes of warfare rarely appear until the fourth century CE. Human sacrifice was a notable aspect of Teotihuacán's public culture. Nearly 200 sacrificial victims, bound and dressed in war regalia, were buried beneath the Temple of Quetzalcoatl, the hub of government, when it was constructed in the early third century.

Teotihuacán's precise grid-like layout reflects a paramount desire to impose human order on an unpredictable natural world. The city's planners aligned its pyramids and plazas with crucial astronomical phenomena to provide a consecrated space to perform sacred rituals at the proper times. The technologies of architecture, astronomy, and calendrical calculation were essential to maintain the orderly structure of the cosmos. Above all, the city's builders intended Teotihuacán to be seen as the Tollan of its day, a ceremonial complex dedicated to perpetuating the power and authority of its ruling class through awesome public rituals. It was for this reason that, centuries later, the Aztecs named the city's massive ruins Teotihuacán, "the place where men become gods."

By 500 CE Teotihuacán's population had swelled to as many as 200,000 inhabitants, surpassed probably only by Constantinople among contemporary cities worldwide. Yet Teotihuacán's rulers pursued imperial expansion only fitfully, if at all. Nevertheless, the city's influence radiated to the entire region through the prestige of its artifacts and culture, both of which were widely imitated throughout Mesoamerica. Visiting merchants and diplomatic missions from the Oaxaca (wah-HAH-kah) highlands, the Gulf coast, and the Maya region inhabited their own special quarters in Teotihuacán. These foreigners' barrios (neighborhoods) were crossroads of cultural and economic exchange that helped disseminate sacred knowledge, ritual culture, political intelligence, and prestige goods throughout Mesoamerica.

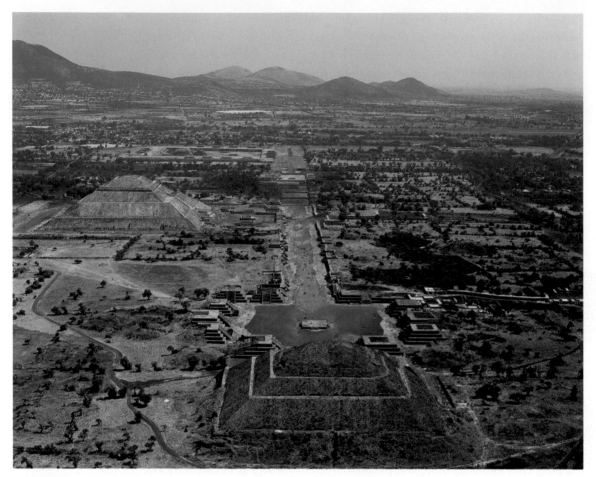

≡ **Teotihuacán** At its peak between 250 and 350, Teotihuacán was one of the largest cities in the world. The Avenue of the Dead stretches for three miles from the Pyramid of the Moon (foreground) to the Temple of Quetzalcoatl and the residences of the elite; the Pyramid of the Sun stands to the left. Some 2,000 apartment compounds housing the city's ordinary inhabitants lined both sides of the avenue.

By the fifth century, the Teotihuacán state exerted a far-reaching influence over the Mesoamerican world through its splendid monuments, its grand public ceremonies, and the abundant output of its craft workshops. At the same time, Teotihuacán's leaders took a more aggressive stance toward rival chiefs and foreign states. This shift would have crucial consequences for the Maya city-states.

The Maya City-State Network

The Maya city-states developed before the rise of Teotihuacán in central Mexico. Like other Mesoamerican cultures, the Maya inherited many features of the ancient Olmec civilization of the Gulf coast, including its monumental architecture, social institutions, calendar, and ritual art. In contrast to the Mexican highlands, however, where the massive scale of Teotihuacán dwarfed all other cities and polities, the Maya region never had a single dominant power.

The period from 250 to 900, the classical age of Maya civilization, witnessed the founding of nearly forty city-states. During these centuries the **Holy Lords**, as the Maya rulers called themselves, engaged in prodigious building of cities and monuments. But this era was also marked by succession struggles, dynastic changes, and perpetual political insecurity. The Holy Lords of powerful city-states frequently resorted to war to subdue neighbors and rivals. Victors rarely established direct rule over vanquished enemies, however. Unlike the Eurasian rulers we studied in earlier chapters, Maya elites did not dream of creating vast empires.

Instead, they were more likely to seek booty and tribute, and above all to seize war captives. Conquerors often brought back skilled craftsmen and laborers to their home city, reserving captives of high rank, such as the unfortunate Eighteen Rabbit, for blood sacrifices. Maya ceramic art often depicts tribute bearers offering cloth, foodstuffs, feathers, and cacao to enthroned rulers. Thus the Maya nobility may have conceived of war as a sacred ritual, but one that also furthered their ambitions for wealth and power.

Maya myths about the origins of the gods and humanity have been preserved in the *Popol Vuh*, or "Book of Council," written down in the Latin alphabet after the Spanish conquest of Mesoamerica in the sixteenth century (see Reading the Past: Maya Hero Twins Vanquish the Lords of the Underworld). The *Popul Vuh* portrays humans as the servants of the all-powerful gods who created them. In return for the gods' gifts of maize and timely rains, humans were obliged to build monuments to glorify the gods, to offer them sacrifices (especially human blood), and to regulate their own lives according to a sacred calendar. The Maya believed that all human beings possess a sacred essence, ***ch'ulel*** (choo-LEL), which is found in blood. The exalted status of kings and nobles endowed them with more potent ch'ulel, and so they were especially prized as blood sacrifices. Women of high birth also participated in the political and ceremonial life of the Maya ruling class, and Maya inscriptions record that several women ruled as Holy Lords. Maya elites thus occupied a unique position at the intersection of the human and the divine, ensuring the world's continuity both by demanding labor and sacrifices from the Maya population and by becoming sacrifices themselves.

On important ritual occasions, the Mesoamerican ballgame—which dates back at least to Olmec times and was no mere spectator sport—became a solemn restaging of the mythical contest in which the Hero Twins triumphed over the lords of the underworld. The object of the ballgame, played by two teams of up to four players each, was to keep a rubber ball up in the air without using hands or feet.

Holy Lord The title given by the Maya to the rulers of their city-states.

ch'ulel In Maya belief, the sacred essence contained in human blood that made it a potent offering to the gods.

READING THE PAST

Maya Hero Twins Vanquish the Lords of the Underworld

The *Popol Vuh* records the myths about the world's creation and the origins of human society as handed down by the Quiché, a late Maya people. Central to the mythology of the *Popol Vuh* is the struggle between the gods and the Xibalba (Shee-BAHL-ba), the lords of the underworld. The narrative focuses mostly on the exploits of the Hero Twins, whose father had been defeated by the Xibalba in a ballgame contest and then decapitated. The Hero Twins travel to the underworld, outwit the Xibalba, and avenge their father's death.

In the following extract, the Hero Twins inform the defeated Xibalba that as punishment for their heinous deed they will no longer receive blood sacrifices—and thus they will lose their power over mortals. Then the Hero Twins resurrect their father and assure him that in the future he will receive worship from the as-yet-unborn humans. Their triumph complete, the twins become transformed into the sun and moon (or, in other versions, the planet Venus), whose daily progressions through the heavens remind humanity of the triumph of the gods over the lords of death.

"Here then is our word that we declare to you. Hearken, all you of Xibalba; for never again will you or your posterity be great. Your offerings also will never again be great. They will be reduced to croton [a shrub] sap. No longer will clean blood be yours. Unto you will be given only worn-out griddles and pots, only flimsy and brittle things.

"You shall surely eat only the creatures of the grass and the creatures of the wastelands. No longer will you be given the children of the light, those begotten in the light. Only things of no importance will fall before you." . . . Thus began their devastation, the ruin of their being called upon in worship. . . .

Here now is the adornment of their father by them. . . . His sons then said to him: "Here you will be called upon. It shall be so." Thus his heart was comforted.

"The child who is born to the light, and the son who is begotten in the light shall go out to you first. Your name shall not be forgotten. Thus be it so," they said to the father when they comforted his heart.

"We are merely the avengers of your death and your loss, for the affliction and misfortune that

Allowing the ball to strike the ground risked incurring the wrath of the underworld gods. After the outcome was decided, the ball court became a sacrificial altar where the losers' heads were impaled on a skull rack alongside the court. These blood sacrifices not only commemorated the victory of the Hero Twins but also renewed the life-giving power of the gods.

were done to you." Thus was their counsel when they had defeated all Xibalba.

Then [the Hero Twins] arose as the central lights. They arose straight into the sky. One of them arose as the sun, and the other as the moon.

Subsequently the Hero Twins' grandmother, Xmucane, fashioned human beings by mixing together maize flour and water. Initially all peoples lived at Tollan, the place of origin. But as they adopted different gods as their patrons, human beings divided into separate tribes speaking different languages and inhabiting their own territories. The ancestors of the Quiché followed the commands of their patron god, Tohil. In return for the god's favor, the Quiché offered Tohil blood sacrifices:

Now when they came from Tulan Zuyva [Tollan], they did not eat. They fasted continuously. Yet they fixed their eyes of the dawn, looking steadfastly for the coming forth of the sun. They occupied themselves in looking for the Great Star, called Icoquih [Venus], which appears first before the birth of the sun. The face of this Green Morning Star always appears at the coming forth of the sun.

When they were there at the place called Tulan Zuyva, their gods came to them. But it was surely not then that they received their ultimate glory or their lordship. Rather it was where the great nations and the small nations were conquered and humiliated when they were sacrificed before the face of Tohil. They gave their blood, which flowed from the shoulders and armpits of all the people.

Straightaway at Tulan came the glory and the great knowledge that was theirs. It was in the darkness, in the night as well, that they accomplished it. . . .

[Tohil spoke to them]: "You shall first give thanks. You shall carry out your responsibilities first by piercing your ears. You shall prick your elbows. This shall be your petition, your way of giving thanks before the face of god."

"Very well," they said. Then they pierced their ears. They wept as they sang of their coming from Tulan.

Source: Dennis Tedlock, *Popol Vuh: The Mayan Book of the Dawn of Life* (New York: Touchstone, 1996), 138–141, 156–157.

Examining the Evidence

1. Why did the Maya believe that human beings must offer blood sacrifices to the gods?

2. Why might the Maya have been so deeply interested in the movements of the sun, moon, and planets?

The intricate Maya calendar determined the timing of war, sacrifice, agricultural work, and markets and fairs. The Maya believed that time and human history moved in elaborate cycles determined by the movements of the sun, moon, and planets—especially Venus, which in Maya belief governed sacrifice and war. To ensure a favorable outcome, the Maya people sought to align major actions in the present, such as attacks on enemies, with heroic events and accomplishments in the past. Thus the Maya took great care to observe and record astronomical phenomena. Maya astronomers calculated eclipses and the movements of planets with astonishing precision: their charts of the movements of Venus, which survive in bark-paper books, are accurate to within one day in 500 years.

Maya society revolved around the activities of the king and the royal clan. Beneath this ruling elite existed a multitiered social order based on class, residence, and kinship. As in many early Eurasian cultures, astrologers, diviners, and especially scribes occupied privileged positions in Maya society. These groups possessed the knowledge crucial to maintaining the royal mystique and to carrying out the tasks of government. The cities also housed large groups of specialized craft-workers in trades such as pottery manufacture, stone and wood carving, weaving, toolmaking, and construction.

Written records from the Maya classical age say little about family life. Although descriptions of Maya society compiled by the Spanish conquerors in the sixteenth century suffer from biases and misrepresentations, they reveal aspects of Maya culture that cannot be gleaned from archaeological evidence. According to these accounts, children were considered members of their fathers' lineage and took their surnames, but they also acquired "house names" from their mothers. Property and status passed from parents to children: sons inherited from fathers, and daughters inherited from mothers. Upon marriage, the husband usually moved in with his wife's family for a period of service lasting six or more years. Thereafter the couple might live with the husband's family or set up their own separate household.

Maize, usually made into steamed cakes known as *tamales*, was the staple of the Maya diet. The lowland Maya practiced both dry-land and intensive wet-land agriculture, growing maize, cotton, beans, squash, chili peppers, root crops, and many other vegetables. Hunting also provided food, but the only domestic animals the Maya possessed were dogs and turkeys.

≡ **Bloodletting by a Maya Queen** Blood sacrifices to the gods occupied a central place in Mesoamerican political life. This stone monument shows the king of Yaxchilan holding a torch over the head of his queen, who is performing a ritual bloodletting by passing a spiked cord through her tongue. The ritual celebrated the birth of the king's son in 709.

During the prosperous classical era the Maya population grew rapidly. In a pattern we have seen repeated around the world, population growth stimulated regular contact and communication throughout the region, and also the specialized production of agricultural and craft goods. The urban ruling elites, while continuing to war against one another, exchanged prestige goods over long distances. The unusual uniformity in spoken languages and pottery manufacture suggests that ordinary people also interacted frequently.

It was during the classical age, too, that Teotihuacán's influence left a clear impression on the Maya world. Obsidian tools, ceramics, stone pyramid architecture, and other artifacts imported into Maya city-states show that cultural interaction and trade with Teotihuacán were well established (see again Map 10.1). Long-distance trade between the central Mexican highlands and the Maya lowlands was complemented by reciprocal gift giving and the dispatch of emissaries among rulers. The circulation of exotic goods charged with sacred power—feathers, pelts, and precious stones—reinforced elite status and helped spread religious practices.

In the fourth century Teotihuacán also became a major political force in the Maya region. Teotihuacán trade and diplomatic missions made forays into Maya. The sudden appearance of Teotihuacán building styles, pottery, and tomb goods suggests that some cities fell under the rule of governors dispatched from Teotihuacán. At the very least, some Maya elites, especially upstart contenders for power seeking to unseat established royal dynasties, emulated certain features of Teotihuacán's political ideology. At Tikal (tee-KAHL) and Copán, mysterious figures identified as "Lords of the West" overthrew previous rulers and founded new royal dynasties. These foreign regimes, however, quickly assimilated into the native ruling elites of their cities.

The Passing of Mesoamerica's Classical Age

Between 550 and 650 Teotihuacán was destroyed. Sacred monuments were cast down, civic buildings were burned, and at least some portion of the population was slaughtered, leaving little doubt that the destruction was politically motivated. Most of Teotihuacán's population scattered, and the city never regained its preeminence. No successor emerged as the dominant power. For the next three or more centuries, the Valley of Mexico was divided among a half-dozen smaller states that warred constantly against one another.

In 562 an alliance of rival states vanquished Tikal, the most powerful Maya city-state, and sacrificed its king. As was Maya practice, however, the allies did not attempt to establish direct rule over Tikal, and by 700 it had recovered, and its kings once again became the paramount lords of an extensive network of allies and trading partners. Interestingly, Maya royal monuments of the eighth century at Tikal (and at Copán during the reign of Eighteen Rabbit and his successors) feature a great revival of Teotihuacán imagery, even though the Mexican city had long been reduced to ruin. The reverence shown to Teotihuacán as a royal capital illustrates the lasting appeal of its ideas and institutions throughout Mesoamerica.

The brilliant prosperity that Tikal and other Maya city-states enjoyed in the eighth century did not last. Over the course of the ninth century, monument building ceased in one Maya city after another. Although there is evidence of internal struggles for power and of interstate warfare, scholars believe that population pressure or an ecological disturbance triggered a more profound economic or demographic crisis. The collapse of the Maya city-state network not only ended individual ruling dynasties but also dismantled the basic economy of the region. Cities and cultivated fields were abandoned and eventually disappeared into the encroaching jungle. The region's population fell by at least 80 percent. New—but much more modest—cities arose along the Gulf coast of the Yucatan peninsula in the following centuries, but the cities of the Maya classical age never recovered.

The crumbling of the entire region's political and economic foundations reveals the tight web of interdependence within the Maya city-state network. The Maya peoples were more culturally uniform than peoples in other parts of Mesoamerica, sharing common languages, material culture, ritual practices, aesthetic values, and political institutions. Yet the competition among many roughly equal city-states also produced an unstable political system rife with conflict. Ultimately the political instability of the Maya city-state network eroded its infrastructure of production, labor, transport, and exchange.

By 900, Mesoamerica's classical age had ended. Yet the region's cosmopolitan heritage endured in the Toltec state that dominated the central Mexican highlands from around 950 to 1150 (see again Map 10.1). Although descended from nomadic foragers from Mexico's northern deserts, the Toltecs resurrected the urban civilization, craft industries, and political culture of Teotihuacán. The Toltec capital of Tula became the new Tollan. Once again, in a pattern we have seen in other parts of the world, a nomadic people had inherited the culture of an urban society.

This era also produced a remarkable synthesis of Mexican and Maya traditions. Chichen Itza (chuh-chen uht-SAH), in the heart of the Yucatan peninsula, dominated the northern Maya region in the tenth century. The art and architecture of Chichen Itza so closely resembles that of Tula that some scholars believe Chichen Itza was a colony of the Toltec state. But Chichen Itza's major monuments are older than those of Tula. Although it is unlikely that the Toltecs ruled over Chichen Itza, there is little doubt that both cities were conceived as reincarnations of ancient

Tollan and shared a political ideology centered on the Feathered Serpent. The striking similarities between Tula and Chichen Itza offer compelling evidence of the growing cultural integration of Mesoamerica.

City and State Building in the Andean Region

↘ **FOCUS** How did environmental settings and natural resources shape livelihoods, social organization, and state building in the Andean region?

At the height of Mesoamerica's classical age, a series of rich and powerful states, centered on spectacular adobe and stone cities, sprouted in both the northwestern coastal lowlands and the Andean highlands of South America (see Map 10.2). But the narrow land bridge of the Isthmus of Panama, covered by thick tropical forests, hampered communication between North and South America. Despite similarities in art, architecture, ritual, and political ideology, there is scant evidence of sustained contact between Mesoamerican and Andean societies during this era. Indeed, their differences are striking. Metalworking, already highly refined in the Andean region in the first millennium BCE, was unknown in Mesoamerica until the seventh century CE. The massive irrigation systems of the Andean region had no parallel in Mesoamerica, but urbanization and trade networks were far more extensive in Mesoamerica than in the Andes. Although the Andean region was characterized by strong states and powerful rulers, they did not develop the traditions of writing and record keeping that became vital to political life in the Maya city-states.

All along the Pacific coast of South America, the abrupt ascent of the Andean mountain chain creates a landscape of distinctive ecological zones. Low coastal deserts give way to steep valleys and high mountain ranges interspersed with canyons and plateaus. The formidable geographical barriers and uneven distribution of resources favored social and cultural diversity and inhibited imperial control by highly centralized states.

Nonetheless, Andean rulers strove to forge regional connections, promoting economic integration by bringing together diverse groups, resources, and technologies. Careful use of the region's material wealth produced impressive achievements, most spectacularly the monumental cities built in both the highlands and lowlands. Yet the challenges of the Andean environment and the resulting fragility of its agriculture continually threatened the social and political institutions that produced these achievements.

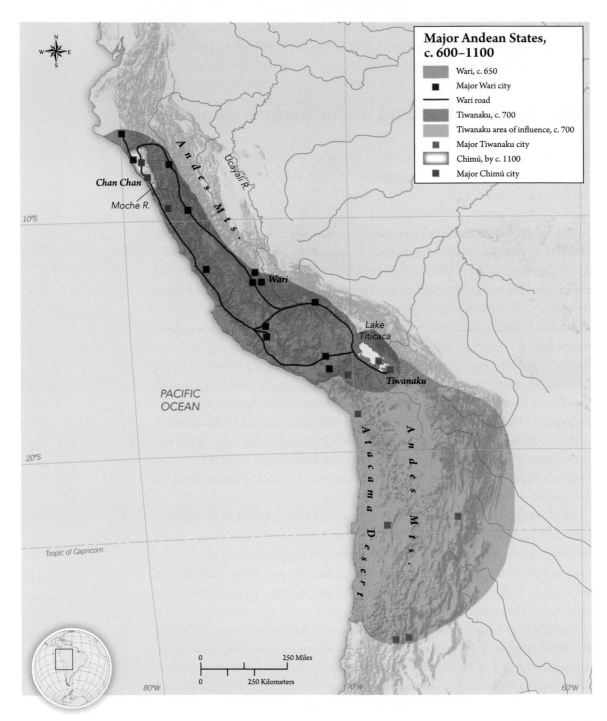

≡ **MAP 10.2** **Major Andean States, c. 600–1100** Despite their radically different ecological habitats, both coastal and highland Andean states relied on sophisticated—but fragile—systems of irrigated agriculture. Coastal Chimú and highland Tiwanaku each developed extensive trade networks. The highland Wari state, in contrast, imposed its military rule by building a series of fortified towns to control local populations.

States and Societies in the Coastal Lowlands

As we saw in Chapter 7, the earliest Andean states, Chavín and Moche, were founded in the arid coastal valleys of northern Peru. But Moche, which had supplanted the earlier Chavín cultures by the first century CE, was beset by climatic and political upheavals. Evidence from tree rings indicates that in the late sixth century the region suffered a drought lasting more than thirty years, followed by decades of unusually heavy rains and severe flooding. Scholars speculate that the El Niño currents might have caused these climatic upheavals. The largest Moche city, Pampa Grande, was burned to the ground in around 700. Whether the city's destruction resulted from domestic unrest or foreign invasion is unclear.

In the late ninth century a new state, Chimú (chee-MOO), arose in the Moche Valley (see again Map 10.2). At its peak, the Chimú capital of Chan Chan comprised a vast maze of adobe-walled enclosures covering eight square miles. The city included at least nine palace compounds, residences for members of the royal clan who shared paramount rulership. There were also some thirty smaller residences of minor nobility and state officials, and densely packed barrios where the city's artisans, laborers, and traders lived in cramped dwellings made of mud-covered cane.

Chan Chan was built on a barren plain near the Peruvian coast. Its inhabitants, and the power of its rulers, were nourished by irrigated agriculture and the construction of a much more extensive network of canals than that of Moche. In the thirteenth and fourteenth centuries the Chimú state expanded into neighboring valleys to tap additional land and water supplies. Military conquest was undoubtedly important in this expansion, but the stability of the Chimú state owed much more to trade and economic integration. Local rulers enjoyed substantial autonomy, and they had access to an enormous range of fine prestige goods produced in Chan Chan's workshops.

States and Societies in the Andean Highlands

Inhabitants of the Andean highlands developed sophisticated agricultural systems to overcome the high altitude, erratic rainfall, and short growing season of the region. Indigenous crops, chiefly potatoes and quinoa (a native cereal), were the staples of the highland diet. Cultivation of raised fields constructed on cobblestone bases and fed by runoff of rain from the surrounding mountains began as early as 800 BCE.

Raised-field agriculture relied on an intricate system of irrigation but did not require complex technology or large-scale organization. Local groups of farmers, known to the Inca as **ayllu** (aye-YOO), constructed the fields well before the

ayllu Groups of farmers (or other specialized occupations) in the Andean highlands who shared claims to common lands and a common ancestry.

SEEING THE PAST

Images of Power in Tiwanaku Art

The lack of written records leaves us with many mysteries about the composition, character, and even the names of the ruling elites who lived in the sumptuous palaces of the city of Tiwanaku. But artistic and architectural evidence gives important clues about the self-image of Tiwanaku's rulers.

Wool Tunic from Tiwanaku, c. 200–400 (Private Collection)

Decorated wool garments and tapestries provide us with rich visual materials of a sort rarely found for other ancient civilizations. The extreme dryness of the Andean highland environment preserved organic materials such as textiles that would have quickly disintegrated in humid climates.

Scholars interpret the dense patterns on the wool tunic shown here as a representation of Tiwanaku and its ruling powers. The face of a god, shown as a many-rayed sun, dominates the center. Below the god's face is a stepped structure that resembles the principal shrine at Tiwanaku. On the lowest tiers of this structure stand two winged figures with feline faces (their heads turned back over their shoulders) and gold ankle bracelets. These figures are probably priests wearing ritual costumes.

Flanking the central images on each side are rows of human figures in elaborate dress holding staffs, arrows, or plants. All of the figures, like the central deity, have vertically divided eyes, which are thought to be a mark of ancestral or divine status. Three upturned animal heads are attached to each headdress, and each figure wears three gold ornaments on its chest. Yet the great variety of headdress styles, facial markings, and garment patterns indicates that each figure represents a specific identity, most likely the heads of the ruling lineages of Tiwanaku or the leaders of subordinate towns and social groups. The array of images suggests a religious festival or procession in which the leaders of human society pay homage to the gods and ancestors.

The Incas who later ruled the Andean region believed that festivals were occasions when the living could connect with their ancestors and invoke divine power to bring life-giving rain to their fields and pastures. The dominant images in Tiwanaku art suggest that the Tiwanaku shared such beliefs.

Source: Margaret Young-Sánchez, ed., *Tiwanaku: Ancestors of the Inca* (Lincoln: University of Nebraska Press, 2004), 47, Figure 2.26a.

Examining the Evidence

1. The figures in the wool tunic hold staffs that take the form of hybrid creatures with serpent bodies and feline (perhaps jaguar) heads. Why did Tiwanaku's leaders choose these animals to represent their power?

2. What does the emphasis on symmetry and repetition in Tiwanaku art, architecture, and urban design tell us about their rulers' ideas of social and cosmic order?

appearance of complex political systems. Ayllu typically owned lands in different locations and ecological zones (valley floors, hillsides, pasture) to minimize risk of crop failures. Groups of ayllu periodically pooled their labor to construct and maintain extensive networks of fields, canals, and causeways.

In contrast to Mesoamerican peoples, who lacked economically useful domesticated animals, Andean peoples used the llama as a beast of burden and the alpaca as a source of meat and wool; the latter was especially important in this bitterly cold environment. Llama caravans traveled up and down the spine of the Andes ranges, trading in local specialties such as woolen cloth, pottery, and bone tools and utensils. Small towns near Lake Titicaca became trading posts that fed this growing interregional exchange. In the fifth century CE the city of Tiwanaku (tee-wah-NAH-coo), at the southern end of Lake Titicaca, became the dominant economic and political center of the region (see again Map 10.2).

≡ **Andean Agriculture** Farmers in the arid Andean highlands irrigated their fields with water stored in stone-lined reservoirs. This depiction of Andean raised-field farming was included in a chronicle written by a native Peruvian around 1615.

Tiwanaku included ceremonial centers with grand temples and public plazas, a large square stone-walled administrative center, and extensive residential barrios. At its peak between 500 and 800 the city may have housed as many as 60,000 inhabitants, so it was roughly the same size as Chan Chan but less than one-third of Teotihuacán's maximum population. Some scholars believe that by this time Tiwanaku had developed from a major metropolis into a highly centralized state led by a small group of priestly clans or perhaps a royal dynasty. The power of the ruling elite rested on a highly ordered cosmology expressed through the precise spatial layout of the city and its lavish culture of rituals and feasting. The prodigious drinking and eating at these events also provided occasions for rulers to demonstrate their generosity and to strengthen social and political bonds with their subjects (see Seeing the Past: Images of Power in Tiwanaku Art). As in Mesoamerica, public ceremony was central to religious and political life. But weapons and images of warfare are rare in Tiwanaku art, suggesting that the city's power derived more from its economic strength and religious ideology than from military aggression.

Tiwanaku was not the only significant political force in the Andean highlands. During the seventh and eighth centuries the city-state of Wari (WAH-ree), 400 miles to the north, established a far-flung network of walled settlements in the highland valleys of modern Peru. In contrast to Tiwanaku, the Wari state set up military outposts to control and extract tribute from local populations. Tiwanaku and Wari shared a common religious heritage but had markedly different forms of religious practice. Wari architecture suggests a more exclusive ceremonial culture restricted to private settings and a small elite, in contrast to the grand temples and public plazas of Tiwanaku.

Archaeological evidence reveals that by the ninth century Wari's colonial empire had collapsed and new building in the city had come to a halt. In around 1000 the same fate befell Tiwanaku. Prolonged drought had upset the fragile ecological balance of raised-field agriculture, and food production declined drastically. The city of Tiwanaku was abandoned, and political power came to be widely dispersed among local chieftains solidly entrenched in hilltop forts. Incessant warfare merely produced a political standoff among local chiefdoms, with no escalation into conquest and expansion until the rise of the Inca Empire in the fifteenth century.

Agrarian Societies in North America

⬊ FOCUS How did the introduction of Mesoamerican crops transform North American peoples?

North America, like the Andean region, long remained isolated from developments in Mesoamerica. The deserts of northern Mexico impeded movement of peoples from the centers of Mesoamerican civilization to the vast landmass to the north. Although North American peoples cultivated some native plants as food sources as early as 2000 BCE, agriculture did not emerge as a way of life in North America until maize was introduced from Mesoamerica around 1000 BCE.

Maize first appeared in North America's southwestern deserts, but the transition to agriculture in this arid region was gradual and uneven. The eastern woodlands had a greater variety of subsistence resources and a longer tradition of settled life, yet here, too, Mesoamerican crops eventually stimulated the emergence of complex societies and expanding networks of communication and exchange (see Map 10.3).

Pueblo Societies in the Southwestern Deserts

Mesoamerican agriculture penetrated the deserts of northern Mexico and the southwestern United States slowly. It was only after 200 CE that yields from growing crops encouraged the southwestern desert peoples to abandon gathering and hunting in favor of settled agriculture. Another important cause of the shift to

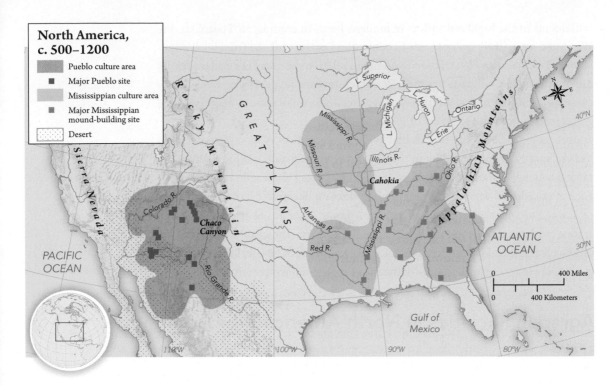

≡ **MAP 10.3   North America, c. 500–1200** After the introduction of Mesoamerican food crops, settled agricultural communities proliferated in both the southwestern deserts and the eastern woodlands of North America.

farming was, ironically, the bow and arrow, introduced by bison hunters of North America's Great Plains, also around 200 CE. By providing more protein from game, use of the bow and arrow made it easier to adopt maize, which supplies ample calories but is very low in protein, as a staple food.

Early agricultural settlements in the southwestern deserts tended to be small, loose clusters of oval pit dwellings. But even these small villages contained special buildings used for ritual purposes. These buildings were the forerunners of the **kivas**, or large ceremonial rooms, of the later pueblo societies in which people lived in large complexes of adjoining adobe buildings. The limited productivity of the land made self-sufficiency difficult. Farmers often traded to obtain food as well as salt, stone for toolmaking, and prestige goods, including hides and precious stones such as turquoise.

Chaco Canyon, in northwestern New Mexico, dramatically illustrates the transformation of social life in the southwestern deserts as its agricultural livelihood matured. The first villages, along with maize and squash agriculture, appeared in the canyon around 500 CE. After 700 CE, population growth and increasing dependence on agriculture led to replacement of the pithouse villages with **pueblos**, in

kiva A large ceremonial chamber located at the center of the pueblo.

pueblo A communal village built by the peoples of southwestern North America, consisting of adjoining flat-roofed stone or adobe buildings arranged in terraces.

which hundreds or even thousands of people lived in contiguous buildings constructed of adobe clay or stone. The dwelling spaces in the pueblos were arranged in semicircular arcs so that each multiroom family unit was equidistant from a central chamber, the kiva that served as the community's ceremonial nucleus.

During the tenth century, Chaco Canyon's population exploded. Much larger pueblos with more than 200 rooms appeared. By the twelfth century the canyon had thirteen of these large pueblos housing a population of approximately 6,000 people.

≡ **Pueblo Bonito, Chaco Canyon** The largest of Chaco Canyon's great houses, Pueblo Bonito rose four stories and contained hundreds of rooms and numerous large circular kivas. The diversity of Pueblo Bonito's burials and artifacts—including trade goods from coastal regions and Mesoamerica—suggests that Chacoan society had a moderately developed social hierarchy. Archaeological research has revealed that over time the pueblo's primary function changed from residential complex to ceremonial center.

Both large and small settlements in Chaco Canyon contained turquoise workshops that manufactured a wide range of ritual ornaments. Exchange networks linked Chaco Canyon with at least seventy communities dispersed across more than 10,000 square miles throughout the Colorado River plateau. These outlying settlements also featured pueblo construction and were connected to Chaco Canyon by a network of rudimentary roads. Although Chaco Canyon may have served as a ritual hub for the entire web of settlements, centralized rule was absent even within the canyon's confines. Each pueblo seems to have pursued similar industrial, trade, and ceremonial activities.

In the early twelfth century prolonged drought weakened the canyon's fragile agricultural base. Many inhabitants migrated elsewhere, and others probably returned to foraging. Pueblo societies continued to flourish in other parts of the southwestern deserts where local conditions remained favorable to farming or trade.

Some scholars believe that regional exchange and the founding of pueblo towns were stimulated by long-distance trade with merchants from the central Mexican highlands. Others contend that trade emerged in the southwestern deserts as a practical response to the unreliability of agriculture in this harsh environment. Environmental changes—especially soil exhaustion and increasingly irregular rainfall—may also have led to the abandonment of concentrated pueblo settlements and the return to more dispersed settlement beginning in the twelfth century. However, a similar trend toward concentration of political power and wider networks of exchange during the period 1000 to 1200, followed by a reversion to smaller and more isolated communities in the centuries before European contact, also occurred in the temperate woodlands of the Mississippi Valley, where livelihoods were less vulnerable to climatic change.

Mound-Building Societies in the Eastern Woodlands

Beginning around 700 CE, the introduction of new technologies radically altered the evolution of eastern woodland societies in North America. The most important innovation was the cultivation of maize, which revolutionized the woodlanders' economic livelihood. At the same time, the flint hoes that accompanied the spread of maize farming made it possible to construct mounds on a much larger scale, and the introduction of the bow and arrow from the Great Plains led to new hunting tactics.

The spread of Mesoamerican agriculture encouraged migration, regional exchange, and the formation of chiefdoms. Unlike the southwestern deserts, where the founding of settled communities followed the transition to agriculture, the eastern woodlands already had permanent villages. Still, population growth triggered by the capacity to produce more food led to greater occupational specialization and social complexity. Favorably located mound settlements conducted a lively trade in stone tools made from chert (a flintlike rock) and obsidian, marine shells from the Gulf of Mexico, and copper from the upper Great Lakes region, as well as salt, pottery, and jewelry.

Mississippian emergence The name scholars give to the spread of common technologies, cultural practices, and forms of social and political organization among a wide range of farming societies in the Mississippi Valley of North America, beginning around 700 and peaking between 1000 and 1500.

As a result of these developments, the middle and lower reaches of the Mississippi River Valley experienced rapid economic and political changes. Scholars have given the name **Mississippian emergence** to the spread of common technologies, cultural practices, and forms of social and political organization among Mississippi Valley farming societies from the eighth century onward (see again Map 10.3).

Although most Mississippian societies remained small, in some cases regional trading centers blossomed into powerful chiefdoms. The most famous is Cahokia (kuh-HOH-kee-uh), at the junction of the Illinois and Mississippi Rivers just east of modern St. Louis. At its fullest extent, the settlement at Cahokia contained at least 10,000 people or perhaps as many as 30,000. Cahokia's physical size and population thus were comparable to those of the city-states of ancient Mesopotamia, as well as Mesoamerica, in their formative stages of development.

☰ **Artist's Reconstruction of Cahokia** Compared to Chaco Canyon (see pages 374–375), Cahokia exhibited a more steeply graded social order. Moreover, in contrast to other mound-building societies—which gradually increased the size of their mounds—construction at Cahokia began with a massive pyramid and great plaza at its core. From the outset Cahokia's rulers displayed an ability to mobilize community labor on a scale unparalleled anywhere else in North America.

Mound building at Cahokia began around 900. By 1200 Cahokia's inhabitants had erected more than one hundred mounds surrounding a four-tiered pyramid set in the middle of four large plazas oriented north, south, east, and west. Some of Cahokia's mounds were used for elite burials, but most served as platforms for buildings. The height of a mound was an index of prestige. The central pyramid, covering fourteen acres and rising over one hundred feet, was crowned by an enormous pole-and-thatch building, which scholars believe was the residence of Cahokia's paramount chief. As was the case with the monuments of Mesoamerican cities, the placement of Cahokia's mounds was apparently determined by observations of crucial celestial events.

Also as in Mesoamerican cities, Cahokia's impressive mounds and plazas displayed the power of its rulers to command labor and resources. The Grand Plaza of Cahokia served as a stage from which the chiefs presided over celebratory feasts, fiercely competitive games played with small stone disks known as *chunkeys*, and solemn death rites in which troops of young women, probably obtained as tribute from outlying areas, were sacrificed. Although Mesoamerican beliefs and rituals may have had some influence on them, Cahokia's elite generated its own distinctive cosmology and ideology.

Following the abrupt and dramatic consolidation of power at Cahokia around 1050, its influence radiated outward throughout the Mississippi Valley. Local chiefs imitated the mound building and sacred ceremonies of the Mississippian culture. Control of prestige goods acquired through trade enhanced the charismatic authority of these chiefs. Still, the power of the paramount chiefs at Cahokia and elsewhere rested on their alliances with lesser chiefs, who were the heads of their own distinct communities, rather than on direct control of the settled population. Political power thus remained fragile—vulnerable to shifts in trade patterns, economic fortunes, and political loyalties.

Cahokia declined after 1250, and its inhabitants gradually abandoned the grand ceremonial center and dispersed. Recent archaeological research has called into question the view that human-caused environmental degradation brought about Cahokia's collapse. Although climate change—including the cooling trend of the Little Ice Age (see Chapter 14)—cannot be overlooked, most likely competition from rival chiefs weakened Cahokia's hegemony. In the wake of Cahokia's demise, long-distance economic and cultural exchanges waned, and incidences of violence grew. The prevalence of warrior imagery, the concentration of the population in fortified towns, and the ample evidence of traumatic death from excavated cemeteries all point to the emergence of warfare as a way of life.

The scale and complexity of the settlements and ritual complexes at Cahokia were unique in North America. Yet its influence as a pan-regional cultural force is reminiscent of other urban centers in the Americas. As in Tiwanaku, feasting, sacrifice, and resettlement of rural inhabitants in the urban core forged a distinctive cultural identity at Cahokia. Also like Tiwanaku, Cahokia apparently served as a ritual center for a group of independent chiefdoms that for a time merged into a single political entity. In this sense, as an economic and political crossroads, Cahokia was central to the emergence of a distinctive Mississippian society.

Habitat and Adaptation in the Pacific Islands

↘ FOCUS In what ways did the habitats and resources of the Pacific Islands promote both cultural unity and cultural diversity?

The Lapita colonization (see Chapter 7) transformed the landscapes and seascapes of the western Pacific, or Near Oceania. After approximately 200 BCE, though, what historians call the "long pause" in transoceanic migrations set in.

Subsequently the cultural unity spawned by the Lapita migrations fragmented as local groups adapted to their diverse island habitats.

The "long pause" may reflect not people's lack of effort, but rather their lack of success in making landfall on the smaller and far more widely dispersed islands of the central and eastern Pacific, or Remote Oceania. But around 300 CE (some scholars would say even several centuries earlier), a new wave of migration began with a leap eastward of more than 1,200 miles from Samoa to the Marquesas and Society Island archipelagoes. This second wave of exploration brought human colonists to virtually every habitable island in the Pacific Ocean by the year 1000 (see Map 10.4).

≡ **Polynesian Sailing Vessel** Although the age of great long-distance voyaging had ceased by the time Europeans reached the Pacific, Polynesians continued to make open-ocean journeys of hundreds of miles. In 1616 a Dutch mariner drew this illustration of a Polynesian double-hulled canoe sailing between Tonga and Samoa. The largest Polynesian canoes were roughly the same length as the sailing vessels of the European explorers.

In Near Oceania, the interaction of the Lapita peoples with the native Papuan societies had generated extraordinary cultural diversity. In contrast, this second wave of migrations into the farthest reaches of Remote Oceania fostered a culturally unified set of islands known as Polynesia. Still, Polynesian settlers did modify their livelihoods and social and political institutions to suit the resources of their island habitats. **Human ecology**—the ways in which people adapt to their natural environment—was as flexible in the Pacific Islands as in the world's great continental landmasses.

Polynesian Expansion

The Pacific Islands are commonly divided into three parts: Melanesia ("Middle Islands"), Micronesia ("Small Islands"), and Polynesia ("Many Islands"). The peoples of Melanesia (if we include New Guinea) make up the most diverse and

human ecology
Adaptation of people to the natural environment they inhabit.

≡ **MAP 10.4   Polynesian Migrations** Between 600 and 1000 Polynesian migrants settled nearly all of the habitable islands of the central and eastern Pacific Ocean. After this wave of migration ebbed, remote islands such as the Hawaiian archipelago and Easter Island lost contact and became isolated from the rest of Polynesia.

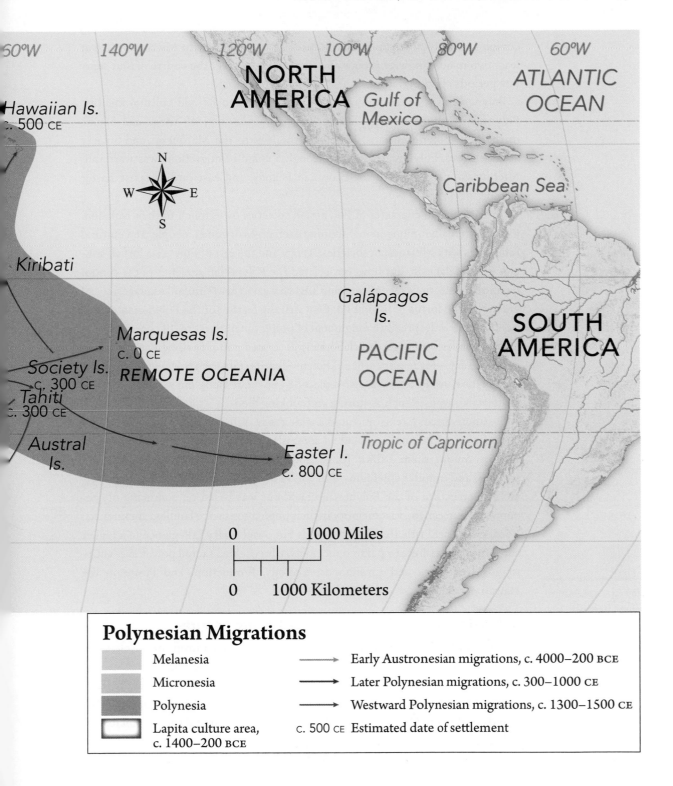

Polynesian Migrations

- Melanesia
- Micronesia
- Polynesia
- Lapita culture area, c. 1400–200 BCE

→ Early Austronesian migrations, c. 4000–200 BCE
→ Later Polynesian migrations, c. 300–1000 CE
→ Westward Polynesian migrations, c. 1300–1500 CE

c. 500 CE Estimated date of settlement

complex assembly of peoples and cultures on earth. Similarly, Micronesia had at least two major language groups and was populated over the course of four separate periods of immigration.

Polynesian societies, in contrast, share a strong social and cultural identity. Polynesian culture emerged from the Lapita settlements of Tonga and Samoa in the first millennium BCE. Following the leap to the Marquesas and Society archipelagoes, Polynesians spread through a chain of migrations westward into Micronesia, northward to the Hawaiian Islands, and eastward as far as Easter Island.

The distinctive character of Polynesian societies owes much to their isolation. Fiji was virtually unique in maintaining exchanges of goods, people, and cultural influences with Melanesian societies; Tonga and the rest of Polynesia lost all contact with Melanesia. But however isolated the Polynesian societies of the central Pacific became, their recent common ancestry gave them similar languages, social practices, and forms of livelihood. One striking feature of the Polynesian expansion was the widespread abandonment of pottery manufacture. In contrast to the Lapita peoples, who regarded elaborately decorated pottery as a sign of high social rank, pottery—for reasons still unknown—lost its status as a prestige good among the Polynesians. Pottery was also replaced by coconut shells and wooden bowls for utilitarian purposes such as storing and cooking food.

Distinctive ecosystems nurtured a wide range of livelihoods and political systems across the Polynesian Pacific. Larger islands with richer and more varied resources, among them Tahiti, Tonga, and Hawaii, gave rise to highly stratified societies and complex chiefdoms with tens of thousands of subjects. The rigid hierarchical structure of the Polynesian chiefdoms was based on command of economic resources. The vast majority in their populations were landless commoners. Local chiefs held title to cultivated lands but owed **fealty** (allegiance to a higher authority) and tribute to paramount chiefs, who wielded sacred power over entire islands (see Lives and Livelihoods: Ecology, Production, and Power in the Hawaiian Islands).

fealty An expression of allegiance to a higher political authority, often verified by swearing an oath of loyalty, giving tribute, and other gestures of submission.

Subsistence and Survival in the Pacific Islands

Counter to the romantic fantasies of nineteenth-century European travelers and twentieth-century anthropologists, the Pacific Islands were not pristine natural worlds undisturbed by their "primitive" human inhabitants. On the contrary, human hands had radically transformed the island ecosystems. For example, the islands of Remote Oceania originally lacked plant and animal species suitable for human food consumption. Polynesian settlers changed all that by bringing with them pigs, dogs, chickens, yams, taro, sugar cane, bananas, coconuts, breadfruit, and various medicinal and fiber plants. The intrusion of these alien species had large and long-lasting consequences for both the environment and its human inhabitants. In many places native bird, turtle, and sea mammal species were hunted to extinction, and **deforestation**, the cutting down of forests, sharply reduced the islands' natural resources.

Most of the tropical food plants transported by colonizers readily thrived in the Pacific Islands. As in Iceland's early history (see Chapter 8), explosive population growth typically followed initial settlement on uninhabited islands. Settlers had a compelling reason—fear of extinction—to have enough children to attain populations large enough to maintain their societies. Population densities on many islands reached 250 persons per square mile. Ecological constraints, however, ultimately curbed unrestricted population growth.

On many islands, population pressure began to strain resources after 1100. Where possible, islanders applied more laborious agricultural methods, building irrigation canals and terraced or walled garden plots. In the Marquesas, swelling population growth increased competition and warfare. More fortified villages were built, and the authority of warrior chiefs rose. A similar pattern of intensified agriculture and warfare in response to population pressure appeared in Fiji. The growing diversity of local ceramic styles in Fiji also suggests a greater demarcation of ethnic groups and political boundaries. Here, too, constant warfare shifted the basis of chiefship from priestly duties to military leadership.

The most striking example of the fragility of island ecosystems and the risk of demographic catastrophe is Easter Island. When Polynesian voyagers originally settled Easter Island sometime after 600 CE, the island was well endowed with fertile soils and abundant forests. These rich resources supported a population that at its peak numbered 10,000 people. Easter Island's famous stone monuments—thirty-ton sculptures believed to be images of ancestors who were transformed into gods—were carved and installed on more than 200 temple platforms across the island between 1100 and 1500. But the clearing of forests for agriculture depleted fuel and construction resources, and erosion and exposure to wind and surf ruined soil fertility. After 1500, the island was plunged into incessant raiding and warfare, accompanied by ritual cannibalism. As the once plentiful flora and fauna of Easter Island were decimated, its human population dwindled to a mere several hundred persons subsisting mainly on fishing, the Pacific Ocean's most reliable resource.

deforestation The cutting down of forests, usually to clear land for farming and human settlement.

LIVES AND LIVELIHOODS

Ecology, Production, and Power in the Hawaiian Islands

Humans first arrived in the Hawaiian Islands during the great wave of Polynesian voyaging of the first millennium CE. The dating of the settlement of Hawaii is disputed, with scholarly opinion ranging from as early as 300 CE to as late as 800. But long-distance voyaging ceased around 1300. For the next five centuries, until the British explorer Captain Cook arrived in 1788, the Hawaiian archipelago remained a world unto itself.

Initially, the human impact on the islands' ecology remained modest. During the thirteenth and fourteenth centuries, however, hierarchical chiefdoms formed in Hawaii, and investment in agricultural production intensified. The construction of

≡ **Hawaiian Landscape** The first European visitors to Hawaii were impressed by the intensive agriculture practiced by the islanders. This village sketch was drawn by a member of the expedition led by the British explorer George Vancouver, who landed at Hawaii in 1792. Cultivated fields lined with stone irrigation channels can be seen in the background. (Village of Macacoupah, Owhyhee [Hawaii]. M. Dubourg, after Thomas Heddington, March 1814. Hand-colored aquatint. 16.14 × 21.66 in.; 41 × 55 cm Bishop Museum)

irrigation systems strengthened the chiefs' authority, allowing them to command more resources and expand their domains through conquest. In the geologically older western islands, the inhabitants constructed taro fields irrigated by stone-lined canals on the valley floors and hillsides. But irrigation was not practicable on the large eastern islands of Hawaii and Maui because they were mostly covered by lava flows. As a result, agriculture in the eastern islands lagged behind that of the western islands.

Population growth and the building of irrigation systems reached their peak in the fifteenth and sixteenth centuries. This was also the period when the *ahupua'a* (ah-HOO-poo-ah-hah) system of land management developed. The ahupua'a consisted of tracts of land running down from the central mountains to the sea, creating wedge-shaped segments that cut across different ecological zones. Each ahupua'a combined a wide range of resources, including forests, fields, fishponds, and marine vegetation and wildlife.

Hawaiian rulers claimed descent from the gods and sharply distinguished themselves from the rest of society. Kings distributed the ahupua'a under their control to subordinate chiefs in return for tribute and fealty, especially in times of war. Local chiefs in turn allocated rights to land, water, and fishing grounds to commoners, who were obliged to work on the personal lands of the chief and to pay tribute in produce. Strict rules of descent and inheritance determined social rank in Hawaiian society, and an elaborate system of **taboos** reinforced social stratification. Taboos also regulated gender differences and boundaries. Women were forbidden to eat many foods, including pork, bananas, and certain kinds of fish, and had to cook their food in separate ovens and eat apart from men.

In the genealogical lore of Hawaii, the oldest royal lineages were in the densely populated western islands of Kauai (kah-WAH-ee) and Oahu. The ruling elites of these islands drew their wealth from irrigated agriculture and focused their religious worship on Kane (KAH-nay), the god of flowing waters and fertility. On the larger islands of Hawaii and Maui, where chiefs and kings instead derived their power from military might, their devotion centered on Ku, the bloodthirsty god of war. From 1400 onward the local rulers in Hawaii and Maui incessantly warred against neighboring rivals. By 1650 single, island-wide kingdoms would be established through conquest on both Maui and Hawaii.

Long before contact with Europeans, then, Hawaiian rulers forged powerful states based on highly stratified systems of social ranking. Private property did not exist. All land and resources belonged to chiefs and kings, who were regarded as gods. Through their monopoly of not only productive resources but also the exchange and use of goods, Hawaiian rulers gained full command over the wealth of their realm and the labor of their subjects.

Questions to Consider

1. How did the sources of wealth and power in the Hawaiian Islands differ from those of market economies elsewhere in the world?

2. In what ways did ecological variations among the Hawaiian Islands foster different patterns of social and political development?

For Further Information:

Hommon, Robert J. *The Ancient Hawaiian State: Origin of a Political Society.* New York: Oxford University Press, 2013.

Kirch, Patrick V. *A Shark Going Inland Is My Chief: The Island Civilization of Ancient Hawai'i.* Berkeley: University of California Press, 2012.

COUNTERPOINT: Social Complexity in Bougainville

➘ FOCUS Why did the historical development of the Melanesian island of Bougainville depart so sharply from that of contemporaneous societies in the Americas and the Pacific?

taboo
In Polynesia, the designation of certain actions or objects as sacred and forbidden to persons because of their social status or gender.

ethnogenesis The formation of separate ethnic groups from common ancestors.

Bougainville (bow-gahn-VEEL), one of the chain of islands stretching in a long arc southeastward from New Guinea, typifies the phenomenon of **ethnogenesis**, the formation of separate ethnic groups from common ancestors. In contrast to the underlying social and cultural unity of many of the societies studied in this chapter, the long-settled islands of Melanesia display extraordinary social and cultural diversity. Here the progress of history fostered not closer interaction and cross-cultural borrowing but rather more acute social differences and strong ethnic boundaries.

Bougainville's Diverse Peoples

Situated slightly below the equator, Bougainville has a tropical climate with virtually no seasonal variation. Yet with four active volcanoes, Bougainville is one of the most geologically unstable places on earth. Volcanic eruptions have periodically

covered major portions of the island with ash and forced the inhabitants to relocate, at least temporarily. The island, roughly the
size of Puerto Rico, is sparsely populated even today. Settlements
are concentrated along streams on the relatively flat terrain of the
northern coast and in the southern interior.

Twenty different languages are spoken on Bougainville today.
Scholars classify twelve of these languages as Austronesian (AW-
stroh-NEE-zhuhn), the language group of the seafarers who settled in the islands of Southeast Asia and the Pacific during the
Lapita colonization. Linguists broadly define the rest as Papuan
(PAH-poo-en), the languages spoken by the ancient inhabitants
of New Guinea. Four of Bougainville's languages are so idiosyn-
cratic that the associations among them confound linguists.

Beyond the striking language differences, Bougainville's inhabitants also vary so much in stature, body type, and biological
chemistry that Bougainville islanders rank among the most ge-
netically diverse populations on the planet. Cultural variation is
similarly striking. Although pottery manufacture on Bougainville
dates back to the pre-Lapita era, some groups apparently have never made pottery.

≡ **Bougainville**

What accounts for such remarkable diversity within the confines of this single
island? One popular theory is that the kind of tropical agriculture practiced in
Bougainville is relatively rich and reliable, and so the islanders have not had to
build trading networks. Traditions of matrilineal descent and local **endogamy**—
marriage within the group—reinforced this pattern of isolated village life. The
social isolation of individual villages also tended to raise language barriers over
time. Further, as modern biological research shows, small populations are more
likely to experience large genetic fluctuations from one generation to the next,
which fosters more, not less, genetic diversity. Not surprisingly, genetic variation
among Bougainville's modern populations correlates strongly with language
groups.

The Historical Roots of Social Difference

Yet the diversity of Bougainville's languages did not result from a long period of
isolation. The island probably experienced a number of separate immigrations
both before and after the Lapita era. The island's Austronesian speakers did not
simply all arrive together at the time of the Lapita migrations. There is clear evidence that some coastal regions were resettled by Austronesian speakers after
volcanic eruptions displaced the previous inhabitants.

endogamy Marriage
within a defined
group, such as a village
or a kinship network.

Further, it is not possible to make neat distinctions between the cultures of "native" Papuan speakers and "immigrant" Austronesian speakers. The Siwai (sih-why), a Papuan-speaking community in southern Bougainville, is noted in anthropological theory as a model of a **big man society,** characterized by an egalitarian social structure and strong communal identity based on sharing and reciprocal exchange. The role of the big man is to redistribute wealth among members of the community to ensure the well-being of all, but the big man does not hold a position above the rest of society. Melanesian big man societies contrast sharply with the stratified social hierarchy of Polynesian chiefdoms, in which a hereditary elite of chiefs monopolized political power and the control of economic resources. Near the Siwai in southern Bougainville, however, is another Papuan-speaking group, the Buin (boo-een), whose society developed the high degree of stratification and inherited rank and privilege typical of Polynesian chiefdoms.

Environmental adaptation does not explain the different social structures of the Siwai and the Buin: the two groups occupy virtually identical habitats, practice similar forms of irrigated taro agriculture, and speak closely related languages. Despite their similar livelihoods, the Siwai and Buin embraced different notions of prestige and status. For example, the Buin regarded pottery making as women's work, whereas the Siwai, uniquely among Melanesian societies, reserved pottery making exclusively for men.

This contrast underscores one important difference between the Buin and their Siwai neighbors. The Buin had access to the coast and, unlike the Siwai, interacted with peoples in neighboring islands. They learned their techniques of pottery making from Austronesian-speaking inhabitants of the nearby Shetland Islands around 1000. Immigrants from the Shetlands may have been absorbed into Buin society.

Yet differences in contact with the outside world cannot fully explain the variations in social practices among Bougainville societies. Some scholars have suggested that in the past, a more pronounced social hierarchy was common in Melanesian societies. In their view, the egalitarian big man societies of Melanesia resulted from the profound changes set in motion by contact with Europeans, including population losses from disease. At the very least, we can no longer attribute the complex human ecology of Bougainville to the former historical interpretation of unchanging island cultures cut off from the march of history by the encircling ocean.

big man society
In modern anthropological theory, an egalitarian society in which a chosen leader, the "big man," supervises the distribution of the community's collective wealth and resources.

Conclusion

During the period 300 to 1200, distinctive regional cultures coalesced in many parts of the Americas and the Pacific Islands. As in Latin Christendom and East Asia, the spread and intensification of agriculture, expanding networks of trade and cultural exchange, and the founding of cities and states led to the formation of common civilizations.

This period marked the classical age in Mesoamerica and the Andean region. There, the development of urban societies and states generated lasting traditions concerning knowledge, livelihoods, and social organization. Rulers such as the Maya Holy Lord Eighteen Rabbit built monumental cities and conducted elaborate public rituals to display their supreme power and bind their subjects to their will.

Permanent towns and long-distance networks of exchange also developed in North America. The spread of prestige goods and ritual art in the eastern woodlands and the southwestern deserts also indicates active cross-cultural borrowing in these regions, at least among elites.

The rapid peopling of the islands of Remote Oceania between 600 and 1000 gave this vast region a common cultural identity as Polynesia. Similar political and social structures and forms of livelihood took root across Polynesia, even though many island populations, such as those of the Hawaiian archipelago and Easter Island, lost contact with the outside world.

Striking, too, are patterns of regional diversity. Different types of social order evolved as new crops and technologies spread and people adjusted institutions and livelihoods to new or transformed habitats. In all of these regions—even among the small village societies of Bougainville, which mostly shunned interaction with their neighbors—social identities and community boundaries changed constantly. Ethnogenesis was a dynamic, continuous process.

By 1200, many of these societies were suffering from economic decline and political fragmentation. Scholars have attributed the collapse of the Maya city-state network, the disintegration of the Tiwanaku state, and the abandonment of Chaco Canyon primarily to ecological causes: either some climatic catastrophe, or the inability of the existing agricultural technologies and political systems to provide for their growing populations. The collapse of these societies reminds us of the fragility of their agricultural systems, still limited to Stone Age technologies, and their vulnerability to long-term ecological and climatic changes. As we shall see in the next chapter, advances in agricultural and industrial technology and the development of new economic institutions in Eurasia during the eleventh to thirteenth centuries laid the foundations for more sustained economic and demographic growth.

review

The major global development in this chapter: The formation of distinctive regional cultures in the Americas and the Pacific Islands between 300 and 1200.

Important Events	
c. 150–300	Building of the city of Teotihuacán in the Valley of Mexico
c. 250–900	Mesoamerica's classical age
c. 500	First permanent settlements in Chaco Canyon
c. 500–1000	Andean state of Tiwanaku
c. 550–650	Fall and destruction of Teotihuacán
c. 600–1000	Polynesian settlement of Pacific Islands
c. 700	Moche city of Pampa Grande destroyed
c. 700–900	Heyday of the Andean state of Wari
c. 800–900	Collapse of the Maya city-states
c. 850–1150	Building of the large pueblos in Chaco Canyon
c. 900	Rise of the Chimú state centered at Chan Chan
c. 950–1150	Toltec state's reign as the dominant power in the Valley of Mexico
c. 1050	Consolidation of Cahokia's dominance in the lower Mississippi Valley region
c. 1100–1500	Construction of Easter Island's stone monuments
c. 1150	Abandonment of the pueblos in Chaco Canyon
c. 1250–1300	Collapse and abandonment of Cahokia

KEY TERMS

ayllu (p. 369)
big man society (p. 388)
chiefdom (p. 356)
ch'ulel (p. 361)
city-state (p. 356)
deforestation (p. 383)

endogamy (p. 387)
ethnogenesis (p. 386)
fealty (p. 382)
Holy Lord (p. 361)
human ecology (p. 379)
kiva (p. 374)

Mississippian emergence (p. 376)
obsidian (p. 356)
prestige good (p. 357)
pueblo (p. 374)
taboo (p. 385)
Tollan (p. 357)

CHAPTER OVERVIEW QUESTIONS

1. How did these societies, equipped with only Stone Age technology, develop the institutions and patterns of exchange to tame often hostile environments and build complex civilizations?
2. How did differences in environment foster or discourage exchanges among adjacent regions?

3. What were the sources of political power in the societies discussed in this chapter, and how were they similar or dissimilar?
4. How did differences in urban design reflect distinctive forms of political and social organization?

MAKING CONNECTIONS

1. Why were the human populations of the regions covered in this chapter more vulnerable to ecological changes than the settled societies of Eurasia?
2. How did the political and social organization of North American chiefdoms compare with those of the Maya city-states?

3. Although North America's eastern woodlands farmers began to cultivate the same food crops as Mesoamerican peoples during the Mississippian emergence, their societies developed in different ways. What might explain these variations?

DOING HISTORY

Sourcing and Situation

Documentary records written by contemporaries provide historians with their most important primary sources. But the societies in the Americas and the Pacific Islands examined in this chapter, with the exception of Mesoamerica, were preliterate and have left no written documents. When historians study other preliterate peoples they rely heavily on the written testimony of outsiders—for example, as we will see in Chapter 11, reports by the Arab geographers, missionaries, and merchants who traveled to sub-Saharan Africa. Consider the sources that have been used in this chapter to study the preliterate societies of the Americas and the Pacific—archaeological remains, linguistic connections, ecological traces, eyewitness accounts by early European visitors, and anthropological research on preliterate societies of the recent past.

1. What are the strengths and weaknesses of each type of evidence?
2. What might be their inherent biases?
3. Look again at the images in this chapter. What can archaeological evidence tell us that written evidence cannot, and vice versa?

For further research into the topics covered in this chapter, see the Bibliography at the end of the book.

The Rise of Commerce in Afro-Eurasia

900–1300

≡ **World in the Making** Arabs and Persians dominated the Indian Ocean trade routes, but by the eleventh century Indian and Malay mariners also plied Asian seas from Africa to China. This thirteenth-century illustration depicts a dhow, the most common type of Indian Ocean sailing vessel, on a voyage from East Africa to Basra, the great port linking Mesopotamia to the Persian Gulf. Indian Ocean trade vastly expanded cultural as well as economic exchange: although the passengers are Arabs, the crew appears to be Indian.

backstory

The collapse of the Han Empire in China and the Roman Empire in the west ended a prolonged era of growth in agriculture and trade in the agrarian heartlands of Eurasia (see Chapters 5 and 6). The steppe nomad invasions devastated many cities in China, India, and the western Roman Empire's former territories. Political disunity hindered efforts to revive agriculture and commerce. Yet the rise of steppe empires such as that of the Turks also fostered trade and cultural exchange across the caravan routes of Central Asia.

In the seventh century, the formation of a vast Islamic empire and the reestablishment of a unified empire in China by the Sui and Tang dynasties created stable political and social foundations for economic recovery (see Chapters 8 and 9). Latin Christendom remained divided into many kingdoms and city-states, and here the reinvigoration of trade and industry came later. The expanding Islamic world also began to reach across the seas and deserts to bring parts of sub-Saharan Africa into its orbit.

EARLY IN THE TWELFTH century, the Jewish merchant Allan bin Hassun wrote home from Aden, in Yemen on the coast of the Arabian Sea, upon his return from India. Allan had been sent to Yemen by his father-in-law, a prominent Cairo cloth merchant, to sell the purple-dyed cloth that was the father-in-law's specialty. But the cloth had proved unprofitable, so Allan persuaded his reluctant father-in-law to supply him with coral and perfume for a trading venture to India. The journey to India and back had been long and dangerous, and Allan's return had been delayed repeatedly by local uprisings, storms, and accidents. Allan intended to return to Cairo, but the high prices that pepper fetched in Aden instead spurred him to set out immediately for India again.

Only fragments of Allan's correspondence survive today, and we do not know how he fared during his return voyage to India. But however successful he was as a businessman, Allan's long sojourns took their toll on his family. In a letter his wife sent to Allan in North Africa, she bitterly chided him for his absence: "We are in great distress, owing to bad health and loneliness." Caring for their sick infant had forced her to sell furniture and rent out the upper story of their house to pay for doctors and medicines. Lamenting that her father was abroad on business at the same time, the wife urged her husband, "By God, do not tarry any longer . . . we remain like orphans without a man."

Allan's last surviving letter, written when he was an old man about to embark on another expedition to India, warned his adult sons not to abandon their families as he had done. He advised his sons, merchants themselves, to form a partnership that would spread the burdens of travel among them. His letter conveyed heartfelt regrets about the personal costs of his life as a merchant: "Had I known how much I would be longing after you, I would not have undertaken this voyage altogether."[1]

In Allan bin Hassun's day, a sustained economic expansion was spreading across Eurasia and Africa. Favorable climatic conditions, improved agricultural efficiency and output, increases in population and growth of cities, and new patterns of consumption led to rapid expansion of the money economy. Long-distance merchants such as Allan opened new trade routes that connected Europe and the Mediterranean with the Islamic lands and the Indian Ocean. Vigorous commercial growth in China stimulated an unprecedented flowering of maritime trade between East Asia and the Indian Ocean world. The thirst for gold brought parts of sub-Saharan Africa into these trade networks as well. In all of these places, commercial wealth reshaped social and political power.

Although the pace and dynamics of economic change varied from region to region, the underlying trends were remarkably consistent. Similarly, in the fourteenth century this surge in economic prosperity suddenly ended across all of Eurasia, from Spain to China. This cycle of economic growth and decline was powered by the progressive integration of local economies into regional and cross-cultural networks of exchange. The benefits of commercial prosperity were unevenly distributed, however. In addition, the wealth generated by the economic success of Jewish communities in Latin Christendom enflamed religious hostilities and led to heavy taxation, persecution, and ultimately exile.

OVERVIEW QUESTIONS

The major global development in this chapter: The sustained economic expansion that spread across Eurasia and Africa between the tenth and fourteenth centuries.

As you read, consider:

1. How did agricultural changes contribute to commercial and industrial growth?

2. What technological breakthroughs increased productivity most significantly?

3. What social institutions and economic innovations did merchants devise to overcome the risks and dangers of long-distance trade?

4. In what ways did the profits of commerce translate into social and economic power?

5. Above all, who benefited most from these economic changes?

Agricultural Innovation and Diffusion

↘ **FOCUS** Which groups took the most active role in adopting new agricultural technologies in the different regions of Eurasia during the centuries from 900 to 1300?

Commercial growth was rooted in an increasingly productive agrarian base. Favorable climatic trends contributed to agricultural expansion across Eurasia. After 900, warmer temperatures set in, lengthening growing seasons and boosting yields. New farming techniques raised yields and encouraged investment in agriculture and specialization of production. Rulers, landowners, and peasants all contributed innovations. With rising agricultural productivity, farmers could feed

READING THE PAST

A Byzantine Gentleman's Advice on Providing for One's Family

Kekaumenos (KEK-ah-meh-noz), a Byzantine official of high social standing, composed his *Advice and Anecdotes* in the closing decades of the eleventh century. Addressed to a son who probably had embarked on a military career, it is a manual for conducting one's life based on personal experience and popular wisdom rather than book learning. Kekaumenos ranges widely over many topics, including military strategy, public service, and household management, and even includes admonitions to a hypothetical emperor. The excerpts here give advice on how to ensure economic security.

Let us suppose you don't hold any public office and that you dwell in your private home. Under such circumstances, you must undertake work on your estate to support your family properly without ever neglecting them because, having nothing else to live on, working the land is your sole resource. Make for yourself things that are self-working—mills, workshops, gardens, and other things that will give you an annual return whether it be in rent or crop. . . .

Plant trees of all kinds and reed beds, which yield an income that doesn't require effort every year. In this way you may live without worry. You must also have livestock—plow oxen, pigs, sheep, and other animals which breed each year, reproducing and multiplying; these animals will ensure the opulence of your table. All these will satisfy your needs, and you will have an abundance of wheat, wine, and everything else, seed and

more people, leading to population expansion and the growth of cities. As urban demand for foodstuffs and industrial raw materials increased, it became more rewarding to produce goods for sale than for household consumption. Increased agricultural production transformed patterns of rural life and community, as well as changed the relationship between peasants working the land and the lords and states that commanded their loyalty and labor.

Retrenchment and Renewal in Europe and Byzantium

The third-century collapse of the unified Roman Empire disrupted economic life in the cities, but it had little direct impact on work and livelihoods in the countryside. In subsequent centuries great lords and peasant smallholders alike livestock, goods to consume yourself or vend in the market. . . .

Be careful not to neglect your patrimony [property inherited from father], else all your riches will end up exhausted. Apply yourself to managing your patrimony prudently: if you are negligent, your servants will appropriate and devour all your grain. Calamitous years will surely come: the earth will be barren and you will find yourself without any reserve of wheat or other cereals to feed your family. . . . Then you will think about going to someone and borrow what you need, but no one will give you anything. . . . As a result, you will experience shame and sorrow: shame, because you

asked and received nothing; sorrow, because you no longer know whom to ask. . . . Worse still: if you find someone to give you a loan, he will claim interest, as most people do, and a mortgage on your property. . . . When your creditor sees you in the market, in the magistrate's court, or in church on a feast day, he will want to show himself rich and superior to you in front of everyone, and will say to you, "Good fellow, what do I owe you when you don't give me back what is mine? Do you want me to ruin you?" . . . If you keep silent, everyone will say, behind your back or in a loud voice, "There goes a debtor who has lost all mettle!" or "How miserable are the days of the insolvent!"

Source: Kékaumenos, *Conseils et récits d'un gentilhomme byzantine*, trans. Paolo Odorico (Toulouse: Éditions Anacharsis, 2016), 113–14.

Examining the Evidence

1. What are Kekaumenos's strategic priorities for securing the family's economic welfare?

2. Why does Kekaumenos regard debt as the worst danger of all?

concentrated on growing food for their own consumption. Even in the tenth and eleventh centuries, when political stability had restored some measure of economic prosperity in the Byzantine Empire and Latin Europe, self-sufficiency was the goal. Kekaumenos, an eleventh-century Byzantine official, instructed his sons that proper household management meant minimizing expenses, diversifying assets, and avoiding dependence on the market (See Reading the Past: A Byzantine Gentleman's Advice on Providing for One's Family).

Great landowners were the main agents of agricultural development and innovation in Europe. The warrior nobility and monastic establishments founded manorial estates that reduced much of the rural population to the condition of **serfs**, who were bound to the soil they tilled as well as to their masters' will. Lords

serf A peasant who was legally bound to the land and who owed goods, labor, and service to the lord who owned the land.

gathered their serfs into compact villages and subjected them to their laws as well as the rules of parish priests. Although free smallholder farmers were probably still the majority, they too sought the protection of local lords.

As lordship came to be defined in terms of control over specific territories and populations, the nobility took greater interest in increasing their revenue. Landowners began to invest in enterprises such as watermills, vineyards, and orchards that required large initial outlays of capital but would yield steady long-term returns. Manorial lords also introduced other new technologies, such as the wheeled moldboard plow. Pulled by horses rather than oxen, this device was better than the light Mediterranean-style plow at breaking up northern Europe's heavy, clayey soils. Still, some fundamental aspects of European agriculture continued unchanged in both the Latin west and the Byzantine east. Wheat and barley remained the dominant crops. Farmers combined livestock raising with cereal cultivation, providing more protein in European diets. The large amount of land needed to pasture animals kept population densities relatively low, however.

The recovery of Byzantium's political fortunes in the tenth and eleventh centuries led to renewed economic growth. Cultivation of olives, grapes, and figs expanded throughout the Mediterranean lands. In Anatolia (modern Turkey), however, the scarcity of labor prompted landowners to replace agriculture with stock-raising—a trend that accelerated when the Seljuk (SEL-juk) Turks, nomadic Muslim warriors from Central Asia, conquered most of Anatolia in the late eleventh century.

Agricultural Transformation in the Islamic World

The Arab conquerors of Syria, Mesopotamia, and Iran had little immediate impact on the already well-established agricultural systems in these regions. Undeveloped areas were another matter, however. The new rulers awarded wilderness lands to Arab governors, who were expected to convert the wastelands to farming and use the revenues to defray the costs of public administration. In the ninth and tenth centuries, as the caliphate began to lose its grip over the provinces,

≡ **A Managerial Landlord** In this illustration from a fifteenth-century French handbook on farming, a landowner personally supervises the agricultural work on his estate. The laborers are engaged in various tasks, including plowing, sowing, and harvesting. The team of horses is pulling a wheeled moldboard plow, which allowed farmers to till the heavy soils of northern Europe more efficiently.

local governors turned to enslaved armies to maintain control. They allocated landed estates, *iqta* (ihk-ta), to military commanders for the upkeep of these enslaved forces. Under the rule of the Seljuk Turks, first in Iran and subsequently in the central Islamic lands, most of the land was held as iqta estates to support the enslaved armies.

Islamic agriculture was transformed by new crops and farming practices. The burgeoning trade with Asia (discussed later in this chapter) introduced into Islamic domains a host of new crops—including rice, cotton, sugar cane, sorghum, and citrus fruits—from the lands surrounding the Indian Ocean. Cultivating these tropical imports as summer crops in the arid Middle East and North Africa required more elaborate irrigation systems. Thus, the spread of Asian crops in Syria, Egypt, and Spain was accompanied by irrigation technologies originally developed in India and Iran. By 1200, Asian tropical crops had been domesticated throughout the Islamic world, from Iran to Spain (see Map 11.1).

iqta In the Islamic world, grants of land made to governors and military officers, the revenues of which were used to pay for administrative expenses and soldiers' salaries.

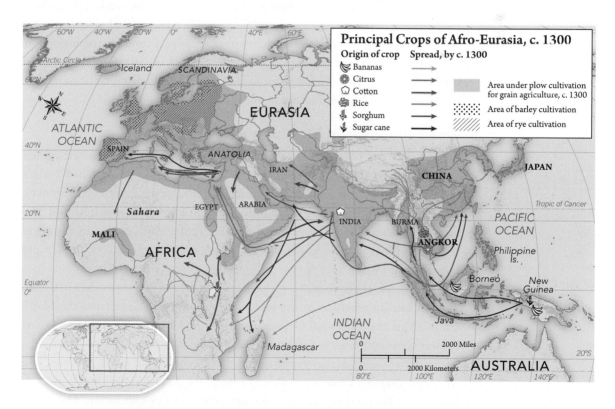

≡ **MAP 11.1   Principal Crops of Afro-Eurasia, c. 1300** The commercial prosperity of this era rested on the population growth made possible by the rising productivity of agriculture. New staple crops expanded the frontiers of agriculture: irrigated rice in Southeast Asia, rye and barley in northern Europe, and bananas in tropical Africa. Techniques of sugar and cotton production developed in India spread west to the Middle East and east to China.

Surprisingly, Europeans adopted few of the new crops and farming practices that were spreading throughout the Islamic world. In northern Europe, climate prevented cultivation of most warm-weather crops. Yet prevailing habits and food preferences also figured significantly in Europeans' lack of interest in Muslim innovations, as the experience of Spain shows. Rice, citrus fruits, and sugar cane were widely grown in Muslim-ruled Spain, whose rulers also invested heavily in irrigation projects. But in the wake of the Christian reconquest of Spain in the thirteenth and fourteenth centuries (discussed in Chapter 13), the new landowners converted the wheat and cotton fields to pasture for sheep and allowed the irrigated rice fields to revert to swamps.

The Seljuk conquests disrupted the agrarian basis of the Islamic world's economic prosperity. As nomadic warriors, the Seljuks were ill-suited to maintaining the fragile ecology of intensive irrigated farming in these arid regions. Moreover, unlike in the manorial order of western Europe, possession of an iqta estate gave the owner no political or legal powers over the peasants who worked it. Lacking ownership of the land and control over the peasants' labor, estate holders had little incentive to try to improve the efficiency of agriculture. Economic regression was most severe in Mesopotamia and Anatolia. Neglect of irrigation systems and heavy taxation prompted massive peasant flight, leading to depopulation and a retreat from farming to pastoralism.

Rice Economies in Monsoon Asia

Between 700 and 1200, an agricultural revolution also transformed economic life and livelihoods throughout monsoon Asia. Earlier Asian farmers had mainly grown dry land cereals such as wheat and millet. Beginning in the eighth century, however, Asian agriculture shifted to irrigated rice as the main staple food. The high efficiency and yields of irrigated rice agriculture, which can feed six times as many people per acre as wheat, generated substantial surpluses and fostered rapid population growth.

Nowhere was the scale of this agricultural transformation greater than in China. The An Lushan rebellion in the mid-eighth century had devastated the North China Plain, the traditional Chinese heartland (see Chapter 9). Refugees fleeing the war-torn north resettled in the south, especially in the well-watered plains of the Yangzi River Valley. Massive investment of labor and capital in dikes, canals, and irrigation channels made it possible to control the annual Yangzi floods, reclaim land in the Yangzi delta, and practice extensive wet rice cultivation. Man-made canals, along with the abundant natural waterways of southern China, also encouraged mobility and trade. Southern products such as tea, sugar, porcelain, and later cotton led to new industries and new patterns of consumption. The imperial state, which gained renewed strength under the Song dynasty (960–1279), strictly limited the social and legal powers exercised by the landed elite. In contrast to other parts of Eurasia during this era, in China small-property owners drove agricultural expansion and economic growth.

In mainland Southeast Asia, rice cultivation became common probably in the first centuries CE; by the eighth century it had spread to Java (see again Map 11.1). Fish and coconuts (a source of fruit, sugar, oil, and wine) also were important staple foods in tropical agriculture. Dried or fermented fish could be stored for lengthy periods, and coconut trees typically yielded fruit four times a year. Tuber crops such as taro and yams provided alternative sources of subsistence.

The development of irrigated rice agriculture from the eighth century onward laid the economic founda-

≡ **Annual Cycle of Rice Cultivation** Rice agriculture fueled Song China's dramatic economic growth. Irrigated rice fields could feed six times as many people per acre as dry-land crops such as wheat or maize. This twelfth-century painting depicts the annual cycle of rice farming in the Yangzi delta (clockwise from top): sowing, irrigation with pedal-powered water pumps, harvesting, threshing, husking, and storing the husked grain in a granary.

tions for the rise of powerful monarchies, most notably Angkor in Cambodia. In contrast to Chinese traditions, the Khmer kings of Angkor never created a centralized bureaucratic state. Instead, they extended their overlordship by recruiting local landowning elites as allies. The Angkor kings established networks of royal temples supported by ample land endowments. In addition to revenue from landholdings, royal and aristocratic patrons gave temples donations of rice, cattle, goats, coconut palms, fruit trees, betel nuts, and clothing. The temples became storehouses of goods shared with the whole community. Java and Burma had similar patterns of intensive rice cultivation, organized by allocating land and labor rights to temple networks. Hence, in Angkor, Java, and Burma, temples acted as hubs for the collection and distribution of resources and as points of connection between rural communities and the king.

Even without a centralized bureaucracy, the Angkor kings retained control over temples and the land and wealth attached to them. The revenues that flowed to

Angkor financed massive construction projects, including irrigation works and new temple complexes. The power and wealth of Angkor reached its peak during the twelfth century, when Angkor Wat was built. The world's largest religious monument, it was originally covered in gold leaf. Designed to represent the world in miniature, it served both as a shrine dedicated to the Hindu god Vishnu and as a royal mausoleum.

In Japan, too, land reclamation efforts organized by aristocratic and religious estates fostered the spread of rice cultivation. Because most large landowners lived in the capital at Kyoto, actual cultivation of the land was divided among tenant farmers and serf-like laborers working under the direction of a village headman. The estate economy remained highly localized and self-sufficient until the early fourteenth century, when double-cropping (combining, as in China, a winter harvest of wheat or soybeans with the summer rice crop) and other technical improvements raised rural incomes. Peasants began to sell their surplus produce at rural markets. Although traders still conducted most exchange through barter, imported Chinese coins began to appear in local markets as well.

Industrial Growth and the Money Economy

> ↘ **FOCUS** How did the composition and organization of the industrial workforce change in different parts of Eurasia during this period?

Economic growth during these centuries was driven by rising agricultural productivity, population increases, and the expansion of markets, rather than revolutionary changes in industrial organization and technology. A world in which labor was cheap and often unfree offered little incentive for investing in labor-saving technology. Although no "industrial revolution" occurred, important strides in technological progress stimulated expansion of manufacturing and transport. Textiles, metallurgy, and shipbuilding were the leading industries in both technical innovation and scale of output. As the volume of transactions increased, so did the demand for money and credit. Money became the lifeblood of urban society and an increasingly important measure of social status.

Technological Change and Industrial Enterprise

Human and animal power continued to serve as the main sources of energy in both agriculture and industry. However, water- and windmills, first used in Europe in Roman times, proliferated rapidly from the tenth to the thirteenth centuries.

People used mills primarily to grind grain, but they also adapted milling techniques to industrial purposes such as crushing ore, manufacturing woolen cloth, and pressing oil seeds.

The production of iron expanded in Europe during these centuries, though no significant technological breakthrough occurred until blast furnace technology using water-driven bellows emerged in Germany sometime after 1300. In China, innovations such as piston-driven blast furnaces and the use of coke (refined coal) as fuel made vigorous growth in iron and steel output possible. In the eleventh century China produced perhaps as much as 125,000 tons of iron per year, more than twice the entire output of Europe.

Probably the farthest-reaching technological advances during this era came in shipbuilding and navigation. Arab seafarers had conquered the monsoon winds of the Indian Ocean by rigging their ships (known as *dhows*) with lateen sails, which allowed them to sail against the wind. By the thirteenth century, Arabian ships were equipped with stern-post rudders that greatly enhanced their maneuverability. Because of the dhow's relatively flimsy hull, though, its range was limited to the placid waters of the Indian Ocean (see World in the Making, page 392).

By the twelfth century, Chinese merchants were sailing to Korea, Japan, and Southeast Asia in ocean-going ships that featured deep keels, stern-post rudders, nailed planking, and waterproofed bulkheads. The magnetic compass had been known in China since ancient times, but the earliest mention of its use as a navigational aid at sea refers to Arab and Persian vessels in the Indian Ocean in the eleventh century.

Important innovations in seafaring and navigation came somewhat later in Europe. The traditional Mediterranean galley, powered by oars, was designed for war rather than commerce, and had little space for cargo. Beginning in the late thirteenth century, the Venetians developed capacious galleys specifically designed as cargo vessels. In addition, a new kind of sailing ship known as the "cog" was introduced from northern Europe in the early fourteenth century. Equipped with square-sail rigging and stern-post rudders, the cogs could be built on a much larger scale, yet they required only one-fifth the crew needed to man a galley.

Equally important to the expansion of European maritime trade were innovations in navigation. The nautical compass came into use in the Mediterranean around 1270. At about the same time, European navigators began to compile sea charts known as "portolans" that enabled them to plot courses between any two points. The combination of compass, portolans, and the astrolabe—an astronomical instrument introduced to Europe via Muslim Spain—vastly broadened the horizons of European seafarers. Mediterranean mariners began to venture beyond the Straits of Gibraltar into the Atlantic Ocean.

In addition to metallurgy and shipbuilding, textile manufacture—the most important industrial enterprise in every premodern society—was also transformed by technological innovation. Egypt, renowned for its linen and cotton fabrics, continued to produce high-quality cloth that was sold across the Islamic world and in Europe as well. Knowledge of silk manufacture, brought to Iran from China by the seventh century, was later passed on to Syria and Byzantium. Woolen cloth manufacture was the largest industry in Europe. The expansion of textile weaving sparked the rise of industrial towns in Flanders (modern Belgium), while Italian cities such as Milan and Florence specialized in dyeing and finishing cloth.

Innovations such as spinning wheels, treadle-operated looms, and water mills sharply increased productivity at virtually every step of textile manufacturing. The new technologies also encouraged a more distinct division of labor. As textile manufacture shifted from a household or manorial activity to an urban, market-oriented industry, skilled tasks such as weaving and dyeing became the exclusive preserve of male artisans. Women were relegated to the low-skilled and laborious task of spinning yarn.

In the twelfth century the Chinese silk industry underwent momentous changes. Previously, silk production had been almost exclusively a northern industry, carried out in state-run workshops or by rural women working at home. However, in 1127 the Jurchen Jin kingdom in Manchuria seized north China, forcing the Song court to take refuge at a new capital at Hangzhou (hahng-jo) in the Yangzi delta. Subsequently China's silk industry shifted permanently to the Yangzi delta, where the humid climate was more conducive to raising silkworms (see Map 11.2).

Like woolen manufacture in Europe, silk production in China steadily ceased to be a cottage industry and moved into urban industrial workshops. Instead of weaving cloth themselves, peasant households increasingly specialized in producing raw silk and yarn for sale to weaving shops. Although state-run silk factories continued to employ some women, private workshops hired exclusively male weavers and artisans.

Indeed, as the role of the market in the household economy grew, men began to monopolize the more skilled and better-paid occupations throughout Eurasia. In European cities especially, women found their entry barred to occupations that had formerly been open to them. Household surveys conducted in Paris around 1300 show that female taxpayers were represented in more than a hundred trades at all levels of income. Many worked as independent artisans, although nearly three-quarters were employed as servants, in preparing and selling food, and in the

≡ **Chinese Silk Weaving** Growing demand for luxury silks with fancy weaves stimulated technological innovations in the Chinese silk industry. This thirteenth-century scroll painting shows various stages of silk production, including sorting cocoons, extracting the silk filaments (right background), and winding yarn on a silk reeling machine (center foreground). At left a female weaver operates a treadle-powered loom. (Sericulture [*The Process of Making Silk*] early thirteenth century. Attributed to Liang Kai [Chinese, mid-1100s–early 1200s]. Handscroll, ink and color on silk, third section: 27.3 × 93.5 cm [10-11/16 × 36-3/4 in.]; second section: 27.5 × 92.2 cm [10-13/16 × 36-1/4 in.]; first section: 26.5 × 92.2 cm [10-3/8 × 36-1/4 in.]. The Cleveland Museum of Art, John L. Severance Collection 1977.5)

textile and clothing industries. Elsewhere in Europe, merchant and artisan guilds (see page 411) almost always excluded women. By the fifteenth century, independent wage-earning women had virtually disappeared from European cities, even in Paris. The majority of women who earned wages were domestic servants. Married women typically worked at family businesses—as innkeepers, butchers, bakers, and clothiers—serving as helpers to their husbands.

Cultural preconceptions about the physical, emotional, and moral weaknesses of women aroused anxieties about their vulnerability in the public realm. The Muslim philosopher and jurist Ibn Hazm (994–1064) warned that men preyed on women working outside the home: "Women plying a trade or profession, which gives them ready access to people, are popular with lovers [men looking for sexual partners]—the lady broker, the coiffeuses, the professional mourner, the singer, the soothsayer, the school mistress, the errand girl, the spinner, the weaver, and the like."[2] At the same time, the segregation of women in Muslim societies conferred high status on women doctors and midwives, which were considered necessary and honorable professions. Muslim women's control over their dowries enabled them to invest in moneylending, real estate, and other commercial activities.

Expanding Circulation of Money

Before 1000 most parts of Eurasia suffered from acute shortages of money. The use of money in Latin Christendom sharply contracted after the demise of the Roman Empire. With gold scarce, the Frankish kings minted silver coins known as pennies. Kings and princes across Europe also frequently granted coinage privileges to various nobles and clerical authorities, and a great profusion of currencies resulted. Silver pennies were still relatively high in value, though, and their use was largely restricted to the nobility and merchants. The great majority of European peasants paid their lords in goods and services rather than money.

Europeans used silver pennies for tax payments and local commerce, but they conducted international trade using the gold coins issued by the Byzantine emperors. The gold *nomisma* (nom-IHS-mah) coin, the cornerstone of Byzantine monetary and fiscal systems, ruled supreme throughout the Mediterranean world from Justinian's time until the end of the eleventh century. The Byzantine state collected taxes in gold coins, which it spent on official salaries, public works, foreign subsidies, the ecclesiastic establishment, and above all its standing army. Byzantium's prominence as the main trading partner of Italy's mercantile cities established the nomisma as the monetary standard in Italy as well.

The Umayyad caliph Abd al-Malik's currency reforms in the 690s had established the silver *dirham* (DEER-im) as the monetary standard for the Islamic world (see Seeing the Past: Imitation and Innovation in Islamic Coinage). The ease with which merchants circulated throughout the Islamic world is demonstrated by a hoard of 900 dirhams buried in Oman around 840, which included coins issued by fifty-nine different mints from Morocco to Central Asia. But the Islamic world suffered from shortages of gold until, as we will see, the rise of trans-Saharan trade in the ninth century.

The revival of gold coinage in Italy in the mid-thirteenth century, first by Florence and Genoa in 1258 and later by Venice, confirms Italian merchants' growing supremacy over Mediterranean trade. The Venetian gold ducat, introduced in 1284, soon established itself as the new monetary standard of Mediterranean commerce. Although gold coins filled the purses of nobles and great merchants throughout Europe, artisans continued to receive their wages in silver coin, and so-called black money (silver debased with lead and other cheap metals that gave it a black color) was widely used for everyday purchases and almsgiving.

The Chinese Empire developed an entirely different monetary system based on low-value bronze coins rather than precious metals. Shortages of bronze coins had forced the Tang government to collect taxes in grain, bolts of cloth, and labor services, with only a few commercial duties paid in coin. In the early eleventh century the Song dynasty launched an ambitious policy of monetary expansion. By the 1020s, the output of Song mints already far surpassed that of earlier dynasties, and it soared to nearly six billion coins per year (requiring 9,600 tons of copper) in the 1070s. Yet even this level of coinage failed to satisfy the combined needs of the state and the private market. Beginning in the early eleventh century, as we will see, the Song government introduced paper money to expand the money supply and facilitate the movement of money across long distances.

Credit and the Invention of Paper Money

Despite the influx of African gold, shortages of gold and silver coin persisted in the Mediterranean world. These shortages, coupled with the high risk and inconvenience of shipping coin over long distances, encouraged the development of credit and the use of substitutes for metallic currency, including bank money, deposit certificates, and bills of exchange. The growing sophistication of business skills and commercial practices during this period was the product of pragmatic solutions to the problems of long-distance trade.

In Muslim and Christian societies, merchants had to overcome strong religious objections to profiting from commercial enterprise, especially the prohibitions against **usury**, the practice of charging interest on debts. The Qur'an, which took shape within the commercial world of Mecca, devotes much attention to codifying ethical principles for merchants. The Qur'an firmly forbids usury, but later Islamic jurists devised means of permitting buying and selling on credit as well as investments aimed at earning a profit. Christian merchants evaded similar prohibitions against usury by drawing up contracts that disguised interest payments as fees or fines.

The global connections created by long-distance trade required institutional support, mechanisms to facilitate the exchanges of goods and wealth between peoples from distant parts of the world. Thus, every major trading city had money-changers to handle the diverse assortment of coins in use. Rudimentary banks that acted primarily as safe deposits but also transferred funds to distant cities were operating in China and the Islamic world by the ninth century and appeared in Genoa and Venice by the early twelfth century.

Long-distance merchants also benefited from new forms of credit such as the **bill of exchange**. The bill of exchange was a written promise to pay or repay a specified sum of money at a future time, which enabled a merchant to deposit money with a bank in one place and collect payment from the bank's agent in another place. Bills of exchange were used in the Islamic world by the tenth century. In Europe, traders at the Champagne fairs, which, as we will see, began in the twelfth century, conducted most of their business on the basis of credit.

The flood of African gold into the Fatimid capital of Cairo in the tenth and eleventh centuries made that city the first great international financial center. The Arab geographer Al-Muqaddasi, writing in about 985, boasted that Cairo "has superseded Baghdad and is the glory of Islam, and is the marketplace for all

usury The practice of charging interest on loans, forbidden under Christian and Muslim legal codes.

bill of exchange A paper note that allowed the bearer to receive money in one place and repay the debt in another currency at another place at a later date.

SEEING THE PAST

Imitation and Innovation in Islamic Coinage

Since their invention in the sixth century BCE, metallic coins have served a variety of purposes. The first goal of Eurasian rulers who issued the coins was to facilitate trade, but coins were also used to pay taxes, and in many cultures coins played an important role in religious ritual and offerings to the gods. Coins also possessed symbolic significance. The stamp or design on a coin became synonymous with the authority of the ruler or state that minted it. Coins thus became vehicles for expressing sovereign power and political and religious beliefs.

During its rapid expansion in the seventh and eighth centuries CE, the Islamic realm spread over two distinct monetary zones: the Mediterranean region, where Byzantine gold coins prevailed as the international monetary standard, and the former Sasanid Empire in Persia and Mesopotamia, where Sasanid silver coins known as *drachm* dominated. At first Muslim rulers imitated the design, weight, and metallic content of Byzantine and Sasanid coins. Thus the first Muslim coins minted in Persia (known as *dirham*, an Arabic rendering of drachm) continued to display a bust of the Sasanid king on one side and a fire altar, the centerpiece of the Zoroastrian religion, on the other side. In 661 the first Umayyad caliph,

Mu'awiya, issued a new coin that retained the imagery of the Sasanid king's bust and the fire altar, but a Persian inscription identified the ruler as Mu'awiya.

Similarly, the first Umayyad gold coins (dinars) portrayed the caliphs in the style of Byzantine emperors (a), but they removed the cross that Byzantine coins prominently displayed atop the tiered platform (b). Moreover, the legend encircling the image of the caliph defiantly proclaims that "Muhammad is the Prophet of God whom He sent with guidance and the religion of truth that he may make it victorious over every other religion" (Qur'an 9.33).

Provoked by this religious broadside, in 692 the Byzantine emperor Justinian II radically changed the design of Byzantine coins. He replaced the emperor's bust with an image of Jesus Christ and made the Christian cross even more obvious.

In response, the caliph Abd al-Malik introduced a change in 696, one that would establish the style for

(a)   (b)

Islamic coins for centuries to come. Abd al-Malik removed all images, including the depiction of the ruler, and replaced them with quotations from the Qur'an (c, d).

The main face of the coin shown here (c) bears the Islamic declaration of faith (*shahada*): "There is no god but God; there is no partner with him." In addition to other quotations from the Qur'an, such coins often state the name of the caliph or provincial governor who issued them. This change reflected Muslim clerics' growing concern that the images of rulers on coins violated the Muslim prohibition against idolatry.

Later Muslim rulers modified this basic model to reflect their political or doctrinal independence. The Fatimid rulers in Egypt, for example, issued coins with legends testifying to their Shi'a affiliation. Thanks to their control over the trans-Saharan gold trade, the Fatimids and the Almoravid dynasty in Morocco began to issue gold dinars in such great quantities that they displaced the Byzantine coin as the international monetary standard of the Mediterranean. Some Christian rulers in Iberia and Italy issued their own copies of Islamic dinars. The gold coin struck by King Alfonso VIII (r. 1158–1214) of Castile imitated the style of the Almoravid dinar but replaced the shahada with professions of Christian faith (still written in Arabic) and the image of a cross (e, f).

Examining the Evidence

1. Why did Muslim rulers at first retain the images of Byzantine and Sasanid rulers on their own coins?

2. How did Muslim and Christian rulers differ in expressing their religious commitments and values through the images on their coins?

mankind."[3] Cairo was home to the Jewish merchant Allan bin Hassun, whose story opened this chapter, and Muslim, Jewish, and Christian merchants in Cairo did business with each other, frequently cooperating in business deals, money transfers, and information sharing. The Cairo Exchange acted as a clearinghouse for moneychanging and the settlement of debts for merchants from Morocco to Persia. The guiding principle of trade was to keep one's capital constantly at work. "Do not let idle with you one dirham of our partnership, but buy whatever God puts into your mind and send it on with the very first ship sailing," wrote a Spanish merchant in Lebanon to his partner in Cairo.[4]

In China, too, merchants used letters of credit to transfer funds to distant regions. In 1024 the Song government replaced private bills with its own official ones, creating the world's first paper money. By the thirteenth century paper money had become the basic currency of China's fiscal administration, and it was widely used in private trade as well. At the same time merchants carried great quantities of Chinese bronze coin overseas to Japan, where by 1300 nearly all Japanese paid their rent and taxes and conducted business using imported Chinese coin.

The flow of money across borders and oceans testified to the widening circulation of goods. Few villagers would ever see a gold coin. Yet the demand for luxury goods and industrial raw materials drew many peasants—however unknowingly—into networks of long-distance trade.

Merchants and Trade Networks in Afro-Eurasia

↘ **FOCUS** How did the commercial revival of 900 to 1300 reorient international trade routes across Afro-Eurasia?

During the period 900 to 1300, major trading centers across Eurasia and Africa came to be linked in a series of regional and international networks of exchange and production. Much of this trade consisted of luxury goods such as spices, silk, and gold intended for a select few—rulers, nobles, and urban elites. Yet bulk products such as grain, timber, and metal ores also became important commodities in maritime trade, and processed goods such as textiles, wine, vegetable oils, sugar, and paper became staple articles of consumption among the urban middle classes. Although the movement of goods would seem sluggish and sporadic to modern eyes, the volume of trade and its size relative to other forms of wealth grew enormously. Genoa's maritime trade in 1293 was three times greater than the entire revenue of the kingdom of France.

Merchant Partnerships and Long-Distance Trade

The expansion of trade required new forms of association and partnership and reliable techniques for communication, payment, credit, and accounting. Notable advances in all of these spheres of trade and finance were made during the "commercial revolution" of the twelfth and thirteenth centuries.

But not all innovations in commercial institutions promoted open access to trade. The **guild** system that took root in European towns during this period reflected the corporate character of urban government and merchant society. Guilds were granted extensive authority to regulate crafts and commerce, restrict entry to a trade, and dictate a wide array of regulations ranging from product specifications to the number of apprentices a master might employ. In the aim of guaranteeing a "just" price and goods of uniform quality, the European guild system also stifled competition and technical innovation. In China and the Islamic world, by contrast, guilds were formed chiefly to supply goods and services to the government, and they had no authority to regulate and control trade. Muslim rulers appointed market inspectors to supervise commerce and craftsmen. These officials upheld Islamic law, adjudicated disputes, and collected taxes and fees.

Merchants who engaged in international trade usually operated as individuals, carrying with them their entire stock of goods and capital, although they often traveled in caravans and convoys for protection against bandits and pirates. As in the case of the Jewish trader Allan bin Hassun, a family firm might dispatch its members to foreign markets, sometimes permanently, to serve as agents. But as the volume of trade grew, more sophisticated forms of merchant organization emerged.

Islamic legal treatises devoted much attention to commercial partnerships. Muslim law permitted limited investment partnerships in which one partner supplied most of the capital, the other traveled to distant markets and conducted their business, and the two shared the profits equally. Italian merchants later imitated this type of partnership in what became known as the *commenda* (coh-MEHN-dah). Chinese merchants likewise created joint trading ventures in the form of limited partnerships for both domestic and international trade.

The commenda partnerships were the forerunners of permanent **joint stock companies,** which were first founded in Italian cities in the thirteenth century. These companies, in which investors pooled their capital for trading ventures, engaged in finance as well as trade and often maintained their own fleets and branch offices in foreign cities. The merchant banks of Florence and other cities of northern Italy gradually became involved in fund transfers, bills of exchange, and moneychanging.

In the late twelfth century, merchants based in Egypt created a commercial association known as the *karimi* (KUH-ree-mee) to organize convoys for trading

guild An association of merchants or artisans organized according to the kind of work they performed.

joint stock company A business whose capital is held in transferable shares of stocks by its joint owners.

expeditions in the Indian Ocean. Cairo's karimi merchants became a powerful **cartel**—a commercial association whose members join forces to fix prices or limit competition—that squeezed small entrepreneurs out of the lucrative spice trade. The karimi merchants cooperated closely with the sultans of Egypt, especially under the Mamluk dynasty (1250–1517), generating substantial tax revenue for the state in exchange for their trade privileges.

Merchants and Rulers

The sumptuous wealth and rising social stature of merchant groups such as the Italian bankers and Cairo's karimi inevitably altered relationships between government and commerce. Rulers who had formerly depended almost exclusively on revenue from the land increasingly sought to capture the scarcely imaginable profits of the money economy. In places as far removed as England and Japan, landowners and governments began to demand payments in money rather than agricultural products or labor services. In Europe the expanding availability of credit was an irresistible temptation to monarchs whose ambitions outgrew their resources. Italian bankers became the chief lenders to the papacy and to the kings and princes of Latin Christendom.

The Italians took the lead in putting private capital to work in service to the state. Merchant communities became closely allied with political leaders in the Italian city-states, most notably in Venice. In the late twelfth century the Venetian government imposed a system of compulsory loans that required contributions from every citizen. Public debt proved to be more efficient than taxation for raising revenue quickly to cope with war and other emergencies. Investment in state debt provided the men, fleets, and arms that enabled Venice to become the great maritime power of the Mediterranean.

As mercantile interests came to dominate the Venetian state, the government took charge of the republic's overseas trade. The state directed commercial expeditions, dictated which merchants could participate, built the vessels at its publicly funded shipyard, and regulated the prices of exports as well as crucial imports such as grain and salt.

Economic regulation was a powerful unifying force elsewhere in Europe as well. For example, the merchant communities of the trading cities along the Baltic seacoast formed an alliance known as the Hanseatic League. The league acted as a cartel to preserve its members' monopoly on the export of furs, grain, metals, and timber from the Baltic region to western Europe.

In most of the Islamic world, merchants—regardless of their religious affiliations—enjoyed high status and close ties to the political authorities. The Fatimid government in Egypt largely entrusted its fiscal affairs to Coptic Christian officials, and Jewish merchant houses achieved prominence as personal bankers

cartel A commercial association whose members join forces to fix prices or limit competition.

to Muslim rulers in Baghdad and Cairo. Private trade and banking were largely free of government interference during the Fatimid dynasty. But state intervention in commerce intensified under the Mamluk sultans, who came to power in Egypt after a palace coup in 1250.

The karimi-controlled spice trade was an especially important source of income for the Mamluk state. Karimi merchants—most of whom were Jewish—also managed the fiscal administration of the Mamluk regime, helping collect provincial revenues, pay military stipends, and administer state-run workshops and trade bureaus. Like European monarchs, the Mamluk sultans became heavily dependent on loans from private bankers to finance wars. Also like their European counterparts, Mamluk sultans were always on the lookout for new sources of revenue. In the fifteenth century the Mamluk government took over many commercial enterprises, most notably the trade in spices and enslaved persons as well as sugar refining, and operated them as state monopolies.

In China, the fiscal administration of the imperial state penetrated deeply into the commercial world. The revenues of the Song Empire far exceeded those of any other contemporary government. The state generated more than half of its cash revenue by imposing monopolies on the production of rice wine and key mineral resources such as salt, copper, and alum. Yet in the most dynamic commercial sectors—iron mining and metallurgy, silk textiles, and the emerging industries of south China such as tea, porcelain, paper, and sugar—private enterprise was the rule. The Song government mainly intervened in private commerce to prevent private cartels from interfering with the free flow of goods.

The Song thus effectively stifled the formation of strong merchant organizations such as the European guilds. Foreign trade was strictly regulated, and the export of strategic goods such as iron, bronze coin, and books was prohibited. Still, Chinese officials recognized the value of international trade as a source of revenue and of vital supplies such as warhorses, and they actively promoted both official trade with foreign governments and private overseas trading ventures.

Merchants in China did not enjoy the social prestige accorded to their Italian or Muslim counterparts. Confucianism viewed the pursuit of profit with contempt and relegated merchants to the margins of respectable society. Yet Confucian moralists applauded prudent management of the household economy and the accumulation of wealth to provide for the welfare of one's descendants. As a minor twelfth-century official named Yuan Cai

The Hanseatic League
● Principal Hanseatic League member
▲ Hanseatic trading partner

≡ **The Hanseatic League**

(you-ahn tsai) wrote in his *Family Instructions*, "Even if the profession of scholar is beyond your reach, you still can support your family through recourse to the arts and skills of medicine, Buddhist or Daoist ministry, husbandry, or commerce without bringing shame upon your ancestors."[5] Like his Byzantine counterpart Kekaumenos, Yuan Cai counseled his peers to be frugal in spending, to invest wisely in land, moneylending, and business ventures, and to never become dependent on the goodwill and honesty of those with whom one does business.

Despite their wealth, merchants led a precarious existence. Long-distance trade offered opportunities to make great profits, but the risks of failure were equally great. To lessen these risks, merchants built communities, negotiated alliances with ruling authorities, and developed reliable methods of communication. Although some rulers coveted the profits of trade for themselves, and others treated merchants as pariahs, traders and rulers usually reached an accommodation that benefited both.

Maritime Traders in the Indian Ocean

The seventh century, when the Tang dynasty in China was at its height (see Chapter 9), marked the heyday of trade and travel along the Silk Road across Central Asia. As we have seen, however, overland commerce between India and China collapsed after the outbreak of the An Lushan rebellion in 755. By the time the Song dynasty was founded in 960, China's principal trade routes had shifted away from Central Asia to the maritime world (see Map 11.2).

Muslim merchants, both Arab and Persian, dominated Indian Ocean trade in the ninth century thanks to their superior shipbuilding and organizational skills. Travel across the Indian Ocean was governed by monsoon winds, which blew steadily from east to west in winter and from west to east in summer, making it impossible to complete a round trip between China and India in a single year. Initially, Muslim seafarers from Persian Gulf ports sailed all the way to China, taking two or three years to complete a round-trip voyage. By the tenth century, merchants more commonly divided the journey to China into shorter segments. By stopping at ports along the Strait of Melaka (Malacca), between Sumatra and the Malay peninsula, Muslim merchants could return to their home ports within a single year. The Srivijaya (sree-vih-JUH-yuh) merchant princes of Sumatra grew wealthy from their share of profits in this upsurge in trade between India and China.

In the eleventh century, however, new maritime powers arose to contest the dominance of Srivijaya and the Muslim merchants in Asian international commerce. The most assertive new entrant into the Indian Ocean trade was the Chola (chohz-ah) kingdom (907–1279), at the southeastern tip of the Indian peninsula. At first Chola nurtured cordial diplomatic and commercial relations with Srivijaya. Yet in 1025

Chola suddenly turned against Srivijaya, and its repeated attacks on Sumatran ports over the next fifty years fatally weakened the Srivijaya princes. But Chola's aggressiveness made many enemies, including the Sinhala kings of Sri Lanka, who stymied its attempt to succeed Srivijaya as the region's supreme maritime power.

Chola's foreign trade was controlled by powerful Tamil merchant guilds that mobilized convoys and founded trading settlements overseas. Tamil merchants carried cargoes of Indian pepper and cotton cloth and Sumatran ivory, camphor, and sandalwood to the southern Chinese ports of Guangzhou and Quanzhou (chwehn-joe).

Silk textiles had long been China's principal export commodity. After the tenth century, however, the growth of domestic silk industries in India and Iran dampened demand for Chinese imports. Although Chinese luxury fabrics such as brocades and satins still were highly prized, porcelain displaced silk as China's leading export. Maritime trade also transferred knowledge of sugar refining and cotton manufacture from India to China, leading to major new industries there.

During the twelfth century Chinese merchants began to mount their own overseas expeditions. Chinese commercial interests increasingly turned toward the Indonesian archipelago in search of fine spices such as clove and nutmeg and other exotic tropical products. Chinese merchants also imported substantial quantities of gold, timber, and sulfur (used in gunpowder and medicines) from Japan in exchange for silk, porcelain, and bronze coin.

The advent of Muslim traders in Indian Ocean trade had stimulated commerce along the east coast of Africa as well. The Swahili peoples of the coasts of Tanzania and Kenya were descended from Bantu settlers who arrived in the region in around 500 CE. Beginning in the ninth century, Swahili merchants transformed the island towns of Shanga and Manda into major trading ports that functioned as regional crossroads, exporting ivory, hides, and quartz and other gems to the Islamic heartland in return for cotton, pottery, glass, and jewelry. When Swahili merchants ventured southward in search of ivory, they discovered an abundance of gold as well.

The reorientation of East African trade networks toward the export of gold had far-reaching political and economic repercussions. In the twelfth century Mapungubwe (Ma-POON-goo-bway), the first identifiable state in southern Africa, arose in the middle Limpopo River Valley, at the junction of the trade routes bringing ivory and copper from the south and gold from the north. The monsoon winds allowed Arab merchants to sail as far south as Kilwa, which eclipsed the older towns of Shanga and Manda as the preeminent trading center along the East African coast (see again Map 11.2). South of Kilwa trade goods were relayed by local merchants from the interior and the Swahili colonies along the coast.

≡ **MAP 11.2 International Commerce in Afro-Eurasia, c. 1150** By 1150 Song China had the world's most dynamic economy thanks to the dramatic growth of its silk, porcelain, iron, and shipbuilding industries. Muslim merchants pioneered trade routes across the Sahara Desert and along the eastern coast of Africa in pursuit of gold, ivory, copper, and other precious goods.

International Commerce in Afro-Eurasia, c. 1150

Trade goods

- Bronze coins
- Camphor
- Cloves
- Copper
- Cotton cloth
- Gems
- Glass
- Gold
- Hides
- Horses
- Ivory
- Nutmeg
- Pepper
- Porcelain
- Refined sugar
- Salt
- Sandalwood
- Silk
- Sulfur
- Swords
- Timber

Trade routes

- Muslim
- Silk Road
- Chinese
- Other

African rain forest

≡ **Kilwa** Kilwa grew rich and powerful thanks to its dominance over the trade in African gold and ivory. The large quantities of Chinese pearls, porcelains, and coins unearthed at Kilwa attest to its prominence in Indian Ocean trade as well. In this German engraving from 1572, the city's domed mosques stand out among a dense cluster of multistory buildings made from stone and coral.

The mid-thirteenth century brought the rise of another powerful state, Great Zimbabwe, that would exert direct control over the main gold-fields and copper mines in the interior. The capital of Great Zimbabwe consisted of a large complex of stone towers and enclosures housing a warrior elite and perhaps as many as 18,000 inhabitants. Many similar but smaller stone enclosures (known as *zimbabwe*), built to shelter livestock as well as protect their inhabitants, sprang up near the gold mines. The abandonment of Mapungubwe at around the same time can probably be attributed to the diversion of commercial wealth to Great Zimbabwe.

Great Zimbabwe's dominance over the export trade could not be sustained indefinitely, however. In the fourteenth century the copper and ivory trade routes shifted to the Zambezi River Valley to the north. The empire fashioned by the rulers of Great Zimbabwe disintegrated in the early fifteenth century, and the capital city was abandoned by the 1450s. The great volume of Chinese coins and porcelain shards that archaeologists have found at Great Zimbabwe and sites along the coast documents East Africa's extensive trade across the Indian Ocean.

Trans-Saharan Traders

The vast Sahara Desert separated most of the African continent from the Mediterranean world, but the thirst for gold breached this seemingly impenetrable barrier in the wake of the Muslim conquest of North Africa. The conversion of the Berbers to Islam and their incorporation into the far-flung Muslim trading world during the seventh century provided the catalyst for the rapid escalation of trans-Saharan trade. Reports of the fabulous gold treasure of al-Sudan ("country of the Blacks"), the Sahel belt of savanna grasslands spanning the southern rim of the Sahara from the Atlantic to the Indian Ocean, lured Berber and Arab merchants across the desert.

Well before the rise of the trans-Saharan trade, growing interaction and exchange among the Sahel societies had begun to generate social differentiation and stratification. The majority of the population, the farmers and herders, remained free people not assigned a caste. In villages, however, communities began to specialize in manufacturing activities such as ironworking, pottery, leather making, and cotton weaving.

By 400 CE clusters of specialized manufacturing villages in the inland delta of the Niger River coalesced into towns trading in iron wares, pottery, copper, salt, and leather goods as well as foodstuffs and livestock. Towns such as Jenne-jeno preserved the independent character of its various artisan communities. But in other Sahelian societies, powerful warrior elites dominated. Originating as clan leaders, these warrior chiefs appropriated ideas of caste status to define themselves as an exclusive and hereditary nobility.

The earliest Muslim accounts of West Africa, dating from around 800, report that a great king—whose title, Ghana, came to be applied to both the ruler's capital and his state—monopolized the gold trade. Ghana's exact location remains uncertain, but its ruler, according to Muslim merchants, was "the wealthiest king on the face of the earth because of his treasures and stocks of gold."[6] The Muslim geographer al-Bakri described the capital of Ghana as consisting of two sizable towns, one in which the king and his court resided and a separate Muslim town that contained many clerics and scholars as well as merchants. Although the king was a pagan, al-Bakri deemed him to have led a "praiseworthy life on account of his love of justice and friendship for Muslims."[7]

At first the impact of Islam on the indigenous peoples was muted. Berber caravans halted at the desert's edge because camels had little tolerance for the humidity and diseases of the savanna belt. Confined to segregated enclaves within the towns, Muslim merchants depended on the favor of local chiefs or the monarchs of Ghana. Yet local rulers found the lucrative profits of trade in gold and enslaved persons irresistible, and the wealth and literacy of Muslim merchants made them valuable allies and advisers. Trade also yielded access to coveted goods such as salt, glass, horses, and swords (see again Map 11.2). The kings of Ghana and other trading cities converted to Islam by the early twelfth century and to varying degrees required their subjects to embrace the new religion as well.

During the twelfth century Ghana's monopoly on the gold trade eroded, and its political power crumbled as well. In the thirteenth century a chieftain by the name of Sunjata (r. 1230–1255) forged alliances among his fellow Malinke to create a new empire known as Mali. Whereas Ghana probably exercised a loose sovereignty within the savanna region, Mali enforced its dominion over a much larger territory by assembling a large cavalry army equipped with horses and iron weapons purchased from Muslim traders. The gold collected as tribute by the Mali kings made them fabulously wealthy.

Sunjata's successors also combined African traditions of divine kingship with patronage of the Islamic faith. The Mali monarch Mansa Musa (MAHN-suh

LIVES AND LIVELIHOODS

The Mande Blacksmiths

In West Africa, ironworking was far more than a useful technology for manufacturing tools and weapons. It also became a fearsome instrument of symbolic power, especially among the Mande peoples inhabiting the Sahelian savanna between the Senegal and Niger River Valleys. Mande society was divided into three principal groups: free persons (including both commoners and the warrior nobility); specialized professional castes (*nyamakala*) such as blacksmiths, leatherworkers, and storytelling bards; and enslaved persons. This three-tiered structure had taken shape at least by the time of the Mali Empire in the thirteenth and fourteenth centuries. But the unique status of blacksmiths in Mande society clearly had more ancient origins.

The nyamakala possessed closely guarded knowledge of technical arts, and this knowledge was tinged with supernatural power. It gave them special abilities that set them apart from the rest of society. The nyamakala were considered alien peoples who married only with their own kind. The right to practice their craft was a hereditary monopoly.

An aura of mystery surrounded the blacksmiths in particular, whose work involved transforming rock into metal through the sublime power of fire. Ordinary people regarded them with a mixture of dread and awe. Similarly, the women of blacksmith clans had the exclusive right to make pottery. Like iron metallurgy, pottery making required mastery of the elemental force of fire.

Armed with secret knowledge and "magical" powers, blacksmiths occupied a central place in the religious life of the community. The right to perform circumcision, a solemn and dangerous ritual of passage to adulthood, was entrusted to blacksmiths. Blacksmiths also manufactured ritual objects, such as the headdresses used in religious ceremonies. They were believed to have healing powers, too. Together with leatherworkers, they made amulets (charms) for protection against demonic attack.

The social distance that separated blacksmiths from the rest of Mande society enhanced their reputation for fairness. Blacksmiths commonly acted as mediators in disputes and marriage transactions. Mande peoples often swore oaths upon a blacksmith's anvil. Most important, only they could hold leadership positions in *komo* associations, initiation societies composed mostly of young men and charged with protecting the community against human and supernatural enemies.

The caste status of blacksmith clans affirmed their extraordinary powers, but it simultaneously relegated them to the margins of society. In Mande origin myths, blacksmiths appear as a powerful force to be tamed and domesticated. The Mande epics trace the founding of the Mali Empire to an intrepid warrior hero, the hunter Sunjata (see page 419), who is said to have overthrown the brutal "blacksmith king" Sumanguru (Soo-mahn-guh-roo) in the mid-thirteenth century. In the new social order of the Mali Empire, the dangerous powers of the blacksmiths were contained by marginalizing them as an occupational caste that was excluded from warfare and rulership and forbidden to marry outside their group. Despite their crucial importance to economic and religious life, the caste identity of the blacksmiths branded them as inferior to freeborn persons in Mande society.

Questions to Consider

1. Why did Mande society regard blacksmiths as exceptional?

2. In what ways was the caste system of West African peoples such as the Mande different from the caste system in India discussed in Chapter 5?

3. Why did the rulers of Mali perceive the Mande blacksmiths as a threat?

For Further Information:

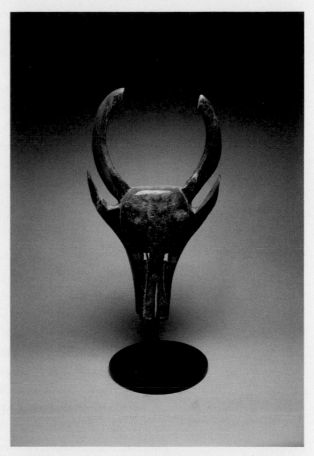

≡ **Komo Mask** Among the Mande peoples of West Africa, komo associations governed many aspects of community life, such as the secret rites of passage that inducted young males into adulthood. Blacksmiths, who worked with wood as well as metal, carved the animal masks used in komo religious rituals.

McIntosh, Roderick. *The Peoples of the Middle Niger: The Island of Gold.* Oxford: Blackwell, 1998.

McNaughton, Patrick R. *The Mande Blacksmiths: Knowledge, Power, and Art in West Africa.* Bloomington: Indiana University Press, 1988.

MOO-suh) (r. 1312–1337) caused a great sensation when he visited Cairo on his pilgrimage to Mecca in 1325. According to a contemporary observer, "Musa flooded Cairo with his benefactions, leaving no court emir nor holder of a royal office without a gift of a load of gold. . . . They exchanged gold until they depressed its value in Egypt and caused its price to fall."[8] Mansa Musa's visit provided evidence of both the power and wealth of Mali and the increasing cultural connections between West Africa and the rest of the Muslim world.

Trade and industry flourished under Mali's umbrella of security. Muslim merchants formed family firms with networks of agents known as *Juula* (meaning "trader" in Malinke), widely distributed among the oasis towns and trading posts of the Sahara. Like other town-dwelling craftsmen and specialists, such as the blacksmiths and leatherworkers, the Juula became a distinct occupational caste and ethnic group whose members lived in separate residential quarters and married among themselves (see Lives and Livelihoods: The Mande Blacksmiths).

Mediterranean and European Traders

The contraction of commerce that followed the fall of the western Roman Empire persisted longer in Europe than did the economic downturn in Asia and the Islamic world. By the twelfth century, however, the rising productivity of agriculture and population growth in western Europe had greatly widened the horizons for trade. Lords encouraged the founding of towns by granting **burghers**—free citizens of towns—certain legal liberties as well as economic privileges such as tax exemptions, fixed rents, and trading rights. In England and Flanders a thriving woolen industry developed. Merchant guilds in both England and Flanders grew so powerful that they chose their own city councils and exercised considerable political independence. In northern Europe, repeating a dynamic we have seen in other parts of the world, commercial expansion altered the political landscape (see Map 11.3).

The prosperity of the woolen industry made Flanders the wealthiest and most densely urbanized region in twelfth-century northern Europe, yet the Flemish towns were dwarfed by the great cities of Italy. Although social tensions often flared between the landed aristocracy and wealthy town dwellers, the political fortunes of the Italian city-states remained firmly wedded to their mercantile interests. By the twelfth century Italian navies and merchant fleets dominated the Mediterranean, with Genoa paramount in the west and Venice the major power in the east.

burgher In Latin Christendom, a free citizen residing in a town who enjoyed certain legal privileges, including the right to participate in town governance.

Europe, c. 1300

Urban population, c. 1300

- Over 80,000
- 40,000–80,000
- 10,000–40,000
- Under 10,000
- Area of high urban development

The Hanseatic League

Danzig   Major member

Riga   Minor member

≡ **MAP 11.3   Europe, c. 1300**   Europe in 1300 boasted three cores of urban development: the mercantile city-states of northern Italy, the wool-manufacturing towns of Flanders, and the former Muslim city-states of southern Spain, which still flourished as centers of trade and industry. Many independent cities in northern Europe banded together to form the Hanseatic League, a trade cartel that monopolized the export of furs, grain, metals, and timber from the Baltic region.

≡ **Fair of Lendit** Dating from the twelfth century, the Lendit fair, held under the auspices of the abbey of St. Denis near Paris for two weeks each June, drew both pilgrims and traders, especially those dealing in cloth, horses, and livestock. In this mid-fifteenth-century illustration, the abbot (center) gives the benediction to mark the opening of the fair. This depiction of the fairgrounds shows (clockwise from upper right) a makeshift tavern, bales of goods, a herder with pigs, moneylenders exchanging sacks of coins, and two women selling merchandise in stalls.

Economic revival in northern and western Europe breathed new life into the long-defunct Roman commercial network. In the twelfth century the counts of Champagne, southeast of Paris, offered their protection and relief from tolls to the growing number of merchants who traveled between the textile manufacturing towns of Flanders and Italy's commercial centers. They established an annual cycle of six two-month fairs that rotated among the towns. Champagne's location midway between Flanders and Italy enhanced its stature as the major crossroads of international commerce and finance in western Europe. Merchants adopted the coins and weights used at the fairs as international standards.

Champagne's heyday as a medieval version of a free-trade zone came to an end in the early fourteenth century. Political tensions between Champagne's counts and the French monarchy frequently interrupted the smooth flow of trade. The Champagne fairs were also victims of their own success: the innovations in business practices spawned by the Champagne fairs, such as transfers of goods and money via agents and bills of exchange, made actual attendance at the fairs unnecessary.

COUNTERPOINT: Jewish Moneylenders in Latin Christendom

> ↘ **FOCUS** How and why did the place of Jews in the society and economy of Latin Christendom differ from their status in Islamic lands?

Jews occupied an anomalous place in Latin Christendom. Officially tolerated by the church and kings, nonetheless, they were forbidden to engage in most crafts and professions. Many Jews earned their living as moneylenders. As we have seen, law codes forbade Christians from charging interest on loans (deemed odious usury) to fellow Christians, but Jews were not subject to this constraint. From the late twelfth century rising anti-Semitism incited violence against Jews, although the destruction or expulsion of Jewish communities followed different paths, as the examples of England and Aragon (in northeastern Spain) show.

England

There is no evidence of Jewish communities in England in Anglo-Saxon times. Jewish merchants probably first arrived in the wake of the Norman conquest of 1066, having been granted rights to mint coins by the new Norman kings. In England, as throughout Latin Christendom, Jews existed outside Christian

≡ **Champagne Trade Fairs**

society and the institutions of lordship and service that governed it. Instead, Jews depended on royal protection, and legally they and their possessions "belonged" to the king. Thus, the English Crown imposed special taxes on Jews, and upon the death of a Jewish householder, the king claimed all his property, including the debts owed to him. It is not true, as commonly supposed, that Jews were barred by law from owning land. However, the law did prohibit Jews from retaining Christian domestics, serfs, or enslaved people. Deprived of the labor necessary to work the land—and excluded from most trades—Jews turned to moneylending.

After 1150 moneylending became virtually an exclusively Jewish enterprise in England, and the most successful, like Aaron of Norwich, became immensely rich. When Aaron died in 1186, his estate—mostly unpaid loans—was valued at 75,000 pounds, at a time when the Crown's annual revenue rarely exceeded 10,000. Most of these debts were owed by prominent nobles, knights, and monasteries. King Henry II's (r. 1154–1189) efforts to collect these debts on his own behalf triggered violent reprisals against Jews, including the massacre of Jewish communities at York and elsewhere in 1190.

To extract more revenues from Jewish moneylenders, Henry's successors instituted registries of all Jews and their property. Because of special taxes levied on Jews, by 1256 the Jewish community had paid over half of its total wealth in royal taxes; the richest, Aaron of York, surrendered his entire fortune and was declared a pauper. This expropriation of Jewish wealth coincided with increasingly menacing anti-Semitic propaganda. Sensational accounts of Jews committing ritual murders of Christian children fanned racial hatred. In a notorious case in London in 1255, false accusations resulted in the execution of nineteen Jews and fueled lurid rumors accusing Jews of diabolical malice against Christians. A series of royal decrees imposed onerous social and religious restrictions, including enforcement of the requirement to wear a visible badge on one's clothing. The Statute on Jewry issued by Edward I in 1275 outlawed usury, denying Jews their main livelihood. In 1290 Edward bowed to the insistent demands of the church and nobility and expelled all Jews from England. At the same time Edward extracted from the barons and churchmen the prodigious sum of 115,000 pounds, or twice his average annual revenue, as compensation for the economic loss of "his Jews."

Aragon

In contrast to England, Iberia had large, long-standing Jewish communities—perhaps 60,000 persons in Aragon alone in the thirteenth century, compared to fewer than 5,000 in England. Jews had enjoyed far greater freedoms and social status under Muslim rule in Iberia than they did in Christian lands, and Jewish statesmen and scholars were fixtures at the court of the Umayyad caliphs. Beginning in the late eleventh century, however, the Christian kingdoms of Castile and Aragon captured large swaths of the former Umayyad caliphate, and by 1248 nearly all of Iberia was under Christian rule (see Chapter 13). Initially the Christian monarchs allowed Muslims and Jews to live as free subjects in self-governing communities (*aljamas*) with considerable religious and legal autonomy. Jews remained free to pursue a wide range of professions. Only a fraction of the Jewish population were moneylenders, but the financial services they provided were integral to Iberia's flourishing prosperity, most notably in Aragon.

By 1300, after conquering Valencia and other Muslim territories as well as the Balearic Islands, Sardinia, and Sicily, Aragon emerged as the dominant power in the western Mediterranean (see again Map 11.3). Despite their contributions to Aragon's booming economy, Jews were excluded from the lucrative maritime trade of the Mediterranean ports and instead gravitated toward moneylending. As in England, nobles and churchmen borrowed heavily from Jewish moneylenders, who in turn were principal sources of royal revenue. As in England, too, Jews and their property were "royal treasure," and the Aragon monarchs upheld the moneylenders' rights to collect debts and foreclose on the estates of insolvent Christians. Indebtedness bred resentment against Jews, compounded by the anti-Semitic propaganda in wide circulation throughout Latin Christendom. *Feudal Customs of Aragon*, a compendium of local laws composed around 1300, repeatedly invokes the "avarice and cupidity" of Jews to justify restrictions on their commercial activities. Absent from this work, however, are the demeaning facial and bodily caricatures of Jews propagated in the art of northern Europe at this time.

The Black Death pandemic that swept across Aragon in 1348 (see Chapter 14) had devastating effects on its economy and the mostly peaceful relations among its Christian, Muslim, and Jewish populations. In the aftermath of the pandemic, toxic mixtures of resentment against royal taxation, indebtedness, and religious prejudice boiled over into sectarian violence. The riots of 1391, when rituals of grievance against Jews routinely performed during Holy Week preceding Easter exploded into wholesale massacres of Jewish communities across Christian Iberia, marked the final rupture of *convivencia*—peaceful coexistence out of convenience, not tolerance.

≡ **Notary Recording Loan** This miniature from *Feudal Customs of Aragon* accompanies a regulation requiring that loans across interfaith lines must be recorded by someone of the creditor's religion. Jewish moneylenders (at right) accept a chalice from a Christian monk (in red) as collateral in exchange for a sack of coins, while a Jewish notary records the transaction. Judaism, Christianity, and Islam all forbade lending at interest among the faithful, hence the frequent recourse to "heathen" creditors. Getty Museum; ms. Ludwig XIV 6 [83.MQ.165], fol. 114.

Conclusion

Beginning in the tenth century, agricultural growth and commercial integration generated a sustained economic expansion across much of Eurasia and Africa. A warmer global climate and the introduction of new crops increased agricultural productivity in both the ancient centers of civilization of the Mediterranean, India, and China and the newly developing areas such as northern and eastern Europe and mainland Southeast Asia. Larger and more stable food supplies nourished population growth in cities and the countryside alike.

The farthest-reaching transformations in economic life and livelihood were the expansion of trade networks and the growing sophistication of commercial practices. Cairo, Venice, Quanzhou, and other leading commercial cities served as the crossroads for enterprising merchants such as Allan bin Hassun; their trade ventures linked the Mediterranean and the Middle East to sub-Saharan Africa, the Indian Ocean, and China. At the same time, the dynamic market economy threatened to subvert the existing social order. The persecution of Jewish moneylenders in Latin Christendom reflected not only religious prejudice but also fears of the power of money. In addition, commercial cities harbored new centers of education and intellectual inquiry, and these too posed challenges to established political and cultural authority, as we will see in the next chapter.

review

The major global development in this chapter: The sustained economic expansion that spread across Afro-Eurasia from 900 to 1300.

Important Events	
850–1267	Chola kingdom in southern India
960–1279	Song dynasty in China
969	Fatimids conquer Egypt
1024	The Song dynasty issues the first paper money in world history
1055	Seljuk Turks capture Baghdad
c. 1120–1150	Construction of Angkor Wat begins
1127	The Jurchen conquer north China; the Song dynasty retains control of southern China
c. 1150–1300	Heyday of the Champagne fairs
c. 1200–1400	Formation of first chiefdoms in the Hawaiian Islands
1230–1255	Reign of Sunjata, founder of the Mali Empire in West Africa
1250–1517	Mamluk dynasty in Egypt

Important Events	
1258	The Italian city-states of Florence and Genoa mint the first gold coins issued in Latin Christendom
1323–1325	Pilgrimage to Mecca of Musa Mansa, ruler of Mali
c. 1400–1450	Great Zimbabwe in southern Africa reaches peak of prosperity

KEY TERMS

bill of exchange (p. 407)   guild (p. 411)   serf (p. 397)

burgher (p. 422)   *iqta* (p. 399)   usury (p. 407)

cartel (p. 412)   joint stock company (p. 411)

CHAPTER OVERVIEW QUESTIONS

1. How did agricultural changes contribute to commercial and industrial growth?
2. What technological breakthroughs increased productivity most significantly?
3. What social institutions and economic innovations did merchants devise to overcome the risks and dangers of long-distance trade?
4. In what ways did the profits of commerce translate into social and economic power?
5. Above all, who benefited most from these economic changes?

MAKING CONNECTIONS

1. In what ways did the spread of new crops and farming technologies during this period have a different impact in the Islamic world and in Asia?
2. How had the principal east-west trade routes between Asia and the Mediterranean world changed since the time of the Han and Roman Empires (see Chapters 5 and 6)?
3. To what extent did the Christian, Jewish, and Muslim merchant communities of the Mediterranean adopt similar forms of commercial organization and business practices during the "commercial revolution" of 900 to 1300? How can we explain the differences and similarities among these groups?

DOING HISTORY

Developments and Processes

A world history perspective enables us to recognize common patterns in long-term developments in different societies, and at the same time it compels us to investigate what processes contributed to these common developments. A striking feature of global historical trends during the period 900 to 1300 was the simultaneous emergence of similar forms of economic development in far-flung areas across Eurasia. These concurrent patterns can partly be explained by the global process of climate change, that is, the earth's warming trend that set in during these centuries. More specifically to this period, greater mobility of people and cross-cultural interaction, especially among merchants, contributed to wider circulation of knowledge.

1. In what ways did the spread of technology—from tools and crops to manufacturing techniques and business practices—lead to economic convergence?

2. Did the political and social trends in Europe, the Islamic world, and Asia that we examined in early chapters favor or hinder economic growth?

3. Did social mobility and the status of the merchant class exhibit similar trends in the different parts of Eurasia during this period?

For further research into the topics covered in this chapter, see the Bibliography at the end of the book.

12

Centers of Learning and the Transmission of Culture

900–1300

≡ **World in the Making** Schools in Latin Christendom organized the learning of ancient Greece and Rome into the seven liberal arts. The trivium (Latin for "three roads") of logic, rhetoric, and grammar endowed the student with eloquence; the quadrivium ("four roads") of arithmetic, geometry, astronomy, and music led to knowledge. This detail from a mural composed between 1365 and 1367 for a Franciscan chapel in Florence depicts the trivium (at right in first row) and the quadrivium (at left) in the persons of the ancient scholars credited with their invention; behind each scholar sits his muse, represented in female form.

backstory

As we saw in Chapters 8 and 9, from 500 to 1000 religious traditions consolidated in the main centers of civilization across Eurasia. Christianity prevailed in many parts of the former Roman Empire, but divisions deepened between the Greek church, which was closely allied with the Byzantine Empire, and the Latin church of Rome. Islam was fully established as the official religion across a vast territory extending from Spain to Persia. In India, the classical Brahminic religion, recast in the form of Hinduism, steadily displaced Buddhism from the center of religious and intellectual life. In contrast, the Mahayana tradition of Buddhism enjoyed great popularity at all levels of society in East Asia. In China, however, Buddhist beliefs clashed with the long-cherished secular ideals of Confucian philosophy. In all of these regions, the study of sacred writings dominated schooling and learning.

IN HER MASTERFUL NOVEL OF court life in Heian Japan, *The Tale of Genji*, Murasaki Shikibu (c. 973–1025) sought to defend the art of fiction and women as readers of fiction. Murasaki's hero, Genji, finds his adopted daughter copying a courtly romance novel and mocks women's passionate enthusiasm for such frivolous writings. Genji protests that "there is hardly a word of truth in all of these books, as you know perfectly well, but here you are utterly fascinated by such fables, taking them quite seriously and avidly copying every word." At the end of his speech, though, Genji reverses his original judgment. Romance novels, he concludes, may be fabricated, but they have the virtue of describing "this world exactly as it is."[1]

Many of Murasaki's contemporaries shared Genji's initial low opinion of the content of courtly romances, but they also rejected such works at least in part because they were written in vernacular Japanese—the language of everyday speech. In Lady Murasaki's day, classical Chinese was the language of politics and religion at the Heian court. Writing in the Japanese vernacular was considered at best a trifling skill, acceptable for letters and diaries but ill-suited to the creation of literature or art.

Like many women of the aristocratic class, Murasaki was also fond of romance tales, which typically revolved around the lives, loves, and marriages of court women. Widowed in her twenties, Murasaki had already acquired some fame as a writer when she was summoned around 1006 to serve as lady-in-waiting to the empress. During her years at the court Murasaki completed her *Tale of Genji*. Manuscript copies circulated widely among court women in Murasaki's lifetime and captivated a sizable male readership as well. From Murasaki's time forward, fiction and poetry written in the Japanese vernacular gained distinction as serious works of literature.

Yet Chinese remained the language of officials, scholars, and priests. The role of Chinese as the language of public discourse and political and religious authority throughout East Asia paralleled that of Latin in western Europe, of Arabic in the Islamic world, and of Sanskrit in South and Southeast Asia. By the twelfth century these cosmopolitan languages—languages that transcended national boundaries—became deeply embedded in new educational institutions, and as a result their intellectual and aesthetic prestige grew. Although writing in vernacular languages gained new prominence as well, the goal was not to address a wider, nonelite audience. Authors writing in the vernacular, like Murasaki, still wrote for elite, learned readers.

The turn toward the vernacular was undoubtedly related to the ebbing authority of vast multicultural empires and the rise of regional and national states. But the emergence of vernacular literary languages did not simply reflect existing regional and national identities; they were instrumental in inventing these identities. Thus, both cosmopolitan and vernacular languages helped create new cultural connections, the former by facilitating the development of international cultural communities, and the latter by broadcasting the idea that nations were defined, in part, by the shared culture of their inhabitants.

OVERVIEW QUESTIONS

The major global development in this chapter: The expansion of learning and education across Eurasia from 900 to 1300 and its relationship to the rise of regional and national identities.

As you read, consider:

1. Did the spread of higher learning reinforce or undermine established political and religious authority?

2. How did educational institutions reshape social hierarchy and elite culture?

3. What were the different uses of cosmopolitan languages (which transcended national boundaries) and vernacular (everyday) languages, and to what degree did they broaden access to written knowledge?

4. How did the different technologies of writing affect the impact of the written word?

Church and Universities in Latin Christendom

↘ **FOCUS** What political, social, and religious forces led to the founding of the first European universities?

Between the tenth and the fourteenth centuries, Latin Christendom witnessed the emergence of a unified learned culture. The values and self-images of clergy and knights increasingly converged. For knights, chivalric virtue and dedication to defense of the Christian faith replaced the wanton lifestyle of the Germanic warriors. At the same time, the clergy became more militant in their promotion of orthodoxy, as reform-minded religious orders devoted themselves to spreading the faith and stamping out heresy.

Schooling created a common elite culture and a single educated class. The career of Peter Abelard (1079–1142) captures this transformation. Abelard's father, a French knight, engaged a tutor to educate young Peter in his future duties as a warrior and lord. Abelard later recalled, "I was so carried away by my love of learning that

I renounced the glory of a soldier's life, made over my inheritance and rights of the elder son to my brothers, and withdrew from the court of Mars [war] in order to kneel at the feet of Minerva [learning]."[2] Abelard's intellectual daring ultimately provoked charges of heresy that led to his banishment and the burning of his books. In the wake of the Abelard controversy, kings and clerics wrestled for control of schools. Out of this contest emerged a new institution of higher learning, the university.

Monastic Learning and Culture

From the time of Charlemagne (r. 768–814), royal courts and Christian monasteries became closely allied. Monasteries grew into huge, wealthy institutions whose leaders came from society's upper ranks. Kings and local nobles safeguarded monasteries and supervised their activities.

Devoted to the propagation of right religion and seeking educated men to staff their governments, Charlemagne and his successors promoted a revival of classical learning consistent with the established doctrines of Latin Christianity. Although Charlemagne never realized his hope that schooling would be widely available, local bishops began to found **cathedral schools**—schools attached to a cathedral and subject to a bishop's authority—as a complement to monastic education.

Elementary schools trained students to speak and read Latin. Advanced education in both monasteries and cathedral schools centered on the "liberal arts," particularly the Roman *trivium* (TREE-vee-um) (Latin for "three roads") of grammar, rhetoric, and logic. Roman educators had championed **rhetoric**—the art of persuasion through writing or speech—and especially oratorical skill as crucial to a career in government service. Monastic teachers likewise stressed the importance of rhetoric and oratory for monks and priests. Unlike the Romans, however, the clergy deemphasized logic; they sought to establish the primacy of revelation over philosophical reasoning. Similarly, the clergy separated the exact sciences of the Greeks—the *quadrivium* (kwo-DRIV-ee-uhm) (Latin for "four roads") of arithmetic, geometry, music, and astronomy—from the core curriculum of the trivium and treated these fields as specialized subjects for advanced study.

Bishops appointed "master scholars" to take charge of teaching at the cathedral schools. The masters in effect had a monopoly on teaching within their cities. The privileged status of these masters and their greater receptivity to logic and the quadrivium caused friction between cathedral schools and monasteries. The Cistercians, a new religious order that spread like wildfire across Europe within fifty years of its founding in 1098 (see Chapter 13), abhorred the growing importance of reasoning and logic in the cathedral schools, instead emphasizing religious education based on memorization, contemplation, and spiritual faith. Thus, the expansion of learning created both new connections and new divisions in Europe's intellectual and cultural elite.

cathedral school In Latin Christendom, a school attached to a cathedral and subject to the authority of a bishop.

rhetoric The art of persuasion through writing or speech.

≡ **Deluxe Illustrated Manuscript** Monastic communities in Latin Christendom created many beautifully illustrated copies of the gospels, the accounts of the life of Christ. The first page of this Gospel of Matthew, produced at a German monastery around 1120 to 1140, shows Saint Matthew writing with a quill pen and sharpening knife. On the next page the first line of the gospel begins with a large letter L (the beginning of the word liber, "book"), set against a background resembling the luxurious Byzantine silks highly prized in Europe.

The Rise of Universities

During the eleventh and twelfth centuries, demand for advanced education rose steadily. Eager young students traveled to distant cities to study with renowned masters. Unable to accommodate all of these students by themselves, masters began to hire staffs of specialized teachers who taught medicine, law, and theology in addition to the liberal arts. Certain schools acquired international reputations for excellence in particular specialties: Montpellier and Salerno in medicine, Bologna in law, Paris and Oxford in theology. These schools also applied higher learning to secular purposes. Montpellier and Salerno incorporated Greek and Arabic works into the study of medicine (see Lives and Livelihoods: Medical Professionals of Latin Christendom).

Christian conquests of Muslim territories in Spain and Sicily in the eleventh century (discussed in Chapter 13) reintroduced Greek learning to Latin Christendom via translations from Arabic. In 1085, King Alfonso VI (r. 1072–1109) of Castile captured Toledo, a city renowned as a center of learning where Muslims, Jews, and

Medical Professionals of Latin Christendom

Economic revival and urban growth in Europe after 1000 spurred major changes in the practice and study of medicine. The rising urban commercial and professional classes increasingly demanded academically trained physicians. The cathedral schools, and later the universities, added medicine as an advanced subject of study. The institutionalization of medicine as an academic discipline transformed learned doctors into a professional class that tightly regulated its membership, practices, and standards.

Around 1173, the Jewish traveler Benjamin of Tudela described Salerno, in southern Italy, as the home of "the principal medical university of Christendom." By *university* Benjamin meant an organized group of scholars, not a formal educational institution. Many of Salerno's skilled doctors hailed from the city's large Jewish and Greek communities and were familiar with Arabic and Byzantine medical traditions. Beginning in the eleventh century, Salerno's doctors produced many medical writings that profoundly influenced medical knowledge and training across Latin Christendom.

Among the notable scholars at Salerno was Constantine the African, a Muslim who arrived from North Africa, possibly as a drug merchant, around 1070. Constantine converted to Christianity and entered the famed Montecassino monastery north of Salerno. His translations of Arabic, Hebrew, and Greek works on medicine became the basis of medical instruction in European universities for centuries afterward.

Salerno's doctors also contributed important writings on gynecology and obstetrics. A local female healer named Trota became a famed authority on gynecology ("women's medicine"). A Salerno manuscript dubiously attributed to Trota justified singling out women's illnesses as a separate branch of medicine:

> Because women are of a weaker nature than men, so more than men they are afflicted, especially in childbirth. It is for this reason also that more frequently diseases abound in them than in men, especially around the organs assigned to the work of nature.[1]

The author attributed women's infirmity to their physical constitution and the trauma of childbirth

≡ **Trota Expounds on the Nature of Women** The *Trotula*, a set of three treatises on gynecology and women's health, was probably composed in Salerno in the twelfth century. All three works were attributed to Trota, although only one is likely to have come from her hand. In this illustration from a fourteenth-century French encyclopedia on natural science, Trota sits before a large open book and instructs a clerk in "the secrets of nature."

but also noted that women were less likely to seek treatment from male doctors. Local authorities, however, typically prohibited women other than midwives from treating patients.

Despite its outpouring of medical treatises, Salerno had no formal institution for medical training until the thirteenth century. By that time the universities of Bologna and Paris had surpassed Salerno as centers of medical learning. Bologna, for example, revived the study of anatomy and surgery and introduced human dissection as part of the curriculum. At the universities, students studied medicine only after completing rigorous training in the liberal arts.

The growing professionalization of medicine nurtured a new self-image of the doctor. Guy de Chauliac, a surgeon trained at Paris in the fourteenth century, wrote,

I say that the doctor should be well mannered, bold in many ways, fearful of dangers, that he should abhor the false cures or practices. He should be affable to the sick, kindhearted to his colleagues, wise in his prognostications. He should be chaste, sober, compassionate, and merciful: he should not be covetous, grasping in money matters, and then he will receive a salary commensurate with his labors, the financial ability of his patients, the success of the treatment, and his own dignity.[2]

The emphasis on high ethical standards was crucial to the effort to elevate medicine's stature as an honorable occupation given the popular image of doctors and pharmacists as charlatans who, in the English poet Chaucer's mocking words, "each made money from the other's guile."[3]

This professional class of doctors steeped in rigorous study and guided by Christian compassion largely served the upper classes, however. Care of the poor and the rural populace was left to uneducated barber-surgeons, bone-setters, and faith healers.

1. Monica H. Green, ed., *The Trotula: An English Translation of the Medieval Compendium of Women's Medicine* (Philadelphia: University of Pennsylvania Press, 2002), 65.

2. Guy de Chauliac, "Inventarium sive chirurgia magna," quoted in Vern L. Bullough, *The Development of Medicine as a Profession: The Contribution of the Medieval University to Modern Medicine* (New York: Hafner, 1966), 93–94.

3. Geoffrey Chaucer, "Prologue," *The Canterbury Tales* (Harmondsworth: Penguin, 1951), 30.

Questions to Consider

1. What kind of education and personal characteristics were deemed necessary to become a professional physician?

2. Why did the public hold doctors in low repute? How did university education aim to improve that image?

For Further Information:

Bullough, Vern L. *The Development of Medicine as a Profession: The Contribution of the Medieval University to Modern Medicine.* New York: Hafner, 1966.

Siraisi, Nancy. *Medieval and Early Renaissance Medicine: An Introduction to Knowledge and Practice.* Chicago: University of Chicago Press, 1990.

Christians freely intermingled, and made it his capital. In the twelfth century Toledo's Arabic-speaking Jewish and Christian scholars translated into Latin the works of Aristotle and other ancient Greek writers as well as philosophical, scientific, and medical writings by Muslim authors. Access to this vast body of knowledge had a profound impact on European intellectual circles. The commentaries on Aristotle by the Muslim philosopher Ibn Rushd (IB-uhn RUSHED) (1126–1198), known in Latin as Averröes (uh-VERR-oh-eez), sought to reconcile the paradoxes between faith and reason. They attracted keen interest from Christian theologians grappling with similar questions.

Ibn Rushd's insistence that faith is incomplete without rational understanding, for which he was persecuted and exiled, added new fuel to the intellectual controversies that flared up in Paris in the 1120s. Peter Abelard, who based his study of theology on the principle that "nothing can be believed unless it is first understood," attracted thousands of students to his lectures. Abelard's commitment to demonstrating the central tenets of Christian doctrine by applying reason and logical proof aroused heated controversy. Church authorities in 1140 found Abelard guilty of heresy and exiled him from Paris. He died a broken man two years later.

The dispute over the primacy of reason or faith continued after Abelard's death. Paris's numerous masters organized themselves into guilds to defend their independence from the local bishop and from hostile religious orders such as the Cistercians, who had led the campaign against Abelard. The popes at Rome, eager to extend the reach of their own authority, placed Paris's schools of theology under their own supervision. In 1215 Pope Innocent III (1198–1216) formally recognized Paris's schools of higher learning as a **university**—a single corporation including masters and students from all the city's schools—under the direction of the pope's representative. Universities at Oxford and Bologna soon gained similar legal status.

In the end, though, chartering universities as independent corporations insulated them from clerical control. European monarchs, eager to enlist educated men in government service, became ardent patrons of established schools and provided endowments to create new ones. Consequently, during the thirteenth century more than thirty universities sprang up in western Europe (see Map 12.1).

Among all the university towns, Paris emerged as the intellectual capital of Latin Christendom in the thirteenth century. Despite a papal ban on teaching Aristotle's works on natural science, the city swarmed with prominent teachers espousing Aristotle's ideas and methods. Thomas Aquinas (c. 1225–1274), a theologian at the University of Paris, incorporated Abelard's methods of logical argument into his great synthesis of Christian teachings, *Summa Theologica*. It stirred turbulent controversy, and much of it was banned until shortly before Aquinas's canonization as a saint in 1323. Academic freedom in the universities, to the extent

university In Latin Christendom, a single corporate body that included teachers and students from a range of different academic disciplines.

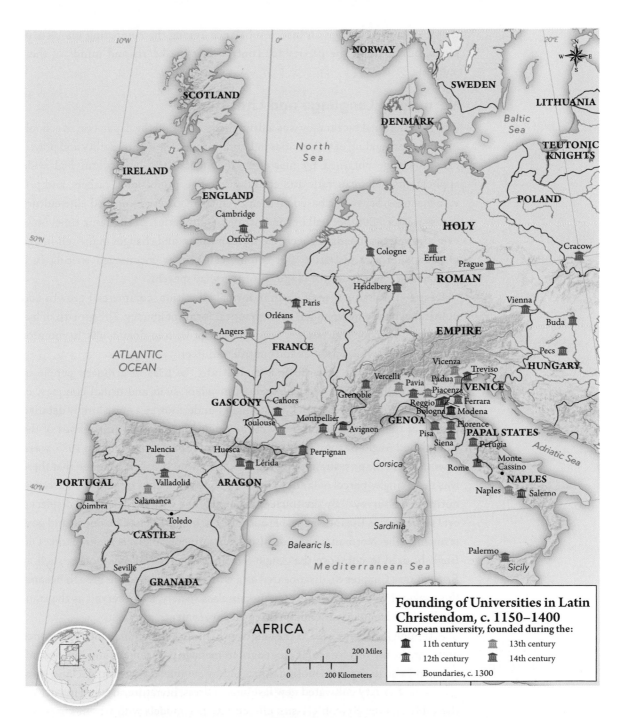

≡ **MAP 12.1   Founding of Universities in Latin Christendom, c. 1150–1400** By the twelfth century universities eclipsed monasteries and cathedral schools as the most prestigious centers of learning in Latin Christendom. They attracted students from many lands and thus helped forge a common elite culture across most of Europe.

that it existed, rested on an insecure balance among the competing interests of kings, bishops, and the papacy for control over the hearts and minds of their students.

Vernacular Language and Literature

The growing need for literacy was a driving force behind the expansion of schooling and the founding of universities in Latin Europe. The mental agility and practical knowledge obtained by mastering the liberal arts curriculum had wide applications in bureaucratic and ecclesiastic office, professional careers, and private business. Schooling based on literacy in Latin fostered a unified elite culture across western Europe, well beyond national boundaries. At the same time, however, the practical needs of government and business and changes in the self-image of the rising administrative and commercial classes encouraged writing in a **vernacular language**—the language of everyday speech.

Despite the dominance of Latin in formal education, commercial growth and political expansion demanded more practical forms of literacy. The growth of bureaucracy developed in tandem with the use of written documents to monitor social and economic activities and control resources.

Government most powerfully intruded into the lives of ordinary people in England. Following the French Norman invaders' swift and brutal conquest of England in 1066, the Norman king William I undertook an astonishingly detailed census of the wealth and property of the English population. In the eyes of the vanquished Anglo-Saxons, the resulting *Domesday Book*, completed in 1087, was a monument to the unrestrained greed of William, who "was not ashamed that there was not a single [parcel of land] . . . not even one ox, or cow, or pig which escaped notice in his survey."[3] By the thirteenth century the written record had displaced oral testimony as the indispensable authority in matters of law, business, and government. The Norman conquest also transformed language in England. Old English, used to compose the Anglo-Saxon law codes and epic poetry such as *Beowulf* (see Chapter 8), disappeared as a written language, while French became the spoken tongue of the court and upper-class society. Latin served as the standard written language of schools and royal government.

Although Latin prevailed as the language of liturgy and scholarship, acceptance grew for the use of vernacular languages to manage government and business affairs, and also to express emotion. Enriched by commercial wealth and land revenues, court society cultivated new fashions in dress, literature, art, and music. Yet the Bible and the Roman classics offered few role models with whom kings and princes, let alone knights and merchants, could identify. Poets and troubadours

vernacular language
The language of everyday speech, in contrast to a language that is mainly literary.

instead used vernacular speech to sing of heroes and heroines who mirrored the ideals and aspirations of their audiences. Tales of King Arthur and his circle, celebrated most memorably in the romances penned (in French) by Chrétien de Troyes in the late twelfth century, mingled themes of religious fidelity and romantic love. Legends of the exploits of the Greek conqueror Alexander the Great, embellished by chivalric ideals, Christian piety, and long-standing fables about "the wonders of the East," also circulated widely in vernacular editions in French, German, and English (see Seeing the Past: Alexander the Great [Iskandar] in Christian and Islamic Legends).

Royal and noble patrons who eagerly devoured vernacular romances also began to demand translations of religious and classical texts. In the early fourteenth century, Dante Alighieri (DAHN-tay ah-lee-JIHR-ee) (1265–1321), composed his *Divine Comedy*, perhaps the greatest vernacular poem of this era, in the dialect of his native Florence. Dante's tale entwined scholastic theology and courtly love poetry to plumb the mysteries of the Christian faith in vivid and captivating language. The influence of Dante was so great that modern Italian is essentially descended from the language of the *Divine Comedy*. Thus, even as the rise of universities promoted a common intellectual culture across Latin Christendom, the growth of vernacular languages led to the creation of distinctive national literary traditions.

Students and Scholars in Islamic Societies

↘ **FOCUS** To what extent did Sunni and Sufi schools foster a common cultural and religious identity among Muslims?

In contrast to Latin Christendom, in the Islamic world neither the caliphs nor dissenting movements such as Shi'ism sought to establish a clergy with sacred powers and formal religious authority. Instead, the task of teaching the faithful about matters of religion fell to the ***ulama*** (oo-leh-MAH), learned persons whose wisdom and holiness earned them the respect of their peers. Ulama could be found in all walks of life. Some earned their living from official duties as judges, tax collectors, and caretakers of mosques. But many ulama were merchants and shopkeepers; the profession of religious teacher was by no means incompatible with pursuit of personal gain. The ulama codified what became the Sunni orthodoxy by setting down formal interpretations of scriptural and legal doctrine, founding colleges, and monopolizing the judgeships that regulated both public and private conduct.

ulama Scholars learned in Islamic scripture and law codes who act as arbiters of Islamic teachings.

SEEING THE PAST

Alexander the Great (Iskandar) in Christian and Islamic Legends

Not surprisingly, the Romans celebrated their fellow empire builder Alexander the Great as a paragon of kingship. Legends about Alexander proliferated in Roman times and remained popular for many centuries after. Thus Geoffrey Chaucer wrote in *The Canterbury Tales*:

> The story of Alexander is so common
> That every wight [person] that hath discretion
> Hath heard somewhat or all of his fortune[1]

In Latin Christendom, Alexander's exploits became a staple feature of vernacular romance literature, alongside the legends of King Arthur and other past heroes. Alexander exemplified the chivalric virtues of "prowess and largesse"—being true to one's cause and generous to one's followers—that were hallmarks of the self-image of Europe's warrior nobility. In contrast to the Persian tyrant Darius, reviled for oppressing his nobles with demands for taxes and services, Alexander is depicted as dividing his empire into fiefs that he distributes to his devoted knights. Another prominent theme in European romances is Alexander's adventures in the exotic lands of Asia, where he vanquishes monstrous peoples and fantastic beasts (a). Such tales spawned lurid depictions of Asia as savage and barbaric.

Legends of Alexander—Iskandar in Arabic—are equally prominent in Islamic traditions, beginning with the Qur'an itself, in which Iskandar is raised up by God to punish the wicked and reward the faithful. The Qur'an also relates that God sent Iskandar to build a wall to seal up the savage tribes of Gog and Magog, who according to both Muslim and Christian prophecy will bring devastation upon the world on the Day of Judgment (b). But Islamic versions of the Alexander/Iskandar legends make no mention of the monstrous peoples of Asia, lands that Muslims themselves inhabited. After their conversion to Islam, the Mongol Ilkhan rulers (see Chapter 13) found in Alexander/Iskandar fitting precedent for their conquest of Iran, legitimated by their submission to the true faith.

Both Christians and Muslim writers portrayed Alexander's conquests as simultaneously quests for knowledge—spurious legend claimed that he was a student of Aristotle—while underscoring the limits of human wisdom. In Islamic accounts this message is voiced by the Jewish and Indian sages he encounters, who warn him that mortals are forbidden to know the secrets of God.

1. Larry D. Benson, ed., *The Riverside Chaucer* (Boston: Houghton Mifflin, 1987), 250 (spelling modernized).

(a)

(b)

Alexander Explores Under the Sea Ordained by God (according to both Christian and Islamic accounts) "lord and master of all the earth," Alexander/Iskandar ventured to the farthest corners of the world in his pursuit of knowledge. Alexander's journey under the sea in a glass diving bell during his travels in Asia appears in both Christian and Islamic legends. *Roman d'Alexandre* (c. 1290s); Staatliche Museen zu Berlin, Kupferstichkabinett, Ms. 78 C 1

Iskandar Builds the Wall to Seal Out Gog and Magog This illustration, taken from a manuscript of Firdausi's *Book of Kings* commissioned by the Mongol Ilkhan rulers of Iran, shows Iskandar directing the artisans of the world to build a wall to hold at bay the savage Gog and Magog (seen in upper-left corner). *Great Mongol Shahnana* (c. 1330s); Smithsonian Freer Gallery and Sackler Gallery of Art, S1986.104 (Detail)

Examining the Evidence

1. How do the creatures Alexander finds under the sea in (a) reinforce the idea of Asia as an alien world?

2. In what ways might the image in (b) of Iskandar as a paragon of kingship appeal to the Mongol rulers of Iran? How does the scene visualize the differences between civilized society and, as represented by Gog and Magog, barbarism?

The Rise of Madrasas

During the Umayyad and Abbasid caliphates, scriptural commentators sought to apply Muhammad's teachings to social life as well as religious conduct. Scholars compiled anthologies of the sayings and deeds of Muhammad, known as **hadith** (hah-DEETH), as guidelines for leading a proper Muslim life. The need to reconcile Islamic ethical principles with existing social customs and institutions resulted in the formation of a comprehensive body of Islamic law, known as *shari'a* (sha-REE-ah). Yet the formal pronouncements of hadith and shari'a did not resolve all matters of behavior and belief.

During the eighth and ninth centuries four major schools of legal interpretation emerged in different parts of the Islamic world to provide authoritative judgments on civil and religious affairs. Yet, as in Latin Christendom, the tension between reason and revelation—between those who emphasized rational understanding of the divine and the free will of the individual and those who insisted on the incomprehensible nature of God and utter surrender to divine will—continued to stir heated debate. The more orthodox schools of law—Hanafi, Maliki, and Shafi'i— were receptive to the rationalist orientation, but the Hanbali tradition firmly rejected any authority other than the revealed truths of the Qur'an and the hadith.

These schools of law became institutionalized through the founding of **madrasas** (MAH-dras-uh), formal colleges for legal and theological studies. Commonly located in mosques, madrasas received financial support from leading public figures or the surrounding community. Higher education was not confined to the madrasas, however. The world's oldest university, in the sense of an institution of higher education combining individual faculties for different subjects, is Al-Qarawiyyin, founded at Fez in Morocco in 859 by the daughter of a wealthy merchant. In 975, the Fatimid dynasty established Al-Azhar University, attached to the main mosque in their new capital at Cairo, as a Shi'a theological seminary. Al-Azhar grew into a large institution with faculties in theology, law, grammar, astronomy, philosophy, and logic. In the twelfth century Al-Azhar was reorganized as a center of Sunni learning, which it remains today.

Islamic education revolved around the master-disciple relationship. A madrasa was organized as a study circle consisting of a single master and his disciples. Several assistants might instruct students in subjects such as Qur'an recitation and Arabic grammar, but Islamic schools had no fixed curriculum like the trivium and quadrivium of Latin Europe. Knowledge of hadith and shari'a law and insight into their application to social life were the foundations of higher education. Because learning the hadith was a pious act expected of all Muslims, schools and study circles were open to all believers, whether or not they were formally recognized as

hadith Records of the sayings and deeds of the Prophet Muhammad.

shari'a The whole body of Islamic law— drawn from the Qur'an, the hadith, and traditions of legal interpretation—that governs social as well as religious life.

madrasa A school for education in Islamic religion and traditions of legal interpretation.

students. Although madrasas rarely admitted women as formal students, women often attended lectures and study groups.

Under the Seljuk sultans (1055–1258), who strictly enforced Sunni orthodoxy and persecuted Shi'a dissidents, the madrasas also became tools of political propaganda. The Seljuks lavishly patronized madrasas in Baghdad and other major cities (see Map 12.2). The Hanafi school became closely allied with the sultanate and largely dominated the judiciary. The Hanbalis, in contrast, rejected Seljuk patronage and refused to accept government positions. The Hanbalis' estrangement from the Seljuk government made them popular among the inhabitants of Baghdad who chafed under Seljuk rule. Charismatic Hanbali preachers frequently mustered common people's support for their partisan causes and led vigilante attacks on

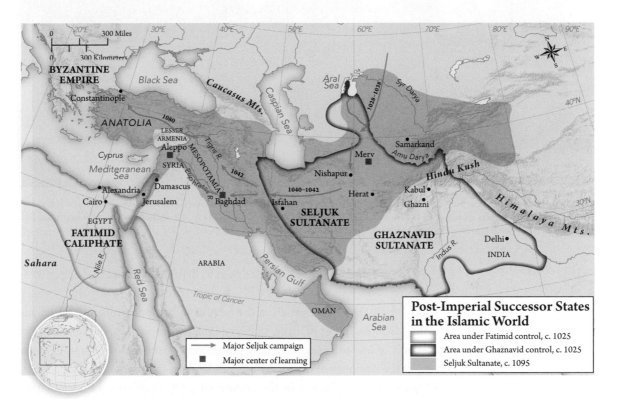

≡ **MAP 12.2   Post-Imperial Successor States in the Islamic World**   By 1000 the Islamic world had fragmented into many regional states, and upstart regimes such as the Shi'a Fatimids in North Africa vied with the Sunni Abbasid caliphs based in Baghdad for supremacy. Nomadic Turkish warriors such as the Seljuks became fierce champions of Islam in Central Asia. After the Seljuk conquest of Baghdad in 1055, the Abbasids ceded political authority to the Seljuk sultans, who strictly upheld Sunni teachings.

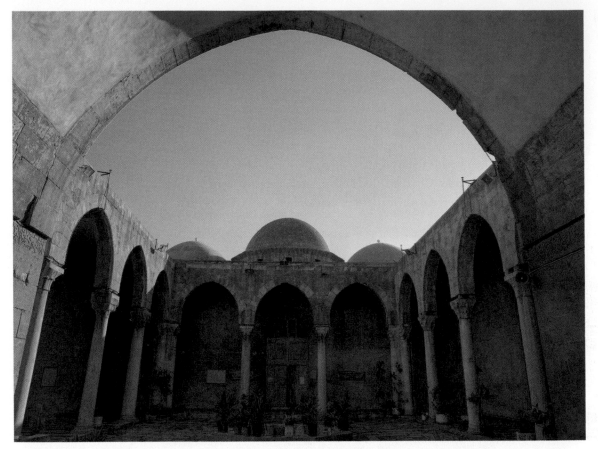

Firdaws Madrasa Far from being cloistered enclaves of students and scholars like Christian universities, madrasas served as the centers of religious life for the whole community. Aleppo in Syria reportedly had forty-seven madrasas, the grandest of which was the Firdaws madrasa, built in 1235.

Shi'a "heretics" and immoral activities such as drinking alcohol and engaging in prostitution.

Turkish military regimes such as the Seljuks in Mesopotamia and Syria, and later the Mamluks in Egypt, came to depend on the cooperation of the ulama and the schools of law to carry out many government tasks and to maintain social order. Yet the authority of the ulama was validated by their reputation for holiness and their personal standing in the community, not by bureaucratic or clerical office. The common people often turned to the neighborhood ulama for counsel, protection, and settlement of disputes, rather than seeking recourse in the official law courts.

The proliferation of madrasas between the tenth and thirteenth centuries promoted the unification of Sunni theology and law and blurred the boundaries between church and state. The Islamic madrasas, like the universities of Latin Christendom, helped to forge a common religious identity. But to a much greater degree than the Christian universities, the madrasas merged with the surrounding urban society and drew ordinary believers, including women, into their religious and educational activities.

Sufi Mysticism and Sunni Orthodoxy

In addition to the orthodox schools of law and the tradition of revelation expressed in hadith, an alternative tradition was **Sufism** (SOO-fiz-uhm)—a mystical form of Islam that emphasizes personal experience of the divine over obedience to scriptures and Islamic law. Sufis cultivated spiritual and psychological awareness through meditation, recitation, asceticism, and personal piety. Over the course of the ninth century Sufi masters elaborated comprehensive programs of spiritual progress that began with intensely emotional expressions of love of God and proceeded toward a final extinction of the self and mystical union with the divine.

Originating as a quest for personal enlightenment, Sufism evolved into a broad social movement. Sufis, like the madrasas, reached out to the common faithful. In their public preaching and missionary work, Sufis addressed everyday ethical questions and advocated a life of practical morality and simplicity. The Sufi ethic of personal responsibility, tolerance and sympathy toward human failings, and moderation in enjoyment of worldly pleasures had broad appeal among all social classes.

Revered as holy persons with a special relationship to God, Sufi masters acquired an aura of sainthood. Tombs of renowned Sufi masters became important pilgrimage sites that drew throngs of believers from near and far, helping forge a sense of community among like-minded devotees. Women played a more prominent role in Sufism than in other Islamic traditions. One of the earliest Sufi teachers Rabi'a al-'Adawiyya (717–801) attracted many disciples, chiefly men, with her fierce asceticism and her insistence that God should be loved for God's own sake, not out of fear of punishment or desire for reward. In the words of her biographer, Rabi'a was "on fire with love and longing, enamored of the desire to approach her Lord," and men accepted her "as a second spotless Mary."[4]

By the eleventh century the Sufi masters' residences, known as *khanaqa* (CON-kah), had developed into lodges where religious teachers lived, taught their disciples, and provided accommodations for traveling Sufis. In the early thirteenth century Sufis began to form brotherhoods that integrated groups of followers into far-flung religious orders. Bonds of Sufi brotherhood cut across national borders and parochial loyalties, restoring a measure of unity sorely lacking in the Islamic world since the Abbasid caliphate's decline.

Sufism A mystical form of Islam that emphasizes personal experience of the divine over obedience to the dictates of scripture and Islamic law.

Ongoing tensions between reason and faith sharply divided the intellectual world of Islam. This dilemma was epitomized by the personal spiritual struggle of Abu Hamid al-Ghazali (AH-boo hah-MEED al-gahz-AHL-ee) (1058–1111), the greatest intellectual figure in Islam after Muhammad himself. Al-Ghazali was appointed to a senior professorship at Baghdad's leading madrasa in 1091, at the young age of thirty-three. Although he garnered great acclaim for his lectures on Islamic law and theology, al-Ghazali was beset by self-doubt and deep spiritual crisis. In 1095, al-Ghazali found himself "continuously tossed about between the attractions of worldly desires and the impulses toward eternal life" until "God caused my tongue to dry up and I was prevented from lecturing."[5] He then resigned his position and spent ten years as a wandering scholar exploring the mystical approach of Sufism.

In the end, al-Ghazali's immersion in Sufism restored his faith in Islamic beliefs and traditions. In the last years of his life, al-Ghazali returned to the academy and wrote a series of major philosophical treatises that reaffirmed the primacy of revelation over rational philosophy in matters of faith and morals. According to al-Ghazali, a proper Muslim life must be devoted to the purification of the soul and the direct experience of God that lay at the core of the Sufi quest. But he also insisted that the personal religious awakening of individuals must not violate the established principles of Islam set down in the Qur'an and the hadith. Al-Ghazali's ideas provided a synthesis of Sunni and Sufi teachings that would come to dominate Islamic intellectual circles.

Oral and Written Cultures in Islam

As the teaching methods of the madrasas reveal, oral instruction took precedence over book learning in Islamic education. Tradition holds that the Qur'an was revealed orally to Muhammad, who was illiterate. The name *Qur'an* itself comes from the Arabic verb "to recite," and recitation of the Qur'an became as fundamental to elementary education as it was to religious devotion. Nonetheless, by the eleventh century books were regarded as indispensable aids to memorization and study, though learning solely from books was dismissed as an inferior method of education.

As the sacred language of scripture, Arabic occupied an exalted place in Islamic literary culture. To fulfill one's religious duty one had to master the Qur'an in Arabic. Arabic became the language of government from Iran to Spain. The Sunni orthodoxy endorsed by the Abbasid caliphs and the Seljuk sultans was also based on codification in Arabic of religious teachings and laws. Thus, the Arabic language came to occupy an important place in the developing Islamic identity.

The breakup of the Abbasid caliphate and the rise of regional states fractured the cultural and linguistic unity of the Islamic world. In the ninth century, Iranian authors began to write Persian in the Arabic script, inspiring new styles of poetry, romance, and historical writing. The poet Firdausi (fur-dow-SEE) (d. c. 1025), for example, drew from Sasanid chronicles and popular legends and ballads in composing his *Book of Kings*. This sprawling history of ancient monarchs and heroes has become the national epic of Iran. The Persian political heritage, in which monarchs wielded absolute authority over a steeply hierarchical society, had always clashed with the radical egalitarianism of Islam and the Arabs. But the reinvigorated Persian poetry of Firdausi and others found favor among the upstart Seljuk sultans.

Court poets and artists drew from the rich trove of Persian literature—ranging from the fables of the sailor Sinbad to the celebrated love story of Warqa and Gulshah—to fashion new literary, artistic, and architectural styles that blended sacred and secular themes. The Seljuks absorbed many of these Persian literary motifs into a reinvented Turkish language and literature, which they carried with them into Mesopotamia and Anatolia. Persian and Turkish gradually joined Arabic as the classical languages of the Islamic world.

In the absence of a formal church, the Islamic schools of law, madrasas, and Sufi khanaqa lodges transmitted religious knowledge among all social classes, broadening the reach of education to a wider spectrum of society than the schools and universities of Latin Christendom. The schools of law and madrasas helped to unify theology and law and to forge a distinct Sunni identity.

Nevertheless, regional and national identities were not completely subsumed by the overarching Islamic culture. Moreover, in the Islamic world—as in Latin Christendom—the tension between reason and revelation remained unresolved. Such conflicts were far more muted in Asia, where no single deity or sacred scripture commanded absolute allegiance. In South and Southeast Asia, as in China, intellectual and spiritual commitments instead were more closely entwined with political authority.

The Cosmopolitan and Vernacular Realms in South and Southeast Asia

↘ **FOCUS** What political and religious forces contributed to the development of a common culture across South and Southeast Asia and its subsequent fragmentation into regional cultures?

Between the fifth and the fifteenth centuries, South and Southeast Asia underwent two profound cultural transformations. In the first phase, from roughly 400 to 900, a new cultural and political synthesis emerged simultaneously across the entire region. Local rulers cultivated a common culture reflecting a new ideology of divine kingship. Sanskrit became a cosmopolitan language for expressing rulers' universal claims to secular as well as sacred authority. In the second phase, from 900 to 1400, rulers instead asserted sovereign authority based on the unique historical and cultural identity of their lands and peoples. The spread of diverse vernacular cultures fragmented the cosmopolitan unity of Sanskrit literary and political discourse.

The Cosmopolitan Realm of Sanskrit

Beginning about the third century CE, Sanskrit, the sacred language of the Vedic religious tradition, became for the first time a medium for literary and political expression as well. The emergence of Sanskrit in secular writings occurred virtually simultaneously in South and Southeast Asia. By the sixth century a common cosmopolitan culture expressed through Sanskrit texts had become fully entrenched in royal courts from Afghanistan to Java. The spread of Sanskrit was not a product of political unity or imperial colonization, however. Rather, it came to dominate literary and political discourse in the centuries after the demise of the Gupta Empire, discussed in Chapter 5, when the Indian subcontinent was divided into numerous regional kingdoms (see Map 12.3).

Sanskrit's movement into the political arena did not originate with the Brahmin priesthood. Instead, the impetus came from the Central Asian nomads, notably the Kushan, who ruled over parts of Afghanistan, Pakistan, and northwestern India from the first century BCE to the fourth century CE. The Kushan kings patronized Buddhist theologians and poets who adopted Sanskrit both to record Buddhist scriptures and to commemorate their royal patrons' deeds in inscriptions and eulogies. Later, the Gupta monarchs used Sanskrit to voice their grand imperial ambitions. The Gupta state collapsed in the mid-sixth century, but subsequent rulers embraced its ideology of kingship centered on the ideal of the *chakravartin*, or universal monarch.

Brahminic colleges attached to temples and Buddhist and Jain monasteries provided formal schooling. These colleges were open to anyone from the "twice-born" (that is, ritually pure) castes of Brahmins, warriors, and *Vaishya* (herders, farmers, and merchants). Beginning in the eighth century, hostels known as *mathas*, often devoted to the worship of a particular deity, became important as meeting places where students, scholars, and pilgrims gathered for religious discussion. Above all, royal courts served as the centers of intellectual life and literary production.

The predominance of Sanskrit was equally strong in the Angkor state in Cambodia and in the Javanese kingdoms. Public display of royal power and virtue through monumental architecture and Sanskrit inscriptions took forms in Angkor

≡ **MAP 12.3   Realm of Sanskrit in South and Southeast Asia, c. 1100**   Despite its political disunity after the collapse of the Gupta Empire around 540, the Indian subcontinent developed a common intellectual culture based on Sanskrit texts. Writings in Sanskrit also gave impetus to state formation and the expansion of Indian religions into Southeast Asia.

identical to those found in the Indian subcontinent. Although Khmer (kih-MAY) served as the language of everyday life, used to record matters such as land grants, tax obligations, and contracts, Sanskrit prevailed as the language of politics, poetry, and religion in Cambodia down to the seventeenth century.

Sanskrit's rise as a cosmopolitan language thus allowed local rulers and intellectual elites to draw on a universal system of values and ideas to establish their claims to authority. Royal mystique was expressed symbolically through courtly epics, royal genealogies, and inscriptions that depicted the ruler as a divinely ordained monarch.

Rival States and Regional Identity

By the tenth century a long period of economic expansion produced a series of powerful states across the Sanskrit realm. Most prominent were Angkor in Cambodia and Chola in southern India (see again Map 12.3), but there were also a number of smaller regional kingdoms. The rulers of these states deemed themselves "great kings" (*maharajas*), the earthly representatives of the gods, particularly Shiva and Vishnu. The maharajas (mah-huh-RAH-juh) sought to affirm and extend their authority through ostentatious patronage of gods and their temples.

A wave of temple building, most of it funded by royal donations, swept across the Sanskrit realm between 1000 and 1250. Affirming the parallels between gods and kings, the builders of these temples conceived of them as palaces of the gods, but the rituals performed in them imitated the daily routines of human monarchs. Dedicated to Shiva, the temple built by royal command at the Chola capital of Tanjavur (tan-JOOR) in 1002 received tribute from more than 300 villages, including some as far away as Sri Lanka, and maintained a staff of 600, in addition to many hundreds of priests and students.

From the tenth century onward, as royal power became increasingly tied to distinct territories, appeals to regional identity replaced Sanskrit claims to universal sovereignty. Kings asserted their rule over local temple networks by stressing their common identity with a distinct territory, people, and culture. Consequently the cosmopolitan cultural community based on Sanskrit writings no longer suited their political goals.

The displacement of Sanskrit by vernacular languages accompanied this political transformation. Between the tenth and fourteenth centuries, political boundaries increasingly aligned with linguistic borders. By the tenth century royal inscriptions began to use local vernacular languages rather than Sanskrit. The Chola kings, for example, promoted a Tamil cultural identity defined as "the region of the Tamil language" to further their expansionist political ambitions. Royal courts, the major centers of literary production, also championed a rewriting of the Sanskrit literary heritage in vernacular languages. The first vernacular versions of the *Mahabharata* epic (discussed in Chapter 5) appeared in the Kannada (kah-nah-DAH) language of southwestern India in the tenth century and in the Telugu (tehl-oo-JOO) and Old Javanese languages in the eleventh

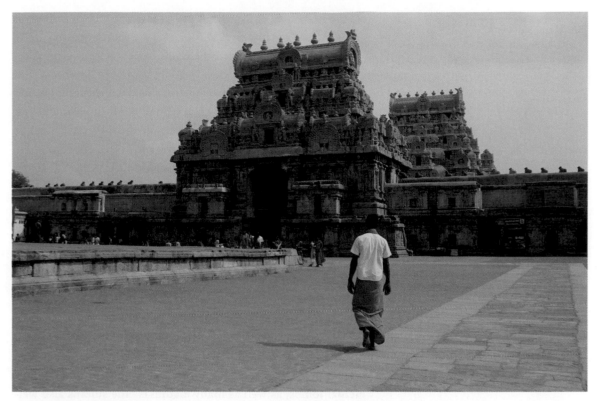

≡ **Tanjavur Temple** The Chola era was marked by a wave of temple building on a grand scale across southern India. Many of these building projects, such as the Rajarajeshvara temple at the Chola capital of Tanjavur seen here, benefited from royal donations intended to link divine authority and kingship. But Hindu temples also attracted patronage from merchant and artisan guilds and obtained revenues from their landholdings, commercial activities, and contributions by village assemblies.

century. Although Sanskrit remained the language of Brahminic religion (and many sacred scriptures were never translated into vernacular languages), after 1400 Sanskrit all but disappeared from royal inscriptions, administrative documents, and courtly literature. The turn toward vernacular literary languages did not broaden the social horizons of literary culture, however. Vernacular literatures relied heavily on Sanskrit vocabulary and rhetoric and were intended for learned audiences, not the common people.

Persianate Literary and Artistic Culture Under the Delhi Sultanate

In the late twelfth century Muhammad Ghuri, the Muslim ruler of Afghanistan, invaded India and conquered the Ganges Valley. After Ghuri's death in 1206, a Turkish slave-general declared himself sultan at Delhi. Over the next three

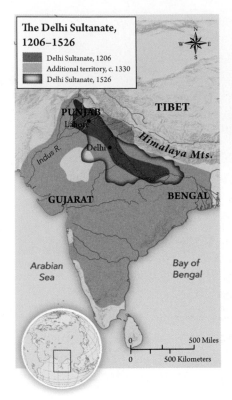

The Delhi Sultanate, 1206–1526

≡ **The Delhi Sultanate, 1206–1526**

centuries a series of five dynasties governed the Delhi sultanate (1206–1526) and imposed Muslim rule over much of India.

The Delhi sultans staffed their government with Muslims, recruiting ulama and Sufis, mostly from Iran and Central Asia. The sultans also founded mosques and madrasas to propagate Islamic teachings, but the ulama and their schools had little impact on the native Hindu population. Instead, it was the missionary zeal of the Sufi orders that paved the way for Islam's spread in South Asia (see Chapter 13, Counterpoint: Sufism in South Asia).

Initially the Delhi sultans cultivated close relations with Sufi masters. Under the dynasty of Muhammad bin Tughluq (r. 1325–1351), however, relations between the sultanate and the Sufi orders chilled. Tughluq enlisted the ulama to condemn unseemly Sufi practices such as religious ceremonies featuring music and dance, and he expelled the Chisti brotherhood, Delhi's dominant Sufi order, from the capital. Deeply versed in philosophy and science, Tughluq became a great patron of Islamic institutions and learning. The Tughluq dynasty fostered a distinctive Islamic-Indian style of architecture adapted to new styles of building, such as congregational mosques and monumental tombs, as well as many madrasas. The sultans also welcomed the influx of Persianized Turks from Central Asia, including scholars, engineers, artisans, and administrators. The famed Moroccan scholar and traveler Ibn Battuta, whom Muhammad bin Tughluq appointed as chief *qadi* (law judge) of Delhi, described the sultan as "of all men, the most addicted to making gifts and shedding blood." Although the sultan awarded him a handsome income—"a number of villages that would produce a revenue of 5000 dinars a year"—Battuta soured on Tughluq's callous cruelty, finding spiritual consolation among the disgraced Sufis, and eventually withdrew from the sultan's service.[6]

In the Persianized political culture introduced by the Ghurids and their successors, the sultan was conceived as a universal monarch who wielded power to ensure worldly justice. As Battuta reported, Muhammad bin Tughluq's subjects addressed him as "Master of the World." The ideas supporting this exalted conception of sovereignty were popularized in Persian poetry, above all the heroic epic of Firdausi as well as the famed romantic verse of Nizami of Ganjeh. Every Muslim prince within the Persianate realm wished to possess copies of Firdausi's *Book of Kings* and Nizami's *Five Treasures*, which were often produced as lavishly illustrated manuscripts. Much of this artistic creation was centered at Delhi. Yet skilled artisans blending Mamluk, Persian, and Indian ornamental styles also composed illustrated manuscripts for both courtly and mercantile patrons in regional centers such as Gujarat, which had close commercial ties with Mamluk Egypt.

The sack of Delhi by Timur in 1398 (see Chapter 14) spelled the demise of effective central control by the Delhi sultans. But Persianate literary and artistic creativity flourished under the patronage of the numerous independent rulers spawned by Timur's conquests in Iran and Afghanistan as well as the sultans at Delhi and regional Indian courts.

Learning, Schools, and Print Culture in East Asia

⬊ FOCUS To what extent did intellectual and educational trends in Song China influence its East Asian neighbors?

Compared to the worlds of Christendom and Islam, in East Asia learning and scholarship were much more tightly yoked to the state and its institutions. Beginning with the Song dynasty (960–1279), the civil service examination system dominated Chinese political life and literary culture. At the same time the political and social rewards of examination success led to a proliferation of schools and broader access to education (see Map 12.4).

The invention and spread of printing transformed written communication and intellectual life in China. Elsewhere in East Asia, however, the spread of printing and vernacular writing had a much more limited impact on government and social hierarchy. In Japan and Korea, literacy and education remained the preserve of the aristocratic elites and the Buddhist clergy.

Civil Service Examinations and Schooling in Song China

Chinese civil service examinations were a complex series of tests based on the Confucian classics, history, poetry, and other subjects. They served as the primary method for recruiting government officials from the eleventh century onward. The examinations also played a crucial role in establishing **Neo-Confucianism**, a revival of Confucian teachings that firmly rejected Buddhism and reasserted the Confucian commitment to moral perfection and the betterment of society, as an intellectual orthodoxy.

Prior to the Song, China's imperial governments recruited their officials mostly through a system of recommendations. Local magistrates nominated promising candidates on the basis of subjective criteria such as literary talent and reputation

Neo-Confucianism
The revival of Confucian teachings beginning in the Song dynasty that firmly rejected Buddhist religion and reasserted the Confucian commitment to moral perfection and the betterment of society.

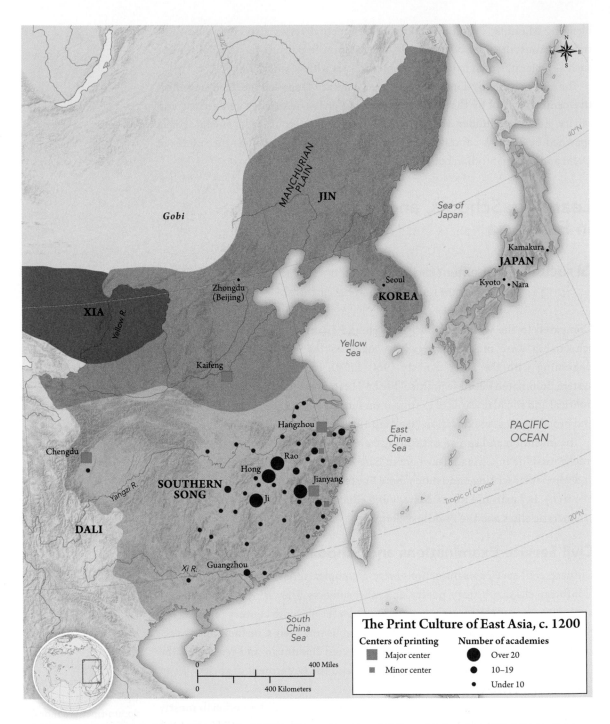

≡ **MAP 12.4   The Print Culture of East Asia, c. 1200**   Chinese literary and philosophical works and Buddhist scriptures written in Chinese provided the foundations of a common East Asian intellectual culture. The prestige of Chinese culture remained intact despite the conquest of north China by the Jin dynasty in 1127. The proliferation of private academies and the greater availability of printed books contributed to the rise of Neo-Confucianism in Southern Song China.

for virtue. Prominent families had enough influence to ensure that their sons received preferential consideration. Family pedigree, secured through wealth, marriage connections, and a tradition of office holding, was the key to continued access to political office.

From the start, however, the Song dynasty was determined to centralize both military and civil power in the hands of the emperor and his ministers. To restore the supremacy of civil authority, the early Song emperors greatly expanded the use of civil service examinations. They sought to create a skilled, ideologically cohesive cadre of officials whose chief loyalty would be to the state rather than to their families. Competitive tests diminished the influence of family prestige in the selection of government officials. The impulse behind the civil service examinations was less democratic than autocratic, however: the final choice of successful candidates rested with the emperor.

By 1250, 400,000 men were taking the triennial civil service examinations. Of this number, only 800 were selected for appointment to office. The enormous number of examination candidates reflected the crucial importance of government office to achieving social and political success. It also testified to the powerful influence of schooling in shaping the lives and outlook of the ruling class. At every level of schooling, the curriculum mirrored the priorities of the civil service examinations. In general the examinations emphasized mastery of the Confucian classics, various genres of poetry, and matters of public policy and statecraft.

For educated men, the power of the examination system was inescapable. Only a few rare individuals would ever pass through, as contemporaries put it, "the thorny gate of learning." Yet examination learning defined the intellectual and cultural values not only of officials but also of the educated public at large. In a poem, a Song emperor exhorted young men to apply themselves to study:

> To enrich your family, no need to buy good land;
> Books hold a thousand measures of grain.
> For an easy life, no need to build a mansion;
> In books are found houses of gold.
> When traveling, be not vexed at the absence of followers;
> In books, carriages and horses form a crowd.
> When marrying, be not vexed by lack of a good matchmaker;
> In books there are girls with faces of jade.
> A boy who wants to become somebody
> Devotes himself to the classics, faces the window, and reads.[6]

The average age of men who passed the highest level of the civil service examinations was thirty-one. Thus China's political leaders commonly underwent a long apprenticeship as students that lasted well into their adult life.

Critics of the civil service examinations complained that the impartiality of the evaluation procedures did not allow for proper assessment of the candidates' moral character. Other critics condemned the examination system and government schools for stifling intellectual inquiry. In their view, the narrow focus of the curriculum and the emphasis on rote knowledge over creative thinking produced petty-minded pedants rather than dynamic leaders.

These various criticisms spurred the founding of private academies. This trend received a major boost from Zhu Xi (jew she) (1130–1200), the most influential Neo-Confucian scholar, who reordered the classical canon to revive humanistic learning and infuse education with moral purpose. Zhu mocked the sterile teaching of government schools and instead championed the private academy as the ideal environment for the pursuit of genuine moral knowledge. His teachings inspired the founding of at least 140 private academies during the twelfth and thirteenth centuries. Moreover, many leading scholars rejected political careers altogether. Withdrawal from public life to devote oneself to literary and aesthetic accomplishment became an alternative path to realizing the Neo-Confucian goal of moral self-cultivation.

Ironically, later dynasties would adopt Zhu Xi's philosophical views and interpretations of the classics as the official orthodoxy of the civil service examinations. Consequently, his Neo-Confucian doctrines were more influential even than

≡ **"Whiling Away the Summer"** The Chinese painter Liu Guandao (active c. 1279–1300) was employed as a court artisan by Qubilai Khan, the Mongol ruler of China (discussed in Chapter 13). In this painting, a scholar holding a fly whisk in one hand and a scroll in the other leisurely reclines on a platform couch, surrounded by artworks and a lute. This scene—mirrored in the standing screen at rear depicting a scholar at his writing table—exemplifies the Neo-Confucian ideal of sagehood, which combined mastery of learning with aesthetic accomplishment. Nelson-Atkins Museum, Kansas City, Purchase: William Rockhill Nelson Trust, 48-5. (Photo © The Nelson Gallery Foundation.)

Thomas Aquinas's synthesis of Christian revelation or al-Ghazali's contributions to Islamic theology.

The Culture of Print in Song China

Just as papermaking originated in China, the Chinese invented the technology of printing. The earliest known example of woodblock printing is a miniature Buddhist charm dating from the first half of the eighth century. By the ninth century printing had developed into a substantial industry in China. The most important use of print was to reproduce Buddhist scriptures and other religious texts. Buddhists regarded the dissemination of scriptures as an act of piety that earned karmic merit for the sponsor. Mass production of religious texts and icons most likely was the original motivation behind the invention of printing.

The founding of the Song dynasty marked the ascendancy of government-sponsored printing. Just as the Song took the lead in education to reinforce their rule, the Song government used printing to help propagate official ideas and values. The state printed collections of statutes, laws, and government procedures and works on medicine, astronomy, and natural history, as well as standard editions of classics, histories, and literary anthologies. In the twelfth century, however, private publishers, including schools as well as commercial firms, surpassed the Song government as the main source of printed books. Schools and academies had the intellectual and financial resources to publish fine-quality, scrupulously edited editions (see again Map 12.4).

Commercial firms usually issued cheaply printed texts that catered to market tastes, especially demand for a wide variety of aids to prepare students for the civil service exams. These works included classical commentaries by famous scholars, dictionaries, school primers, writing manuals, phrase books, and collections of examination essays by the highest-ranked candidates. Books largely for personal

≡ **Chinese Woodblock Printing** The religious merit earned for spreading Buddhist teachings appears to have been the motivating force behind the invention of printing in China. This copy of the *Diamond Sutra*, a popular digest of Mahayana Buddhist teachings, bears the date 868, making it the oldest known dated example of block printing.

enjoyment, such as poetry and prose anthologies by famous authors and works of drama and fiction, also became staples of commercial publishing, along with medical and fortune-telling texts purveying practical knowledge.

Despite the advantages of printing as a means of mass reproduction, the technology of printing spread slowly. Elsewhere in East Asia, state and religious institutions monopolized printing. Although Muslims were aware of printing by the eleventh century, they felt deep reverence for the handwritten word and fiercely opposed mechanical reproduction of the sacred words of the Qur'an and other religious texts. No printing presses were established in the Islamic world before the eighteenth century. The printing press invented by the goldsmith Johannes Gutenberg in the German city of Mainz in the 1440s appears to have been a separate invention unrelated to Chinese printing technology.

Classical and Vernacular Traditions in East Asia

Just as Latin endured as the common literary language of Latin Christendom, the classical Chinese language unified East Asian intellectual life. Korean and Japanese writers at first composed their works in classical Chinese. Although works of popular entertainment such as drama and fiction begin to include colloquial speech during the Song period, classical Chinese prevailed as the dominant literary language of East Asia down to modern times.

In Korea, mastery of Chinese literary forms, especially poetry, became an essential mark of accomplishment among aristocrats. The advent of the Koryŏ (KAW-ree-oh) dynasty (918–1392) signaled the dominance of Confucianism in Korean political culture. The Koryŏ state preserved aristocratic rule, but it also instituted civil service examinations. Schooling and the examination system were highly centralized in the capital of Kaesong, and they were largely restricted to aristocratic families.

Confucian culture became even more deeply entrenched in the ruling class during the succeeding Yi dynasty (1392–1910). The Yi monarch Sejong (SAY-johng) (r. 1418–1450) took the initiative in creating a native writing system, known as *han'gul* (HAHN-goor), to enable his people to express themselves in their everyday tongue. But the Korean aristocracy, determined to preserve its monopoly over learning and social prestige, resisted the new writing system. As in Japan, it was women of aristocratic families who popularized the native script by using it extensively in their correspondence and poetry.

In Japan, too, Chinese was the learned, formal, written language of public life. Aristocratic men studied the Chinese classics, history, and law and composed Chinese poetry. By 850 the Japanese had developed a phonetic system for writing

Japanese, but they rarely used it in public life. The Japanese kana script instead was relegated to the private world of letters and diaries; it became so closely associated with women writers that it was called "woman's hand." Women of the Heian aristocracy were expected to be well versed in poetry and composition, and this era witnessed a remarkable outpouring of great literature by women writing vernacular Japanese. In fact, women composed much of the memorable writing of this era such as the *Pillow Book* of Sei Shōnagon (SAY SHON-nah-gohn) and Lady Murasaki's *Tale of Genji*. Although the world immortalized by Murasaki was narrowly self-centered, she and her fellow women writers gave birth to Japanese as a written language (see Reading the Past: Lady Murasaki on Her Peers Among Women Writers).

To different degrees, the spread of vernacular writing broadened access to written knowledge throughout East Asia. In China, the classical language retained its preeminence as a literary language, but the early development of printing and public schools fostered a relatively high level of literacy. In Mesoamerica, by contrast, writing remained a jealously guarded prerogative of the ruling class.

COUNTERPOINT: Writing and Political Power in Mesoamerica

↘ **FOCUS** How did the relationship between political power and knowledge of writing in Mesoamerica differ from that in the other civilizations studied in this chapter?

The Greeks coined the word *hieroglyph* (priestly or sacred script) for the Egyptian language, whose signs differed radically from their own alphabetic writing. In ancient societies such as Egypt, writing and reading were skills reserved for rulers, priests, and administrators. Writing was both a product and an instrument of political control. Rulers denied ordinary people access to books and other forms of written knowledge.

This monopoly over the written word vanished in the major civilizations of Eurasia and Africa during the first millennium BCE. Subsequently the evangelical zeal of Buddhists, Christians, and Muslims encouraged the spread of literacy and written knowledge. But in more isolated parts of the world, such as Mesoamerica, writing, like ritual, served to perpetuate the profound social gulf that separated the rulers from the common people.

READING THE PAST

Lady Murasaki on Her Peers Among Women Writers

In addition to her great novel *Tale of Genji*, Lady Murasaki composed a memoir, covering a brief period from 1008 to 1010, that reflects on events and personalities at the Heian court. Among its more personal elements are Murasaki's observations about other women writers of her day, such as Izumi Shikibu (EE-zoo-mee SHEE-kee-boo), who earned the scorn of many for the frankly amorous tone of her poems and her flamboyant love affairs, and Sei Shōnagon, renowned author of the *Pillow Book*, a collection of writings on taste and culture. Murasaki's tart judgments reveal the intense rivalry for literary fame among women in the court's status-conscious circles.

> Now someone who did carry on a fascinating correspondence was Izumi Shikibu. She does have a rather unsavory side to her character but she has a talent for tossing off letters with ease and seems to make the most banal statement sound special. Her poems are most interesting. Although her knowledge of the canon and her judgments of other people's poetry leave something to be desired, she can produce poems at will and always

manages to include some clever phrase that catches the attention. Yet when it comes to criticizing or judging the works of others, well, she never really comes up to scratch—the sort of person who relies on a talent for extemporization, one feels. I cannot think of her as a poet of the highest rank.

> Sei Shōnagon, for instance, was dreadfully conceited. She thought herself so clever and littered her writings with Chinese words; but if you examined them closely, they left a great deal to be desired. Those who think of themselves as being superior to everyone else in this way will inevitably suffer and come to a bad end.[1]

Yet Murasaki is no less harsh in her self-appraisal:

> Thus do I criticize others from various angles— but here is one who has survived this far without having achieved anything of note. . . . Pretty yet shy, shrinking from sight, unsociable, fond of old tales, conceited, so wrapped up in poetry that other people hardly exist, spitefully looking down on the whole world—such is the unpleasant opinion that people have of me.[2]

1. Ivan Morris, *The World of the Shining Prince: Court Life in Ancient Japan* (New York: Knopf, 1964), 251.

2. *The Diary of Lady Murasaki*, trans. Richard Bowring (London: Penguin, 1996), 53–54.

Examining the Evidence

1. Although women writers such as Murasaki did not compose their major works in Chinese, they still held literary skill in Chinese in high regard. Why?

2. Why might Lady Murasaki have believed that a woman writer's talent was best expressed by poetry? (Consider the chapter narrative as well as this excerpt in formulating your response.)

Mesoamerican Languages: Time, History, and Rulership

In Mesoamerica, written languages took the form of symbols with pictorial elements, much like the hieroglyphs of ancient Egypt. Mesoamerican texts also display many parallels with Egyptian writings. Most surviving texts are inscriptions on monuments that commemorate the great feats and divine majesty of rulers. Knowledge of astronomical timekeeping, divination and prophecy, and rituals intended to align human events with grand cycles of cosmic time were indispensable to political power.

The earliest writing in Mesoamerica was the Zapotec (sah-po-TEHK) script of the Monte Alban state in southern Mexico, which was in use at least as early as 400 BCE. The Zapotec language achieved its mature form in 300–700 CE, the Monte Alban state's heyday. Unfortunately, the Zapotec language remains undecipherable. Nonetheless, Zapotec inscriptions display many of the same themes found in later Mesoamerican literary traditions. For example, the earliest Zapotec monuments with writing depict slain enemies and captives, a common motif in Maya monuments.

Maya rulers wielded the written word to consolidate their power, using it to display both divine approval of their reign and the fixed course of human history. Maya scribes used calendrical calculation to create genealogical histories organized around the crucial events and persons—birth, marriage, ancestors, offspring—in the lives of royal and noble persons. Maya inscriptions also commemorated the rulers' accomplishments by portraying them as reenacting the triumphs of ancient heroes (see Reading the Past: Maya Hero Twins Vanquish the Lords of the Underworld, pages 362–363). The regular destruction of monuments testifies to the power of the visible word in Mesoamerican societies. The Zapotecs at Monte Alban plastered over or reused old monuments in new construction. The Maya frequently defaced, sawed, buried, or relocated monuments of defeated enemies or disgraced persons.

In addition to stone inscriptions on monuments, temples, and dwellings, a handful of Maya bark-paper books have survived. Whereas stone monuments served as public propaganda, the bark-paper books contained the technical knowledge of astronomy, calendrical science, divination, and prophecy that governed the lives of the Maya elite.

The tradition of monument building lapsed almost entirely after the demise of the classic Maya city-states in the ninth and tenth centuries. Yet the nobility preserved knowledge of the Maya script down to the Spanish conquests in the sixteenth century. Spanish missionaries deliberately destroyed nearly all of the bark-paper books, which they condemned as works of the devil.

≡ **Mesoamerican Scripts**

≡ **Maya Scribe** In the Maya classical age, the power of the pen often was mightier than that of the sword. Court scribes combined writing ability, artistic skill, and esoteric knowledge of such fields as astronomy to create the monuments and artifacts that perpetuated royal authority. Scribes were also associated with divine figures, as in this painted vase from the period 600 to 900, which depicts a scribe in the guise of the maize god.

In their place the Spanish taught the Maya to write their language using the Roman alphabet. The *Popul Vuh*, the "Book of Council" that has served as a rich mine of information about Maya mythology and religion, was composed in Roman script in the mid-sixteenth century (see Chapter 10). After an alphabet was adopted, however, knowledge of the Maya hieroglyphic script died out.

The Legacy of Mesoamerican Languages

Although the classical Maya language became extinct, scholars today can decipher as much as 80 percent of surviving Maya texts. Linguists have found that the political institutions and cultural values embedded in the Maya literary legacy also appear, in altered form, in the later written records of the Mixtecs and Aztecs of central Mexico. All of these languages, as well as Zapotec, were part of a broader Mesoamerican tradition that used writing to enhance rulers' prestige and power. Although command of writing was restricted to a tiny elite, Mesoamerican rulers addressed the mass of the populace through public monuments. Here, as in many cultures, the sacred and imperishable character of writing, in contrast to the fleeting nature of ordinary speech, endowed the ruler's words with a powerful aura of truth.

Yet it was precisely because of such tight control that written languages like classic Maya became extinct once the social and political systems that created them disappeared. In the cosmopolitan civilizations of Eurasia, by contrast, rulers and religious authorities were powerless to maintain a monopoly over the power of the written word, especially when vernacular tongues displaced classical languages as the chief media of written communication.

Conclusion

The tenth to the fourteenth centuries witnessed a remarkable expansion of learning and schooling across Eurasia. This expansion of knowledge and education was fostered by the growing penetration of religious institutions and values in local society and by the creation of formal institutions of higher learning. The languages of sacred texts and religious instruction—Latin, Arabic, Sanskrit, and Chinese—achieved new prominence in higher education and intellectual discourse. The growing prestige of these cosmopolitan languages led them to be adopted in government and literary expression as well.

The deepening infusion of religious faith into traditions of learning thus produced more distinct and coherent cultural identities in each of the major civilizations of Eurasia. At the same time the friction between sacred and secular learning—between faith and reason—intensified. In Latin Christendom, struggles erupted among the Roman church, monarchs and city councils, and guilds of masters, each seeking to dictate the structure and content of university education. In the Islamic world, in the absence of an ordained clergy, individual ulama and madrasas aligned themselves with one of several separate traditions of Islamic law and theological study. Sufis proposed a radically different understanding of Islam. In China, a resurgent, secular Neo-Confucianism dominated public discourse through the state-run civil service examinations and schools, pushing Buddhism to the margins of intellectual life. In the Maya world, by contrast, the rulers' monopoly of the written word ensured their domination over all aspects of political, social, and religious life.

Yet the emergence of vernacular literary languages undercut the unity of learned culture. Writing in the vernacular was stimulated by political fragmentation and rivalry and by the flowering of local and regional literary and artistic expression in an era of vigorous economic prosperity. Despite this proliferation of vernacular literature like Lady Murasaki's *Tale of Genji*—written by and for the elite—the cultural and social gulf between the literate and the illiterate remained as wide as ever.

The intense struggles over the definition of religious truth and social values in the major regions of Eurasia during these centuries aggravated conflicts between different civilizations and ways of life. As we will see in the next chapter, the launch of the Crusades and the Mongol conquests inflamed the already smoldering tensions between Christians and Muslims and between nomadic and settled peoples.

review

The major global development in this chapter: The expansion of learning and education across Eurasia from 900 to 1300 and its relationship to the rise of regional and national identities.

Important Events	
918–1392	Koryŏ dynasty in Korea
960–1279	Song dynasty in China
c. 1010	Lady Murasaki's *Tale of Genji* begins to circulate among the Japanese court aristocracy
1055	Seljuk Turks capture Baghdad and establish their rule over Mesopotamia and Syria
1066	Norman conquest of England
1130–1200	Life of Neo-Confucian scholar Zhu Xi
1140	Catholic church authorities convict theologian Peter Abelard of heresy
c. 1150	First university founded at Paris
1206–1526	Delhi sultanate in India
1215	Pope Innocent III bans the teachings of Aristotle and Ibn Rushd
1273	Publication of Thomas Aquinas's *Summa Theologica*
c. 1313–1321	Dante Alighieri composes his epic poem *Divine Comedy*
1382	Ibn Khaldun becomes professor of Islamic law at Cairo
1392–1910	Yi dynasty in Korea

KEY TERMS

cathedral school (p. 436)
hadith (p. 446)
madrasa (p. 446)
Neo-Confucianism (p. 457)

rhetoric (p. 436)
shari'a (p. 446)
Sufism (p. 449)
ulama (p. 443)

university (p. 440)
vernacular language (p. 442)

CHAPTER OVERVIEW QUESTIONS

1. Did the spread of higher learning reinforce or undermine established political and religious authority?
2. How did educational institutions reshape social hierarchy and elite culture?

3. What were the different uses of cosmopolitan languages and vernacular languages, and to what degree did they broaden access to written knowledge?
4. How did the different technologies of writing affect the impact of the written word?

MAKING CONNECTIONS

1. In what ways did the cathedral schools and universities of Latin Christendom modify the classical traditions of learning of ancient Greece and Rome?
2. How did the madrasas of the Islamic world differ from European universities in their curricula,

their teachers, and their relationships with political and religious authorities?

3. How can we explain the failure of printing technology to spread from China to neighboring societies such as Japan, India, or the Islamic world until centuries later?

DOING HISTORY

Contextualization

The law of unseen consequences applies over and over again throughout history, and the evolution of schools and educational institutions certainly provides many examples. For instance, in Latin Christendom bishops established cathedral schools to gain more control over the content of formal education, but they found themselves in a losing struggle with monasteries, kings, municipal authorities, and even the Roman popes over who gets to teach, what should be taught, and how students should learn.

1. How did competing priorities among religious and political authorities lead to the creation of the institution of the university?
2. Do we find similar struggles over educational institutions and the content of learning in the Islamic world and China?
3. How did the different political, religious, and intellectual contexts of Latin Christendom, the Islamic world, and the Chinese Empire not only influence the content and purpose of schooling but also reshape the social elites in each society?

For further research into the topics covered in this chapter, see the Bibliography at the end of the book.

Crusaders, Mongols, and Eurasian Integration

1050–1350

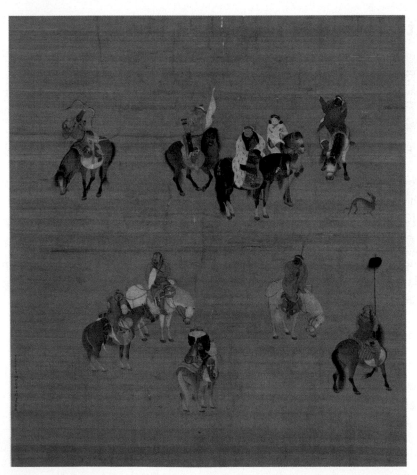

≡ **World in the Making** Qubilai, grandson of the great conqueror Chinggis, cemented his claim as Great Khan of all the Mongols only after a bloody struggle against one of his brothers. In his quest to become the first foreign emperor of China, Qubilai sought to bridge the pastoral heritage of the Mongols and the political and cultural traditions of the Chinese. This detail from a painting of a Mongol hunting party depicts Qubilai (center) wearing Chinese robes under his Mongol fur coat, accompanied by his wife, Chabi (also in white).

backstory

By the twelfth century, economic revival and commercial integration had begun to stimulate unprecedented cultural contact and exchange across Eurasia (see Chapters 11 and 12). But economic prosperity did not necessarily translate into political strength. The weakened Abbasid caliphs, already challenged by rival caliphates in Egypt and Spain, had become pawns of the Seljuk (Saljuk) Turks, invaders from Central Asia. In China, the Song dynasty was also vulnerable to invasion by its northern neighbors. In 1127 Jurchen invaders from Manchuria seized the northern half of the empire, forcing the Song court to flee to the south. Within Christendom, the division between the Latin west and the Byzantine east widened into outright hostility, and the Roman and Byzantine churches competed against each other to convert the pagan peoples of eastern Europe and Russia to Christianity.

WHILE ON A DIPLOMATIC MISSION to the Christian kingdom of Jerusalem, the Syrian courtier Usamah ibn Minqidh (oo-SAW-mah ib-in-moon-KEED) (1095–1188) visited the shrine to Saint John the Baptist near Nablus. Upon entering, he found a group of white-haired Christians bent over in prayer. "The sight of their piety touched my heart," Usamah later wrote, "but at the same time it displeased and saddened me, for I had never seen such zeal and devotion among the Muslims." After returning to the Syrian capital Damascus, however, Usamah chanced upon a Sufi hospice, where he "saw about a hundred prayer-mats, and on each a Sufi, his face expressing peaceful serenity, and his body humble devotion. This was a reassuring sight, and I gave thanks to Almighty God that there were among the Muslims men of even more zealous devotion than those Christian priests."

Born in the year Pope Urban II proclaimed the "crusade" to wrest the Holy Land from Muslim dominion and dying a year after the sultan Saladin recaptured Jerusalem, Usamah spent his long career in service to several Muslim rulers, fighting battles against the "Franks" (the Christian Crusaders) but even more often becoming ensnared in political intrigues and military struggles among his Muslim patrons. Usamah admired the military prowess of the Crusaders, yet he was appalled that "among the Franks, the knights have a monopoly of the positions of honor and importance . . . and no one else has any prestige."[1] For Usamah, the Crusaders were conspicuously lacking in *adab*—the quality of refinement expressed through genteel manners, wit, and literary elegance that defined the upper rank of Muslim society. Best known as a poet, Usamah was steeped in Arabic literary culture, but he was not a man of deep piety like his father, who made forty-three handwritten copies of the Qur'an. He deplored the uncouth mores and lust for warmongering of the Franks more than their faith, and he developed cordial relations with some Christians who sheltered and protected him.

Usamah ibn Minqidh bore witness to an era in which the tense hostility that had divided Christians and Muslims exploded into a succession of religious wars. Although the Crusaders ultimately failed in their quest, the Crusades marked a crucial moment in the definition of Europe as the realm of Latin Christendom. At the same time, centralization of ecclesiastic control and theological orthodoxy under the Roman papacy brought about a final rupture between Rome and the Christian churches of Byzantium and Asia. But the papacy's drive to create a united Latin Christendom under clerical leadership foundered, and national monarchies enhanced their power throughout Europe.

Shortly after Usamah's death, another clash of cultures erupted when Mongol armies began to sweep across Eurasia. From humble origins among the nomadic herders of Central Asia, the Mongols became world conquerors. They terrified populations from Korea to Hungary, laid waste to dozens of cities, and toppled many rulers. For all their violence, the Mongols built bridges that connected diverse civilizations rather than walls that divided them. But ultimately the contradictions between the political and cultural traditions of the nomadic Mongols and the settled lives of the peoples they conquered proved too great, and the Mongol Empires collapsed. By 1400 Europe and Asia had once again grown distant from each other.

OVERVIEW QUESTIONS

The major global development in this chapter: The Eurasian integration fostered by the clashes of culture known as the Crusades and the Mongol conquests.

As you read, consider:

1. In what ways did the growing economic and cultural unity of Latin Christendom promote the rise of powerful European national monarchies?

2. To what degree did the expansion of Latin Christendom remake eastern Europe in the image of western Europe?

3. In what ways did the Mongol conquests foster cultural and economic exchange across Eurasia?

4. How and why did the Mongol rulers of China, Iran, and Russia differ in their relationships with the settled societies they ruled?

The Crusades and the Imperial Papacy 1050–1350

⟆ FOCUS In what ways did the Roman popes seek to expand their powers during the age of the Crusades?

The **Crusades** are generally understood as an effort to reclaim control of the sacred sites of the Christian religion from Muslim rule. More broadly, the Crusades developed into an evangelical movement to Christianize the world. The summons to rescue Jerusalem from the "heathen" Muslims, announced at a church council in 1095, escalated to include campaigns to recover Islamic Spain; to impose

Crusades The series of military campaigns instigated by the Roman papacy with the goal of returning Jerusalem and other holy places in Palestine to Christian rule.

Christianity on the pagan Celtic, Slavic, and Baltic peoples of Europe; and to eradicate heresy—doctrines contrary to the church's official teachings—from within Latin Christendom. The era of the Crusades also witnessed the temporary rise of an "imperial" papacy as administrative reforms within the church broadened the Roman popes' authority over secular affairs as well as the spiritual life of the Christian faithful.

The Papal Monarchy

The transformation of Latin Christendom that led to the crusading movement began with initiatives to reform the church from within. In the eyes of both lay and clerical critics, abuses such as violations of celibacy and the sale of church offices had compromised the clergy's moral authority. The reformers also sought to renew the church's commitment to spread the teachings of Christ to all peoples of the world. Pope Gregory VII (r. 1073–1085) was the staunchest advocate of the primacy of the pope as the leader of all Christian peoples. Within the church, Gregory campaigned to improve the moral and educational caliber of the clergy and demanded strict conformity to the standard religious services authorized by the church hierarchy. Thus, under Gregory VII, the movements for clerical reform and centralization of authority within the church merged. As a result, clerical reform became a force for the religious and cultural unification of Europe.

Long before Gregory VII's papacy, the rivalry between the Roman and Byzantine churches had resulted in bitter division in the Christian world. Half-hearted efforts at reconciliation came to an end in 1054, when the Roman pope and the patriarch at Constantinople expelled each other from the church. This mutual excommunication initiated a formal break between the Latin and Orthodox churches that came to be known as the **Great Schism**. As the split between the Christian leadership widened, Rome and Constantinople openly competed for the allegiance of new converts in eastern Europe and Russia.

The popes faced competition from within Europe as well as from without. Secular leaders in many parts of Europe had the right to make appointments to key church positions in their domains. In effect, this gave them control over church lands and officials. Pope Gregory demanded an end to such secular control. In a deliberately public disagreement with the Holy Roman emperor Henry IV (r. 1056–1106) known as the **investiture controversy** (*investiture* refers to the appointment of church officials), Gregory challenged the emperor's authority to appoint bishops within his domains. Gregory invalidated Henry's right to rule over his territories, provoking the emperor's enemies among the German princes to rise against him. Henry was forced to prostrate himself before the pope and beg

Great Schism The separation of the Latin Catholic and Greek Orthodox churches following the mutual excommunication by the Roman pope and the Byzantine patriarch in 1054.

investiture controversy Conflict between the pope and the Holy Roman emperor over who had the authority to appoint bishops and other church officials.

forgiveness. Ultimately, a compromise gave kings and princes some say in appointments to major church offices in their territories but ceded leadership of the church to the papacy.

Deprived of control over the church, the Holy Roman emperors lost their primary base of support. The German princes consolidated their power over their own domains, reducing the emperorship to a largely ceremonial office. The Roman papacy, in contrast, increasingly resembled a royal government, with its own law courts, fiscal officers, and clerical bureaucracy.

Papal success and the church's growing immersion in worldly affairs gave rise to a new round of calls for change within the church. The Cistercian order, founded in France in 1098, epitomized the renewed dedication to poverty, chastity, and evangelism among the Latin clergy. Passionate defenders of Roman orthodoxy, the Cistercians worked tirelessly to uproot what they perceived as the heresies of their fellow Christians. It was the Cistercians who secured the papal condemnation that ended the career of the Parisian theologian Peter Abelard in 1140 (discussed in Chapter 12).

The Crusades 1095–1291

Upon receiving an appeal from the Byzantine emperor for aid against the advancing armies of the Seljuk Turks in 1095, Pope Urban II (r. 1088–1099) called upon "the race of Franks [Latin Christians] . . . beloved and chosen by God" to "enter upon the road to the Holy Sepulcher; wrest that land from the wicked race, and subject it to yourselves."[2] Urban II's summons for a crusade to liberate Jerusalem drew inspiration from the reform movements within the church and from a desire to transform the warrior rulers of Latin Christendom, constantly fighting among each other, into a united army of God. A papal dispensation granted to the Crusaders by Urban II transformed participation in the crusade into a form of penance, for which the Crusader would receive a full absolution of sins. This helped create enthusiasm for crusading among the knightly class, which saw the crusade as a means of erasing the heavy burden of sin that inevitably saddled men of war and violence.

The Crusader forces, more a collection of ragtag militias under the command of various minor nobles than a united army, suffered setbacks, yet achieved surprising success in capturing Jerusalem in 1099 (see Map 13.1). But the victors lacked strong leadership and failed to follow up their initial success by establishing unified political and military institutions. Spurning the Byzantine emperor's claims to sovereignty, the Crusaders divided the conquered territories among themselves and installed a French duke as king of Jerusalem and defender of the Holy Land.

≡ **Crusaders Voyaging to Holy Land** Pope Urban's summons for a crusade to recapture Jerusalem was directed at knights, but people of all walks of life—including women and the urban poor—rallied to the Crusader cause. This Spanish illustration from 1283 shows the Crusaders embarking for the Holy Land aboard galleys powered chiefly by oars, the typical type of warship used in the Mediterranean Sea.

Perhaps the greatest beneficiaries of the crusading movement were Venice and Genoa, whose merchants rushed to secure trading privileges in the Crusader kingdoms along the eastern shores of the Mediterranean.

At first Muslims did not understand the religious aspirations of the Crusaders and failed to rally against the Christian invaders. Nearly a century elapsed before a serious challenge arose to Christian rule over Jerusalem. In 1169 the Seljuk emir of Damascus dispatched one of his lieutenants, Saladin (c. 1137–1193), to Egypt to shore up defenses against a possible Christian attack. Saladin soon seized power from the much-weakened Fatimid caliphate and declared himself an independent sultan. He sought to muster support by declaring a holy war against the Christian occupiers of Jerusalem. In 1187 Saladin conquered Jerusalem and most of the Crusader principalities.

This unexpected reversal prompted Christendom's leading monarchs—the kings of England and France and the Holy Roman emperor—to join together in what became known as the Third Crusade (1189–1192). Dissension among the Christian kings hobbled the military campaign, however, and the crusade ended with a truce under which the Christian armies withdrew in exchange for a Muslim pledge to allow Christian pilgrims access to holy sites.

Over the next century new crusades were repeatedly launched, with little success. Moreover, the original religious motivations of the Crusaders came to be overshadowed by political and economic objectives. The army mustered under the banner of the Fourth Crusade initially set sail for Egypt, only to be diverted to Constantinople. The Venetians, who financed the Fourth Crusade, decided that seizing the capital of their fellow Christian, the Byzantine emperor, offered more immediate rewards than the uncertain prospects of war against the Muslims

≡ **MAP 13.1 The Crusader Movement, 1096–1204** The Crusader movement was fueled by a mix of motives, including religious piety, personal ambition, and the lure of booty. Despite the success of the First Crusade in capturing Jerusalem in 1099, unity among the Crusaders proved elusive. The Venetian captains of the Fourth Crusade diverted their fleet away from Muslim-occupied territories and instead sacked Constantinople, the capital of the Byzantine Empire.

(see again Map 13.1). The capture of Constantinople in 1204 catapulted Venice to dominance over commerce throughout the eastern Mediterranean and the Black Sea. The Byzantine emperor recovered his capital in 1260 thanks to the naval support of Genoa, Venice's perennial rival. After the Venetian seizure—with the

SEEING THE PAST

The Mappaemundi of Latin Christendom

More than any other sources, biblical stories and popular legends about the Greek conqueror Alexander the Great shaped the geographic imagination of Latin Christendom. The influence of these writings is especially apparent in the medieval *mappaemundi* ("maps of the world") that frequently embellished the margins of illuminated manuscripts. Some mappaemundi were much larger, intended for public display in churches.

The basic format of mappaemundi derived from the so-called T-O map designed by Isidore (c. 560–636), the bishop of Seville in the seventh century, and is illustrated here. Isidore showed the world divided into three parts and apportioned among the three sons of Noah as recorded in the Book of Genesis: Asia was given to Shem, Europe to Japeth, and Africa to Ham. The T-O maps are so named because the three continents are separated by T-shaped bodies of water (the Mediterranean Sea forming one axis, and the Black Sea and the Nile River the other), surrounded by a circular ocean. The maps are oriented with the

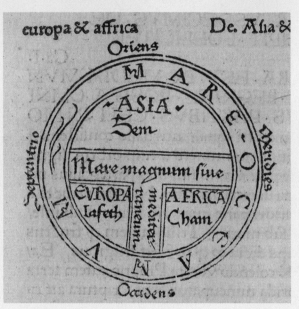

Isidore of Seville's T-O Map

east at top, the direction of the Garden of Eden and the paradise that awaits the Christian faithful at the time of the final judgment.

pope's tacit approval—of Constantinople, the schism between the Roman Catholic and Greek Orthodox churches became irreparable.

The Crusades also intensified the cultural divide between Christians and Muslims. The militant rhetoric and propaganda of holy war rendered any lasting peace between Christians and Muslims inconceivable. Chronicles from both sides are filled with grotesque caricatures and misconceptions of each other's beliefs

The basic outline of the T-O map reappears in this small but detailed map from a psalter (prayer book) dating to about 1260. Jerusalem is located at the center of the world. At the top in the east, the Garden of Eden is indicated by a circle framing Adam, Eve, and the Tree of Knowledge. An image of Jesus Christ (holding a T-O globe in his left hand) stands above the Garden of Eden. Many places noted on the map refer to popular stories taken from the Bible and the legends of Alexander the Great. On the right edge of the world are figures representing monstrous and fabulous races such as one-legged or headless peoples whom Alexander was said to have encountered in his journey through Asia. The combination of biblical lore and Alexandrian myths portrayed Asia as the land of the future paradise but also as a forbidding, barbaric wilderness beyond the pale of civilization.

Examining the Evidence

1. What can the psalter map tell us about the limits of Europeans' actual geographic knowledge in the age of the Crusades?

2. How do the purpose and features of this map differ from those of a road map today?

Psalter Mappamundi, c. 1260

and customs. In reality, not all interactions between Christians and Muslims were hostile, as the testimony of Usamah ibn Minqidh, who we met at the beginning of this chapter, reveals. The Muslim pilgrim Ibn Jubayr, passing through the Crusader-ruled territories in 1184, observed that "the soldiers occupied themselves in their war, while the people remained at peace."[3] Plentiful trade flowed across the battle lines, and the Crusaders acquired an appetite for sugar (previously unknown in Europe) and the spices of Asia that would later prompt Portuguese seafarers to seek a new maritime route to Asia. However, the increased contact between Muslims and Christians that resulted from the Crusades only intensified religious and ethnic differences.

Papal Supremacy and the Christian People

The reorientation of the Crusades toward political aims originated within the papacy itself. Pope Innocent III (r. 1198–1216) tried to capitalize on the crusading spirit to strengthen papal authority both within the church and over secular society. The Crusaders had rallied together under the sign of the cross, the common symbol of all Christians regardless of national origins and allegiances. Innocent likewise invoked the Crusaders' language of universal brotherhood to redefine Christendom as an empire of "the Christian people" subject to the authority of the pope in both spiritual and worldly matters (see Seeing the Past: The Mappaemundi of Latin Christendom). Legislation enacted at Innocent's instigation created a more centralized Christian church and deprived bishops of much of their independence. Innocent also established a judicial body, the **Inquisition**, to investigate and punish anyone who challenged the pope's supreme authority. The Inquisition expanded, with the eager support of lay monarchs, into a broad-based campaign directed against heretics and nonbelievers alike. Thus, it became, in many ways, an internal Crusade.

Jewish communities in Christian Europe were early targets of Innocent's Inquisition. Many Christians regarded Jews as an alien race whose presence corrupted Christian society. As we have seen in Chapter 11, Jews were often vilified because of their prominence in trades such as moneylending, which tainted them with the stigma of usury. Innocent's new orders, which compelled Jews to wear distinctive forms of dress such as special badges or hats, were intended to reinforce existing laws forbidding marriage between Christians and Jews.

Efforts to impose religious conformity on Latin Christendom received further impetus from the formation of new religious orders, most notably the Franciscans and the Dominicans. Like the Cistercians, these new orders dedicated themselves to the principles of poverty and evangelism. Unlike the Cistercians, who remained confined to their monasteries, Franciscan and Dominican friars traveled widely, preaching to the populace and depending on almsgiving for their needs. The new preaching orders sought to carry out the church's mission to regulate and reform the behavior of lay believers. The Franciscan and Dominican orders were also in the forefront of campaigns to convert the non-Christian peoples of eastern Europe.

Inquisition A system of courts and investigators set up by the Roman papacy in the early thirteenth century to identify and punish heretics.

During the thirteenth century the precarious position of the Christian outposts along the coast of Palestine and Syria became dire. The rise of a powerful Islamic state under the Mamluk dynasty in Egypt (discussed later in this chapter) after 1250 sealed the fate of the crusading movement. In 1291 the Mamluks captured Acre, the last Christian stronghold in Palestine.

The Making of Christian Europe 1100–1350

⬊ **FOCUS** How did the efforts to establish Christianity in Spain and eastern Europe compare with the Crusaders' quest to recover Jerusalem?

Despite their ultimate failure, the Crusades had profound consequences for the course of European history. Among the most important was their role in consolidating the social and cultural identity of Latin Christendom. Even as the movement to retake the Holy Land from the Muslim occupiers foundered and sank, the crusading spirit provided the crucial momentum for Christendom to expand into northern and eastern Europe.

The crusading ideal also encouraged assimilation of the warrior class into the monastic culture of the Christian church. This merger produced the culture of **chivalry**—the knightly class's code of behavior, which stressed honor, piety, and devotion to one's ideals. The code of chivalry confirmed the moral as well as social superiority of the warrior nobility. Knights played at least as great a role as clerical evangelists in spreading Christian culture.

In the thirteenth and fourteenth centuries Christian kings and knights conquered and colonized territories from Spain in the west to the Baltic Sea in the east. Europe took form out of the processes of military conquest, migration, and cultural colonization that would later also characterize European expansion into the Americas.

The Reconquest of Spain 1085–1248

Under its Umayyad dynasty (756–1030), Muslim-ruled Spain had enjoyed relative religious peace. Although religious toleration was often compromised by sharp differences in social standing among Muslims, Jews, and Christians, the Umayyad rulers fostered a tradition of mutual accommodation. Yet the subjection of Christian peoples to Muslim rulers in Spain, as in Palestine and Syria, became increasingly intolerable to Christian rulers and church leaders alike. At the same

chivalry The code of behavior, stressing honor, piety, and devotion to one's ideals, of the knightly class of medieval Europe.

time that he issued his summons for the First Crusade, Pope Urban II urged Christian rulers in northern Spain to take up arms against their Muslim neighbors. The *Reconquista* ("reconquest" of Spain) thus became joined to the crusading movement.

In its heyday the Umayyad caliphate in Spain was the most urbanized and commercially developed part of Europe. In the early eleventh century, however, the Umayyad caliphate disintegrated and splintered into dozens of feuding city-states. The conquest of Toledo, Spain's second-largest city, by King Alfonso of Castile in 1085 lifted Castile into a preeminent position among Spain's Christian kingdoms. The Muslim emirs turned to the Almoravid (al-moe-RAH-vid) rulers of North Africa for protection. The Almoravids, fervently devoted to the cause of holy war, halted the Christian advance but imposed their own authoritarian rule over the Muslim territories in Spain.

The Almohad (AHL-moh-had) dynasty, which supplanted the Almoravids in North Africa and Spain in 1148, was even more fiercely opposed to the Umayyad heritage of tolerance toward non-Muslims. Almohad policies, which included the expulsion of all Jews who refused to convert to Islam, were highly unpopular. Despite a major victory over Castile in 1195, the Almohads were unable to withstand intensified Christian efforts to "reconquer" Spain. Between 1236 and 1248 the major Muslim cities of Spain—Córdoba, Valencia, and finally Seville—fell to Castile and its allies, leaving Granada as the sole remaining Muslim state in Spain.

After capturing Toledo in 1085, the kings of Castile made the city their capital. Toledo was renowned as a cultural and intellectual crossroads and, despite the rhetoric of holy war, the Castilian kings preserved Toledo's multicultural character. But Toledo's intellectual and religious tolerance steadily eroded as the Reconquista advanced. At first, the Christian kings allowed their Muslim subjects, known as Mudejars (mu-DAY-hahr), to own property, worship in mosques, and be judged by Islamic law before *qadi* jurists. After 1300, however, judicial autonomy eroded, and Mudejars accused of crimes against Christians were tried in Christian courts under Christian law. Christian rulers also converted the great mosques of Córdoba, Seville, and Toledo into Christian cathedrals.

The place of Jews also deteriorated in a European world that had come to define itself as the realm of "the Christian people." Attacks on Jews escalated dramatically with the onset of the

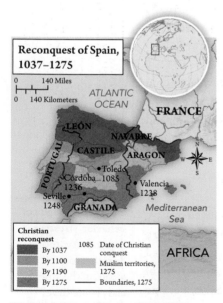

≡ **Reconquest of Spain, 1037–1275**

Crusades. In 1190, as we have seen, Jews were expelled from England. In the 1230s, when the Inquisition began a deliberate persecution of Jews, many fled from France and Germany to seek sanctuary in Spain. Yet in Spain, too, Jews occupied an insecure position. In the fourteenth century, as in other parts of Latin Christendom, violence against Jews swept Spain. In 1391 wholesale massacres of Jews in Spain's major cities dealt a catastrophic blow to Jewish communities from which they never recovered. Rigid intolerance had replaced the vibrant multiculturalism of Umayyad Spain.

Christianizing Eastern Europe 1150–1350

In 1145 Pope Eugene III invited the knights of Christendom to launch a crusade against the non-Christian populations of northern and eastern Europe—collectively referred to as the Wends. The pope acted at the instigation of his teacher Bernard of Clairvaux (d. 1153), the Cistercian abbot who had put Peter Abelard on trial for heresy. Bernard had urged Christian knights to take up arms against pagan peoples everywhere (see Reading the Past: Bernard of Clairvaux's Summons to the Wendish Crusade). In the three centuries following the Wendish Crusade of 1147, Latin Christendom steadily encroached upon the Baltic and Slavic lands through a combination of conquest and colonization.

The fissure that split the Latin and Greek Christian churches also ran through eastern Europe. In the tenth and eleventh centuries, the rulers of Poland and Hungary had chosen to join the Roman church, but Christian converts in the Balkans such as the Serbs and Bulgars as well as the Rus princes had adopted the Greek Orthodoxy of Constantinople. In subsequent centuries, Latin and Greek clerics waged war against each other for the allegiance of the eastern European peoples along a frontier stretching from the Adriatic Sea to the Baltic Sea (see Map 13.2).

Freebooting nobles enthusiastically joined the Wendish Crusade and were the first to profit from its military successes. Small groups of knights subjugated the Wendish peoples in piecemeal fashion, built stoutly fortified castles to control them, and recruited settlers from France and the Low Countries to clear the forests for cultivation. The colonists were accompanied by missionaries, led by the Cistercians, seeking to "civilize" the Slavs by converting them to Latin Christianity.

Many Slavic princes opted to embrace Latin Christianity and to open their lands to settlement by immigrants from the west. To attract settlers, local lords usually exempted homesteaders from feudal obligations and the legal condition of serfdom. For example, a charter issued by the king of Hungary in 1247 to new settlers in a sparsely populated corner of his realm declared, "Let the men gathered

READING THE PAST

Bernard of Clairvaux's Summons to the Wendish Crusade

In March 1147, the Cisterican abbot Bernard of Clairvaux came to Frankfurt to promote what would become the Second Crusade. Few German knights expressed enthusiasm for a new crusade in the Holy Land, but they clamored to attack their pagan Slavic and Baltic neighbors in eastern Europe. Eager to capitalize on this fervor, Bernard secured the pope's permission to launch the part of the Second Crusade known as the Wendish Crusade. In this letter—addressed "to all Christians"—Bernard seeks to drum up recruits.

> [Satan] has raised up evil seed, wicked pagan sons, whom, if I may say so, the might of Christendom has endured too long, shutting its eyes to those who with evil intent lie in wait, without crushing their poisoned heads under its heel. . . . Because the Lord has committed to our insignificance the preaching of this crusade, we make known to you that at a council of the king, bishops, and princes who had come together at Frankfurt, the might of Christians was armed against them, and that for the complete wiping out or, at any rate, the conversion of these peoples, they have put on the Cross, the sign of our salvation. And we by virtue of our authority promised them the same spiritual privileges as those enjoy who set out toward Jerusalem. Many took the Cross on the spot, the rest we encouraged to do so, so that all Christians who have not yet taken the Cross for Jerusalem may know that they will obtain the same spiritual privileges by undertaking this expedition, if they do so according to the advice of the bishops and princes. We utterly forbid that for any reason whatsoever a truce should be made with these peoples, either for the sake of money or for the sake of tribute, until such a time as, by God's help, they shall be either converted or erased. . . . The uniform of this army, in clothes, in arms, and in all else, will be the same as the uniform of the other, for it is fortified with the same privileges.

Source: Bernard of Clairvaux, *Letters*, trans. Bruno Scott James (London: Burns, Oates, 1953), 466–68.

Examining the Evidence

1. In Bernard's view, who is the real enemy of the Christian faithful?

2. Why might German knights have preferred to join a crusade against the pagan Wends rather than the Muslims threatening Jerusalem?

Expansion of Christianity in Eastern Europe, c. 1300

Latin Christendom
Orthodox Christendom
Islamic lands
Pagan
● Newly founded German town
■ Member of the Hanseatic League

0   140 Miles
0   140 Kilometers

≡ **MAP 13.2** **Expansion of Christianity in Eastern Europe, c. 1300** The Crusader movement spearheaded the expansion of Latin Christendom into eastern Europe and the Baltic Sea region. In the wake of the Wendish Crusade of 1147, the Cistercians and other religious orders zealously pursued the conversion of pagan peoples to Latin Christianity.

there, of whatever status or language, live under one and the same liberty."[4] Perhaps as many as 200,000 immigrants, mostly from Germany and Flanders, had already settled east of the Elbe River by 1200.

Local princes, both conquerors and natives, also promoted the founding of cities. To attract merchants and artisans, princes granted city charters that guaranteed considerable political and economic autonomy. In the thirteenth century, the loose confederation of independent Christian trading colonies ringing the Baltic known as the Hanseatic League (discussed in Chapter 11) rapidly expanded (see again Map 13.2). In addition to regulating trade, the Hanseatic League provided a counterweight against rulers seeking to extort heavy customs duties from traders passing through their lands. Throughout eastern Europe, cities and towns became oases of foreign colonists who differed sharply from the rural inhabitants in language and culture as well as wealth and status.

≣ **Peasants Receiving Land Title** New peasant settlers brought fresh labor and superior farming technology that transformed the landscape of eastern Europe. This illustration from the *Sachsenspiegel* (c. 1220), the first major law code written in German rather than Latin, shows homesteaders receiving titles of ownership to the lands they cleared for farming.

By 1350, Latin Christianity was firmly implanted in all parts of Europe except the Orthodox Balkan peninsula. But the rise of strong national monarchies had thwarted the Roman popes' ambitions to create a unified Christendom under papal rule. Kings and princes increased their demands for tax revenue, extended the jurisdiction of royal courts, and convened assemblies (known as "parliaments") of leading nobles, clergy, and townsmen to rally support for their policies. Europe's patchwork of feudal domains and independent cities began to merge into unified national states, especially in England and France. The French philosopher Nicole Oresme (c. 1323–1382) expressed the spirit of his age when he rejected a "universal monarchy" as "neither just nor expedient."[5] Instead, Oresme argued, practical necessity dictated that separate kingdoms, each with its own laws and customs, should exercise sovereign power over their own people.

Neither did the Muslims' success in repelling the Crusaders restore unity to the Islamic world. After enduring for sixty years, the Ayyubid dynasty founded by Saladin was overthrown in 1250 by Turkish slave soldiers, the Mamluks. At that same time, the Islamic world faced a new challenge, the Mongol invasions, that would have a far more lasting impact on the development of Islamic societies than did the Crusades.

The Mongol World Empire 1100–1368

⬐ **FOCUS** How did the organization of Mongol society and government change from the time of Chinggis Khan to that of his grandson Qubilai, the ruler of China?

The era of Mongol domination marked a watershed in world history. Although the Mongols drew on long-standing traditions of tribal confederation, warfare, and tribute extraction, the Mongol Empire was unprecedented in its scope and influence. Historians give much of the credit for the Mongols' swift military triumphs and political cohesion to the charismatic authority of the empire builder Chinggis Khan. Later generations of Mongol rulers built upon Chinggis's legacy, seeking to adapt steppe traditions of rulership to the complex demands of governing agrarian societies.

Despite the brutality and violence of the Mongol conquests, the Mongol Empire fostered far-reaching economic and cultural exchanges. The Mongols encouraged the free movement of merchants throughout their domains and embraced religious and intellectual diversity. Wherever they went the Mongols sought to impose their own political, social, and military institutions, but the Mongol conquerors of Iran and central Asia adopted the Islamic religion of their subjects. The Mongols transformed the world—and were themselves transformed by the peoples they subjugated.

Rise of the Mongols

In the several centuries before the rise of the Mongols, the dynamics of state formation in the Eurasian steppe underwent dramatic transformation. In the early tenth century, the Khitans (kee-THANS) of eastern Mongolia annexed Chinese territories around modern Beijing and established a Chinese-style dynasty, Liao (lee-OW) (937–1125). The new dynasty was a hybrid state that incorporated elements of Chinese bureaucratic governance while retaining the militarized tribal social structure and nomadic lifestyle of the steppe.

≡ **Liao and Jin States**

In the 1120s the Jurchens, a seminomadic group from northern Manchuria, overran the Liao and the rest of northern China and founded their own state of Jin (1115–1234). The Jin state largely retained the dual administrative structure of the Liao. But in contrast to the Liao, the Jin conquerors were dwarfed by the enormous Chinese population under their rule. The Jin rulers struggled to preserve their cultural identity in the face of overwhelming pressures to assimilate to Chinese ways.

Temujin (teh-MU-jihn) (c. 1162–1227), the future Chinggis Khan, was born into one of the numerous tribes living in eastern Mongolia, on the margins of the Jin realm. Tribal affiliations were unstable, however, and at that time the "Mongol people" was not a clearly defined group. The pastoral livelihood of the steppe nomads was vulnerable to catastrophic disruptions, such as prolonged drought, severe winters, and animal diseases. Scarcity of resources often provoked violent conflict among neighboring tribes. The constant violence of the steppe produced permanently militarized societies. For most of the male population, warfare became a regular profession, and women took charge of tending herds and other activities usually reserved for men in the premodern world (see Lives and Livelihoods: Mongol Women in the Household Economy and Public Life).

Orphaned at age nine and abandoned by his father's tribe, Temujin gained a following through his valor and success as a warrior. Building on this reputation, he proved extraordinarily adept at constructing alliances among chiefs and transforming tribal coalitions into disciplined military units. By 1206 Temujin had forged a confederation that unified most of the tribes of Mongolia, which recognized him as Chinggis (meaning "oceanic"), the **Great Khan**, the universal ruler of the steppe peoples.

Creation and Division of the Mongol Empire 1206–1259

Maintaining unity among the fractious coalition of tribal leaders required a steady stream of booty in the form of gold, silk, slaves, and horses. Thus, once installed as Great Khan, Chinggis led his army in campaigns of plunder and conquest. In 1218, Chinggis's attention turned toward the west after the Turkish shah of Khwarazam (in Transoxiana) massacred a caravan of Muslim merchants traveling under the Mongol khan's protection. Enraged, Chinggis laid waste to Samarkand, the shah's capital, and other cities in Transoxiana and eastern Iran in what was perhaps the most violent of the Mongol campaigns. After deposing the Khwarazam shah, Chinggis returned to the east and renewed his campaign to conquer China.

By the time of Chinggis's death in 1227, Mongol conquests stretched from eastern Iran to Manchuria (see Map 13.3). Up to this point, the impact of the Mongol invasions had been almost wholly catastrophic. Solely interested in plunder,

Great Khan "Lord of the steppe"; the Great Khan of the Mongols was chosen by a council of Mongol chiefs.

Chinggis had shown little taste for the daunting task of ruling the peoples he vanquished.

Throughout Central Asian history the death of a khan almost always provoked a violent succession crisis. But Chinggis's charisma sufficed to ensure an orderly transition of power. Before he died, Chinggis parceled out the Mongol territories among his four sons or their descendants, and he designated his third son Ogodei to succeed him as Great Khan.

The Mongol state under Chinggis Khan was a throwback to the Turkish-Uighur practice of allowing conquered peoples to maintain their autonomy in exchange for tribute. Ogodei, in contrast, began to adopt features of the Liao-Jin system of dual administration under the direction of a Khitan statesman and former Jin official, Yelu Chucai. Under Ogodei's leadership the Mongols steadily expanded their dominions westward into Russia, and they completed the conquest of the Jin. Mongol armies had invaded Hungary and Poland and were threatening to press deeper into Europe when Ogodei's death in 1241 halted their advance.

After Ogodei's nephew Mongke was elected Great Khan in 1251, he radically altered Chinggis's original allocation of Mongol territories, assigning the richest lands, China and Iran, to his brothers Qubilai and Hulegu. Mongke's dispensation outraged the other descendants of Chinggis. By the end of his reign, the Mongol realm had broken into four independent and often hostile khanates (see again Map 13.3).

Qubilai Khan and the Yuan Empire in China 1260–1368

The death of Mongke in 1259 sparked another succession crisis. After four years of bitter struggle Mongke's brother Qubilai secured his claim as Great Khan. Qubilai devoted his energies to completing the conquest of China. In 1271 he adopted the Chinese-style dynastic name Yuan and moved the Great Khan's capital from Mongolia to China, where he built a massive city, Dadu, at the former Jin capital of Zhongdu (modern Beijing). Five years later, Mongol armies captured the Southern Song capital of Hangzhou, and by 1279 Chinese resistance to Mongol rule had ceased. The Yuan Empire (1271–1368) would last only about one hundred years, but for the first time all of China had fallen under foreign rule.

Qubilai envisioned himself not merely as first among the Mongol princes but also as an exalted "Son of Heaven" in the style of the Chinese emperors. Building on the precedents of the Liao and Jin states, Qubilai created a highly centralized administration designed to extract the maximum revenue from China's land, people, and commerce. The Venetian merchant Marco Polo (1254–1324), astonished at the splendor of the Great Khan's capital, proclaimed that Qubilai was "the

≡ **MAP 13.3** **Mongol Conquests and Division** Chinggis Khan—far more interested in amassing booty than governing an empire—divided the territories conquered by the Mongol armies among his four sons and named his third son Ogodei as his successor as Great Khan. Disputes over succession created hostility among Chinggis's descendants. By 1260 the Mongol Empire had split into four independent—and sometimes rival—khanates.

most powerful man in men, land, and treasure that the world has ever seen, or who ever will be, from Adam our first father until now."[6]

tax farming The assignment of tax collection powers to private individuals or groups in exchange for fixed payments to the state.

Although Qubilai was a conscientious and diligent ruler, his successors gave little attention to the tasks of maintaining the infrastructure of the agrarian economy or protecting people's welfare. Instead, they relied on a system of **tax farming** that delegated tax collection privileges to private intermediaries, mostly Muslim merchants. Many of these tax farmers abused their authority and demanded exorbitant payments from an increasingly disgruntled agrarian population. At the same time, however, the Mongols strongly encouraged commerce, and international trade

≡ **The Khan's Paper Money** Marco Polo's *Description of the World*, completed in 1298, became an international "best-seller"; over 140 manuscripts in Latin and numerous vernacular languages survive. This illustration from a French version dated 1410 shows merchants exchanging goods for Mongol paper money (in boxes) under Qubilai's watchful eye. Most European readers regarded Polo's reports of the great riches of Qubilai's realm, including using mere paper as money, as outlandish fabrications—hence the common Italian name for his book, *Il milione* ("The million" [falsehoods]). Livre des merveilles du monde (Bibliothèque nationale de France, Ms. fr. 2810, fol. 45)

flourished. The Mongols created a vast network of post stations and issued passports to merchants to ensure safe passage throughout the Mongol realm. Marco Polo reported that the paper money issued by Qubilai is "distributed through all the provinces, kingdoms, and lands under his rule; and no one dares refuse them, in pain of losing his life. . . . All the people and populated regions under his rule willingly take these notes in payment, because with them they'll go and make all their payments for merchandise, pearls, precious stones, gold and silver."[7]

LIVES AND LIVELIHOODS

Mongol Women in the Household Economy and Public Life

The prominent roles of women in the life of the pastoral nomads of the Eurasian steppe contrasted starkly with women's reclusive place in most settled societies. Under Chinggis Khan's permanently militarized society, nearly all adult men had to embark on lengthy campaigns of conquest far from home. The women left behind were compelled to shoulder even the most arduous tasks. Kinship and gender relations among the pastoral nomads also differed in many ways from the practices of settled societies. Mongol women remained subservient to their husbands, but royal and noble women participated vigorously in public life and political affairs.

European travelers to the Mongol domains expressed surprise at women's key roles in the pastoral economy. John of Plano Carpini, a papal envoy dispatched to the Mongol court in 1245, claimed that productive labor fell entirely to the Mongol women:

> The men do not make anything at all, with the exception of arrows, and they sometimes tend the flocks, but they hunt and practice archery. . . . Their women make everything, including leather garments, tunics, shoes, and everything made of leather. They also drive the carts and repair them. They load the camels, and in all tasks they are very swift and energetic. All the women wear breeches, and some of them shoot like the men.[1]

Despite women's vital contributions to the family's economic welfare, however, Mongol society was based on a patrilineal system of inheritance in which men controlled property and wealth. Mongol women had no property of their own. Women who lacked the protection of a husband often found themselves abandoned and destitute. Such was the fate that befell Chinggis's mother Hoelun, whose husband was murdered when Chinggis was nine years old. Deserted by her husband's kinfolk, Hoelun doggedly raised her sons on her own, at times forced to forage for roots and berries to survive.

Nonetheless, royal Mongol women were outspoken figures whose voices carried much weight in court deliberations. When Ogodei died in 1241, his widow ruled over the Mongol confederation for five years before ceding power to one of her sons. Qubilai's mother, Sorqaqtani-Beki, likewise played a decisive role in the history of the Mongol Empire. The pastoral nomads of the Eurasian steppe commonly protected widows by remarrying them to younger male relatives of their deceased husbands, and when Sorqaqtani-Beki's husband Tolui died in 1232, Ogodei offered to marry her to one of his sons. She firmly declined Ogodei's proposal and instead demanded a fiefdom to provide for her upkeep. Ogodei reluctantly granted her a fief of 80,000 households in northern China, which Sorqaqtani-Beki insisted on governing herself. In keeping with the policies of Ogodei's minister Yelu Chucai, Sorqaqtani-Beki instituted a Chinese-style civil administration and engaged Chinese scholars to tutor her sons. Qubilai's upbringing thus turned his attention, and the direction of the Mongol Empire, away from the Mongols' steppe homeland and toward China.

Sorqaqtani-Beki proved to be a shrewd politician who earned wide admiration among Mongols and foreigners alike. In 1251, her popularity and political agility paid off when she succeeded in elevating her son Mongke to the position of Great Khan, displacing the lineage of Ogodei. Sorqaqtani-Beki died the following year, but the supreme authority of the Great Khans remained with her sons, including Qubilai, the future emperor of China.

1. Christopher Dawson, ed., *Mission to Asia: Narratives and Letters of the Franciscan Missionaries of Mongolia and China in the Thirteenth and Fourteenth Centuries* (New York: Harper & Row, 1966), 18.

≡ **Mongol Empress Chabi** Mongol leaders often had multiple wives, each of whom took charge of her own household. Chabi, the second of Qubilai's four wives, became one of the most powerful figures at the Mongol court after Qubilai's election as Great Khan. Her ambition to become empress of China was a driving force behind Qubilai's conquest of the Southern Song.

Questions to Consider

1. How did the division of household work in pastoral societies such as the Mongols differ from that found among settled farming peoples?

2. How might the role of women in the Mongol household economy explain the power they wielded in tribal affairs?

For Further Information:

Lane, George. *Daily Life in the Mongol Empire.* Westwood, CT: Greenwood Press, 2006.

Rossabi, Morris. *Khubilai Khan: His Life and Times.* Berkeley: University of California Press, 1988.

The Yuan Empire maintained the Central Asian tradition of a social structure based on tribal loyalties. Political, legal, and economic privileges rested on an ethnic hierarchy that favored the Mongol tribes and the "affiliated peoples"—non-Chinese who had served the Mongols since the time of Chinggis, including Turks, Tibetans, Persians, and above all Uighurs. The Yuan state largely drew its administrators from merchants and scholars among the "affiliated peoples." The Mongols forbade Chinese to possess firearms, ride horses, learn the Mongol language, or intermarry with Mongols.

Qubilai aspired to be a truly universal monarch. In his quest for an appropriate model, he turned to Phags-pa (pak-pa) Lama (1235–1280), the spiritual leader of the Saskya sect of Tibetan Buddhism. As a transnational faith, Buddhism helped unite the diverse peoples of eastern Asia under Mongol rule. At the same time, Qubilai's support enabled Phags-pa and the Saskya Lamas to gain supreme authority over Tibet, a position they would hold until the rival lineage of Dalai Lamas displaced them in the sixteenth century.

Still, the Mongols accorded full tolerance to all religions. Muslim, Jewish, and Nestorian Christian communities flourished in China under Mongol rule. John of Montecorvino, a Franciscan missionary dispatched by the pope, arrived at the Yuan capital in 1294. John erected a church near the khan's palace and by his own estimate attracted 6,000 converts—mostly non-Chinese—to Christianity. Pleased with John's reports of the progress of his missionary work, in 1308 the pope consecrated him as the first Latin bishop of Beijing.

Under Qubilai's leadership the Mongol Empire in China departed from the practices of the early steppe empires, which relied on plunder and extraction of tribute from settled societies. Instead the Yuan state, like its Liao and Jin predecessors, developed institutions for imposing direct rule on its Chinese subjects, even if it did not penetrate local society to the extent that native Chinese empires had. At the same time, the Mongols in China turned their backs on their steppe homeland. By 1300 the Yuan emperors were raised exclusively within the confines of the capital at Dadu and had largely severed their connections with the independent Mongol khanates in central and western Asia.

The Mongol Khanates and the Islamic World 1240–1350

◥ **FOCUS** In what respects did the Turkish Islamic states of the Mamluks and Ottomans pursue policies similar to those of the Mongol regimes in Iran and Russia?

In 1253 the Great Khan Mongke assigned his brother Hulegu (HE-luh-gee) responsibility for completing the Mongol conquest of Iran and Mesopotamia. In 1258 Baghdad fell to Hulegu's army. In their hunger for booty, the Mongol victors utterly destroyed the city of Baghdad, the official capital of Islam. By Hulegu's own estimate, 200,000 people perished. Survivors of the Mongol conquest fled to Cairo, where the Mamluk (MAM-luke) sultanate, a regime of military slave origins, had overthrown the dynasty of Saladin and was consolidating its power over Egypt and Syria. The Mamluks became the new political leaders of the Islamic world, rallying their fellow Muslims to the cause of holy war against the Mongol onslaught.

The conquest of Baghdad was the last great campaign conducted jointly by the Mongol princes. As we have seen, by the time of Qubilai's succession in 1263 as Great Khan, rivalry among Chinggis's heirs had fractured the Mongol Empire into four independent khanates: the Golden Horde along the frontiers of Russia; the Chagadai (shah-gah-TY) khanate in Central Asia; the Ilkhanate based in Iran; and the khanate of the Great Khan in China (see again Map 13.3).

Mongol Rule in Iran and Mesopotamia

After conquering Iran and Mesopotamia, Hulegu's army suffered a decisive defeat at the hands of the Mamluks in Palestine in 1260 and withdrew. At around this time Hulegu adopted the Turkish title of *Ilkhan* ("subordinate khan"), implying submission to his brother Qubilai, the Great Khan. Hulegu and his successors as Ilkhan (il-con) also made diplomatic overtures to the Christian monarchs of Europe with the goal of forming an alliance against their common enemy, the Mamluks, to no avail.

The Ilkhans ruled over their domains from a series of seasonal capitals in Azerbaijan, a region in the northwestern corner of Iran where good pastureland was plentiful. The Ilkhans followed the nomadic practice of moving their camps in rhythm with the seasonal migrations of their herds. The Mongol conquests of Iran and Mesopotamia had caused immense environmental and economic harm. Abandonment of farmlands and the deterioration of irrigation systems sharply curtailed agricultural production. Much land was turned over to pasture or reverted to desert.

As in China, Mongols composed a tiny minority of the Ilkhanate's population. Like the Yuan state, the Ilkhanate initially recruited its administrative personnel from foreigners and members of minority groups. Christian communities, notably the Nestorians and Armenians, had been quick to side with the Mongol invaders against their Muslim overlords. But the Mongols in Iran increasingly turned toward the faith of the Muslim majority. The proselytizing efforts of Sufi sheikhs attracted many converts, especially among the Mongol and Turkish horsemen who were the backbone of the Ilkhanate's military strength. By the late thirteenth century, escalating religious tensions and the familiar pattern of violent succession disputes among the Mongol leaders threatened to tear apart the Ilkhan state. The ascension of Ghazan (haz-ZAHN) (r. 1295–1304) as Ilkhan revived the Ilkhanate and marked a decisive turning point in Mongol rule in Iran.

A convert to Islam, Ghazan took pains to show his devotion to the faith of the great majority of his subjects. Ghazan reduced Christians and Jews to subordinate status and banished Buddhist monks from the Ilkhan realm. He also placed the Ilkhanate government on sounder footing by reforming the fiscal system, investing greater resources in agriculture, instituting a new currency, and reducing taxes.

≡ **Mongol Siege of Baghdad** The Mongol conquest of Baghdad in 1258 ended the caliphate, the main political institution of the Islamic world since the death of Muhammad. In this illustration of the siege, a group of Mongols at lower right beat a flat drum; the archers and soldiers are all in Persian dress. At upper left the last Abbasid caliph makes a futile attempt to escape by boat.

Ghazan broke with the practice of seasonal migration and constructed a permanent capital at Tabriz appointed with palaces, mosques, Sufi lodges, a grand mausoleum for himself, and baths and caravanserais to accommodate traveling merchants.

Rashid al-Din (ra-SHEED al-DEEN) (1247–1318), a Jewish doctor who converted to Islam, served as chief minister and architect of Ghazan's program of reform. Rashid al-Din also carefully embellished Ghazan's image as ruler, forging a new ideology of sovereignty that portrayed Ghazan as a devout Muslim, a Persian philosopher-king, and a second Alexander the Great. Under Rashid al-Din's direction, court scholars compiled the *Compendium of Chronicles*, a history of the world that glorified the Mongol rulers as rightful heirs to the legacies of the Persian kings and the Abbasid caliphate.

The Ilkhans became great patrons of arts and letters. Rashid al-Din boasted that "in these days when, thank God, all corners of the earth are under our rule and that of Chinggis Khan's illustrious family, philosophers, astronomers, scholars, and historians of all religions and nations—Cathay and Machin (north and south

China), India and Kashmir, Tibetans, Uighurs, and other nations of Turks, Arabs, and Franks—are gathered in droves at our glorious court."[8] Manuscript painting, luxury silks, architectural decoration, metalworking, and ceramics all reflected the impact of new aesthetic ideas and motifs, with Chinese influences especially prominent.

Under Rashid al-Din's stewardship, the ideological basis of the Ilkhanate shifted away from descent from Chinggis Khan and toward the role of royal protector of the Islamic faith. In the early fourteenth century, a renewal of cordial relations among the leaders of the four Mongol khanates eased the passage of caravans and travelers across the Silk Road. Conversion to Islam did not alienate their fellow Mongols, but neither did it repair the breach with the Mamluk regime.

Ghazan's reforms failed to ensure the long-term stability of the Ilkhanate regime, however. Ghazan's attempt to recast the Ilkhanate as a monarchy in the tradition of the Islamic caliphate ran into strong opposition among Mongol leaders accustomed to tribal independence and shared sovereignty. The reign of Ghazan's nephew Abu Said (r. 1316–1335) was wracked by factional conflicts that sapped the Ilkhan leadership and cost Rashid al-Din his life. After Abu Said died without an heir in 1335, the Ilkhanate's authority steadily disintegrated. In 1353 members of a messianic Shi'a sect murdered the last Ilkhan.

The Golden Horde and the Rise of Muscovy

The Golden Horde in Central Asia and Russia proved more durable than the Ilkhanate. In 1237 a Mongol army led by Chinggis's grandson Batu conquered the Volga River Valley and sacked the main cities of the Bulgars and the Rus princes, including the fortified outpost of Moscow. In 1240 Kiev succumbed to a Mongol siege, and the Mongol armies quickly pushed westward into Poland and Hungary, prompting the Roman pope to declare a crusade against this new menace. But feuding among the Mongol princes after the death of Ogodei in 1241 halted the Mongol advance into Europe. Instead, Batu created an independent Mongol realm known as the Golden Horde, with its capital at Sarai in the lower Volga River Valley (see again Map 13.3). Batu's successor, Berke (r. 1257–1267), was the first of the Mongol khans to convert to Islam.

In the Rus lands, as in Iran, the Mongols instituted a form of indirect governance that relied on local rulers as intermediaries. The Mongols required that the Rus princes conduct censuses, raise taxes to support the Mongol army, maintain post stations, and personally appear at the khan's court at Sarai to offer tribute. The Golden Horde and the Ilkhanate both adopted the Persian-Turkish institution of *iqta*, land grants awarded to military officers to feed and supply the soldiers under their command. The administrative structure of the Golden Horde and its system of military estates were subsequently adopted by the expanding Muscovy state in the fifteenth century.

As elsewhere in the Mongol realms, the khans of the Golden Horde strongly encouraged commerce, from which the Rus princes and the Christian church benefited enormously. Moscow flourished as the capital of the fur trade. As a result of this commercial prosperity, the first Grand Prince of Muscovy, Ivan I (r. 1328–1340), nicknamed "Moneybags" by his subjects, was able to build the stone churches that became the heart of the Kremlin, the seat of future Russian governments. The wealth accumulated by the Orthodox Christian clerics and the protection they enjoyed under the traditional Mongol respect for religious institutions strengthened the church's position in Rus society and fostered greater independence from the Byzantine patriarch.

Despite its commercial expansion, Rus was marginal to the khanate, which focused its attention instead on controlling the steppe pasturelands and trade routes. In contrast to Qubilai's Yuan dynasty, the Golden Horde retained its connections to the steppe and the culture of pastoral nomadism. Nor did conversion to Islam bring about substantial changes in the Golden Horde culture comparable to those that occurred in the Ilkhanate. Not until the 1310s did the Golden Horde adopt Islam as its official religion. Although conversion to Islam pulled the Mongols of the Golden Horde more firmly into the cultural world of their Turkish subjects (and away from that of Christian Rus), it did not lead them to abandon their pastoral way of life.

Retrenchment in the Islamic World: The Mamluk and Ottoman States

The fall and destruction of Baghdad in 1258 delivered a devastating blow to the Islamic world. The sack of Baghdad and the execution of the Abbasid caliph left the Islamic confederacy leaderless and disorganized. Out of this political crisis emerged two new dynastic regimes, the Mamluks in Egypt and the Ottomans in Anatolia (modern Turkey). Together, these two dynasties restored order to the Islamic lands of the eastern Mediterranean and halted further Mongol advances (see Map 13.4). Both the Mamluks and the Ottomans were warrior states, but they owed their political longevity to their ability to adapt to the requirements of governing large settled populations. The Mamluk sultanate ruled from 1250 to 1517, nearly three times as long as the Yuan dynasty. The Ottoman Empire would prove to be one of the most enduring in world history, stretching from its origins in the late thirteenth century to final eclipse in 1923, following World War I.

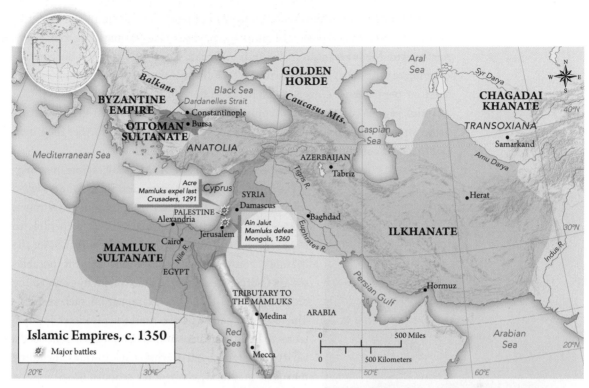

≡ **MAP 13.4   Islamic Empires, c. 1350**   The Mongol leader Hulegu captured Baghdad in 1258, but his attempt to conquer Syria and Palestine was repelled by the Mamluk sultanate based in Egypt. Later rulers of the Ilkhanate founded by Hulegu converted to Islam, as did the Mongol chiefs of the Golden Horde in Russia. The disruptions caused by the Mongol invasions eventually led to the rise of another warrior sultanate, the Ottomans, in the early fourteenth century.

In 1250 the Mamluks, a regiment of enslaved Turkish soldiers, overthrew the Ayyubid dynasty in Egypt and chose one of their officers as sultan. The Mamluk regime gained enormous stature among Muslims when it repelled the Mongol incursions into Syria in 1260. Its prestige was further burnished after it expelled the last of the Crusader states from Palestine in 1291.

The Mamluk elite consisted solely of foreigners, predominantly Turks, who had been purchased as slaves and raised in Egypt for service in the Mamluk army or administrative corps. Sons of Mamluk soldiers were excluded from government and military service, which therefore had to be replenished in each generation by fresh imports of enslaved persons from the steppe. The Mamluk soldiers and administrators were bound to the state by personal allegiance to their officers and the sultan.

The Mamluk regime devoted itself to promoting the Islamic faith and strengthening state wealth and power. Mamluk Egypt sat astride the maritime routes connecting the Mediterranean to the Indian Ocean. Revenues from the burgeoning commerce with Asia, driven especially by Europeans' growing appetite for spices such as pepper and ginger, swelled the coffers of the Mamluk treasury. The Mamluk regime cultivated close commercial and political ties with Venice, setting aside intense religious differences with their Christian allies to further their own political and commercial interests.

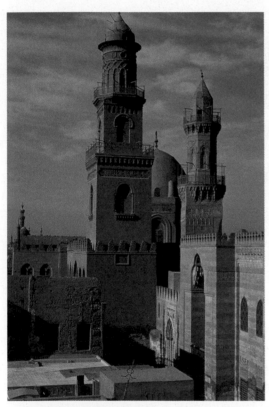

≡ **Qala'un Complex in Cairo** Because Mamluk leaders could not pass on their status to their sons, they turned to creating monuments and charitable foundations—whose property could not be confiscated by the state—that remained under the control of family members. The Mamluk sultan Qala'un (r. 1280–1290) incorporated a madrasa and a hospital into the ornate mausoleum he built for himself (center). A similar complex built by Qala'un's son stands in the right foreground.

Despite the stability of the Mamluk regime, membership in the ruling class was insecure. Sons of the enslaved soldiers were excluded from military and government service. Family fortunes were also often vulnerable to confiscation amid the factional conflicts that beset the Mamluk court. Sultans and other affluent notables sought to preserve control of their wealth by establishing charitable trusts that were exempt from such seizures. The founding patrons often used the resources of these trusts to build large ceremonial complexes that housed a variety of religious and charitable institutions, including mosques, madrasas, elementary schools, hospitals, and Sufi hospices, as well as their own tombs.

Another Islamic warrior state, one that would ultimately contest the Mamluks' leadership within the Islamic world, emerged in Anatolia. The Ottomans traced their origins to Osman (d. 1324), who arose as the leader of an expanding confederation of nomadic warriors in the late thirteenth century. In Osman's day, Anatolia was the frontier between the Byzantine Empire and the Ilkhanate (see again Map 13.4). Like other nomadic confederations, the Ottoman alliance was based on political expediency rather than permanent ethnic allegiances, and Osman's first invasions targeted neighboring Turks. Then, in 1302, after bad weather decimated their herds, Osman turned against the Byzantine towns of Anatolia. Osman's son and successor Orkhan (r. 1324–1362) led the Ottoman army in conquests of the major cities of Anatolia and made Bursa, a prosperous center of silk manufacture, his capital in 1331.

Although the tribal society of the Turkish nomads was a flexible institution in which loyalty and service counted far more than lineage and faith, it was poorly suited to the needs of governing a large agrarian population. Osman granted pasturelands to his followers, but he also cultivated the support of Christian farmers and town folk and protected their property rights. The stable revenue base provided by agriculture could support a greater number of warriors than the booty obtained from raiding.

Early on Orkhan began to transform himself from a tribal chief into a Muslim sultan at the head of a strongly centralized state. The rapid growth of Ottoman military power was propelled by the incorporation into the army's ranks of bands of Muslim holy warriors—**gazis**, who combined the qualities of frontier bandits and religious zealots. Under Orkhan's leadership the Ottoman army also underwent a metamorphosis from horse-riding archers into large infantry units capable of sophisticated siege tactics. In 1354, Ottoman forces crossed the Dardanelles to seize Byzantine territories in the Balkans, the first step toward the conquest of Constantinople and the fall of the Byzantine Empire in 1453.

The hardening of religious identities and rivalries during the age of the Crusades persisted long afterward. But in South Asia, interactions across confessional lines promoted by Sufi brotherhoods stimulated ecumenical tolerance and mutual respect between Muslims and Hindus.

COUNTERPOINT: Sufism in South Asia

↘ FOCUS Why was Sufism more successful than orthodox Islam in building bridges between Muslims and Hindus in India?

Sufism—a mystical tradition that stresses self-mastery, practical virtues, and spiritual growth through personal experience of the divine—had already emerged by 1200 as a major expression of Islamic values and social identity (see Chapter 12). Sufism appeared in many variations and readily assimilated local cultures to its beliefs and practices. In sharp contrast to the orthodox scholars and teachers known as *ulama*, who made little effort to convert nonbelievers, Sufi preachers were inspired by missionary zeal and welcomed non-Muslims to their lodges and sermons. This made them ideal instruments for the spread of Islam to new territories.

At the outset of the Delhi sultanate (1206–1526), the sultans presided over an unruly elite of Turkish warriors, Persian-speaking courtiers and administrators,

gazis "Holy warriors"; in Islam, fighters who declare war against nonbelievers.

Sufism A mystical form of Islam that emphasizes personal experience of the divine over obedience to the dictates of scripture and Islamic law.

and Hindu Brahmins and landowners. Implicitly recognizing the practical limits of their authority, the Delhi sultans sought to strengthen their control by striking alliances with revered Sufi masters, or *shaykhs*.

In the wake of Muslim conquests in South Asia, the Sufi orders established khanaqa lodges in the countryside as well as in the cities, reaching more deeply into local society. Sufism affirmed the special role of the saint or holy man as an earthly representative of God, insisting that it was the blessing of a Sufi saint that conferred sovereign authority on monarchs. Sufi shaykhs presided over the khanaqas much like princes over their courts. For example, they welcomed local people seeking justice, mediation of disputes, and miraculous cures. Learned dignitaries, both Muslim and Hindu, sought out Sufi masters for spiritual counsel and instruction. The monumental tombs of renowned saints became cultural and religious crossroads as they attracted steady streams of both Hindu and Muslim worshippers and pilgrims.

Sufis used vernacular language to address local audiences. In the Delhi region they adopted Hindi as a spoken language, and it was Sufis who developed Urdu, a literary version of Hindi, as the common written language among Muslims in South Asia. Leading Sufis often sought spiritual accommodation between Islamic and Hindu beliefs and practices. In their quest for a more direct path to union with the divine, many Sufis were attracted to the ascetic practices, yoga techniques, and mystical knowledge of Hindu yogis. Similarly, Hindus assimilated the Sufi veneration of saints into their own religious lives without relinquishing their Hindu identity. Most important, the Sufi ethic of practical piety in daily life struck a responsive chord among Hindus. Nizam ad-din Awliya (1236–1325), head of the Chishti brotherhood, the leading Sufi order, ministered to the spiritual needs of Hindus as well as Muslims. His message—forgive your enemies, enjoy worldly pleasures in moderation, and fulfill your responsibilities to family and society—was closely aligned with the basic principles of Hindu social life. Thus, Sufism served as a bridge between the two dominant religious traditions of India.

Awliya's followers saw him as the leader of a spiritual kingdom parallel to the domain of secular rulers. But Awliya and other Chishti shaykhs avoided politics and court life, advocating a humble ethic of poverty and charity and openness to all ranks of society. When a disciple asked if an enslaved person could be initiated into the order, Awliya replied, "There is no such thing as slavery and dominion in this Way; all who enter properly into the world of love do God's work."[9] Awliya not only spurned possession of wealth but also insisted that his initiates abstain from any form of earning a livelihood, which he regarded as enslavement that compromised spiritual freedom. Lay followers showered Awliya with donations, which he immediately dispensed to the poor. The Chishti order's free kitchens became an important source of public charity.

Not all Sufis were so inclined. The Suhrawardi brotherhood, second to the Chishti in influence, amassed great wealth from royal and mercantile patrons at their main lodge at Multan (in modern Pakistan) and enjoyed an affluent lifestyle. The Suhrawardi collaborated with the Delhi sultanate and often mediated between the sultans and local rulers. In contrast to the universalism of the Chishti order, the Suhrawardi shaykhs believed that Muslim rulers should strive for the prosperity and welfare of orthodox Sunni Muslims above all others. The Chishti and Suhrawardi orders also diverged in their religious practices. In their quest for mystical union with the divine, for example, Chishti masters encouraged inducing spiritual bliss through ecstatic performance of music, song, and dance—rites denounced as misguided and potentially dangerous by Suhrawardi shaykhs and orthodox ulama alike.

As the Sufi orders became established institutions in South Asian society, wandering mendicant Sufis known as **dervishes** pursued more austere forms of worldly renunciation. Like the Chishti, dervishes honored self-denial and deemed ecstatic visions—stimulated by music, dance, and even mood-altering drugs—central to spiritual growth. But the dervishes went further than the Chishti in their uncompromising hostility not only to temporal rulers but also to any form of social discipline, including the usual Islamic strictures on personal conduct.

In 1398 the Turkic-Mongol conqueror Timur sacked Delhi and massacred its population before abruptly departing, leaving the sultanate's political dominion in tatters. Timur himself became a great patron of the Sufi movement in his Central Asian domains (see Chapter 14). The Sufi orders continued to enjoy popular support in the territories of the sultanate, now carved up into regional

dervishes Wandering mendicant Sufis known for ecstatic rituals such as whirling dances.

≡ **Dancing Sufis** This painted miniature illustrated a 1602 manuscript of a collection of poems by Amir Hasan Dihlavi (d. 1328), a lay disciple of the renowned Sufi master Nizam ad-din Awliya. To the consternation of orthodox Muslims, Awliya, like many Sufi masters, endorsed music and dance as means to heighten one's ecstatic experience of the divine. Illuminated Manuscript, Divan, Walters Art Museum Ms. W.650, fol. 62a kingdoms. As part of their project of imperial reunification, the sixteenth-century Mughal emperors sought out Sufi masters as spiritual advisers and renewed royal patronage of the Sufi brotherhoods.

Conclusion

The initial waves of the Mongol invasions spread fear and destruction across Eurasia, and the political and cultural repercussions of the Mongol conquests would resound for centuries. Adapting their own traditions to vastly different local settings, the Mongols reshaped the societies and cultures of Iran, Russia, and China as well as Central Asia.

The Mongol incursions most profoundly affected the Islamic states and societies of Iran and Mesopotamia and the Rus lands. Many areas never recovered from the disruption of irrigated agriculture and reverted to pasture for stock raising and in some cases even to barren desert. The Mongol invasions also erased the last of the Seljuk emirates, clearing the ground for the rise of new Turkish sultanates, the Mamluks and the Ottomans.

Like the Ilkhans in Iran, the Mongols of the Golden Horde converted to Islam, although their Rus subjects remained Christians. The rising Muscovy state would retain Mongol military and political institutions in building its own Russian empire. In China, by contrast, the Mongols failed to adapt their style of rule to the requirements of a large agrarian empire. The Yuan regime in China had badly deteriorated by the 1330s and collapsed into civil war and rebellion in the 1350s.

The Mongols brought the worlds of pastoral nomads and settled urban and agrarian peoples into collision, but a different kind of clash of cultures had been triggered by the Crusades. Although the Crusaders failed to achieve their goal of establishing Christian rule over Jerusalem, the crusading movement expanded the borders of Latin Christendom by advancing the "reconquest" in Spain and by bringing the Slavic and Baltic peoples of eastern Europe within the Christian fold. At the same time, the political and cultural abyss between Latin Christendom and the Islamic world deepened. By contrast, the proliferation of Sufi brotherhoods in South Asia mitigated tensions between Muslims and Hindus.

The crusading movement figured decisively in the formation of Europe as the realm of "the Christian people" obedient to the Roman papacy. But the growing power of national monarchies frustrated the popes' efforts to establish supreme rule over secular as well as spiritual affairs. The unity imposed by the Mongol conquests also was short-lived. The unprecedented movement of people, goods, and ideas throughout Eurasia during the Mongol heyday vanished almost completely after the collapse of the Ilkhan and Yuan states in the mid-fourteenth century. By then, as the next chapter will reveal, both Europe and the Islamic lands had plunged into a new era of crisis following the devastating catastrophe of the Black Death.

review

The major global development in this chapter: The Eurasian integration fostered by the clashes of culture known as the Crusades and the Mongol conquests.

Important Events	
1054	Great Schism between the Roman and Byzantine churches
1085	Christian capture of Muslim-ruled Toledo
1095	Pope Urban II issues summons for First Crusade
1098	Founding of the Cistercian order
1099	First Crusade concludes with the Christian capture of Jerusalem
1147	Wendish Crusade (part of the Second Crusade)
1187	Saladin recaptures Jerusalem
1198–1216	Papacy of Innocent III
1206	Temujin (Chinggis) becomes Great Khan
1240	Mongol conquest of Kiev
1250–1517	Mamluk sultanate in Egypt and Syria
1258	Mongols sack Baghdad
1271–1368	Rule of Mongols over China as the Yuan dynasty
1291	Mamluks recapture Acre, last Christian stronghold in Palestine
1295–1304	Rule of Ghazan as Ilkhan; conversion of Ilkhan Mongols to Islam

KEY TERMS

chivalry (p. 481)

Crusades (p. 473)

dervishes (p. 503)

gazis (p. 501)

Great Khan (p. 488)

Great Schism (p. 474)

Inquisition (p. 480)

investiture controversy (p. 474)

Sufism (p. 501)

tax farming (p. 490)

CHAPTER OVERVIEW QUESTIONS

1. In what ways did the growing economic and cultural unity of Latin Christendom promote the rise of powerful European national monarchies?

2. To what degree did the expansion of Latin Christendom remake eastern Europe in the image of western Europe?

3. In what ways did the Mongol conquests foster cultural and economic exchange across Eurasia?

4. How and why did the Mongol rulers of China, Iran, and Russia differ in their relationships with the settled societies they ruled?

MAKING CONNECTIONS

1. How did the relationship between the Roman popes and the Christian monarchs of western Europe change from the reign of Charlemagne (see Chapter 8) to the papacy of Innocent III?

2. In what ways did the Crusades contribute to the definition of Europe as the realm of Latin Christendom?

3. To what extent were the policies of the Mongols similar to those of earlier Central Asian nomad empires such as the Khazars and the Turks (see Chapter 9)?

DOING HISTORY

Claims and Evidence in Sources

Eyewitness testimonies can be especially valuable historical sources. But the authors of such "saw with my own eyes" accounts had their own personal motives and beliefs. These biases may be especially acute in cases of cross-cultural encounters in which writers describe strangely unfamiliar—and potentially hostile—societies, religions, and cultural practices. Historians must consider both the subjective and objective features of such testimonies to determine their reliability as historical sources. As we saw

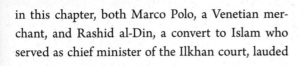

in this chapter, both Marco Polo, a Venetian merchant, and Rashid al-Din, a convert to Islam who served as chief minister of the Ilkhan court, lauded the Mongol khans as the greatest and most powerful rulers of all time—claims that surely jarred their Christian and Muslim readers.

1. Given their disparate backgrounds and audiences, why might these authors make similar claims about the Mongol khans?
2. Consider the motives of Marco Polo and Rashid al-Din. In what ways were they similar or different?
3. What can such testimony tell us about both the Mongols and the audiences these writers were addressing?

For further research into the topics covered in this chapter, see the Bibliography at the end of the book.

14

Collapse and Revival in Afro-Eurasia

1300–1450

≡ **World in the Making** The fall of Constantinople to the Ottoman Turks in 1453 marked the end of the Byzantine Empire and heralded the coming age of gunpowder weapons. The Ottoman forces under Sultan Mehmed II breached the triple walls of Constantinople using massive cannons known as bombards. The Turkish cannons appear in the center of this book illustration of the siege of Constantinople, published in France in 1455.

backstory

In the fourteenth century, a number of developments threatened the connections among Afro-Eurasian societies. The collapse of the Mongol empires in China and Iran in the mid-1300s disrupted caravan traffic across Central Asia, diverting the flow of trade and travel to maritime routes across the Indian Ocean. Although the two centuries of religious wars known as the Crusades ended in 1291, they had hardened hostility between Christians and Muslims. As the power of the Christian Byzantine Empire contracted, Muslim Turkish sultanates—the Mamluk regime in Egypt and the rising Ottoman dynasty in Anatolia (modern Turkey)—gained control of the eastern Mediterranean region. Yet the Crusades and direct contact with the Mongols (subjects of Chapter 13) had also whetted European appetites for luxury and exotic goods from the Islamic world and Asia. Thus, despite challenges and obstacles, the Mediterranean remained a lively crossroads of commerce and cross-cultural exchange.

IN AUGUST 1452, AS THE ARMIES of the Ottoman sultan Mehmed II encircled Constantinople, the Byzantine emperor Constantine XI received a visit from a fellow Christian, a Hungarian engineer named Urban. Urban had applied metallurgical skills acquired at Hungary's rich iron and copper mines to the manufacture of large cannons known as *bombards*. He came to the Byzantine capital to offer his services to repel the Ottoman assault. But although Urban was a Christian, he was a businessman, too. When Constantine could not meet his price, Urban quickly left for the sultan's camp. Facing the famed triple walls of Constantinople, Mehmed promised to quadruple the salary Urban requested and to provide any materials and manpower the engineer needed.

Seven months later, in April 1453, Ottoman soldiers moved Urban's huge bronze bombards—with barrels twenty-six feet long, capable of throwing 800-pound shot—into place beneath the walls of Constantinople. Although these cumbersome cannons could fire only seven rounds a day, they battered the walls of Constantinople, which had long been considered impenetrable. After six weeks of siege the Turks breached the walls and swarmed into the city. The vastly outnumbered defenders, Emperor Constantine among them, fought to the death.

The fall of Constantinople to the Ottomans marks a turning point in world history. After perpetuating ancient Rome's heritage and glory for a thousand years, the Byzantine Empire came to an end. Islam continued to advance; in the fourteenth and fifteenth centuries, it expanded most dramatically in Africa and Asia. Italian merchants and bankers lost their dominance in the eastern Mediterranean and turned westward toward the Atlantic Ocean in search of new commercial opportunities. The bombards cast by the Hungarian engineer for the Ottoman sultan heralded a military revolution that would decisively alter the balance of power among states and transform the nature of the state itself.

The new global patterns that emerged after Constantinople changed hands had their roots in calamities of the fourteenth century. The Ottoman triumph came just as Europe was beginning to recover from the catastrophic outbreak of plague known as the Black Death. The demographic and psychological shocks of epidemic disease had severely tested Europe's political and economic institutions—indeed, even its Christian faith. The Black Death also devastated the Islamic world. Economic depression struck hard in Egypt, Syria, and Mesopotamia, the heartland of Islam. However, Europe's economy recovered more quickly.

In Asia, the fourteenth century witnessed the rise and fall of the last Mongol empire, that of Timur (also known as Tamerlane). The end of the Mongol era marked the passing of nomadic rule, the resurgence of agrarian bureaucratic states such as Ming China and the Ottoman Empire, and the shift of trade from the overland Silk Road to maritime routes across the Indian Ocean. Commerce attained unprecedented importance in many Asian societies. The flow of goods across Eurasia and Africa created new concentrations of wealth, fostered new patterns of consumption, and reshaped culture. The European Renaissance, for example, although primarily understood as a rebirth of the classical culture of Greece and Rome, also drew inspiration from the wealth of goods that poured into Italy from the Islamic world and Asia. By contrast, Japan remained isolated from this global bazaar, and this isolation contributed to the birth of Japan's distinctive national culture. For most Afro-Eurasian societies, however, the maritime world increasingly became the principal crossroads of economic and cultural exchange.

OVERVIEW QUESTIONS

The major global development in this chapter: Crisis and recovery in fourteenth- and fifteenth-century Afro-Eurasia.

As you read, consider:

1. In the century after the devastating outbreak of plague known as the Black Death, how and why did Europe's economic growth begin to surpass that of the Islamic world?

2. Did the economic revival across Eurasia after 1350 benefit the peasant populations of Europe, the Islamic world, and East Asia?

3. How did the process of conversion to Islam differ in Iran, the Ottoman Empire, West Africa, and Southeast Asia during this period?

4. What political and economic changes contributed to the rise of maritime commerce in Asia during the fourteenth and fifteenth centuries?

Fourteenth-Century Crisis and Renewal in Eurasia

✘ FOCUS How did the Black Death affect society, the economy, and culture in Latin Christendom and the Islamic world?

No event in the fourteenth century had such profound consequences as the **Black Death** of 1347–1350. The unprecedented loss of life that resulted from this **pandemic** abruptly halted the economic expansion that had spread throughout Europe and the Islamic heartland in the preceding three centuries. Although the

Black Death The catastrophic outbreak of plague that spread from the Black Sea to Europe, the Middle East, and North Africa in 1347–1350, killing a third or more of the population in afflicted areas.

population losses were as great in the Islamic world as in Latin Christendom, the effects on society, the economy, and ideas diverged in important ways.

Largely spared the ravages of the Black Death, Asian societies and economies faced different challenges following the collapse of the Mongol empires in the fourteenth century. Expanding maritime trade and the spread of gunpowder weapons gave settled empires a decisive edge over nomadic societies, an edge that they never again relinquished. The founder of the Ming dynasty (1368–1644) in China rejected the Mongol model of "universal empire" and strove to restore a purely Chinese culture and social order. The prestige, stability, and ruling ideology of the Ming state powerfully influenced neighbors such as Korea and Vietnam—but had far less effect on Japan.

The "Great Mortality": The Black Death of 1347–1350

On the eve of the Black Death, Europe's agrarian economy already was struggling under the strain of climatic change. Around 1300 the earth experienced a shift in climate. The warm temperatures that had prevailed over most of the globe for the previous thousand years gave way to a **Little Ice Age** of colder temperatures and shorter growing seasons; it would last for much of the fourteenth century. The expansion of agriculture that had occurred in the Northern Hemisphere during the preceding three centuries came to a halt. Unlike famine, though, the Black Death pandemic struck the ruling classes as hard as the poor. Scholars estimate that the Black Death and subsequent recurrences of the pandemic killed approximately one-third of the population of Europe.

Although the catastrophic mortality (death rates) of the Black Death is beyond dispute, the causes of the pandemic remain mysterious. The Florentine poet Giovanni Boccaccio (1313–1375), an eyewitness to the "great mortality," described the appearance of apple-sized swellings, first in the groin and armpits, after which these "death-bearing plague boils" spread to "every part of the body, wherefrom the fashion of the contagion began to change into black or livid blotches . . . in some places large and sparse, and in others small and thick-sown." The spread of these swellings, Boccaccio warned, was "a very certain token of coming death."[1] The prominence of these glandular swellings, or buboes, in eyewitness accounts has led modern scholars to attribute the Black Death to bubonic plague, which is transmitted by fleas to rats and by rats to humans. The populations of western Eurasia had no previous experience of the disease, and hence no immunity to it. Outbreaks of plague continued to recur every decade or two for the next century and intermittently thereafter.

Boccaccio and other eyewitnesses claimed that the Black Death had originated in Central Asia and traveled along overland trade routes to the Black Sea. The first outbreak among Europeans occurred in 1347 at the Genoese port of Caffa, on the

pandemic An outbreak of epidemic disease that spreads across an entire region.

Little Ice Age Name applied by environmental historians to periods of prolonged cool weather in the temperate zones of the earth.

Crimean peninsula. The Genoese seafarers then spread the plague to the seaports they visited throughout the Mediterranean. By the summer of 1350 the Black Death had devastated nearly all of Europe (see Map 14.1).

Epidemiological studies have confirmed that the Black Death was a byproduct of the Mongol conquests. Mongol horsemen carried the plague bacillus from the remote highland forests of Southeast Asia into Central Asia and then west to the Black Sea. The impact of the plague on China remains uncertain, however. The Mongol Yuan dynasty already was losing its hold on China in the 1330s, and by the late 1340s China was afflicted by widespread famine, banditry, and civil war. By the time the Ming dynasty took control in 1368, China's population had fallen substantially. Yet Chinese sources make no mention of the specific symptoms of

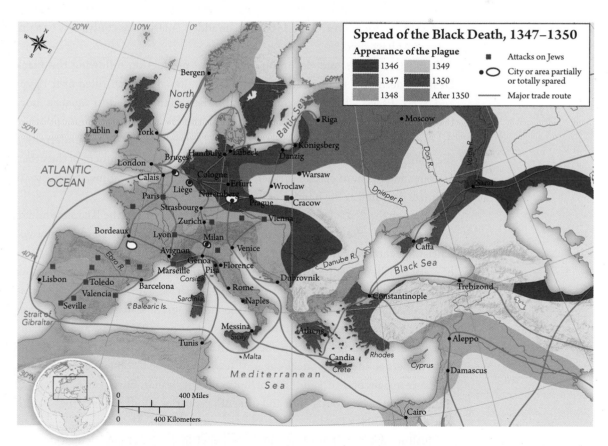

Spread of the Black Death, 1347–1350

Appearance of the plague

1346	1349
1347	1350
1348	After 1350

■ Attacks on Jews
●◯ City or area partially or totally spared
— Major trade route

≡ **MAP 14.1   Spread of the Black Death, 1347–1350**   From Caffa on the shores of the Black Sea, Genoese merchant ships unwittingly carried the plague to Constantinople and other Mediterranean ports in the summer of 1347. Over the next four years the Black Death advanced across the Mediterranean Sea and throughout central and northern Europe. Hundreds of Jewish communities were attacked or destroyed by Christians who blamed the pandemic on the Jews.

the Black Death, and there is no evidence of pandemic in the densely populated areas of South and Southeast Asia.

The demographic collapse resulting from the Black Death was concentrated in Europe and the Islamic lands ringing the Mediterranean. In these regions population growth halted for over a century. In the Islamic world, as in Europe, the loss of human lives and livestock seriously disrupted agriculture. While rural inhabitants flocked to the towns in search of food and work, urban residents sought refuge in the countryside from the contagion that festered in crowded cities. The scarcity of labor following the pandemic prompted a return to pastoral nomadism in many rural areas, and the urban working classes who survived benefited from rising wages. "The wages of skilled artisans, wage workers, porters, servants, stablemen, weavers, masons, construction workers, and the like have increased manyfold," wrote the Egyptian historian al-Maqrizi (al-mak-REE-zee), who served as Cairo's market inspector from 1399 to 1405. But, he added, "of this class only a few remain, since most have died."[2]

Population losses and declining agricultural production following the Black Death undermined the Mamluk (MAM-luke) sultanate, which ruled over Egypt and Syria. Faced with decreasing revenues, the sultanate tried to squeeze more taxes from urban commerce and industry. But the creation of state monopolies in the spice trade and the sugar industry throttled private enterprise and undermined the commercial vitality of Cairo and Damascus. The impoverishment of the urban artisan and merchant classes further weakened the Mamluk regime, leading to its ultimate downfall at the hands of Ottoman conquerors in 1517.

Although the Black Death afflicted Latin Christendom and the Islamic world in equal measure, their responses to the epidemic diverged in significant ways. Christians interpreted the plague as divine punishment for humanity's sins. Acts of piety and atonement proliferated, most strikingly in the form of processions of flagellants (from *flagella*, a whip used by worshippers as a form of penance), whose self-mutilation was meant to imitate the sufferings of Christ. In many places Christians blamed vulnerable minorities—such as beggars, lepers, and especially Jews—for corrupting Christian society. Although the Roman church, kings, and local leaders condemned attacks against Jews, their appeals often went unheeded. Macabre images of death and the corruption of the flesh in European painting and sculpture in the late fourteenth and fifteenth centuries vividly convey the anguish caused by the Black Death.

Muslims did not share the Christian belief in "original sin," which deemed human beings inherently sinful, and so they did not see the plague as a divine punishment. Instead, they accepted it as an expression of God's will and even a blessing for the faithful. Muslim cleric Ibn al-Wardi (IB-unh al-wahr-dee), who

≡ **Dance of Death** The scourge of the Black Death dramatically influenced attitudes toward death in Latin Christendom. Literary and artistic works such as this woodcut of skeletons dancing on an open grave vividly portrayed the fragility of life and the dangers of untimely death. For those unprepared to face divine judgment, the ravages of disease and death were only a prelude to the everlasting torments of hell.

succumbed to the disease in 1349, wrote that "this plague is for Muslims a martyrdom and a reward, and for the disbelievers a punishment and rebuke."[3] The flagellants' focus on atonement for sin and the scapegoating of Jews seen in Christian Europe were wholly absent in the Islamic world.

Rebuilding Societies in Western Europe 1350–1492

Just as existing religious beliefs and practices shaped Muslim and Christian responses to the plague, underlying conditions influenced political and economic recovery in the two regions. Latin Christendom recovered more quickly than

Islamic lands. In Europe, the death toll caused an acute labor shortage. Desperate to find tenants to cultivate their lands, the nobility had to offer generous concessions, such as release from labor services, that liberated the peasantry from the conditions of serfdom. The incomes of the nobility and the church declined by half or more, and many castles and monasteries fell into ruin. The shortage of labor enabled both urban artisans and rural laborers to bargain for wage increases. Many nobles, unable to find tenants, converted their agricultural land into pasture. Hundreds of villages were abandoned. In much of central Europe, farmlands reverted to forest.

Economic change brought with it economic conflict, and tensions between rich and poor triggered insurrections by rural peasants and the urban lower classes throughout western Europe. In England, King Richard II's attempt to shift the basis of taxation from landed wealth to a head tax on each subject incited the Peasant Revolt of 1381. Led by a radical preacher named John Ball, the rebels presented a petition to the king that went beyond repeal of the head tax to demand freedom from the tyranny of noble lords and the Christian church.

> Henceforward, that no lord should have lordship but that there should be proportion between all people, saving only the lordship of the king; that the goods of the holy church ought not to be in the hands of men of religion, or parsons or vicars, or others of holy church, but these should have their sustenance easily and the rest of the goods be divided between the parishioners, . . . and that there should be no villeins [peasants subject to a lord's justice] in England or any serfdom or villeinage, but all are to be free and of one condition.[4]

In the end the English nobles mustered militias to suppress the uprising. This success could not, however, reverse the developments that had produced the uprising in the first place. A new social order began to form, one based on private property and entrepreneurship rather than nobility and serfdom, but equally extreme in its imbalance of wealth and poverty.

Perhaps nowhere in Europe was this new social order more apparent than in Italy. In the Italian city-states, the widening gap between rich and poor was reflected in their governments, which increasingly benefited the wealthy. Over the course of the fifteenth century, the ideals and institutions of republican (representative) government on which the Italian city-states were founded steadily lost ground. A military despot wrested control of Milan in 1450. Venice's **oligarchy**— rule by an exclusive elite—strengthened its grip over the city's government and commerce. In Florence, the Medici family of bankers dominated the city's political affairs. Everywhere, financial power was increasingly aligned with political power.

oligarchy Rule by a small group of individuals or families.

In the wake of the Black Death, kings and princes suffered a drop in revenues as agricultural production fell. Yet in the long run, royal power grew at the expense of the nobility and the church. In England and France, royal governments gained new sources of income and established bureaucracies of tax collectors and administrators to manage them. The rulers of these states transformed their growing financial power into military and political strength by raising standing armies of professional soldiers and investing in new military technology. The French monarchy, for instance, capitalized on rapid innovations in gunpowder weapons to create a formidable army and to establish itself as the supreme power in continental Europe. Originally developed by the Mongols, these weapons had been introduced to Europe via the Islamic world by the middle of the fourteenth century.

The progress of the Hundred Years' War (1337–1453) between England and France reflected the changing political landscape. The war broke out over claims to territories in southwestern France and a dispute over succession to the French throne. In the early years of the conflict, the English side prevailed, thanks to the skill of its bowmen against mounted French knights. By 1400, combat between knights conducted according to elaborate rules of chivalry had yielded to new forms of warfare. Cannons, siege weapons, and, later, firearms undermined both the nobility's preeminence in war and its sense of identity and purpose. An arms race between France and its rivals led to rapid improvements in weaponry, especially the development of lighter and more mobile cannons. Ultimately the French defeated the English, but the war transformed both sides. The length of the conflict, the propaganda from both sides, and the unified effort needed to prosecute the increasingly costly war all contributed to the evolution of royal governments and the emergence of a sense of national identity.

New economic conditions contributed to the growth of monarchical power (see Map 14.2). To strengthen their control, the rulers of France, England, and Spain relied on new forms of taxation, as well as financing from bankers. The French monarchy levied new taxes on salt, land, and commercial transactions, wresting income from local lords and town governments. The marriage of Isabella of Castile and Ferdinand of Aragon in 1469 created a unified monarchy in Spain. This expansion of royal power in Spain depended heavily on loans from Genoese bankers. In their efforts to consolidate power, Ferdinand and Isabella, like so many rulers in world history, demanded religious conformity. In 1492 they conquered Granada, the last Muslim foothold in Spain, and ordered all Jews and Muslims to convert to Christianity or face banishment. With the *Reconquista* (Spanish for "reconquest") of Spain complete, Ferdinand and Isabella turned their crusading energies toward exploration. That same year, they sponsored the first of Christopher Columbus's momentous transatlantic voyages in pursuit of the fabled riches of China.

≡ **MAP 14.2 Europe and the Greater Mediterranean, 1453** The century following the Black Death witnessed the growth of royal power and territorial consolidation across Europe, most notably in England and France. But central Europe and Italy remained politically fragmented. The Ottoman conquest of Constantinople in 1453 extinguished the Byzantine Empire and sharpened the conflict between Christendom and the Islamic world in southeastern Europe.

Ming China and the New Order in East Asia 1368–1500

State building in East Asia, too, fostered the development of national states. The Yuan dynasty established in China by the Mongol khan Qubilai had foundered after his death in 1294. Qubilai's successors wrung as much tribute as they could from the Chinese population, but they neglected the infrastructure of roads, canals, and irrigation and flood-control dikes that the Chinese economy depended on. When peasant insurrections and civil wars broke out in the 1350s, the Mongol leaders abandoned China and retreated to their steppe homeland. After a protracted period of war and devastation, a Chinese general of peasant origin restored native rule, founding the Ming dynasty in 1368 (see Map 14.3).

The Ming founder, Zhu Yuanzhang (JOO yuwen-JAHNG) (r. 1368–1398)—better known by his imperial title, Hongwu (hoong-woo)—resurrected the basic Chinese institutions of civil government. But throughout his life Hongwu viewed the scholar-official class with suspicion. Born a peasant, Hongwu saw himself as a populist crusading against the snobbery and luxurious lifestyle of the rich and powerful. Once in command, he repeatedly purged high officials and exercised despotic control over his government. Hongwu reinstituted the civil service examinations system to select government officials, but he used the examinations and the state-run school system as tools of political indoctrination, establishing the teachings of twelfth-century Neo-Confucian philosopher Zhu Xi (JOO shee) as the standard for the civil service exams. Zhu shared the Neo-Confucian antipathy toward Buddhism as a foreign religion and sought to reassert the Confucian commitment to moral perfection and the betterment of society. **Neo-Confucianism** advocated a strict moral code and a patriarchal social hierarchy, and the Ming government supported it with the full force of imperial law.

The Neo-Confucian ideology of Hongwu emphasized the patriarchal authority of the lineage, and his law code deprived women of many rights, including a share in inheritance. It outlawed the remarriage of widows. By 1300 many elite families practiced foot binding, which probably originated among courtesans and entertainers. From around age six the feet of girls were tightly bound with bandages, deforming the bones and crippling them. The feet of adult women ideally were no more than three or four inches long; they were considered a mark of feminine beauty and a symbol of freedom from labor. Foot binding accompanied seclusion in the home as a sign of respectable womanhood.

Despite the strictures of patriarchal society, women performed essential economic roles in the nonelite households. Women worked alongside men in rice cultivation and performed most tasks involved in textile manufacture. The spread of cotton, introduced from India in the thirteenth century, gave peasant women new economic opportunities. Most cotton was grown, ginned (removing the seeds), spun into yarn, and woven into cloth within a single household, principally by women. Confucian moralists esteemed spinning, weaving, and embroidery as "womanly work" that would promote industriousness and thrift; they became dismayed, however, when women displayed entrepreneurial skill in marketing their wares.

Hongwu rejected the Mongol model of a multiethnic empire and turned his back on the world of the steppe nomads. He located his capital at Nanjing, on the south bank of the Yangzi River, far from the Mongol frontier. Foreign embassies were welcome at the Ming court, which offered trading privileges in return for

Neo-Confucianism
The revival of Confucian teachings beginning in the Song dynasty that firmly rejected Buddhist religion and reasserted the Confucian commitment to moral perfection and the betterment of society.

≡ **MAP 14.3** **The Ming Empire, c. 1500** Emperor Yongle moved the Ming capital from Nanjing to Beijing and launched expeditions commanded by his trusted aide Zheng He that voyaged throughout Southeast Asia and the Indian Ocean. After a disastrous campaign against the Mongols in 1449, the Ming established nine garrison commands to defend China's northern frontier. In the 1540s the Ming rebuilt the Great Wall to guard against the revived Mongol menace.

tribute and allegiance to the Chinese emperor. But Hongwu distrusted merchants as much as he did intellectuals. In 1371 he forbade Chinese merchants from engaging in overseas commerce and placed foreign traders under close government scrutiny.

Hongwu's son, the Emperor Yongle (r. 1402–1424), reversed his father's efforts to sever China from the outside world. Instead, Yongle embraced the Mongol vision of world empire and rebuilt the former Mongol capital of Dadu, creating the modern city of Beijing. Throughout his reign Yongle campaigned to subdue the Mongol tribes along the northern frontier, but with little success. He also wanted to expand southward. In 1405 he launched, as we will see, a series of naval expeditions under Admiral Zheng He (JUNG-huh), and in 1407 he invaded and conquered Vietnam (see again Map 14.3). Like his father, however, Yongle was an autocrat who promoted Neo-Confucian policies, even as he sought to reestablish some of the global connections Hongwu had tried to sever.

The Ming dynasty abandoned its designs for conquest and expansion after the death of Yongle in 1424. Yet the prestige, power, and philosophy of the Ming state continued to influence its neighbors, with the significant exception of Japan (see Counterpoint: Age of the Samurai in Japan 1185–1450). Vietnam regained its independence from China in 1427, but under the long-lived Le dynasty (1428–1788), Vietnam retained Chinese-style bureaucratic government. The Le rulers oversaw the growth of an official class schooled in Neo-Confucianism and committed to forcing its cultural norms, kinship practices, and hostility to Buddhism on Vietnamese society as a whole. In Korea, the rulers of the new Yi dynasty (1392–1910) also embraced Neo-Confucian ideals of government. Under Yi rule the Confucian-educated elite acquired hereditary status with exclusive rights to political office. In both Vietnam and Korea, aristocratic rule and Buddhism's dominance over daily life yielded to a "Neo-Confucian revolution" modeled after Chinese political institutions and values.

Islam's New Frontiers

⬊ **FOCUS** Why did Islam expand dramatically in the fourteenth and fifteenth centuries, and how did new Islamic societies differ from established ones?

In the fourteenth and fifteenth centuries, Islam continued to spread to new areas, including central and maritime Asia, sub-Saharan Africa, and southeastern Europe. In the past, Muslim rule had often preceded the popular adoption of

Islamic religion and culture. Yet the advance of Islam in Africa and Asia came about not through conquest, but through slow diffusion via merchants and missionaries. The universalism and egalitarianism of Islam appealed to rising merchant classes in both West Africa and maritime Asia.

During this period, Islam expanded by adapting to older ruling cultures rather than seeking to eradicate them. Timur, the last of the great nomad conquerors, and his descendants ruled not as Mongol khans but as Islamic sultans. The culture of the Central Asian states, however, remained an eclectic mix of Mongol, Turkish, and Persian traditions, in contrast to the strict adherence to Muslim law practiced under the Arab regimes of the Middle East and North Africa. This pattern of cultural adaptation was even more evident in West Africa and Southeast Asia.

Islamic Spiritual Ferment in Central Asia 1350–1500

As we saw in Chapter 13, the spread of **Sufism** played a significant role in the process of cultural assimilation in Central and South Asia. One of Sufism's most important royal patrons was Timur (1336–1405), the last of the Mongol emperors. Born near the city of Samarkand (SAM-ar-kand) when the Mongol Ilkhanate in Iran was on the verge of collapse (see Chapter 13), Timur—himself a Turk—grew up among Mongols who practiced Islam. He rose to power in the 1370s by reuniting quarreling Mongol tribes in common pursuit of conquest.

From the early 1380s, Timur's armies relentlessly pursued campaigns of conquest, sweeping westward across Iran into Mesopotamia and Russia and eastward into India. In 1400–1401 Timur seized and razed Aleppo and Damascus, the principal Mamluk cities in Syria. Rather than trying to consolidate his rule in West Asia, however, Timur turned his attention eastward. He was preparing to march on China when he fell ill and died in 1405. Although Timur's empire quickly fragmented, his triumphs would serve as an inspiration to later empire builders, such as the Mughals in India and the Manchus in China. Moreover, his support of Sufism would have a lasting impact, helping lay the foundation for a number of important Islamic religious movements in Central Asia.

The institutions of Timur's empire were largely modeled on the Ilkhan synthesis of Persian civil administration and Turkish-Mongol military organization. While Timur allowed local princes a degree of autonomy, he was determined to make Samarkand a grand imperial capital. The citadel and enormous bazaar built by Timur have long since perished, but surviving mosques, shrines, and tombs illuminate Timur's vision of Islamic kingship: all-powerful, urbane and cosmopolitan, and ostentatious in its display of public piety.

After Timur's death in 1405, his sons carved the empire into independent regional kingdoms. Yet Sufi brotherhoods and the veneration of Sufi saints exerted

Sufism A mystical form of Islam that emphasizes personal experience of the divine over obedience to the dictates of scripture.

an especially strong influence over social life and religious practice in Central Asia. Timur had lavished special favor on Sufi teachers and had strategically placed the shrines of his family members next to the tombs of important Sufi leaders. The relics of Timur in Samarkand, along with the tombs of Sufi saints, attracted pilgrims from near and far.

Elsewhere in the Islamic world, a number of religious movements combined the veneration of Sufi saints and belief in miracles with unorthodox ideas derived from Shi'ism, the branch of Islam that maintains that only descendants of Muhammad's son-in-law Ali have a legitimate right to serve as caliph. One of the most militant and influential of these radical Islamic sects was the Safavid (SAH-fah-vid) movement founded by a Sufi preacher, Safi al-Din (SAH-fee al-dean) (1252–1334). Like other visionary teachers, Safi preached the need for a purified Islam cleansed of worldly wealth, urban luxury, and moral laxity. The Safavids roused their followers to attack Christians in the Caucasus region, but they also challenged Muslim rulers such as the Ottomans and Timur's successors. At the end of the fifteenth century, a charismatic leader, Shah Isma'il (shah IS-mah-eel), combined Safavid religious fervor with Shi'a doctrines to found a **theocracy**—a state subject to religious authority. It would rule Iran for more than two centuries and shape modern Iran's distinctive Shi'a religious culture.

≡ **Timur Enthroned** We can glean some sense of Timur's self-image from the *Book of Victories*, a chronicle of Timur's campaigns commissioned by one of his descendants in the 1480s. This scene portrays the ceremony in 1370 when Timur declared himself successor to the Chagadai khans. (The John Work Garrett Library, The Sheridan Libraries, Johns Hopkins University)

Ottoman Expansion and the Fall of Constantinople 1354–1453

The spread of Islam in Central Asia would have profound consequences for the region. In the eyes of Europeans, however, the most significant—and alarming—advance was the Ottoman expansion into the Balkan territories of southeastern Europe. The Byzantine state was severely shaken by the Black Death, and in 1354 the Ottomans took advantage of this weakness to invade the Balkans. After a

theocracy A state ruled by religious authorities.

janissary corps
Enslaved soldiers who
served as the principal
armed forces of the
Ottoman Empire
beginning in the
fifteenth century; also
staffed much of the
Ottoman state
bureaucracy.

decisive victory in Kosovo in 1389, the Ottoman Empire annexed most of the Balkans except the region around Constantinople itself, reducing it to an isolated enclave.

The growing might of the Ottoman Empire stemmed from two military innovations: (1) the formation of the **janissary corps**, elite army units composed of enslaved soldiers, and (2) the use of massed musket fire and cannons, such as the bombards of Urban, the Hungarian engineer whom we met at the start of this chapter. In the late fourteenth century the Ottomans adopted the Mamluk practice of organizing slave armies that would be more reliably loyal to the sultan than the unruly *ghazi* ("holy warrior") bands that Osman (r. 1280–1324), the founder of the Ottoman state, had gathered as the core of his army. At first, prisoners and volunteers made up the janissary corps. Starting in 1395, however, the Ottomans imposed a form of conscription known as *devshirme* (dev-SHEER-may) on the Christian peoples of the Balkans to supplement Turkish recruits. Adolescent boys conscripted through the devshirme were taken from their families, raised as Muslims, and educated at palace schools for service in the sultan's civil administration as well as the army.

Practical concerns dictated Ottoman policies toward Christian communities. Where Christians were the majority of the population, the Ottomans could be quite tolerant. Apart from the notorious devshirme slave levy, Ottoman impositions were less burdensome than the dues the Balkan peoples had owed the Byzantine emperor. The Ottomans allowed Balkan Christians freedom to practice their religion, and they protected the Greek Orthodox Church, which they considered indispensable to maintaining social order. In Anatolia and other places where Christians were a minority, however, the Ottomans took a much harder line. By 1500 Christian society in Anatolia had nearly vanished; most Christians had converted to Islam.

Despite their own nomadic origins, the Ottomans regarded nomadic tribes, like religious minorities, as a threat to stability. Many nomads were forcibly deported and settled in the Balkans and western Anatolia, where they combined farming with stock raising. Due to heavy taxes imposed on animal herds, nomads had to earn additional income through transport, lumbering, and felt and carpet manufacture. Strong demand

≡ **Ottoman Expansion, c. 1200–1453**

from European customers and the imperial capital of Istanbul (the name Mehmed II gave to Constantinople) stimulated carpet weaving by both peasants and herders.

The patriarchal family, in which the wife is subject to her husband's control, was a pillar of Ottoman law, just as it was in Ming China. Although men usually controlled property in the form of land and houses, women acquired wealth in the form of money, furnishings, clothes, and jewelry. Women invested in commercial ventures, tax farming, and moneylending. Because women were secluded in the home and veiled in public—long-established requirements to maintain family honor and status in the central Islamic lands—women used servants and trusted clients to help them conduct their business activities.

The final defeat of the Byzantine Empire by Ottoman armies in 1453 shocked the Christian world. Mehmed II's capture of Constantinople also completed a radical transformation of the Ottoman enterprise. The Ottoman sultans no longer saw themselves as roving ghazi warriors, but as monarchs with absolute authority over a multinational empire at the crossroads of Europe and Asia. A proudly Islamic regime, the Ottoman sultanate aspired to become the centerpiece of a broad cosmopolitan civilization, a new Roman Empire, spanning Europe, Asia, and Africa.

Commerce and Culture in Islamic West Africa

West African trading empires and the merchants they supported had long served as the vanguard of Islam in sub-Saharan Africa. The Mali Empire's adoption of Islam as its official religion in the late thirteenth century encouraged conversion to Islam throughout the West African savanna. Islam continued to prosper despite the collapse of Mali's political dominion in the mid-fourteenth century.

Merchants of many nationalities still braved the perilous journey across the Sahara Desert in their quest for gold (see Reading the Past: A Genoese Merchant on Commercial Prospects in a Saharan Oasis Town). The towns of Jenne and Timbuktu, founded along the Niger River by Muslim merchants in the thirteenth century, emerged as the new crossroads of trans-Saharan trade. Jenne benefited from its access to the gold mines and rain forest products of coastal West Africa. Timbuktu's commercial prosperity rose as trade grew between West Africa and Mamluk Egypt. Islamic intellectual culture thrived among the merchant families of Timbuktu, Jenne, and other towns.

As elsewhere in the Islamic world, West African trader families readily combined religious scholarship with mercantile pursuits. Since the eleventh century, disciples of renowned scholars had migrated across the Sahara and founded schools and libraries. The Moroccan Muslim scholar and traveler Ibn Battuta (IB-uhn ba-TOO-tuh), who visited Mali in 1352–1353, voiced approval of the people's

READING THE PAST

A Genoese Merchant on Commercial Prospects in a Saharan Oasis Town

In 1447 the Genoese merchant Antonio Malfante was dispatched to Tuat, in the heart of the Sahara Desert in central Algeria, to gather commercial information on behalf of his company. Malfante's letter to his superiors is the earliest record by a Latin Christian of the Saharan oasis towns and the lands beyond.

This locality is a mart of the Moors, to which merchants come to sell their goods: gold is carried hither, and bought by those who come up from the coast. . . . The generality, however, are very poor, for they do not sow, nor do they harvest anything, save the dates upon which they subsist. They eat no meat but that of castrated camels, which are scarce and very dear. . . .

There are many Jews, who lead a good life here, for they are under the protection of the several rulers, each of whom defends his own clients. Thus they enjoy very secure social standing. Trade is in their hands, and many of them are to be trusted with the greatest confidence. . . .

In the lands of the blacks, as well as here, dwell the Philistines [Tuareg nomads], who live, like the Arabs, in tents. . . . The states which are under their rule . . . have inhabitants of the faith of Muhammad. In all, the great majority are blacks, but there are a small number of whites. [Malfante then lists over a dozen cities, including Takedda, Gao, Timbuktu, Jenne, and Mali.] All these are great cities, capitals of extensive lands.

"eagerness to memorize the great Qur'an: they place fetters on their children if they fail to memorize it and they are not released until they do so."[5] The Muslim diplomat Hasan al-Wazzan (hah-SAHN al-wah-zan), whose *Description of Africa* (published in Italian in 1550) became a best-seller in Europe, wrote that in Timbuktu "the learned are greatly revered. Also, many book manuscripts coming from the Berber [North African] lands are sold. More profits are realized from sales of books than any other merchandise."[6]

Islam wielded considerable influence in the towns. Clerics presided over worship and festival life and governed social behavior by applying Muslim law and cultural traditions. Yet away from the towns the majority of the population remained attached to ancestral beliefs in nature spirits, especially the spirits of rivers and thunder. Healer priests, clan chiefs, and other ritual experts shared

To the south of these are innumerable great cities and territories, the inhabitants of which are all blacks and idolators, continually at war with each other in defense of their law and the faith of their idols. Some worship the sun, others the moon, the seven planets, fire, or water; others a mirror which reflects their faces, which they take to be images of the gods; others groves of trees, which they take to be seats of a spirit to whom they make sacrifice; others again, statues of wood and stone with which, they say, they commune by incantations. . . .

The place where I am is good for trade, as the Egyptians and other merchants come hither from the land of the blacks bringing gold, which they exchange for copper and other goods. Thus everything sells well, until there is nothing left for sale. The people here will neither sell nor buy unless at a profit of one hundred percent. For this reason I have lost—Praise be God!—on the goods I have brought here, two thousand dinars.

Source: G. R. Crone (trans.), *The Voyages of Cadamosto and Other Documents on Western Africa in the Second Half of the Fifteenth Century* (London: Hakluyt Society, 1937), 86–90.

Examining the Evidence

1. What do Malfante's remarks suggest about the relationships among government, commerce, and religion in the Saharan oasis towns?

2. Does Malfante indicate that Tuat would be a profitable place for his company to do business? Why or why not?

responsibility for making offerings to the spirits, providing protection from evil demons and sorcerers, and honoring the dead.

Advance of Islam in Maritime Southeast Asia

Muslim Arab merchants had dominated maritime commerce in the Indian Ocean and Southeast Asia since the seventh century. Not until the thirteenth century, however, did Islam begin to gain converts in Malaysia and the Indonesian archipelago. By 1400 Arab and Gujarati traders and Sufi teachers had spread Islam throughout maritime Asia. The dispersion of Muslim merchants took the form of a **trade diaspora**, a network of merchant settlements dispersed across foreign lands but united by common origins, religion, and language, as well as by business dealings.

trade diaspora A network of merchants from the same city or country who live permanently in foreign lands and cooperate with one another to pursue trading opportunities.

≡ **Timbuktu Manuscript** Timbuktu became a hub of Islamic culture and intellectual life during the thirteenth and fourteenth centuries. Scholars and students assembled impressive libraries of Arabic texts, such as this Qur'an. Written mostly on paper imported from Europe, Timbuktu's manuscripts were preserved in family collections after the city's leading scholars were deported to North Africa by Moroccan invaders in 1591.

Political and economic motives strongly influenced official adoption of Islam. In the first half of the fourteenth century, the Majapahit (mah-jah-PAH-hit) kingdom (1292–1528), a bastion of Hindu religion, conquered most of Java and forced many local rulers in the Indonesian archipelago to submit tribute (see Map 14.4). In response, many of these rulers adopted Islam as an act of resistance to dominance by the Majapahit kings. By 1428 the Muslim city-states of Java's north coast, buoyed by the profits of trade with China, secured their independence from Majapahit. Majapahit's dominion over the agricultural hinterland of Java lasted until 1528, when a coalition of Muslim princes forced the royal family to flee to Bali, which remains today the sole preserve of Hinduism in Southeast Asia.

Cosmopolitan port cities, with their diverse merchant communities, were natural sites for religious innovation. The spread of Islam beyond Southeast Asia's port cities, however, was slow and uneven. Because merchants and Sufi teachers overshadowed the orthodox ulama in the spread of Islam in Southeast Asia, relatively open forms of Islam flourished. The Arab shipmaster Ibn Majid (IB-uhn maj-jid), writing in 1462, bemoaned the corruption of Islamic marriage and dietary laws among the Muslims of Melaka (mah-LAK-eh): "They have no culture at all. The infidel marries Muslim women while the Muslim takes pagans to wife. . . . The Muslim eats dogs for meat, for there are no food laws. They drink wine in the markets and do not treat divorce as a religious act."[7] Enforcement of Islamic law often was suspended where it conflicted with local custom. Southeast Asia never adopted some features of Middle Eastern culture often associated with Islam, such as the veiling of women.

Local pre-Islamic religious traditions persisted in Sumatra and Java long after the people accepted Islam. The most visible signs of conversion to Islam were giving up the worship of idols and the consumption of pork and adopting the practice of male circumcision. In addition, the elaborate feasting and grave goods, sacrifice of enslaved people, and widow sacrifice (*sati*) that normally accompanied the burials of chiefs and kings largely disappeared. Malays and Javanese readily adopted veneration of Sufi saints and habitually prayed for assistance from the spirits of deceased holy men. Muslim restrictions on women's secular and religious activities met with spirited resistance from Southeast Asian women, who were accustomed to active participation in public life. Even more than in West Africa, Islam in Southeast Asia prospered not by destroying traditions, but by assimilating them.

In regions such as West Africa and Southeast Asia, then, Islam diffused through the activities of merchants, teachers, and settlers rather than through conquest. The spread of Islam in Africa and Asia also followed the rhythms of international trade. While Europe recovered slowly from the Black Death, thriving commerce across the Indian Ocean forged new economic links among Asia, Africa, and the Mediterranean world.

The Global Bazaar

◥ **FOCUS** How did the pattern of international trade change during the fourteenth and fifteenth centuries, and how did these changes affect consumption and fashion tastes?

Dynastic changes, war, and the Black Death roiled the international economy in the fourteenth century. Yet the maritime world of the Indian Ocean, largely spared both pandemic and war, displayed unprecedented commercial dynamism. Pepper and cotton textiles from India, porcelain and silk from China, spices and other exotic goods from Southeast Asia, and gold, ivory, and copper from southern Africa circulated through a network of trading ports that spanned the Indian Ocean, Southeast Asia, and China. These trading centers attracted merchants and artisans from many lands, and the colorful variety of languages, dress, foods, and music that filled their streets gave them the air of a global bazaar (see Map 14.4).

The crises of the fourteenth century severely disrupted the European economy, but by 1450 Italy regained its place as the center within Latin Christendom of finance, industry, and trade. Italian production of luxury goods surpassed Islamic competitors' in both quantity and quality. Wealth poured into Italy, where it found new outlets in a culture of conspicuous consumption.

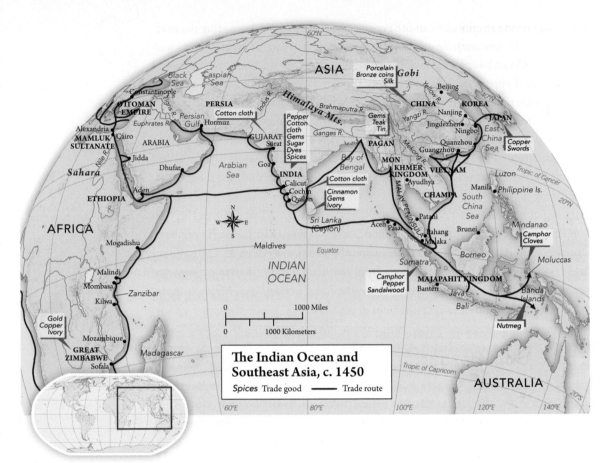

≡ **MAP 14.4   The Indian Ocean and Southeast Asia, c. 1450**   Spared the devastation of the Black Death, maritime Asia flourished in the fourteenth and fifteenth centuries. But travel across the Asian seas still had to follow the rhythms of the seasonal monsoon winds. The Islamic sultanate of Melaka on the Malay peninsula emerged as a great commercial crossroads where merchants from the Indian Ocean and the China seas gathered to trade.

Economic Prosperity and Maritime Trade in Asia 1350–1450

In Qubilai Khan's day, hostility among the Mongol khanates disrupted Central Asian caravan trade. After 1300 maritime commerce largely replaced inland trade over the ancient Silk Road. Asian merchants from India to China would seize the opportunities presented by the new emphasis on maritime trade.

In India, improvements in spinning wheels and looms, and above all the invention of block printing of fabrics in the fourteenth century, led to a revolution in cotton textile manufacture. Using block printing (carved wooden blocks covered with dye), Indian weavers produced colorful and intricately designed fabrics—later known in Europe as chintz, from the Hindi *chint* ("many-colored")—that were far cheaper than luxury textiles such as silk or velvet. Although cotton cultivation and weaving spread to Burma, Thailand, and China, Indian fabrics dominated Eurasian markets (see Lives and Livelihoods: Urban Weavers in India).

Along with textiles, India was famous for its pepper, for which Europeans had acquired a taste during the age of the Crusades. Muslim merchants from Gujarat controlled both cotton and pepper exports from the cities of Calicut and Quilon (KEE-lon). By 1500 Gujarati merchants had created a far-flung trade network across the Indian Ocean from Zanzibar to Java. Gujarati *sharafs* (from the Persian word for "moneylender") and Tamil *chettis* ("traders") acted as bankers for merchants and rulers alike in nearly every Indian Ocean port.

China's ocean-going commerce also flourished in the fourteenth century. Silk had long dominated China's export trade, but by the eleventh century domestic silk-weaving was flourishing in Iran, the Byzantine Empire, and India. Instead, China retained its preeminent place in world trade by exporting porcelain, which became known as "chinaware." Chinese ceramics already had become an important item of Asian maritime trade in the tenth century, when Chinese potters perfected the techniques for making porcelain wares, which were harder and whiter than previous types of ceramics. In the thirteenth century, artisans at Jingdezhen (JING-deh-JUHN) in southern China began to produce blue-and-white porcelains decorated with cobalt metallic pigment imported from Central Asia, which Chinese potters called "Mohammedan blue." By 1500, Jingdezhen had become the largest manufacturing city in the world, housing more than 1,000 kilns with some 70,000 craftsmen engaged in several dozen specialized tasks.

The most avid consumers of Chinese porcelains were in the Islamic world, reflecting the global nature of the Chinese ceramics industry. Muslims used Chinese porcelains both as eating and drinking vessels and to decorate mosques, tombs, and other holy places. Imports of Chinese porcelain devastated local ceramic manufacturing in many parts of maritime Asia, from the Philippines to East Africa.

In mainland Southeast Asia, the shift in political power from the inland rice-growing regions toward coastal port cities reflected the new prominence of maritime trade in the region's economic life. Burma exported cotton to China as early as 1400 and became an important source of metals, gems, and teak for shipbuilding. The profits of maritime commerce fueled the emergence of Ayudhya (a-YOOD-he-ya) in Thailand as the dominant power in mainland Southeast Asia in the late fourteenth century. By 1400 Ayudhya was challenging Majapahit for control of the Southeast Asian trade routes between India and China.

China influenced patterns of international trade not only as a producer, as with ceramics, but as a market for exported goods. It was Chinese demand that drove

LIVES AND LIVELIHOODS

Urban Weavers in India

Industry and commerce in India, especially in textiles, grew rapidly beginning in the fourteenth century. Specialized craftsmen in towns and regional groups of merchants formed guilds that became the nuclei of new occupational castes, *jati* (JAH-tee). Ultimately these new occupational castes would join with other forces in Indian society to challenge the social inequality rooted in orthodox Hindu religion.

It was growth in market demand and technological innovations such as block printing that drove the rapid expansion of India's textile industries. Luxury fabrics such as fine silks and velvet remained largely the province of royal workshops or private patronage. Mass production of textiles, by contrast, was oriented toward the manufacture of cheaper cotton fabrics, especially colorful chintz garments. A weaver could make a woman's cotton *sari* in six or seven days, whereas a luxury garment took a month or more.

Weaving became an urban industry. It was village women who cleaned most of the cotton and spun it into yarn; they could easily combine this simple if laborious work with other domestic chores. But weaving, bleaching, and dyeing cloth were skilled tasks performed by professional urban craftsmen, or in some cases by artisans living in separate weavers' settlements in the countryside.

Increased affluence brought further social and economic differentiation to the ranks of weavers. Although guild leaders negotiated orders from merchants and princes, artisans could freely sell their own wares through urban shops and country fairs. The most successful weavers became merchants and

≡ **Indian Block-Printed Textile, c. 1500**
Block-printed textiles with elaborate designs were in great demand in India and throughout Southeast Asia, Africa, and the Islamic world. This cotton fabric with geese, lotus flower, and rosette designs was manufactured in Gujarat in western India.

brokers, buying more looms and hiring others to work under their supervision. By the fourteenth century some weavers had begun to add the honorific title *chetti* (merchant) to their names.

The rising prosperity of weavers whetted their aspirations for social recognition. Enforcing laws governing caste purity amid the whirl and congestion of city life was far more difficult than in the villages. As a fourteenth-century poet wrote about the crowded streets of his hometown of Jaunpur in the Ganges Valley, in the city "one person's caste-mark gets stamped on another's forehead, and a brahmin's holy thread will be found hanging around an untouchable's neck."[1] Brahmins objected to this erosion of caste boundaries, to little avail. Weavers became influential patrons of temples and often served as trustees and accountants in charge of managing temple endowments and revenues.

In a few cases the growing economic independence of weavers and like-minded artisans prompted complete rejection of the caste hierarchy. Sufi preachers and *bhakti* (BAHK-tee)—devotional movements dedicated to patron gods and goddesses—encouraged the disregard of caste distinctions in favor of a universal brotherhood of fellow believers. The fifteenth-century bhakti preacher Kabir, who was strongly influenced by Sufi teachings, epitomized the new social radicalism coursing through the urban artisan classes. A weaver himself, Kabir joined the dignity of manual labor to the purity of spiritual devotion, spurning the social pretension and superficial piety of the Brahmins and Muslim clerics.

By the seventeenth century, such ideas had coalesced into a separatist religious movement, Sikhism, centered on a trinity of labor, charity, and spiritual devotion. The Sikhs, who gained a following principally among traders and artisans in the northwestern Punjab region, drew an even more explicit connection between commerce and piety. In the words of a hymn included in a sixteenth-century anthology of Sikh sacred writings,

> The true Guru [teacher] is the merchant;
> The devotees are his peddlers.
> The capital stock is the Lord's Name, and
> To enshrine the truth is to keep His account.[2]

Sikh communities spurned the distinction between pure and impure occupations. In their eyes, holiness was to be found in honest toil and personal piety, not ascetic practices, book learning, or religious rituals.

1. Vidyapati Thakur, *Kirtilata*, quoted in Eugenia Vanina, *Urban Crafts and Craftsmen in Medieval India (Thirteenth–Eighteenth Centuries)* (New Delhi: Munshiram Manoharlal, 2004), 143.

2. *Sri Guru Granth Sahib*, trans. Gophal Singh (Delhi: Gur Das Kapur & Sons, 1960), 2:427.

Questions to Consider

1. In what ways did the organization of textile production reinforce or challenge the prevailing social norms of Hindu society?

2. In what ways did religious ideas and movements reflect the new sense of dignity among prosperous Indian merchants and craftsmen?

For Further Information:

Ramaswamy, Vijaya. *Textiles and Weavers in Medieval South India*. Delhi: Oxford University Press, 1985.

Vanina, Eugenia. *Urban Crafts and Craftsmen in Medieval India (Thirteenth–Eighteenth Centuries)*. New Delhi: Munshiram Manoharlal, 2004.

≡ **Jingdezhen Porcelains from a Philippines Shipwreck**   These porcelain bowls from Jingdezhen were part of the cargo of a Chinese junk that sank around 1490 near Palawan Island, probably en route to Muslim communities in the southern Philippines. The ship also carried ceramics from Thailand, Vietnam, and Burma, tin ingots and bronze bracelets, and many elephant tusks, evidence of the diversity of Asian maritime trade.

the rapid expansion of pepper cultivation in Southeast Asia, in particular Sumatra, during the fifteenth century. In return for exports of pepper, sandalwood, tin and other metals, fine spices, and exotic products of the tropical rain forests, Southeast Asia imported cotton cloth from India and silks, porcelain, and bronze coins from China. In the wake of this trade boom, Indian and Chinese merchant communities sprouted across maritime Southeast Asia. The trade diasporas of Gujarati Muslims and Chinese from Guangzhou (Canton) and Quanzhou (CHYWAN-joe) created networks of cultural as well as economic influence, ultimately altering the balance of political power as well (see again Map 14.4).

China's Overseas Overture: The Voyages of Zheng He 1405–1433

The growth of South Asian maritime trade attracted the attention of the Chinese government, and in the early fifteenth century, the Ming dynasty in China took a more active role in maritime Southeast Asia. From the 1390s

Malay princes in Sumatra appealed to the Ming court for protection against the demands of the Majapahit kings. In 1405 the Ming emperor Yongle decided to intervene by sending a naval expedition to halt the expansionist aggression of Majapahit and Ayudhya and to assert Chinese authority over the maritime realm.

Yongle entrusted the fleet to the command of his closest confidant, a young military officer named Zheng He (1371–1433). Zheng, born into a Muslim family who had served the Mongol rulers of the Yuan dynasty, was conscripted into the eunuch corps (castrated males employed as guardians of the imperial household) and placed in the retinue of the prince who would become Emperor Yongle.

For his mission to Southeast Asia, Yongle equipped Zheng He with a vast armada, a fleet of sixty-three ships manned by nearly 28,000 sailors, soldiers, and officials. Zheng's seven-masted flagship, more than 400 feet long, was a marvel of Chinese nautical engineering. His fleet later became known as the "treasure ships" because of the cargoes of exotic goods and tribute they brought back from Southeast Asia, India, Arabia, and Africa. But Zheng's primary mission was political, not economic.

Departing in November of 1405, Zheng's fleet sailed first to Java in a show of force designed to intimidate Majapahit. He then traveled to Sumatra and Melaka and across the Indian Ocean to Ceylon and Calicut. No sooner had Zheng He returned to China in the autumn of 1407 than Yongle dispatched him on another voyage. Yongle had recently launched his invasion of Vietnam, and the purpose of the second voyage was to curtail Ayudhya's aggression and establish a Chinese presence at strategic ports such as Melaka along the Straits of Sumatra. Altogether Yongle commissioned six expeditions under Zheng He's command. During the fourth and subsequent voyages, Zheng He sailed beyond India to Arabia and down the east coast of Africa.

The projection of Chinese power over the sea lanes of maritime Asia led to far-reaching economic and political changes. The close relations Zheng He cultivated with rulers of port cities strengthened their political independence and promoted commercial growth. Under the umbrella of Chinese protection, Melaka flourished as the great crossroads of Asian maritime trade.

The high cost of building and equipping the treasure ships depleted the Ming treasury, however. In 1430, Yongle's successor dispatched Zheng He on yet another voyage, his seventh. After traveling once again to Africa, Zheng died during his return home. With the passing of the renowned admiral, enthusiasm for the expeditions evaporated. Moreover, the Ming court faced a new threat: a resurgent Mongol confederation in the north. In 1449 a foolish young Ming emperor led a military campaign against the Mongols, only to be taken captive. The Ming court obtained the emperor's release by paying a huge ransom, but its strategic priorities had been completely transformed. Turning its back on the sea, the Ming state devoted its energies and revenues to rebuilding the Great Wall, much of which had crumbled to dust, as a defense against further Mongol attacks.

The shift in Chinese policy did not mean the end of Chinese involvement in maritime trade. Chinese merchants continued to pursue trading opportunities in defiance of the imperial ban on private overseas commerce. Melaka's rulers converted to Islam but welcomed merchants from every corner of Asia. The population probably reached 100,000 before Melaka was sacked by the Portuguese in 1511. Spurred by the growing European appetite for Asian spices, the violent intrusion of the Portuguese would transform the dynamics of maritime trade throughout Asia.

Commerce and Culture in the Renaissance

European expansion in the late fourteenth and early fifteenth centuries was preceded and influenced by a period of dramatic change, the sweeping transformation in European culture known as the **Renaissance**. In its narrow sense *Renaissance* (French for "rebirth") refers to the revival of ancient Greek and Roman philosophy, art, and literature that originated in fourteenth-century Italy. Scholars rediscovered classical learning and began to emulate the language and ideas of Greek and Roman philosophers and poets; these individuals became known as humanists, students of the liberal arts or humanities. The new intellectual movement of **humanism** combined classical learning with Christian piety and dedication to civic responsibilities.

At the same time, the Renaissance inaugurated dramatic changes in the self-image and lifestyle of the wealthy. The new habits of luxurious living and magnificent display diverged sharply from the Christian ethic of frugality. Innovations in material culture and aesthetic values reflected crucial changes in the Italian economy and its relationship to the international trading world of the Mediterranean and beyond.

The Black Death had hit the Italian city-states especially hard. Diminishing profits from trade with the Islamic world prompted many Italian merchants to abandon commerce in favor of banking. Squeezed out of the eastern Mediterranean by the Turks and Venetians, Genoa turned its attention westward. Genoese bankers became financiers to the kings of Spain and Portugal and supplied the funds for their initial forays into the Atlantic in search of new routes to African gold and Asian spices. European monarchs' growing reliance on professional armies, naval fleets, and gunpowder weapons forced them to borrow money to meet the rising costs of war, further stimulating demand for banking services.

Renaissance A period of intense intellectual and artistic creativity in Europe, beginning in Italy in the fourteenth century as a revival of the classical civilization of ancient Greece and Rome.

humanism The study of the humanities (rhetoric, poetry, history, and moral philosophy), based on the works of ancient Greek and Roman writers, that provided the intellectual foundations for the Renaissance.

Italy became the primary producer of luxury goods for Europe, displacing the Islamic world and Asia. Before 1400, Islamic craftsmanship had far surpassed that of Latin Christendom. The upper classes of Europe paid handsome sums to obtain silk and linen fabrics, ceramics, rugs, glass, metalwork, and jewelry imported from the Mamluk Empire. "The most beautiful things in the world are found in Damascus," wrote Simone Sigoli, a Florentine who visited the city in 1386. "Such rich and noble and delicate works of every kind. . . . Really, all Christendom could be supplied for a year with the merchandise of Damascus."[8] But the Black Death, Timur's invasions, and Mamluk mismanagement devastated industry and commerce in Egypt and Syria.

Seizing the opportunity these developments created, Italian entrepreneurs first imitated and then improved on Islamic techniques and designs for making silk, tin-glazed ceramics known as *maiolica* (my-OH-lee-kah), glass, and brassware. By 1450 these Italian products had become competitive with or eclipsed imports from Egypt and Syria. Italian firms captured the major share of the international market for luxury textiles and other finished goods, and the Islamic lands were reduced to being suppliers of raw materials such as silk, cotton, and dyestuffs.

Along with Italy's ascent in finance and manufacturing came a decisive shift in attitudes toward money and its use. The older Christian ethics of frugality and disdain for worldly gain gave way to prodigal spending and consumption. Much of this torrent of spending was lavished on religious art and artifacts, and the Roman papacy stood out as perhaps the most spendthrift of all. Displaying personal wealth and possessions affirmed social status and power. Civic pride and political rivalry fueled public spending to build and decorate churches and cathedrals. Rich townsmen transformed private homes into palaces, and artisans fashioned ordinary articles of everyday life—from rugs and furniture to dishes, books, and candlesticks—into works of art. Public piety blurred together with personal vanity. Spending money on religious monuments, wrote the fifteenth-century Florentine merchant Giovanni Rucellai (ROO-chel-lie) in his diary, gave him "the greatest satisfaction and the greatest pleasure, because it serves the glory of God, the honor of Florence, and my own memory."[9]

"Magnificence" became the watchword of the Renaissance. Wealthy merchants and members of the clergy portrayed themselves as patrons of culture and learning. Worldly goods gave tangible expression to spiritual refinement. The paintings of Madonnas and saints that graced Renaissance mansions were much more than objects of devotion: they were statements of cultural and social values. New commercial wealth created an expanded market for art, which was in turn shaped by the values associated with commerce.

SEEING THE PAST

Leonardo da Vinci's *Virgin of the Rocks*

While living in Milan in the early 1480s, Leonardo accepted a commission to paint an altarpiece for the chapel of Milan's Confraternity of the Immaculate Conception, a branch of the Franciscan order. Leonardo's relationship with the friars proved to be stormy. His first version of the painting (now in the Louvre), reproduced here, apparently displeased his patrons and was sold to another party. Only after a fifteen-year-long dispute over the price did Leonardo finally deliver a modified version in 1508.

In portraying the biblical encounter between the child Jesus and the equally young John the Baptist during the flight to Egypt, Leonardo replaced the traditional desert setting with a landscape filled with rocks, plants, and water. Leonardo's dark grotto creates an aura of mystery and foreboding, from which the figures of Mary, Jesus, John, and the angel Uriel emerge as if in a vision. A few years before, Leonardo had written about "coming

Virgin of the Rocks, c. 1483–1486

As with Islam in West Africa, the intellectual ferment of the Renaissance was nurtured in an urban environment. Humanist scholars shunned the warrior culture of the old nobility while celebrating the civic roles and duties of townsmen, merchants, and clerics. Despite their admiration of classical civilization, the humanists did not reject Christianity. Rather, they sought to reconcile Christian faith and doctrines with classical learning. By making knowledge of Latin and to the entrance of a great cavern, in front of which I stood for some time, stupefied and uncomprehending. . . . Suddenly two things arose in me, fear and desire: fear of the menacing darkness of the cavern; desire to see if there was any marvelous thing within."[1] The scene's ambiguity may have been the reason the friars rejected this version. The painting they eventually took added features such as a halo for Jesus and a cross-like staff for John that clarified their identities.

Fantastic as the scene might seem, Leonardo's meticulous renderings of rocks and plants were based on close observation of nature. Geologists have praised Leonardo's highly realistic sandstone rock formations and his precise placement of plants where they would most likely take root.

Masterpieces such as the *Virgin of the Rocks* display Leonardo's careful study of human anatomy, natural landscapes, and botany. Although he admired the perfection of nature, Leonardo also celebrated the human mind's rational and aesthetic capacities, declaring, "We by our arts may be called the grandsons of God."[2]

1. Arundel ms. (British Library), p. 115 recto, cited in Martin Kemp, *Leonardo da Vinci: The Marvelous Works of Nature and Man* (Oxford: Oxford University Press, 2006), 78.

2. John Paul Richter, ed., *The Notebooks of Leonardo da Vinci* (reprint of 1883 ed.; New York: Dover, 1970), Book IX, 328 (para. 654).

Examining the Evidence

1. How does Leonardo express the connection between John (at left) and Jesus through position, gesture, and their relationships with the figures of Mary and the angel Uriel?

2. The friars who commissioned the painting sought to celebrate the sanctity and purity of their patron, the Virgin Mary. Does this painting achieve that effect?

Greek, history, poetry, and philosophy the mark of an educated person, the humanists transformed education and established models of schooling that would endure down to modern times.

Nowhere was the revolutionary impact of the Renaissance felt more deeply than in visual arts such as painting, sculpture, and architecture. Artists of the Renaissance exuded supreme confidence in the human capability to equal or even surpass the works of nature. The new outlook was exemplified by the development of the techniques of perspective, which artists used to convey a realistic, three-dimensional quality to physical forms, most notably the human body.

Above all, the Renaissance transformed the idea of the artist. No longer mere tradesmen, artists now were seen as possessing a special kind of genius that enabled them to express a higher understanding of beauty. In the eyes of contemporaries, no one exemplified this quality of genius more than Leonardo da Vinci (1452–1519), who won renown as a painter, architect, sculptor, engineer, mathematician, and inventor. Leonardo spent much of his career as a civil and military engineer in the employ of the Duke of Milan, and developed ideas for flying machines, tanks, robots, and solar power that far exceeded the engineering capabilities of his time. Leonardo sought to apply his knowledge of natural science to painting, which he regarded as the most sublime art (see Seeing the Past: Leonardo da Vinci's *Virgin of the Rocks*).

The flowering of artistic creativity in the Renaissance was rooted in the rich soil of Italy's commercial wealth and nourished by the flow of goods from the Islamic world and Asia. International trade also invigorated industrial and craft production across maritime Asia and gave birth there to new patterns of material culture and consumption. In Japan, however, growing isolation from these cross-cultural interactions fostered the emergence of a national culture distinct from the Chinese traditions that dominated the rest of East Asia.

COUNTERPOINT: Age of the Samurai in Japan 1185–1450

⬊ **FOCUS** How and why did the historical development of Japan in the fourteenth and fifteenth centuries differ from that of mainland Eurasia?

samurai Literally, "those who serve"; the hereditary warriors who dominated Japanese society and culture from the twelfth to the nineteenth century.

In Japan as in Europe, the term *Middle Ages* brings to mind an age of warriors, a stratified society governed by bonds of loyalty between lords and vassals. In Japan, however, the militarization of the ruling class intensified during the fourteenth and fifteenth centuries, a time when the warrior nobility of Europe was crumbling. Paradoxically, the rise of the **samurai (sah-moo-rye)** ("those who serve") warriors as masters of their own estates was accompanied by the increasing independence of peasant communities.

In contrast to the regions explored earlier in this chapter, Japan became more isolated from the wider world during this era. After the failed Mongol invasion of Japan in 1281, ties with continental Asia became increasingly frayed. Thus, many Japanese see this era as the period in which Japan's unique national identity— expressed most distinctly in the ethic of *bushidō* (boo-shee-doe), the "way of the warrior"—took its definitive form. A culture based on warriors, rather than Confucian scholars, created a different path for the development of Japanese society.

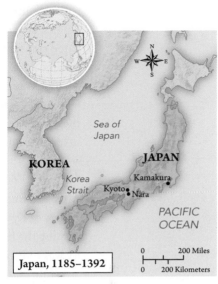

≡ **Japan, 1185–1392**

"The Low Overturning the High"

During the Kamakura period (1185–1333), the power of the **shogun**, or military ruler, of eastern Japan was roughly in balance with that of the imperial court and nobility at Kyoto in the west. Warriors dominated both the shogun's capital at Kamakura (near modern Tokyo) and provincial governorships, but most of the land remained in the possession of the imperial family, the nobility, and religious institutions based in Kyoto. After the collapse of the Kamakura government in 1333, Japan was wracked by civil wars. In 1336 a new dynasty of shoguns, the Ashikaga (ah-shee-KAH-gah), came to power in Kyoto. Unlike the Kamakura shoguns, the Ashikaga aspired to become national rulers. Yet not until 1392 did the Ashikaga shogunate gain uncontested political supremacy, and even then it exercised only limited control over the provinces and local samurai.

In the Kamakura period, the samurai had been vassals subordinated to warrior clans to whom they owed allegiance and service. But wartime disorder and Ashikaga rule eroded the privileges and power of the noble and monastic landowners. Most of their estates fell into the hands of local samurai families.

Just as samurai were turning themselves into landowners, peasants banded together in village associations to resist demands for rents and labor service from their new samurai overlords. These village associations created their own autonomous governments to defy outside control while requiring strict conformity to the collective will of the community. As one village council declared, "Treachery, malicious gossip, or criminal acts against the village association will be punished by excommunication from the estate."[10] Outraged lords bewailed this reversal of the social hierarchy, "the low overturning the high," but found themselves powerless to check the growing independence of peasant communities.

shogun The military commander who effectively exercised supreme political and military authority over Japan during the Kamakura (1185–1333), Ashikaga (1336–1573), and Tokugawa (1603–1868) shogunates.

The political strength of the peasants reflected their rising economic fortunes. Japan's agrarian economy improved substantially with the expansion of irrigated rice farming. The village displaced the manorial estate as the basic institution of rural society. Japan in the fifteenth century had little involvement in foreign trade, and there were few cities apart from the metropolis of Kyoto, which had swelled to 150,000 inhabitants by midcentury. Yet the prosperity of the agrarian economy generated considerable growth in artisan crafts and trade in local goods.

The New Warrior Order

After the founding of the Ashikaga shogunate, provincial samurai swarmed the streets of Kyoto seeking the new rulers' patronage. In this world of "the low overturning the high," warriors enjoyed newfound wealth while much of the old nobility was reduced to abject poverty.

While derided by courtiers as uneducated and boorish, the shoguns and samurai became patrons of artists and cultural life. The breakdown of the traditional social hierarchy allowed greater intermingling among people from diverse backgrounds. The social and cultural worlds of the warriors and courtiers merged, producing new forms of social behavior and artistic expression.

In the early years of the Ashikaga shogunate, the capital remained infatuated with Chinese culture. As the fourteenth century wore on, however, this fascination with China was eclipsed by new fashions drawn from both the court nobility and Kyoto's lively world of popular entertainments. Accomplishment in poetry and graceful language and manners, hallmarks of the courtier class, became part of samurai self-identity as well. A new mood of simplicity and restraint took hold, infused with the ascetic ethics of Zen Buddhism, which, as we saw in Chapter 9, stressed introspective meditation as the path to enlightenment.

The sensibility of the Ashikaga age was visible in new kinds of artistic display and performance, including poetry recitation, flower arrangement, and the complex rituals of the tea ceremony. A new style of theater known as *nō* reflected this fusion of courtly refinement, Zen religious sentiments, and samurai cultural tastes. Thus, the rise of warrior culture in Japan did not mean an end to sophistication and refinement. It did, however, involve a strong focus on cultural elements that were seen as distinctly Japanese.

In at least one area, developments in Japan mirrored those in other parts of the world. The warriors' dominance over Ashikaga society and culture led to a decisive shift toward patriarchal authority. Women lost rights of inheritance as warrior houses consolidated landholdings in the hands of one son who would continue the family line. The libertine sexual mores of the Japanese aristocracy depicted in Lady Murasaki's *Tale of Genji* (c. 1010) (see Chapter 12) gave way to a new emphasis on female chastity as an index of social order. The profuse output of novels, memoirs, and diaries written by court women also came to an end by 1350.

By 1400, then, the samurai had achieved political mastery in both the capital and the countryside and had eclipsed the old nobility as arbiters of cultural values. This warrior culture, which combined martial prowess with austere aesthetic tastes, stood in sharp contrast to the veneration of Confucian learning by the Chinese literati and the classical ideals and ostentatious consumption prized by the urban elite of Renaissance Italy.

Conclusion

The fourteenth century was an age of crisis across Eurasia and Africa. Population losses resulting from the Black Death devastated Christian and Muslim societies and economies. In the long run Latin Christendom fared well: the institution of serfdom largely disappeared from western Europe, new entrepreneurial energies were released, and the Italian city-states recovered their commercial vigor and stimulated economic revival in northern Europe. However, the once great Byzantine Empire succumbed to the expanding Ottoman Empire and, under fire by Urban's cannon, came to an end in 1453. Despite the Ottoman conquests, the central Islamic lands, from Egypt to Mesopotamia, never regained their former economic vitality. Still, the Muslim faith continued to spread, winning new converts in Africa, Central Asia, and Southeast Asia.

The fourteenth century also witnessed the collapse of the Mongol empires in China and Iran, followed by the rise and fall of the last of the Mongol empires, that of Timur. In China, the Ming dynasty spurned the Mongol vision of a multinational empire, instead returning to an imperial order based on an agrarian economy, bureaucratic rule, and Neo-Confucian values. New dynastic leaders in Korea and Vietnam imitated the Ming model, but in Japan the rising samurai warrior class forged a radically different set of social institutions and cultural values.

The Black Death redirected the course of European state-making. Monarchs strengthened their authority, aided by advances in military technology, mercenary armies, and fresh sources of revenue. The intensifying competition among national states would become one of the main motives for overseas exploration and expansion in the Atlantic world. At the same time, the great transformation in culture, lifestyles, and values known as the Renaissance sprang from the ruin of the Black Death.

review

The major global development in this chapter: Crisis and recovery in fourteenth- and fifteenth-century Afro-Eurasia.

Important Events	
1325–1354	Travels of Ibn Battuta in Asia and Africa
1336–1573	Ashikaga shogunate in Japan
1337–1453	Hundred Years' War between England and France
1347–1350	Outbreak of the Black Death in Europe and the Islamic Mediterranean
c. 1351–1782	Ayudhya kingdom in Thailand
1368–1644	Ming dynasty in China
1381	Peasant Revolt in England
1392–1910	Yi dynasty in Korea
1405	Death of Timur; breakup of his empire into regional states in Iran and Central Asia
1405–1433	Chinese admiral Zheng He's expeditions in Southeast Asia and the Indian Ocean
1421	Relocation of Ming capital from Nanjing to Beijing
1428–1788	Le dynasty in Vietnam
1453	Ottoman conquest of Constantinople marks fall of the Byzantine Empire

KEY TERMS

Black Death (p. 511)
humanism (p. 536)
janissary corps (p. 524)
Little Ice Age (p. 512)
Neo-Confucianism (p. 519)

oligarchy (p. 516)
pandemic (p. 511)
Renaissance (p. 536)
samurai (p. 540)
shogun (p. 541)

Sufism (p. 522)
theocracy (p. 523)
trade diaspora (p. 527)

CHAPTER OVERVIEW QUESTIONS

1. How and why did Europe's economic growth begin to surpass that of the Islamic world in the century after the Black Death?

2. Did the economic revival across Eurasia after 1350 benefit the peasant populations of Europe, the Islamic world, and East Asia?

3. How did the process of conversion to Islam differ in Iran, the Ottoman Empire, West Africa, and Southeast Asia during this period?

4. What political and economic changes contributed to the rise of maritime commerce in Asia during the fourteenth and fifteenth centuries?

MAKING CONNECTIONS

1. What social, economic, and technological changes strengthened the power of European monarchs during the century after the Black Death?
2. How and why did the major routes and commodities of trans-Eurasian trade change after the collapse of the Mongol Empires in Central Asia?

3. In what ways did the motives for conversion to Islam differ in Central Asia, sub-Saharan Africa, and the Indian Ocean during this era?
4. In this period, why did the power and status of the samurai warriors in Japan rise while those of the warrior nobility in Europe declined?

DOING HISTORY

Argument

Historical sources speak, but in many voices. Historians must seek coherent explanations for historical developments by assessing the evidence of sources and constructing arguments that provide sound interpretations of the phenomena they are analyzing. Consider the consequences of the Black Death crisis discussed in this chapter. The pandemic was equally devastating to the populations of both Latin Christendom and the Islamic Mediterranean world. Yet we see different outcomes in European and Muslim societies in terms of religious beliefs about the meaning of the pandemic, its consequences for economic livelihoods and later economic development, and its impact on social structure.

1. What arguments do historians make to explain these differences?
2. Do you find these arguments persuasive? Why or why not?
3. Are there other issues that you think should be considered in trying to explain the different outcomes of the Black Death in Christian and Muslim societies?

For further research into the topics covered in this chapter, see the Bibliography at the end of the book.

The Early Modern World, 1450–1750

≡ In this exquisite miniature painting from the 1590s, the Mughal emperor Akbar receives the Persian ambassador Sayyid Beg in 1562. The painting is an illustration commissioned for Akbar's official court history, the *Akbarnama*, and thus would have been seen and approved by the emperor himself. The meeting is emblematic of the generally amiable relationship between the Mughals and their Safavid neighbors in Iran.

Between 1450 and 1750, regional societies gave way to multiethnic empires, and horse-riding warriors gave way to cannon and long-distance sailing craft. Historians call this era "early modern" because it was marked by a shift toward centralized, bureaucratic, monetized, and technologically sophisticated states. Yet most of these "modern" states also clung to divine kingship and other remnants of the previous age, and most sought to revive and propagate older religious or philosophical traditions. Some states embraced tolerance, whereas others fought bitterly over matters of faith.

A striking novelty was the creation of permanent linkages between distant regions, most notably the Americas and the rest of the world. Early globalization accelerated changes in everything from demography to commerce to technology, allowing populations to grow and individuals to get rich. Yet globalization also enabled the spread of disease, and some innovations made warfare more deadly; early modernity did not promise longer and better lives for everyone.

Beginning around 1450, Iberians—the people of Spain and Portugal—used new ships and guns to venture into the Atlantic, where they competed in overseas colonization, trade, and conquest. They did so at the expense of millions of native peoples, first in Africa and the East Atlantic and then throughout the Americas and beyond. Other Europeans followed in the Iberians' wake, but the silver of Spanish America became the world's money.

Modernity affected Africa most deeply via the slave trade. The older flow of captive workers to the Muslim Middle East and Indian Ocean basin continued into early modern times, but it was displaced by a more urgent European demand in the Atlantic. The desire for enslaved persons to staff distant plantations and mines fueled existing antagonisms within Africa even as it spawned new ones.

In the Indian Ocean basin a freer model of interaction developed. By 1450 Islamic merchants had come to dominate these seas by establishing trading networks from East Africa to Southeast Asia. After 1500, European interlopers discovered that in such a thriving, diverse, and politically decentralized region, they would have to compete fiercely for space. This they did, first by establishing coastal trading forts, then by moving inland.

On the Eurasian mainland, with the aid of modern firearms, powerful Ottoman, Russian, Safavid, and Mughal leaders turned from regional consolidation to imperial expansion by 1500. Unlike the Safavids and Mughals, the Ottomans sought to extend their empire overseas, taking on rivals in the Mediterranean and the Indian Ocean. Russia would venture abroad under Peter the Great.

Europe remained mostly embroiled in religious and political conflict. The religious schism known as the Protestant Reformation touched off bloody wars, and doctrinal disputes persisted. Warfare itself was transformed from knightly contests and town sieges to mass infantry mobilization and bombardment of strategic fortresses. Europe's political fractures enabled the rise of market economies, with more states sponsoring overseas colonizing ventures. New forms of government emerged, along with a questioning of ancient authorities. From this came a new science, emphasizing empirical observation and secular reasoning.

In early modern East Asia, by contrast, introversion was the rule. Although both China and Japan had strong seafaring traditions by 1450, state policies from the fifteenth to the sixteenth century discouraged external affairs. Despite official isolation, both regions proved to be dynamic. Political consolidation and population growth were matched with a shift from tributary to money economies. In the Chinese Ming and Qing Empires, this led to a rise in demand for silver, stimulating global circulation of this mostly American-produced metal. Porcelain and silk, much of it produced by poor women working in the household, were sent abroad in exchange. With the patronage of newly wealthy merchants and bureaucrats, the arts flourished on a scale not seen before.

By 1700, the American colonies were not the neo-Europes their first colonizers had envisioned. Centuries of ethnic and cultural mixture, forced labor regimes, frontier expansion, and export-oriented economies all led to the formation of distinct societies. In much of the Americas, the different outlooks of European colonizers and colonists would prove irreconcilable.

Despite these profound transformations, many people remained largely unaffected by the currents of early modernity. Most of North and South America, Polynesia, Oceania, central and southern Africa, and highland Asia remained beyond the zone of sustained contact with foreigners. New commodities and biological transfers were only beginning to be felt in many of these places at the end of the early modern era. As a result of their long isolation, inhabitants of these regions would be among the most drastically affected by modernity's next wave. ∎

Empires and Alternatives in the Americas

1430–1530

≡ **World in the Making** Perched on a granite ridge high above Peru's Urubamba River, the Inca site of Machu Picchu continues to draw thousands of visitors each year. First thought to be the lost city of Vilcabamba, then a convent for Inca nuns, Machu Picchu is now believed to have been a mid-fifteenth-century palace built for the Inca emperor and his mummy cult. It was probably more a religious site than a place of rest and recreation.

backstory

By the fifteenth century the Americas had witnessed the rise and fall of numerous empires and kingdoms, including the classic Maya of Mesoamerica, the wealthy Sicán kingdom of Peru's desert coast, and the Cahokia mound builders of the Mississippi Basin. Just as these cultures faded, there emerged two new imperial states that borrowed heavily from their predecessors. The empires discussed in this chapter, the Aztec and Inca, were the largest states ever to develop in the Americas, yet they were not all-powerful. About half of all native Americans, among them the diverse peoples of North America's eastern woodlands, lived outside their realms.

IN 1995, ARCHAEOLOGISTS discovered a tomb on a peak overlooking Arequipa, Peru. Inside was the mummified body of an adolescent girl placed there some 500 years earlier. Evidence suggests she was an *aclla* (AHK-yah), or "chosen woman," selected by Inca priests from among hundreds of regional headmen's daughters. Most aclla girls became priestesses dedicated to the Inca emperor or the imperial sun cult. Others became the emperor's concubines or wives. Only the most select, like the girl discovered near Arequipa, were chosen for the "debt-payment" sacrifice, or *capacocha* (kah-pah-KOH-chah), said to be the greatest honor of all.

According to testimonies collected after the Spanish conquest of the Incas in 1532 (discussed in the next chapter), the capacocha sacrifice was a rare event preceded by rituals. First, the victim, chosen for her (and rarely, his) physical perfection, trekked to Cuzco, the Inca capital. The child's father brought gifts from his province and in turn received fine textiles from the emperor. Following an ancient Andean tradition, ties between ruler and ruled were reinforced through such acts of reciprocity. The girl, too, received skirts and shawls, along with votive objects. These adorned her in her tomb, reached after a long journey on foot from Cuzco.

As suggested by later discoveries, at tomb-side the aclla girl was probably given a beaker of maize beer. In a pouch she carried coca leaves. Coca, chewed throughout the Andes, helped fend off altitude sickness, whereas the maize beer induced sleepiness. Barely conscious of her surroundings, the girl was lowered into her grass-lined grave, and, according to the forensic anthropologists who examined her skull, struck dead with a club.

Why did the Incas sacrifice children, and why in these ways? By combining material, written, and oral evidence, scholars are beginning to solve the riddle of the Inca mountain mummies. It now appears that death, fertility, reciprocity, and imperial links to sacred landscapes were all features of the capacocha sacrifice. Although such deadly practices may challenge our ability to empathize with the leaders, if not the common folk, of this distant culture, with each new fact we learn about the child mummies, the closer we get to understanding the Inca Empire and its ruling cosmology.

The Incas and their subjects believed that death occurred as a process, and that proper death led to an elevated state of consciousness. In this altered state a person could communicate with deities directly, and in a sense join them. If the remains of such a person were carefully preserved and honored, they could act as an oracle, a conduit to the sacred realms above and below the earth. Mountains, as sources of springs and rivers, and sometimes fertilizing volcanic ash, held particular significance.

In part, it was these beliefs about landscape, death, and the afterlife that led the Incas to mummify ancestors, including their emperors, and to bury chosen young people atop mountains that marked the edges, or heights, of empire. Physically perfect noble children such as the girl found near Arequipa were thus selected to communicate with the spirit world. Their sacrifice unified the dead, the living, and the sacred mountains, and also bound together a far-flung empire that was in many ways as fragile as life itself.[1]

But this fragility was not evident to the people gathered at the capacocha sacrifice. By about 1480, roughly half of all native Americans were subjects of two great empires, the Aztec in Mexico and Central America and the Inca in South America. Both empires subdued neighboring chiefdoms through a mix of violence, forced relocation, religious indoctrination, and marriage alliances. Both empires demanded allegiance in the form of tribute. Both the Aztecs and Incas were greatly feared by their millions of subjects. Perhaps surprisingly, these last great native American states would prove far more vulnerable to European invaders than their nonimperial neighbors, most of whom were gatherer-hunters and semi-sedentary villagers. Those who relied least on farming had the best chance of getting away.

OVERVIEW QUESTIONS

The major global development in this chapter: The diversity of societies and states in the Americas prior to European invasion.

As you read, consider:

1. In what ways was cultural diversity in the Americas related to environmental diversity?

2. Why was it in Mesoamerica and the Andes that large empires emerged around 1450?

3. What key ideas or practices extended beyond the limits of the great empires?

Many Native Americas

↘ **FOCUS** What factors account for the diversity of native American cultures?

Scholars once claimed that the Western Hemisphere was sparsely settled prior to the arrival of Europeans in 1492, but we now know that by then the population of the Americas had reached some 60 million or more. Although vast open spaces remained, in places the landscape was more intensively cultivated and thickly populated than western Europe (see Map 15.1). Fewer records for nonimperial groups survive than for empire builders such as the Incas and Aztecs, but scholars have recently learned much about these less-studied cultures. Outside imperial boundaries, coastal and riverside populations were densest. This was true in the Caribbean, the Amazon, Paraguay-Paraná, and Mississippi River basins, the Pacific Northwest, and parts of North America's eastern seaboard.

Ecological diversity gave rise in part to political and cultural diversity. America's native peoples, or Amerindians, occupied two ecologically diverse continents. They also inhabited tropical, temperate, and icy environments that proved more or less suitable to settled agriculture. Some were members of egalitarian gatherer-hunter bands; others were subjects of rigidly stratified imperial states. In between were traveling bands of pilgrims led by prophets; chiefdoms based on fishing, whaling, or farming; regional confederacies of chiefdoms; and independent city-states.

Political diversity was more than matched by cultural diversity. The Aztecs and Incas spread the use of imperial dialects within their empires, but elsewhere hundreds of distinct Amerindian languages could be heard. Modes of dress and adornment were even more varied, ranging from total nudity and a few tattoos to highly elaborate ceremonial dress. Lip and ear piercing, tooth filing, and molding of the infant skull between slats of wood were but a few of the many ways human appearances were reconfigured. Architecture was just as varied, as were ceramics and other arts. In short, the Americas' extraordinary range of climates and natural resources both reflected and encouraged diverse forms of material and linguistic expression. Perhaps only in the realm of religion, where shamanism persisted, was a unifying thread to be found.

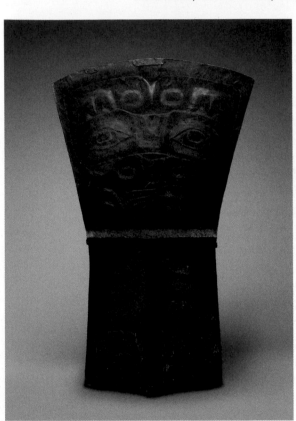

≡ **Tlingit Ceremonial Copper**   Many indigenous nations in North America prized copper as a trade good and prestige item. Much of the metal originated in Upper Michigan, home of the world's largest native (unalloyed) copper deposits. Copper sources were also found in the Pacific Northwest, however, and this decorated copper "shield" was a symbol of chiefly wealth among the Tlingit of Alaska's Pacific coast. Along with other valuable items such as blankets and skins, "coppers" were exchanged at potlatch feasts, which dumbfounded outsiders for their extreme generosity. The copper's upper design element identifies its owner's lineage and the T-shaped ridges below represent ancestral vertebrae.

≡ **MAP 15.1   Main Settlement Areas in the Americas, c. 1492**   Most native Americans settled in regions that supported intensive agriculture. The trade routes shown here linked peoples from very different cultures, mostly to exchange rare items such as shells, precious stones, and tropical bird feathers, but seeds for new crops also followed these paths.

Legend from map:

Main Settlement Areas in the Americas, c. 1492

- Main areas of settlement, c. 1492
- Major trade route

Principal crops

- Amaranth
- Beans
- Cacao
- Chilies
- Cotton
- Maize
- Manioc
- Potatoes, sweet potatoes
- Quinoa
- Squash, pumpkins, gourds
- Sunflowers
- Tobacco
- Tomatoes
- Peanuts

Shamanism consisted of reliance on healer-visionaries for spiritual guidance. In imperial societies shamans constituted a priestly class. Both male and female, shamans had functions ranging from fortune teller to physician, with women often acting as midwives. Still, most native American shamans were males. The role of shaman could be inherited or determined following a vision quest. This entailed a solo journey to a forest or desert region, prolonged physical suffering, and controlled use of hallucinogenic substances. In many respects Amerindian shamanism resembled shamanistic practices in Central Asia and sub-Saharan Africa.

Often labeled "witch doctors" by Christian Europeans, shamans maintained a body of esoteric knowledge that they passed along to apprentices. Some served as historians and myth keepers. Most used powerful hallucinogens to communicate with the spirits of predatory animals, which were venerated almost everywhere in the Americas. Animal spirits were regarded as the shaman's alter ego or protector, and were consulted prior to important occasions. Shamans also mastered herbal remedies for all forms of illness, including emotional disorders. These rubs, washes, and infusions were sometimes effective, as shown by modern pharmacological studies. Shamans nearly always administered them along with chants and rituals aimed at expelling evil spirits. Shamans, therefore, combined the roles of physician and religious leader, using their knowledge and power to heal both body and spirit.

The many varieties of social organization and cultural practice found in the Americas reflect both creative interactions with specific environments and the visions of individual political and religious leaders. Some Amerindian gatherer-hunters lived in swamplands and desert areas where subsistence agriculture was impossible using available technologies. Often such gathering-hunting peoples traded with—or plundered—their farming neighbors. Yet even farming peoples did not forget their past as hunters. As in other parts of the world, big-game hunting in the Americas was an esteemed, even sacred activity among urban elites.

Just as hunting remained important to farmers, agriculture could be found among some forest peoples. Women in these societies controlled most agricultural tasks and spaces, periodically making offerings to spirits associated with human fertility. Amerindian staple foods included maize, potatoes, and manioc, a lowland tropical tuber that could be ground into flour and preserved. With the ebb and flow of empires, many groups shifted from one mode of subsistence to another, from planting to gathering-hunting and back again. Some, such as the Kwakiutl (KWAH-kyu-til) of the Pacific Northwest, were surrounded by such abundant marine and forest resources that they never turned to farming. Natural abundance combined with sophisticated fishing and storage systems allowed the Kwakiutl to

shamanism
Widespread system of religious belief and healing originating in Central Asia.

build a settled culture of the type normally associated with agricultural peoples. Thus, the ecological diversity of the Americas helped give rise to numerous cultures, many of which blurred the line between settled and nomadic lifestyles.

Tributes of Blood: The Aztec Empire 1325–1521

⬊ **FOCUS** What core features characterized Aztec life and rule?

Mesoamerica, made up of modern southern Mexico, Guatemala, Belize, El Salvador, and western Honduras, was a land of city-states after about 800 CE. Following the decline of Teotihuacán (tay-oh-tee-wah-KAHN) in the Mexican highlands and the classic Maya in the greater Guatemalan lowlands, few urban powers, with the possible exception of the Toltecs, managed to dominate more than a few neighbors.

This would change with the arrival in the Valley of Mexico of a band of former gatherer-hunters from a northwestern desert region they called Aztlán (ost-LAWN), or "place of cranes." As newcomers these "Aztecs," who later called themselves Mexica (meh-SHE-cah, hence "Mexico"), would suffer humiliation by powerful city-dwellers centered on Lake Texcoco, now overlain by Mexico City. The Aztecs were at first regarded as barbarians, but as with many conquering outsiders, in time they would have their revenge (see Map 15.2).

Humble Origins, Imperial Ambitions

Unlike the classic Maya of preceding centuries, the Aztecs did not develop a fully phonetic writing system. They did, however, preserve their history in a mix of oral and symbolic, usually painted or carved, forms. Aztec elders maintained chronicles of the kind historians call master narratives, or state-sponsored versions of the past meant to glorify certain individuals or policies. These narratives related foundation myths, genealogies, tales of conquest, and other important remembrances. Though biased and fragmentary, many Aztec oral narratives were preserved by young native scribes writing in Nahuatl (NAH-watt), the Aztec language, soon after the Spanish Conquest of 1519–1521 (discussed in the next chapter).

Why is it that the Spanish victors promoted rather than suppressed these narratives of Aztec glory? In one of history's many ironic twists, Spanish priests arriving in Mexico in the 1520s taught a number of noble Aztec and other Mesoamerican youths to adapt the Latin alphabet and Spanish phonetics to various local languages,

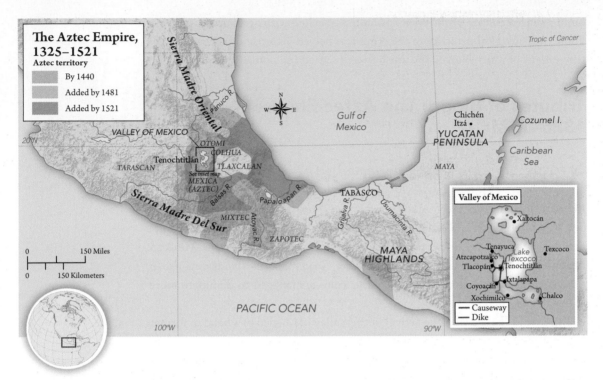

≡ **MAP 15.2 The Aztec Empire, 1325–1521** Starting from their base in Tenochtitlán (now Mexico City), the Aztecs quickly built the most densely populated empire in the Americas. Their first objective was the Valley of Mexico itself. Although a line of kings greatly extended the empire, not all peoples fell to the Aztec war machine, including the Tlaxcalans to the east of Tenochtitlán and the Tarascans to the west. Also unconquered were the many nomadic peoples of the desert north and the farming forest peoples of the southeast.

most importantly Nahuatl. The Spanish hoped that stories of Aztec rule and religion, once collected and examined, would be swiftly discredited and replaced with Western, Christian versions. Not only did this quick conversion not happen as planned, but an unintended consequence of the information-gathering campaign was to create a vast body of Mesoamerican literature written in native languages.

The Aztecs were a quick study in the production of written historical documents, and most of what we know of Aztec history relies heavily on these hybrid, sixteenth-century sources (see Seeing the Past: An Aztec Map of Tenochtitlán). Aside from interviews with the elders, several painted books, or codices, marked with precise dates, names, and other symbols, survive, along with much archaeological and artistic evidence. In combining these sources with Spanish eyewitness accounts of the conquest era, historians have assembled a substantial record of Aztec life and rule.

An Aztec Map of Tenochtitlán

Named for Mexico's first Spanish viceroy, the *Codex Mendoza* was painted by Aztec artists about a dozen years after the Spanish Conquest of 1519–1521. It was commissioned by the viceroy as a gift for the Holy Roman emperor and king of Spain, Charles V. After circulating among the courts of Europe, the *Codex Mendoza* landed in the Bodleian Library in Oxford, England, where it remains. Much of the document consists of tribute lists, but it also contains an illustrated history of Aztec conquests, crimes and punishments, and even a map of Tenochtitlán, the Aztec capital. This symbol-filled map is reproduced here.

According to legend, the Aztec capital came into existence when an eagle landed on a cactus in the middle of Lake Texcoco. This image, now part of the Mexican national flag, is at the center of the map. Beneath the cactus is a picture of a stone carving of a cactus fruit, a common Aztec symbol for the human heart, emblem of sacrifice. Beneath this is a third symbol labeled afterward by a Spanish scribe "Tenochtitlán."

The city, or rather its symbol, marks the meeting of four spatial quarters. In each quarter are various Aztec nobles, only one of whom, Tenochtli (labeled "Tenuch" on the map), is seated on a reed mat, the Aztec symbol of supreme authority. He was the Aztecs' first emperor; the name "Tenochtli" means "stone cactus fruit."

The lower panel depicts the Aztec conquests of their neighbors in Colhuacan and Tenayuca. Framing

Tenochtitlán, from the *Codex Mendoza* (Granger)

the entire map are symbols for dates, part of an ancient Mesoamerican system of timekeeping and prophesying retained by the Aztecs. Finally, barely legible in the upper left-hand corner is the somewhat jarring signature of André Thevet, a French priest and royal cosmographer who briefly possessed the *Codex Mendoza* in the late sixteenth century.

Examining the Evidence

1. What does this map reveal about the Aztec worldview?

2. How might this document have been read by a common Aztec subject?

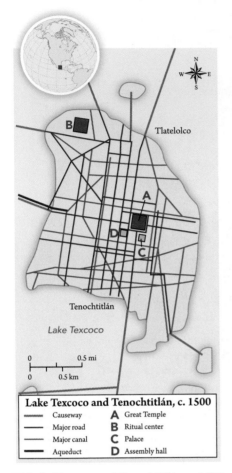

Tlatelolco

Tenochtitlán

Lake Texcoco

| 0 | 0.5 mi |
| 0 | 0.5 km |

Lake Texcoco and Tenochtitlán, c. 1500

———	Causeway	**A**	Great Temple
———	Major road	**B**	Ritual center
———	Major canal	**C**	Palace
———	Aqueduct	**D**	Assembly hall

≡ **Lake Texcoco and Tenochtitlán, c. 1500**

The Aztecs apparently arrived in the Valley of Mexico sometime in the thirteenth century, but it was not until the early fourteenth that they established a permanent home. The most fertile sites in the valley were already occupied, but the Aztecs were not dissuaded; they had a reputation for being tough and resourceful. Heeding an omen in the form of an eagle perched on a cactus growing on a tiny island near the southwest edge of Lake Texcoco, the refugees settled there in 1325. Reclaiming land from the shallow lakebed, they founded a city called Tenochtitlán (teh-noach-teet-LAWN), or "cactus fruit place." Linked to shore by three large causeways, the city soon boasted stone palaces and temple-pyramids.

The Aztecs transformed Tenochtitlán into a formidable capital. By 1500 it was home to some 200,000 people, ranking alongside Nanjing and Paris among the world's most populous cities at the time. At first the Aztecs developed their city by trading military services and lake products such as reeds and fish for building materials, including stone, lime, and timber from the surrounding hillsides. They then formed marriage alliances with regional ethnic groups such as the Colhua, and by 1430 initiated imperial expansion.

Intermarriage with the Colhua, who traced their ancestry to the warrior Toltecs, lent the lowly Aztecs a new, elite cachet. At some point the Aztecs tied their religious cult, focused on the war god Huitzilopochtli (weetsy-low-POACH-tlee), or "hummingbird-on-the-left," to cults dedicated to more widely known deities, such as the water god Tlaloc. A huge, multilayered pyramid faced with carved stone and filled with rubble, now referred to by archaeologists as the Templo Mayor, or "Great Temple," but called by the Aztecs Coatepec, or "Serpent Mountain," became the centerpiece of Tenochtitlán. At its top, some twenty stories above the valley floor, sat twin temples, one dedicated to Huitzilopochtli, the other to Tlaloc. Coatepec was built to awe and intimidate. In the words of one native poet,

Proud of itself
Is the City of Mexico-Tenochtitlán
Here no one fears to die in war
This is our glory
This is Your Command
Oh Giver of Life

Have this in mind, oh princes
Who could conquer Tenochtitlán?
Who could shake the foundation of heaven?[2]

The Aztecs saw themselves as both stagehands and actors in a cosmic drama centered on their great capital city.

Enlarging and Supplying the Capital

With Tenochtitlán surrounded by water, subsistence and living space became serious concerns amid imperial expansion. Fortunately for the Aztecs, Lake Texcoco was shallow enough to allow an ingenious form of land reclamation called *chinampa* (chee-NAHM-pah). **Chinampas** were long, narrow terraces built by hand from dredged mud, reeds, and rocks, bordered by interwoven sticks and live trees. Chinampa construction also created canals for canoe transport. Building chinampas and massive temple-pyramids such as Coatepec without metal tools, wheeled vehicles, or draft animals required thousands of workers. Their construction, therefore, is a testimony to the Aztecs' power to command labor.

Over time, Tenochtitlán's canals accumulated algae, water lilies, and silt. Workers periodically dredged and composted this organic material to fertilize maize and other plantings on the island terraces. Established chinampa lands were eventually used for building residences, easing urban crowding. By the mid-fifteenth century the Aztecs countered problems such as chronic flooding and high salt content at their end of the lake with dikes and other public works.

Earlier, in the fourteenth century, an adjacent "twin" city called Tlatelolco (tlah-teh-LOLE-coe) had emerged alongside Tenochtitlán. Tlatelolco was the Aztec marketplace. Foods, textiles, and exotic goods were exchanged here. Cocoa beans from the hot lowlands served as currency, and products such as turquoise and quetzal feathers arrived from as far away as New Mexico and Guatemala, respectively. Though linked by trade, these distant regions fell well outside the Aztec domain. All products were transported along well-trod footpaths on the backs of human carriers. Only when they arrived on the shores of Lake Texcoco could trade goods be shuttled from place to place in canoes. Tlatelolco served as crossroads for all regional trade, with long-distance merchants, or *pochteca* (poach-TEH-cah), occupying an entire precinct.

Aztec imperial expansion began only around 1430, less than a century before the arrival of Europeans. An alliance between Tenochtitlán and the city-states of Texcoco and Tlacopan led to victory against a third, Atzcapotzalco (otts-cah-poat-SAUL-coh) (see again Map 15.2). Tensions with Atzcapotzalco extended back to the Aztecs' first arrival in the region. The Aztecs used the momentum of this victory to overtake their allies and lay the foundations of a regional, tributary empire.

chinampa A terrace for farming and house building constructed in the shallows of Mexico's Lake Texcoco by the Aztecs and their neighbors.

≡ **Aztec Chinampa** The Aztec capital of Tenochtitlán was one of several cities occupying the huge basin of the Lake of Mexico, a complex tropical environment located at roughly 7,000 feet above sea level. The Aztecs and their subjects learned to efficiently farm lake margins by way of so-called floating gardens, or *chinampas*. The chinampa, as diagrammed here, took advantage of lake water, compost, and interwoven reeds to maximize crop yields, resist winter frosts, and produce food year-round. Canals allowed passage of large dugout canoes loaded with produce, wood, rocks, and soil.

Within a generation they controlled the entire Valley of Mexico, exacting tribute from several million people. The Nahuatl language helped link state to subjects, although many subject groups retained local languages. These persistent forms of ethnic identification, coupled with staggering tribute demands, would eventually help bring about the end of Aztec rule.

Holy Terror: Aztec Rule, Religion, and Warfare

A series of six male rulers, or *tlatoque* (tlah-TOE-kay, singular *tlatoani*), presided over Aztec expansion. When a ruler died, his successor was chosen by a council of elders from among a handful of eligible candidates. Aztec kingship was sacred in that each tlatoani traced his lineage back to the Toltecs. For this, the incorporation of the Colhua lineage had been essential. In keeping with this Toltec legacy, the Aztec Empire was characterized by three core features: human sacrifice, warfare, and tribute. All were linked to Aztec and broader Mesoamerican notions of cosmic order, specifically the human duty to feed the gods.

≡ **Aztec Human Sacrifice** This image dates from just after the Spanish Conquest of Mexico, but it was part of a codex about Aztec religious practices and symbols. Here a priest is removing the beating heart of a captive with a flint knife as an assistant holds his feet. The captive's bloody heart, in the form of a cactus fruit, ascends, presumably to the gods (see the same icon in Seeing the Past: An Aztec Map of Tenochtitlán, page 559). At the base of the sacrificial pyramid lies an earlier victim, apparently being taken away by noble Aztec men and women responsible for the handling of the corpse.

Like most Mesoamericans, the Aztecs traced not only their own but also all human origins to sacrifices made by deities. In origin stories male and female gods threw themselves into fires, drew their own blood, and killed and dismembered one another, all for the good of humankind. These sacrifices were considered essential to the process of releasing and renewing the generative powers that drove the cosmos.

According to Aztec belief, humans were expected to show gratitude by following the example of their creators in an almost daily ritual cycle. Much of the sacred calendar had been inherited from older Mesoamerican cultures, but the Aztecs added many new holidays to celebrate their own special role in cosmic history. The Aztecs' focus on sacrifice also appears to have derived from their sense that secular and spiritual forces were inseparable. Affairs of state were affairs of heaven, and vice versa. Tenochtitlán was thought to be the foundation of heaven, its enormous temple-pyramids the center of human-divine affairs. Aztec priests and astrologers believed that the universe, already in its fifth incarnation after only 3,000 years, was unstable, on the verge of chaos and collapse. Only human intervention in the form of sustained sacrificial ritual could stave off apocalypse.

As an antidote, the gods had given humans the "gift" of warfare. Human captives, preferably young men, were to be hunted and killed so that the release of their blood and spirits might satisfy the gods. Warrior sacrifice was so important to the Aztecs that they believed it kept the sun in motion.

Devout Aztec subjects also took part in nonlethal cosmic regeneration rituals in the form of personal bloodletting, or **autosacrifice**. According to sources, extremities and genitals were bled using thorns and stone blades, with public exhibition of suffering as important as blood loss. Blood offerings were absorbed by thin sheets of reed paper, which were burned before an altar. These bloodlettings, like captive sacrifices, emphasized the frailty of the individual, the pain of life, and indebtedness to the gods. Human blood fueled not only the Aztec realm but also the cosmos.

Given these sacrificial obligations, Aztec warfare aimed not at the annihilation but rather at live capture of enemies. Aztec combat was ideally a stylized and theatrical affair similar to royal jousts in contemporary Eurasia, with specific individuals paired for contest. Aztec warriors were noted for their fury, a trait borrowed from their patron deity, Huitzilopochtli. Chronic enemies such as the Tlaxcalans apparently learned to match the ferocious Aztec style, and some enemies, such as the Otomí, were eventually incorporated into Aztec warrior ranks.

Mesoamerican warriors considered death on the battlefield the highest honor. But live capture was the Aztecs' main goal, and most victims were marched naked and bound to the capital to be sacrificed. Although charged with religious meaning, Aztec warrior sacrifices were also intended to horrify enemies; visiting diplomats were made to watch them. Aztec imperial expansion depended in part on religious terror, or the ability to appear chosen by the gods for victory.

In addition to sacrificial victims, the Aztecs demanded **tribute** of conquered peoples. There were periodic labor drafts for public works, and tribute lists included food, textiles, and craft goods for the empire's large priestly and warrior classes. Other tribute items were redistributed to favored subjects of lower status to help cement loyalties. Yet other tribute items were purely symbolic. Some new subjects were made to collect filth and inedible insects, for example, just to prove their unworthiness. As an empire that favored humiliation over co-optation and promotion of new subjects, the Aztecs faced an ever-deepening reservoir of resentment.

autosacrifice The Mesoamerican practice of personal bloodletting as a means of paying debts to the gods.

tribute Taxes paid to a state or empire, usually in the form of farm produce or artisan manufactures but sometimes also human labor or even human bodies.

Daily Life Under the Aztecs

Aztec society was stratified, and Mexica nobles regarded commoners as uncouth. In between were bureaucrats, priests, district chiefs, scribes, merchants, and artisans. Although elites displayed the fruits of their subordinates' labors, most Aztec art seems to have been destined not for wealthy people's homes but for temples, tombs, and religious shrines. Despite heavy emphasis on religious ceremonies, the Aztecs also maintained a civil justice system. Quite unlike most of the world's imperial cultures, Aztec nobles sometimes received harsher punishments than commoners for similar misdeeds.

Class hierarchy was reinforced by dress and speech codes, along with many other rules and rituals. The tlatoani, for example, could not be touched or even looked in the face by any but his closest relatives, consorts, and servants. Even ranking nobles were supposed to lie face down on the ground and put dirt in their mouths before him. Nobles guarded their own rank by using a restricted form of speech. Chances for social advancement were limited, but some men gained status on the battlefield.

At the base of the social pyramid were peasants and enslaved persons. Some peasants were ethnic Aztecs, but most belonged to city-states and clans that had been conquered after 1430. In either case, peasants' lives revolved around producing food and providing overlords with tribute goods and occasional labor. Slavery usually took the form of crisis-driven self-indenture; it was not an inherited social status. Slavery remained unimportant to the overall Aztec economy.

Merchants, particularly the mobile *pochteca* responsible for long-distance trade, occupied an unusual position. Although the pochteca sometimes accumulated great wealth, they remained resident aliens. They had no homeland but made a good living supplying elites with exotic goods. Nonetheless, there is no evidence of complex credit instruments, industrial-style production, or real estate exchange of the sort associated with early merchant capitalism in other parts of the world at this time. The Aztec state remained tributary, the movement of goods mostly a reflection of power relations. Merchants, far from influencing politics, remained ethnic outsiders. Thus, both the Aztec economy and social structure reinforced the insularity of Aztec elites.

The life of an Aztec woman was difficult even by early modern standards. Along with water transport and other heavy household chores, maize grinding and tortilla making became the core responsibilities of most women in the Valley of Mexico and indeed throughout Mesoamerica. Without animal- or water-driven grain mills, food preparation was an arduous, time-consuming task, particularly for the poor. Only noblewomen enjoyed broad exemption from manual work.

Sources suggest that some women assumed minor priestly roles. Others worked as surgeons and herbalists. Midwifery was also a fairly high-status, female

LIVES AND LIVELIHOODS

The Aztec Midwife

In Aztec culture, childbirth was a sacred and ritualized affair. Always life threatening for mother and child, giving birth and being born were both explicitly compared to the battlefield experience. Aside from potential medical complications, the Aztecs considered the timing of a child's birth critical in determining her or his future. This tricky blend of physical and spiritual concerns gave rise to the respected and highly skilled livelihood of midwife. It is not entirely clear how midwives were chosen, but their work is well described in early post-conquest records, particularly the illustrated books of Aztec lore and history collectively known as the *Florentine Codex*. The following passage, translated directly from sixteenth-century Nahuatl, is one such description. Note how the midwife blends physical tasks, such as supplying herbs and swaddling clothes, with shamanistic cries and speeches.

≡ **Aztec Midwife** This image accompanies a description in Nahuatl, the Aztec language, of the midwife's duties written soon after the Spanish Conquest. (Firenze, Biblioteca Medicea Laurenziana, Ms. Med. Palat. 219, f. 132v. Su concessione del MiBACT)

And the midwife inquired about the fate of the baby who was born.

When the pregnant one already became aware of [pains in] her womb, when it was said that her time of death had arrived, when she wanted to give birth already, they quickly bathed her, washed her hair with soap, washed her, adorned her well. And then they arranged, they swept the house where the little woman was to suffer, where she was to perform her duty, to do her work, to give birth.

If she were a noblewoman or wealthy, she had two or three midwives. They remained by her side, awaiting her word. And when the woman became really disturbed internally, they quickly put her in a sweat bath [a kind of sauna]. And to hasten the birth of the baby, they gave the pregnant woman cooked *ciuapatli* [literally, "woman medicine"] herb to drink.

And if she suffered much, they gave her ground opossum tail to drink, and then the baby was quickly born. [The midwife] already had all that was needed for the baby, the little rags with which the baby was received.

And when the baby had arrived on earth, the midwife shouted; she gave war cries, which meant the woman had fought a good battle, had become a brave warrior, had taken a captive, had captured a baby.

Then the midwife spoke to it. If it was a boy, she said to it: "You have come out on earth, my youngest one, my boy, my young man." If it was a girl, she said to it: "My young woman, my youngest one, noblewoman, you have suffered, you are exhausted." . . . [and to either:] "You have come to arrive on earth, where your relatives, your kin suffer fatigue and exhaustion; where it is hot, where it is cold, and where the wind blows; where there is thirst, hunger, sadness, despair, exhaustion, fatigue, pain. . . ."

And then the midwife cut the umbilical cord.

Source: Selection from the *Florentine Codex* in *Mesoamerican Voices: Native-Language Writings from Colonial Mexico, Oaxaca, Yucatan, and Guatemala,* ed. Matthew Restall, Lisa Sousa, and Kevin Terraciano (New York: Cambridge University Press, 2005), 216–17.

Questions to Consider

1. Why was midwifery so crucial to the Aztecs?
2. How were girls and boys addressed by the midwife, and why?

For Further Information:

Carrasco, Davíd, and Scott Sessions. *Daily Life of the Aztecs, People of the Sun and Earth.* 2nd ed. Indianapolis: Hackett, 2008.

Clendinnen, Inga. *Aztecs: An Interpretation.* New York: Cambridge University Press, 1994.

occupation (see Lives and Livelihoods: The Aztec Midwife). These were exceptions; women's lives were mostly hard under Aztec rule. Scholars disagree, however, as to whether male political and religious leaders viewed women's duties and contributions as complementary or subordinate. Surviving texts do emphasize feminine mastery of the domestic sphere and its social value. However, this emphasis may simply reflect male desire to limit women's actions, since female reproductive capacity was also highly valued as an aid to the empire's perpetual war effort.

Indeed, Aztec society was so militarized that giving birth was referred to as "taking a captive." This comparison reflects the Aztec preoccupation with pleasing their gods: women were as much soldiers as men in the ongoing war to sustain human life. Women's roles in society were mostly domestic rather than public, but the home was a sacred space. Caring for it was equivalent to caring for a temple. Sweeping was a ritual, for example, albeit one with hygienic benefits. Hearth tending, maize grinding, spinning, and weaving were also ritualized tasks. Insufficient attention to these daily rituals put families and entire lineages at risk.

Aztec children, too, lived a scripted existence, their futures predicted at birth by astrologers. Names were derived from birthdates and served as a public badge of fate. Sources affirm that Aztec society at all levels emphasized duty and good comportment rather than rights and individual freedom. Parents were to police their children's behavior and to help mold all youths into useful citizens. Girls and boys were assigned tasks considered appropriate for their sex well before adolescence. By age fourteen, children were engaged in adult work. One break from the chores was instruction between ages twelve and fifteen in singing and playing instruments, such as drums and flutes, for cyclical religious festivals. Girls married at about age fifteen, and boys nearer twenty, a pattern roughly in accordance with most parts of the world at the time. Elder Aztec women served as matchmakers, and wedding ceremonies were elaborate, multiday affairs. Some noblemen expanded their prestige by retaining numerous wives and siring dozens of children.

At around harvest time in September, Aztec subjects ate maize, beans, and squash seasoned with salt and ground chili peppers. During other times of the year, and outside the chinampa zone, food could be scarce, forcing the poor to consume roasted insects, grubs, and lake scum. Certain items, such as frothed cocoa, were reserved for elites. Stored maize was used to make tortillas year-round, but two poor harvests in a row, a frequent occurrence in highland Mexico, could reduce rations considerably.

In addition to periodic droughts, Aztec subjects coped with frosts, plagues of locusts, volcanic eruptions, earthquakes, and floods. This ecological uncertainty restricted warfare to the agricultural off-season. Without large domesticated animals and metal tools, agricultural tasks throughout Mesoamerica demanded virtual armies of field laborers equipped only with fire-hardened digging sticks and obsidian or flint knives.

Animal protein was scarce, especially in urban areas where hunting opportunities were limited and few domestic animals were kept. Still, the people of Tenochtitlán raised turkeys and plump, hairless dogs (the prized Xolo breed of today). Even humble beans, when combined with maize, could constitute a complete protein, and indigenous grains such as amaranth were also nutritious. Famines still occurred, however, and one in the early 1450s led to mass migration out of the Valley of Mexico. Thousands sold themselves into slavery to avoid starvation.

The Limits of Holy Terror

As the Aztec Empire expanded, sacrificial debts became a consuming passion among pious elites. Calendars filled with sacrificial rites, and warfare was ever more geared toward satisfying a ballooning cosmic debt.

By 1500 the Aztec state had reached its height, and some scholars have argued that it had even begun to decline. Incessant captive wars and tribute demands had reached their limits, and old enemies such as the Tlaxcalans and Tarascans remained belligerent. New conquests were blocked by difficult terrain, declining tributes, and resistant locals. With available technologies, there was no place else for the empire to grow, and even with complex water works in place, agricultural productivity barely kept the people fed. Under the harsh leadership of Moctezuma II ("Angry Lord the Younger") (r. 1502–1520), the future did not look promising. Although there is no evidence to suggest the Aztec Empire was on the verge of collapse when several hundred bearded, sunburned strangers of Spanish descent appeared on Mexico's Gulf coast shores in 1519, points of vulnerability abounded.

Tributes of Sweat: The Inca Empire 1430–1532

⟍ FOCUS What core features characterized Inca life and rule?

At about the same time as the Aztec expansion in southernmost North America, another great empire emerged in the central Andean highlands of South America. There is no evidence of significant contact between them. Like the Aztecs, the Incas burst out of their highland homeland in the 1430s to conquer numerous neighbors and huge swaths of territory. They demanded tribute in goods and labor, along with allegiance to an imperial religion. Also like the Aztecs, the Incas based their expansion on a centuries-long inheritance of technological, religious, and political traditions.

By 1500 the Incas ruled one of the world's most extensive, ecologically varied, and rugged land empires, stretching nearly 3,000 miles along the towering Andean mountain range from the equator to central Chile. Like most empires ancient and modern, extensive holdings proved to be a mixed blessing (see Map 15.3).

From Potato Farmers to Empire Builders

Thanks to archaeological evidence and early post-conquest narratives, much is known about the rise and fall of the Inca state. Still, like the early Ottoman, Russian, and other contemporary empires, numerous mysteries remain. As in those cases, legends of the formative period in particular require skeptical analysis. The Inca case is somewhat complicated by the fact that their complex knotted-string records, or *khipus* (also *quipus*, KEY-poohs), have yet to be deciphered.

Scholars agree that the Incas emerged from among a dozen or so regional ethnic groups living in the highlands of south-central Peru between 1000 and 1400 CE. Living as potato and maize farmers, the Incas started out as one of many similar groups of Andean mountaineers. Throughout the Andes, clans settled in fertile valleys and alongside lakes between 8,500 and 13,000 feet above sea level. Though often graced with fertile soils, these highland areas suffered periodic frosts and droughts, despite their location within the tropics. Even more than in the Aztec realm, altitude (elevation above sea level), not latitude (distance north or south of the equator), was key.

Anthropologist John Murra described Inca land use as a "**vertical archipelago**," a stair-step system of interdependent environmental "islands." Kin groups occupying the altitudes best suited to potato and maize farming established settlements in cold uplands, where thousands of llamas and alpacas—the Americas' only large domestic animals—were herded, and also in hot lowlands, where cotton, peanuts, chilis, and the stimulant coca were grown. People, animals, and goods traveled between highland and lowland ecological zones using trails and hanging bridges.

Other Andeans inhabited Peru's desert coast, where urban civilization was nearly as old as that of ancient Egypt. Andean coast dwellers practiced large-scale irrigated agriculture, deep-sea fishing, and long-distance trade. Trading families outfitted large balsawood rafts with cotton sails and plied the Pacific as far as Guatemala. Inland trade links stretched over the Andes and into the Amazon rain forest. Along the way, coast-dwelling traders exchanged salt, seashells, beads, and copper hatchets for exotic feathers, gold dust, and pelts. The Incas would exploit all of these regions and their interconnections, replacing old exchange systems and religious shrines with their own. Around 1200 CE they established a base near Cuzco (KOOS-coh), in Peru's highlands not far from the headwaters of the Amazon, and soon after 1400 they began their drive toward empire (see again Map 15.3).

vertical archipelago
Andean system of planting crops and grazing animals at different altitudes.

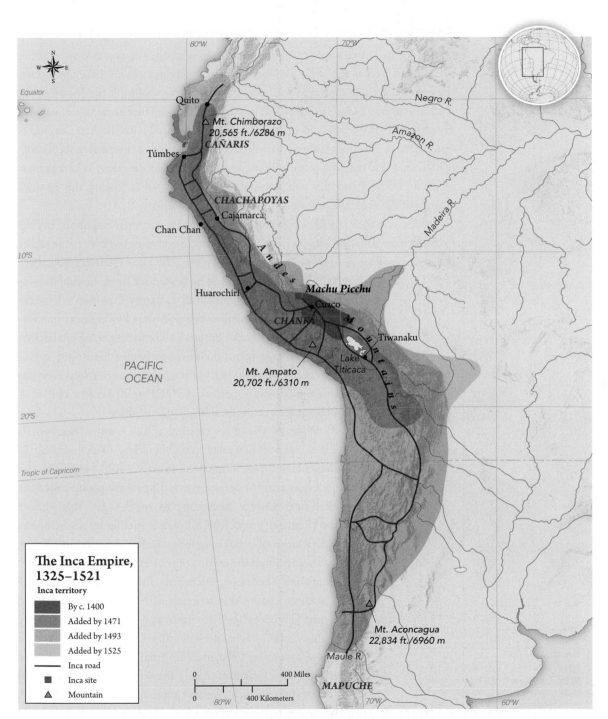

≡ **MAP 15.3 The Inca Empire, 1325–1521** Starting from their base in Cuzco, high in the Andes, the Incas built the most extensive empire in the Americas, and the second most populous after that of the Aztecs. They linked it by a road system that rivaled that of the ancient Romans. Some groups, such as the Cañaris and Chachapoyas, resisted Inca domination for many years, and the Mapuche of Chile were never conquered.

The Great Apparatus: Inca Expansion and Religion

Cuzco, located in a narrow valley at a breathtaking altitude of over two miles above sea level, served as the Incas' political base and religious center. Like the Aztecs, the Incas saw their capital as the hub of the universe, calling it the "navel of the world." Paths and roads radiated out in all directions and tied hundreds of subsidiary shrines to the cosmically ordained center. Compared with the Aztec capital of Tenochtitlán, however, Cuzco was modest in size, perhaps home to at most 50,000. Still, Cuzco had the advantage of being stoutly built of hewn stone. Whereas most of Tenochtitlán's temples and palaces were dismantled following the Spanish Conquest, Cuzco's colossal stone foundations still stand.

The Incas in the early fifteenth century began conquering their neighbors. In time each emperor, or Sapa ("Unique") Inca, would seek to add more territory to the realm, called Tawantinsuyu (tuh-wahn-tin-SUE-you), or, "The Four Quarters Together."

The Sapa Inca was thought to be descended from the sun and was thus regarded as the sustainer of all humanity. Devotion to local deities persisted, however, absorbed over time by the Incas in a way reminiscent of the Roman Empire's assimilation of regional deities and shrines. This religious inclusiveness helped the empire spread quickly even as the royal cult of the sun was inserted into everyday life. In a similar way, Quechua (KETCH-wah) became the Incas' official language even as local languages persisted.

Inca expansion was so rapid that the empire reached its greatest extent within a mere four generations of its founding. In semi-legendary times, Wiracocha Inca (r. 1400–1438) was said to have led an army to defeat an invading ethnic group called the Chankas near Cuzco. According to royal sagas, this victory spurred Wiracocha to defend his people further by annexing the fertile territories of other neighbors. Defense turned to offense, and thus was primed the engine of Inca expansion.

Wiracocha's successor, Pachacuti Inca Yupanki (r. 1438–1471), was more ambitious, so much so that he is widely regarded as the true founder of the Inca Empire. Archaeological evidence backs this claim. Pachacuti (literally "cataclysm") took over much of what is today Peru, including many coastal oases and the powerful Chimú kingdom. Along the way, Pachacuti perfected the core strategy of Inca warfare: amassing and mobilizing such overwhelming numbers of troops and backup forces that fighting was often unnecessary.

Cuzco, c. 1500

Upper Cuzco	**A** Main plaza
Lower Cuzco	**B** Temple of the Sun
Residential Area	**C** Assembly Hall
—— Road	**D** Palace of the Virgins of the Sun

≡ **Cuzco, c. 1500**

Thousands of peasants were conscripted to bear arms, build roads, and carry food. Others herded llamas, strung bridges, and cut building stone. With each new advance, masonry forts and temples were constructed in the imperial style, leaving an indelible Inca stamp on the landscape. Even opponents such as the desert-dwelling Chimú capitulated in the face of the Inca juggernaut. Just after the Spanish Conquest, Pachacuti was remembered by female descendants:

> As [Pachacuti] Inca Yupanki remained in his city and town of Cuzco, seeing that he was lord and that he had subjugated the towns and provinces, he was very pleased. He had subjugated more and obtained much more importance than any of his ancestors. He saw the great apparatus that he had so that whenever he wanted to he could subjugate and put under his control anything else he wanted.[3]

These remembrances underscore the Sapa Inca's tremendous power.

Pachacuti's successors extended conquests southward deep into what are today Chile and Argentina, and also eastward down the slope of the Andes and into the upper Amazon Basin. It is from this last region, the quarter the Incas called Antisuyu (auntie-SUE-you), that we derive the word *Andes*. On the northern frontier, the Incas fought bitterly with Ecuadorian ethnic groups to extend Inca rule to the border of present-day Colombia (see again Map 15.3). Here the imperial Inca conquest machine met its match: many native highlanders fought to the death.

According to most sources, Inca advances into new territory were couched in the rhetoric of diplomacy. Local headmen were told they had two options: (1) to retain power by accepting Inca sovereignty and all the tributary obligations that went with it, or (2) to defy the Inca and face annihilation. Most headmen went along, particularly once word of the Incas' battlefield prowess spread. Those who did not were either killed in battle or exiled, along with their subject populations, to remote corners of the empire.

The Incas dominated agricultural peoples and their lands, but they also spread their imperial solar cult. Whatever their motives, like the Aztecs they defined domination in simple terms: tribute payment. Conquered subjects showed submission by rendering portions of their surplus production—and also labor—to the emperor. Tribute payment was a grudgingly accepted humiliation throughout the Andes, one that many hoped to shake off at the first opportunity.

Inca religion is only starting to be understood. As the chapter-opening description of child sacrifice suggests, spirit and body were deemed inseparable despite permanent loss of consciousness. Likewise, features in the landscape, ranging from springs and peaks to boulders, were thought to emit spiritual energy (see Reading

READING THE PAST

An Andean Creation Story

The small Peruvian town of Huarochirí (wahr-oh-chee-REE), located in the high Andes east of Lima, was the target of a Spanish idolatry investigation at the end of the sixteenth century. The Spanish conquest of the Incas had little effect on the everyday life of Andean peasants, and many clung tenaciously to their religious beliefs. In Huarochirí, Spanish attempts to replace these beliefs with Western, Christian ones produced written testimonies from village elders in phonetically rendered Quechua, the most commonly spoken language in the Inca Empire. Like the Aztec codices, the resulting documents—aimed at eradicating the beliefs they describe—have unwittingly provided modern researchers with a rare window on a lost mental world. The passage here, translated directly from Quechua to English, relates an Andean myth that newly arrived or converted Christians considered a variation on the biblical story of Noah and the Great Flood. In the Christian story, God, angered by the wickedness of man, resolves to send a flood to destroy the earth. He spares only Noah, whom he instructs to build an ark in which Noah, his family, and a pair of every animal are to be saved from the Great Flood.

> In ancient times, this world wanted to come to an end. A llama buck, aware that the ocean was about to overflow, was behaving like somebody who's deep in sadness. Even though its owner let it rest in a patch of excellent pasture, it cried and said, "In, in," and wouldn't eat. The llama's owner got really angry, and he threw a cob from some maize he had just eaten at the llama. "Eat, dog! This is some fine grass I'm letting you rest in!" he said. Then that llama began speaking like a human being. "You simpleton, whatever could you be thinking about? Soon, in five days, the ocean will overflow. It's a certainty. And the whole world will come to an end," it said. The man got good and scared. "What's going to happen to us? Where

the Past: An Andean Creation Story). Even human-made landforms, such as irrigation canals, were described as "alive." These sacred **wakas** (or *huacas*) received offerings in exchange for good harvests, herd growth, and other bounties.

Andeans also venerated their ancestors' corpses. As long as something tangible remained of the deceased, they were not regarded as entirely dead. It helped that the central Andes' dry climates were ideal for mummification: preservation often required little more than removal of internal organs. It would have been fairly common in Inca times to encounter a neighbor's "freeze-dried" grandparents

waka A sacred place or thing in Andean culture.

can we go to save ourselves?" he said. The llama replied, "Let's go to Villca Coto mountain. There we'll be saved. Take along five days' food for yourself." So the man went out from there in a great hurry, and himself carried both the llama buck and its load. When they arrived at Villca Coto mountain, all sorts of animals had already filled it up: pumas, foxes, guanacos [wild relatives of the llama], condors, all kinds of animals in great numbers. And as soon as that man had arrived there, the ocean overflowed. They stayed there huddling tightly together. The waters covered all those mountains and it was only Villca Coto mountain, or rather its very peak, that was not covered by the water. Water soaked the fox's tail. That's how it turned black. Five days later, the waters descended and began to dry up. The drying waters caused the ocean to retreat all the way down again and exterminate all the people. Afterward, that man began to multiply once more. That's the reason there are people until today.

Source: Excerpt from *The Huarochirí Manuscript: A Testament of Ancient and Colonial Andean Religion*, trans. and ed. Frank Salomon and George L. Urioste (Austin: University of Texas Press, 1991), 51–52.

Examining the Evidence

1. What do the similarities and differences between the Andean and Judeo-Christian flood stories suggest?

2. What do the differences between them reveal?

For Further Information:

Spalding, Karen. *Huarochirí: An Andean Society Under Inca and Spanish Rule.* Stanford, CA: Stanford University Press, 1988.

Urton, Gary. *Inca Myths.* Austin: University of Texas Press, 1999.

hanging from the rafters, still regarded as involved in household affairs. Andeans sometimes carried ancestor mummies to feasts and pilgrimages as well. Thus, Inca society included both past and present generations.

The Incas harnessed these and other core Andean beliefs, yet like the Aztecs they put a unique stamp on the region they came to dominate. Though warlike, the Incas rarely sacrificed captive warriors, a ritual archaeologists now know was practiced among ancient coastal Peruvians. Cannibalism was something the Incas associated with barbaric forest dwellers. Inca stone architecture, though borrowing from older forms, is still identifiable thanks to the use of trapezoidal (flared) doors, windows, and niches (see World in the Making, page 550). Even so, the Incas' imperial sun cult proved far less durable than local religious traditions once the empire fell. And despite the Incas' rhetoric of diplomacy, most Andeans appear to have associated their rule with tyranny. Like the Aztecs, they failed to inspire loyalty in their subjects, who saw Inca government as a set of institutions designed to exploit, rather than protect, the peoples of the empire.

Daily Life Under the Incas

Inca society, like Aztec society, was stratified, with few means of upward mobility. Along with class gradations tied to occupation, the Incas divided society according to sex, age, and ethnic origin. Everyday life thus varied tremendously among the Inca's millions of subjects, although the peasant majority probably had much in common with farming folk the world over. Seasonal work stints for the empire were a burden for men, whereas women labored to maintain households. Unlike that of the Aztec, the Inca legal system appears to have been harder on commoners than nobles. Exemplary elite behavior was expected, but not so rigidly enforced.

At the pinnacle of society was the Sapa Inca himself, the "son of the Sun." He was also believed to be the greatest warrior in the world, and everyone who came before him was obliged to bear a symbolic burden, such as a load of cloth or large water vessel. Only the Inca's female companions had intimate contact with him. Although the ideal royal couple according to Inca mythology was a sibling pair, in fact dozens of wives and concubines assured that there would be heirs. Unlike monarchs in Europe and parts of Africa, the Sapa Incas did not practice primogeniture, that is, the automatic inheritance of an estate or title by the eldest son. Neither did they leave succession to a group of elders, the method preferred by the Aztecs. Violent succession struggles predictably ensued. Though barred from the role of Inca themselves, ambitious noblewomen exercised considerable behind-the-scenes power over imperial succession.

Just beneath the Inca imperial line were Cuzco-based nobles, identifiable by their huge ear spools and finely woven tunics. Rather like their Aztec counterparts, they spoke a dialect of the royal language forbidden among commoners. Among this elite class were decorated generals and hereditary lords of prominent clans. Often drawn from these and slightly lower noble ranks was a class of priests and astrologers who maintained temples and shrines.

Many noblewomen and girls deemed physically perfect, like the sacrificial victim described at the start of this chapter, were also selected for religious seclusion. Seclusion was not always permanent, because some of these women were groomed for marriage to the Inca. Still more noblewomen, mostly wives and widows, maintained the urban households and country estates of the Incas, dead and alive.

Next came bureaucrats, military leaders, and provincial headmen. Bureaucrats kept track of tribute obligations, communal work schedules, and land appropriations. Following conquest, up to two-thirds of productive land was set aside in the name of the ruling Inca and the cult of the sun. Bureaucrats negotiated with headmen as to which lands these would be, and how and when subjects would be put to work on behalf of their new rulers. If negotiations failed, the military was called in for a show of force. Lower-ranking Inca military men, like bureaucrats, faced service at the hostile fringes of empire. They had little beyond the weak hold of local power to look forward to. As a result, in sharp distinction with the Aztecs, death in battle was not regarded as a glorious sacrifice among the Incas. Furthermore, many officers were themselves provincial in origin and thus had little hope of promotion to friendlier districts closer to the imperial core.

The Inca and his retinue employed numerous artisans, mostly conquered provincials. Such specialists included architects, record keepers, civil engineers, metalworkers, weavers, potters, and many others. Unlike the Aztecs, the Incas did not tolerate free traders, instead choosing to manage the distribution of goods and services as a means of exercising state power. Partly as a result, market-oriented slavery appears not to have existed under the Incas, although some conquered young men and women spared from death or exile worked as personal servants. Most Inca subjects were peasants belonging to kin groups whose lives revolved around agriculture and rotational labor obligations. For them, the rigors of everyday life far outweighed the extra demands of Inca rule. Only in the case of recently conquered groups, or those caught in the midst of a regional rebellion or succession

Inca Mummy The Incas did not sacrifice humans as often as the Aztecs did, but headmen in newly conquered regions were sometimes required to give up young sons or daughters for live burial on high mountains. Such sacrifices were known as *capacocha*, or "debt payment." The victims, including this adolescent girl found in a shallow tomb atop 20,000-foot Mount Lullaillaco in the Argentine Andes, died of exposure after the long climb, but the Incas believed them to remain semiconscious and in communication with the spirit world.

conflict, was this not true. Even then, subsistence remained the average Andean's most pressing concern.

Artisans produced remarkable textiles, metalwork, and pottery, but the empire's most visible achievements were in the fields of architecture and civil engineering. The Incas' extensive road systems, irrigation works, and monumental temples were unmatched by any ancient American society. No one else moved or carved such large stones or ruled such a vast area. Linking coast, highlands, and jungle, the Incas' roads covered nearly 10,000 miles. Many road sections were paved with stones, and some were hewn into near-vertical mountainsides by hand. Grass weavers spanned gorges with hanging bridges strong enough to sustain trains of pack llamas. These engineering marvels enabled the Incas to communicate and move troops and supplies with amazing speed, yet they also served the important religious function of facilitating pilgrimages and royal processions. Massive irrigation works and stone foundations, though highly practical, were similarly charged with religious power. Thus, the Inca infrastructure not only played an important practical role in imperial government, but it also expressed the Incas' belief in the connection between their own rule and the cosmic order.

The Incas appropriated Andean metalworking techniques, which were much older and more developed than those of Mesoamerica. Metal forging was as much a religious as an artistic exercise in the Andes, and metals themselves were regarded as semi-divine. Gold was associated with the sun in Inca cosmology and by extension with the Sapa Inca and his solar cult. Silver was associated with the moon and with several mother goddesses and Inca queens and princesses. Copper and bronze, considered less divine than gold and silver, were put to more practical uses.

Another ancient Andean tradition inherited by the Incas was weaving. Inca cotton and alpaca-fiber textiles were of extraordinary quality, and cloth became the coin of the realm. Following Andean norms of reciprocity, cooperative regional lords were rewarded by the Incas with gifts of blankets and ponchos, which they could then redistribute among their subjects. Unlike some earlier coastal traditions, Inca design favored geometric forms over representations of humans, animals, or deities. Fiber from the vicuña, a wild relative of the llama, was reserved for the Sapa Inca. Some women became master weavers, but throughout most of the Inca Empire men wove fibers that had been spun into thread by women, a gendered task division later reinforced by the Spanish.

khipu Knotted cotton or alpaca-fiber strings used by the Incas and other Andeans to record tributes, troop numbers, and possibly narratives of events.

With such an emphasis on textiles, it may come as no surprise that the Incas maintained a record-keeping system using knotted strings. Something like an accounting device in its most basic form, the **khipu** enabled bureaucrats to keep track of tributes, troop movements, ritual cycles, and other important matters.

Like bronze metallurgy, the khipu predates the Inca Empire, but it served the empire well. Although its capabilities as a means of data management are a subject of intense debate, the khipu was sufficiently effective to remain in use for several centuries under Spanish rule, long after alphabetic writing was introduced.

Throughout the Andes, women occupied a distinct sphere from that of men, but not a subordinate one. For example, sources suggest that although the majority of Andeans living under Inca rule were patrilineal, or male centered, in their succession preferences, power frequently landed in the hands of sisters and daughters of headmen. Inca descendants described a world in which both sexes participated equally in complementary agricultural tasks, and also in contests against neighboring clans. Women exempted from rotational labor duties handled local exchanges of food and craft goods. Women's fertility was respected, but never equated with warfare, as in Aztec society. Interestingly, Andean childbirth was almost regarded as a nonevent and rarely involved midwives.

As in most early modern societies, parents treated Inca children much like miniature adults and dressed them accordingly. Parents educated children by defining roles and duties early, using routine chores deemed appropriate to one's sex and status as the primary means of education. Girls and boys also participated in most work projects. The expectation of all children was not to change society but to reproduce and maintain it through balanced relations with deities and neighbors. Contact with the Inca himself was an extremely remote possibility for most children living in the empire. A rare exception was capacocha sacrificial victims, such as the headman's daughter described at the opening of this chapter.

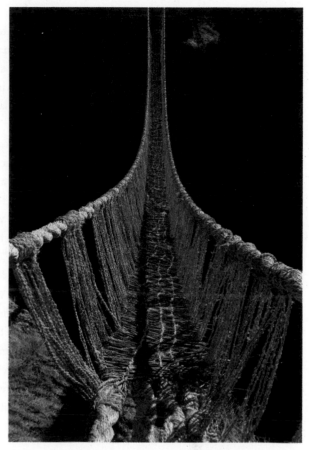

Inca Hanging Bridge Among the great challenges facing the Incas as they expanded their empire across the rugged Andes Mountains of South America were deep canyons cut by swift rivers. Drawing on ancestral techniques, the Incas spanned these chasms with braided-grass bridges of remarkable strength and durability. Such bridges, carefully maintained, allowed passage of heavily burdened people as well as llama trains, linking up a road system that spanned tens of thousands of kilometers. These Indigenous bridge-building technologies survived throughout the colonial period in Peru and Ecuador, supplemented by Spanish pulleys and straps for transporting large livestock. In some places, old-style hanging footbridges survived well into the twentieth century.

Just as maize was native to highland Mesoamerica and served as the base for urban development, the potato was the indigenous staple of the central Andes. A hearty, high-yield tuber with many varieties, the potato could be roasted, stewed, or naturally freeze-dried and stored for long periods. Maize could also be stored dry or toasted, but among Andeans it was generally reserved for beer making. Along with maize, many lowland dwellers subsisted on manioc, peanuts, beans, and chili peppers.

Andean pastoralism played a critical role in Inca expansion. Domesticated animals included the llama, alpaca, and guinea pig. Llamas, in addition to carrying loads, were sometimes eaten, and alpacas provided warm cloth fiber. Slaughter of domestic animals, including fertilizer-producing guinea pigs, usually accompanied ritual occasions such as weddings or harvest festivals. The average Andean diet was overwhelmingly vegetarian. Nevertheless, a common component of Inca trail food was *charqui* (hence "jerky"), bits of dried and salted llama flesh. Llamas and alpacas were never milked. Like many other peoples, Andeans restricted consumption of and even contact with certain animal fluids and body parts.

The high Inca heartland, though fertile, was prone to droughts and frosts. The warmer coast was susceptible to periodic floods. Only by developing food storage techniques and exploiting numerous microenvironments were the Incas and their subjects able to weather such events. Added to these cyclical catastrophes were volcanic eruptions, earthquakes, mudslides, tsunamis, and plagues of locusts. Still, the overall record suggests that subsistence under the Incas, thanks to the "vertical archipelago," was much less precarious than under the Aztecs.

The Great Apparatus Breaks Down

Inca expansion derived from a blend of religious and secular impulses. As in Aztec Mexico, religious demands seem to have grown more and more urgent, possibly even destabilizing the empire by the time of the last Sapa Inca. As emperors died, their mummy cults required extravagant maintenance. The most eminent of mummies in effect tied up huge tracts of land. Logically, if vainly, successive emperors strove to make sure their mummy cults would be provided for in equal or better fashion. Each hoped his legacy might outshine that of his predecessor. Given the extraordinary precedent set by Pachacuti Inca, some scholars have argued that excessive mummy veneration effectively undermined the Inca Empire.

Too, as with the Aztecs, rapid growth by violent means sowed seeds of discontent. On the eve of the Spanish arrival both empires appear to have been contracting rather than expanding, with rebellion the order of the day. The Incas had never done well against lowland forest peoples, and some such enemies kept up chronic raiding activities. Highlanders such as the Cañaris of Ecuador and the Chachapoyas of northern Peru had cost the Incas dearly in their conquest, only just completed in 1525 after more than thirty years. Like the Tlaxcalans of Mexico, both of these recently conquered groups would ally with Spanish invaders in hopes of establishing their independence once and for all.

The Inca state was demanding of its subjects, and enemy frontiers abounded. Yet it seems the Incas' worst enemies were ultimately themselves. A nonviolent means of royal succession had never been established. This was good for the empire in that capable rather than simply hereditary rulers could emerge, but bad in that the position of Sapa Inca was always up for grabs. In calmer times, defense against outside challengers would not have been difficult, but the Spanish had the good fortune to arrive in the midst of a civil war between two rivals to the throne, Huascar and Atawallpa (also "Atahualpa"). By 1532 Atawallpa defeated his half-brother, only to fall prey to a small number of foreign interlopers.

COUNTERPOINT: The Peoples of North America's Eastern Woodlands 1450–1530

➤ **FOCUS** How did the Eastern Woodlanders' experience differ from life under the Aztecs and Incas?

By 1450 several million people inhabited North America's eastern woodlands. Forests provided raw materials for building as well as habitat for game. Trees also yielded nuts and fruits and served as fertilizer for crops when burned. The great mound-building cultures of the Mississippi Basin had faded by this time, their inhabitants having returned to less urban, more egalitarian ways of life. Villages headed by elected chiefs were typical (see Map 15.4).

Most of what we know about native eastern North Americans at this time derives from contact-era (1492–1750) European documents, plus archaeological studies. Although less is known about them than about the Aztecs or Incas, it appears that Eastern Woodlands peoples faced significant changes in politics and everyday life just prior to European arrival. Climate change may have been one important factor spurring conflict and consolidation.

Eastern Woodlands peoples were like the Aztecs in at least one sense. Most were maize farmers who engaged in seasonal warfare followed by captive sacrifice. According to archaeological evidence, both maize planting and warrior sacrifice spread into the region from Mesoamerica around the time of the Toltecs

(800–1100 CE). The century prior to European contact appears to have been marked by rapid population growth, increased warfare, and political reorganization. Multisettlement alliances or leagues, such as the Powhatan Confederacy of tidewater Virginia, were relatively new. Some confederacies were formed for temporary defensive purposes, and others were primarily religious. Some villages housed over 2,000 inhabitants, and confederacies counted up to 20,000 or more.

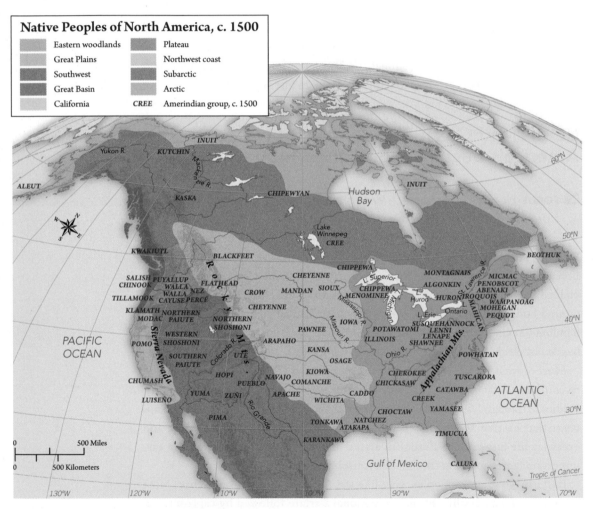

Native Peoples of North America, c. 1500

- Eastern woodlands
- Great Plains
- Southwest
- Great Basin
- California
- Plateau
- Northwest coast
- Subarctic
- Arctic
- *CREE* Amerindian group, c. 1500

≡ **MAP 15.4** **Native Peoples of North America, c. 1500** To the north of Mesoamerica, hundreds of native American groups, most of them organized as chiefdoms, flourished in a wide array of climate zones, from the coldest Arctic wilderness to the hottest subtropical deserts. Populations were highest where maize and other crops could be grown, as in the Rio Grande and Mississippi Valleys, Great Lakes, and eastern woodlands regions.

As in the Andes, clan divisions were common, but population densities were lower.

Smaller gathering-hunting groups occupied more challenging landscapes, yet thanks to their varied diet, they seem to have suffered fewer vitamin and mineral deficiencies than settled maize eaters. Even maize farmers, however, were generally taller than their European (or Mesoamerican) contemporaries. Throughout the eastern forests, including the Great Lakes region, metallurgy was limited to hammering native copper. Copper was regarded as a sacred substance associated with chiefly power. Beads made from polished seashells, or **wampum**, were similarly prized.

≡ **Huron Wampum Belt** For many Eastern Woodlands peoples such as the Huron, seashells like the New England quahog (a variety of clam) were sacred trade goods. Shell beads, or wampum, were woven into ceremonial belts whose geometrical designs and color schemes represented clans and sometimes treaties between larger groups. The linked-hands motif in this belt suggests a treaty or covenant.

Chiefs, usually warriors or shamans elected by popular agreement, headed most Eastern Woodlands groups. They retained power, however, only by redistributing goods such as surplus food or war booty; generosity was the hallmark of leadership. Few chiefdoms were hereditary, and chiefs could be deposed at any time. Individual Eastern Woodlanders, particularly young men, yearned for independence even as circumstances forced them to cooperate and subordinate their wills to others. If the chief's generosity was a centripetal force, egalitarian desires formed a centrifugal one.

Some agricultural peoples, such as the Huron of central Ontario, Canada, had male chiefs or headmen but were organized matrilineally. This meant that society was built around clans of mothers, daughters, and sisters. Matrilineal clans occupied **longhouses**, or wooden multifamily residential buildings. Elder women consulted with chiefs, and all women played a part in urging men to war. Agriculture was a strictly female preserve among the Huron, closely linked to human fertility. Huron men handled risky activities such as hunting, warfare, and tree felling. Their sphere of influence lay largely outside the village. Men's exploits abroad, including adolescent vision quests, conferred status. Among all Eastern Woodlanders, public speech making was as prized

wampum Beads made of seashells; used in eastern North America as currency and to secure alliances.

longhouse A wooden communal dwelling typical of Eastern Woodlands peoples.

among adult men as martial expertise. Only the most esteemed men participated in councils.

Children's lives were difficult among Eastern Woodlanders (keeping in mind that this was true of early modern childhood generally). Due to a multitude of vermin and pathogens, inadequate nutrition, smoky residences, and hazards of war and accident, relatively few children survived to adulthood. Partly for these reasons, Eastern Woodlands cultures discouraged severe discipline for children, instead allowing them much freedom.

Playtime ended early, however, as children were schooled before puberty in their respective arts and responsibilities. Girls learned to farm and cook, boys to hunt and make war. Soon after puberty young people began to "try out" mates until a suitable match was found. Though this and the seemingly casual practice of divorce among Eastern Woodlanders were considered scandalous by early modern European standards, stable monogamy prevailed.

Warfare was endemic throughout the eastern woodlands in the summer season, when subsistence itself was less of a battle. In form, these wars resembled blood feuds, or vengeance cycles. According to European witnesses, wars among the Iroquois, Mahicans, and others were spawned by some long-forgotten crime, such as the rape or murder of a clan member. As such, they were not struggles over land, but rather male contests intended to prove courage and preserve honor.

Warfare closely resembled hunting in that successful warriors were expected to ambush and capture their equivalents from the opposite camp. These unlucky individuals were then brought to the captor's longhouse for an excruciating ordeal, nearly always followed by slaughter and ritual consumption. (Female and child captives, by contrast, were "adopted" as replacements for lost kin.) The religious significance of captive sacrifice among Eastern Woodlanders has been less clearly explained than that of the Aztecs, but it seems to have been tied to subsistence anxieties.

Eastern Woodlands religions varied, but there were commonalities. Beyond the realm of everyday life was a complex spirit world. Matrilineal societies such as the Huron traced their origins to a female spirit whose grandsons invented the essential techniques of civilized life. The sky itself was often more important than the sun or moon in Eastern Woodlands mythologies, and climatic events were associated with bird spirits, such as the thunderbird.

Like Andean peoples, many Eastern Woodlanders believed that material things such as boulders, islands, and personal charms contained life essences, or "souls."

Traders and warriors, in particular, took time to please spirits and "recharge" protective amulets with offerings and incantations. Periodic feasts were also imbued with spiritual energy. On the whole, religious life was an everyday affair, not an institutionalized one. Instead of priesthoods, liturgies, and temples, most Eastern Woodlands peoples relied on elders and shamans to maintain traditions and remind juniors of core beliefs.

Most Eastern Woodlanders did not regard death as a positive transition. They believed that souls lived on indefinitely and migrated to a new home, usually a recognizable ethnic village located in the western distance. Even dogs' souls migrated, as did those of wild animals. The problem with this later existence was that it was unsatisfying. Dead souls were said to haunt the living, complaining of hunger and other insatiable desires. The Huron sought to keep their dead ancestors together and send them off well through elaborate burial rituals, but it was understood that ultimately little could be done for them.

Conclusion

By the time Europeans entered the Caribbean Sea in 1492, the Americas were home to over 60 million people. Throughout the Western Hemisphere, native American life was vibrant and complex, divided by language, customs, and sometimes geographical barriers, but also linked by religion, trade, and war. Cities, pilgrimage sites, mountain passes, and waterways served as crossroads for the exchange of goods and ideas, often between widely dispersed peoples. Another uniting factor was the underlying religious tradition of shamanism.

The many resources available in the highland tropics of Mesoamerica and the Andes Mountains promoted settled agriculture, urbanization, and eventually empire building. Drawing on the traditions of ancestors, imperial peoples such as the Aztecs and Incas built formidable capitals, road systems, and irrigation works. As the Inca capacocha and Aztec warrior sacrifices suggest, these empires were driven to expand at least as much by religious beliefs as by material desires. In part as a result of religious demands, both empires were in crisis by the first decades of the sixteenth century, when Europeans possessing steel-edged weapons, firearms, and other deadly technologies first encountered them. Other native peoples, such as North America's Eastern Woodlanders, built chiefdoms and confederacies rather than empires, and to some degree these looser structures would prove more resilient in the face of European invasion.

review

The major global development in this chapter: The diversity of societies and states in the Americas prior to European invasion.

Important Events	
c. 900–1600	Period of dispersed farming and hunting in the Eastern Woodlands
c. 1200	Incas move into Cuzco region
c. 1270	Aztecs settle in Valley of Mexico
c. 1320	Aztecs ally with Colhua
c. 1325	Tenochtitlán founded at Lake Texcoco's edge
c. 1437	Incas defeat Chankas
c. 1440–1471	Sapa Inca Pachacuti expands empire into Ecuador and Bolivia
1450–1451	Great famine in Valley of Mexico
1471–1493	Incas conquer northern Chile and Argentina
1487–1502	Aztecs dedicate Coatepec (Templo Mayor) and expand sacrificial wars
1493–1525	Incas conquer northern Peru and highland Ecuador
1502–1519	Reign of Moctezuma II, conquered by Spanish
1525–1532	Inca succession war, followed by arrival of the Spanish
c. 1570	Formation of Huron Confederacy north of Lake Ontario and of Iroquois League south of Lake Ontario

KEY TERMS

autosacrifice (p. 564)   longhouse (p. 583)   vertical archipelago (p. 570)
chinampa (p. 561)   shamanism (p. 556)   waka (p. 574)
khipu (p. 578)   tribute (p. 564)   wampum (p. 583)

CHAPTER OVERVIEW QUESTIONS

1. In what ways was cultural diversity in the Americas related to environmental diversity?

2. Why was it in Mesoamerica and the Andes that large empires emerged in around 1450?

3. What key ideas or practices extended beyond the limits of the great empires?

MAKING CONNECTIONS

1. Compare the Aztec and Inca Empires with the Ming (see Chapter 14 and/or Chapter 20). What features did they share? What features set them apart?

2. How did Aztec and Inca sacrificial rituals differ, and why?

3. What were the main causes of warfare among native American peoples prior to the arrival of Europeans?

DOING HISTORY

Making Connections

Studying the past at global scale enables historians to *make connections* that would not otherwise be visible, or conspicuous. One of the enduring mysteries of world history is why people began building cities in some places rather than others, and how urbanism spread (or did not spread) from these original sites to new ones. In the case of the Americas, it may be that urbanism developed independently in Mesoamerica and South America despite some communication by sea or land between them. In any event, it seems that how cities developed was not quite the same in each continental region.

1. In comparing the Aztec and Inca Empires, as well as their capital cities of Tenochtitlán and Cuzco, what aspects of urbanism stand out?

2. Were there other significant cities in the Aztec and Inca realms? Were there conquered "enemy" cities that were transformed in fundamental ways?

3. What general observations result from making connections?

For further research into the topics covered in this chapter, see the Bibliography at the end of the book.

Notes

Chapter 1

1. Charles Darwin, *On the Origin of Species*, ed. Joseph Carroll (Peterborough, Ontario, Canada: Broadview, 2003), 432.

2. J. C. Beaglehole, ed., *The Voyage of the Endeavour 1768–1771: The Journals of Captain James Cook on His Voyages of Discovery* [Series] (Cambridge: Cambridge University Press, 1955), 1:399.

Chapter 2

1. H. L. J. Vanstiphout, ed., *Epics of Sumerian Kings: The Matter of Aratta* (Atlanta, GA: Society of Biblical Literature, 2004), 85.

2. Martha T. Roth, *Law Collections from Mesopotamia and Asia Minor* (Atlanta, GA: Society of Biblical Literature, 1997), 121.

3. J. A. Black, et al., *The Literature of Ancient Sumer* (Oxford: Oxford University Press, 2004), 319.

4. Translated from E. Edel, *Die ägyptisch-hethitische Korrespondenz aus Boghazkoy* (Opladen, Germany: Westdeutscher Verlag, 1994), 40–41.

Chapter 3

1. Burton Watson, trans., *Records of the Grand Historian by Sima Qian: Han Dynasty II* (New York: Columbia University Press, 1993), 129.

2. *The Laws of Manu*, trans. Georg Bühler (New York: Dover, 1969), 327–28.

3. Wendy Doniger O'Flaherty, *The Rig Veda: An Anthology* (New York: Penguin Books, 1981), 10.90, 30–31.

4. Burton Watson, trans., in Wm. Theodore de Bary and Irene Bloom, eds., *Sources of Chinese Tradition*, 2nd ed. (New York: Columbia University Press, 1999), 1:38.

Chapter 4

1. Translated from Florence Malbran-Labat, *La version akkadienne de l'inscription trilingue de Darius à Behistun* (Rome: GEI, 1994), 93–103.

2. Yasna 30:3, in S. Insler, *The Gathas of Zarathustra* (Leiden, Netherlands: Brill, 1975), 33.

Chapter 5

1. Susan Sherwin-White and Amélie Kuhrt, *From Samarkhand to Sardis: A New Approach to the Seleucid Empire* (Berkeley: University of California Press, 1993), 179.

2. Ainslie T. Embree, ed., *Sources of Indian Tradition*, 2nd ed. (New York: Columbia University Press, 1988), 1:282.

3. *Sources of Indian Tradition*, 1:148.

4. Leonard Nathan, *The Transport of Love* (Berkeley: University of California Press, 1976), 83.

5. Confucius, *Analects* 15, 17, *Chinese Civilization: A Sourcebook*, 2nd ed., trans. Patricia Buckley Ebrey (New York: Free Press, 1993), 18.

6. *Sophocles I*, trans. Elizabeth Wyckoff (Chicago: University of Chicago Press, 1954), 174.

Chapter 6

1. H. Mattingly, trans., *Tacitus on Britain and Germany* (Harmondsworth, Middlesex, UK: Penguin Books, 1978), 72.
2. Horace, *Epistles* 2.1, lines 156–57.
3. Herbert Musurillo, ed. and trans., *The Acts of the Christian Martyrs* (Oxford: Clarendon Press, 1972), 119.
4. Ammianus Marcellinus, 24.6.7, quoted in M. Brosius, *The Persians* (London: Routledge, 2006), 187.
5. Josef Wiesehöfer, *Ancient Persia from 550 BC to 650 AD* (London: Tauris, 1996), 199.

Chapter 7

1. *The Endeavour Journal of Joseph Banks, 1768–1771*, ed. J. C. Beaglehole (Sydney, Australia: Halstead Press, 1962), 1:368. Spellings retained from the original source.
2. *The Endeavour Journal of Joseph Banks, 1768–1771*, 2:37. Spellings retained from the original source.
3. Martin West, trans., "A New Sappho Poem," *The Times Literary Supplement*, June 24, 2005.

Chapter 8

1. Jo Ann McNamara and John E. Halborg, eds. and trans., *Sainted Women of the Dark Ages* (Durham, NC: Duke University Press, 1992), 65, 72, 75.
2. Procopius, *The Secret History*, trans. G. A. Williamson (London: Penguin, 1966), 106.
3. Alcuin, "Letter 8" (to Charlemagne), in Stephen Allott, *Alcuin of York, c. A.D. 732 to 804: His Life and Letters* (York, UK: Sessions, 1974), 11.
4. Gregory, *Pastoral Care*, 1.1, trans. Henry Davis, in *Ancient Christian Writers* (New York: Newman Press, 1950), 11:21.
5. S. H. Cross and O. P. Sherbovitz-Wetzor, *The Russian Primary Chronicle, Laurentian Text* (Cambridge, MA: Medieval Academy of America, 1953), 53, referring to the Poliane people inhabiting modern-day Ukraine.
6. Procopius, *History of the Wars*, trans. H. B. Dewing (Cambridge, MA: Harvard University Press, 1924), 7:14, 22–30.
7. Quoted in Gaston Wiet, *Baghdad: Metropolis of the Abbasid Caliphate* (Norman: University of Oklahoma Press, 1971), 11.
8. Sufyan al-Thawri, quoted in Francis Robinson, ed., *The Cambridge Illustrated History of the Islamic World* (Cambridge: Cambridge University Press, 1996), 22.
9. Charles Plummer, ed., *Two of the Saxon Chronicles* (Oxford: Clarendon Press, 1892), 57.
10. *Beowulf*, lines 4–11, from *Beowulf: A Verse Translation*, trans. Michael Alexander (London: Penguin, 1973), 3.

Chapter 9

1. Xuanzang, *Da Tang xiyu ji* [*Record of the Western Regions*] (Shanghai: Shanghai renmin chubanshe, 1977), 108.
2. *Nihon shoki* [*The Chronicles of Japan*], ed. Inoue Mitsusada (Tokyo: Chuo koronsha, 1987), 2:70.
3. Xuanzang, *Da Tang xiyu ji* [*Record of the Western Regions*], 41.
4. Xuanzang, *Da Tang xiyu ji* [*Record of the Western Regions*], 149.
5. Translated in Munshi Debiprasad, "Ghatayala Inscription of the Pratihara Kakkuka of [Vikrama-]Samvat 918," *Journal of the Royal Asiatic Society* (1895): 519–20.
6. Cosmas Indicopleustes, *Christian Topography* (c. 547–550) (London: Hakluyt Society, 1897), Book II, 47.

Chapter 11

1. Quotations from S. D. Goitein, "Portrait of a Medieval India Trader: Three Letters from the Cairo Geniza," *Bulletin of the School of Oriental and African Studies*, 50, no. 3 (1987): 461; S. D. Goitein, *A Mediterranean Society: The Jewish Communities of the World as Portrayed in the Documents of the Cairo Geniza* (Berkeley: University of California Press, 1978–1988), 3:194; 5:221.

2. Ibn Hazm, *The Ring of the Dove: A Treatise on the Art and Practice of Arab Love* (London: Luzac, 1953), 74.

3. Al-Muqaddasi, *The Best Divisions for Knowledge of the Regions*, trans. Basil Anthony Collins (Reading, UK: Garnet, 1994), 181.

4. Quoted in Goitein, *A Mediterranean Society*, 1:200.

5. Translation adapted from Yuan Ts'ai, *Family Instructions for the Yuan Clan*, quoted in Patricia Buckley Ebrey, *Family and Property in Sung China: Yuan Ts'ai's* Precepts for Social Life (Princeton, NJ: Princeton University Press, 1984), 267.

6. Ibn Hawqal, *The Picture of the Earth*, translated in N. Levtzion and J. F. P. Hopkins, eds., *Corpus of Early Arabic Sources for West African History* (Cambridge: Cambridge University Press, 1981), 49.

7. Al-Bakri, *Kitab al masalik wa-'l-mamalik*, translated in Levtzion and Hopkins, eds., *Corpus of Early Arabic Sources*, 79.

8. Al-Umari, "The Kingdom of Mali and What Appertains to It" (1338), cited in Levtzion and Hopkins, eds., *Corpus of Early Arabic Sources*, 270–71.

Chapter 12

1. Lady Murasaki, *The Tale of Genji*, quoted in Ivan Morris, *The World of the Shining Prince: Court Life in Ancient Japan* (New York: Knopf, 1964), 308–9.

2. *The Letters of Abelard and Heloise*, trans. Betty Radice (Harmondsworth, UK: Penguin, 1974), 58.

3. *The Anglo-Saxon Chronicle*, trans. G. N. Garmonsway (London: J. M. Dent, 1954), 216.

4. Farid al-Din Attar, *Tadhkirat al-Awliya*, quoted in Margaret Smith, *Rabi'a the Mystic and Her Fellow Saints in Islam* (Cambridge: Cambridge University Press, 1928), 3–4.

5. W. Montgomery Watt, *The Faith and Practice of al-Ghazali* (London: George Allen & Unwin, 1967), 57.

6. *The Travels of Ibn Battutah*, ed. Tim Cakintosh-Smith (London: Picador, 2002), 167, 187.

7. Quoted in Ichisada Miyazaki, *China's Examination Hell: The Civil Service Examinations of Imperial China* (New Haven, CT: Yale University Press, 1981), 17.

Chapter 13

1. Quotations from Usamah ibn Munqidh, *The Book of Learning by Example*, translated in Francesco Gabrieli, ed., *Arab Historians of the Crusades* (Berkeley: University of California Press, 1969), 73, 84.

2. *The Deeds of the Franks and the Other Pilgrims to Jerusalem*, cited in James Harvey Robinson, ed., *Readings in European History* (Boston: Ginn, 1904), 1:312.

3. Ibn Jubayr, "Relation de voyages," *Voyageurs arabes: Ibn Fadlan, Ibn Jubayr, Ibn Battuta et un auteur anonyme*, trans. Paul Charles-Dominique (Paris: Éditions Gallimard, 1995), 310.

4. Cited in Robert Bartlett, *The Making of Europe: Conquest, Colonization, and Cultural Change, 950–1350* (Princeton: Princeton University Press, 1993), 132.

5. Nicole Oresme, "Le Livre de Politiques d'Aristotle," *Transactions of the American Philosophical Society*, new series, vol. 60, part 6 (1970): 292.

6. *Marco Polo: The Description of the World*, trans. Sharon Kinoshita (London: Hackett, 2016), 67.

7. *Marco Polo*, 87.

8. *Rashiduddin Fazullah's* Jami'u't-tawarikh [Compendium of Chronicles]: *A History of the Mongols*, trans. W. M. Thackston (Cambridge, MA: Harvard University, Department of Near Eastern Languages and Civilizations, 1998), Part I, 6.

9. *Nizam ad-din Awliya: Morals for the Heart*, trans. Bruce B. Lawrence (New York: Paulist Press, 1992), 83.

Chapter 14

1. Giovanni Boccaccio, *The Decameron* (New York: Modern Library, 1931), 8–9.

2. Quoted in Adel Allouche, *Mamluk Economics: A Study and Translation of Al-Maqrizi's* Ighathah (Salt Lake City: University of Utah Press, 1994), 75–76 (translation slightly modified).

3. Quoted in Michael W. Dols, "Ibn al-Wardi's *Risalah al-naba' 'an al'waba'*: A Translation of a Major Source for the History of the Black Death in the Middle East," in *Near Eastern Numismatics, Iconography, Epigraphy and History: Studies in Honor of George C. Miles*, ed. Dickran K. Kouymjian (Beirut, Lebanon: American University of Beirut, 1974), 454.

4. *Anonimalle Chronicle*, in *The Peasants' Revolt of 1381*, ed. R. B. Dobson (London: Macmillan, 1970), 164–65.

5. Ibn Battuta, "The Sultan of Mali," in *Corpus of Early Arabic Sources for West African History*, trans. J. F. P. Hopkins, ed. N. Levtzion and J. F. P. Hopkins (Cambridge: Cambridge University Press, 1981), 296.

6. Leo Africanus, *History and Description of Africa*, trans. John Poy (London: Hakluyt Society, 1896), 3:825.

7. Shihab al-Din Ahmad ibn Majid, "Al'Mal'aqiya," in *A Study of the Arabic Texts Containing Material of South-East Asia*, ed. and trans. G. R. Tibbetts (Leiden, Netherlands: Brill, 1979), 206.

8. Simone Sigoli, "Pilgrimage of Simone Sigoli to the Holy Land," in *Visit to the Holy Places of Egypt, Sinai, Palestine and Syria in 1384 by Frescobaldi, Gucci, and Sigoli*, trans. Theophilus Bellorini and Eugene Hoade (Jerusalem: Franciscan Press, 1948), 182.

9. Quoted in Lisa Jardine, *Worldly Goods: A New History of the Renaissance* (New York: Doubleday, 1996), 126.

10. Declaration of Oshima and Okitsushima shrine association, dated 1298, quoted in Pierre François Souyri, *The World Turned Upside Down: Medieval Japanese Society* (New York: Columbia University Press, 2001), 136.

Chapter 15

1. For the archaeologist's own account of these discoveries, see Johan Reinhard, *The Ice Maiden: Inca Mummies, Mountain Gods, and Sacred Sites in the Andes* (Washington, DC: National Geographic, 2005).

2. Miguel León-Portilla, *Pre-Columbian Literatures of Mexico* (Norman: University of Oklahoma Press, 1969), 87.

3. Juan de Betanzos, *Narrative of the Incas*, c. 1557, trans. Roland Hamilton and Dana Buchanan (Austin: University of Texas Press, 1996), 92.

Chapter 16

1. Christopher Columbus, *The Four Voyages*, trans. J. M. Cohen (New York: Penguin, 1969), 300.

2. Gomes Eannes de Azurara, quoted in John H. Parry and Robert G. Keith, *New Iberian World: A Documentary History of the Discovery of Latin America to the Seventeenth Century* (New York: Times Books, 1984), 1:256.

3. Alfred Crosby, *The Columbian Exchange: Biological and Cultural Consequences of 1492*, 2nd ed. (Westport, CT: Praeger, 2003).

4. Quoted in Ross Hassig, *Aztec Warfare: Imperial Expansion and Political Control* (Norman: University of Oklahoma Press, 1992), 124.

Chapter 17

1. The story of Domingo Angola is reconstructed from notary documents found in the Ecuadorian National Archive in Quito (Archivo Nacional del Ecuador, Protocolos notariales 1:19 FGD, 1-x-1601, ff. 647–746, and 1:6 DLM, 5-x-1595, f. 287v) and various studies of the early slave trade, especially Linda Heywood and John Thornton, *Central Africans, Atlantic Creoles, and the Foundation of the Americas, 1585–1660* (New York: Cambridge University Press, 2007). On the Jesuits in Luanda and their involvement in the slave trade at this time, see Dauril Alden, *The Making of an Enterprise: The Society of Jesus in Portugal, Its Empire, and Beyond, 1540–1750* (Stanford, CA: Stanford University Press, 1996), 544–46.

2. Joseph Miller, *Way of Death: Merchant Capitalism and the Angolan Slave Trade, 1730–1830* (Madison: University of Wisconsin Press, 1988), 4–5.

3. George E. Brooks, *Landlords and Strangers: Ecology, Society, and Trade in Western Africa, 1000–1630* (Boulder, CO: Westview Press, 1994).

4. This and other letters are published in António Brásio, ed., *Monumenta Missionaria Africana*, vol. 1, *África Ocidental (1471–1531)* (Lisbon: Agência Geral do Ultramar, 1952), 470–71. (Special thanks to José Curto of York University, Canada, for pointing out this reference.)

5. Olaudah Equiano, *The Interesting Narrative of the Life of Olaudah Equiano, Written by Himself*, 2nd ed., introduction by Robert J. Allison (Boston: Bedford/St. Martin's, 2007).

Chapter 18

1. Marshall Hodgson, *The Venture of Islam* (Chicago: University of Chicago Press, 1974), 2:34.

2. Robert Sewell, *A Forgotten Empire (Vijayanagar): A Contribution to the History of India* (London: Sonnenschein, 1900), 245.

3. Thackston Wheeler, ed. and trans., *The Baburnama: Memoirs of Babur, Prince and Emperor* (Washington, DC: Smithsonian Institution, 1996), 326, 384.

4. Vasco da Gama, *The Diary of His Travels Through African Waters, 1497–1499*, ed. and trans. Eric Axelson (Somerset, UK: Stephan Phillips, 1998), 45.

Chapter 19

1. Richard Kagan, *Lucrecia's Dreams: Politics and Prophecy in Sixteenth-Century Spain* (Berkeley: University of California Press, 1990), 66.

2. Richard Kagan, *Lucrecia's Dreams: Politics and Prophecy in Sixteenth-Century Spain* (Berkeley: University of California Press, 1990); Anne Marie Plane, Leslie Tuttle, and Anthony Wallace, eds., *Dreams, Dreamers, and Visions: The Early Modern Atlantic World* (Philadelphia: University of Pennsylvania Press, 2013); Mustafa Celalzade, *Selim-name* [In praise of Selim], ed. Ahmet Uđur, Mustafa Huhadar, as it appears in Halil Berktay and Bogdan Murgescu, *The Ottoman Empire* (Thessaloniki: CDRSEE, 2005), 53.

3. Habsburg ambassador Ghiselin de Busbecq, quoted in Gérard Chaliand, ed., *The Art of War in World History from Antiquity to the Nuclear Age* (Berkeley: University of California Press, 1994), 457.

Chapter 20

1. Tonio Andrade, *Lost Colony: The Untold Story of China's First Great Victory over the West* (Princeton, NJ: Princeton University Press, 2011); Robert Antony, *Elusive Pirates, Pervasive Smugglers: Violence and Clandestine Trade in the Greater China Seas* (Hong Kong: Hong Kong University Press, 2010); Xing Hang, *Conflict and Commerce in Maritime East Asia: The Zheng*

Family and the Shaping of the Modern World, 1620–1720 (New York: Cambridge University Press, 2016); Bashō, "The Records of a Weather-Exposed Skeleton" (c. 1685), ed. and trans.

Nobuyuki Yuasa, *The Narrow Road to the Deep North and Other Sketches* (London: Penguin, 1966).

Chapter 21

1. Sor Juana Inés de la Cruz, quoted in Irving Leonard, *Baroque Times in Old Mexico: Seventeenth-Century Persons, Places, and Practices* (Ann Arbor: University of Michigan Press, 1959), 189.

2. Saramakan elder Lántifáya, quoted in Richard Price, *First-Time: The Historical Vision of an Afro-American People* (Baltimore, MD: Johns Hopkins University Press, 1983), 71.

Chapter 22

1. Luis Peru de Lacroix, *Diario de Bucaramanga* (Caracas: Comité ejecutivo del Bicentenario de Simón Bolívar, 1982), 67, quoted in Charles Minguet, ed., *Simon Bolivar: Unité impossible* (Paris: La Découverte, 1983), 13.

2. Voltaire, *Essai sur les moeurs et l'esprit des nations*, ed. René Pomeau, 2 vols. (Paris: Garnier, 1963 [1756/1761]) 2: 806.

3. Quoted in Hilda L. Smith and Berenice A. Carroll, eds., *Women's Political and Social Thought* (Bloomington: Indiana University Press, 2000), 133.

4. "Political Testament," in *Europe in Review*, ed. George I. Mosse et al. (Chicago: Rand McNally, 1957), 111–12.

5. Quoted in Richard Wortman, *Scenarios of Power: Myth and Ceremony in Russian Monarchy, Volume 1: From Peter the Great to the Death of Nicholas I* (Princeton, NJ: Princeton University Press, 1995), 130.

6. *Seminario Económico de México*, 1811, quoted in Silvia Marina Arrom, *The Women of Mexico City, 1790–1857* (Palo Alto, CA: Stanford University Press, 1985), 18.

7. Edward Long, quoted in Barbara Bush, *Slave Women in the Caribbean, 1650–1838* (London: Heinemann, 1990), 15, 51.

8. Alexander Hamilton, *Federalist Papers*, Number 15.

9. Letter to John Jay, March 14, 1779, http://www.c250.columbia.edu/c250_celebrates/remarkable_columbians/alexander_hamilton.html.

10. Quoted in Ron Chernow, *Alexander Hamilton* (New York: Penguin, 2004), 316.

11. Quoted in Lynn Hunt, *The French Revolution and Human Rights: A Brief Documentary History* (Boston: Bedford/St. Martins, 1996), 65.

12. Quoted in Annie Jourdan, *Napoléon: Héros, Imperator, Mécène* (Paris: Aubier, 1998), 34.

13. Quoted in Albert Hourani, *Arabic Thought in the Liberal Age, 1798–1939* (London: Oxford University Press, 1962); "Address to the National Assembly, to Our Lords the Representatives of the Nation," quoted in Laurent Dubois and John D. Garrigus, eds., *Slave Revolution in the Caribbean, 1789–1804: A Brief History with Documents* (Boston: Bedford/St. Martins, 2005), 69.

14. Quoted Dubois and Garrigus, *Slave Revolution*, 77.

15. "Notes [from Napoleon Bonaparte] to Serve as Instructions to Give to the Captain General Leclerc," quoted in Dubois and Garrigus, *Slave Revolution*, 176.

16. "Proclamation of 1809," quoted in Peter Bakewell, *A History of Latin America: Empires and Sequels, 1450–1930* (Oxford: Blackwell, 1997), 362.

17. Juan Ruiz de Apodaca, quoted in Richard Boyer and Geoffrey Spurling, eds., *Colonial Lives: Documents on Latin American History, 1550–1850* (New York: Oxford University Press, 2000), 305.

18. Quoted in George Reid Andrews, *Afro-Latin America, 1800–2000* (New York: Oxford University Press, 2004), 57.

19. Quoted in John Lynch, "The Origins of Spanish American Independence," in *The Cambridge History of Latin America* (Cambridge: Cambridge University Press, 1985), 3:32.
20. Quoted in Martyn Lyons, *Napoleon Bonaparte and the Legacy of the French Revolution* (London: Macmillan, 1994), 232.
21. Quoted in Lyons, *Napoleon Bonaparte*, v.
22. Quoted in Sujit Sivasundaram, *Waves Across the South: A New History of Revolution and Empire* (London: William Collins, 2020), 92.

23. William Briggs, quoted in Phyllis Mack, *Heart Religion in the British Enlightenment: Gender and Emotion in Early Methodism* (New York: Cambridge University Press, 2008), 2.
24. John Esposito, *Islam: The Straight Path* (New York: Oxford University Press, 1991).
25. "Letter from Jamaica," 1815, http://faculty.smu.edu/bakewell/bakewell/texts/jamaica-letter.html.

Chapter 23

1. James R. Simmons Jr., ed., *Factory Lives: Four Nineteenth-Century Working-Class Autobiographies* (Peterborough, Ontario: Broadview, 2007), 110.
2. Simmons, *Factory Lives*, 123.
3. Quoted in Brian Dolan, *Wedgwood: The First Tycoon* (New York: Viking, 2004), 54.
4. Quoted in Sally and David Dugan, *The Day the World Took Off: The Roots of the Industrial Revolution* (London: Macmillan, 2000), 54.
5. Quoted in Ken Alder, *Engineering the Revolution: Arms and Enlightenment in France, 1763–1815* (Princeton, NJ: Princeton University Press, 1997), 223.
6. Quoted in Tessa Morris-Suzuki, *The Technological Transformation of Japan from the Seventeenth to the Twenty-First Century* (Cambridge: Cambridge University Press, 1994), 65.
7. Quoted in Morris-Suzuki, *The Technological Transformation*, 73.
8. Quoted in T. R. Havens, "Early Modern Farm Ideology and Japanese Agriculture," in *Meiji Japan: Political, Economic and Social History*, ed. Peter Kornicki (Routledge: New York, 1998), 1:235.
9. Quoted in Edward Beatty, *Institutions and Investment: The Political Basis of Industrialization in Mexico Before 1911* (Stanford, CA: Stanford University Press, 2001), 59.
10. Thomas Munro, quoted in Romash Chunder Dutt, *The Economic History of India* (Delhi: Low Price, 1990 [orig. pub. 1902–1904]), 185–86.

11. "The Land System of the Heavenly Dynasty" (1853), quoted in *China: Readings in the History of China from the Opium War to the Present*, ed. J. Mason Gentzler (New York: Praeger, 1977), 56.
12. Quoted in Michael E. Meeker, *A Nation of Empire: The Ottoman Legacy of Turkish Modernity* (Berkeley: University of California Press, 2002), 103.
13. Afaf Lutfi Al-Sayyid Marsot, *Egypt in the Reign of Muhammad Ali* (Cambridge: Cambridge University Press, 1984), 169–71.
14. Quoted in Carolyn Brown, "We Were All Slaves" in *African Miners, Culture, and Resistance at the Enugu Government Colliery* (Portsmouth, NH: Heinemann, 2003), 36.
15. Mr. Laird, quoted in Joseph Inicori, *Africans and the Industrial Revolution in England: A Study in International Trade and Economic Development* (New York: Cambridge University Press, 2002), 394.
16. Debendranath Tagore, quoted in Blair B. Kling, *Partner in Empire: Dwarkanath Tagore and the Age of Enterprise in Eastern India* (Berkeley: University of California Press, 1976), 184.
17. Quoted on the Tata Group website, http://www.tata.com/0_about_us/history/pioneers/quotable.htm.
18. Quoted in Susie Tharu and K. Lalita, eds., *Women Writing in India: 600 BC to the Early Twentieth Century* (London: Pandora, 1991), 1:214.
19. Quoted in Caroline Arscott, "'Without Distinction of Party': The Polytechnic Exhibitions

in Leeds, 1839–1945," in *The Culture of Capital: Art, Power, and the Nineteenth-Century Middle Class*, ed. Janet Wolff and John Seed (Manchester, UK: Manchester University Press, 1988), 145.

20. Quoted in Susie Porter, *Working Women in Mexico City: Public Discourse and Material Conditions, 1879–1931* (Tucson: University of Arizona Press, 2003), 3–4.

21. Quoted in E. Patricia Tsurumi, *Factory Girls: Women in the Thread Mills of Meiji Japan* (Princeton, NJ: Princeton University Press, 1990), 139.

22. Quoted in Ivy Pinchbeck, *Women Workers and the Industrial Revolution, 1750–1850* (London: Virago, 1981 [orig. pub. 1930]), 195.

23. Quoted in Eric Hobsbawm and George Rudé, *Captain Swing: A Social History of the Great English Agricultural Uprising of 1830* (New York: Norton, 1968), 208.

24. Quoted in Victoria E. Bonnell, *The Russian Worker: Life and Labor Under the Tsarist Regime* (Berkeley: University of California Press, 1983), 197.

25. Judith A. Carney, *Black Rice: The African Origins of Rice Cultivation in the Americas* (Cambridge, MA: Harvard University Press, 2001), 31.

26. Carney, *Black Rice*, 147.

Chapter 24

1. Anne Walthall, *The Weak Body of a Useless Woman: Matsuo Taseko and the Meiji Restoration* (Chicago: University of Chicago Press, 1998), 98, 107.

2. Quoted in John Armstrong Crow, *The Epic of Latin America*, 4th ed. (Berkeley: University of California Press, 1992), 542.

3. Quoted in George Reid Andrews, *Afro-Latin America, 1800–2000* (New York: Oxford University Press, 2004), 113.

4. Quoted in Sarah C. Chambers, *From Subjects to Citizens: Honor, Gender, and Politics in Arequipa, Peru, 1780–1854* (University Park: Pennsylvania State University Press, 1999), 234–235.

5. Quoted in Chambers, *From Subjects to Citizens*, 184.

6. "Alexander Nikitenko Responds to the Emancipation of the Serfs, 1861," http://artsci.shu.edu/reesp/documents/nikitenko.htm.

7. Quoted in Jasper Ridley, *Garibaldi* (London: St. Martins, 2001), 443.

8. Ridley, *Garibaldi*, 448.

9. German Historical Institute, http://ghdi.ghi-dc.org/sub_document.cfm?document_id=250.

10. Quoted in James L. Roark et al., *The American Promise: A History of the United States*, 4th ed. (Boston: Bedford/St. Martins, 2009), 537.

11. Quoted in Frank Linderman, *Pretty-Shield: Medicine Woman of the Crows* (Lincoln: University of Nebraska Press, 1972), 83.

12. Daklugie quoted in Colin G. Calloway, *First Peoples: A Documentary Survey of American Indian History*, 3rd ed. (Boston: Bedford/St. Martins, 2008), 312.

13. Quoted in Mikiso Hane, *Peasants, Rebels, and Outcastes: The Underside of Modern Japan* (New York: Pantheon, 1982), 24.

14. Quoted in Richard Slotkin, *The Fatal Environment: The Myth of the Frontier in an Age of Industrialization* (Norman: University of Oklahoma Press, 1985), 339.

15. Quoted in Slotkin, *The Fatal Environment*, 347.

16. "The Race Problem: An Autobiography: A Southern Colored Woman," *Independent*, 56 (1904): 586–89.

17. Quoted in Stephen Oates, *A Woman of Valor: Clara Barton and the Civil War* (New York: Free Press, 1994), 157–58.

18. Ida B. Wells, *Crusade for Justice: The Autobiography of Ida B. Wells*, ed. Alfreda M. Duster (Chicago: University of Chicago Press, 1970), 49.

19. Eliezer Perlman (Ben Yehuda), quoted in Howard M. Sachar, *A History of the Jews in the Modern World* (New York: Random House, 2006), e-Book, n.p.

20. Grete Meisel-Hess, *The Sexual Crisis*, trans. Eden and Cedar Paul (New York: Critic and Guide, 1917), 6.

21. Paul Leroy-Beaulieu, quoted in *Histoire de la colonisation française* (Paris: Fayard, 1991), 2:149.

22. Rachel Fell McDermott et al., eds., *Sources of Indian Traditions: Modern India, Pakistan, and Bangladesh* (New York: Columbia University Press, 2014), 99.

23. Quoted in Rudrangshu Mukherjee, "The Sepoy Mutinies Revisited," in *War and Society in Colonial India, 1807–1945*, ed. Kaushik Roy (Delhi: Oxford University Press, 2006), 121.

24. Quoted in Charles Lee Keeton, *King Thebaw and the Ecological Rape of Burma: The Political and Commercial Struggle Between British India and French Indo-China in Burma, 1878–1886* (Delhi: Manohar Book Service, 1974), 202.

25. Phan Chau Trinh, in Truong Buu Lam, *Colonialism Experienced: Vietnamese Writing on Colonialism, 1900–1931* (Ann Arbor: University of Michigan Press, 2000), 130.

26. William Morton Fullerton, *In Cairo*, quoted in Max Rodenbeck, *Cairo: The City Victorious* (New York: Knopf, 1999), 136.

27. Letter from the king of Daboya to governor of the Gold Coast, July 8, 1892, quoted in A. Adu Boahen, *African Perspectives on Colonialism* (Baltimore, MD: Johns Hopkins University Press, 1987), 37.

28. Cecil Rhodes, "Confession of Faith" (1877), in John E. Flint, *Cecil Rhodes* (Boston: Little Brown, 1974), 248–50.

29. Ramon Hawley Myers and Mark R. Peattie, eds., *The Japanese Imperial Colonial Empire, 1895–1945* (Princeton, NJ: Princeton University Press, 1984), 15.

30. Quoted in Mike Davis, *Late Victorian Holocausts: El Niño Famines and the Making of the Third World* (London: Verso, 2001), 46.

31. Jack Kelly, *Gunpowder: Alchemy, Bombards, and Pyrotechnics: The History of the Explosive That Changed the World* (New York: Basic Books, 2004), 233.

32. Davis, *Late Victorian Holocausts*, 139.

33. Quoted in Jennifer W. Cushman, *Family and State: The Formation of a Sino-Thai Tin-Mining Dynasty, 1797–1832* (Singapore: Oxford University Press, 1991), 62.

34. Khayr al-Din al-Tunisi, "The Surest Path to Knowledge Concerning the Condition of Countries," quoted in *Colonial Rule in Africa: Readings from Primary Sources*, ed. Bruce Fetter (Madison: University of Wisconsin Press, 1979), 57.

35. Quoted in Fetter, *Colonial Rule in Africa*, 117.

36. Quoted in Robert O. Collins, ed., *Eastern African History*, vol. 2, *African History: Text and Readings* (New York: Markus Wiener, 1990), 124.

37. Quoted in Sumanta Banerjee, "Women's Popular Culture in Nineteenth Century Bengal," in *Recasting Women: Essays in Indian Colonial History*, ed. Kumkum Sangari and Sudesh Vaid (New Brunswick, NJ: Rutgers University Press, 1990), 142.

38. Quoted in David Robinson, *Muslim Societies and French Colonial Authorities in Senegal and Mauritania, 1880–1920* (Athens: Ohio University Press, 2000), 204.

39. Quoted in Irokawa Daikichi, *The Culture of the Meiji Period*, ed. and trans. Marius B. Jansen (Princeton, NJ: Princeton University Press, 1985), 56.

40. Mary Antin, *The Promised Land* (Boston: Houghton Mifflin, 1912), 8.

41. "Song of Revolution," in Gungwu Wang, *Community and Nation: China, Southeast Asia and Australia* (St. Leonards, Australia: Allen and Unwin, 1992), 10.

Chapter 25

1. Chief Segale, quoted in Peter Warwick, *Black People and the South African War, 1899–1902* (Cambridge: Cambridge University Press, 1983), 177.

2. General Sir Ian Hamilton, *A Staff-Officer's Scrap-Book During the Russo-Japanese War* (New York: Longman's Green, 1907), 2:64.

3. Quoted in Paul A. Cohen, *History in Three Keys: The Boxers as Event, Experience, and Myth* (New York: Columbia University Press, 1997), 80.

4. Bal Gangadhar Tilak, "Address to the Indian National Congress, 1907," https://sourcebooks.fordham.edu/mod/1907tilak.asp.

5. Albert Sarraut, 1913, quoted in Tim Harper, *Underground Asia: Global Revolutionaries and the Assault on Empire* (Cambridge, MA: Harvard University Press, 2021), 147.

6. Emiliano Zapata, "Plan de Ayala," quoted in Manuel Plana, *Pancho Villa et la Révolution Mexicaine*, trans. Bruno Gaudenzi (Florence, Italy: Castermann, 1993), 28.

7. Wang Jingwei, quoted in Prasenjit Duara, *Rescuing History from the Nation: Questioning Narratives of Modern China* (Chicago: University of Chicago Press, 1995), 141.

8. Quoted in Isabel V. Hull, *The Entourage of Wilhelm II, 1888–1918* (New York: Cambridge University Press, 1982), 266.

9. Quoted in Michael S. Neiberg, *The World War I Reader* (New York: New York University Press, 2006), 212.

10. Anonymous letter, February 17, 1915, in David Omissi, ed., *Indian Voices of the Great War: Soldiers' Letters, 1914–1918* (London: Macmillan, 1919), 38.

11. Philip Sauvain, *Key Themes of the Twentieth Century* (Cheltenham, UK: Stanley Thornes, 1996), 32.

12. "This Day in History," https://www.history.com/this-day-in-history/international-congress-of-women-opens-at-the-hague.

13. Yigit Akin, "War, Women, and the State: The Politics of Sacrifice in the Ottoman Empire During the First World War," *Journal of Women's History*, 26, no. 3 (Fall 2014): 13.

14. Laura Engelstein, *Russia in Flames: War, Revolution, Civil War, 1914–1921* (New York: Oxford University Press, 2017), 96.

15. Quoted in Oscar J. Martinez, *Fragments of the Mexican Revolution: Personal Accounts from the Border* (Albuquerque: University of New Mexico Press, 1983), 52.

16. Quoted in Margaret Macmillan, *Paris 1919: Six Months That Changed the World* (New York: Random House, 2001), 403.

17. "The Black Soldier," *Crisis*, 16, no. 2 (June 1918): 60.

18. Quoted in Merrill Peterson, *"Starving Armenians": America and the Armenian Genocide, 1915–1930* (Charlottesville: University of Virginia Press, 2004), 48.

19. Quoted in Andrew Mango, *Atatürk: The Biography of the Founder of Modern Turkey* (Woodstock, NY: Overlook, 1999), 278.

20. Quoted in Mango, *Atatürk*, 219.

21. Irfan Organ, *Portrait of a Turkish Family* (London: Eland, 1993), 223.

22. Quoted in Macmillan, *Paris 1919*, 340.

23. Quoted in Geoffrey Hodges, "Military Labour in East Africa," in *Africa and the First World War*, ed. Melvin Eugene Page (New York: St. Martin's Press, 1987), 146.

24. Quoted in Sally Marks, *The Ebbing of European Ascendancy: An International History of the World, 1914–1945* (London: Arnold, 2002), 219.

25. Quoted in Babacar Fall, *Le travail forcé en Afrique occidentale française (1900–1946)* (Paris: Karthala, 1993), 181.

26. Quoted in Michael Tsin, *Nation, Governance, and Modernity in China: Canton, 1900–1927* (Palo Alto, CA: Stanford University Press, 1999), 151.

27. Quoted in Wang Zheng, *Women in the Chinese Enlightenment: Oral and Textual Histories* (Berkeley: University of California Press, 1999), 196.

28. Quoted in Lynn Thomas, "The Modern Girl and Racial Respectability in South Africa," *Journal of African History*, 47, no. 3 (2006): 487.

29. Mohandas Gandhi, "Hind Swaraj," in *The Collected Works of Mahatma Gandhi* (Ahmedabad: Navjivan Trust, Government of India, Publications Division, 1963), 23.

30. Quoted in Jochen Hellbeck, *Revolution on My Mind: Writing a Diary Under Stalin* (Cambridge, MA: Harvard University Press, 2006), 146.

31. Jorge Luis Borges, "Things That Might Have Been," in *Selected Poems*, ed. Alexander Coleman (New York: Viking, 1999), 405.

Chapter 26

1. J. B. Priestley, *English Journey; being a rambling but truthful account of what one man saw and heard and felt and thought during a journey through England during the autumn of the year 1933* (London: Harper & Brothers, 1934), 319.

2. Ana Núñez Machin, quoted in Angel Santana Suárez, "Angel Santana Suárez: Cuban Sugar Worker," in *The Human Tradition in Latin America: The Twentieth Century*, ed. William H. Beezley and Judith Ewell (Wilmington, DE: Scholarly Resources, 1987), 85, 86.

3. Quoted in Piers Brendon, *The Dark Valley: A Panorama of the 1930s* (London: Jonathan Cape, 2000), 175.

4. Quoted in Ann Farnsworth-Alvear, *Dulcinea in the Factory: Myths, Morals, Men, and Women in Colombia's Industrial Experiment, 1905–1960* (Durham, NC: Duke University Press, 2000), 124, 125.

5. Quoted in James L. Roark et al., *The American Promise: A History of the United States*, 4th ed. (Boston: Bedford/St. Martins, 2009), 856.

6. Quoted in John Eric Marot, *The October Revolution in Prospect and Retrospect: Interventions in Russian and Soviet History* (Leiden, Netherlands: Brill, 2012), 54.

7. Barbara Evans Clements et al., *Russia's Women: Accommodation, Resistance, Transformation* (Berkeley: University of California Press, 1991), 270.

8. Quoted in Eric Weitz, *A Century of Genocide: Utopias of Race and Nation* (Princeton, NJ: Princeton University Press, 2015), 58.

9. "Requiem," https://the-eye.eu/public/Books/Poetry/Anna%20Akhmatova%20-%20Poems.pdf.

10. Edvard Radzinsky, *Stalin: The First In-Depth Biography Based on Explosive New Documents from Russia's Secret Archives*, trans. H. T. Willetts (New York: Doubleday, 1996), 363.

11. Jiang Jieshi, quoted in Patricia Buckley Ebrey, *Cambridge Illustrated History of China* (Cambridge: Cambridge University Press, 1996), 277.

12. Herbert Bix, *Hirohito and the Making of Modern Japan* (New York: HarperCollins, 2000), 274–76.

13. Adolf Hitler, *My Struggle* (London: Hurst and Blackett, 1939 [1926]) vol. 1, chapter 6, Project Gutenberg, http://gutenberg.net.au/ebooks02/0200601.txt.

14. Claudia Koonz, *Mothers in the Fatherland: Women, the Family and Nazi Politics* (London: Routledge, 2013 [orig. pub. 1987]), 157.

15. Edward Keynes and David W. Adamany, eds., *Borzoi Reader in American Politics* (New York: Knopf, 1971), 111.

16. Quoted in David Clay Large, *Between Two Fires: Europe's Path in the 1930s* (New York: Norton, 1991), 162.

17. Matsuoka Yosuke, quoted in Bix, *Hirohito*, 374.

18. Primo Levi, *Survival in Auschwitz and The Reawakening*, trans. Stuart Woolf (New York: Summit, 1985), 122.

19. Amartya Sen in Arjo Klamer, "Interview with Amartya Sen," *Journal of Economic Perspectives*, 3, no. 1 (Winter 1989): 136.

20. Quoted in John Lancaster, "An Indian Revolutionary Gains Favor Posthumously," *Washington Post*, May 23, 2005.

21. Quoted in Neil Macmaster, *War in the Mountains: Peasant Society and Counter-Insurgency in Algeria, 1918–1958* (New York: Oxford University Press 2020), 53–54.

22. Carla Capponi, interviewed in Shelley Saywell, *Women in War: From World War II to El Salvador* (New York: Penguin, 1986), 82.

Chapter 27

1. Timothy Dunmore, *Soviet Politics, 1945–1953* (London: Macmillan, 1984), 129.

2. Harry S. Truman, "Truman Doctrine Speech," March 12, 1947.

3. Katherine Verdery, *Transylvanian Villagers: Three Centuries of Political, Economic, and Ethnic Change* (Berkeley: University of California Press, 1983), 33–34.

4. Dwight D. Eisenhower, press conference, April 7, 1954.

5. Quoted in Ronald J. Spector, *In the Ruins of Empire: The Japanese Surrender and the Battle for Postwar Asia* (New York: Random House, 2007), 78.

6. Quoted in Alex von Tunzelmann, *Indian Summer: The Secret History of the End of an Empire* (New York: Henry Holt, 2007), 225.

7. Everette Lee DeGoyler, quoted in Daniel Yergin, *The Prize: The Epic Quest for Oil, Money, and Power* (New York: Simon & Schuster, 1991), 393.

8. Golda Meir, *My Life* (New York: Putnam, 1975).

9. Gamal Abdel Nasser, "Nationalization Speech, 1956," in *Middle East in Crisis: A Historical and Documentary Review*, ed. Carol A. Fisher and Fred Krinsky (Syracuse, NY: Syracuse University Press, 1959), 136ff.

10. "Africa Must Unite" (1963), quoted in Michael Hunt, *The World Transformed, 1945 to the Present* (Boston: Bedford/St. Martin's, 2004), 144.

11. Superintendent of Police Philip, quoted in Carolyn A. Brown, *"We Were All Slaves": African Miners, Culture, and Resistance at the Enugu Government Colliery* (Portsmouth, NH: Heinemann, 2003), 310.

12. "Proclamation of the Algerian National Liberation Front (FLN), November 1, 1954,"

Cornell Middle East Library, https://middleeast.library.cornell.edu/content/proclamation-algerian-national-liberation-front-fln-november-1-1954.

13. W. O. Baker, "Computers as Information-Processing Machines in Modern Science," *Daedalus*, 99, no. 4 (Fall 1970): 1120.

14. Norman Borlaug, "Nobel Prize Acceptance Speech," 1970, http://www.nobel.se.

15. Jean Monnet, quoted in Ghita Ionescu, ed., *The New Politics of European Integration* (London: Palgrave Macmillan, 1972), 38.

16. "Mao Zedong on War and Revolution," Asia for Educators, http://afe.easia.columbia.edu/special/china_1900_mao_war.htm.

17. Anne Frank, *Diary of a Young Girl*, trans. B. M. Mooyaart (New York: Simon & Schuster, 1953), 237.

18. Quoted in Paula Giddings, *Where and When I Enter: The Impact of Black Women on Race and Sex in America* (New York: William Morrow, 1984), 316.

19. David Caute, *Sixty-Eight* (London: Hamilton, 1988), 165.

20. Richard Wright, *The Color Curtain: A Report on the Bandung Conference* (Jackson, MS: Banner, 1995).

21. Jawaharlal Nehru, "Speech to Bandung Conference Political Committee, 1955," Fordham Modern History Sourcebook, https://sourcebooks.fordham.edu/halsall/mod/1955nehru-bandung2.html.

Chapter 28

1. *Small Fires: Letters from Soviet Citizens to Ogonyok Magazine, 1887–1990*, eds. Christopher Cerf and Marina Albee (New York: Summit, 1990), 178; author interview with Russian citizen, July 1994.

2. Quoted in Orville Schell, "China's Spring," in *The China Reader: The Reform Era*, ed. Orville Schell and David Shambaugh (New York: Vintage, 1999), 194.

3. Quoted in *Guardian Weekly*, September 19–25, 2002.

4. Quoted in James C. McKinley Jr., "Mexican Farmers Protest End of Corn-Import Taxes," *New York Times*, February 1, 2008.

5. William H. Worger, *Africa and the West: A Documentary History: From Colonialism to Independence, 1875 to the Present* (New York: Oxford University Press, 2010), 204.

6. Soutik Biswas, "India's Architect of Reforms," BBC News, May 22, 2004.

7. Quoted in Yvonne Corcoran-Nantes, "Female Consciousness or Feminist Consciousness:

Women's Consciousness-Raising in Community-Based Struggles in Brazil," in *Global Feminisms Since 1945*, ed. Bonnie G. Smith (London: Routledge, 2000), 89.

8. Quoted in Michael Dutton, et al., *Beijing Time* (Cambridge, MA: Harvard University Press, 2008), 10.

9. Saranya Sukumaran, quoted in Saritha Rai, "India Is Regaining Contracts with the U.S.," *New York Times*, December 25, 2002, W7.

10. Georges Quioc, "La 'consomania' de l'Europe de l'Est électrise les distributeurs de l'Ouest," *Le Figaro Économie*, January 13, 2003.

11. Quoted in *Le Monde*, June 2, 2002.

12. Quoted in *Le Monde*, January 17, 2003.

13. Quoted in *Libération*, January 20 and 21, 2002.

14. "Fourth World Conference on Women Beijing Declaration, 1995," http://www.un.org/ womenwatch/daw/beijing/platform/declar.htm.

15. Quoted in Amitav Ghosh, *The Nutmeg's Curse: Parables for a Planet in Crisis* (Chicago: University of Chicago Press, 2021), 71.

16. Quoted in Ayse Saktanber, "'We Pray Like You Have Fun': New Islamic Youth in Turkey Between Intellectualism and Popular Culture," in *Fragments of Culture: The Everyday of Modern Turkey* (London: I. B. Tauber, 2006), 254.

17. Quoted in "Nobel Peace Prize for Woman of 30m Trees," *Guardian*, October 9, 2004.

18. Quoted in "At Birth Control Class, Mullahs Face New Reality," *International Herald Tribune*, November 12, 2009.

19. Lisa Drummond and Mandy Thomas, eds., *Consuming Urban Culture in Contemporary Vietnam* (London: Routledge, 2003), 115.

20. Excerpted from "Mandato de la Primera Cumbre Continental de Mujeres Indigenas de Abya-Yala," posted on Abya-Yala Net, http://www.abyay-alanet.org/index.php (no longer available), translated by Pamela Murray in Pamela Murray, ed., *Women and Gender in Modern Latin America: Historical Sources and Interpretations* (New York: Routledge, 2014), 328–30.

21. "Wangari Maathai, Nobel Laureate," Marion Institute, https://www.marioninstitute.org/ wangari-maathai-nobel-laureate/.

22. Wu Guanzhong, "Preface by the Artist," in Anne Farrer, *Wu Guanzhong: A Twentieth-Century Chinese Painter* (London: British Museum, 1991), 9.

Bibliography (Resources for Research)

Chapter 1

The study of the earliest stages of world history relies to a great extent on archaeological sources, but because the evolution of natural species, including humans, is involved, the disciplines of anthropology, genetics, and linguistics also contribute. The literature is extensive, and ideas change rapidly due to new finds.

Bahn, Paul G. *The Cambridge Illustrated History of Prehistoric Art*. New York: Cambridge University Press, 1997.

Barker, Graeme. *The Agricultural Revolution in Prehistory: Why Did Foragers Become Farmers?* Oxford: Oxford University Press, 2009.

Bellwood, Peter. *First Farmers: The Origins of Agricultural Societies*. Malden, MA: Blackwell 2005.

Fagan, Brian, and Nadia Durrani. *World Prehistory: A Brief Introduction*, 10th ed. New York: Routledge, 2020.

Human origins. http://humanorigins.si.edu

Humphrey, Louise and Stringer, Chris. *Our Human Story*. London: Natural History Museum, 2018

Lascaux: A Visit to the Cave. https://archeologie. culture.fr/lascaux/en/visit-cave/salle-taureaux/

Roberts, Alice. *Evolution: The Human Story*, 2nd ed. New York: Dorling Kindersley, 2018.

Scarre, Chris, ed. *The Human Past*, 4th ed. New York: Thames & Hudson, 2018.

Stringer, Chris, *Lone Survivors: How We Came to Be the Only Humans on Earth*. New York: Henry Holt and Company, 2013.

Stringer, Chris, and Andrews, Peter, *The Complete World of Human Evolution*, 2nd ed. London: Thames & Hudson, 2017.

Tattersall, Ian. *Masters of the Planet: The Search for Our Human Origins*. New York: Palgrave Macmillan, 2012.

Wenke, Robert J., and Deborah I. Olszewski. *Patterns in Prehistory: Humankind's First Three Million Years*, 5th ed. New York: Oxford University Press, 2007.

Chapter 2

Early developments in Mesopotamia interest historians, archaeologists, and anthropologists because they present the first appearance in world history of many aspects of human culture, such as cities, states, empires, and laws.

Aruz, Joan, ed. *Beyond Babylon: Art, Trade, and Diplomacy in the Second Millennium B.C.* New York: Metropolitan Museum of Art; New Haven: Yale University Press, 2008.

Cline, Eric H. *1177 B.C.: The Year Civilization Collapsed*, rev. and exp. ed. Princeton: Princeton University Press, 2021.

Collins, Paul. *The Sumerians: Lost Civilizations*. London: Reaktion Books, 2021.

*George, Andrew. *The Epic of Gilgamesh*. London: Penguin Books, 2000.

*Roth, Martha T. *Law Collections from Mesopotamia and Asia Minor*, 2nd ed. Atlanta: Scholars Press, 1997.

Uluburun shipwreck. https://nauticalarch.org/projects/ uluburun-late-bronze-age-shipwreck-excavation/

Van De Mieroop, Marc. *The Eastern Mediterranean in the Age of Ramesses II*. Malden, MA: Blackwell, 2007.

Van De Mieroop, Marc. *A History of the Ancient Egypt*, 2nd rev. ed. Chichester, West Sussex: Wiley-Blackwell, 2021.

Van De Mieroop, Marc. *A History of the Ancient Near East ca. 3000–323 B.C.*, 3rd rev. ed. Chichester, West Sussex: Wiley-Blackwell, 2016.

Wenke, Robert J., and Deborah I. Olszewski. *Patterns in Prehistory: Humankind's First Three Million Years*, 5th ed. New York: Oxford University Press, 2007.

*Primary source

Chapter 3

Most histories of early South and East Asia treat the periods before the appearance of written sources. They tend to focus on urban cultures, but pastoral aspects also draw attention. Several websites provide access to translations of primary sources.

Anthony, David W. *The Horse, the Wheel, and Language: How Bronze-Age Riders from the Eurasian Steppes Shaped the Modern World*. Princeton: Princeton University Press, 2007.

Beckwith, Christopher I. *Empires of the Silk Road: A History of Central Eurasia from the Bronze Age to the Present*. Princeton: Princeton University Press, 2009.

Ebrey, Patricia Buckley. *The Cambridge Illustrated History of China*, 2nd ed. Cambridge: Cambridge University Press, 2010.

Hansen, Valerie. *The Open Empire: A History of China to 1800*, 2nd ed. New York: W. W. Norton, 2015.

Indus Civilization. http://www.harappa.com/har/har0.html

*Internet East Asian Sourcebook. http://www.fordham.edu/halsall/eastasia/eastasiasbook.html

*Internet Indian History Sourcebook. http://www.fordham.edu/halsall/india/indiasbook.html

Li, Feng. *Early China: A Social and Cultural History*. Cambridge: Cambridge University Press, 2013.

Lyonnet, Bertille, and Dubova, Nadezhda A. eds. *The World of the Oxus Civilization*. Abingdon, Oxon: Routledge, 2021

Robinson, Andrew. *The Indus. Lost Civilizations*. London: Reaktion Books, 2015.

Thapar, Romila. *Early India from the Origins to A.D. 1300*. Berkeley: University of California Press, 2002.

*Visual Sourcebook of Chinese Civilization. http://depts.washington.edu/chinaciv/index.htm

*Primary source

Chapter 4

In their general surveys of the culture, many of the plentiful books on ancient Egypt treat the New Kingdom's imperial period and the period when Nubians ruled Egypt. The empires of Assyria and ancient Persia are often discussed in general surveys of ancient Near Eastern history. There are a vast number of books on Greek history that include surveys of the periods studied here.

*Achaemenid Persia. http://www.achemenet.com/en/

Ancient Egypt. http://www.ancient-egypt.co.uk

British Museum on Mesopotamia. http://www.mesopotamia.co.uk

Cline, Diane Harris. *The Greeks: An Illustrated History*. Washington, DC: National Geographic, 2016.

*Kuhrt, Amélie. *The Persian Empire: A Corpus of Sources from the Achaemenid Period*. London: Routledge, 2007.

Morkot, Robert G. *The Black Pharaohs: Egypt's Nubian Rulers*. London: Rubicon, 2000.

Radner, Karen. *Ancient Assyria: A Very Short Introduction*. Oxford: Oxford University Press, 2015.

Theban Mapping Project. http://www.thebanmappingproject.com

Van De Mieroop, Marc. *A History of the Ancient Egypt*, 2nd rev. ed. Chichester, West Sussex: Wiley-Blackwell, 2021.

Waters, Matt. *Ancient Persia: A Concise History of the Achaemenid Empire, 550–330 BCE*. New York: Cambridge University Press, 2014.

*Primary source

Chapter 5

The ancient cultures of India, China, Greece, Israel, and Judah are discussed in numerous historical surveys and more specialized publications. Because Buddhism and Hinduism had a lasting influence, many books treat the early developments of these religions within a long-term context. The scholarly literature on ancient Greece and on the Hebrew Bible is vast and additions to it are continuous.

Avari, Burjor. *India: A History of the Indian Sub-Continent from c. 7000 B.C. to A.D. 1200*. 2nd ed. New York: Taylor and Francis, 2016.

Cartledge, Paul. *Ancient Greece: A Very Short Introduction*. Oxford: Oxford University Press, 2011.

Chapman, Stephen B., and Marvin A. Sweeney, eds. *The Cambridge Companion to the Hebrew Bible/Old Testament*. New York: Cambridge University Press, 2016.

Erskine, Andrew, ed. *A Companion to the Hellenistic World*. Malden, MA: Blackwell, 2003.

Gascoigne, Bamber. *A Brief History of the Dynasties of China*. London: Robinson, 2003.

Hansen, Valerie. *The Open Empire: A History of China to 1800*, 2nd ed. New York: W. W. Norton, 2015.

*Ivanhoe, Philip J., and Bryan W. Van Norden, eds. *Readings in Classical Chinese Philosophy*, 2nd ed. Indianapolis: Hackett. 2005.

Kinzl, Konrad H., ed. *A Companion to the Classical Greek World*. Malden, MA: Blackwell, 2006.

Knott, Kim. *Hinduism: A Very Short Introduction*. Oxford: Oxford University Press, 1998.

Prebish, Charles S. and Damien Keown. *Buddhism: The Ebook: An Online Introduction*, 4th ed. State College, PA: Journal of Buddhist Ethics Online Books, 2010.

Puett, Michael, and Christine Gross-Loh. *The Path: What Chinese Philosophers Can Teach Us About the Good Life*. New York: Simon & Schuster, 2016.

Ska, Jean-Louis. *A Basic Guide to the Old Testament*. New York: Paulist Press, 2019.

*Sources of Indian Tradition. http://www.columbia.edu/itc/mealac/pritchett/00sources/#one

*Primary source

Chapter 6

Ancient Rome is the subject of a vast amount of research and writing and works continue to be published on every aspect of its history and culture. In contrast, publications on the empires of Persia that existed alongside the Roman were highly specialized until recently.

Beard, Mary. *SPQR: A History of Ancient Rome*. New York: Liveright Publishing Corporation, a division of W. W. Norton, 2015.

Bontty, Monica M. *Ancient Rome: Facts and Fictions*. Santa Barbara, CA: ABC-CLIO, 2020.

Bowersock, G. W., Peter Brown, and Oleg Grabar, eds. *Late Antiquity: A Guide to the Postclassical World*. Cambridge, MA: Belknap Press of Harvard University Press, 1999.

Ellerbrock, Uwe. *The Parthians: The Forgotten Empire*. London: Routledge, 2021.

Green, Bernard. *Christianity in Ancient Rome: The First Three Centuries*. London: T & T Clark International, 2010.

Harris, William V. *Roman Power: A Thousand Years of Empire*. Cambridge: Cambridge University Press, 2016.

*Internet Ancient History Sourcebook. Rome. http://www.fordham.edu/halsall/ancient/asbook09.html

Lee, A. D. *From Rome to Byzantium AD 363 to 565: The Transformation of Ancient Rome*. Edinburgh: Edinburgh University Press, 2013.

Matyszak, Philip. *Chronicle of the Roman Republic: The Rulers of Ancient Rome from Romulus to Augustus*. London: Thames & Hudson, 2008.

Parker, Geoffrey, and Brenda Parker. *The Persians: Lost Civilizations*. London: Reaktion Books, 2017.

Parthian Empire. http://parthia.com/

*Perseus digital texts. http://www.perseus.tufts.edu

Scarre, Chris. *Chronicle of the Roman Emperors: The Reign-by-Reign Record of the Rulers of Imperial Rome*. London: Thames & Hudson, 2012.

Vermes, Geza. *Christian Beginnings: From Nazareth to Nicaea (AD 30–325)*. New Haven: Yale University Press, 2013.

*Primary source

Chapter 7

In the absence of written sources, historians draw deeply on works from the archaeological perspective. The varied cultures discussed in this chapter are spread all over the world and are unevenly studied. There are many more studies of those on the American continent, for example, than on those of the Pacific.

African Archaeology. http://www.african-archaeology.net

Cochrane, Ethan E., and Terry L. Hunt, eds. *The Oxford Handbook of Prehistoric Oceania*. New York: Oxford University Press, 2018.

Connah, Graham. *African Civilizations: An Archaeological Perspective*, 3rd ed. New York: Cambridge University Press, 2016.

Ehret, Christopher. *The Civilizations of Africa: A History to 1800*. 2nd ed. Charlottesville: University of Virginia Press, 2016.

Houston, Stephen D., ed. *The First Writing: Script Invention as History and Process*. Cambridge: Cambridge University Press, 2004.

Milleker, Elizabeth J., ed. *The Year One: Art of the Ancient World East and West*, New York: Metropolitan Museum of Art; New Haven: Yale University Press, 2000.

Moche culture. http://www.huacas.com

Nichols, Deborah L., and Christopher A. Pool, eds. *The Oxford Handbook of Mesoamerican Archaeology*. Oxford: Oxford University Press, 2012.

Scarre, Chris, ed. *The Human Past*, 4th ed. New York: Thames & Hudson, 2018.

Snow, Dean R., Nancy Gonlin, and Peter E. Siegel. *The Archaeology of Native North America*, 2nd ed. Abingdon, Oxon: Routledge, 2019.

Stone, Rebecca. *Art of the Andes: From Chávin to Inca*, 3rd ed. London: Thames & Hudson, 2012.

Wenke, Robert J., and Deborah I. Olszewski. *Patterns in Prehistory: Humankind's First Three Million Years*, 5th ed. New York: Oxford University Press, 2007.

Chapter 8

Both Christianity and Islam spread across vast regions of Eurasia and Africa during this era, yet these religious traditions also assumed a multitude of forms in different societies. Recent research emphasizes the enduring influence of Roman culture and institutions on both Latin and Byzantine Christianity, and the ways in which Muhammad's teachings and the Islamic movement were shaped by interactions among the complex mosaic of cultures in Arabia and surrounding regions.

Al-Azmeh, Aziz. *The Emergence of Islam in Late Antiquity: Allāh and His People*. Cambridge: Cambridge University Press, 2014.

Barraclough, Eleanor Rosamund. *Beyond the Northlands: Viking Voyages and the Old Norse Sagas*. Oxford: Oxford University Press, 2016.

Bessard, Fanny. *Caliphs and Merchants: Cities and Economies of Power in the Near East, 700–950*. Oxford: Oxford University Press, 2020.

Bowerstock, G. W. *The Crucible of Islam*. Cambridge, MA: Harvard University Press, 2017.

Brown, Peter. *The Rise of Western Christendom*, rev. ed. Oxford: Blackwell, 2013.

Catlos, Brian A. *Kingdoms of Faith: A New History of Islamic Spain*. New York: Basic Books, 2018.

Christiansen, Eric. *The Norsemen in the Viking Age*. Oxford: Blackwell, 2006.

Donner, Fred. *Muhammad and the Believers: At the Origins of Islam*. Cambridge, MA: Harvard University Press, 2010.

Global Middle Ages. http://globalmiddleages.org

Heather, Peter. *Empires and Barbarians: The Fall of Rome and the Birth of Europe*. Oxford: Oxford University Press, 2010.

Herrin, Judith. *Byzantium: The Surprising Life of a Medieval Empire*. Princeton: Princeton University Press, 2007.

Hoyland, Robert, *In God's Path: The Arab Conquests and the Creation of an Islamic Empire*. Oxford: Oxford University Press, 2015.

Islamic Studies on the Internet. http://www.fordham. edu/halsall/islam/islamsbook.html

Kreuger, Derek, ed. *Byzantine Christianity*. Minneapolis: Fortress, 2006.

Lapidus, Ira M. *A History of Islamic Societies*, 3rd ed. Cambridge: Cambridge University Press, 2014.

McNamara, Jo Ann, and John E. Halborg, eds. and trans. *Sainted Women of the Dark Ages*. Durham: Duke University Press, 1992.

Nelson, Janet L. *King and Emperor: A New Life of Charlemagne*. Berkeley: University of California Press, 2019.

Price, Neil. *Children of Ash and Elm: A New History of the Vikings*. New York: Basic Books, 2020.

Wickham, Chris. *Framing the Early Middle Ages: Europe and the Mediterranean, 400–800*. Oxford: Oxford University Press, 2005.

Worlds of Late Antiquity (post-Roman Mediterranean): http://www9.georgetown.edu/faculty/jod/wola. html

Chapter 9

The spread of religious ideas and practices, political ideologies and institutions, and written languages and literary traditions shaped the formation of common civilizations in East, South, and Southeast Asia during the first millennium CE. Much scholarly attention has focused on the role of the overland Central Asian "Silk Road" in stimulating cultural and economic interaction across Asia, but maritime routes also fostered such exchanges and promoted regional integration.

A Visual Sourcebook of Chinese Civilization. http:// depts.washington.edu/chinaciv/

Adshead, S. A. M. *T'ang China: The Rise of the East in World History*. Houndmills: Palgrave Macmillan, 2004.

Ali, Daud. *Courtly Culture and Political Life in Early Medieval India*. Cambridge: Cambridge University Press, 2004.

Bentley, Jerry H. *Old World Encounters: Cross-Cultural Contacts and Exchanges in Pre-Modern Times*. Oxford: Oxford University Press, 1993.

Chattopadhyaya, Brajadulal. *The Making of Early Medieval India*. Bombay: Oxford University Press, 1994.

Doniger, Wendy. *On Hinduism*. Oxford: Oxford University Press, 2014.

Farris, William Wayne. *Sacred Texts and Buried Treasures: Issues in the Historical Archaeology of Ancient Japan*. Honolulu: University of Hawai'i Press, 1998.

Hall, Kenneth R. *A History of Early Southeast Asia: Maritime Trade and Societal Development, 100–1500*. Lanham, MD: Rowan and Littlefield, 2011.

Hansen, Valerie. *The Silk Road: A New History with Documents*. Oxford: Oxford University Press, 2016.

Higham, Charles. *The Civilization of Angkor*. Berkeley: University of California Press, 2002.

Holcombe, Charles. *The Genesis of East Asia, 221 B.C.–A.D. 907*. Honolulu: University of Hawai'i Press, 2001.

International Dunhuang Project. http://idp.bl.uk/

Liu, Xinru. *The Silk Road in World History*. New York: Oxford University Press, 2010.

Lockard, Craig A. *Southeast Asia in World History*. New York: Oxford University Press, 2009.

Pai, Hyung-Il. *Constructing "Korean" Origins: A Critical Review of Archaeology, Historiography, and Racial Myth in Korean State-Formation Theories*. Cambridge, MA: Harvard University Asia Center, 2000.

Skaff, Jonathan. *Sui-Tang China and Its Turko-Mongol Neighbors: Culture, Power and Connections, 580–800*. Oxford: Oxford University Press, 2012.

Thapar, Romila. *Early India: From the Origins to A.D. 1300*. Berkeley: University of California Press, 2002.

de la Vaissière, Étienne. *Sogdian Traders: A History*. Leiden: Brill, 2005.

Whitfield, Susan, and Ursula Sims-Williams, eds. *Silk Road: Trade, Travel, War, and Faith*. Chicago: Serindia, 2004.

Wolters, O. W. *History, Culture, and Region in Southeast Asian Perspectives*. Ithaca: Cornell University Southeast Asia Program Publications, 1999.

Chapter 10

Our knowledge of the history of all the societies in this chapter except the Maya depends on research in fields such as archaeology and linguistics rather than written sources. Comparative and interdisciplinary research has revealed common features in the formation of social identity and political power, the broad reach of the cultural heritage of Mesoamerica, and human responses to ecological crises and the collapse of social systems.

Cahokia Mounds historical site. https://cahokia-mounds.org

Coe, Michael D., and Stephen D. Houston. *The Maya*, 9th ed. London: Thames & Hudson, 2015.

Cowgill, George L. *Ancient Teotihuacan: Early Urbanism in Central Mexico*. New York: Cambridge University Press, 2015.

Diamond, Jared. *Collapse: How Societies Choose to Fail or Succeed*. New York: Viking, 2004.

Drew, David. *The Lost Chronicles of the Maya Kings*. Berkeley: University of California Press, 1999.

Earle, Timothy. *How Chiefs Come to Power: The Political Economy in Prehistory*. Stanford: Stanford University Press, 1997.

Fagan, Brian. *Chaco Canyon: Archaeologists Explore the Lives of an Ancient Society*. New York: Oxford University Press, 2005.

Homman, Robert J. *The Ancient Hawaiian State: Origins of a Political Society*. New York: Oxford University Press, 2013.

Howe, K. R., ed. *Vaka Moana, Voyages of the Ancestors: The Discovery and Settlement of the Pacific*. Honolulu: University of Hawai'i Press, 2007.

Janusek, John Wayne. *Ancient Tiwanaku*. New York: Cambridge University Press, 2008.

Kirch, Patrick V. *On the Road of the Winds: An Archaeological History of the Pacific Islands Before European Contact*, rev ed. Berkeley: University of California Press, 2017.

Kirch, Patrick V. *A Shark Going Inland Is My Chief: The Island Civilization of Ancient Hawai'i*. Berkeley: University of California Press, 2012.

Kolata, Alan. *The Tiwanaku: Portrait of an Andean Civilization*. Cambridge, MA: Blackwell, 1993.

Milner, George R. *The Moundbuilders: Ancient Peoples of Eastern North America*. London: Thames & Hudson, 2005.

Pauketat, Timothy R. *Cahokia: Ancient America's Great City on the Mississippi*, New York: Viking, 2010.

Quilter, Jeffrey, and Mary Miller, eds. *A Pre-Columbian World*. Washington, DC: Dumbarton Oaks Research Library, 2006.

Sahlins, Marshall. *Social Stratification in Polynesia*. Seattle: University of Washington Press, 1958.

Sharer, Robert J. *Daily Life in Maya Civilization*, 2nd ed. Westfield, CT: Westview, 2009.

Spriggs, Matthew. *The Island Melanesians*. Oxford: Blackwell, 1997.

Stanish, Charles. *Lake Titicaca: Legend, Myth, and Science*. Los Angeles: Cotsen Institute of Archaeology, 2011.

Chapter 11

The diffusion of crops, technological innovations, and new commercial institutions and practices gave impetus to major advances in agricultural productivity, industrial growth, and commercial exchange across Eurasia between 900 and 1300. Far-flung merchant networks not only fostered the spread of goods and ideas but also gave birth to multicultural trading communities in the great port cities and major commercial centers.

Abu-Lughod, Janet. *Before European Hegemony: The World System, A.D. 1250–1350*. Oxford: Oxford University Press, 1989.

Austen, Ralph A. *Trans-Saharan Africa in World History*. New York: Oxford University Press, 2010.

Chaffee, John W. *The Muslim Merchants of Premodern China: The History of a Maritime Asian Trade Diaspora, 750–1400*. Cambridge: Cambridge University Press, 2018.

Chaudhuri, K. N. *Asia Before Europe: Economy and Civilization of the Indian Ocean from the Rise of Islam to 1750*. Cambridge: Cambridge University Press, 1990.

Epstein, Steven A. *An Economic and Social History of Later Medieval Europe, 1000–1500*. Cambridge: Cambridge University Press, 2009.

Fauvelle, François-Xavier. *The Golden Rhinoceros: Histories of the African Middle Ages*. Princeton: Princeton University Press, 2018.

Favier, Jean. *Gold and Spices: The Rise of Commerce in the Middle Ages*. New York: Holmes and Meier, 1998.

Goldberg, Jessica L. *Trade and Institutions in the Medieval Mediterranean: The Geniza Merchants and their Business World*. Cambridge: Cambridge University Press, 2012.

Gomez, Michael. *African Dominion: A New History of Empire in Early and Medieval West Africa*. Princeton: Princeton University Press, 2018.

Herlihy, David. *Opera Muliebria: Women and Work in Medieval Europe*. Philadelphia: Temple University Press, 1990.

Laiou, Angeliki E., and Cécile Morrison. *The Byzantine Economy*. Cambridge: Cambridge University Press, 2007.

Medieval Europe. http://sourcebooks.fordham.edu/Halsall/sbook1j.asp

Verhulst, Adriaan. *The Carolingian Economy*. Cambridge: Cambridge University Press, 2002.

Von Glahn, Richard. *The Economic History of China from Antiquity to the Nineteenth Century*. Cambridge: Cambridge University Press, 2016.

Watson, A. M. *Agricultural Innovation in the Early Islamic World: The Diffusion of Crops and Farming Techniques, 700–1100*. Cambridge: Cambridge University Press, 1983.

Chapter 12

In contrast to the control that religious and legal institutions wielded over educational institutions and intellectual life in Islamic and Christian societies, in China the civil service examinations implanted secular Confucian ideas and values in the ruling elite. This era witnessed both the circulation of knowledge across cultural and religious boundaries—for example, the rediscovery of Greek philosophy and science in Latin Christendom via translations from Arabic—and increasing regional diversity in vernacular languages and literary cultures.

Asher, Catherine B., and Cynthia Talbot. *India Before Europe*. Cambridge: Cambridge University Press, 2006.

Asia for Educators: 1000 to 1450, Intensified Hemispheric Interactions (see sections on Neo-Confucianism). http://afe.easia.columbia.edu/tps/1000ce.htm

Berkey, Jonathan. *The Transmission of Knowledge in Medieval Cairo: A Social History of Islamic Education*. Princeton: Princeton University Press, 1992.

Bol, Peter K. *Neo-Confucianism in History*. Cambridge, MA: Harvard University Asia Center, 2008.

Clanchy, M. T. *Abelard: A Medieval Life*. Oxford: Blackwell, 1997.

Cobban, A. B. *The Medieval Universities: Their Development and Organization*. London: Methuen, 1975.

Coe, Michael D. *Breaking the Maya Code*, 3rd. ed. New York: Thames & Hudson, 2012.

Ephrat, Daphna. *A Learned Society in a Period of Transition: The Sunni Ulama of Eleventh-Century Baghdad*. Albany: SUNY Press, 1995.

Kornicki, Peter Francis. *Languages, Scripts, and Chinese Texts in East Asia*. Oxford: Oxford University Press, 2018.

Miyazaki, Ichisada. *China's Examination Hell: The Civil Service Examinations of Imperial China*. New Haven: Yale University Press, 1981.

Moore, R. I. *The First European Revolution, c. 970–1215*. Oxford: Blackwell, 2000.

Morris, Ivan. *The World of the Shining Prince: Court Life in Ancient Japan*. New York: Knopf, 1964.

Orme, Nicholas. *Medieval Schools: From Roman Britain to Renaissance England*. New Haven: Yale University Press, 2006.

Pollock, Sheldon. *The Language of the Gods in the World of Men: Sanskrit, Culture, and Power in Premodern India*. Berkeley: University of California Press, 2006.

Ridgeon, Lloyd, ed. *The Cambridge Companion to Sufism*. Cambridge: Cambridge University Press, 2015.

Schele, Linda, and Peter Mathews. *The Code of Kings: The Language of Seven Sacred Maya Temples and Tombs*. New York: Scribners, 1998.

Starr, S. Frederick. *Lost Enlightenment: Central Asia's Golden Age from the Arab Conquest to Tamerlane*. Princeton: Princeton University Press, 2015.

Tedlock, Dennis. *2000 Years of Mayan Literature*. Berkeley: University of California Press, 2010.

Wink, André. *The Making of the Indo-Islamic World*. Cambridge: Cambridge University Press, 2020.

Chapter 13

The era of the Crusades sharpened the boundaries between the Christian and Islamic worlds, launched Latin Christendom's expansion into eastern and northern Europe and Spain, and gave rise to more distinctive religious, political, and cultural identities among Christians and Muslims alike. Although the Mongol conquests unleashed widespread destruction, Mongol rule had a transformative influence on many societies, including Russia, Iran, and China, and sparked a cultural renaissance in Central Asia.

Barber, Malcolm. *The Crusader States*. New Haven: Yale University Press, 2012.

Bartlett, Robert. *The Making of Europe: Conquest, Colonization, and Cultural Change, 950–1350*. Princeton: Princeton University Press, 1993.

Biran, Michal. *Chinggis Khan*. Oxford: Oneworld, 2007.

Biran, Michal, et al., ed. *Along the Silk Roads in Mongol Eurasia: Generals, Merchants, and Intellectuals*. Berkeley: University of California Press, 2020.

Bisson, Thomas N. *The Crisis of the Twelfth Century: Power, Lordship, and the Origins of European Government*. Princeton: Princeton University Press, 2009.

Christiansen, Eric. *The Northern Crusades: The Baltic and the Catholic Frontier, 1100–1525*, 2nd ed., London: Penguin, 1997.

Crusades: Introduction. http://www.theorb.net/encyclop/religion/crusades/crusade_intro.html

Ernst, Carl W., and Bruce B. Lawrence. *Sufi Martyrs of Love: The Chishti Order in South Asia and Beyond*. New York: Palgrave Macmillan, 2002.

Favreau, Marie. *The Horde: How the Mongols Changed the World*. Cambridge, MA: Harvard University Press, 2021.

France, John. *The Crusades and the Expansion of Catholic Christendom, 1000–1714*. London: Routledge, 2005.

Heng, Geraldine. *The Invention of Race in the European Middle Ages*. Cambridge: Cambridge University Press, 2018.

Hillenbrand, Carole. *The Crusades: Islamic Perspectives.* New York: Routledge, 2000.

Islam, Riazul. *Sufism in South Asia: Impact on Fourteenth Century Muslim Society.* Karachi: Oxford University Press, 2002.

Kafadar, Cemal. *Between Two Worlds: The Construction of the Ottoman State.* Berkeley: University of California Press, 1995.

Lane, George. *Early Mongol Rule in Thirteenth-Century Iran: A Persian Renaissance.* Abingdon, UK: Routledge, 2003.

Larner, John. *Marco Polo and the Discovery of the World.* New Haven: Yale University Press, 1999.

May, Timothy. *The Mongol Conquests in World History.* London: Reaktion, 2012.

Ostrowski, Donald. *Muscovy and the Mongols: Cross-Cultural Influences on the Steppe Frontier, 1304–1589.* Cambridge: Cambridge University Press, 1998.

Riley-Smith, Jonathan. *The Crusades: A History,* 3rd ed. Basingstoke, UK: Bloomsbury, 2014.

Tyerman, Christopher. *The Invention of the Crusades.* Toronto: University of Toronto Press, 1998.

Wickham, Chris. *Medieval Europe.* New Haven: Yale University Press, 2016.

Chapter 14

The Black Death pandemic that erupted in the mid-fourteenth century had devastating consequences in Europe and the Islamic world, bringing an abrupt halt to the rising prosperity of the previous centuries. Despite the fall of the Mongol-ruled Yuan Empire in China, maritime Asia was spared the ravages of the Black Death and continued to enjoy robust cultural and economic interchange. By 1400 economic recovery in Italy gave birth to a new age of intellectual and artistic vigor—the Renaissance—which was shaped by transformative changes in trade, industry, material culture, and lifestyles.

Aberth, John. *The Black Death, the Great Mortality of 1348–1350: A Brief History with Documents,* 2nd ed. Boston: Bedford/St. Martin's, 2016.

Adolphson, Mikael S. *The Gates of Power: Monks, Courtiers, and Warriors in Premodern Japan.* Honolulu: University of Hawai'i Press, 2000.

Barker, Juliet R. V. *1381: The Year of the Peasants' Revolt.* Cambridge, MA: Harvard University Press, 2014.

Brook, Timothy. *The Confusions of Pleasure: Commerce and Culture in Ming China.* Berkeley: University of California Press, 1998.

Campbell, Bruce M. S. *The Great Transition: Climate, Disease, and Society in the Late Medieval World.* Cambridge: Cambridge University Press, 2016.

Dreyer, Edward L. *Zheng He: China and the Oceans in the Early Ming Dynasty.* New York: Pearson Longman, 2007.

Dunn, Ross E. *The Adventures of Ibn Battuta: A Muslim Traveler of the 14th Century,* rev. ed., Berkeley: University of California Press, 2012.

Eaton, Richard M. *India in the Persianate Age, 1000–1765.* Princeton: Princeton University Press, 2019.

Gerritsen, Anne. *The City of Blue and White: Chinese Porcelain and the Early Modern World.* Cambridge: Cambridge University Press, 2020.

Goldthwaite, Richard A. *Wealth and the Demand for Art in Italy, 1300–1600.* Baltimore: Johns Hopkins University Press, 1993.

Green, Monica H., ed. *Pandemic Disease in the Medieval World: Rethinking the Black Death.* Kalamazoo: Arc Medieval Press, 2015.

Jardine, Lisa. *Worldly Goods: A New History of the Renaissance.* New York: Doubleday, 1996.

Manz, Beatrice Forbes. *The Rise and Rule of Tamerlane.* Rpt. Cambridge: Cambridge University Press, 1999.

Medieval Japan Through Art: Samurai Life in Medieval Japan. http://www.colorado.edu/cas/tea/curriculum/imaging-japanese-history/medieval/index.html

Meloy, John L. *Imperial Power and Maritime Trade: Mecca and Cairo in the Later Middle Ages,* 2nd ed. Chicago: University of Chicago Press, 2015.

Reid, Anthony. *Southeast Asia in the Age of Commerce, 1350–1750. Vol. 2, The Land Below the Winds;*

Vol. 2, Expansion and Crisis. New Haven: Yale University Press, 1989, 1993.

Robinson, David. *Muslim Societies in African History.* Cambridge: Cambridge University Press, 2004.

Souyri, Pierre-François. *The World Turned Upside Down: Medieval Japanese Society.* New York: Columbia University Press, 2001.

Wakita, Haruko. *Women in Medieval Japan: Motherhood, Household Economy, and Sexuality.* Tokyo: University of Tokyo Press, 2006.

Chapter 15

The "pre-contact" cultures of the Americas are no longer considered "prehistoric." Scholars from many disciplines have combined resources and methods to explain the rise of empires such as those of the Incas and Aztecs as well as the far more common appearance of regional chiefdoms from Canada to Patagonia.

Alconini, Sonia, and Alan Covey, eds. *The Oxford Handbook of the Incas.* New York: Oxford University Press, 2018.

Berdan, Frances F. *The Aztecs.* London: Reaktion Books, 2021.

Boone, Elizabeth, and Gary Urton. *Their Way of Writing: Scripts, Signs, and Pictographies in Pre-Columbian America.* Cambridge, MA: Harvard University Press, 2011.

Carrasco, Davíd. *The Aztecs: A Very Short Introduction.* New York: Oxford University Press, 2011.

Carrasco, Davíd. *Religions of Mesoamerica*, 2nd ed. Long Grove, IL: Waveland Press, 2013.

Clendinnen, Inga. *Aztecs: An Interpretation.* New York: Cambridge University Press, 2014.

D'Altroy, Terrence. *The Incas*, 2nd ed. New York: Wiley-Blackwell, 2014.

Matos Moctezuma, Eduardo. *Aztecs.* London: Royal Academy of Arts, 2002.

Richter, Daniel K. *Facing East from Indian Country: A Native History of Early America.* Cambridge, MA: Harvard University Press, 2003.

Sauer, Jacob J. *The Archaeology and Ethnohistory of Araucanian Resilience.* Cham, NY: Springer, 2015.

Shimada, Izumi, ed. *The Inka Empire: A Multidisciplinary Approach.* Austin: University of Texas Press, 2015.

Schwaller, John F. *The Fifteenth Month: Aztec History in the Rituals of Panquetzaliztli.* Norman: University of Oklahoma Press, 2019.

Townsend, Camilla. *Fifth Sun: A New History of the Aztecs.* New York: Oxford University Press, 2019.

Trigger, Bruce, ed. *The Cambridge History of the Native Peoples of the Americas.* 3 vols. New York: Cambridge University Press, 1999.

Trigger, Bruce. *The Children of Aataentsic: A History of the Huron People to 1660*, 2nd ed. Montreal: McGill-Queen's University Press, 1987.

Urton, Gary. *Inka History in Knots: Reading Khipus as Primary Sources.* Austin: University of Texas Press, 2017.

Chapter 16

Europe's transatlantic expansion in the wake of Columbus's 1492 voyage was audacious and often violent, but scholars have reexamined evidence that points to a complex range of interactions with native peoples as well as enslaved and free Africans. Early American colonialism was no picnic, but even in resistance it was a shared and also global project.

Altman, Ida. *Life and Society in the Early Spanish Caribbean: The Greater Antilles, 1493–1550.* Baton Rouge: LSU Press, 2021.

Bakewell, Peter J. *A History of Latin America to 1825*, 3rd ed. New York: Wiley-Blackwell, 2009.

Benton, Lauren, and Nathan Perl-Rosenthal, eds. *A World at Sea: Maritime Practices and Global History.* Philadelphia: University of Pennsylvania Press, 2020.

Burnard, Trevor G. *The Atlantic in World History, 1490–1830.* London: Bloomsbury Academic, 2020.

Cañizares-Esguerra, Jorge, and Erik R. Seeman, eds. *The Atlantic in Global History, 1500–2000*. New York: Routledge, 2018.

Covey, Alan R. *Inca Apocalypse: The Spanish Conquest and the Transformation of the Andean World*. New York: Oxford University Press, 2020.

Crosby, Alfred. *The Columbian Exchange*, 2nd ed. New York: Praeger, 2003.

Dillehay, Tom. *Monuments, Empires, and Resistance: The Araucanian Polity and Ritual Narratives*. New York: Cambridge University Press, 2012.

Disney, Anthony. *A History of Portugal and the Portuguese Empire*. New York: Cambridge University Press, 2009.

Fernández-Armesto, Felipe. *Straits: Beyond the Myth of Magellan*. Oakland: University of California Press, 2022.

Gómez, Pablo F. *The Experiential Caribbean: Creating Knowledge and Healing in the Early Modern Atlantic*. Chapel Hill: University of North Carolina Press, 2017.

Lane, Kris. *Potosí: The Silver City That Changed the World*. Oakland: University of California Press, 2019.

Mangan, Jane E. *Trading Roles: Gender, Ethnicity, and the Urban Economy in Colonial Potosí*. Durham: Duke University Press, 2005.

Metcalf, Alida. *Go-Betweens in the History of Brazil, 1500–1600*. Austin: University of Texas Press, 2005.

Phillips, William D., and Carla Rahn Phillips. *The Worlds of Christopher Columbus*. New York: Cambridge University Press, 1993.

Restall, Matthew. *Seven Myths of the Spanish Conquest*, 2nd ed. New York: Oxford University Press, 2021.

Restall, Matthew. *When Montezuma Met Cortés: The True Story of the Meeting That Changed History*. New York: Ecco, 2018.

Schwartz, Stuart B., ed. *Tropical Babylons: Sugar and the Making of the Atlantic World, 1450–1680*. Chapel Hill: University of North Carolina Press, 2004.

Thornton, John K. *A Cultural History of the Atlantic World, 1250–1820*. New York: Cambridge University Press, 2012.

Townsend, Camilla. *Malintzin's Choice: An Indian Woman in the Conquest of Mexico*. Albuquerque: University of New Mexico Press, 2006.

Walvin, James. *Sugar: The World Corrupted, from Slavery to Obesity*. New York: Pegasus, 2018.

Chapter 17

Scholars of precolonial Atlantic Africa have made great strides in recent years by using a blend of written, material, and oral sources to build narratives similar to those for the pre-Columbian Americas. We now know a great deal about Atlantic Africa's diverse array of chiefdoms, kingdoms, and gatherer-hunter bands.

Boeston, Koen, and Inge Brinkman, eds. *The Kongo Kingdom: The Origins, Dynamics and Cosmopolitan Culture of an African Polity*. New York: Cambridge University Press, 2018.

Brooks, George E. *Eurafricans in Western Africa: Commerce, Social Status, Gender and Religious Observance from the Sixteenth to the Eighteenth Century*. Athens: Ohio University Press, 2003.

Carney, Judith, and Richard N. Rosomoff. *In the Shadow of Slavery: Africa's Botanical Legacy in the Atlantic World*. Oakland: University of California Press, 2011.

Ehret, Christopher. *The Civilizations of Africa: A History to 1800*. 2nd ed. Charlottesville: University of Virginia Press, 2016.

Fromont, Cécile. *The Art of Conversion: Christian Visual Culture in the Kingdom of Congo*. Chapel Hill: University of North Carolina Press, 2014.

Gomez, Michael. *African Dominion: A New History of Empire in Early and Medieval West Africa*. Princeton: Princeton University Press, 2018.

Green, Toby. *A Fistfull of Shells: West Africa from the Rise of the Slave Trade to the Age of Revolution*. Chicago: University of Chicago Press, 2019.

Heywood, Linda. *Njinga of Angola: Africa's Warrior Queen*. Cambridge, MA: Harvard University Press, 2017.

Heywood, Linda, and John Thornton. *Central Africans, Atlantic Creoles, and the Foundation of the Americas, 1585–1660*. New York: Cambridge University Press, 2007.

Kane, Ousmane. *Beyond Timbuktu: An Intellectual History of Muslim West Africa*. Cambridge, MA: Harvard University Press, 2016.

Newitt, Maylin. *The Portuguese in West Africa, 1415–1670: A Documentary History*. New York: Cambridge University Press, 2010.

Silva, Filipa Ribeira da. *Dutch and Portuguese in Western Africa: Empires, Merchants and the Atlantic System, 1580–1674*. Leiden: Brill, 2011.

Sweet, James H. *Domingos Álvares, African Healing, and the Intellectual History of the Atlantic World*. Chapel Hill: University of North Carolina Press, 2013.

Thornton, John K. *A History of West Central Africa to 1850*. New York: Cambridge University Press, 2020.

Wheat, David. *Atlantic Africa and the Spanish Caribbean, 1570–1640*. Chapel Hill: University of North Carolina Press, 2016.

Chapter 18

Once seen as static and "despotic," the diverse polities and empires of the Middle East and South Asia are now understood to have been stunning in their complexity, dynamism, and material wealth. Scholars have recovered many new sources in local languages to give voice to numerous peoples until recently seen only through European eyes.

Alpers, Edward. *The Indian Ocean in World History*. New York: Oxford University Press, 2014.

Barendse, R. J. *The Arabian Seas: The Indian Ocean World of the Seventeenth Century*. New York: Routledge, 2002.

Barrow, Ian J. *The East India Company, 1600–1858: A Short History with Documents*. Indianapolis: Hackett, 2017.

Beaujard, Philippe. *The Worlds of the Indian Ocean: A Global History*. New York: Cambridge University Press, 2019.

Biedermann, Zoltán. *(Dis)Connected Empires: Imperial Portugal, Sri Lankan Diplomacy, and the Making of a Habsburg Conquest in Asia*. New York: Oxford University Press, 2018.

Clulow, Adam, and Tristan Mostert, eds. *The Dutch and English East India Companies: Diplomacy, Trade, and Violence in Early Modern Asia*. Amsterdam: University of Amsterdam Press, 2018.

Faroqhi, Suraiya. *The Ottoman and Mughal Empires: Social History in the Early Modern World*. New York: I.B. Tauris, 2019.

Floor, Willem. *The Persian Gulf: A Political and Economic History in Five Port Cities, 1500–1730*. Odenton, MD: Mage Publishers, 2006.

Matthee, Rudi. *Persia in Crisis: Safavid Decline and the Fall of Isfahan*. London: I.B. Tauris, 2012.

Nath, Pratyay. *Climate of Conquest: War, Environment, and Empire in Mughal North India*. New Delhi: Oxford University Press, 2019.

Newitt, Malyn. *A History of Portuguese Overseas Expansion, 1400–1668*. New York: Routledge, 2005.

Prange, Sebastian. *Monsoon Islam: Trade and Faith on the Medieval Malabar Coast*. New York: Cambridge University Press, 2018.

Reid, Anthony. *A History of Southeast Asia: Critical Crossroads*. New York: Wiley-Blackwell, 2015.

Stein, Burton. *Vijayanagara*. New York: Cambridge University Press, 2005.

Stern, Philip J. *The Company-State: Corporate Sovereignty and the Early Modern Foundations of the British Empire in India*. New York: Oxford University Press, 2012.

Stoker, Valerie. *Polemics and Patronage in the City of Victory: Vyāsatīrtha, Hindu Sectarianism, and the*

Sixteenth-Century Vijayanagar Court. Oakland: University of California Press, 2016.

Subrahmanyam, Sanjay. *Empires Between Islam and Christianity, 1500–1800.* Albany: SUNY Press, 2019.

Chapter 19

The early modern period in European history has been transformed by the rise of world history, forcing scholars to resituate this dynamic and often warring region in a broader context, linking overseas expansion back to internal transformations. By including the Ottoman Empire in this narrative, we begin to see the larger dimensions of an age of regional struggle before nation-states.

Barnett, Lydia. *After the Flood: Imagining the Global Environment in Early Modern Europe.* Baltimore: Johns Hopkins University Press, 2019.

Biedermann, Zoltán, Anne Gerritsen, and Giorgio Riello, eds. *Global Gifts: The Material Culture of Diplomacy in Early Modern Eurasia.* New York: Cambridge University Press, 2018.

Burke, Edmund, and Kenneth Pomeranz, eds. *The Environment and World History.* Berkeley: University of California Press, 2009.

Casale, Giancarlo. *Prisoner of the Infidels: The Memoir of an Ottoman Muslim in Seventeenth-Century Europe.* Oakland: University of California Press, 2021.

Casale, Giancarlo. *The Ottoman Age of Exploration.* New York: Oxford University Press, 2010.

Clines, Robert. *A Jewish Jesuit in the Eastern Mediterranean: Early Modern Conversion, Mission, and the Construction of Identity.* New York: Cambridge University Press, 2020.

Davis, Natalie Zemon. *Women on the Margins: Three Seventeenth-Century Lives.* Cambridge, MA: Harvard University Press, 1995.

Davis, Robert C. *Holy War and Human Bondage: Tales of Christian-Muslim Slavery in the Early-Modern Mediterranean.* Santa Barbara: ABC-CLIO, 2009.

Faroqhi, Suraiya. *Subjects of the Sultan: Culture and Daily Life in the Ottoman Empire.* London: I.B. Tauris, 2005.

Fattori, Niccolò. *Migration and Community in the Early Modern Mediterranean: The Greeks of Ancona, 1510–1595.* New York: Palgrave Macmillan, 2019.

Ferguson, Heather. *The Proper Order of Things: Language, Power, and Law in Ottoman Administrative Discourses.* Stanford: Stanford University Press, 2018.

Findlen, Paula, ed. *Early Modern Things: Objects and their Histories, 1500–1800.* New York: Routledge, 2013.

Jamieson, Alan G. *Lords of the Sea: A History of the Barbary Corsairs.* London: Reaktion, 2012.

Matar, Nabil. *Britain and Barbary, 1589–1689.* Gainesville: University Press of Florida, 2005.

Parker, Geoffrey. *Global Crisis: War, Climate Change, and Catastrophe in the Seventeenth Century.* New Haven: Yale University Press, 2013.

Pettigrew, William A., and David Veevers, eds. *The Corporation as a Protagonist in Global History, c. 1550–1750.* Leiden: Brill, 2019.

Richards, John F. *The Unending Frontier: An Environmental History of the Early Modern World.* Berkeley: University of California Press, 2003.

Schwartz, Stuart B. *All Can Be Saved: Religious Tolerance and Salvation in the Iberian Atlantic World.* New Haven: Yale University Press, 2008.

Chapter 20

Scholars of East and Southeast Asia have long known how important this region was in producing technical innovations and driving global trade, even as it suffered its own internal upheavals. As with Europe, the region has come to be seen as core to understanding the world's first era of genuine globalization, linked by silver, silk, porcelain, and many other commodities, if also divided by gunpowder.

Andaya, Barbara Watson, and Leonard Y. Andaya. *A History of Southeast Asia, 1400–1830*. New York: Cambridge University Press, 2014.

Andrade, Tonio. *The Gunpowder Age: China, Military Innovation, and the Rise of the West in World History*. Princeton: Princeton University Press, 2017.

Andrade, Tonio, and Xing Hang, eds. *Sea Rovers, Silver, and Samurai: Maritime East Asia in Global History, 1550–1700*. Honolulu: University of Hawai'i Press, 2016.

Brewer, Carolyn. *Shamanism, Catholicism, and Gender Relations in the Colonial Philippines, 1521–1685*. Burlington, VT: Ashgate, 2004.

Brook, Timothy. *The Troubled Empire: China in the Yuan and Ming Dynasties*. Cambridge, MA: Belknap, 2010.

Clulow, Adam. *The Company and the Shogun: The Dutch Encounter with Tokugawa Japan*. New York: Columbia University Press, 2014.

Clunas, Craig. *Pictures and Visuality in Early Modern China*. London: Reaktion, 2005.

Elvin, Mark. *The Retreat of the Elephants: An Environmental History of China*. New Haven: Yale University Press, 2006.

Engel, Barbara. *Women in Russia, 1700–2000*. New York: Cambridge University Press, 2004.

Haneda, Masashi, and Mihoko Oka. *A Maritime History of East Asia*. Nagano: Kyoto University Press, 2019.

Hang, Xing. *Conflict and Commerce in Maritime East Asia: The Zheng Family and the Shaping of the Modern World, c. 1620–1720*. New York: Cambridge University Press, 2016.

LeDonne, John. *The Grand Strategy of the Russian Empire, 1650–1831*. New York: Oxford University Press, 2004.

Marcon, Federico. *The Knowledge of Nature and the Nature of Knowledge in Early Modern Japan*. Chicago: University of Chicago Press, 2015.

Parker, Geoffrey. *Global Crisis: War, Climate Change, and Catastrophe in the Seventeenth Century*. New Haven: Yale University Press, 2013.

Rawski, Evelyn S. *Early Modern China and Northeast Asia: Cross-Border Perspectives*. New York: Cambridge University Press, 2015.

Roberts, Luke S. *Performing the Great Peace: Political Space and Open Secrets in Tokugawa Japan*. Honolulu: University of Hawai'i Press, 2012.

Seth, Michael J. *A Concise History of Korea from the Neolithic Period Through the Nineteenth Century*, 3rd ed. Boulder, CO: Rowman & Littlefield. 2006.

Sunderland, Willard. *Taming the Wild Field: Colonization and Empire on the Russian Steppe*. Ithaca: Cornell University Press, 2006.

Swope, Kenneth. *The Military Collapse of China's Ming Dynasty, 1618–1644*. New York: Palgrave, 2014.

Vaporis, Constantine Nomikos. *Voices of Early Modern Japan: Contemporary Accounts of Daily Life During the Age of the Shoguns*, 2nd ed. New York: Routledge, 2021.

Von Glahn, Richard. *Fountain of Fortune: Money and Monetary Policy in China, 1000–1700*. Berkeley: University of California Press, 1996.

Chapter 21

The early modern Americas were something new under the sun, whole continental regions claimed by distant European monarchs, yet clearly these colonies were on their own paths of social, political, and economic development. Once seen as mere dependencies with derivative cultures, the Americas before independence are now regarded as serious gravitational forces in world history as well as sites of cautionary tales of environmental transformation.

Alchon, Suzanne Austin. *A Pest in the Land: New World Epidemics in Global Perspective*. Albuquerque: University of New Mexico Press, 2003.

Brown, Vincent. *The Reaper's Garden: Death and Power in the World of Atlantic Slavery*. Cambridge, MA: Harvard University Press, 2008.

Candiani, Vera. *Dreaming of Dry Land: Environmental Transformation in Colonial Mexico City*. Stanford: Stanford University Press, 2014.

Englebert, Robert, and Andrew Wegman, eds. *French Connections: Cultural Mobility in North America and the Atlantic World, 1600–1875*. Baton Rouge: Louisiana State University Press, 2020.

Hämäläinen, Pekka. *The Comanche Empire*. New Haven: Yale University Press, 2009.

Myscofski, Carole. *Amazons, Wives, Nuns, and Witches: Women and the Catholic Church in Colonial Brazil, 1500–1822*. Austin: University of Texas Press, 2013.

Ponce-Vázquez, Juan José. *Islanders and Empire: Smuggling and Political Defiance in Hispaniola, 1580–1690*. New York: Cambridge University Press, 2019.

Schwartz, Stuart B. *Blood and Boundaries: The Limits of Religious and Racial Exclusion in Early Modern Latin America*. Waltham, MA: Brandeis University Press, 2020.

Schwartz, Stuart B. *Sea of Storms: A History of Hurricanes in the Greater Caribbean from Columbus to Katrina*. Princeton: Princeton University Press, 2015.

Rediker, Marcus. *The Slave Ship: A Human History*. New York: Penguin, 2008.

Reséndez, Andrés. *The Other Slavery: The Uncovered Story of Indian Enslavement in America*. New York: Houghton Mifflin, 2016.

Rushforth, Brett. *Bonds of Alliance: Indigenous and Atlantic Slaveries in New France*. Chapel Hill: University of North Carolina Press, 2014.

Seijas, Tatiana. *Asian Slaves in Colonial Mexico: Chinos to Indios*. New York: Cambridge University Press, 2015.

Smallwood, Stephanie. *Saltwater Slavery: A Middle Passage from Africa to American Diaspora*. Cambridge, MA: Harvard University Press, 2008.

Skopyk, Bradley. *Colonial Cataclysms: Climate, Landscape, and Memory in Mexico's Little Ice Age*. Tucson: University of Arizona Press, 2020.

Townsend, Camilla. *Annals of Native America: How the Nahuas of Colonial Mexico Kept Their History Alive*. New York: Oxford University Press, 2017.

White, Sam. *A Cold Welcome: The Little Ice Age and Europe's Encounter with North America*. Cambridge, MA: Harvard University Press, 2017.

Chapter 22

The age of revolutions is rich in biographies and histories of uprisings that covered a vast area of the globe. There were both historical "winners" and "losers" not to mention dramatic change. New studies emphasize the African background to pivotal uprisings and the relationship of these uprisings to support or lack thereof for the American Revolution.

Brown, Vincent. *Tacky's Revolt: The Story of an African Slave War*. Cambridge: Harvard University Press, 2020.

Burnard, Trevor. *Jamaica in the Age of Revolution*. Philadelphia: University of Pennsylvania Press, 2020.

Chambers, Sarah C., and John C. Chasteen. *Latin American Independence: An Anthology of Sources*. Indianapolis: Hackett, 2010.

Colley, Linda. *The Gun, the Ship, and the Pen: War, Constitutions, and the Making of the Modern World*. New York: W. W. Norton, 2021.

Girard, Philippe. *Toussaint Louverture: A Revolutionary Life*. New York: Basic Books, 2016.

Hunt, Lynn. *Inventing Human Rights: A History*. New York: W. W. Norton, 2007.

Jasanoff, Maya. *Liberty's Exiles: American Loyalists in the Revolutionary World*. New York: Penguin-RandomHouse, 2011.

Landers, Jane G. *Atlantic Creoles in the Age of Revolutions*. Cambridge: Harvard University Press, 2010.

Lovejoy, Paul. *Jihad in West Africa in the Age of Revolutions*. Athens: Ohio University Press, 2017.

Lynch, John. *Simón Bolívar: A Life*. New Haven: Yale University Press, 2006.

Massie, Robert K. *Catherine the Great: Portrait of a Woman*. New York: Random House, 2011.

May, Cedrick. *Evangelism and Resistance in the Black Atlantic, 1760–1835*. Athens: University of Georgia Press, 2008.

Napoleonic Empire. http://www.bbc.co.uk/history/historic_figures/bonaparte_napoleon.shtml

Popkin, Jeremy. *You Are All Free: The Haitian Revolution and the Abolition of Slavery*. New York: Cambridge University Press,2010.

Qadhi, Abu Ammar Yasir. *A Critical Study of Shirk: Being a Translation and Commentary of Muhammad b. Abd al-Wahhab's Kashf al-Shubuhat*. Birmingham: Al Hidayyah, 2002.

Robertson, Ritchie. *The Enlightenment: The Pursuit of Happiness 1680–1790*. London: Allen Lane, 2021.

Rucker, Walter. *Gold Coast Diasporas: Culture, Identity, and Power*. Bloomington: Indiana University Press, 2015.

Shovlin, John. *Trading with the Enemy: Britain, France, and the Quest for a Peaceful World Order*. New Haven: Yale University Press, 2021.

Wheatley, Phillis. *The Writings of Phillis Wheatley*. Edited by Vincent Carretta. New York: Oxford University Press, 2019.

Walker, Charles. *Tupac Ameru*. Cambridge: Harvard University Press, 2014.

Chapter 23

World history allows us to think differently about the Industrial Revolution, understanding it less as a radical departure and more as a burst of productivity and inventiveness taking place in many parts of the world. Its success depended on a wide variety of people and their ingenuity, not to mention hard work.

Banerjee, Swapna M. *Men, Women, and Domestics: Articulating Middle-Class Identity in Colonial Bengal*. New York: Oxford University Press, 2004.

Bezis-Selfa, John. *Forging America: Ironworkers, Adventurers, and the Industrious Revolution*. Ithaca: Cornell University Press, 2004.

Carney, Judith A., and Richard N. Rosomoff. *In the Shadow of Slavery: Africa's Botanical Legacy in the Atlantic World*. Berkeley: University of California Press, 2009.

Darwin, John. *Unlocking the World: Port Cities and Globalization in the Age of Steam. 1830–1930*. London: Allen Lane, 2020.

Dolan, Brian. *Wedgwood: The First Tycoon*. New York: Viking, 2004.

Gelvin, James L., and Nile Green, eds. *Global Muslims in the Age of Steam and Print*. Berkeley: University of California Press, 2014.

Inikori, Joseph. *Africans and the Industrial Revolution in England: A Study in International Trade and Economic Development*. Cambridge: Cambridge University Press, 2002.

Izzard, Sebastian. *Hiroshige/Eisen: The Sixty-Nine Stations of the Kisokaido*. New York: George Braziller, 2008.

Jones, Gareth Stedman. *Karl Marx: Greatness and Illusion*. Cambridge: Harvard University Press, 2016.

Lowe, Lisa. *Intimate Relations Across Four Continents*. Durham: Duke University Press, 2015.

Mulholland, James L. *Before the Raj: Writing Early Anglophone India*. Baltimore: Johns Hopkins University Press, 2021.

Platt, Stephen R. *Autumn in the Heavenly Kingdom: China, the West, and the Epic Story of the Taiping Civil War*. New York: Vintage, 2012.

Porter, Susie. *Working Women in Mexico City: Public Discourses and Material Conditions, 1879–1931*. Tucson: University of Arizona Press, 2003.

Rappaport, Erica. *A Thirst for Empire: How Tea Shaped the Modern World*. Princeton: Princeton University Press, 2017.

Riello, John. *Cotton: The Fabric That Made the Modern World*. Cambridge: Cambridge University Press, 2013.

Rocchi, Fernando. *Chimneys in the Desert: Industrialization in Argentina During the Export Boom Years*. Palo Alto: Stanford University Press, 2006.

Russell, Lynette. *Roving Mariners: Australian Aboriginal Whalers and Sealers in Southern Oceans*. Albany: State University of New York Press, 2012.

Sarkar, Tanika, and Sumit Sarkar. *Women and Social Reform in Modern India: A Reader*. Indianapolis: Indiana University Press, 2008.

Scanlan, Padraic X. *Slave Empire: How Slavery Built Modern Britain*. London: Robinson, 2021.

Sivasundaram, Sujit. *Waves Across the South: A New History of Revolution and Empire*. Chicago: University of Chicago Press, 2020.

Shepherd, Verene A. *A Maharani's Misery: Narratives of a Passage from India to the Caribbean*. Kingston: University of West Indies Press, 2002.

Taylor, Michael. *The Interest: How the British Establishment Resisted the Abolition of Slavery*. London: Bodley Head, 2021l

Chapter 24

Walthall and Steele's collection of primary sources gives an intimate look at nation-building in Japan, while Judson shows nations deriving from empires and the process as the work of culture and grass-roots actors.

Bay, Mia. *To Tell the Truth Freely: The Life of Ida B. Wells*. New York: Hill and Wang, 2009.

Burbank, Jane, and Frederick Cooper. *Empires in World History: Power and the Politics of Difference*. Princeton: Princeton University Press, 2010.

Chapdelaie, Robin Phylisia. *The Persistence of Slavery. An Economic History of Trafficking in Nigeria*. Amherst: University of Massachusetts Press, 2021.

Delay, Brian. *War of a Thousand Deserts: Indian Raids and the U.S.-Mexican War*. New Haven: Yale University Press, 2008.

DeVries, Annalise. *Maadi: The Making and Unmaking of a Cairo Suburb, 1878–1962*. Cairo: Cairo University Press, 2021.

Doyle, Dan. *The Cause of All Nations: An International History of the American Civil War*. New York: Basic Books, 2015.

Feifer, George. *Breaking Open Japan: Commodore Perry, Lord Abe and the American Imperialism of 1853*. Washington, DC: Smithsonian, 2006.

Fenn, Elizabeth. *Encounters at the Heart of the World: A History of the Mandan People*. New York: Macmillan, 2014.

Fisher, Michael. *Migration: A World History*. New York: Oxford University Press, 2014.

Forment, Carlos. *Democracy in Latin America, 1760–1900: Civic Selfhood and Public Life in Mexico and Peru*. Chicago: University of Chicago Press, 2003.

Gounder, Farzana et al., eds. *Gender and the Legacy of Slavery and Indenture*. London: Routledge, 2021.

Judson, Pieter M. *The Habsburg Empire: A New History*. Cambridge: Harvard University Press, 2016.

Khaled, Adeeb, *Central Asia: A New History from Imperial Conquests to the Present*. Princeton: Princeton University Press, 2021.

Lynch, John. *Argentine Caudillo: Juan Manuel de Rosas*. Lexington: Rowman and Littlefield, 2001.

Mathew, Johan. *Margins of the Market: Trafficking and Capitalism Across the Arabian Sea*. Cambridge: Cambridge University Press, 2016.

Minawi, Mostafa. *The Ottoman Scramble for Africa: Empire and Diplomacy in the Sahara and the Hijaz*. Palo Alto: Stanford University Press, 2016.

Morrison, Alexander. *The Russian Conquest of Central Asia: A Study in Imperial Expansion.* Cambridge: Cambridge University Press, 2021.

National Park Service: Frederick Douglass. https://www.nps.gov/frdo/learn/historyculture/frederickdouglass.htm

*Nikitenko, Alexander. *Up from Serfdom: My Childhood and Youth in Russia, 1804–1824.* Translated by Helen Saltz Jacobson. New Haven: Yale University Press, 2001.

Osborne, Myles, and Susan Kingsley Kent. *Africans and Britons in the Age of Empires, 1660–1980.* London: Routledge, 2015.

Tuna, Mustafa O. *Imperial Russia's Muslims: Islam, Empire, and European Modernity, 1788–1914.* Cambridge: Cambridge University Press, 2015.

*Walthall, Anne and Steele M. William, eds. *Politics and Society in Japan's Meiji Restoration: A Brief History with Documents.* Boston: Bedford, 2017.

*Primary source

Chapter 25

Studies of the wars and revolutions of the early twentieth century and their global impact abound. The following selections are among the best at providing either a broad picture or an individual account.

Akin, Yigit. *When the War Came Home: The Ottomans' Great War and the Devastation of an Empire.* Palo Alto: Stanford University Press, 2018.

Allawi, Ali A. *Faisal I of Iraq.* New Haven: Yale University Press, 2014.

Callahan, Michael D. *Mandates and Empire: The League of Nations and Africa, 1914–1931.* East Sussex: Sussex Academic Press, 2008.

Engelstein, Laura. *Russia in Flames: War, Revolution, and Civil War, 1914–1921.* New York: Oxford University Press, 2017.

Feigenbaum, Anna. *Tear Gas: From the Battlefields of World War I to the Streets of Today.* London: Verso, 2017.

Gerwarth, Robert and Erez Manela. *Empires at War 1911–1923.* New York: Oxford University Press, 2014.

Gibbons, Ivan. *How and Why Ireland Was Divided.* Chicago: University of Chicago Press, 2021.

Gingeras, Ryan. *Mustafa Kemal Atatürk: Heir to an Empire.* New York: 2016.

Gordon, David B. *Sun Yatsen: Seeking a Newer China.* New York: Prentice Hall, 2009.

Hajdarpasic, Edin. *Whose Bosnia: Nationalism and Political Imagination in the Balkans, 1840–1914.* Ithaca: Cornell University Press, 2015.

Harper, Tim. *Underground Asia: Global Revolutionaries and the Assault on Empire.* Cambridge: Harvard University Press, 2021.

Hart, Paul. *Emiliano Zapata.* New York: Oxford University Press, 2018.

Hart, Peter. *Gallipoli.* New York: Oxford University Press, 2011.

Hunt, Nancy Rose. *A Nervous State: Violence, Remedies, and Reverie in Colonial Congo.* Durham: Duke University Press, 2016.

Jones, Mark. *Founding Weimar: Violence and the German Revolution of 1918–1919.* Cambridge: Cambridge University Press, 2016.

Keller, Kathleen. *Colonial Suspects: Suspicion, Imperial Rule, and Colonial Society in Interwar French West Africa.* Lincoln: University of Nebraska Press, 2018.

King, Charles. *Midnight at the Pera Palace: The Birth of Modern Istanbul.* New York: W. W. Norton, 2014.

Leonhard, Jörn. *Pandora's Box: A History of the First World War.* Cambridge: Harvard University Press, 2018.

Pederson, Susan. *The Guardians: The League of Nations and the Crisis of Empire.* New York: Oxford University Press, 2015.

Romero, Luis Alberto. *A History of Argentina in the Twentieth Century.* Translated by James P. Brennan. College Station: Penn State University Press, 2002.

*Wasserman, Mark. *The Mexican Revolution: A Brief History in Documents.* Boston: Bedford, 2012.

Weinbaum, Alys Eve, et al. *Modern Girl Around the World: Consumption, Modernity, and Globalization.* Durham: Duke University Press, 2008.

Williamson, Edwin. *Borges: A Life.* New York: Viking 2004.

*Primary source

Chapter 26

This grim period in human history has yielded an ever-growing crop of excellent works, some of them clearly examining the worst aspects of the Great Depression and World War II globally and others looking at resistance, survival, and intellectual breakthroughs.

Belogurova, Anna. *The Nanying Revolution: The Comintern and Chinese Networks in Southeast Asia, 1890–1957.* Cambridge: Cambridge University Press, 2019.

Browning, Christopher. *Remembering Survival: Inside a Nazi Slave Labor Camp.* New York: W. W. Norton, 2010.

Byfield, Judith A., Carolyn A. Brown, Timothy Parsons, and Ahmad Alawad Sikainga, eds. *Africa and World War II.* Cambridge: Cambridge University Press, 2015.

Danke, Li. *Echoes of Chongqing: Women in Wartime China.* Champaign Urbana: University of Illinois Press, 2010.

Driscoll, Marc. *Absolute Erotic, Absolute Grotesque: The Living, Dead, and Undead in Japan's Imperialism, 1895–1945.* Durham: Duke University Press, 2010.

Feinstein, Charles H., et al. *The World Economy Between the World Wars.* New York: Oxford University Press, 2008.

Haggai, Erlich. *Haile Sellassie: His Rise and Fall.* Boulder: Lynne Rienner, 2019.

Hanebrink, Paul. *A Specter Haunting Europe: The Myth of Judeo-Bolshevism.* Cambridge: Harvard University Press, 2018.

Hanson, David. *Mussolini's War: Fascist Italy from Triumph to Collapse.* London: Allen Lane, 2020.

Hellbeck, Jochen. *Stalingrad: The City That Defeated the Third Reich.* New York: Public Affairs, 2015.

Khan, Yasmin. *The Raj at War: A People's History of India's Second World War.* London: Bodley Head, 2015.

Kotkin, Stephen. *Stalin: Waiting for Hitler, 1929–1941.* Princeton: Princeton University Press, 2017.

Krylova, Anna. *Soviet Women in Combat: A History of Violence on the Eastern Front.* New York: Cambridge University Press, 2010.

Kushner, Barak. *The Thought War: Japanese Imperial Propaganda.* 2006.

Matera, Marc, and Susan K. Kent. *The Global 1930s: The International Decade.* London: Routledge, 2017.

Naimark, Norman. *Genocide: A World History.* New York: Oxford University Press, 2016.

*Pa, Chin. *Family.* Beijing: Foreign Languages Press, 1958 [1931].

Slezkine, Yuri. *The House of Government: A Saga of the Russian Revolution.* Princeton: Princeton University Press, 2017.

Snyder, Timothy. *Bloodlands: Europe Between Hitler and Stalin.* New York: Basic Books, 2010.

Teicher, Amir. *Social Mendelism: Genetics and the Politics of Race in Germany, 1900–1948.* Cambridge: Cambridge University Press, 2020.

Tidrick, Kathryn. *Gandhi: A Political and Spiritual Life.* London: Verso, 2007.

Van de Ven Hans. *China at War: Triumph and Tragedy in the Emergence of the New China, 1937–1952.* London: Profile, 2017.

Wildt, Michael. *An Uncompromising Generation: The Nazi Leadership of the Reich Security Main Office.* Madison: University of Wisconsin Press, 2009.

*Primary source

Chapter 27

The Cold War transformed world politics amid the often violent accomplishment of decolonization. Amid the postwar world recovery, notable leaders of new nations worked to overcome colonialism's legacy of poverty, illiteracy, and lingering factionalism.

Brown, Jonathan C. *Cuba's Revolutionary World.* Cambridge: Harvard University Press, 2017.

Cumings, Bruce. *The Korean War: A History.* New York: Penguin Random House, 2011.

Feinberg, Melissa. *Curtain of Lies: The Battle over Truth in Stalinist Eastern Europe.* New York: Oxford University Press, 2017.

Florvil, Tiffany. *Mobilizing Black Germany: Afro-German Women and the Making of a Transnational Movement.* Champaign: University of Illinois Press, 2020.

Fontaine, Darcie. *Decolonizing Christianity: Religion and the End of Empire in France and Algeria, 1940–1965.* Cambridge: Cambridge University Press, 2016.

Grant, Colin. *Homecoming: Voices of the Windrush Generation.* London: Jonathan Cape, 2019.

Halleiner, Eric. *Forgotten Foundations of Bretton Woods: International Development and the Making of the Postwar Order.* Ithaca: Cornell University Press, 2014.

Hirsch, Francine. *Soviet Judgment at Nuremberg: A New History of the International Military Tribunal After World War II.* New York: Oxford University Press, 2021.

Hong, Young-Sun. *Cold War Germany, the Third World, and the Global Humanitarian Regime.* Cambridge: Cambridge University Press, 2015.

Jobs, Richard I. *Backpack Ambassadors: How Youth Travel Integrated Europe.* Chicago: University of Chicago Press, 2017.

Macmaster, Neil. *War in the Mountains: Peasant Society and Counterinsurgency in Algeria, 1918–1955.* New York: Oxford University Press, 2020.

Matera, Marc. *Black London: The Imperial Metropolis and Decolonization in the Twentieth Century.* Berkeley: University of California Press, 2015.

Nasta, Susheila and Mark Stein, eds. *Black and Asian British Writing.* Cambridge: Cambridge University Press, 2020.

Paynes, Les and Tamara Payne. *The Dead Are Arising: The Life of Malcolm X.* New York: Liveright, 2020.

Phạm, Quỳnh N., and Robbie Shilliam, eds. *Meanings of Bandung: Post-Colonial Orders and Decolonial Visions.* Lexington: Rowman and Littlefield, 2016.

Prakash, Gyan. *Emergency Chronicles: Indira Gandhi and Democracy's Turning Point.* Princeton: Princeton University Press, *2018.*

Robson, Laura. *The Politics of Mass Violence in the Middle East.* New York: Oxford University Press, 2020.

Sanos, Sandrine. *Simone de Beauvoir: Creating a Feminist Existence in the World.* New York: Oxford University Press, 2017.

Shepard, Todd. *Voices of Decolonization: A Brief History with Documents.* Boston: Bedford, 2015.

White, Luise. *Fighting and Writing: The Rhodesian Army at War and Postwar.* Durham: Duke University Press, 2021.

Yang, Jisheng. *The World Turned Upside Down: A History of the Chinese Cultural Revolution.* London: Swift, 2021.

Zhou, Xun. *Forgotten Voices of Mao's Great Famine, 1958–1961.* New Haven: Yale University Press, 2014.

Chapter 28

The decades around the turn of the twenty-first century were full of events that shifted balances of economic and political power. More than that, violence, pandemic, and suffering litter the world, making globalization hotly debated and contested. This selection of works shows why.

Alexievich, Svetlana. *Secondhand Time: The Last of the Soviets.* New York: Random House, 2016.

Andrews, Kehinde. *The New Age of Empire: How Racism and Colonialism Still Rule the World*. New York: Bold Type Books, 2021.

Bayly, Susan. *Asian Voices in a Post-Colonial Age: Vietnam, India and Beyond*. Cambridge: Cambridge University Press, 2007.

Benjamin, Thomas. "A Time of Reconquest: History, the Maya Revival, and the Zapatista Rebellion." *American Historical Review* 105, no. 2 (April 2000), 417–50.

Dickson, Bruce J. *The Party and the People: Chinese Politics in the 21st Century*. Princeton: Princeton University Press, 2021.

Fong, Mei. *One Child: The Story of China's Most Radical Experiment*. Boston: Mariner, 2015.

Ghosh, Amitav. *The Nutmeg's Curse: Parable for a Planet in Crisis*. Chicago: University of Chicago Press, 2021.

Haass, Richard. *The World: A Brief Introduction*. New York: Penguin, 2020.

Kandiyoti, Deniz, and Ayse Saktanber. *Fragments of Culture: The Everyday of Modern Turkey*. London: Bloomsbury, 2020.

Khair, Tabish. *The New Xenophobia*. New York: Oxford University Press, 2016.

Mahler, Anne Garland. *From the Tricontinental to the Global South Race, Radicalism, and Transnational Solidarity*. Durham: Duke University Press, 2018.

Myers, Steven Lee. *The New Tsar: The Rise and Reign of Vladimir Putin*. New York: Penguin Random House, 2016.

Narayanan, Vidya, Vlad Barash, John Kelly, Lisa-Maria Neudert, Bence Kollanyi, and Philip N. Howard. *Polarisation, Partisanship and Junk News Consumption over Social Media in the US. Data Memo No. 2018*. Ithaca: Cornell University, 2018

Smith, Raymond A., and Patricia Siplon. *Drugs into Bodies: Global AIDS Treatment Activism*. Westport: Praeger, 2006.

South African Government. http://www.info.gov.za/documents/constitution/1996/96cons2.htm

Stent, Angela. *Putin's World: Russia Against the West and with the Rest*. New York: Twelve, 2019.

Stovall, Tyler. *White Freedom: The Racial History of an Idea*. Princeton: Princeton University Press, 2021.

Taubman, William. *Gorbachev: His Life and Times*. New York: W. W. Norton, 2017.

United Nations. http://www.un.org/womenwatch/. Provides ample information on women around the world and on the UN's programs for women.

Wasserstrom, Jeffrey. *Vigil: Hong Kong on the Brink*. New York: Columbia Global Reports, 2020.

Wagner, Dierdre Howard. *Indigenous Invisibility in the City: Successful Resurgence and Community Development Hidden in Plain Sight*. New York: Routledge, 2020.

Zarate, Joseph. *Wars of the Interior*. London: Granta, 2021.

Credits

Part 1

NYPL/Science Source, p. 2

Chapter 1

Fine Art Images/Heritage Images/Getty Images, p. 6; John Reader/Science Source, p. 12; (left) National Museum of Tanzania, Dar es Salaam. © 1985 David L. Brill, humanoriginsphotos.com, p. 21; (right) © Werner Forman Archive/British Institute of History and Archaeology, Dar-es-Salam/HIP/Art Resource, NY (right), p. 21; © CM Dixon/Heritage Image/agefotostock, p. 22; Erich Lessing/Art Resource, NY, p. 24; Caves of Lascaux, Dordogne, France/Bridgeman Images, p. 25; xefstock/iStockphoto, p. 30; © Dorling Kindersley, p. 36; Photo by Ludo Kuipers, ozoutback.com.au, p. 40.

Chapter 2

NYPL/Science Source, p. 44; bpk Bildagentur/National Museum, Baghdad, Iraq/Art Resource, NY, p. 52; (left) Image copyright © The Metropolitan Museum of Art. Image source: Art Resource, NY, p. 53; (right) © RMN-Grand Palais/Art Resource, NY, p. 53; © RMN-Grand Palais/Art Resource, NY, p. 58; Courtesy of the Penn Museum, image #295918, object #B16665, p. 62; Markus Lange/Robert Harding, p. 66; nisudapi/flickr, p. 69; Image copyright © The Metropolitan Museum of Art. Image source: Art Resource, NY, p. 73; © Raga Jose Fuste/Prisma/agefotostock, p. 76.

Chapter 3

State Hermitage Museum, St. Petersburg, Russia/Bridgeman Images, p. 80; Guang Niu/Getty Images, p. 86; The State Hermitage Museum, St. Petersburg. Photograph © The State Hermitage Museum/photo by Vladimir Terebenin, p. 88; Borromeo/Art Resource, NY, p. 91; (top) Alfredo Dagli Orti/Shutterstock, p. 93; (bottom) Scala/Art Resource, NY, p. 93; © Werner Forman Archive/Private Collection London. Location: 07/HIP/Art Resource, NY, p. 104; © Lowell Georgia/Corbis/Getty Images, p. 108; Kenneth Garrett, p. 114; "Seated female," Bronze Age. Gift of Norbert Schimmel Trust, 1989, The Metropolitan Museum of Art, p. 115.

Chapter 4

Diego Delso, delso.photo, License CC-BY-SA https://creativecommons.org/licenses/by-sa/4.0/legalcode, p. 120; Scala/Art Resource, NY, p. 125; © Kenneth Garrett, p. 129; Nigel Pavitt/AWL Images Ltd, p. 132; Werner Forman Archive/Bridgeman Images, p. 133; © The Trustees of the British Museum/Art Resource, NY, p. 140; akg images/Suzanne Held, p. 144; Charles O'Rear/Getty Images, p. 145; © RMN-Grand Palais/Art Resource, NY, p. 149.

Chapter 5

De Agostini via Getty Images, p. 158; "Fasting Buddha Shakyamuni," 3rd–5th c. Samuel Eilenberg Collection, Ex Coll.: Columbia University, Purchase, Rogers, Dodge, Harris Brisbane Dick and Fletcher Funds, Joseph Pulitzer Bequest, and Lila Acheson Wallace Gift, 1987, The Metropolitan Museum of Art, p. 164; © The Trustees of the British Museum/Art Resource, NY, p. 168; © N Sharma/Dinodia Photo/Dinodia Photo Library/agefotostock, p. 171; Werner Forman/Art Resource, NY, p. 176; © Xiaoyang Liu/Getty Images, p. 177; Album/Art Resource, NY, p. 183; British Library, London, UK. © British Library Board. All Rights Reserved/Bridgeman Images, p. 185; Louvre, Paris, France/Bridgeman Images, p. 188.

Chapter 6

© Raimund Koch/Getty Images, p. 196; Album/Art Resource, NY, p. 201; © The Trustees of the British Museum/Art Resource, NY, p. 202; akg-images/Bildarchiv Steffens, p. 211; Erich Lessing/Art Resource, NY, p. 212; Somerset County Museum, Taunton Castle, UK/Bridgeman Images, p. 213; Peter Horree/Alamy Stock Photo, p. 216; Album/Alamy Stock Photo, p. 220; Album/Art Resource, NY, p. 228.

Chapter 7

Private Collection. Photo © Boltin Picture Library/Bridgeman Images, p. 234; Museum of Fine Arts, Houston, Texas, USA. © Museum of Fine Arts, Houston/Museum purchase funded by Brown Foundation Accessions Endowment Fund/Bridgeman Images, p. 244; Catalogo Digital, Museo de Antropologia de Xalapa, Universidad Veracruzana, p. 248; George Stuart, p. 251; Private Collection. © Paul Maeyaert/AISA/Bridgeman Images, p. 255; HIP/Art Resource, NY, p. 257; © OUP, p. 263; "A New Sappho Papyrus"(recto), 3rd to 2nd c. BC. © Institute for Classical Studies at the University of Cologne. Kölner Papyri, https://papyri.uni-koeln.de/stueck/tm68983, CC BY 4.0, https://creativecommons.org/licenses/by/4.0/, p. 266.

Part 2

Werner Forman Archive/Bridgeman Images, p. 270.

Chapter 8

Erich Lessing/Art Resource, NY, p. 274; Cameraphoto Arte, Venice/Art Resource, NY, p. 281; Erich Lessing/Art Resource, NY, p. 282; © The Trustees of the British Museum, p. 285; © Ayhan Altun/Alamy Stock Photo, p. 287; Erich Lessing/Art Resource, NY, p. 294; Ketan Gajria, p. 302; Arthur M. Sackler Gallery, Smithsonian Institution, Washington, DC: Purchase—Smithsonian Unrestricted Trust Funds, Smithsonian Collections

Acquisition Program, and Dr. Arthur M. Sackler, S1986.104, Detail, p. 304; Bungemuseet AB, photo by Helena Duveborg, p. 309.

Chapter 9

From the Collection of the Fujita Museum, Osaka, Japan. First section, tenth chapter of the painted scroll, Genjo sanzo e (Japanese National Treasure), p. 314; Produced by the Institute of Digitization of Cultural Relics of the Dunhuang Academy, provided by the Dunhuang Academy, p. 321; © Artokoloro Quint Lox Limited/agefotostock, p. 323; Arthur M. Sackler Museum, Harvard University Art Museums, USA. © Harvard Art Museums/Bequest of Grenville L. Winthrop/Bridgeman Images, p. 325; © Pictures From History/AGB/agefotostock, p. 330; © Vanni Archive/Art Resource, NY, p. 332; Erich Lessing/Art Resource, NY, p. 337; Hemis/Alamy Stock Photo, p. 343; robert-harding/Alamy Stock Photo, p. 344.

Chapter 10

Werner Forman Archive/Bridgeman Images, p. 352; © Gloria & Richard Masc/Pacific Stock/agefotostock, p. 358; © Herb Lingl/aerialarchives.com, p. 360; © The Trustees of the British Museum/Art Resource, NY, p. 364; Private collection, p. 370; akg-images/De Agostini Picture Lib./G. Dagli Orti, p. 372; R. Perron/Art Resource, Art Resource, NY, p. 375; Cahokia Mounds State Historic Site. Artist William Iseminger, p. 377; "This Bay we named Maria's Bay . . ." from James Burney, *A Chronological History of The Voyages and Discoveries in the South Sea or Pacific Ocean*, vol. 3 (London: Luke Hansard & Sons, 1803), p. 84, p. 379; "Village of Macacoupah, Owhyhee", M. Dubourg, after Thomas Heddington, 1814. Bishop Museum Archives, www.bishopmuseum.org, p. 384.

Chapter 11

© BnF, Dist. RMN-Grand Palais/Art Resource, NY, p. 392; © British Library Board. All Rights Reserved/Bridgeman Images, p. 398; © ChinaStock, p. 401; The Cleveland Museum of Art. John L Severance Collection

1977.5, p. 405; (top) © The Trustees of the British Museum/Art Resource, NY, p. 408, 409; (bottom) Courtesy of the American Numismatic Society, p. 409; Pictures from History/Bridgeman Images, p. 418; Barakat Gallery, barakatgallery.com, p. 421; Snark/Art Resource, NY, p. 424; The J. Paul Getty Museum, Los Angeles, p. 428.

Chapter 12

Scala/Art Resource, NY, p. 432; The J. Paul Getty Museum, Los Angeles, p. 437; The J. Paul Getty Museum, Los Angeles, p. 437; Thomas de Maubeuge, Trotula (Paris, ca. 1304). Bibliotheque de Rennes Metropole, p. 438; bpk Bildagentur/Kupferstichkabinett/Staatliche Museen, Berlin, Germany/Jörg P. Anders/Art Resource, NY, p. 445; Freer Gallery of Art, Smithsonian Institution, Washington, D.C.: Purchase—Charles Lang Freer Endowment, F1952.11 (Detail), p. 445; B.O'Kane/Alamy Stock Photo, p. 448; sunilkumar c s sunil/Alamy Stock Photo, p. 455; Liu Guandao, Chinese (active 1279–1300). *Whiling Away the Summer, Yuan Dynasty (1279–1368)*. Handscroll, ink and color on silk, 12 x 268 inches (30.5 x 680.7 cm). The Nelson-Atkins Museum of Art, Kansas City, Missouri. Purchase: William Rockhill Nelson Trust, 48-5. Photo © The Nelson Gallery Foundation, p. 460; British Library, London, UK/Bridgeman Images, p. 461; Photograph K1185, Justin Kerr, p. 466.

Chapter 13

The Picture Art Collection/Alamy Stock Photo, p. 470; Biblioteca Monasterio del Escorial, Madrid, Spain/Bridgeman Images, p. 476; Saint Isidore of Seville, from *Isidori Iunioris Hispalensis Episcopi Liber etimologiarum ad Braulionem Cesar Augustanum Episcopum scriptus incipit foeliciter* (Augsburg, Germany: Günther Zainer, 1472). Incunabula Collection and Otto Vollbehr Collection, https://www.loc.gov/item/ca18000702/, p. 478; © British Library Board/Robana/Art Resource, NY, p. 479; akg-images, p. 486; Pictures from History/Bridgeman Images, p. 491; © Bibliotheque Nationale,

Paris/HIP/Art Resource, NY, p. 493; bpk Bildagentur/Staatsbibliothek zu Berlin, Stiftung Preussicher Kulturbesitz, Berlin, Germany/Art Resource, NY, p. 496; akg-images/Gerard Degeorge, p. 500; "Dancing Sufis," from Ḥasan Dihlavī, *Collection of Poems (Divan)*, Walters Art Museum Ms. W.650, fol. 62a, p. 503.

Chapter 14

Erich Lessing/Art Resource, NY, p. 508; akg-images, p. 515; Bihzad, "Timur granting audience on the occasion of his accession," from Sharaf al-Din 'Ali Yazd, Zafaranama (ca. 1467), plate 2. The John Work Garrett Library, The Sheridan Libraries, Johns Hopkins University. https://www.flickr.com/photos/hopkinsarchives/albums/72157632108344242, CC BY 2.0, https://creativecommons.org/licenses/by-sa/2.0/, p. 523; Ariadne Van Zandbergen/Alamy Stock Photo, p. 528; Ashmolean Museum, University of Oxford, UK. © Ashmolean Museum/Bridgeman Images, p. 532; Photo: F. Osada ©Franck Goddio/Hilti Foundation. Franck Goddio et al., *Lost at Sea—The strange route of the Lena shoal Junk* (London: Periplus, 2002), p. 534; Erich Lessing/Art Resource, p. 538.

Part 3

V&A Images, London/Art Resource, NY, p. 546.

Chapter 15

Bridgeman Images, p. 550; Image copyright © The Metropolitan Museum of Art. Image source: Art Resource, NY, p. 554; Granger, p. 559; Image by Joaquín Enríquez from Pixabay, p. 562; Scala/Art Resource, NY, p. 563; Bernardino De Sahagún, *General History of the Things of New Spain by Fray Bernardino de Sahagún: The Florentine Codex. Book VI: Rhetoric and Moral Philosophy* (1577). https://www.loc.gov/item/2021667851/, p. 566; AP Photo/Natacha Pisarenko, p. 577; imageBROKER/Alamy Stock Photo, p. 579; National Museum of the American Indian, Smithsonian Institution (1/2132). Photo by Katherine Fogden, p. 583.

Chapter 16

Museo Naval, Madrid, Spain/Bridgeman Images, p. 588; Patrick Landmann/Science Source, p. 594; Lorenz Fries, "Cannibals on a Caribbean Island" (cropped), from Uslegung der Mercarthen oder Cartha marina (Strasbourg: Johannes Grieninger, 1525). ©John Carter Brown Library. Accession no. 17183. https://jcb.lunaimaging.com/, CC BY 4.0, https://creativecommons.org/licenses/by/4.0/, p. 601; Leonhart Fuchs, De historia stirpium commentarii insignes, illus. Albrecht Meyer, Heinricus Fullmaurer and Veit Rudolph Speckle (1542). Houghton Library, Harvard University, p. 605; Francisco de Xerez, Title Page (cropped), from Uerdadera relacion de la conquista del Peru (Seville: Bartholome Perez, 1534). ©John Carter Brown Library. Accession no. 7649. https://jcb.lunaimaging.com/, CC BY 4.0, https://creativecommons.org/licenses/by/4.0/, p. 610; Granger, p. 611; Courtesy of The Hispanic Society of America, New York, p. 614; "Praefecturae Paranambucae Pars Borealis, una cum Praefectura de Itâmaracâ" (map) (Amsterdam: Joan Bleu, 1662). ©John Carter Brown Library. Accession no. 03171. https://jcb.lunaimaging.com/, CC BY 4.0, https://creativecommons.org/licenses/by/4.0/, p. 620; Diego de Ocaña, from Relación del viaje de Fray Diego de Ocaña por el Nuevo Mundo (1605). Library of the University of Oviedo, M-215. https://digibuo.uniovi.es/dspace/handle/10651/27859CC, CC BY-NC-ND 3.0, https://creativecommons.org/licenses/by-nc-nd/3.0/legalcode, p. 623.

Chapter 17

Image copyright © The Metropolitan Museum of Art. Image source: Art Resource, NY, p. 628; © National Maritime Museum, Greenwich, London, p. 634; Aldo Tutino/Art Resource, NY, p. 638; Image copyright © The Metropolitan Museum of Art. Image source: Art Resource, NY, p. 640; Fr. Giovanni Antonio Cavazzi, "King Ndongo Forging Weapons," from Istorica descrizione de' tre' regni Congo, Matamba et Angola (Bologna, 1687). Biblioteca Estense, Modena, Italy, p. 643; Fr. Giovanni Antonio Cavazzi, "Baptism of Queen Nzinga," from Istorica descrizione de' tre' regni Congo, Matamba et Angola (Bologna, 1687). Biblioteca Estense, Modena, Italy, p. 652; Johannes Kip, "A. Fishing Cannoes of Mina 5 or 600 at a Time/B. Negro's Cannoes Carrying Slaves on Board of Ships Att Mansfoe," from Awnsham Churchill, A Collection of Voyages and Travels . . ., Vol. V, Pl. g. (London, 1744–46). Beinecke Rare Book and Manuscript Library, Yale University, p. 656; British Library, London, UK. © British Library Board. All Rights Reserved/Bridgeman Images, p. 660; Fr. Giovanni Antonio Cavazzi, "Queen Nzinga with Military Entourage," from Istorica descrizione de' tre' regni Congo, Matamba et Angola (Bologna, 1687). Biblioteca Estense, Modena, Italy, p. 664.

Chapter 18

V&A Images, London/Art Resource, NY, p. 668; By permission of the Biblioteca Casanatense, Rome, MiC, Ms 1889, p. 675; Colin McPherson/Corbis via Getty Images, p. 677; © British Library Board, Add Or 3129, f.20, p. 683; Private Collection. Photo © Christie's Images/Bridgeman Images, p. 686; V&A Images, London/Art Resource, NY, p. 690; Sarin Images/Granger, p. 697; Collection Het Scheepvaartmuseum, Amsterdam, p. 699.

Chapter 19

Prado, Madrid, Spain. Index Fototeca/Bridgeman Images, p. 706; isa özdere/Alamy Stock Photo, p. 714; The Picture Art Collection/Alamy Stock Photo, p. 716; © A. Dagli Orti/© NPL - DeA Picture Library/Bridgeman Images, p. 717; CBL T 439.9 (recto) © The Trustees of the Chester Beatty Library, Dublin, p. 718; © ChinaStock, p. 728; akg-images, p. 732; Prado, Madrid, SpainPhoto © Fine Art Images/Bridgeman, Images, p. 737; akg-images/Universal Images Group, p. 738; Heritage Images/Fine Art Images/akg-images, p. 742; Private Collection/Bridgeman Images, p. 747.

Chapter 20

© ChinaStock, p. 752; Tretyakov Gallery, Moscow, Russia/Bridgeman Images, p. 759; Golestan Palace, Tehran, Iran/Bridgeman Images, p. 762; G.Dagli Orti/© NPL - DeA Picture Library/Bridgeman Images, p. 764; Pictures from History/Bridgeman Images, p. 767;

Granger, p. 773; Granger, p. 775; © RMN-Grand Palais/Art Resource, NY, p. 777; Sino-Spanish codex (Boxer codex), ca. 1590. Boxer mss. II. Indiana University, Bloomington, Indiana, p. 786.

Chapter 21

Fundação Biblioteca Nacional—Brasil. BNDIGITAL I: Carlos Julião, "Cena romântica," from *Notícia summaria do gentilismo da Asia* (1700s). https://bdlb.bn.gov.br/acervo/handle/20.500.12156.3/36129?locale-attribute=en, p. 790; Corsham Court, Wiltshire/Bridgeman Images, p. 796; Hoberman Publishing/Alamy Stock Photo, p. 798; Museo de América, Madrid, p. 800; Album/Alamy Stock Photo, p. 802; © A. Dagli Orti/© NPL - DeA Picture Library/Bridgeman Images, p. 805; Daniel Defoe and Charles Johnson, *A general history of the pyrates* . . . (London: T. Warner, 1724), Boston Public Library via The Internet Archive, p. 811; Private Collection/Bridgeman Images, p. 817; The New York Public Library/Art Resource, NY, p. 824.

Part 4

© Illustrated London News Ltd/Mary Evans, p. 828.

Chapter 22

© NPL - DeA Picture Library/M. Seemuller/Bridgeman Images, p. 832; Private Collection/Bridgeman Images, p. 838; Hillwood Estate, Museum & Gardens, photographed by Edward Owen, p. 840; Samuel Jennings, "Liberty Displaying the Arts and Sciences," 1792. Library Company of Philadelphia, p. 846; Photo © CCI/Bridgeman Image, p. 849; Gainew Gallery/Alamy Stock Photo, p. 854; Private Collection/Bridgeman Images, p. 857; akg-images, p. 862; G. Dagli Orti/© NPL - DeA Picture Library/Bridgeman Images, p. 867.

Chapter 23

Private Collection Photo © Christie's Images/Bridgeman Images, p. 872; Cotehele House, Cornwall, UK/Bridgeman Images, p. 879; Niday Picture Library/Alamy Stock Photo, p. 884; Brooklyn Museum of Art, New York, USA. © Brooklyn Museum of Art/Gift of Dr. and Mrs. Maurice Cottle/Bridgeman Images, p. 888; *Bulletin of the Pan American Union*, 42 (1916). Benson Latin American Collection, University of Texas Libraries, p. 889; Shiva Lal, "Opium being weighed on scales," c. 1857–60. © Victoria and Albert Museum, London, p. 892; © Jehangir Sorabjee/Dinodia Photo, p. 898; akg-images, p. 899; akg-images, p. 906.

Chapter 24

History and Art Collection/Alamy Stock Photo, p. 910; akg-images/De Agostini Picture Lib./G. Dagli Orti, p. 917; Sovfoto/Universal Images Group/Getty Images, p. 920; STUDIO MELANGE/Shutterstock, p. 924; National Portrait Gallery, Smithsonian Institution, p. 927; Korneli Kekelidze Georgian National Centre of Manuscripts, p. 931; © British Library Board. All Rights Reserved/Bridgeman Images, p. 940; © Art Media/Heritage Image/agefotostock . . ., p. 941; akg-images, p. 942; © Tetra Images/Corbis/Getty Images, p. 946.

Chapter 25

Schalkwijk/Art Resource, NY/© 2022 Banco de México Diego Rivera Frida Kahlo Museums Trust, Mexico, D.F./Artists Rights Society (ARS), New York (ARS), p. 952; Private Collection/Bridgeman Images, p. 958; Science History Images/Alamy Stock Photo, p. 964; Walter Trier-Archiv, Konstanz, p. 966; Corbis via Getty Images, p. 967; © A. Dagli Orti/© NPL - DeA Picture Library/Bridgeman Images, p. 973; Gamma-Keystone via Getty Images, p. 975; Granger, p. 982; Still from Zi Mei Mua, directed by Zheng Zhengqiu, p. 985; "The Argentine (tango)" (London: Chappell & Co., 1912). From The New York Public Library, https://digitalcollections.nypl.org/items/510d47da-52e2-a3d9-e040-e00a18064a99, p. 989.

Chapter 26

bpk Bildagentur/Art Resource, NY, p. 992; Schalkwijk/Art Resource, NY. © 2022 Banco de México Diego Rivera Frida Kahlo Museums Trust, Mexico, D.F./Artists Rights Society (ARS), New York, p. 999; akg-images, p. 1002; Bettmann Archive/Getty Images, p. 1005; American Photo Archive/Alamy Stock Photo, p. 1017;

Index

Note: Page numbers followed by *f, t, m,* or *b* refer to figures or illustrations, tables, maps, and boxes, respectively.

Egyptian influences in, 123,
132*b*–33*b*, 132*f*
gold mines of, 127
Kingdom of Meroe, 130*m*, 130–31,
132*b*–33*b*
Number systems:
"Arabic," 171
in classical India, 171
in Mesopotamia, 59, 63
Nuns, 276, 338
Nut, 72

Oahu, 385*b*
Obsidian, 37*b*, 261, 356, 357
Oceania:
in early modern era, 549
resources of remote, 379*f*, 382–83
Octavian (Augustus), 198, 205–9, 212*b*,
212*f*, 216
Odoacer, German king, 226, 289
Oedipus the King (Sophocles), 182
Ogodei, 489, 492*b*–93*b*, 497
Oikumene, 213*b*, 212*f*
Old English language, 442
Old Javanese language, 340
Old Kingdom (ancient Egypt), 71–72
Old Persian language, 122, 144
Old Testament, 190
Oligarchy, 150, 152, 516
Olmecs, 246–49, 356
Omens, 140*b*–41*b*, 140*f*
On Architecture (Vitruvius), 210*b*
Ontario, Canada, 583–84
On the Origin of Species (Darwin), 8
Oracle bones, 103, 105–10, 108*b*–9*b*,
108*f*, 264
Oral history, Aztec, 557
Oresme, Nicole, 486
Oresteia (Aeschylus), 182–83
Orkhan, 500–501
Orthodox Church, 287
Charlemagne's protection of, 291
Cistercians and, 475
Great Schism and, 474, 475
Greek, 483
wealth accumulation under
Mongols, 498
Osiris, 73, 126, 127, 189, 216
Osman, 500–501, 524
Ostrogoths, 289–90
Otomi, 564
Ottoman Empire, 498, 500–501, 523–25,
524*m*
armies of, 273, 510, 524, 525

in early modern era, 548
fall of Constantinople to, 510
Safavid challenge of, 523
Oxford, university at, 437, 440
Oxus people, 82, 113*m*, 113–16, 114*f*, 115*f*

Pachacuti Inca Yupanki, 572–73, 580
Pacific Islands:
agricultural livelihoods in, 258–59
Austronesians in, 259–61
Bougainville, 387*m*, 387–88
cross-cultural exchange in, 355
habitat and adaptation in, 378–83
histories of peoples of, 354
Lapita culture in, 261, 261*m*
peopling of, 259–61
political and religious authority
in, 355
Polynesia, 236
Polynesian expansion/migrations,
379–82, 380*m*–81*m*
in post-classical era, 272
prehistoric cultures of, 258–62, 259*m*
subsistence and survival in, 382–83
Pacific Northwest cultures, 554,
556–57
Pacific Ocean, 258
Pacifism, in Jainism, 163
Paekche, 328, 329
Pagan societies, in post-classical world,
276, 283
Painting(s):
by Aztecs, 559*b*, 559*f*
cave paintings, 23, 25, 25*f*, 243
during Renaissance, 539–40
wall paintings, 25*f*, 65, 66*f*, 125
Palaces:
in Alexandria, 188
of ancient Egypt, 72
of ancient Mesopotamia, 72
in Andean region, 369
Assyrian, 135
Aztec, 560
Cretan, 65, 66*f*
as trade centers, 65
underground, of Shi Huangdi,
176, 177*f*
Palaiologos, Maria, 287*f*
Palembang, 344
Paleolithic, 19–20
art of, 23–25, 24*b*, 24*f*
community life in, 21–25
gatherer-hunter economy in, 20–21
stone tools in, 20

Palestine:
Byzantine Empire's loss of, 286
Christian outposts along coast
of, 481
Christian peoples in, 481
Judaism in, 217, 217
Mongol defeat in, 495
Pallava dynasty, 336*b*
Pampa Grande, 369
Pandemics, 272 (*See also* Plague)
Panini, 171
Pan-Islamic empire, 302–3
Pantheon, 210*b*
Papacy, 283
bank lending to, 412
bond between secular rulers and, 291
Crusades and, 475–80
Great Schism and, 474
investiture controversy, 474–75
as monarchy, 474–75
political aims of Crusades and,
480–81
spending and consumption by, 537
See also Popes
Papermaking, 305
Paper money, 410
Papuan societies, 379, 387
Paracas, 254
Paraguay-Paraná, 554
Paris, university at, 437, 439*b*, 440
Parliaments, in eastern Europe, 486
Parthenon, 183*f*
Parthian Empire, 103, 139, 143*m*, 146,
227–28
Pastoralism, 83, 87, 240, 488, 492*b*,
514, 580
Pater familias, 200
Patriarchy:
in India, 338
in Japan, 542–43
Mesopotamian society as, 58
under Neo-Confucianism, 519
in Ottoman law, 525
Patricians, 200–202, 201*f*, 205
Patrilineal system:
in Bantu society, 242–43
in Byzantium, 397*b*
in Inca Empire, 579
in Mongol society, 492*b*
Patronage:
Christian, 283, 284*b*
in early modern era, 549
by Ilkhans, 496–97
in India's textile industries, 532*b*